Acknowledgements

This collection of essays grew out of the 2011 WG Hart Legal Workshop entitled 'Sovereignty in Question'. As the academic directors of the Workshop and now editors of the volume we would like to thank Professor Avrom Sherr, Director of the Institute of Advanced Legal Studies in London, and Belinda Crothers, Academic Programmes Manager at IALS, for their support in hosting the Workshop. We would also like to thank Lord Hope of Craighead for encouraging the project and, of course, all the participants at the Workshop and our contributors.

For their support in bringing this book to fruition, we thank Alex Flach, Natasha Flemming, Clare Kennedy, and their colleagues at Oxford University Press, and also our 'in-house' researchers Stephen Dimelow and Binesh Hass.

Particular words of thanks go to Putachad for her very special jacket painting. As a professional artist, she naturally thought about the meaning and place of sovereignty in our contemporary world when visualizing the subject in paint. For Putachad, 'the juxtaposition of pyramids denotes the distinct ambit and limits, while also suggesting interdependence'.

Richard Rawlings
Peter Leyland
Alison L Young

April 2013

Contents

List of Contributors ix

1. Introduction: Sovereignty in Question 1
   Richard Rawlings
2. Sovereignty Frames and Sovereignty Claims 18
   Neil Walker
3. Why Sovereignty? 34
   Martin Loughlin
4. Parliamentary Sovereignty and Constitutional Change in the United Kingdom 50
   Jeffrey Goldsworthy
5. Parliamentary Sovereignty Re-defined 68
   Alison L Young
6. Is the Rule of Law now the Sovereign Principle? 89
   Lord Hope of Craighead
7. Changing the United Kingdom Constitution: The Blind Sovereign 98
   Richard S Kay
8. 'A Sort of Farewell': Sovereignty, Transition, and Devolution in the United Kingdom 120
   John Morison
9. Referendums, Popular Sovereignty, and the Territorial Constitution 145
   Peter Leyland
10. The United Kingdom, the European Union, and Sovereignty 165
    Paul Craig
11. European Restatements of Sovereignty 186
    Damian Chalmers
12. Sovereignties in Strasbourg 213
    David Feldman
13. Sovereignty, Constitutional Dialogues, and Political Networks: A Comparative and Conceptual Study 236
    Margit Cohn
14. Sovereignty: A View from the International Bench 251
    Sir Christopher Greenwood
15. Territorial Sovereignty and Territorial Extension in an Inter-Connected World 269
    Joanne Scott

16. Sovereignty and Private Corporate Power: The Case of Multinational Enterprises 286
Peter Muchlinski

17. Sovereignty and Liberty in the Internet Era 305
Perry Keller

Index 325

List of Contributors

Damian Chalmers, Professor of European Union Law, London School of Economics and Political Science

Margit Cohn, Senior Lecturer, Faculty of Law and Federmann School of Public Policy and Government, Hebrew University of Jerusalem

Paul Craig, Professor of English Law, St John's College, University of Oxford

David Feldman, Rouse Ball Professor of English Law, University of Cambridge

Jeffrey Goldsworthy, Professor of Law, Monash University

Sir Christopher Greenwood, Judge, International Court of Justice

Lord Hope of Craighead, Former Deputy President of the Supreme Court of the United Kingdom

Richard S Kay, Wallace Stevens Professor of Law, University of Connecticut School of Law

Perry Keller, Senior Lecturer, Dicksoon Pool School of Law, King's College London

Peter Leyland, Professor of Public Law, London Metropolitan University

Martin Loughlin, Professor of Public Law, London School of Economics and Political Science

John Morison, Professor of Law, School of Law, Queen's University Belfast

Peter Muchlinski, Professor of International Commercial Law, School of Oriental and African Studies, University of London

Richard Rawlings, Professor of Public Law, University College London

Joanne Scott, Professor of European Law, University College London

Neil Walker, Regius Professor of Public Law and the Law of Nature and Nations, University of Edinburgh

Alison L Young, Fellow and Lecturer in Law, Hertford College, University of Oxford

1

Introduction: Sovereignty in Question

*Richard Rawlings**

A. Hart to Hart, via MacCormick

Forty years ago in one of England's ancient universities it all seemed pretty straightforward. Term 1, week 1 featured the Great Victorian AV Dicey on the sovereignty of the Westminster Parliament. In a (legal) nutshell: Parliament could do anything save bind its successors (= 'positive aspect'); no body (and certainly not judges) could trump Westminster (= 'negative aspect').[1] After which, the ignoble thought occurred, what remained for three more years of legal studies?

We learned—again virtually by rote—two classic distinctions. A necessary element in rendering Dicey's account credible even to callow youth, attention was drawn to the competing legal and political conceptions of sovereignty: *de jure* and *de facto.* Though, one already mused, complacently given the blood-soaked years of the twentieth century, the answer to why Parliament did not command the killing of blue-eyed babies apparently still lay in the sweet reasonableness of MPs and their constituents.[2] The distinction between the internal aspect of sovereignty as expressed in terms of ultimate authority in a constitution, and the external aspect involving the relationship between sovereign States, had also to be factored in. Such an approach conveniently echoed the traditionally strong dualist view of international law in the British constitution and hence the centrality of Parliament.[3]

'Sovereignty' was here being inscribed in large letters on a small cover. A distinctive constitutional tradition of the absolute legal authority of Queen-in-Parliament answered in terms of one conception of sovereignty, the character of the highest organ of the State, and effectively crowded out discussion of sovereignty in terms of the supreme quality of State power or of the entirety of the powers included in the State's authority.[4] Perhaps mention was made of sovereignty in the further

* Professor of Public Law, University College London.

[1] AV Dicey, *Introduction to the Study of the Law of the Constitution* (ECS Wade ed, 10th edn, Macmillan 1962) 39–40.

[2] Dicey (n 1) 81.

[3] To this effect, authorities such as *Cheney v Conn* [1968] 1 WLR 242 (Ch D) would have featured prominently.

[4] For a recent discussion of these different conceptualizations, founded on the work of R Carré de Malberg, *Contribution à la théorie générale de l'Etat, spécialement d'après les données fournies par le droit*

sense of imputation, a republican-style dash of Parliament exercising a sovereignty that belonged to the people, but somehow I doubt it.[5]

Conditions had been ripe for Dicey's brilliant evocation of legislative supremacy of, by, and for, the English gentleman to continue to dominate the local syllabus. Let us recall first, that English law was at the time recovering from a period of exceptional formalism. Only ten years earlier, a distinguished American visitor had described judicial review in England as restricted by an old-fashioned, positivist corset.[6] Second and related, so much in the application and study[7] of legal principle in England had become determinedly insular in character. As the leading English judge of his generation would later lament, there was a certain conceit—familiarly associated with Dicey—about the superiority of the English common law and its institutions.[8]

Not that the Oxford law student was lacking for theory (or so we thought). Herbert Hart's *The Concept of Law*[9] is not usually put together with Mao's contemporaneous *Little Red Book*,[10] yet in this case too there was a sense of requisite 'thoughts' being contained in one slim volume.[11] Hart's *Concept of Law*, after all, has been described as the most successful work of analytical jurisprudence ever to appear in the common law world.[12] The discussion by Hart of sovereignty was typically clear and concise and full of easily remembered nostrums. Generations of undergraduates never would forget his rules-based demolition of Austin's positivist conception of law as simply the commands of an identifiable, indivisible, and illimitable sovereign.[13] As regards the external dimension of a State's independence in the international community, Hart's concise view[14] of international law as problematic in light of missing or limited elements of legislation, adjudication, and centralized sanctions was also easy on the eye.

constitutionnel français (2 vols, Dalloz 2004), see M Toper, 'The Survival of Sovereignty' in H Kalmo and Q Skinner (eds) *Sovereignty in Fragments: The Past, Present and Future of a Contested Concept* (CUP 2010). See also Chapter 2 of this volume by Walker.

[5] For later efforts, see A Tomkins, *Our Republican Constitution* (Hart Publishing 2005) and R Bellamy, *Political Constitutionalism: A Republican Defence of the Constitutionality of Democracy* (CUP 2007).

[6] KC Davis, 'The Future of Judge-made Public Law in England: A Problem of Practical Jurisprudence' (1961) 61 *Col Law Rev* 201. For the then high point of the recovery, see *Anisminic Ltd v Foreign Compensation Commission* [1969] 2 AC 147 (HL).

[7] W Twining, *Blackstone's Tower: The English Law School* (Sweet & Maxwell 1994).

[8] T Bingham, '"There is a World Elsewhere": The Changing Perspectives of English Law' (1992) 41 *ICLQ* 513, 514.

[9] HLA Hart, *The Concept of Law* (OUP 1961).

[10] *Quotations from Chairman Mao Tse-Tung* (Government of the People's Republic of China 1964). Recently rediscovered on the top shelf, my student copies of both books appear reasonably well-thumbed.

[11] Hans Kelsen (and in view of his Nazi past emphatically not Carl Schmitt) would have been the leading exception: H Kelsen, *General Theory of Law and State* (Harvard University Press 1949). For the avoidance of doubt, Ronald Dworkin was a recent arrival in Oxford and the huge influence of his interpretive theory had yet to percolate.

[12] AWB Simpson, *Reflections on 'The Concept of Law'* (OUP 2011) 1. See also N Lacey, *A Life of H. L. A. Hart, The Nightmare and the Noble Dream* (OUP 2004).

[13] J Austin, *The Province of Jurisprudence Determined* (J Murray 1832); Hart (n 9) esp chs 2–4.

[14] Hart (n 9) ch 10.

Of course in saying all this I exaggerate a little. Had not Sir Ivor Jennings warned that sovereignty 'is a word of quasi-theological origin which may easily lead us into difficulties'?[15] In the words of one slightly subversive don, 'at the inmost centre of English legal education there were ominous signs of fission'.[16] Given the carnage then being wreaked on the streets of Belfast, it was not so easy for example to gloss over Dicey's polemically Unionist approach in relation to sovereignty.[17] The distinctive Scots tradition[18] encompassing ideas of popular sovereignty provided an altogether more welcome diversion, though ultimately, amid a still prevailing Anglo-centric view of the unitary State,[19] only that. Meanwhile, in the academic home of (Cecil) Rhodes scholarships the old white Dominions—and the United States—were never to be ignored. The famous preamble to the Statute of Westminster 1931, effectively rebalancing the State of legislative relations with the old Imperial Parliament, was an inspiration for some and a source of puzzlement to others.[20]

The (not so) 'new view'[21] of parliamentary sovereignty, concerning the 'manner and form' in which legislation is enacted, fell to be grappled with. For a doctrine with 'the attraction of being couched in the calm, hard, tightly knit style of the common lawyer rather than in the vague and emotional language of the political scientist',[22] how could it be otherwise? A well-known list of Commonwealth authorities met the demands of the case law method.[23] When push came to shove, however, suggesting such legal restraints on the United Kingdom Parliament did not, in personal experience, go down well.[24]

There were whispers in the library of a seemingly far-off court in Luxembourg claiming that what the British firmly referred to as 'common market law' could somehow have supremacy over national legislation.[25] However, only limited light was shed on this since the broader constitutional implications of British accession via the European Communities Act 1972 were being glossed over by ministers.[26] Meanwhile, those few of us not put off by the apparent damp squib of limited sanctioning powers found ourselves confronted, on the one hand, by a rigidly State-centred approach

[15] Sir Ivor Jennings, *The Law and the Constitution* (5th edn, University of London Press 1959) 147.

[16] RVF Heuston, *Essays in Constitutional Law* (Stevens 1961) 1–2. And for what we might have been reading, see now J McLean, *Searching for the State in British Legal Thought: Competing Conceptions of the Public Sphere* (CUP 2012) esp ch 3.

[17] RA Cosgrove, *The Rule of Law: Albert Venn Dicey, Victorian Jurist* (Macmillan 1980) esp chs 6 and 10.

[18] *MacCormick v Lord Advocate* 1953 SC 396 (Ct of Sess). See Chapter 6 of this volume by Lord Hope.

[19] A familiar theme in subsequent historical writing, eg, L Colley, *Britons: Forging the Nation 1707–1837* (Yale University Press 1992).

[20] See also in the context of empire's end, *Madzimbamuto v Lardner-Burke* [1969] 1 AC 645 (PC).

[21] RTE Latham, *The Law and the Commonwealth* (OUP 1949) 523; Jennings (n 15) 152–6.

[22] Heuston (n 16) 6.

[23] *Attorney-General for New South Wales v Trethowan* [1932] AC 526 (PC); *Harris v Minister of the Interior* 1952 (2) SA 428; and *Bribery Commissioner v Ranasinghe* [1965] AC 172 (PC).

[24] For the then prevailing wisdom, see H Wade, 'The Legal Basis of Sovereignty' (1955) 13 *CLJ* 172. The matter is taken up in Chapters 4 and 5 of this volume by Jeffrey Goldsworthy and Alison L Young respectively.

[25] Case C -6/64 *Costa v ENEL* [1964] ECR 585.

[26] D Nicol, *EC Membership and the Judicialization of British Politics* (OUP 2001).

to public international law[27] and, on the other hand, all those haunting TV images of the Vietnam war. Measured words on the external dimension to sovereignty were all very well, but might not public international law have more to say on behalf of the victims of Agent Orange?[28]

Twenty years ago at Britain's most determinedly modern law school things appeared a little more complicated, even rather exciting. In the 1992 Chorley Lecture delivered at the London School of Economics and Political Science, Neil MacCormick spoke of somewhere 'Beyond the Sovereign State'.[29] A cheery farewell was the not so subliminal descriptive and normative message: 'sovereignty and sovereign states, and the inexorable linkage of law with sovereignty and the State, have been but the passing phenomena of a few centuries'; their passing is 'by no means regrettable'; 'current developments in Europe exhibit the possibility of going beyond all that'.[30] In later work, MacCormick would indeed speak of 'post-sovereignty'.[31]

MacCormick's contribution struck a chord. It chimed locally with the rich LSE tradition of treating law as a social phenomenon and of engaging with the economically and socially relevant[32] and, as indicated, with a range of contemporary legal and political occurrences in this part of the globe. In the domestic sphere, not only had judicial review advanced considerably, in part under the shadow of the European Convention on Human Rights ('ECHR').[33] But also, as illustrated by a broadly-based Claim of Right declaring 'the sovereign right of the Scottish people to determine the form of Government best suited to their needs',[34] the United Kingdom's old Celtic lands were stirring afresh in the face of Dicey's English doctrine and a famously radical Conservative Government.[35] The well-known metaphor of 'hollowing out of the State' would soon be coined to highlight the way that central government functions had apparently been depleted or transferred including 'upwards' to the EU.[36]

The contemporaneous *Factortame*[37] saga—involving 'a hitherto unprecedented non-application of parliamentary statute by a judicial tribunal'—naturally featured

[27] In the guise of state recognition and self-defence, diplomatic immunities and all that: Nuremberg, as I recall, featured as the proverbial exception that proves the rule.

[28] See in this regard, R Falk (ed) *The Vietnam War and International Law* (4 vols) (Princeton University Press 1968–76).

[29] N MacCormick, 'Beyond the Sovereign State' (1993) 56 *MLR* 1.

[30] MacCormick (1993) (n 29) 1.

[31] See N MacCormick, *Questioning Sovereignty: Law, State and Nation in the European Commonwealth* (OUP 1999) ch 8. Many of the themes in his Chorley Lecture are elaborated in this volume.

[32] R Rawlings (ed) *Law, Society and Economy: Centenary Essays for the London School of Economics and Political Science* (Clarendon Press 1997).

[33] C Harlow and R Rawlings, *Law and Administration* (3rd edn, CUP 2009) ch 3.

[34] *A Claim of Right for Scotland: Campaign for a Scottish Assembly, Constitutional Steering Committee* (Polygon 1989), as crafted by the unofficial Scottish Constitutional Convention.

[35] Notwithstanding the previous failures to achieve devolution represented by the Scotland Act 1978 and the Wales Act 1978. Northern Ireland, meanwhile, had been subject to 'Direct Rule' from London.

[36] R Rhodes, 'The Hollowing Out of the State: The Changing Nature of the Public Service in Britain' (1994) 65 *Pol Q* 138. See also M Majone, 'The Rise of the Regulatory State in Europe' (1994) 17 *West European Politics* 77. For subsequent enlargement of the theme, see N Bamforth and P Leyland (eds) *Public Law in a Multi-Layered Constitution* (Hart Publishing 2003).

[37] Case C-213/89 *R v Secretary of State for Transport, ex p. Factortame Ltd* [1990] ECR I-2433; *R v Secretary of State for Transport, ex p. Factortame Ltd (No 2)* [1991] AC 603 (HL).

early in the lecture. While MacCormick recognized that this development might be thought what Parliament had commanded in the European Communities Act 1972,[38] the affair clearly served to bring home the huge practical implications of United Kingdom membership; and the more so, in light of the Community's vibrant Single Market programme.[39] Maximizing the historical significance, these were still the days of the fall of the Berlin Wall and associated prospects for democracy in Central and Eastern Europe under the rubric of EU Enlargement.[40] Conversely however, the then travails of the Maastricht Treaty as demonstrated not only in a burst of British Euroscepticism[41] but also in seemingly widespread concerns about national sovereignty and 'democratic deficit' in the evolving European project,[42] cast a long shadow.

The argument was pitched in an attractive manner. RIP the Westphalian model: MacCormick was 'unwaveringly opposed to the road back [to] universal sovereign statehood' in the light of two world wars.[43] Equally, however, and at one with the belief in 'a diffusion of political power centres as well as of legal authorities', our lecturer did not wish 'to go forward to a situation in which there is a massively centralised European Community which takes over the dominant place in legal imagination'.[44] Presaging much in the literature of European governance,[45] MacCormick advocated a determinedly non-hierarchical and pluralist approach: a 'sideways move' to 'a world in which our normative existence and our practical life are anchored in, or related to, a variety of institutional systems', one perhaps hopefully dependent 'on a high degree of relatively willing co-operation'.[46] Nor was it surprising to hear MacCormick—a committed Scottish nationalist—emphasizing the need to 'create space for a real and serious debate about the demands of subsidiarity' in the European context.[47] Notwithstanding the potentially flattening

[38] *R v Secretary of State for Transport, ex p. Factortame Ltd* [1990] and *R v Secretary of State for Transport, ex p. Factortame Ltd (No 2)* [1991]. And see latterly, *Thoburn v Sunderland City Council* [2003] QB 151; and the European Union Act 2011.

[39] European Commission, 'Completing the Internal Market' (White Paper) COM (85) 310 final; Single European Act 1986.

[40] And see F Fukuyama, *The End of History and the Last Man* (Penguin 1992).

[41] R Rawlings, 'Legal Politics: The United Kingdom and Ratification of the Treaty on European Union: Part 1' (1994) *PL* 254: R Rawlings, 'Legal Politics: The United Kingdom and Ratification of the Treaty on European Union: Part 2' (1994) *PL* 367.

[42] Customarily associated with the 1992 Danish referendum; for a convenient overview see R Corbett, *The Treaty of Maastricht: From Conception to Ratification: A Comprehensive Reference Guide* (Longman 1993). 'Accountability' (or the lack of it) would subsequently feature prominently in the literature: C Harlow, *Accountability in the European Union* (OUP 2002).

[43] MacCormick (n 29) 17.

[44] MacCormick (n 29).

[45] For early illustration, see F Scharpf, 'Community and Autonomy: Multi-level Policy-making in the European Union' (1994) 1 *Journal of European Public Policy* 219. The distance subsequently travelled may be traced in N Krisch, *Beyond Constitutionalism: The Pluralist Structure of Postnational Law* (OUP 2010).

[46] MacCormick (n 29) 17. On the varying conceptions of pluralism in MacCormick's work, see N Krisch, 'Who is Afraid of Radical Pluralism? Legal Order and Political Stability in the Postnational Space' (2011) 24 *Ratio Juris* 386.

[47] MacCormick (n 29). Formally introduced by the Maastricht Treaty, the subsidiarity principle would quickly suffer a stunted growth: A Estella, *The EU Principle of Subsidiarity and its Critique* (OUP 2002).

effects on diversity, 'a common interpretative tradition [as] yielded by the now well-developed jurisprudence of human rights in Europe'[48] was another major thread in the rich tapestry woven here.

For those of us of a more cautious disposition, however, parts of the argument were troubling, even heretical. The hitherto strict conceptual canon of sovereignty[49] could not simply be wished away. One need not be dying in the ditch with Dicey to insist that State and sovereignty exist in a reciprocal relationship; on sovereignty as a juridical concept which symbolizes a unity of ordering; and that sovereignty and government should not be conflated.[50] Moreover, in actively seeking the interest of many in some re-configuration of sovereignty better to fit the age, MacCormick had laid it on thick, to the extent of proclaiming that 'no State in Western Europe any longer is a sovereign State'.[51]

Fast forwarding another twenty years, we arrive at the Institute of Advanced Legal Studies in London, the venue of the annual WG Hart Legal Worksop.[52] As heralded by MacCormick, there was by now a sense in much of the literature of the meaning of sovereignty being 'open to change across time and space'.[53] Against this backdrop, using the generous format of Hart Workshops to revisit the subject appeared opportune.[54] In accordance with established convention, the Workshop would consider both legal theoretical and practical implications. A play on his book *Questioning Sovereignty* (1999), the Workshop title *Sovereignty in Question* was chosen as a mark of respect to Sir Neil MacCormick, who died in 2009.[55]

The hosting of *Sovereignty in Question* in one of the world's two most global cities[56] was especially apt. If, according to an ever more colourful lexicon, sovereignty could be 'pooled', 'differentiated', 'diversified', 'fragmented', etc.,[57] where better to consider the causes and consequences or indeed the misconceptions? While the proceedings would naturally have a strong UK element, London is today a veritable crossroads of the legal world. This is so not just in terms of the gleamingly

[48] MacCormick (n 29) 18. For comparative analysis of the reception of the ECHR regime, see H Keller and A Stone Sweet (eds) *A Europe of Rights: The Impact of the ECHR on National Legal Systems* (OUP 2008). The proper role of an international human rights institution such as the European Court of Human Rights ('ECtHR') is discussed in this volume by David Feldman.

[49] As inaugurated by J Bodin, *The Six Books of a Commonweale* (R Knolles trans, first published 1576 and translated 1606, Harvard University Press 1962) Book 1, ch 10.

[50] M Loughlin, 'Ten Tenets of Sovereignty' in N Walker (ed) *Sovereignty in Transition* (Hart Publishing 2003). Martin Loughlin pursues the argument in Chapter 3 of this volume.

[51] MacCormick (n 29) 16.

[52] The two Harts should not be confused. WG Hart was an otherwise obscure benefactor of the University of London.

[53] J Bartelson, 'The Concept of Sovereignty Revisited' (2006) 17 *European Journal of International Law* 463. Leading illustrations are provided by Walker (n 50) and Kalmo and Skinner (n 4).

[54] The Workshop, which featured seven plenary sessions and fifteen panels, took place over three days in June 2011. The full programme is available at <http://events.sas.ac.uk/support-research/events/view/9235> (last accessed 18 April 2013).

[55] For MacCormick, see the Oxford Dictionary of National Biography entry by Neil Walker available at <http://www.oxforddnb.com/view/article/101976> (last accessed 18 April 2013).

[56] As measured in the Global Cities Index across the five dimensions of business activity, human capital, information exchange, cultural experience and political engagement. See <http://www.atkearney.com/documents/10192/dfedfc4c-8a62-4162-90e5-2a3f14f0da3a> (last accessed 18 April 2013).

[57] Martin Loughlin provides a fuller listing in Chapter 3 of this volume.

towered offices of the City of London, but of the historical legacy of empire as represented in 'the common law globe', of the twin regional rubrics of EU law and the ECHR, and of the United Kingdom's still major role on the broader international stage.[58] Londoners themselves were already counting down to the 2012 Olympic and Paralympic Games. Global reach and organization, all those national anthems: what better symbolic representation of countervailing trends in relation to sovereignty?

MacCormick's 1992 Chorley Lecture can now be seen as ahead of its time in certain respects. The process of economic globalization is further advanced,[59] with multiple effects on the capacities of government in nation-states. The related rise and rise of supranational regulation shows no sign of abating, not least under the auspices of another 1990s creation, the World Trade Organization ('WTO'), and is apt to take novel and controversial forms.[60] More particularly, in the wake of the introduction of a single currency and latter-day global financial crisis, a new wave of fiscal coordination now informs the Eurozone.[61] Meanwhile, the inter-connected age of information and communications technology has dawned, with the Internet promptly emerging as a chief global phenomenon with which, for better or worse, all States must cope.[62]

Conversely, by today's standards MacCormick's designedly broad canvas may be accounted unduly narrow: no longer Diceyan Anglo-centricity, but in its place Europe, Europe, Europe.[63] Though it would have fitted the general thrust, his Chorley Lecture did not engage with what a Judge of the International Court of Justice would promptly identify as the 'The Reformation in International Law':[64] a set of intellectual and practical developments marked by more generous, less State-centred, conceptualizations of the subject and by the explosive growth of international institutions. Nor indeed has this broad dynamic been played out: witness the happy view of the trajectory of the discipline towards strengthening the entire international community by protecting human security, the global environment, and human rights.[65] Alternatively, take MacCormick's concluding flourish that 'beyond the sovereign State is where we are now'.[66] Some testing outside a very special regional framework would surely have been appropriate. Reflecting and

[58] See, for further elaboration, R Rawlings, 'Modelling Judicial Review' (2008) 61 *Current Legal Problems* 95.

[59] Chapter 16 of this volume, by Peter Muchlinski, reflects this theme.

[60] A key departure point for Chapters 15 and 17 of this volume by Joanne Scott and Perry Keller respectively. See also, for a classic account, A-M Slaughter, *A New World Order* (Princeton University Press 2004).

[61] Damian Chalmers discusses the implications as regards sovereignty in Chapter 11 of this volume.

[62] The revolution in ICT is duly represented in Chapter 17 of this volume by Perry Keller.

[63] The subtitle to MacCormick's *Questioning Sovereignty* (n 31) serves to underscore the point: *Law, State and Nation in the European Commonwealth.*

[64] R Higgins, 'The Reformation in International Law' in R Rawlings (ed) *Law, Society, and Economy* (n 32) 207.

[65] U Fastenrath, R Geiger, D-E Khan, A Paulus, S von Schorlemer, and C Vedder (eds) *From Bilateralism to Community Interest: Essays in Honour of Judge Bruno Simma* (OUP 2011). See also J Cohen, *Globalization and Sovereignty: Rethinking Legality, Legitimacy and Constitutionalism* (CUP 2012).

[66] MacCormick (n 29) 18.

reinforcing global shifts of power, the so-called BRIC States—Brazil, Russia, India, and China—attest a different view.[67]

Sovereignty in Question had some particular prompts. On the domestic stage, the great wave of devolution to Scotland, Wales, and Northern Ireland at the turn of the century[68] had not served to stabilize the internal constitutional architecture of the 'Union State': quite the reverse.[69] The immediate prospect was a referendum on Scottish independence and hence some very practical issues pertaining to the meaning of 'sovereignty' and, more particularly, the exercise of 'popular sovereignty'.[70] Related in part to the Human Rights Act 1998, the continued advance of judicial review in the domestic courts also commanded attention. After all, senior judges had recently ventured the possibility of a head-on clash with parliamentary sovereignty under the attractive banner of the rule of law: a putative move beyond the thinner use of interpretative principle to direct constitutional review of statute[71] at common law.[72]

Then there was the enticing prospect of revisiting some of MacCormick's assumptions against the backdrop of the huge developments in the EU: from the practical realities of enlargement into Central and Eastern Europe to the ongoing crisis in the Eurozone, via the failure of a 'Constitutional Treaty' and eventual adoption of its close cousin the Lisbon Treaty.[73] In particular, 'Beyond the Sovereign State' needed reconsideration in the light of a substantial and difficult jurisprudence in the national courts on the limits to EU competence.[74] An added twist was provided by domestic legislation for a mass of so-called 'referendum locks' on further transfers of power to Brussels: the paradoxical invocation of popular sovereignty in defence of the practical exercise of parliamentary sovereignty.[75]

[67] For discussion, see C Roberts (ed) *Challengers or Stakeholders? BRICs and the Liberal World Order* (2010) 42 *Polity* (Special Issue) 1–129.

[68] R Hazell and R Rawlings (eds) *Devolution, Law Making and the Constitution* (Imprint Academic 2005). See further V Bogdanor, *The New British Constitution* (Hart Publishing 2009).

[69] A point underscored by P Leyland, 'The Multifaceted Constitutional Dynamics of UK Devolution' (2011) 9 *International Journal of Constitutional Law* 251.

[70] S Tierney, *Constitutional Referendums: A Theory and Practice of Republican Deliberation* (OUP 2012). See also Chapter 9 of this volume by Peter Leyland.

[71] See respectively, *R v Secretary of State for the Home Department, ex p. Simms* [2000] 2 AC 115 (HL), and the speeches of Lords Steyn and Hope and Lady Hale in *R (Jackson) v Attorney General* [2005] UKHL 56. Lord Hope revisits the matter in Chapter 6 of this volume, including by reference to *AXA General Insurance v Lord Advocate* [2011] UKSC 46.

[72] Much has been heard in this context of so-called 'common law constitutionalism': for the advanced version, see TRS Allan, *Constitutional Justice: A Liberal Theory of the Rule of Law* (OUP 2001).

[73] J-C Piris, *The Constitution for Europe: A Legal Analysis* (CUP 2006); J-C Piris, *The Lisbon Treaty: A Legal and Political Analysis* (CUP 2010).

[74] Generated especially in Germany in cases such as *Brunner v European Union Treaty* (1994) 1 CMLR 57 and, latterly, as Damian Chalmers relates in Chapter 11 of this volume, in a growing number of countries. For MacCormick's critical response to *Brunner*, see N MacCormick, 'The Maastrict-Urteil: Sovereignty Now' (1995) 1 *European Law Journal* 259.

[75] See now the European Union Act 2011. While the editors could not claim to have anticipated an 'in/out' referendum on EU membership, the British Prime Minister's recent suggestion of one underwrites the point; see <http://www.number10.gov.uk/news/eu-speech-at-bloomberg> (last accessed 18 April 2013). The general theme is pursued by Paul Craig in Chapter 10 of this volume.

Adopting the standpoint of the international lawyer, we were naturally of the opinion that 'reports of the death of sovereignty are much exaggerated'.[76] After all, transiting within living memory from vast tracks of 'imperial sovereignty'[77] to today's cast of nearly 200 'sovereigns' on the UN stage is no mean historical fact. Our discussion would, however, focus on the challenges presented to classical international law understandings of sovereignty in the twin contexts of the rise of global industry and the vertical dimension to the spread of law through supranational or transnational adjudicative and regulatory frameworks and networks.[78] One special prompt was the burgeoning interest in constitutional and judicial 'dialogues' in many countries[79] and across jurisdictions;[80] indeed, this would prove a notably popular item in the call for papers.[81] Countervailing concerns associated with sovereignty as a legal value commanded further attention, it being increasingly observed that, while power is 'billeted' and powers are 'bounded' in the modern sovereign State, in global space the hard-won controls of democratic government and public law are the more notable by their absence.[82]

As the discussion at the Workshop confirmed, the interplay of the twin elements of continuity and change provides a convenient angle of approach to the subject. In particular, the proceedings highlighted, first, sovereignty's enduring role as a central concept in legal thought and constitutional discourse, and, second, a common sense of unease about (how to deal with) it.[83] In the second decade of the twenty-first century a suitably telling juxtaposition lay close to hand: on the one hand, a great outpouring of academic writings on sovereignty in the last few years, fuelled in large measure by post-national views of State sovereignty as obfuscating and even distorting; and, on the other hand, the practical reality of multitudinous demands by peoples in different parts of the world who aspire to (something called) sovereignty.[84] On from Dicey's peculiarly English doctrine, and on from MacCormick's

[76] J Crawford, 'Sovereignty as a Legal Value' in J Crawford and M Koskenniemi, *The Cambridge Companion to International Law* (CUP 2012). See too Chapter 14 of this volume by Sir Christopher Greenwood.

[77] Broadly defined by R Jackson, 'Sovereignty in World Politics: A Glance at the Conceptual and Historical Landscape' (1999) 67 *Political Studies* 431, 441, as the exercise of supreme authority over 'somebody else's homeland'.

[78] Epitomized in so-called 'global administrative law'; for this perspective, see B Kingsbury, N Krisch, and R Stewart, 'The Emergence of Global Administrative Law' (2005) 68 *Law and Contemporary Problems* 15.

[79] As heralded in the Canadian context by P Hogg and A Bushell, 'The Charter Dialogue between Courts and Legislators (Or Perhaps the Charter of Rights Isn't a Bad Thing after All)' (1997) 35 *Osgoode Hall Law Journal* 75. For a British view, see AL Young, *Parliamentary Sovereignty and the Human Rights Act* (Hart Publishing 2009).

[80] As earlier observed by A-M Slaughter, 'Judicial Globalization' (2000) 40 *Virginia Journal of International Law* 1103.

[81] A dimension represented in Chapter 13 of this volume by Margit Cohn.

[82] See, eg, P Cerny, 'Globalization and the Erosion of Democracy' (1999) 36 *European Journal of Political Research* 1 and C Harlow, 'Global Administrative Law: The Quest for Principles and Values' (2006) 17 *European Journal of International Law* 187.

[83] An increasingly familiar departure point in writings on European integration: N Walker 'Late Sovereignty in the European Union' in Walker (n 50).

[84] See further in this regard, O Dahbour, *Self-Determination without Nationalism: A Theory of Postnational Sovereignty* (Temple University Press 2013).

brave European vision: the conditions were ripe for some careful reassessment of sovereignty and the law.

In devising the Workshop programme, we also wished to avoid 'the twentieth century gap between the discourses of internal and external' sovereignty.[85] This was not to reject the distinction, but rather to explore the points of contact or correlations and mutual complications. As reflected in the title of this resulting volume, the aim was to approach sovereignty in a non-compartmentalized way, so viewing it as neither a purely domestic/internal concept nor a wholly international/external one. The idea of London as a legal crossroads played well here, effectively enabling a suitably broad range of national, European, and international experience to be brought to bear. The approach, with its evident synergies, was one we thought particularly appropriate for our inter-connected age.

Self-evidently no conference and certainly no book could encompass the entirety of the contemporary debates on sovereignty. Better to structure our discussions in terms of continuity and change in an inter-connected (legal) world, the call for papers asked for contributions on five key themes. Naturally the first one was the evolution (or otherwise) of the concept and conceptions of sovereignty. The way in which traditional views of sovereignty continue to be called into question by the evolving nature of State forms provided the starting point. In the event, a rubric that encompassed the purpose and role of sovereignty engendered a set of lively debates, which extended to the design (or otherwise) of the process of constitutional change[86] and to radical attempts at 'decentring' sovereignty in mainstream legal discourse.[87] Reflecting the more prominent role of the courts in so many jurisdictions today, 'the judicial challenge' was the second main theme. The formula was carefully chosen to encompass both challenges by the courts to pre-conceived notions of legislative sovereignty, most obviously in the domestic context with the Diceyan inheritance, and challenges for the courts in navigating multiple sovereignties, for example at the regional level in respect of human rights.

So-called 'bottom-up' challenges to sovereignty were contained in the third main theme of 'plurinational democracies and jurisdiction'.[88] This reflected the powerful pull of ideas about identity or imagined community, not least in an age of globalization.[89] Predictably perhaps, in the light of (impending) events, the discussion remained largely focused on a certain Atlantic archipelago, and more especially on Scotland and Northern Ireland. As a law-based vehicle for expressions of popular sovereignty, the constitutional device of the referendum featured prominently here. Highlighting the sense in which the various themes overlapped, the fourth

[85] R Prokhovnik, 'Internal/External: The State of Sovereignty' (1996) 2 *Contemporary Politics* 7, 9.

[86] See Chapter 7 of this volume by Richard Kay.

[87] A strand in the proceedings epitomized in Chapter 8 of this volume by John Morison.

[88] See the pioneering work of J Tully, *Strange Multiplicity, Constitutionalism in an Age of Diversity* (CUP 1995); and, for a comparative overview, F Requejo and M Badia (eds) *Federalism, Plurinationality and Democratic Constitutionalism: Theory and Cases* (Routledge 2011).

[89] For the link with the construction of territorial societies, see M Keating, *Plurinational Democracy. Stateless Nations in a Post-Sovereignty Era* (OUP 2001) and S Tierney, 'Reframing Sovereignty? Sub-State National Societies and Contemporary Challenges to the Nation-State' (2005) 54 *ICLQ* 161.

one of 'sovereignty and European integration' straddled developments in both the politico-legislative and the judicial spheres. As against the spectre of a new legal order with the potential further to transcend traditional views of sovereignty and the sovereign State, the distinctive United Kingdom experience would be both centre-stage at the Workshop, and one part of a broader narrative concerning the relationship for example between conceptions of sovereignty and conceptions of legal and constitutional pluralism.[90]

The fifth theme, 'sovereignty and the international order', followed on naturally. Inside this expansive rubric our proceedings focused on two key elements. On the one hand, the question of the relationship between the work of international or regional courts and the internal as well as the external aspect of sovereignty linked back to the theme of 'the judicial challenge'. On the other hand, and in part engaging with MacCormick's pioneering contribution, the place and role of legal conceptions of 'sovereignty' fell to be re-examined in the light of cutting-edge corporate, regulatory, and technological developments happening on a global scale.

As will be explained in more detail, the five main themes of the Hart Workshop 2011 are all well-represented in this book.[91] The general scheme of the chapters, which is one of theoretical overviews followed by successive clusters of chapters with State and substate, European and international perspectives, also reflects the Workshop design. It helps to illuminate the interplay of the twin elements of continuity and change and, in particular, the interconnections between the different levels in terms of the internal and external aspects of sovereignty.

B. Domestic, European, and International Perspectives

Chapters 2 and 3 go to the heart of the conceptual debate by examining whether sovereignty is in transition, has been revised, or has remained the same. Given the provenance of the book in the Hart Workshop 2011, it is surely appropriate that the first one is by Neil MacCormick's successor-in-title at the University of Edinburgh, Neil Walker. With a view to clearing up much of the confusion and controversy about the meaning and utility of the concept of sovereignty, Walker sets about elaborating the distinction between sovereignty as 'framing' (a conceptual device for making sense of the modern legal and political world) and—reflecting the invocation of the label by a wide range of different actors seeking or asserting power and authority within, or among, States—sovereignty as 'claiming'. Against the backdrop of what he sees as 'the stability of the former' and 'the fluidity of the latter' during the ascendancy of the modern State, Walker plays up the challenging effects of the contemporary wave of globalization and, with particular

[90] As illustrated by Krisch (n 45) and N Walker, J Shaw, and S Tierney (eds) *Europe's Constitutional Mosaic* (Hart Publishing 2011).

[91] Chapter 16 of this volume by Peter Muchlinski was specially commissioned by the editors. Other chapters have been revised and on occasion reconstituted in the light of subsequent developments.

reference to the United Kingdom, the now 'evolving state' of both sovereignty framing and claiming. The bottom line of Chapter 2, however, is the great difficulty of discarding such a foundational concept and the fertile tendencies for new claims to sovereignty. Set in these terms, earlier notions of 'post-sovereignty'[92] appear overly simple, even somewhat old-fashioned.

Martin Loughlin is likewise concerned to discipline discussions of sovereignty, but in a more austere fashion. His determinedly State-centred view serves as an important counterpoint to some highly flexible views of sovereignty in an age of globalization theory and practice. Believing that the concept of sovereignty 'is today much misunderstood', Loughlin underwrites the correlation between the internal aspect of supreme law-making authority within the territory, and the external aspect of autonomous and equal entity on the international plane. His task, as Loughlin freely admits, is a daunting one in view of the great weight of literature in recent times devoted to sovereignty as a contested concept. His advantage is that, being firmly rooted in the great historical experience of modernity, the approach is in its own terms coherent and viable. Sovereignty, as we are elsewhere reminded, reflects and reinforces the existence of territorial communities to which 'government should be (and sometimes is) accountable'.[93]

Chapter 4 by Jeffrey Goldsworthy is the first in a cluster of chapters building on recent domestic debates about the distinctive constitutional tradition of parliamentary sovereignty. Goldsworthy's chapter considers ways of reforming the United Kingdom's uncodified constitution so as to control or limit Parliament's law-making authority. As the leading historian of the doctrine,[94] Goldsworthy is naturally interested to explore approaches which go with the grain of (official) consensus about Parliament's continuing sovereign power. These include comparatively mild requirements as to the procedure and form of legislative enactment: requirements for example of express amendment, repeal or override that are consistent with Parliament retaining full substantive power to change the law. Turning to more radical approaches, not least a self-entrenched referendum requirement protecting a written constitution, Goldsworthy stresses the importance of consensual change founded on the expressed will of the people: in practical terms, the referendum requirement legitimated by the approval of the electorate in a referendum.

Alison L Young adopts a different angle of approach. She considers the normative justification for the view of 'continuing parliamentary legislative supremacy' that Parliament should have legally unlimited law-making power but should not be able to bind its successors on substantive matters, nor (despite those good old Commonwealth authorities) via 'manner and form', nor (contrary to Goldsworthy's view) as to the procedures through which legislation is made. Chapter 5, therefore, looks at the extent to which sovereignty entails the ability to determine the sphere

[92] Even in its moderated version: N MacCormick, 'Sovereignty and After' in Kalmo and Skinner (n 4).

[93] Crawford (n 76) 132.

[94] J Goldsworthy, *The Sovereignty of Parliament: History and Philosophy* (Clarendon Press 1999); J Goldsworthy, *Parliamentary Sovereignty, Contemporary Debates* (CUP 2010).

of one's own competences. The author here invokes the increasingly fashionable idea in the domestic debates of 'bipolar sovereignty':[95] Parliament and judiciary as sharers in the uncodified UK Constitution. In Young's view, empowering Parliament to bind its successors could upset what is a delicate balance of powers.

In an essay that will surely attract considerable attention, Lord Hope of Craighead, the first Deputy President of the United Kingdom Supreme Court, tackles 'the judicial challenge' head on. While he finds little reason to doubt the positive aspect of Dicey's famous doctrine, Lord Hope thus questions the negative aspect (of no competing authority), suggesting that, especially from the Scottish viewpoint, the relationship between Westminster and the domestic courts is less clear. In so taking issue with certain other leading judges, Lord Hope emphasizes the need for a constitutional long-stop in the Westminster model of parliamentary government: the courts as the ultimate guardians of the rule of law. To mix the metaphors, this is the realm of the nuclear option. Lord Hope wants the Executive to understand that the absence of a general strike down power does not rule out the fashioning of a legal remedy should that constitutional long-stop ever be legislatively threatened.

In Chapter 7, Richard Kay introduces a valuable comparative element. His interest is the process by which, in his view, the traditional doctrine of parliamentary sovereignty is being transformed. The metaphor is that of 'the blind sovereign', wherein the basic constitutional format is not consciously designed but rather is revealed over time in the famously British pragmatic fashion of ad hoc and piecemeal development. Rightly concerned not to over-egg the pudding, Kay qualifies the evident contrast with the classic comparative form of wholesale and deliberated constitutional revision by reference to the often messy forms of supplementary development—interpretation—in a codified constitution like that of the United States. Equally, however, the chapter may be thought to ground the case for a UK-wide constitutional convention: dare one say it, 'a sovereign with spectacles'. It may just possibly herald one.[96]

Turning to developments at the substate level, it would be strange indeed if Scotland and Northern Ireland did not feature in this volume given the contemporary history. Following in the footsteps of Michel Foucault,[97] and engaging with the theme of plurinational democracies in terms of the transition in Northern Ireland, John Morison attempts the radical agenda of developing a governmentality approach that relegates sovereignty and the State from a central position in public law. This is the stuff both of broad perspective—for Morison a move beyond the myopia of hierarchies and supremacy—and of careful examination of the many micro-developments in the workings of power in constitutional spaces beneath the formal architecture of the Belfast Agreement.[98] Ranging through policing, justice,

[95] See, eg, C Knight, 'Bi-polar Sovereignty Restated' (2009) *CLJ* 361.

[96] See House of Commons Political and Constitutional Reform Committee, 'Do We Need a Constitutional Convention for the UK?' (HC Paper (2012–13) no 371).

[97] M Foucault, 'Governmentality' in G Burchell, C Gordon, and P Miller (eds) *The Foucault Effect: Studies in Governmentality* (Harvester Wheatsheaf 1991).

[98] *The Belfast Agreement: An Agreement Reached at the Multi-Party Talks on Northern Ireland* (Cm 3883, 1998).

and security to issues of identity and culture, and on into rights, equality, and good relations, the piece attests the sheer vibrancy of the 'technologies of governance' happening under the broad banner of 'the peace process'. In typically bold fashion, Morison concludes by referring us back to Neil MacCormick and suggesting that ideas of 'non-sovereignty' elaborated in relation to the European legal order could usefully inform our understanding of the continuing devolution process in the United Kingdom.

The account by Peter Leyland of 'Referendums, Popular Sovereignty, and the Territorial Constitution' in Chapter 9 adopts the impending vote on Scottish independence as a starting point. Leyland is concerned, however, to place the role of referendums as an instrument of popular sovereignty in a broader constitutional perspective, historically with reference both to Ireland and to 'home rule' or devolution, and latterly in relation to England and local government. While recognizing that referendums have a part to play in determining important constitutional matters, the author highlights the dangers for the wider democratic process from their growing use. A sense of the intricate balance between, on the one hand, contemporary demands to exercise popular sovereignty and, on the other hand, a need to discipline the practice in the name of good governance values of fairness and propriety, infuses the chapter. To combat the potential for abuse, Leyland envisions a dedicated set of rules to determine when constitutional referendums can be held.

The referendum technique also looms large in Chapter 10 by Paul Craig, which neatly combines the domestic and European perspectives. His focus is the United Kingdom's notably equivocal relationship with the EU—which the author sees as becoming more troubled in recent years—and the conception of sovereignty that shapes, and is shaped by, it. The chapter thus discusses a series of contemporary initiatives designed to reassert the central role of the (Member) State against the backdrop of a still rapidly evolving supranational regime: the 'summoning of the people' through referendum requirements that place very real limits on the giving of new powers to the EU; a quest for repatriated powers in the classically core field of State activity that is criminal justice; and—of course—the prospect of an in/out referendum now conjured by Prime Minister David Cameron. The particular value of the piece lies in Craig's engagement with (British) Euroscepticism, a species of ideas of which much is heard and rather less is explained. The analysis also connects with the earlier set of chapters on parliamentary sovereignty, the continuing nature of which is, in Craig's words, 'the blessing and curse for those minded to repatriate power'.

Craig's 'pair' on the theme of sovereignty and European integration is Damian Chalmers, who contributes a wide-ranging comparative study grounded in a host of high level judicial decisions. Chalmers discusses three competing models or 'restatements' of sovereignty that embrace the idea of EU law as a government order. Protective in nature, the first model sees sovereignty as encompassing a series of public and collective activities which help make up a domestic human order that transcends and constrains (EU) government. The second one sees sovereignty as 'ordaining' EU law, so granting it authority while maintaining a requirement for democratic quality including respect for human rights. In contrast, in the third model, which Chalmers sees being underwritten in official responses to the Eurozone crisis, sovereignty is adopted by the Union machinery as a legitimation strategy, with its claim to involve sovereigns (parliaments or peoples) grounding a largely unfettered power of rule to realize its own governmental objectives. Far from the optimism of MacCormick's European vision twenty years ago, Chalmers sees this development as reaching into 'a darker tradition' of sovereignty associated with Carl Schmitt.[99]

Chapter 12 by David Feldman takes us firmly into the realm of human rights, that great talisman of the vertical spread of law in the post-Second World War period, and more particularly to the role and workings of the European Court of Human Rights ('ECtHR'). The piece should be of broad comparative interest since it eschews the many accounts of domestic constitutional machinery for controlling the impact of international law to examine what the author identifies as the 'reverse process' whereby international courts and tribunals take into account the practical realities of State, constitutional, and legislative sovereignties. Illuminating the matter with some major examples of tension between national authorities and the Strasbourg Court, Feldman suggests that there can be good reasons of prudence and principle for European and international judges to cogitate before extending the scope of States' obligations. Perhaps, hopefully, allowing 'morally sound' and 'socially persuasive' concerns of national governments into the equation 'could enhance the effectiveness and perceived legitimacy of an international institution's decisions and judgments'.

Chapter 13 by Margit Cohn is a most contemporary variation on the theme of the judicial challenge. The author conducts us on an international and comparative tour of constitutional or democratic 'dialogue', showing how this fashionable discourse is commonly part of a normative effort at blunting concerns about judicial supremacy in the light of judicial review of legislation. Viewed in this way, it links with a conception of domestic sovereignty that revolves around similar questions of power-allocation. In adopting a distinction between classical-hierarchical and political versions of sovereignty, Cohn further highlights two distinct kinds of structural arrangement for 'dialogue': 'formal' mechanisms such as override clauses, and 'implied' forms as in network analyses of decision-making in both the legal and political spheres. The golden thread of the argument is the subtly different ways in which the hierarchical vision of sovereignty is challenged according to the particular form of 'dialogue' that is in play.

Who better to explore the theme of 'sovereignty and the international order' than a Judge of the International Court of Justice? From his viewpoint on the Bench, sovereignty in Sir Christopher Greenwood's words is 'neither totem nor torment but an inescapable fact of life'. Recalling the distinction between sovereignty in the internal and international senses of power and authority within and between States, Sir Christopher explains how the relationship has become ever more complicated.

[99] C Schmitt, *Political Theology: Four Chapters on the Concept of Sovereignty* (G Schwab trans, University of Chicago Press 2005).

To this effect, Chapter 14 engages with some classic case law on the effects, or otherwise, of State sovereignty on substance and jurisdiction in international law; highlights the mirror image developments of increasing international law obligations regarding States' behaviour within their own territories, and of States increasingly seeking to apply their law to extra-territorial activities; and points up the phenomenon of international law being drawn into debates over the allocation of power within States. The piece epitomizes the broader interest at the Hart Workshop in continuity and change and, just as with David Feldman's chapter in relation to international courts, in pursuing a non-compartmentalized approach.

The door is opened to a final trio of chapters expounding an international perspective. From the standpoint of the collection, these constitute representative case studies: each one engages with contemporary developments associated with global industry while presenting different takes on the implications for sovereignty and the law. Squarely focused on what may be termed 'legal geography', Chapter 15 by Joanne Scott pursues the issue of international jurisdictional reach. The focus is so-called 'territorial extension', a growing phenomenon which itself presents a challenge to the classical concept of (the) territorial sovereignty (of States). Using the example of EU regulation of the aviation industry, she thus demonstrates the potential for powerful States and/or regional groupings to invoke a (perhaps fleeting) territorial connection so as to shape conduct and circumstances abroad by extending a regulatory perimeter. This, for Scott, is nothing less than 'a source of global power'. Further, however, she argues that an understanding of sovereignty conceived as territorial supremacy without the possibility for territorial extension 'would be ill-suited to our profoundly inter-connected world'. The chapter is a pioneering one: Scott aims to begin the process of specifying the criteria for contextual evaluations of the practice.

In Chapter 16, Peter Muchlinski recalls MacCormick's pluralistic approach for the purpose of examining the relationship between State sovereignty and the facilitation of good corporate activity. In engaging with the role of transnational corporate power, Muchlinski thus seeks to move away from contractarian ideas of sovereignty, based on traditional State institutions, with a view to limiting the legitimation of elite power. Broadening the canvas, this chapter examines the trade-off between non-market goals and market-facilitating ones in the contemporary debate surrounding multinational enterprises and State sovereignty. The author argues that as legally conferred economic liberties create increasing disparities in wealth, so equal respect for individuals and their human rights may be limited. The chapter ends, however, on a more positive note. Invoking ideas of subsidiarity developed in part by MacCormick, Muchlinski considers that newer forms of cooperative action between firms, communities, and civil society present a more hopeful avenue for reconciling corporate power and public interests.

Perry Keller rounds off the volume by tackling the thorny subject of 'Sovereignty and Liberty in the Internet Era'. The departure point is the fracturing by the global revolution in ICT of the historic relationship between the media and the State that was first framed by the territorial authority of sovereigns and later found new legitimacy in terms of popular sovereignty with the rise of the modern liberal democratic State.[100] Keller, however, takes issue with the view of supranational constitutionalism as the answer to the waning of State power and authority in this field, contending that there is no core understanding of freedom of expression sufficiently 'thin' to be universally shared and sufficiently 'thick' to determine when and how States ought to limit harmful or offensive expression. The argument is effectively grounded in a broad-ranging comparative analysis: from the US Supreme Court to the ECtHR, and on through the UN Human Rights Committee to the increased potential involvement of the WTO. Undaunted, Keller sets about demonstrating the primary importance of community and locality in finding solutions to the challenges of public expression, and hence the continuing vitality of bonded territorial and popular sovereignty in delivering freedom of speech.

C. Conclusion

Enough has been said to show the thinking behind, and the richness of, this sample of contemporary essays on sovereignty. Twenty years more and perhaps the collection will itself serve as a useful historical benchmark. After all, the essays have been written at a time of very great testing of the institutional frameworks at every level: domestic, European, international, or global. So far have we since travelled, not just from the oh-so-English Oxford of the early 1970s, but also from those heady days of MacCormick's intervention at LSE towards the end of the last century.

Sovereignty and the Law serves on the domestic front to illuminate an evermore contested constitutional doctrine and settlement. For which read parliamentary sovereignty: as yet unbowed, but bloodied and perhaps somewhat battle-weary. Territorial relations will surely feature prominently here in the next period, whatever the result of the referendum on Scottish independence. Looking more broadly, easy assumptions about the withering of (State) sovereignty in the light of EU integration and globalization do not find favour in this volume, and in my view rightly so. A more subtle set of understandings is on show reflecting, at one and the same time, the enduring strength of a foundational concept, the continuing widespread appeal of an idea, and the myriad contemporary dynamics epitomized in the vertical dimension to the spread of law. In the realm of sovereignty, the capacities for regeneration, reinvention, and restatement are not to be gainsaid.

[100] See further, P Keller, *European and International Media Law* (OUP 2011).

2

Sovereignty Frames and Sovereignty Claims

*Neil Walker**

A. Introduction

Why are we constantly 'questioning sovereignty'?[1] Why are we inclined to accuse sovereignty of 'hypocrisy'[2] or to reduce it to a 'game'?[3] Why are we concerned to 'relocate'[4] sovereignty or to search for its 'fragments'?[5] Why do we consider sovereignty to be 'in transition',[6] perhaps even in 'in crisis'?[7] Why do we feel ourselves in such danger of losing focus on sovereignty that we must strive, as in the present volume, to keep it 'in perspective'? Frankly, if sovereignty is such trouble and if sovereignty is *in* such trouble—so incoherent, so illusory, so recondite, so degraded, so superannuated, so dispersed and diffuse—then why bother with it?

The reason, I believe, is actually quite straightforward, though its detailed explanation quickly becomes quite complicated. Sovereignty has long held a dual significance in legal thought. It has been part of the deep and often taken-for-granted conceptual structure through which law is authorized and organized *as* law and in terms of which we are able to conceive of legal order in general. Yet it has also been the label invoked by, attributed to, or claimed on behalf of, a wide range of different actors, entities, and mechanisms associated with the legal and political architecture of the State and of inter-State relations. That is to say, sovereignty has inhabited both the silent (and relatively still) depths and the vocal (and relatively volatile) surfaces of legal thought. It has supplied a stable *frame* through which the legal world as a whole is apprehended and shaped as well as the discursive form of

* Regius Professor of Public Law and the Law of Nature and Nations, University of Edinburgh.

[1] N MacCormick, *Questioning Sovereignty* (OUP 1999).

[2] S Krasner, *Sovereignty: Organized Hypocrisy* (Stanford University Press 1999).

[3] R Adler-Nissen and T Gammeltoft-Hansen (eds), *Sovereignty Games: Instrumentalizing State Sovereignty in Europe and Beyond* (Palgrave 2008).

[4] N Walker (ed) *Relocating Sovereignty* (Dartmouth 2006).

[5] H Kalmo and Q Skinner (eds) *Sovereignty in Fragments: The Past, Present and Future of a Contested Concept* (CUP 2010).

[6] N Walker (ed), *Sovereignty in Transition* (Hart Publishing 2003)

[7] J Fischer, 'Europe's Sovereignty Crisis', *Social Europe Journal*, 2 August 2011, available at <http://www.social-europe.eu/2011/08/europes-sovereignty-crisis> (last accessed 19 April 2013).

a *claim* variously, and sometimes speculatively or contentiously, made in respect of a State, a federal province, a nation, a people, a supra-State, a constitution, a constitutive rule or rule-set, a governmental complex, or a specific institution of government or governance.[8]

Sovereignty, therefore, has always been a concept as fundamental as it is contentious, as difficult to give up as it is to pin down. Today, however, there is something of a shift in both registers of sovereignty—in sovereignty as frame as well as sovereignty as claim. In each case this shift is associated with the gradual decentring of the State within the global matrix of legal and political authority. On the one hand, as the basic idea of sovereignty has been closely bound up with the form of the modern State, it is unsurprising that the challenge posed by the forces of globalization to the dominant centrality of the modern State form has also led to greater questioning of sovereignty even at the level of deep structure. On the other hand, the more diverse and densely interconnected institutional and regulatory architecture of a less State-centred world also challenges our understanding—already less settled and more fragile at this level—of where and how, if at all, specific sovereignty claims may be persuasively articulated and vindicated.

Sovereignty as frame and sovereignty as claim alike, therefore, occupy a more precarious position today than they did in the period of high political modernity ushered in by the late eighteenth-century constitutional settlements in the United States and France. But it is hardly a more marginal position, for the very factors that challenge the centrality or appropriateness of the sovereignty paradigm also provide the occasion for its re-emphasis. If sovereignty is one of the very building blocks of modern legal thought and organization, then it cannot lightly be discarded; its vulnerability, therefore, is as likely to provoke efforts towards its reassertion or refinement as towards its abandonment. Equally, the increasing fluidity and interconnectedness of governmental relations, which challenges particular claims to sovereignty and complicates their assessment, also provides a fertile field for new claims to sovereignty or the refinement of old claims. The very factors that make sovereignty an increasingly troubled and troubling concept, in other words, also serve to intensify efforts and to extend opportunities to resort to it.

In what follows, I begin by providing a basic account of the difference between sovereignty as framing and sovereignty as claiming, setting out how, during the ascendancy of the modern State, the stability of the former has contrasted with the fluidity of the latter. I continue by analysing why, and how, this has changed in the contemporary wave of globalization. I conclude with some brief remarks about the distinctive ways in which the evolving State of sovereignty framing and claiming plays out in the specific context of the United Kingdom and of its external and internal legal and constitutional relations today. How do 'sovereignty as frame' and 'sovereignty as claim' continue to structure the British Constitution, for better or for worse?

[8] See, eg, R Jackson, 'Sovereignty in World Politics: A Glance at the Conceptual and Historical Landscape' (1999) 67 *Political Studies* 431.

B. The Sovereignty Frame

Our modern notion of sovereignty derives from the medieval figure of the sovereign—the ruler who holds absolute authority over his subjects and who is under no legal obligation to any higher power.[9] The figure of the sovereign already involved a process of abstraction—the King possessing a 'politic body or capacity' in addition to his 'natural body'.[10] Gradually, as the early modern sovereign sought or acquired more extensive and more intensive resources and responsibilities of government, the abstract quality of the office became more pronounced. Both the ruler and the ruled became more formalized and detached categories. Sovereignty came to acquire its mature sense, referring to the existence of a singular ruling power, however institutionalized and internally differentiated, in which inheres final and absolute authority over the political community as a whole. Sovereignty thus understood as an ideal of indivisible but impersonal authority, as developed by early modern thinkers such as Grotius, Bodin, and Hobbes, resolved two key problems that had confounded medieval political theory. Authority no longer needed to be concentrated in the hands of the one, or the few, in order to be considered a unity. Equally, its separation from a particular personage or personal office allowed for its continuity over space and time.[11]

The development of this more encompassing conception of sovereignty also begins to account for sovereignty's Janus-faced quality in the modern order—its simultaneous reference to the internal relations of the State polity and to its external relations. Let us recall that, as distinct from the overlapping and interlocking pattern of influence among dynastically sovereign, imperial, clerical, feudal, and other forms that were characteristic of medieval authority, modern sovereignty denotes the finality, comprehensive remit, and indivisibility of the ruling power within a territory. It follows that modern sovereignty's interior and exterior dimensions become closely mutually conditioned and enabled. For the monopolistic authority of a State within its territory to be achieved and maintained, recognition from other polities and their commitment to non-interference was necessary. Equally, for States to exercise their external sovereignty as actors capable of entering into international legal commitments, the indivisibility and finality of their internal authority was required.[12]

How might we summarize the significance of this profound shift from pre-modern to modern understandings of sovereign authority? In general terms, we may consider the deep structure of the emergent sovereignty frame along

[9] See, eg, M Loughlin, *Foundations of Public Law* (OUP 2010) ch 7.

[10] *Calvin's Case* (1608) 7 Co Rep 1 10a; 77 ER 378 (Coke CJ).

[11] See, eg, J Bertelson, 'On the Indivisibility of Sovereignty' [2011] 2 *Republics of Letters: A Journal for the Study of Knowledge, Politics and the Arts* 2, available at <http://arcade.stanford.edu/journals/rofl/articles/on-indivisibility-sovereignty-by-jens-bartelson> (last accessed 19 April 2013).

[12] On the self-conscious linkage of internal and external sovereignty in the making of the United States, see D Armitage, *The Declaration of Independence: A Global History* (Harvard University Press 2007).

two dimensions.[13] In the first place, and most fundamentally, there is an *epistemic* shift. Sovereignty in its mature form consists of a new 'social imaginary'[14]—a novel way of knowing and ordering the world that 'silently frames the conduct of much of modern politics'.[15] Sovereignty's mature frame is first and foremost a presuppositional frame that shapes perception, understanding and, in turn, practical reason. It involves the constructive assumption of an ultimately authoritative 'unity (out) of a manifold'.[16] It is a representational and ordering device which envisages and identifies discrete polities that can act in the name of an undifferentiated collective notwithstanding an internal diversity of interests, values, and wills. Importantly, as Martin Loughlin has argued,[17] in this deep framing sense sovereignty is conceptually prior both to positive law, including constitutional law, and to the governmental and wider political system, and does not necessarily privilege either. Like politics, law, or at least the domain of public law,[18] is predicated upon sovereignty. The security of law's commitments, its construction of a bounded order, its durability, and its expansive capacity for reflexive self-reproduction are all dependent on the axiomatic frame of sovereign power.

Secondly, the mature age of sovereignty also involves a *systemic* shift. International relations theorists tend to talk in the language of 'system'—as in the 'system of States' or the 'Westphalian system'.[19] The template of mature sovereignty, with its symbiotically related internal and external aspects, presupposes and requires a general type rather than a unique instance. It imagines a world of sovereign States, mutually recognizing, mutually supportive, and mutually exclusive in their claims to the plenitude of internal authority. That is to say, mature sovereignty can only be understood in a systemic context, sustained through a path-dependent and self-reproductive cycle of formally identical polities operating according to certain uniform norms of engagement.

Of course, the 'real world' is much different from this idealized world of international law and relations, and always has been. The sovereign system in the high modern age was a partial and precarious accomplishment, denied to many conquered or aspiring peoples in the name of empire or the self-interest of the already self-chosen, and more generally vulnerable to State aggression in a global system then, as now, lacking any central monopoly of legitimate violence. Yet, the systemic dimension obtained sufficient purchase—enough of a 'framing effect'—to provide a powerful and sustained logic of reproduction in global political relations.

[13] See N Walker, 'The Variety of Sovereignty' in Adler-Nissen and Gammeltoft-Hansen (n 3) 21–32; see also Walker (n 4) xi–xxi.

[14] C Taylor, *Modern Social Imaginaries* (Duke University Press 2004).

[15] Jackson (n 8) 431.

[16] H Lindahl, 'Sovereignty and Symbolization' (1997) 28 *Rechtstheorie* 347, 348.

[17] See, eg, M Loughlin, 'In Defence of *Staatslehre*' (2009) 48 *Der Staat* 1. See also Loughlin (n 9).

[18] For discussion of alternative historical frames for the modern legal universe (in whole or in part), in particular the fluid tradition of 'common law(s)', see P Glenn, *On Common Laws* (OUP 2005). See also N Walker, 'On the Necessary Publicness of Law' in C Michelon, G Clunie, C McCorkindale, and H Psarras (eds) *The Public in Law* (Ashgate 2012).

[19] See, eg, Jackson (n 8).

C. The Sovereignty Claim

Jean Bodin famously spoke of the 'marks of sovereignty' to convey the idea that modern sovereignty in its abstract and encompassing sense possesses no singular phenomenal form, but instead is made visible or perceptible to us through its diverse manifestations.[20] The construction of a unity out of the manifold that is so vital to the deep epistemic frame of sovereignty is, and cannot but be, an artificial unity—one which is only empirically observed and reconstituted through 'scattered signs'.[21] These marks and signs are not self-evident or self-selecting. They are a matter of active construction and reception, and beneath, before, and after that construction and reception may lie speculation and disagreement, struggle and contention, endorsement and rejection of any particular site and image of sovereign power.

The invocation of sovereignty, in other words, involves a 'speech act' possessing not only locutionary and illocutionary force but also perlocutionary force.[22] That is to say, sovereignty claims are not merely utterances conveying a set meaning, but have real and variable effects on social and political practice through persuading, threatening, enlightening, inspiring, or otherwise shaping behaviour or expectations. These effects are inseparable from the history of a particular set of sovereign arrangements and the constellation of meaning associated with that history. The British idea of the Queen-in-Parliament, the historical French attachment to the dual notions of national sovereignty and popular sovereignty, and the importance of the residual 'sovereign' powers of the states as consecrated in the Tenth Amendment of the United States Constitution, for example, all refer to quite different marks of sovereignty which only make sense in their own particular context. Yet each speaks to the distribution of the same underlying unity of sovereign power, and each shows sovereignty at the symbolic level to be of a deeply ideological character—a vehicle through which meaning is constructed to shape and allocate power.

In expressive terms, therefore, sovereignty is a 'virtual' category, one that has no phenomenal presence in its capacious entirety and so must always, and can only, manifest itself through iterative and more-or-less creative symbolic acts of representation.[23] This symbolic work, sometimes speculative or contentious in its claims, may involve either, in the one direction, specification of the detailed framework of operationalization and application of sovereignty; or, in the other direction, the identification of its source or pedigree. That is to say, it may involve, in the former more concrete vein, claims to the rightful possession or appropriate articulation of some or all aspects of the sovereign power on behalf of particular institutional

[20] J Bodin, *The Six Books of a Commonweale* (R Knolles trans first published 1576 and translated 1606, Harvard University Press 1962) Book 1, ch 10.

[21] D Baranger, 'The Apparition of Sovereignty' in Kalmo and Skinner (n 5) 53.

[22] WG Werner and JH de Wilde, 'The Endurance of Sovereignty' [2001] 7 *European Journal of International Relations* 283, 287.

[23] See Lindahl (n 16).

forms or regulatory complexes—legislative, executive, or judicial organs or some combination of these, federated levels of government, constitutive instruments, etc. Or it may involve, in the latter more abstract vein, the 'imputation' of the 'true' seat or source of sovereign power to other 'virtual' entities themselves capable of being made apparent only through representation, such as 'the people' or 'the nation'.[24]

It is unsurprising that sovereignty in its expressive dimension is used to such various and open-ended effect. Its wide range of reference is not just the obverse, but also the price of its underlying unity, and a reflection of the importance of the ideological stakes involved. According to the prominent French constitutional scholar Carré de Malberg, moreover, the unwieldy range of the sovereignty term, and the consequent danger of conceptual confusion, is exacerbated by the lack of sufficient discrimination in our natural language.[25] And what is the case for French also applies in English. Unlike the German language, for example, both French and English use the 's' word to refer not only to the supreme ordering power in the deep framing sense considered above—which is the only meaning of *Souveranitat* in German—but, in addition, to both the entire range of powers embraced within the State's authority (*Staatsgewalt*) and the power of the highest organ of State authority (*Herrschaft*).

We should not, however, overstate the indeterminacy of the claim-language of sovereignty. It is far from true that 'anything goes' in the bidding war over what counts as a sovereignty mark. Claims to sovereignty are more or less compelling and their persuasiveness depends, amongst other things, upon the embedded familiarity of their invocation in their immediate symbolic context, or the persuasiveness of their asserted or implied resemblance to, or analogy with, other contexts of use, as well as the plausibility of their corroboration of existing architectures of authority. For example, one standard version of 'foundational constitutionalism' typically invokes sovereignty as a recurrent link in an extended chain of authority.[26] Sovereignty may, as in the American version of the foundational constitutional story, appear in one and the same narrative in various guises and iterations—as the collective will and constituent power of the people or nation; as the spirit animating and authorizing the basic form of a written constitution; as a quality imbuing some of the organs named in the written constitution; and as a remainder or residual power left to other constitutional actors. Other constitutional heritages possess their own variations on this conventional symbolical wisdom[27] but in all cases the marks of sovereignty tend to fit together in patterns whose intelligibility and acceptability turns on their clear resonance with a dominant narrative of political authority current in that polity or more generally.

[24] See, eg, M Troper, 'The Survival of Sovereignty' in Kalmo and Skinner (n 5) 147.

[25] R Carré de Malberg, *Contribution à la théorie générale de l'Etat, spécialement d'après les données fournies par le droit constitutionnel français* (2 vols, Dalloz 2004) vol 1, 79.

[26] See, eg, N Krisch, *Beyond Constitutionalism: The Pluralist Structure of Postnational Law* (OUP 2010) ch 2.

[27] For discussion of the main modern constitutional traditions, including their use of sovereignty discourse, see M Rosenfeld, *The Identity of the Constitutional Subject: Selfhood, Citizenship, Culture and Community* (Routledge 2009).

D. Sovereignty in a Post-Westphalian Age

If the high modern world emphasized 'sovereign' comprehensiveness of authority, universality of form, and mutual exclusivity of claims, our late modern world in, which the continuing adequacy of sovereignty as a framing and claiming device stands to be assessed, looks quite different. While the State remains the focus of political organization—and its continuing prominence is one reason why talk of a return to a medieval configuration is inaccurate—the State is now merely first amongst equals. In place of a universal and uniform template of sovereign statehood we have a highly differentiated European and, indeed, global 'mosaic' of legal and political capacities.[28] In place of internal sovereignty as comprehensive and monopolistic, authority is typically partial—distributed between various political sites and levels, States and otherwise. And in place of mutual exclusivity as the default condition of external sovereignty, we have overlap, interlock, and mutual interference.

How so? No single factor explains the gradual and continuing movement from universality, comprehensiveness, and mutual exclusivity to differentiation, partiality, and overlap. Rather, there is a combination and accumulation of forces. Some tendencies challenge States and their borders as effective containers of power. The long post-Second World War development of transnational markets, communication media, and cultural forms gradually eroded the material capacity of the nation State as the axis of economic power and political authority and, to a lesser extent, its symbolic locus as the core of political identity. Institutional responses to these changes underscored the State-decentring trend. Globally inclusive entities such as the United Nations and exclusive groupings such as the G8, as well as regional institutions like the EU, both tracked and reinforced the development of forms of collective action and public goods (and 'bads') beyond the State. Their remit ranges far and wide, from the provision of security to the protection of human rights, and from the making of transnational markets to market 'correction' in spheres as diverse as food safety, environmental protection, energy efficiency, and criminal justice cooperation. Overlapping these umbrella institutions there is a dense network of powerful, functionally specialist transnational organizations, from State-controlled public bodies such as the World Trade Organization ('WTO') and the International Atomic Energy Agency, through hybrid public/private entities such as the Internet Corporation for Assigned Names and Numbers, to purely non-State organs such as the International Olympic Committee.[29] To repeat, none of these changes implies that the sovereign State is redundant. They simply generate new and supplementary tiers of transnationally connected legal and political authority, in so doing

[28] See, eg, N Walker, J Shaw, and S Tierney (eds) *Europe's Constitutional Mosaic* (Hart Publishing 2011). For discussion of sovereign-like forms in the wider global mosaic, see, eg, JL Dunoff and J Trachman (eds) *Ruling the World? Constitutionalism, International Law and Global Governance* (CUP 2009).

[29] For discussion, see for example N Walker, 'Postnational Constitutionalism and Postnational Public Law: A Tale of Two Neologisms' [2012] 3 *Transnational Legal Theory* 61.

challenging the generality of the framework of State authority. Particular States retain considerable power, though, tellingly, these tend to be of a size or regional prominence—whether the United States or newly emergent regional powers such as Brazil, Russia, India, and China—that allows them to operate on the same global scale as many of the new transnational entities.

But the challenge to State sovereignty is not simply a matter of the emergence of a higher scale of authority. Alongside these global and transnational tendencies, other disturbances to the sovereignty of the State emanate from below.[30] Ironically, the seeds of this challenge to the modem system were sown in the American constitutional settlement of 1789. As well as the first constitutionally baptized modern State, the United States was also the first mature federation. It gave novel constitutional form to the idea of territorially distributed power *within* the polity. However, it did so in a way which—even if it required a Civil War to settle the matter definitively—understood the allocation of jurisdiction between federal government and provincial or 'State' institutions as an expression of the sovereign authority of the United States as an integrated whole, rather than as a challenge to the very idea of a sovereign frame.[31]

Federalism US-style was designed and rolled out in a particular way, involving a clear division between the two levels of authority and their respective policy spheres; a high degree of ethnic or cultural homogeneity between the different State units; and uniform and symmetrical legal and institutional treatment of these units. Contemporary federalism, or quasi-federalism, has gradually diverged from that classical norm. Most newer federations, such as Germany, are 'cooperative' rather than 'dual' arrangements, involving a significant degree of policy overlap and institutional interlocking between central and local levels. Many, such as Canada, Spain, or Belgium, with the United Kingdom's 'Union State' as an untidy outlier even of this sub-category of quasi-federations, are also multinational or multi-ethnic rather than merely territorial compacts, with some constituencies retaining aspirations towards stronger forms of constitutional recognition.[32] And such multinational or multi-ethnic federations tend, in addition, towards uneven or asymmetrical treatment of their provinces; those with the clearest or most longstanding traditions of distinctiveness, or the strongest claim to national identity, are accorded more ample recognition of cultural goods such as language or religion, greater regional governmental autonomy, or disproportionate influence at the federal centre. All these factors combine to create a looser and more fluid political form, challenging the earlier conception of the federal State as a mere variation of the sovereigntist ideal of a well-ordered and permanently settled unity.[33]

[30] See, eg, S Tierney, 'Reframing Sovereignty? Sub-State National Societies and Contemporary Challenges to the Nation-State' (2005) 54 *ICLQ* 161.

[31] On the relationship between a fragmented notion of internal sovereignty and a unitary notion of external sovereignty in the US, see R Keohane, 'Ironies of Sovereignty: The European Union and the United States' (2002) 40 *Journal of Common Market Studies* 743.

[32] See S Rokkan and D Urwin, *The Politics of Territorial Identity: Studies in European Regionalism* (Sage 1982).

[33] See, eg, S Choudry (ed) *Constitutional Design for Divided Societies: Integration or Accommodation?* (OUP 2008).

So when considering the overall challenge to the universality, comprehensiveness, and mutual exclusivity of the modern system of States and its sovereigntist frame, we must look to both flanks—to pressures from the substate interior as well as from the transnational beyond. Furthermore, the two dynamics feed off one another. Claims to substate national recognition or protection are powerfully sponsored through global and regional mechanisms for the promotion of individual or collective rights, while supranational institutions such as the EU provide a scale of policy and economic support which makes the ambition of greater regional autonomy within existing States more viable. By the same token, just because existing States have gradually ceded authority and capacity upwards to other territorial or functional institutions, they may become less attractive magnets for substate nations and less well-equipped to maintain their sovereign integrity.[34]

In all of this, it is evident how the challenge to the high modern paradigm of sovereignty gathers pace. The development of new and unfamiliar forms and sites of authority alongside, and often interlocking with, the State means that the expressive language of sovereignty is no longer so clearly suited to the 'marks' of our global institutional architecture, many parts of which bear only a tenuous relationship to anything resembling a unitary polity. Systemically too these new forms and combinations of authority disturb the self-reproductive cycle of sovereign mutual exclusion and recognition. And the fundamental question whether the sovereigntist worldview, with its predilection to picture legal authority as a plurality of unities, is even epistemically adequate to the task of providing a basic grid for the changing world order, is posed ever more insistently and challengingly.

In earlier work, I sought to address and answer this challenge by resort to the idea of 'late sovereignty'.[35] Late sovereignty is still sovereignty and so remains connected to the modernist paradigm to the extent that sovereignty language and its associated ideas of ultimate authority continue to be used across existing States and, indeed, are increasingly endorsed across other non-State sites of political or legal community, whether in sub-national contexts or in supranational or transnational contexts such as the EU or the WTO. Yet late sovereignty is both a distinctive and probably an irreversible phase in the history of modern sovereignty. It is distinctive in the sense that the claim to authority as flowing from and through some underlying unity is no longer combined with the notion that it need be monopolistic within the territorial boundaries of the polity. Rather, what we observe, for example, in the relations of the EU to its Member States, each of which makes sovereigntist or supremacy-based claims in respect of the other,[36] is an emerging sense of 'autonomy without territorial exclusivity'.[37] In turn, this break in the connection between

[34] See, eg, Tierney (n 30). See more generally S Tierney, *Constitutional Law and National Pluralism* (OUP 2006); M Keating, *Stateless Nations: Plurinational Democracy in a Post-Sovereignty Era* (OUP 2004).

[35] N Walker, 'Late Sovereignty in the European Union' in Walker (n 6). For a recent refinement and application, see C MacAmhlaigh, 'Late Sovereignty in Post-integration Europe: Continuity and Change in a Constitutive Concept' in R Adler-Nissen and U Grad (eds) *European Integration and Postcolonial Sovereignty Games: The EU Overseas Countries and Territories* (Routledge 2013)

[36] See, eg, M Claes, *The National Courts' Mandate in the European Constitution* (Hart Publishing 2006).

[37] Walker (n 35) 23. See also Chapter 11 of this volume by Damian Chalmers.

ultimate authority and exclusivity of authority undermines the systemic conservatism of the older matrix. If the power of any and each sovereign entity is no longer conditioned by an attitude of mutual forbearance and recognition on the part of all such entities then, in a self-reinforcing fashion, the system as a whole becomes less resistant against new claims and new mutations of sovereignty. This structural shift is reflected and reinforced at the level of the sociology of political power. Non-State political forms may have been the creation of sovereign States, but over time they become much more than the sum of their antecedents and may transcend the conditions of their formation. Particular non-State polities may come and go—in 2013 we can no longer even be sure that the world's most advanced non-State polity, the EU, will survive in recognizable form. Yet given the continuing economic, technological, cultural, and institutional forces of transnationalism, and given continuing indication of the pliability of the sovereign form, the possibility of rewinding to an age of high modernity in which no non-State juridical entity challenges the exclusive authority of the State seems remote.

But if the logic of sovereignty is no longer one of conservative reproduction but of variable reiteration, will we not in time arrive at a tipping point where sovereignty loses its grip as a plausible way of imagining and adjusting our global political arrangements? Will we not reach a stage where States are so qualified and compromised in their internal and external normative authority, yet non-State entities are so deficient or otherwise unfamiliar in terms of our conventional template of the sovereign polity, that sovereignty no longer serves as a viable frame for the whole? Even to pose the question raises three related imponderables, and it is our inability to resolve these imponderables which should make us unwilling to 'wish away' our sovereigntist frame.

A first imponderable is starkly empirical. We cannot predict the course of global history, and so cannot tell whether the trend away from the State system may nevertheless re-stabilize in a new equilibrium. Secondly, for the same reason, we cannot predict or control for the degree of latent flexibility in the language and presuppositions of sovereignty. Thirdly, we cannot easily answer the relevant counterfactual question; namely, if there is a sovereignty-shaped hole emerging in our understanding of the legal and political universe, how do we begin to conceive of an alternative matrix of political agency? For sovereignty will not fade and become irrelevant in a conceptual vacuum, but only to the extent that such an alternative emerges and 'catches on'. Yet precisely because we still tend to think, however implicitly, within a sovereigntist frame and perspective, we lack the means to assess how likely the emergence of such an alternative paradigm might be or what shape it might take.

But what of those, such as Neil MacCormick, who have nevertheless confidently hailed the end of sovereignty?[38] It is surely instructive that in so doing they have tended to concentrate on surfaces rather than depths, institutional appearances rather than formative premises, claims rather than frames. It is undeniable, and

[38] See, eg, MacCormick (n 1). For a more qualified later view, see N MacCormick, 'Sovereignty and After' in Kalmo and Skinner (n 5); see also Keating (n 34).

well-illustrated by MacCormick, that governmental power, whether in federations, in our own Union State, at supranational sites, or in international contexts, tends to be divided, pooled, shared, or otherwise redistributed in ever more novel and manifold ways. But the logic of modern sovereignty has always depended upon the contrast and facilitative relationship between underlying unity of form and diversity of application, and indeed the energy of modern sovereign power lies in the versatile and renewable capacity of the former to prompt and contain the latter. It simply begs the question, therefore, to point to an unprecedented pattern of institutional diversity as evidence of sovereignty's broken unity.

E. The Changing UK Context: Parliamentary Sovereignty and its Reductions

As other chapters in this volume make abundantly clear,[39] discussion of sovereignty in the British context continues to be dominated by the doctrine of parliamentary sovereignty.[40] It naturally follows that contemporary British debate over the challenge to sovereignty in general should also focus on the ways in which parliamentary sovereignty in particular has recently been subjected to new threats, provocations, and qualifications. The questioning of parliamentary sovereignty, which in its canonical Diceyan version holds that Parliament can make and unmake any law and that no other body can override or set aside its legislation, has come from quite different corners of the legal universe.[41] The integrity of the doctrine is challenged from the perspective of EU law and its own self-understanding as a supreme and self-contained legal order. It is interrogated through the prism of the Human Rights Act 1998 and, in particular, its strong section 3(1) direction to interpret statute in conformity with the rights contained in the European Convention on Human Rights. It is also queried from the standpoint of the United Kingdom's constituent nations—for a long time Ireland and, more recently, Scotland, with Wales some way behind—and their claim, buttressed by the recent growth of devolved systems of government, to possess or develop their own seat of sovereign authority.[42]

Closely bound up with these challenges, a more general scepticism towards the parliamentary sovereignty doctrine as an unqualified attribution of power to the

[39] See especially the contributions from Goldsworthy, Young, and Hope in this volume.

[40] See, eg, the classic studies J Goldsworthy, *The Sovereignty of Parliament: History and Philosophy* (OUP 1999) and J Goldsworthy, *Parliamentary Sovereignty: Contemporary Debates* (CUP 2010).

[41] For a good overview, see AW Bradley, 'The Sovereignty of Parliament: Form or Substance?' (7th edn, OUP 2011).

[42] See, eg, MacCormick (n 1) chs 11 and 12; M Keating, *The Independence of Scotland* (OUP 2009). The continuing power of the sovereignty metaphor is vividly demonstrated by the tone and content of the Scottish Government's recent document setting out its timetable for constitutional change in view of the referendum on independence intended for the autumn of 2014. In a double-spaced document of a mere sixteen pages there are no fewer than nine references to the Scottish people as 'sovereign' or as possessing a claim to 'sovereignty'; see *Scotland's Future; from the Referendum to Independence and a Written Constitution* (Scottish Government: February 2013) available at <http://www.scotland.gov.uk/Resource/0041/00413757.pdf/>.

institutional complex of the Queen-in-Parliament has recently gained a firm foothold within both academic and judicial circles. We are advised from a position of 'common law constitutionalism'[43]—or, perhaps more accurately, 'common law radicalism'[44]—that the role of the courts in providing the last legal word on the meaning of the Constitution is no mere institutional inference. It is not simply that, as the branch of government concerned with interpretation and application in disputed instances, they have an unavoidable voice in the recognition and mobilization of our constitutional fundamentals, yet in using that voice should do no more than passively acknowledge and register parliamentary sovereignty as an unassailable political fact. Rather, the enduring involvement of the courts is deemed to have a more profound significance. It indicates that parliamentary sovereignty is itself a dual or 'bipolar' principle,[45] or a common law rule of a kind that is open to refinement or qualification by the judges. In turn, this power of qualification, as has been suggested in a number of recent cases,[46] may enable, indeed oblige, the judges to impose certain substantive constraints in the name of the Rule of Law or a more general attachment to a principled rather than a policy-based foundation for legal rules.[47] In this broader movement, the challenge to a Westminster-centred concentration of power from Brussels, from Strasbourg, and from the Celtic nations is understood both as an opportunity and as a reason to rethink an old doctrine for new times.

How does this distinctive developmental track fit with our general understanding of sovereignty as providing a dual significance in legal thought—as concerned both with framing and with claiming? Most strikingly, what we observe in the British context, through the telescoping of the sovereignty debate onto the institutional complex of the Queen-in-Parliament, is a tendency to elide or blur the very distinction between the underlying frame and the sovereign mark which I have sought to emphasize. In a nutshell, parliamentary sovereignty tends to be approached less as a sign of sovereignty than as the thing itself. Let me conclude by suggesting why and how this tendency occurs, and outlining some of its consequences.

This is not the place to rehearse the history of Parliament and its struggle with the Crown, and how this struggle was won over the course of the seventeenth century and consolidated in the eighteenth.[48] It suffices to say that the early success of parliamentary sovereignty, at a point where the full conceptual apparatus of

[43] See, eg, TRS Allan, 'In Defence of the Common Law Constitution: Unwritten Rights as Fundamental Law' (2009) 22 *CLJ* 187.

[44] See, eg, C Turpin and A Tomkins, *British Government and the Constitution* (6th edn, CUP 2007) 66.

[45] S Sedley, 'Human Rights: A Twenty-First Century Agenda' [1995] *PL* 386, 389.

[46] See in particular, *Robinson v Secretary of State for Northern Ireland* [2002] UKHL 32 (HL) (Lord Bingham and Lord Hoffmann); *R (Jackson) v Attorney General* [2005] UKHL 56, [2006] 1 AC 262 (Lord Steyn and Lord Hope of Craighead); *AXA General Insurance v Lord Advocate* [2011] UKSC 46 (Lord Hope of Craighead and Lord Reed).

[47] See, eg, Allan (n 43).

[48] See, eg, Loughlin (n 9) ch 9 and A Tomkins, *Our Republican Constitution* (Hart Publishing 2005) ch 3.

modern constitutionalism was not yet in place, shaped and constrained the way in which ideas of ultimate authority could be imagined and pursued within the British polity. If we recall the history of sovereignty as one of progressive abstraction from the personal, dynastic, and singular to the impersonal, corporate, and internally differentiated, the idea of parliamentary sovereignty occupies a midpoint on this continuum. Only with the development of foundational constitutional settlements in the late eighteenth century was the distinction between sovereignty in general—now seen as an attribute of 'the people' as constituent power—and its particular institutional manifestations and applications fully developed and clarified in political theory and symbology. The English, and later the British, State was in this regard a case of arrested development. The part became the whole, the surrogate the original, the application the source.

Other ideas of sovereignty did of course emerge or were preserved alongside parliamentary sovereignty, both in terms of pedigree and institutionalization. On the one hand, in terms of pedigree, an alternative and in some measure complementary tradition of popular sovereignty grew and persisted alongside parliamentary sovereignty without ever receiving the endorsement of a constitutional moment of self-founding or otherwise achieving widespread recognition as the dominant source of constitutional legitimacy.[49] On the other hand, in terms of institutionalization—and indeed providing one of the counterpoints to the idea of popular sovereignty—even after the struggles of the seventeenth century the Crown retained a residual final authority apart from Parliament. This was particularly evident in the persistence of prerogative powers, but also as one dimension of the resilient authority of the courts and, perhaps, one remote form of corroboration of the contemporary revival of the judicial claim to co-sovereignty.[50] Yet throughout, Parliament continued to provide the magnetic centre of the constitutional order, its assertion of sovereignty supplying the symbolic and authoritative point of reference and limiting condition for other claims, both innovatory and renovatory.

This narrow vision of sovereignty supplied many advantages of institutional unity and, in time, of democratic focus. Indeed, much of the force of the contemporary case for the United Kingdom as a distinctively 'political constitution',[51] as one more responsive to the will of the legislature than to the reason of doctrine, depends on that vision of sovereignty. But narrowness of outlook and concentration of institutional authority also has a downside, not least its failure to unpack sovereignty into a fuller constitutional vision. In particular, the 'single mark' of parliamentary sovereignty has always occupied the space and pre-empted the adoption of just that constitutional framework of higher law which would allow a popular designation and broaden distribution of the marks of sovereignty. Instead, concentrated in the single institutional complex of the Queen-in-Parliament, the domain of

[49] See, eg, Tomkins (n 48).

[50] On the resilience of the Crown in British constitutional law generally, see M Sunkin and S Payne (eds) *The Nature of the Crown: A Legal and Political Analysis* (OUP 1999).

[51] For an astute overview of political constitutionalism and its relationship to so-called 'legal constitutionalism' see G Gee and GC Webber, 'What is a Political Constitution?' (2010) 30 *OJLS* 273.

sovereignty becomes a congested zone. This has a number of challenging consequences. From its narrow point of ultimate authority parliamentary sovereignty tends to be conceptually overburdened as our constitutional lodestar, to be competed over as a prize rather than treated as a common resource of constitutional authority, and to invite a backward-looking rather than a forward-looking approach to constitutional construction and justification. Let us briefly examine each of these related tendencies.

First there is the question of conceptual overload. There are many examples of the reductive and distorting effect of too narrow a focus on parliamentary sovereignty. Take, for instance, the matter of statutory interpretation. Until recent years, the idea that the first and only responsibility of the Courts was to give effect to the intention of Parliament had the effect of chilling meaningful discussion of the nature and purpose of the judicial role in areas where statute offered insufficient guidance or might even be absent—notably in human rights cases and in judicial review of administrative action. Indeed, some of the early success of a common law constitutionalist approach is owed to its candid approach to the insufficiency of existing protocols of judicial interpretation and the inordinate weight these placed on the narrow principle of parliamentary sovereignty.[52]

Or take, for example, the question of Britain's relationship with the EU. In most constitutional orders, internal sovereignty (the location of ultimate authority within the polity) and external sovereignty (the authority of the polity as a whole in relation to the rest of the world) are clearly concerned with distinct aspects. This is often reflected in a written constitution, where different provisions will deal with the internal allocation of authority amongst the branches and levels of government on the one hand, and external relations on the other, including the place of international law, supranational law, or other forms of foreign law vis-à-vis domestic law in the hierarchy of sources of law-making.[53] In the British case, however, there is no such clear distinction between internal and external sovereignty and their limits, at least as regards legislative authority.[54] Accordingly, the question of the standing of EU law, which by encroaching on many areas of domestic authority curtails the international legal sovereignty of the United Kingdom, is treated in the same perspective, and as part of the same stream of constitutional reasoning and judicial authority, as any internal challenge to the sovereign location of power from the perspective, say, of human rights or the devolution of power.[55]

[52] For an enduringly excellent statement of the legal and political circumstances of the early growth of common law constitutionalism, see M Hunt, *Using Human Rights Law in English Courts* (Hart Publishing 1997).

[53] See, eg, Claes (n 36).

[54] Of course, external sovereignty also refers, more positively, to the continuing right of the executive to participate in international relations and to make international agreements on behalf of the United Kingdom in those areas where such a right has not already been curtailed or qualified (by the operation of parliamentary sovereignty). In that respect, external sovereignty continues to be treated quite apart from the doctrine of parliamentary sovereignty.

[55] See, eg, *R v Secretary of State for Transport, ex p. Factortame (No 1)* [1990] 2 AC 85; *R v Secretary of State for Transport, ex p. Factortame (No 2)* [1991] 1 AC 603; *Thoburn v Sunderland City Council* [2003] QB 151; read alongside the (non EU-related) cases cited at n 46.

Parliamentary sovereignty is considered as a single reference point and conceptual prism for internal and external relations alike, even though the stakes are quite different—the proper distribution and self-imposed limits of internal legislative authority on the one hand, and the balance of UK authority with Europe and the world on the other. Again, the reduction of the whole to the part, the idea to one of its manifestations, has a cramping effect on constitutional language and thought. Parliamentary sovereignty is in danger of having to explain and justify too much and to collapse different questions into a single answer.

Secondly, there is the prize-fighting dimension. If sovereignty in the British Constitution exists only, or predominantly, through its parliamentary mark, then the key to constitutional authority and the realization of any particular vision of the constitutional good lies in control of the meaning or operationalization of that mark. The reason why disagreements between different conceptions of the nature and reach of parliamentary sovereignty are so hotly contested between political and legal, legislative and judicial, Parliament-centred and common-law-centred, therefore, is that these disagreements concern occupation of the narrow access route to the commanding heights of our unwritten constitutional system. What is more, there is a self-reinforcing intractability to the debate. As there is no Archimedean point beyond parliamentary sovereignty where the debate over the meaning of parliamentary sovereignty can be definitively resolved, the contest threatens to become perpetual.[56] And as some parties, the various institutional parties in particular, who argue for this or that understanding of parliamentary sovereignty have both an authoritative presence in the negotiation and a significant stake in the outcome—that is to say, they are seeking to declare the rules of the very game in which they are active players—this further militates against settlement.

In turn, this is connected to a third limiting tendency associated with the centrality of parliamentary sovereignty. The focus on the past and its struggles rather than the future that is so characteristic of our leading narratives of constitutionalism also stems from the difficulty of thinking or acting beyond parliamentary supremacy as the apex of authority. Just as there is no likelihood of easy resolution of disputes over the provenance, status, meaning, and extent of parliamentary sovereignty, so too the resilience of the doctrine militates against the adoption of the kind of written constitutional prospectus enjoyed by virtually all other States. There is little political will to depart from a framework which has become so embedded within our political heritage and which, in its open-ended empowerment of the government of the day, suits the beliefs and the interests of the key institutional actors who have been shaped by that heritage and on whom any initiative to change would depend. Nor, especially in an age where the territorial integrity of the polity is under challenge from nationalist quarters, would the prospects be promising of

[56] For a typical recent example of such contestation, see the articles by R Bellamy, P Craig, C Forsyth, NW Barber, TRS Allan, and AL Young on the prospects or otherwise of parliamentary sovereignty and the relative merits and robustness of the 'political' and 'legal' dimensions of British constitutionalism in a special 'Symposium on the changing landscape of British constitutionalism' in (2011) 9 *International Journal of Constitutional Law* 86.

a successful conclusion if any broader project of refounding and resettlement were to be attempted.[57]

The absence of a viable alternative horizon inevitably redirects our constitutional visionaries and engineers backwards. If there can be no constitutional resource to draw upon in determining and finessing the ground-rules for steering constitutional adjustment and reform other than the resource we already possess, then that resource has to be mined exhaustively for the nuggets of meaning and practice which support our preferred reading. Ironically, therefore, despite its very different origins and centre of institutional gravity, and despite its much more permissive consequences in terms of legislative policy, the root idea of parliamentary sovereignty, with its venerable standing and self-reproductive tendencies, ends up performing the same kind of symbolic function as some of the older written constitutions, most notably the United States Constitution. Over time, its foundational precepts, just like their foundational texts, come to assume an almost sacred quality and so supply a non-negotiable point of departure for anyone who wants to be taken seriously in the constitutional conversation.

It is certainly the case, we may therefore conclude, that the sovereignty frame is still entrenched within the deep structure of British constitutionalism, even for those who might be critical about its scope or absolute quality. Yet the reduction of that frame to the particular and partial claim of parliamentary sovereignty adds a peculiar texture to our constitutional debate. Sovereignty does indeed remain very much 'in perspective' in the United Kingdom today, but it is often through a rather narrow focus.

[57] On the difficulties associated with fundamental constitutional reform in the United Kingdom, and on some recently suggested surrogate proposals, see A McHarg, 'Reforming the United Kingdom Constitution: Law, Convention, Soft Law' (2008) 71 *MLR* 853.

3

Why Sovereignty?

Martin Loughlin[*]

A. Introduction

The concept of sovereignty enters the vocabulary of public law only with the formation of the modern institution of the State. Although medieval political formations possessed 'a very strong sense of that concrete thing, hierarchy, they lacked the idea of that abstract thing, sovereignty'. [1] This abstract idea of sovereignty exists alongside the similarly abstract entity of the State, an impersonal institution that maintains supreme governing authority over a defined territory and is differentiated both from its constituent people and its office-holders.[2] State and sovereignty exist in a reciprocal relationship: the State assumes sovereignty just as sovereignty assumes the State. State and sovereignty emerge as concepts of modern Western rationalism.[3]

The primary function of the concept of sovereignty is to signify in jural form the nature and quality of political relationships with respect to modern regimes. One set of relations concerns the position of the State in the international arena. A regime is recognized as a sovereign State when its governing authority is in no way legally dependent on any higher authority, whether that of pope or emperor. The sovereign State is an autonomous entity that acknowledges other similar entities in the sphere of international relations on the basis of formal equality. Correlating with this external aspect is the internal dimension. From the internal perspective, sovereignty expresses the conviction that the State is the ultimate source of law. There can be no fetter on the law-making authority of the State, whether deriving from divine law or natural law. The law made by the authorized institutions of the State is supreme. Sovereignty is a concept which expresses the State's independent status as a politico-legal entity in the world and its absolute authority to make law.

* Professor of Public Law, London School of Economics and Political Science.

[1] B de Jouvenel, *Sovereignty: An Inquiry into the Political Good* (JF Huntington trans, CUP 1957) 171.

[2] Q Skinner, 'The State' in T Ball, J Farr, and RL Hanson (eds) *Political Innovation and Conceptual Change* (CUP 1989) 90–131.

[3] Q Skinner, *The Foundations of Modern Political Thought* (CUP 1978); A Osiander, *Before the State: Systemic Political Change in the West from the Greeks to the French Revolution* (OUP 2007).

B. Confusion over Sovereignty

This concept of sovereignty is today much misunderstood.[4] The main reason derives from its intrinsic political and legal dimensions. Sovereignty is a fundamental concept of both political and legal thought, expressing the autonomous nature of the State's political power and its specific mode of operation in a distinctively juristic form. In this way, sovereignty symbolizes the specific character of political and legal authority within modernity.

During the twentieth century, this dual legal and political dimension became a source of deep discomfort for scholars in the emerging academic disciplines of law and political science. In their quest for scientific credibility, political scientists sought to specify causal laws of political behaviour and in this empiricist frame sovereignty was felt only to express the metaphysics of a bygone era.[5] At the same time, legal philosophers were determined to establish the autonomous normative authority of law. They, therefore, felt obliged to sever any connection between law and political power concluding that 'the sovereignty concept obviously must be radically displaced'.[6]

Together, these academic developments have subverted the foundations of the discipline of public law. From the perspective of public law, these scholarly developments have led only to confusion and obfuscation. Contemporary jurists, now wedded to the idea of the autonomy of law, seem unable to relate the legal to the political in a sensible manner. But the problems of sovereignty in political science are, if anything, even more acute. Maintaining a scientific idiom but refusing fully to abandon the term, political scientists fail to acknowledge the essentially juristic character of the concept. As a result, they confuse sovereignty with a quite different phenomenon: that of governmental power. From this elementary error, it is a short step to assume that sovereignty can be equated with absolutism and is incompatible with constitutionalism, federalism, rights, and myriad other liberal values.

Given this State of affairs, it is tempting to join the chorus of scholars who, at various points during the twentieth century, called for abandonment of any further

[4] From this introductory statement, it is evident that much of the literature on sovereignty goes wrong in assuming (a) that sovereignty is not linked to the concept of the State, (b) that it existed in the ancient and medieval world, (c) that it is inherent in any notion of political authority, (d) that sovereignty is not absolute, and (e) that sovereignty can be delegated, distributed, and shared. For an account that makes all these elementary errors see A de Benoist, 'What is Sovereignty?' (1999) 116 *Telos* 99.

[5] See, eg, JP Nettl, 'The State as a Conceptual Variable' (1968) 20 *World Politics* 559, 560: 'Nowadays, the problem of sovereignty is, for social scientists, a dead duck.'

[6] H Kelsen, *Das Problem der Souveränität und die Theorie des Völkerrechts* (Mohr 1920) 320: 'Die Souveränitätsvorstellung freilich muss radikal verdrängt werden.' See also H Kelsen, *Introduction to the Problems of Legal Theory* (BL Paulson and SL Paulson trans of first edn [1934] of *Reine Rechtslehre*, Clarendon Press 1992) 124: 'The theoretical dissolution of the dogma of sovereignty, the principal instrument of imperialistic ideology directed against international law, is one of the most substantial achievements of the Pure Theory of Law.'

use of the term.[7] But for at least three reasons this is not an option.[8] The first is that many who wish to jettison the concept are under a misapprehension as to its nature,[9] and if we are confused about what is being rejected, abandonment is unlikely to improve the situation. The second is that its rejection seems to be part of a strategy for overthrowing the modern discourse of public law in its entirety.[10] But if the argument is that sovereignty is an anachronism, those making the case must offer an alternative conceptual framework to explain the workings of governing power today. This is a challenge few have recognized, let alone risen to.

The third reason why sovereignty cannot be abandoned is just as serious. Far from being allowed to wither, the term is nowadays much in vogue. It is back in fashion because of changes taking place in the nature of governing relations which have placed in question the existing global order of nation-states. We are living through what has been called an 'age of fracture',[11] in which many of the certainties that anchored modern understandings of government and law have become unhinged. As is often the case in such moments, scholars return to fundamentals to offer an explanation of the impact of these changes. The hitherto neglected concept of sovereignty has come to the forefront of scholarly attention, though only to exacerbate the sense of disorientation with respect to its nature.

Evidence of this disorientation is the remarkable growth in scholarly publications on the subject of sovereignty, virtually all of which seek some re-specification of the concept.[12] Some of these accounts qualify the concept by severing its integral parts. We have long been familiar with the distinction between legal and political conceptions of sovereignty, between *de jure* and *de facto* sovereignty, or between internal and external aspects.[13] This type of division has recently been added to by the use of such expressions as negative and positive conceptions of sovereignty or

[7] See, eg, L Duguit, *Law in the Modern State* (F Laski and H Laski trans, Allen & Unwin 1921) esp ch 1; J Maritain, 'The Concept of Sovereignty' (1950) 44 *American Political Science Review* 343 ('It is my contention that political philosophy must get rid of the word, as well as the concept, of Sovereignty—not because it is an antiquated concept...but because...this concept is intrinsically wrong', 344); SI Benn, 'The Uses of Sovereignty' (1955) 3 *Political Studies* 109 ('In the light of this analysis it would appear a mistake to treat "sovereignty" as denoting a genus of which the species can be distinguished by suitable adjectives, and there would seem to be a strong case for giving up so Protean a word', 122).

[8] There are others, not least of which is the fact that the newly emerging powers—the so-called BRIC nations (Brazil, Russia, India, and China)—remain protective of their status as sovereign States.

[9] See, eg, Maritain (n 7) 355: 'In order to think in a consistent manner in political philosophy, we have to discard the concept of Sovereignty, which is but one with the concept of Absolutism.' On the confusions in Benn's analysis see WJ Stankiewicz, *In Defense of Sovereignty* (OUP 1969) 11–20.

[10] See, eg, L Duguit, 'The Law and the State' (1917) 31 *Harv L Rev* 1 (which rejects all prior theories of public law on the assumption that they rest on metaphysical foundations and seeks to replace them with a conception of public law erected on purely empirical foundations). For analysis, see M Loughlin, *Foundations of Public Law* (OUP 2010) ch 13.

[11] DT Rodgers, *Age of Fracture* (Belknap Press 2011).

[12] Panu Minkkinen has recently noted that, according to British Library records, around 330 books with sovereignty in the title had been published during the previous decade: P Minkkinen, *Sovereignty, Knowledge, Law* (Routledge 2009) 6.

[13] See, eg, AV Dicey, *Introduction to the Study of the Law of the Constitution* (8th edn, Macmillan 1915) 425 (legal–political and *de jure–de facto*); R Prokhovnik, 'Internal/External: the State of Sovereignty' (1996) 2 *Contemporary Politics* 7.

'sovereignty-in-principle' and 'sovereignty-in-practice'.[14] But the most significant—if confounding—development has been an explosion in the number of studies that use adjectival qualifiers. Terms such as 'shared sovereignty', 'mixed sovereignty', 'divided sovereignty', 'pooled sovereignty', or 'cooperative sovereignty' have recently become fashionable.[15] Yet these are now being supplemented by much more exotic terms, such as 'floating sovereignty', 'multiple sovereignty', 'perforated sovereignty', 'fragmented sovereignty', 'reconfigured sovereignty', 'complex sovereignty', 'decentralized sovereignty', 'agonal sovereignty', and 'polymorphous sovereignty'.[16] There has even been a variation on this theme through the method of temporalization: implicitly recognizing sovereignty as a modern concept, scholars have responded to contemporary uncertainties with 'late-sovereignty' or 'post-sovereignty'.[17]

In light of these developments, it is evident that the concept of sovereignty cannot simply be abandoned. But in these febrile times, it is essential that some effort is made to specify its meaning. If the overall aim is to explain more precisely the phenomenon of political power, its nature, the manner of its exercise, and the means available for holding power-wielders to account, then we need a coherent account of this concept. Before doing so, however, I should examine how the confusions over sovereignty have been generated.

C. Socio-economic Change

There is little doubt that we are experiencing a period of significant change in the form of governing arrangements. Recent economic, technological, and cultural developments have eroded a number of the foundations of the modern system

[14] RH Jackson, *Quasi-States: Sovereignty, International Relations and the Third World* (CUP 1990) 26–31 (positive and negative); E Grande and LW Pauly (eds) *Complex Sovereignty: Reconstituting Political Authority in the Twenty-first Century* (University of Toronto Press 2005) 9–10 (principle and practice).

[15] See S Besson, 'Review of *Sovereignty in Transition*' (2005) 3 *International Journal of Constitutional Law* 147.

[16] See T Kostakopoulou, 'Floating Sovereignty: A Pathology or a Necessary Means of State Evolution' (2002) 22 *OJLS* 135; J Přibáň, 'Multiple Sovereignty: On Europe's Self-Constitutionalization and Legal Self-Reference' (2010) 23 *Ratio Juris* 41; ID Duchacek, D Latouche, and G Stevenson (eds) *Perforated Sovereignties and International Relations* (Greenwood Press 1988); H Kalmo and Q Skinner (eds) *Sovereignty in Fragments: The Past, Present and Future of a Contested Concept* (CUP 2010); TL Ilgen (ed) *Reconfigured Sovereignty: Multi-layered Governance in the Global Age* (Ashgate 2003); E Grande and LW Pauly (eds) *Complex Sovereignty: Reconstituting Political Authority in the Twenty-first Century* (University of Toronto Press 2005); A Stone Sweet, 'A Cosmopolitan Legal Order: Constitutional Pluralism and Rights Adjudication in Europe' (2012) 1 *Global Constitutionalism* 53 ('decentralized sovereignty'); AD Barder and F Debrix, 'Agonal Sovereignty: Rethinking War and Politics with Schmitt, Arendt and Foucault' (2011) 37 *Philosophy and Social Criticism* 775; S Humphreys, 'Polymorphous Sovereignty' in C Barbour and G Pavlich (eds) *After Sovereignty: On the Question of Political Beginnings* (Routledge 2010) 146.

[17] See, eg, MC Bateson, 'Beyond Sovereignty: An Emerging Global Civilization' in RBJ Walker and SH Mendlovitz (eds) *Contending Sovereignties: Redefining Political Community* (Lynne Reinner Publishers 1990) 145; N MacCormick, 'Beyond the Sovereign State' (1993) 56 *MLR* 1; JA Camillieri and J Falk, *The End of Sovereignty? The Politics of a Shrinking and Fragmented World* (Edward Elgar 1992); N Walker, 'Late Sovereignty in the European Union' in N Walker (ed) *Sovereignty in Transition* (Hart Publishing 2003) 3–32.

of nation-states. Increased global flows of capital, intensified networks of social interaction, and the emergence of transnational regulatory regimes on a significant scale have combined to create the perception that the capacity of national governments to control their economies is diminishing and that the conditions for meeting their citizens' well-being have considerably altered. The activity of governing has become, in certain respects at least, less centralized and more dispersed and this is experienced as a diminution in the efficacy of the main levers of command and control.

All this may be true. But it is not self-evident that such governmental developments have had dramatic effects on the concept of sovereignty. Many writers believe—indeed, assume—that they have. It is true that the concept of sovereignty was forged under conditions in which rulers were turning their attention inwards, seeking to increase the intensity of their powers of rule. It is also true that today governments increasingly feel obliged to turn their attention outwards, to engage in cooperative inter-State ventures in order to provide collective goods. This reorientation might suggest a shift in political relations that could ultimately affect sovereignty. But it is not clear that those who believe that socioeconomic developments affecting the conditions of governing are undermining sovereignty have adequately grasped its nature.

Sovereignty is the concept on which received ideas of legitimate domination are founded. That those ideas have always been contested is not at all surprising: it is a direct consequence of the continuous struggle to establish the conditions of political authority in regimes founded on collective self-actualization. But the contest over the conditions of legitimate domination is now equated with the contestability of the concept of sovereignty itself.[18] And this leads to an important misuse of language, generating analytical confusion, misdiagnosis of the issues, and occasionally even incoherence of the proposed solution. There are two main types of confusion and they concern the attempt to sever the political and legal dimensions of sovereignty. These are best explained separately.

D. Sovereignty and Government

The first source of confusion, located mainly within contemporary political science, arises because scholars are increasingly conflating sovereignty and government. This results from a failure to maintain the distinction between the concept of sovereignty itself and its particular 'marks'.[19] Sovereignty expresses a principle of unity: it is

[18] Various authors have argued, to my mind erroneously, that sovereignty is an 'essentially contested concept'; see, eg, S Besson, 'Sovereignty in Conflict' in C Warbrick and S Tierney (eds) *Towards an 'International Legal Community'? The Sovereignty of States and the Sovereignty of International Law* (BIICL 2006) 138–9, 144–64; D Sarooshi, 'The Essentially Contested Nature of the Concept of Sovereignty: Implications for the Exercise by International Institutions of Delegated Powers of Government' (2004) 25 *Michigan Journal of International Law* 1107.

[19] See J Bodin, *The Six Bookes of a Commonweale* ([1576], R Knolles trans [1606], KD McRae ed, Harvard University Press 1962) Book 1, ch 10.

an expression of illimitability, perpetuity, and indivisibility. Any limit on sovereignty eradicates it, any division of sovereignty destroys it. Yet the powers of rule, the 'marks of sovereignty', can be divided and limited. Indeed, for the purpose of maintaining political authority they must be so divided and limited. But this maxim relates to the phenomenon of governing not to the concept of sovereignty.

The distinction between sovereignty and government forms a central pillar of public law thought. It was first expressed by Jean Bodin in Book II of his *Six livres de la république*, in which he explained that there is a 'great difference between the State and the government of the State'.[20] It has since, until recently, been treated as a commonplace of public law thought. Bodin contended that the distinction 'seems to me more than necessary for the good understanding of the State of every commonwealth, if a man will not cast himself headlong into an infinite labyrinth of errors'.[21] Having lost the sense of this distinction, this is precisely what is now happening.[22]

Some of these errors are of the most elementary kind, as in the claim that federalism is incompatible with—or (the same thing) requires a division of—sovereignty.[23] But this type of error mostly arises because political scientists fail to acknowledge that sovereignty is a juridical concept. As a result, they confuse sovereignty with governmental competence, and therefore with ideas such as autarky, that is, with the ability of a nation-State to control its own material conditions and destiny. This stems from a blurring of the distinction between the *ability* to govern and the *right* to govern. This distinction relates to two different concepts of power: the former is *potentia*, the actual ability to control things, while the latter is *potestas*, the exercise of rightful authority. Political scientists tend to focus only on the former, whereas the concept of sovereignty is concerned primarily with *potestas* (and in its most sophisticated presentation requires a dialectical engagement between *potestas* and *potentia*).

One obvious source of current disarray thus derives from the fact that a concept formed within the framework of public law and used to explain the structure of legal authority in the modern world is now being confused with the ability of governments of nation-states to control the conditions of their material existence. Given the ubiquity of this usage, it is not easy to see what is to be done. Confusion between the conceptual and the actual is one reason for the huge literature exploring what

[20] Bodin (n 19) 199. [21] Bodin (n 19) 249–50.

[22] One illustration is P Eleftheriadis, 'Law and Sovereignty' (2010) 29 *Law and Philosophy* 535, who suggests (on the basis of limited analysis) that Bodin's arguments on sovereignty 'now seem quaint and irrelevant' (535). Eleftheriadis argues that 'if we take sovereignty seriously, we cannot have constitutional law' (538) and that 'the survival of sovereignty is what it appears to be, just a mistake. It is the result of some kind of absent-mindedness on the part of some constitutional lawyers and political thinkers' (539).

[23] See, eg, Dicey (n 13), who was guilty of conflating the specifically British legal doctrine of sovereignty (that of the absolute legal authority of the Crown-in-Parliament) with the more general political claim of the necessity for there to be a clearly determined ultimate political authority. This confuses the abstract concept of sovereignty with the more concrete phenomenon of the sovereign. In this respect, Dicey's position is close to that of C Schmitt, *Political Theology: Four Chapters on the Concept of Sovereignty* (G Schwab trans, University of Chicago Press 2005).

appear to be ambiguities of sovereignty. This type of confusion leads to the perception that sovereignty is, in the formulation of one leading international relations scholar, a form of 'organized hypocrisy'.[24] That is, it presents itself an ideological smokescreen preventing us from seeing clearly the way power works in the contemporary world. If this actually is the way the term is now being used, there is indeed a case for jettisoning it, not least because political scientists who use the term invariably end up asking the wrong sort of questions. Yet if the term is suppressed in the cause of promoting objective social science, will this enable scholars to identify the workings of power more clearly and formulate more precisely questions of legitimacy, control, and accountability in the exercise of governing authority? I have no answer. But it is not obvious that the problems concerning power agglomeration in the world will be clarified once the concept of *potestas* has been absorbed into that of *potentia*.

E. Sovereignty and Law

What can be said with greater confidence is that abandonment of the sovereignty concept will lead to an epistemological crisis in public law. This brings us to the second type of confusion: obfuscation over the nature of the concept within contemporary jurisprudence. Jurists continue to recognize sovereignty as a legal concept but they have grown increasingly concerned about its political dimension, often conceiving it in a purely metaphorical sense, as the 'sovereignty of law'. This is in reality an attempt to overthrow it.

This process has been in train for quite some time. During the 1920s, for example, Hans Kelsen argued that the purity of legal science can be preserved only by presenting an entirely normative theory of sovereignty. In Kelsen's worldview, any attempt to connect the legal and the political—law and State—leads only to incoherence. Many jurists have since followed his lead in seeking systematically to jettison the concepts of State and sovereignty. From the juridical point of view, they argue, State and law are the same thing: the idea of the State must be equated with that of legal order. To the extent that we continue to talk about sovereignty, it can only mean the sovereignty of legal ordering. In place of State and sovereignty, they assert the autonomy of law or constitution. This amounts to more or less the same thing since, in this formulation, constitution stands as an ideal representation of legal form.

At the core of this type of argument is the claim to the autonomy of law. For Kelsen, this amounted to a formal science of normative ordering which sought to remove all forms of value judgment from the explanatory account, thereby presenting itself as a science 'purified of all political ideology' and of 'every element of the natural sciences'.[25] Of particular significance is the fact that many jurists opposed

[24] SD Krasner, *Sovereignty: Organized Hypocrisy* (Princeton University Press 1999).
[25] Kelsen (n 6) 1.

to Kelsen's pure theory have since adopted his central claim of legal autonomy. These anti-positivist scholars elevate it into a claim about something abstract called 'legality'. Law is now not only autonomous but also contains its own intrinsic morality, from which it derives its own source of authority.[26] Those who assert the autonomy of constitution rather than legality draw a distinction without a difference: these theories are variants of normativism, united in the abstract and ideal character of the directing idea of the autonomy of normative ordering.

This line of argument is implicit in the arguments of Ronald Dworkin and his followers, who bolster 'law's empire', 'freedom's law', and 'sovereign virtue'.[27] The case is presented in its most explicit form by Mattias Kumm, who recognizes that this line of argument must bring about a 'paradigm shift' in public law.[28] Arguing that public lawyers remain in the thrall of 'the conventional statist paradigm', Kumm seeks to reconceptualize the discipline from the perspective of what he calls the 'cosmopolitan paradigm'. At the centre of his argument is a 'practice-conception of constitutionalism'.[29] This conception rejects the argument that the State is the source of law. It is also a direct assault on the sovereignty principle. Constitutionalism, he contends, 'does not require the framework of a State to be meaningful'. It is, instead, the other way round: 'The meaning of the institutional framework of the State is to be determined by principles of constitutionalism.'[30] The entire edifice of State and sovereignty must be overthrown in favour of a cosmopolitan claim of adherence to the authority of self-standing principles of constitutionalism.

In this mode of thought, the concepts of State and constitution are equated with legal order, legal ordering is claimed to be autonomous, and the intrinsic qualities that make up legal ordering have moral standing. This moral standing of legal ordering thus provides its own criterion of authority. What unites the claims of these theorists is their belief in law as a structure of norms.

If law is to be conceived as a normative system whose authority comes not from the State but from its intrinsic moral properties, then no clear distinction can be drawn between the law of a State and international law. Such an argument undermines the idea of State sovereignty and postulates a monist system of law. The argument is explicit in Kelsen's theory. Kelsen argues that legal norms acquire their validity from an original constitution,[31] but he then suggests that this founding norm of the State's legal order itself derives from a basic norm of public international law.[32] There is,

[26] See, eg, D Dyzenhaus, 'Constitutionalism in an Old Key: Legality and Constituent Power' (2012) 1 *Global Constitutionalism* 229; D Dyzenhaus, 'The Question of Constituent Power' in M Loughlin and N Walker (eds) *The Paradox of Constitutionalism: Constituent Power and Constitutional Form* (OUP 2007).

[27] R Dworkin, *Law's Empire* (Harvard University Press 1986); R Dworkin, *Freedom's Law: The Moral Reading of the American Constitution* (Harvard University Press 1996); and R Dworkin, *Sovereign Virtue: The Theory and Practice of Equality* (Harvard University Press 2000).

[28] M Kumm, 'The Cosmopolitan Turn in Constitutionalism: On the Relationship between Constitutionalism in and beyond the State' in JL Dunoff and JP Trachtman (eds) *Ruling the World? Constitutionalism, International Law and Global Governance* (CUP 2009).

[29] M Kumm, 'The Best of Times and the Worst of Times: Between Constitutional Triumphalism and Nostalgia' in P Dobner and M Loughlin (eds) *The Twilight of Constitutionalism?* (OUP 2010) ch 10.

[30] Kumm (n 28) 263. [31] Kelsen (n 6) 57. [32] Kelsen (n 6) 61–2, 113–25.

in other words, a single universal legal order from which the validity of municipal legal orders derive. Kumm's cosmopolitan theory also defends this position. Kumm argues that sovereignty is now merely 'an empty rhetorical gesture',[33] and should be replaced with a federated scheme on a global basis, entailing an overarching principle of subsidiarity with its notion of graduated authority.

This is highly controversial, not least in being a theory of law far removed from the world we inhabit. But it contains a more basic theoretical difficulty. It postulates a system of law as a normative scheme that somehow carries its own authority. The difficulty here is that norms do not of themselves act; legal norms acquire their authority only within the frame of a political power that ensures their application and enforcement. This political aspect of sovereignty—that which normativists seek to suppress—expresses the essential factual conditions that underpin legal validity. As constitutional scholars have long recognized, governmental power has to exist before any legal norms that regulate the exercise of that power can be made operational.[34] The political domain is not constituted merely through some elaborate scheme of norms.

F. The Concept of Sovereignty

Having identified the confusions and challenges, the meaning of this foundational public law concept of sovereignty can now be clarified.[35] Though conceptually distinct, the concept of sovereignty has its historic roots in the figure of the sovereign. But in order to avoid conflating the terms sovereign and sovereignty—itself a major source of confusion today[36]—the way in which this concept of sovereignty has evolved through the early-modern to the modern period needs iteration.

The term 'sovereign' originally denoted the office of the ruler, and signified the authority of that office. The 'sovereign' ruler was not legally obligated to any other power and, since the ruler's 'sovereignty' expressed independence from any higher authority, sovereignty itself came to signify the quality of the legal relationship between ruler and subject. The *potestas* of the sovereign ruler was conceived as absolute. But this was never conceived as a personal power. The ruler held a representative office equipped with power and jurisdiction for the purpose of establishing a system of rule in the common interest.[37] Once the representative character of the office was

[33] Kumm (n 28) 292.

[34] See, eg, J Madison, A Hamilton, and J Jay, *The Federalist Papers* ([1788] I Kramnick ed, Penguin 1987) no 51 (Madison) p 320: 'you must first enable the government to control the governed; and in the next place oblige it to control itself.'

[35] This account is drawn from a section of my paper; see M Loughlin, 'In Defence of *Staatslehre*' (2009) 48 *Der Staat* 1, 3–5.

[36] This conflation of sovereign and sovereignty is exhibited by Maritain (n 7). This is the reason he comes to the erroneous view that sovereignty is to be defined as a right of supreme and independent power which is maintained as a natural and inalienable right.

[37] Even apparently authoritarian scholars such as Hobbes recognized the representative nature of the office of the sovereign: T Hobbes, *Leviathan* (first published 1651, CUP 1996) ch 30 (Of the office of the sovereign representative).

generally accepted, the claim that this ruling must take an institutional form could be pressed.

Institutionalization of the office of the sovereign became the precondition of its corporatization. This was effected through internal differentiation. As governing tasks increased in scale and complexity, the sovereign powers of office—what Bodin had called the 'marks of sovereignty'[38]—could no longer be exercised by the ruler personally. Initially, the diffusion was rudimentary with, for example, the King's leading ministers acting as custodians of the great seals of State. But eventually these sovereign powers came to be exercised variously through the king's courts, the King's ministers, the King-in-Council, and the King-in-Parliament. The powers of rule were exercised not only through an institutionalized office but also in a corporate form.

Institutionalization, internal differentiation, and corporatization of the office of the sovereign made it possible to distinguish between the sovereign powers of rule and the concept of sovereignty itself. Sovereignty came to be understood as an expression of the absolute legal authority of the ruling power in its corporate capacity. This point was implicit in early-modern writing on the State, in which it was acknowledged that although the powers of rule could be divided, sovereignty—the absolute authority of the collective ruling power—could not.[39]

But the most profound shift in meaning took place when it was accepted that sovereign right was not bestowed from above (by God), but conferred from below (by 'the people'). The problem was that 'the people' can claim to possess an ultimate authority only once institutional arrangements of governing have been established, and this appears paradoxical.[40] This difficulty is overcome, however, if the claim to ultimate authority is recognized as symbolic: the political pact that symbolizes the transition from natural to civil existence is a virtual act whose meaning is manifest only in retrospect. It is through this type of virtual exercise that the symbolic world of the political—the world of public law—is created. In this formulation, sovereignty vests neither in the ruler, nor in the office of government, nor in the people: sovereignty vests in the relationship itself. Sovereignty stands as a representation of the autonomy of a political domain and as a symbol of the absolute authority of that domain.

The claim to absolute authority in the political domain is intrinsically juristic. This is so in two senses. First, the world of absolute authority—of sovereignty—must assume an institutional form, conferring the office of government with a rightful power. Secondly, the power so conferred equips the constituted authorities with unlimited competence to govern through the instrumentality of law. Two different concepts of law are used here: the law that constitutes, and the law that is created as a consequence of that constitution. The latter is positive law. The former is that which is created by the secularization, historicization, and positivization of the

[38] Bodin (n 19).

[39] This is the point of the distinction made by Bodin between sovereignty and government; see Bodin (n 19).

[40] P Ricoeur, 'The Political Paradox' in his *History and Truth* (C Kelbley trans, Northwestern University Press 1965) 247.

medieval natural law idea of fundamental law. The former concept—public law in the technical sense (the law that constitutes the public domain)—can accurately be rendered in French as *droit politique* or in German as *Staatsrecht*: that which confers the right to govern by way of positive law. In English, it is the constitutive aspect of public law.

Sovereignty, then, is both a political and a legal concept. It is the regulatory idea that enables us to conceive of an autonomous political domain in jural terms. As a representation of this autonomous domain, sovereignty might be compared to the double helix of DNA, in which the political and legal run as anti-parallel strands. The essential coding information of the political domain is contained within this structure, in which the political strand is power-generational and the legal is power-distributive. This configuration of coding information constitutes the basic elements of State formation. The type of power with which we are here concerned is political power; this is power generated *inter homines*, power created as a result of the drawing together of a multitude into a 'people' or a 'nation' and harnessed through institutional forms. The most basic institutional formation is the State, a complex juristic entity comprising three essential aspects: territory, people, and ruling authority.[41]

Sovereignty expresses the principles of external independence, internal authority, and ultimate legal supremacy of the State. A people occupying a defined territory and equipped with institutions of self-rule, presents itself to the rest of the world as a sovereign entity, signifying independence from subjection to any higher authority. This principle forms the basis of international law, a sphere in which States contract with one another to regulate inter-State relations.[42] Although it is sometimes said that the existence of a body of international law itself amounts to a limitation on State sovereignty, this is confused and confusing. States may have pledged to restrict the exercise of some of their governmental powers—their 'sovereign rights'—but this is not the same as a restriction on sovereignty. States sign and ratify treaties as sovereign entities: international law, far from being a limitation on, is in reality an explication of State sovereignty.

A similar point can be made with respect to internal authority. Sovereignty is an essential characteristic of a State. Every State possesses supreme, unlimited, and indivisible authority. There can be no limitations on a State's authority to rule by means of law. In most regimes, the constitutional rules allocate the 'sovereign rights' of rule among particular institutions of government, generally between legislature, executive, and judiciary. Since the jurisdictional competence of each of these governmental institutions is established and limited by a formal constitution, none possess ultimate authority to rule. But this does not amount to a limitation on sovereignty. British scholars wedded to the traditional principle of the absolute legal authority of the Crown-in-Parliament, in particular, have a tendency to become confused on this matter. In modern constitutional regimes, the ultimate sovereign authority becomes an abstract entity: 'the

41 See Loughlin (n 10) ch 7.

42 See, eg, UN Charter, Art 2, which recognizes the sovereign equality, territorial integrity, and political independence of all States.

people' or 'the Nation' which is the bearer of 'constituent power'.[43] Constitutional arrangements do not limit or restrict sovereignty. They are exemplifications of the existence of sovereignty.

G. Sovereignty and the European Union

These confusions in the treatment of sovereignty have mainly arisen through the distortions of realists in international relations and their allies in the domestic sphere, the legal positivists. They have acquired a particular prominence today in analyses of the nature of relations between Member States and the European Union. This is illustrated in the pioneering work of Neil MacCormick. In *Questioning Sovereignty*, MacCormick provides an account of the relationship between State, law, and politics which, from the public law perspective I have outlined, is unconvincing and which leads him to make an erroneous argument about sovereignty. Building on distinctions between legal and political sovereignty and between internal and external sovereignty, he makes a case for limited or divided sovereignty—a position that makes no sense—and suggests that the arrangement of European nation-states today is best characterized as one of 'post-sovereignty'.[44]

Many of these errors are traceable to his Chorley Lecture of 1992, in which MacCormick argued that 'sovereignty and sovereign states, and the inexorable linkage of law with sovereignty and the State, have been but the passing phenomena of a few centuries'; that 'jurisprudence has lately by-passed sovereignty'; that those legal theorists who make 'the tacit assumption of the paradigmatic quality of the State and its law' are distorting experience; that sovereignty leads to a 'monocular view of these things'; and that 'our passing beyond the sovereign State is... a good thing, an entirely welcome development in the history of legal and political ideas'.[45]

It is apparent that his understanding of sovereignty derives almost entirely from John Austin's nineteenth century empiricist theory of legal positivism. Following Austin, MacCormick conflates the idea of sovereignty with that of a sovereign, believing it to entail the notion 'that all law must originate in a single power source, like a sovereign'.[46] This results in some contrived analysis in which, having defined the sovereign State as 'a territorial political order coupled with a legally defined position of near-absolute legislative power' he questions whether this is 'intelligible and satisfactory'.[47] We might agree that it is not, but it is a conundrum of his own

[43] I here set to one side the complicated question about the existence of a sovereign in this type of constitutional regime. The constitutional arrangements may govern in normal times, but that does not cover the situation of an exception in which extraordinary action must be taken as a matter of the State's self-preservation. Only at these moments does the sovereign reveal itself, hence Schmitt's claim that the sovereign 'is he who determines on the exception' (Schmitt (n 23) 5).

[44] N MacCormick, *Questioning Sovereignty: Law, State, and Nation in the European Commonwealth* (OUP 1999) esp 126 (internal–external), 127–31 (legal–political), 95, and 142 (post-sovereignty).

[45] N MacCormick, 'Beyond the Sovereign State' (1993) 56 *MLR* 1. The quotations are to be found at 1, 2, 2, 5, and 1 respectively.

[46] MacCormick (n 45) 8.

[47] MacCormick (n 45) 14.

devising. Yet from this unsound presumption MacCormick argues that it necessarily follows that sovereign States not only 'have a monopoly of legitimate political power' but also possess 'a monopoly of normative power', which in turn leads to the marginalization of international law, primitive law, church law, and other types of so-called 'living law'.[48] If by State MacCormick means—as is implied—some central authority, none of this follows from the concept of sovereignty I have outlined. Neither does his conclusion that, since no nation-State in the EU is in 'a position such that all the power exercised internally in it, whether politically or legally, derives from purely internal sources' none can be regarded any longer as a sovereign State.[49] This is a clear illustration of the conflation of sovereignty and government.

MacCormick later amplifies this analysis, claiming that 'absolute or unitary sovereignty is entirely absent from the legal and political setting of the European Community' on the ground that '[n]either politically nor legally is any member State in possession of ultimate power over its own internal affairs'.[50] Yet one can accept the fact that the EU 'exercises political power on some matters over member states' and the fact that EU legislation 'binds member states and overrides internal state-law within the respective criteria of validity' without it following that 'ultimate' authority ceases to remain within the Member States.[51] The elaborate inter-governmental arrangements of the EU have been created by its Member States to meet the collective interests of their citizens. Unless the argument is that this arrangement is now so fixed and permanent that it is no longer within the political authority of a Member State to withdraw from these treaty arrangements, then no issue of ultimate authority—and no question of sovereignty—is involved. This is an argument that, to my knowledge, no jurist has yet made.

The persistence of these claims about 'divided sovereignty' or about evolution 'beyond the sovereign State' in the EU context partly derives from British jurists working with a highly parochial, positivist concept of legal sovereignty. They confuse the foundational concept of sovereignty with a particular political conviction: that the State cannot persist without the continued existence of a specific governmental institution equipped with unlimited legal competence. This makes no sense. It suggests that sovereignty is destroyed whenever a State adopts a federal system of government, or even when it adopts a modern fundamental constitution that allocates governmental competences across a variety of institutions. It also suggests the absence of even an elementary grasp of the science of public law.

Alongside this peculiarly British confusion, there exists a more general ambiguity in the European literature concerning sovereignty and government. Much of this stems from an early ruling of the Court of Justice which claimed that the European Community 'creates a new legal order...for the benefit of which the States have limited their sovereign rights, albeit within limited fields'.[52] The first part of this

[48] MacCormick (n 45). [49] MacCormick (n 45) 16. [50] MacCormick (n 44) 132.
[51] MacCormick (n 44) 132.
[52] Case 26/62, *Van Gend en Loos v Nederlandse Administratie der Berlastingen* [1963] ECR 1, 12.

statement presents no conceptual difficulties. A number of legal orders can exist within the frame of a sovereign State. This is, after all, exemplified in the United Kingdom as well as being a central feature of federal systems. All that is required is the existence of procedures for determining spheres of competence and rules of priority. The more general source of confusion here concerns the Court's reference to 'sovereign rights'. But this term simply means 'powers of government'. Certain powers of government—governmental competences—have undoubtedly been limited and restricted as a consequence of EU membership, just as certain powers of government are limited and restricted whenever a State enters into any treaty. But this has no bearing on sovereignty.[53]

The distinction between competences and sovereignty must be kept clear: competences can be limited, whereas sovereignty cannot. Sovereign authority resides in the ultimate power of the people to determine the form of constitution of the State, and this can entail membership of the EU or withdrawal from it. Those who argue that the existence of EU law imposes a limit on sovereignty have it the wrong way round. Rather, as successive rulings of the German Federal Constitutional Court have indicated, it is the sovereignty of Member States that impose limits on the competence of the EU.[54] Far from limiting, dividing, or decentralizing sovereignty, the obligations that a State takes on through treaties are manifestations of its sovereign authority.

H. Conclusions

In this chapter, I have tried to show how sovereignty is misunderstood and misused both in legal theory and political science. This concept, which underpins the modern discourse of public law, serves as the symbolic representation of the autonomy of the political domain and is the medium through which the idea of absolute legal authority can be grasped. Much of the confusion over the use of this term stems from a failure of scholars to distinguish the concept of sovereignty from the figure

[53] The Court of Justice of the EU has stated that, given the principle of the supremacy of EU law, it is for EU law to determine the relationship between national law and member law. But this remains purely at the level of interaction of legal orders. Those who claim that it affects sovereignty are in reality adopting a normativist position which seeks altogether to displace the concept. For an illustration, albeit with respect to the European Convention of Human Rights, see Stone Sweet (n 16). Sensing that something is not quite right with his analysis with respect to sovereignty he states: 'I define *sovereignty* in narrow, juridical terms, as the formal capacity to make and enforce legal norms' (61). In that sentence, Stone Sweet accentuates sovereignty, whereas I would accentuate 'narrow', 'formal', and 'legal norms'. He later returns to this problem, finally conceding the implications: 'From the point of view of centralized sovereignty, the notion of "decentralized sovereignty" may seem nonsense, an oxymoron. At the very least, how the regime has evolved... requires us to reconsider the concept of sovereignty, perhaps rejecting it altogether' (62).

[54] *Brunner v European Union Treaty* [1994] 1 CMLR 57; Lisbon Treaty decision of 30 June 2008 (2 BvE 2/08); *Honeywell* decision of 6 July 2010 (2 BvR 2661/06); Monetary Union Financial Stabilization Act decision of 7 Sept 2011 (2 BvR 987/10). See JE Murkens, '"We Want Our Identity Back": The Revival of National Sovereignty in the German Federal Constitutional Court's Decision on the Lisbon Treaty' [2010] *PL* 530–50.

of the sovereign. The construction of an omnicompetent figure of the sovereign was an essential transitional step in the formation of the practice of public law. But idealization of the office of the sovereign ruler was merely the precondition of its destruction. The modern State has invariably assumed a constitutional form in which the sovereign rights of government are allocated among a variety of institutions. The formation of an elaborate institutional apparatus of rule has thus become the means by which the concept of sovereignty maintains its authority. It is often stated that 'the people' is sovereign, that is, that the people now acts as the ultimate authority and bearer of 'constituent power'. This is not wrong, but since the concept of 'the people' is itself one of symbolic representation, it is more accurate to say that sovereignty has no locus: it is the set of relations through which our ideas of authority are conceived.[55]

The current malaise stems from a failure to grasp the nature of this evolution. The errors present themselves differently in political science and law. In political science, it is the refusal to acknowledge the legal character of sovereignty as a concept which expresses the idea of political power in juridical terms, as is highlighted by the common assumption that it mainly concerns the ability of a nation-state to control its own material conditions. In legal theory, the error arises from a failure to differentiate between sovereignty and sovereign. Conflating the two, legal theorists have assumed that the apportionment of sovereign rights of governing among a variety of institutions, far from being an explication of sovereignty, actually results in the limitation, division, or destruction of sovereignty. Sovereignty is a juridical not a material concept, and as a juridical concept it symbolizes a unity of ordering, not an aggregation of competences.

So why does it matter if this term is given a variety of discrepant meanings in different frames of thought? Is this analysis concerned only with the technicalities of the vocabulary and grammar of public law? When MacCormick claims that the EU offers the prospect of the emergence of a new kind of commonwealth 'with new possibilities of imagining, and thus of subsequently realizing, political order on the basis of a pluralistic rather than a monolithic conception of the exercise of political power and legal authority',[56] nothing in my account of sovereignty inhibits that realization. When he says that by 'creating a framework of political and economic order across many states and national cultures... Europe necessarily weakens somewhat the idea of the exclusive territoriality of its parts' and this does not 'derogate unacceptably from internal jurisdictions and democratic institutional authorities within the parts',[57] this account in no way contradicts that assessment.

Yet there is an issue of substance underpinning this analysis. A serious threat to the concept of sovereignty does presently exist and it has not been precisely identified by many scholars who now invoke the term. That threat concerns the *erosion* of sovereignty. This threat stems from a growing belief that the intricacy of the new patterns of governmental arrangements is leading to the establishment of

[55] M Loughlin, *The Idea of Public Law* (OUP 2003) ch 5.
[56] MacCormick (n 44) 191.
[57] MacCormick (n 44).

new technologies of governing that cannot adequately be grasped in the modern discourse of public law. That discourse, erected on the foundation of sovereignty and expressing the idea of collective self-actualization rendered in the language of liberty, equality, and solidarity, may be both fluid and ambiguous and now is undoubtedly under strain. It nonetheless contains within it a notion of political freedom that is worthy of preservation. There is, to be sure, no guarantee that it can be preserved. But what is clear is that the labyrinth of errors that riddles contemporary usage of sovereignty and which is leading to the corruption of this discourse of public law does absolutely nothing either to bolster the prospect of its retention or to establish an alternative discourse better able to grasp in juristic terms the nature of this newly-emerging governing regime.

4

Parliamentary Sovereignty and Constitutional Change in the United Kingdom

Jeffrey Goldsworthy[*]

A. Parliamentary Sovereignty as an Obstacle to Constitutional Change

In this chapter I will examine ways of reforming the United Kingdom's so-called 'unwritten'—uncodified and partly common law or customary—constitution. This requires addressing a notorious conundrum, posed by the constitution's most fundamental 'unwritten' doctrine, which maintains that Parliament possesses sovereign law-making authority—authority that is legally (but not morally or practically) unlimited.[1] The conundrum is this: can Parliament use its sovereign authority to limit its authority? If it cannot, it is not easy to see how the British constitution can be legally reformed to provide Britons with the supposed benefits of modern constitutionalism, such as the protection of a strong bill of rights, a separation of judicial power, or a federal division of powers between its component parts.

The conundrum arises because: (a) any such constitutional reform must be enacted by Parliament, given that it is the supreme law-maker within the United Kingdom and no other institution possesses the requisite authority; (b) the efficacy of such a reform would depend on its being constitutionally 'entrenched', in the sense of being legally impervious to violation, amendment, or repeal by subsequent legislation passed through the ordinary legislative process; but (c) according to one influential interpretation of the doctrine of parliamentary sovereignty, Parliament cannot entrench legislation to prevent it being later amended or repealed by ordinary legislation.

Sovereignty understood in this way is sometimes called 'continuing sovereignty'; this is distinguished from 'self-embracing sovereignty', which could be used by

* Professor of Law, Monash University. I thank Dale Smith, Patrick Emerton, and Stuart Lakin for helpful comments on Section B.

[1] J Goldsworthy, *The Sovereignty of Parliament: History and Philosophy* (Clarendon Press 1999).

Parliament to control or limit its law-making authority in the future. But this terminology is ambiguous and potentially confusing. If Parliament could subject the exercise of its legislative authority to purely procedural or formal requirements but not substantive limits, it could be said to possess procedural self-embracing sovereignty and substantive continuing sovereignty.

If Parliament possesses full continuing sovereignty (substantive and procedural) then any statutory provision purporting to prohibit new constitutional limits to its authority being overridden by ordinary legislation could itself be repealed by ordinary legislation, possibly even by implication, which would mean that in practice it could be ignored. The efficacy of implied repeal was robustly affirmed by the Judicial Committee of the Privy Council in *McCawley v R*,[2] on the ground that an 'uncontrolled constitution', such as the United Kingdom's, can be amended or repealed in the same way as any other law:

> Where the constitution is uncontrolled the consequences of its freedom admit of no qualification whatever... If it were uncontrolled, it would be an elementary commonplace that in the eye of the law the legislative document or documents which defined it occupied precisely the same position as a Dog Act or any other Act, however humble its subject-matter.[3]

Their Lordships held that, because Queensland's Constitution Act 1916 was uncontrolled, it was 'embarrassing and even ridiculous' for the respondents to maintain that the State legislature had to amend or repeal the instrument by express provision before being able to legislate inconsistently with it.[4] The efficacy of implied repeal followed inexorably from 'the spirit and genius' of the British constitution, on which that of Queensland was modelled; it made no difference that the former was 'constituted by historic development' while the latter was set out in 'an originating document'.[5]

This mind-set has made it difficult for some constitutional lawyers to conceive of how Parliament's sovereign authority could ever, by lawful rather than revolutionary means, be subordinated to entrenched constitutional limits. For example, Peter Oliver has written that if Parliament's sovereignty is not self-embracing, then 'Parliament as presently constituted... is frozen for all time as a legally untouchable and prior rule',[6] and that 'the dominant approach in the United Kingdom was to assume that Parliament's sovereignty was continuing *and that it must forever be so*'.[7]

A solution to the conundrum will not be found by brooding about the concept of sovereignty to determine whether a true sovereign can or cannot limit itself, or whether true sovereignty is necessarily continuing or self-embracing.[8] Any attempt to derive substantive legal conclusions from purely conceptual or metaphysical analysis must lead to a dead-end. It is true that sixteenth and seventeenth century theories of sovereignty influenced the development of the doctrine of parliamentary

[2] [1920] AC 691 (PC). [3] *McCawley* (n 2) 704. [4] *McCawley* (n 2) 705.

[5] *McCawley* (n 2) 703–4.

[6] PC Oliver, *The Constitution of Independence: The Development of Constitutional Theory in Australia, Canada, and New Zealand* (OUP 2005) 87.

[7] Oliver (n 6) 9 (emphasis added). [8] See the second paragraph of Section A.

sovereignty. But there were many other influences, and the word 'sovereignty' came to be used as a convenient label for a long-accepted, if partly under-determinate doctrine, with no assumption that it necessarily replicates some *a priori* concept of sovereignty.[9] Instead, it is necessary to examine the nature of the unwritten constitution, or at least, of the unwritten doctrine of parliamentary sovereignty.

The doctrine is 'unwritten' because it is not set out in a written constitution or statute. It is well known that it is not a creature of statute law. It was not, and could not have been, enacted into law by Parliament, because Parliament could not have conferred its law-making authority upon itself. As has often been observed, that would have been boot-strapping, question-begging, and so on. The source of Parliament's authority to make statutes must be deeper than its own statutes.[10]

It should by now be equally well known that the doctrine is not a matter of common law, in the popular modern sense of judge-made law. Among other problems, such as historical absurdity, that would raise embarrassing questions about the source of the judges' authority to make law. Their authority, like that of Parliament, must come from somewhere, and the judges, like Parliament, cannot 'pull themselves up by their own bootstraps', by conferring authority on themselves.[11]

So someone's legal authority—Parliament's, the judges', or both—must be grounded in a kind of law that was made neither by Parliament nor by the judges unilaterally. Enquiries into the nature of that kind of law, which constitutes the very foundation of the British legal system, cannot avoid grappling with difficult and contentious questions in the philosophy of law.

B. The Nature of the Doctrine of Parliamentary Sovereignty

Over the last two decades the doctrine of parliamentary sovereignty has been subjected to a crescendo of criticisms, either for being normatively unattractive, legally erroneous, or both. The criticisms have persuaded several senior judges to express scepticism about the doctrine, although others have responded by reaffirming it.[12]

[9] For the same reason, I am not greatly troubled by arguments that the word 'sovereignty' is inappropriate and misleading; see, eg, P Eleftheriadis, 'Law and Sovereignty' (2010) 29 *Law and Philosophy* 535, 547–53. The word, or something similar such as 'supremacy', is useful and perhaps indispensable in order to convey the core idea that Parliament's law-making authority is not subject to any substantive limit. In that respect the US Congress is clearly distinguishable, although even there the idea of legislative 'supremacy' that is limited only by written constitutions is regularly used: see J Goldsworthy, *Parliamentary Sovereignty: Contemporary Debates* (CUP 2010) 226–8.

[10] Goldsworthy (n 1) 238–9; Goldsworthy (n 9) 51.

[11] Goldsworthy (n 9) 51 (quoting Lord Lester); Goldsworthy (n 1) 240–3.

[12] For scepticism see, eg, *R (Jackson) v Attorney General* [2005] UKHL 56, [2006] 1 AC 262 [102] (Lord Steyn), [104], [107], [126] (Lord Hope), [159] (Baroness Hale); *Thoburn v Sunderland City Council* [2002] EWHC 195 (Admin), [2003] QB 151 [60] (Laws LJ). For reaffirmation see, eg, *Jackson*, [9] (Lord Bingham), [168] (Lord Carswell); Lord Bingham of Cornhill, 'The Rule of Law and the Sovereignty of Parliament' (2008) 19 *King's College LJ* 223, reprinted in T Bingham, *The Rule of Law* (Allen Lane 2010); Lord Neuberger, 'Who are the Masters Now?', Second Lord Alexander of Weedon Lecture, 6 April 2011, available at <http://www.judiciary.gov.uk/Resources/JCO/Documents/Speeches/mr-speech-weedon-lecture-110406.pdf> (last accessed 8 April 2013).

Consequently, it may no longer be supported by a consensus among the senior judiciary, which necessarily gives rise to some uncertainty about its current status.[13]

The significance of this judicial disagreement about the very foundation of the British legal system depends on philosophical questions about the nature and basis of law. Why is it that equally experienced judges can disagree about such a basic legal issue, and how can their disagreement be resolved? While supporters of the doctrine of parliamentary sovereignty have tended to seek succour from legal positivism, most of its leading critics have embraced Ronald Dworkin's interpretive theory of law.[14] This simultaneously exemplifies the practical relevance of analytical legal philosophy to real legal problems, and provides a concrete example of deep theoretical disagreement that should be grist for the philosophers' mill.

For many legal positivists, the most important function of a legal system, at least in a pluralistic community, is to enable its members to cooperate with one another despite their chronic and interminable disagreements about what is morally required of them in their mutual dealings.[15] A legal system performs that function by authoritatively establishing what norms of behaviour will be promulgated and enforced on behalf of the community as a whole, notwithstanding the continuing dissent of some individuals or groups. But a legal system can do this only if there is widespread consensus, at least among most senior legal officials, about the location and scope of the law-making authority needed to promulgate those norms.[16] Without such a consensus, a viable legal system can be neither established nor maintained.[17] It is important to note that the parties to the requisite consensus must include not only the senior judiciary, but senior officials of the political branches of government.[18]

The term 'widespread consensus' is deliberately vague. There must be a general congruence in the behaviour of officials in recognizing what laws are valid and in enforcing them. That surely depends partly on general agreement as to deeper norms (rules or principles) by which that behaviour is publicly justified, although there does not need to be agreement about the deepest reasons that motivate different officials publicly to endorse those norms.[19] The allegiance of some officials to those norms might to some extent be feigned: they might have private reservations about

[13] M Elliott, 'Interpretative Bills of Rights and the Mystery of the Unwritten Constitution' [2011] *NZL Rev* 591, 622.

[14] See, eg, Goldsworthy (n 1) ch 10; TRS Allan, *Constitutional Justice: A Liberal Theory of the Rule of Law* (OUP 2001); J Jowell, 'Parliamentary Sovereignty under the New Constitutional Hypothesis' [2006] *PL* 562; S Lakin, 'Debunking the Idea of Parliamentary Sovereignty: The Controlling Factor of Legality in the British Constitution' (2008) 28 *OJLS* 709; MD Walters, 'Written Constitutions and Unwritten Constitutionalism' in G Huscroft (ed) *Expounding the Constitution: Essays in Constitutional Theory* (CUP 2008) 245.

[15] Goldsworthy (n 1) 254–6.

[16] Goldsworthy (n 1) 254–6.

[17] Goldsworthy (n 1) 240–1, 254–6.

[18] Goldsworthy (n 1) 240–6; Goldsworthy (n 9) 54–6.

[19] Goldsworthy (n 1) 256–8. Adam Tucker attributes to me the opposite view, that there must be official consensus as to the ultimate reasons for this behaviour, in A Tucker, 'Uncertainty in the Rule of Recognition and in the Doctrine of Parliamentary Sovereignty' (2011) *OJLS* 61, 69 fn 34. This stems from a misquotation that omits the concluding words of the passage he quotes (italicized in what follows), in which I say that according to Hart legal practices are constituted not only by officials' behaviour but 'also by their reasons for engaging in it, *at least in so far as those reasons*

some aspects of the norms, which lead to occasional surreptitious disobedience.[20] Moreover, these norms are likely to be under-determinate, in that they do not provide clear solutions to some possible 'hard cases'. For that reason, disagreements among officials about the appropriate resolution of these cases must be resolved through moral and political reasoning.[21] Whether or not the doctrine of parliamentary sovereignty permits Parliament to bind itself to comply with requirements as to the form of, or procedure for, future legislation—in other words, whether or not Parliament possesses procedural self-embracing sovereignty—is an example.[22] But the core of the doctrine, that Parliament's law-making authority is not subject to any substantive limits, should not be in doubt.[23]

On this view, the doctrine of parliamentary sovereignty is a kind of customary but partly under-determinate law, constituted by the long-standing custom of legal officialdom, which neither Parliament nor the judges created, or can change, unilaterally. This is consistent with HLA Hart's theory that the fundamental 'secondary' rules in any legal system are constituted by the practices of senior legal officials. The existence of secondary rules of change and recognition depends, in large part, on their being publicly accepted as binding by the most senior officials of all branches of government.[24] They do not—and could not—owe their existence to acceptance by the judiciary alone.[25]

Dworkin's interpretive theory of law, at least as expounded by Trevor Allan, does not seem to acknowledge the need for this official consensus. Allan insists that parliamentary sovereignty is a creature of the common law, which he regards not as judicially posited law,[26] but as a generally coherent body of norms based on fundamental principles of political morality that the judges enunciate and expound through 'interpretation' but have no authority to change. The identity of these principles is supposedly an objective matter: they are whatever principles provide the best moral justification of the legal system as a whole. The process of interpretation by which they are identified requires that they satisfy two inter-related criteria: they must 'fit' enough

constitute rules'. See Goldsworthy (n 1) 248. See also Goldsworthy (n 1) 256–7. Tucker says exactly the same thing: see A Tucker (n 19) 64.

[20] See J Goldsworthy, 'The Limits of Judicial Fidelity to Law: The Coxford Lecture' (2011) 24 *Canadian Journal of Law & Jurisprudence* 305.

[21] Goldsworthy (n 1) 259. Adam Tucker also erroneously attributes to me a 'simplistic' thesis that ignores indeterminacies in the doctrine of parliamentary sovereignty as a rule of recognition. See Tucker (n 19) 62. Tucker's emphasis on indeterminacies in the doctrine of parliamentary sovereignty was anticipated in Oliver (n 6), which is discussed in Goldsworthy (n 9) ch 5.

[22] Goldsworthy (n 1) 2, 14–15, 244–5, 259; Goldsworthy (n 9) chs 5–7, 289–90, 298.

[23] Tucker argues that whether or not an 'odious' statue would be legally valid is indeterminate, because the rule of recognition must be inferred strictly from officials' past behaviour and not their 'hypothetical beliefs' about their own future behaviour if confronted with an unprecedented statute. See Tucker (n 19) 69. This is difficult to reconcile with (a) the rule of recognition being constituted partly by officials' 'standing disposition' to take 'patterns of conduct as guides to their own future behaviour' (Tucker (n 19) 70, quoting HLA Hart); (b) the rule of recognition being a general rule, which entails that it must transcend the particular past behaviour from which it is partly inferred; (c) his own footnote 24; and (d) occasional odious statutes, far from being unprecedented, having been enacted and accepted as valid in the past.

[24] HLA Hart, *The Concept of Law* (2nd edn, Clarendon Press 1994) ch 6.

[25] Goldsworthy (n 1) 240–6; Goldsworthy (n 9) 54–6.

[26] See text following n 10.

of the other putative norms of the system to count as an interpretation of it (that is, only a limited number of those norms may be rejected as erroneous), and also provide the best available moral justification of the system as a whole. The most fundamental principles change only if other parts of the system change.

Those, like Allan, who apply Dworkinian interpretation to the British constitution usually conclude that its most fundamental principles either always limited Parliament's law-making authority, or given recent changes to the constitution, do so now.[27] They argue, for example, that Parliament today is recognized as having authority to enact statutes largely due to general acceptance of the principle of democracy, and that this could not justify allegiance to a statute that undermined democracy because 'the statute would violate the political principle which the doctrine [of parliamentary sovereignty] itself enshrines'.[28]

A major problem for this interpretive theory is that the vagueness of the 'fit' criterion, and the epistemic difficulties of the moral justification criterion, are likely to make very different interpretations of a legal system plausible. If radically different interpretations of the location and scope of law-making authority were endorsed by different groups of senior legal officials (say, by judges on the one hand and legislators on the other), there would be a real threat to the continuing efficacy or stability of the system. This is not a fanciful possibility: something like this happened in South Africa in the 1950s.[29]

Allan's interpretation of the contemporary British constitution is highly contestable. It can plausibly be argued that a better interpretation, especially in terms of the dimension of 'fit', accommodates the doctrine of parliamentary sovereignty.[30] Rival theories of the British constitution are sometimes grouped into two categories, labelled 'legal constitutionalism' and 'political constitutionalism'.[31] Parliamentary sovereignty is a crucial element of political constitutionalism, but is rejected by strong versions of legal constitutionalism.[32] Political constitutionalism can be defended on the basis of either a legal positivist analysis, or a Dworkinian interpretation, of the constitution. If conflicting interpretations led legislators to endorse political constitutionalism, and judges to endorse a strong version of legal constitutionalism, there would be a serious risk of a destabilizing conflict between them.

In Dworkinian theory, interpretation is the method by which judges resolve disagreements about the content of ordinary (statute and common) law. But even

[27] For Trevor Allan's most recent enunciation of this view see TRS Allan, 'Questions of Legality and Legitimacy: Form and Substance in British Constitutionalism' (2011) 9 *International Journal of Constitutional Law* 155. See also Jowell (n 14); Lakin (n 14); Walters (n 14).

[28] TRS Allan, *Law, Liberty and Justice: The Legal Foundations of British Constitutionalism* (Clarendon Press 1993) 282.

[29] See Hart (n 24) 122–3, discussed in Goldsworthy (n 1) 241. See also the account of the nineteenth-century dispute over parliamentary privilege between the Houses of Parliament and the courts in Goldsworthy (n 1) 242.

[30] Goldsworthy (n 1) 254, 271.

[31] For a description of political constitutionalism and references to the literature, see R Bellamy, 'Political Constitutionalism and the Human Rights Act' (2011) 9 *International Journal of Constitutional Law* 86, esp 89–94.

[32] Bellamy (n 31) 89–94.

if the theory is right about this, it is surely because there is a rule established by a general consensus among senior officials that judges have authority to do so. If officials disagreed about whether the judges had such authority, the disagreement could surely not be settled by the judges' interpretation of their own authority. That would be question-begging.[33] It is hard to see how interpretation could, for practical purposes, resolve disagreements between rival interpretations of a constitution in which the authority of the interpreters is itself in dispute. To suggest that the legally correct interpretation is whichever of the contenders (that of the legislators or that of the judges) is truly the best would hardly be helpful. Both groups could plausibly claim that their interpretation is the best, in terms of either 'fit', or moral justification, or both.

As Jeremy Waldron has put it, 'the prescription most commonly advanced by the [moral] realist, "*Choose the objectively right answer*", is, though metaphysically admirable, politically impotent'.[34] His point is corroborated by the fact that when judges disagree among themselves about the best interpretation of ordinary law, for practical purposes their disagreement is not, and could not be, resolved by the criterion of objective rightness or truth. That is precisely what is in dispute. Their disagreement is settled, instead, by a universally accepted decision procedure whereby the interpretation of the majority prevails.

If identifying the foundations of a legal system depended ultimately on establishing objective moral truths, and two powerful groups of officials disagreed with one another about those truths, we would be plunged back into the very predicament from which we need to be rescued by law: that of chronic and interminable moral disagreement.[35] Without consensus between the two groups as to whose interpretation is legally authoritative, it is hard to see how potentially destructive conflict could be avoided. Resolution of the disagreement through mutually respectful dialogue could not be guaranteed. The predicament can be escaped only if there is official consensus either as to the location and scope of law-making authority, or as to the location of authority to resolve disagreements about those matters (which would sooner or later amount to the same thing). Dworkinians appear simply to assume that judges possess authority of the second kind, but such an assumption is question-begging.

Of course, there can be no guarantee that the requisite official consensus, once established, can be sustained. My point is not that a legal positivist analysis of a constitution makes official consensus more likely (although if all officials acknowledge the need for consensus, they might be more likely to achieve it). It is merely that Dworkinian interpretation cannot replace official consensus as an essential foundation for any viable legal system. Even if an interpretation of the constitution were 'correct' according to Dworkinian criteria, in the absence of official consensus either as to its correctness or as to the authority of the interpreter to affirm it, it could not provide the stable foundation that any legal system needs to function effectively. If the

[33] Goldsworthy (n 9) 52–3.

[34] J Waldron, 'Moral Truth and Judicial Review' (1998) 43 *American Journal of Jurisprudence* 75, 81.

[35] Goldsworthy (n 1) 254–6.

requisite official consensus breaks down, there is no alternative to political contestation or possibly more dangerous kinds of conflict. That disturbing prospect should be kept in mind whenever the future of parliamentary sovereignty is discussed.

Has the official consensus that traditionally supported the doctrine of parliamentary sovereignty already broken down? The expression of dissenting opinions by a few senior judges in *R (Jackson) v Attorney General* does not prove that it has.[36] This is because, first, their opinions are either based on demonstrable falsehoods or are highly questionable;[37] secondly, they can be overridden by a majority of their peers; and thirdly, they can be sidelined by retirement and replacement.

C. Changing a Customary Rule

HLA Hart pointed out that one defect of a system of purely customary law is the lack of a 'rule of change'—a rule that permits the deliberate making of changes.[38] This is a problem for Britain's unwritten constitution. Although the customary doctrine of parliamentary sovereignty allows Parliament to change all other parts of the constitution, this rule of change does not apply to the doctrine itself.

It was not logically impossible for the official consensus that constitutes this customary doctrine to include a rule of change allowing either Parliament, or the courts, unilaterally to limit Parliament's sovereignty. Such a rule of change could have been adopted in Britain. As for Parliament, this would have amounted to the official consensus accepting substantive, as well as procedural, self-embracing sovereignty. As for the courts, it would have amounted to the consensus accepting a positivist version of common law constitutionalism, which regards parliamentary sovereignty in the same way as ordinary common law doctrines of tort or contract—as judge-made law that is subject to judicial modification and development.[39] But there is scant evidence that the actual official consensus does accept either of these rules of change, or indeed, any particular rule of change.

Moreover, there are powerful reasons of democratic principle for officials not accepting these particular rules of change. If the courts had authority unilaterally to modify or repudiate the doctrine of parliamentary sovereignty, they could impose all kinds of limits on Parliament's authority with no democratic input or warrant. That would be a profoundly undemocratic method of constitutional change. Common law constitutionalists might prefer not to have to persuade their

[36] *Jackson* (n 12).

[37] Lord Steyn's assertion that the judges created the principle of parliamentary sovereignty (*Jackson* (n 12) [102]) is a demonstrable falsehood, as is Lord Hope's related assertion that the principle was 'created by the common law' (*Jackson* (n 12) [126]), if he means judge-made law. See Goldsworthy (n 1); Goldsworthy (n 9) ch 2. Lord Hope's suggestion that the Acts of Union 1707, the ECA 1972, and the HRA 1998 have all qualified or limited parliamentary sovereignty ([104]–[106]) are highly questionable: Goldsworthy (n 9) ch 10. See also Lord Hope's more cautious remarks in *AXA General Insurance Ltd v Lord Advocate* [2011] UKSC 46, [2012] AC 868 [46]–[51]; and Chapters 6 and 5 in this volume by Lord Hope and Alison L Young respectively.

[38] Hart (n 24) 90–3.

[39] See n 11.

fellow citizens of the merits of their particular vision of constitutionalism, but they should be required to nonetheless.

If Parliament had authority unilaterally to limit its own authority—if it had substantive as well as procedural self-embracing sovereignty—a political party with temporary control of both Houses could protect its partisan policies, enacted into law, from amendment or repeal by majorities in later Parliaments, which would also be undemocratic. Or it could include in a particular statute a requirement that the assent of some private body, such as a corporation, be obtained in order to amend or repeal the statute. This might seem far-fetched, but a corporation entering into an agreement with the government involving the investment of a large amount of money for the sake of long-term returns might seek binding guarantees that the agreement will not be unilaterally changed by either the government or Parliament.[40]

It is not inconsistent for me, having argued on other occasions that it is reasonable to entrust Parliament with legislative sovereignty, to warn against possible abuses of substantive self-embracing sovereignty. One of the reasons for entrusting Parliament with substantive continuing sovereignty is that mistakes and injustices can be corrected by future Parliaments. But if Parliament had substantive self-embracing sovereignty it could make this very difficult or impossible.

The doctrine of parliamentary sovereignty surely can be changed or even repudiated: any suggestion that Britain, alone among all the nations in the world, is incapable of adopting an entrenched written constitution would surely be absurd. But the doctrine can be changed or repudiated only by a change in the consensus among senior legal officials in general, which is what currently constitutes and sustains the doctrine.[41] Requiring such a change builds some checks and balances into the process of constitutional reform, because power to change the doctrine is not vested in a single institution or a small group of officials.[42]

Of course, any such change must start somewhere: someone must initiate the necessary change in consensus. The courts could attempt to initiate change, but could succeed only if the other branches of government were willing to accept it. Similarly, Parliament could attempt to initiate such a change, by enacting legislation that purports to limit or abdicate part of its authority, but would succeed only if the courts were willing to endorse it.[43]

It has been argued that any change to this official consensus must amount to a revolution, even if it is an amicable, 'legal' revolution. Sir William Wade took this view, and argued that such revolutionary changes have already taken place.[44] But why describe a wholly consensual change in the official consensus as extra-legal and revolutionary? One possible reason is that the official consensus itself positively forbids such a change. On this view, officials share a consensus that their consensus must never change: that they and their successors must *forever* accept that Parliament is sovereign. But it would surely be implausible to attribute this to the official

[40] Here and in the next paragraph I borrow my own words from Goldsworthy (n 9) 116, 137–8.
[41] See Section B. [42] See Section E. [43] See Section E.
[44] HWR Wade, 'Sovereignty—Revolution or Evolution?' (1996) 112 *LQR* 568.

consensus, because it would be foolish and futile to purport to forbid constitutional change in perpetuity. Officials today cannot effectively prevent themselves from changing their own minds, let alone prevent other officials in the future from doing so. And it would be foolishly arrogant to condemn in advance possible changes that, in the unforeseeable circumstances of the future, might be desirable or even necessary.[45]

Customary law is not static: it evolves along with the consensus that constitutes it. Abrupt changes to fundamental legal rules, imposed on many officials by coercion or removal from office, can be described as revolutionary. But gradual, consensual change in response to broader social developments may be regarded as entirely lawful.[46]

An abrupt change from one system of government to a radically different one—say, from parliamentary sovereignty to an entrenched, written constitution—might aptly be described as revolutionary, even if it were brought about by a peaceful and voluntary change in the consensus among senior officials and the community more broadly. But that is of little importance. It is, and must be, possible for such a change to be made and, if so, the important question is how it should be made.

Non-coercive constitutional change in contemporary societies requires appealing to the principles of political morality that are the source of modern constitutional legitimacy, such as popular sovereignty and the rule of law. Such changes require political as much as legal processes and decision-making. Officials who favour constitutional change must persuade other officials, and the public at large, that it is desirable. The more important the proposed change, the more necessary is public consultation, perhaps in the form of a Citizens Assembly or Convention, or even participation in decision-making by way of a referendum.[47] If sections of the public regard themselves as members of different sub-national communities with some distinctive interests—as they do in the United Kingdom—and the proposed change is likely to affect those interests in significantly different ways, a more complex decision-making procedure may be required. It might, for example, be necessary to obtain the agreement of a majority within each affected community, rather than just a majority of the public as a whole.[48] Negotiating such issues may require considerable political skill and tact.

Officials can, of course, pretend that no change is needed, because the constitution already includes something that it really does not. Or they can pretend, or convince themselves, that they have authority to implement some change unilaterally. But that is fraught with danger. Consider, for example, the judiciary. Any attempt by the judiciary unilaterally to change the most fundamental rules of the system is hazardous. They can use all the usual techniques of the common law, including gradualism

[45] Goldsworthy (n 9) 112–13.

[46] Goldsworthy (n 9) 123–5. See also JWF Allison, *The English Historical Constitution: Continuity, Change and European Effects* (CUP 2007) 110–19, 127; P Eleftheriadis, 'Parliamentary Sovereignty and the Constitution' (2009) 22 *Canadian Journal of Law & Jurisprudence* 267, 289; Tucker (n 19) 75.

[47] V Bogdanor and S Vogenauer, 'Enacting a British Constitution: Some Problems' [2008] *PL* 38, 52–4.

[48] S Tierney, *Constitutional Referendums: The Theory and Practice of Republican Deliberation* (OUP 2012) 76–7, 138ff.

and even a little subterfuge.[49] They can try to disguise their radical law-making as the discovery of pre-existing law. Or they can describe an increasing number of principles or even statutes as 'constitutional', and then later on, announce that 'of course, if these principles are constitutional, they must by definition control even the power of Parliament'. Parliament *might* be bluffed or bamboozled into accepting this. The gradual judicial construction of a common law constitution is, therefore, one possible future for parliamentary sovereignty.

On the other hand, Parliament might not succumb so easily. It might resent and resist the judicial attempt to change the rules that were previously generally accepted, and take strong action to defeat it.[50] If the judges tear up the consensus that constitutes the basic rules of the system, they are poorly placed to complain if it is replaced by a power struggle they are ill-equipped to win. In the absence of official consensus, their own authority as well as Parliament's would be up for grabs. So they can attempt to initiate constitutional change, but would be well advised to ensure that the other branches of government are likely to acquiesce. Otherwise they would be wise to wait for Parliament to initiate change.

D. Entrenching Purely Procedural or Formal Requirements for Law-making

Constitutional changes might be more or less radical, in terms of controlling or limiting Parliament's powers. Less radical change would, presumably, be easier to achieve because it would be more likely to be acceptable. An example may be the enactment by Parliament of mild requirements as to the procedure or form by which new statutes must be enacted.

At present, long-standing official and community consensus—a form of customary law—determines that Parliament is composed of the two Houses and the sovereign, and that the assent of all three is generally required for the enactment of legislation.[51] This is now qualified by the Parliament Acts 1911 and 1949, which in effect provide that in some cases Parliament can act without the assent of the Lords.[52] But Parliament's law-making procedures and legislative forms are currently governed not by law, but by the non-justiciable Standing Orders of each House. A yet unresolved question is whether Parliament could enact binding rules governing these procedures and forms, applicable either to all or only to special legislation. The customary

[49] Goldsworthy (n 20).

[50] See the discussion in D Oliver, 'Parliamentary Sovereignty: A Pragmatic or Principled Doctrine?', *UK Constitutional Law Group Blog*, 3 May 2012, available at <http://ukconstitutionallaw.org/2012/05/03/dawn-oliver-parliamentary-sovereignty-a-pragmatic-or-principled-doctrine/> (last accessed 13 September 2012).

[51] Pavlos Eleftheriadis greatly exaggerates the extent to which this customary law is equivalent to a written constitution, such as that of the United States, and limits Parliament's sovereignty: see Eleftheriadis (n 46) and Eleftheriadis (n 9). See also Goldsworthy (n 1) 14–15.

[52] R Ekins, 'Acts of Parliament and the Parliament Acts' (2007) 123 *LQR* 91.

law that constitutes the doctrine of parliamentary sovereignty does not provide an unequivocal answer to that question.

A requirement that Parliament follow a particular procedure in order to enact legislation of a special kind, or that such legislation take or include some particular form (such as a particular form of words), can have various purposes including:

- To protect very important legislation from inadvertent or ill-considered amendment or repeal, by prompting more careful or extensive deliberation within Parliament than is needed to enact ordinary legislation.
- To make it more probable that a bill likely to be controversial will be brought to public attention.
- To differentiate between the respective functions of the two Houses.
- To ensure that Parliament expresses its intentions with unmistakable clarity to avoid subsequent misunderstandings (in the case of requirements as to form).

There are many possible requirements that are worth considering. When thinking about procedural requirements within Parliament, we usually envisage super majority requirements. But many other, much milder, procedural requirements are possible, including: (a) satisfaction of a special quorum; (b) passage by an absolute majority of all the members in one or both Houses; (c) giving of reasons to Parliament for some particular legislative change; (d) origination and amendment of specific categories of legislation (such as taxation and appropriation bills) only in the lower House. Possible requirements as to the form of legislation include: (a) express rather than implied amendment or repeal of special laws; (b) use of a particular verbal formula such as a 'notwithstanding' clause to enact certain laws; and (c) dealing only with one subject-matter (a common requirement in Australia for taxation and appropriation bills).

It is well known that such requirements might not effectively protect legislation unless they, themselves, are protected from amendment or repeal by legislation passed in the ordinary way. If they are not, they are not strictly binding because Parliament can repeal them by ordinary legislation, which exposes the formerly protected legislation to amendment or repeal in the same way.[53] Worse still, Parliament might not need to use this two-step procedure: it might be able directly to amend or repeal the protected legislation by enacting ordinary legislation, on the ground that this would amount to an implied amendment or repeal of the special manner or form requirements by virtue of being inconsistent with them.[54]

It is sometimes said that, in order to protect legislation more effectively, it is necessary to employ 'double' entrenchment, whereby legislation is protected by a special requirement as to procedure or form that is itself protected by a second special requirement.[55] However, double entrenchment would not be effective unless the second special requirement were protected by a third special requirement; in

[53] Hence, the referendum requirements in the European Union Act 2011, ss 2, 3, and 6 do not bind Parliament in the requisite sense.

[54] See the discussion of *McCawley* (n 2) in Section A.

[55] G Carney, *The Constitutional Systems of the Australian States and Territories* (CUP 2006) 191.

other words, 'triple' entrenchment would be required. This is because if the second special requirement could be, and were, amended or repealed by ordinary legislation, then the first special requirement would no longer be protected and could be amended or repealed in the same way, followed by the originally protected legislation. For the same reason, the effectiveness of triple entrenchment would require 'quadruple entrenchment' and so on potentially to infinity.

The only way of providing legally effective entrenchment without generating this potentially infinite regress of entrenchments is to adopt a particular kind of double entrenchment, which is usually called 'self-entrenchment'. A special requirement as to manner or form is 'self-entrenched' when it provides that it must be complied with not only to amend or repeal the primary legislation it is designed to protect, but also to amend or repeal itself. This creates a circular or self-referential mode of entrenchment that obviates the need for an infinite regress of entrenchments. Usually there is only one special requirement, which is self-entrenched. But it is possible for one special requirement to be protected by a second, or even third, special requirement that is self-entrenched. At some point, self-entrenchment must be used to break the need for an on-going sequence of entrenchments.

Self-entrenched requirements as to form or procedure are consistent with substantive continuing sovereignty,[56] provided that they do not substantively limit Parliament's law-making authority, or make it so difficult for it to legislate that its power to do so is diminished. A self-entrenched referendum requirement is an example of a requirement that clearly violates this proviso, for reasons that will be explained in Section E. This proviso, admittedly, gives rise to questions of degree, best exemplified by super-majority requirements (three-fifths, two-thirds, three quarters, etc).[57] But if it is satisfied, purely procedural or formal requirements are consistent with Parliament retaining full, continuing power to change the substance of the law however, and whenever, it sees fit.

Purely procedural or formal requirements are not only consistent in principle with parliamentary sovereignty, but could enhance it. To take just one of the purposes mentioned earlier, Parliament may want to protect itself from its own ignorance or negligence, by requiring that some important statute can be amended or repealed only by express words, or even a specific verbal formula, rather than by implication. In this way Parliament can ensure that future legislators must be given clear notice of any proposal to change the statute. This would involve overriding the doctrine of implied repeal. But why should the doctrine of implied repeal be regarded as sacrosanct? It is essential to Parliament's sovereignty that it can amend or repeal its own earlier statutes however, and whenever, it chooses. But why must it always be able to do so by implication, rather than by using express words? Parliament is more, rather than less, sovereign if it can subject itself to such requirements, because it then has more control over its own deliberative and decision-making processes. If the courts were prepared to enforce such requirements, by invalidating any statute enacted contrary to them, Parliament would no longer be fully sovereign in Dicey's

[56] See the third paragraph of Section A.

[57] I briefly discuss this issue in Goldsworthy (n 9) 198.

sense (which specified that no court or other body could lawfully override or set aside any statute).[58] But so what? It would still be fully sovereign in the more important sense of being free to change the substance of the law however and whenever it should, with due deliberation, choose.

Similar arguments can be made with respect to other requirements of a procedural or formal nature, such as quorum or absolute majority requirements. No statutory requirements currently govern the British Parliament's standard legislative procedures: these are determined by the Standing Orders of each House. But why should Parliament not have the power to replace Standing Orders with legislative requirements? Its power to determine the procedures by which it is to be taken to have acted is the reason why the Parliament Acts 1911 and 1949 are legally valid and effective.[59] It does not, of course, logically follow that Parliament could also impose requirements on the internal proceedings of each House. But to deny that it could, one must argue that immutable custom dictates that the two Houses must always have unfettered discretion to regulate their own internal procedures. That would be a surprising substantive restriction on Parliament's sovereign power to legislate, since it could not be justified by the overriding need to preserve that very power. Surely Parliament has power to alter the traditional privileges of its Houses; if so, why should that power not extend to altering their ability to regulate their own internal proceedings?

Parliament's sovereign power should, therefore, be regarded as including power to regulate by statute its own internal decision-making procedures, subject to the over-riding proviso that its substantive continuing sovereignty may not be destroyed or diminished. The crucial question should be, not whether Parliament can 'bind' itself, but whether it can do so in a way that does not destroy or diminish that continuing substantive power.

It has often been recognized that a self-entrenched procedural requirement could be so difficult—perhaps even impossible—to comply with, that in substance it would amount to a restriction of Parliament's substantive power to legislate. If Parliament purported to enact such a requirement, it could be repealed, perhaps even by implication (meaning that it could simply be ignored), by a subsequent Parliament. And its validity might be successfully challenged on the ground that, in substance, it violates this limit to the power used to enact it.

I do not maintain that it is currently generally accepted that Parliament can enact mild requirements as to procedure or form. My argument is that it could, and should be, because this is not only consistent in principle with Parliament's sovereignty but enhances it.[60] This should involve a relatively minor change in the customary official consensus that constitutes the doctrine of parliamentary sovereignty. Moreover, there is evidence that the courts have already changed their position on this question.

[58] AV Dicey, *Introduction to the Study of the Law of the Constitution* (ECS Wade ed, 10th edn, Macmillan 1962) 40.

[59] Ekins (n 52) 115.

[60] Goldsworthy (n 9) 114 fn 27, 139, 181–2, 201.

First, they have recently claimed authority to impose on Parliament what amount to requirements as to form. Take the interpretive rule that Parliament is presumed not to have intended to override common law freedoms unless its intention to do so is expressed with unmistakable clarity. This and other presumptions were, until recently, ostensibly concerned to ensure that the courts can be certain that Parliament intended that consequence. But lately, other rationales have been suggested. In *R v Secretary of State for the Home Department, ex p Simms*,[61] Lord Hoffman said that 'Parliament must squarely confront what it is doing and accept the political costs.'[62] Lord Bingham observed extra-judicially that:

> if... legislation... would strike ordinary people as unfair or disproportionate or immoral, the need to spell out that intention explicitly on the face of the bill must operate as a discouragement, not least because of the increased risk of media criticism and parliamentary and popular resistance.[63]

This rationale has little to do with legislative intention: it would be more appropriate as a reason for imposing a mandatory requirement as to form. But if the courts now treat interpretive presumptions as, in effect, requiring express words before they will accept that a statute has certain effects, surely they should accept that Parliament can subject itself to a similar requirement in other contexts.

The decision in *R v Secretary of State for Transport, ex p Factortame (No 2)* [64] can also be interpreted as accepting that Parliament has the power to bind itself by an express repeal requirement.[65] On this view, the European Communities Act 1972 ('the ECA') was construed as imposing a requirement as to the form of future legislation—namely, that any breach of applicable EC law must be authorized by express words clearly communicating Parliament's intention to do so. This is not a limitation of substance: Parliament remains at liberty at any time to override EC laws. It merely requires that Parliament use express words to do so, or else provisions inconsistent with those laws will be inoperative. One justification for holding provisions of the latter kind inoperative is that Parliament may have enacted them inadvertently, without appreciating that they are inconsistent with EC law.

In *Thoburn v Sunderland City Council*,[66] Lord Justice Laws suggested that the ECA is just one of a number of 'constitutional statutes' that can now be amended or repealed only by express words, and not mere implication. What is remarkable is his repeated claim that this is due, not to Parliament's own intentions in enacting those statutes, but to 'the common law'. 'The ECA is, *by force of the common law*, a constitutional statute.'[67] I regard this as fundamentally mistaken,[68] but let us put that aside. For present purposes, the significance of his suggestion is this. If the judiciary is willing to regard a statute such as the ECA as not subject to implied repeal, it has conceded that Parliament may be bound by a mild requirement as to the form of legislation that is needed for the amendment or repeal of older statutes.

[61] [2000] 2 AC 115 (HL).
[62] *Simms* (n 61) 131.
[63] Lord Bingham of Cornhill, 'Dicey Revisited' [2002] *PL* 39, 48.
[64] [1991] 1 AC 603 (HL).
[65] See Goldsworthy (n 9) 289–90, 298.
[66] [2002] EWHC 195 (Admin), [2003] QB 151.
[67] *Thoburn* (n 66) [62] (emphasis added).
[68] Goldsworthy (n 9) 312–14.

The conclusion that a requirement of the use of express words, or even of a particular verbal formula, is merely a requirement as to form that could be made binding and justiciable, has profound practical implications. A 'notwithstanding' clause such as section 33 of the Canadian Charter, providing that a statute inconsistent with statutory rights can validly operate only if it uses a particular verbal formula, is a requirement as to form.[69] Section 33 is limited in scope, and does not preserve the law-making powers previously enjoyed by Canadian Parliaments.[70] Nevertheless, it provides a model that could be developed in some future attempt to reconcile parliamentary sovereignty with more robust judicial protection of rights or other constitutional principles. For example, the United Kingdom Human Rights Act 1998 could be amended to authorize courts to invalidate any legislation inconsistent with the rights it protects, except for legislation expressly declaring Parliament's intention to override them or (better still) judicial interpretations of them.[71] Judicial review under the Canadian Charter is sometimes classified as 'strong' judicial review, like review under the United States Constitution. So it may seem paradoxical that the inclusion of a 'notwithstanding' clause is sufficient to make this consistent with parliamentary sovereignty. But it would be consistent, because Parliament would retain full substantive power to change the law however and whenever it pleases. It would have bound itself only with respect to the form of the legislation needed to do so. Any obstacles to its use of that form to exercise its power would be political rather than legal.

A requirement of express amendment, repeal or override is just one example of requirements as to procedure or form that are consistent with Parliament retaining full substantive power to change the law—that is, substantive continuing sovereignty. But any attempt by Parliament to subject itself to such a requirement should also comply with the political principle known as symmetric entrenchment.[72] That principle holds that the enactment of any such requirement should itself comply with that same requirement. One Parliament should not require its successors to comply with requirements that it is unable or unwilling to comply with itself. If the argument presented came to be accepted, it would be possible for Parliament to enact the requirement of symmetric entrenchment, and protect it by a second, self-entrenched, procedural requirement.[73]

E. Enacting Self-entrenched Referendum Requirements

My conclusions so far cannot accommodate every desirable reform. A self-entrenched referendum requirement, despite being perfectly democratic, cannot logically be

[69] Section 33 provides that Canadian legislation 'may expressly declare…that the Act or a provision thereof shall operate notwithstanding a provision included in section 2 or sections 7 to 15 of this Charter'.

[70] See Goldsworthy (n 9) 202.

[71] See Goldsworthy (n 9) 219–20 for an explanation of the words 'better still'.

[72] JO McGinnis and MB Rappaport, 'Symmetric Entrenchment: A Constitutional and Normative Theory' (2003) 89 *Virginia L Rev* 385.

[73] T Roszkowski and J Goldsworthy, 'Symmetric Entrenchment of Manner and Form Requirements' (2012) 23 *Public Law Review* 216.

classified as a purely procedural or formal requirement. It limits Parliament's substantive power, and is inconsistent with the very core of the doctrine of parliamentary sovereignty.

Any self-entrenched requirement that legislation may be passed only with the assent of a body outside Parliament, whether it is a private body or the electorate as a whole, is a requirement as to the procedure by which a law is made. The difficulty is that it is not a requirement as to the procedure by which laws must be made *by Parliament*, exercising *its* continuing sovereign power to make laws. It allows Parliament to make those laws only with the assent of an external body, and by prohibiting Parliament from legislating without that assent it radically diminishes Parliament's sovereignty. The British writers who have embraced what is called the 'manner and form' or 'procedurally self-embracing' theory of parliamentary sovereignty have often ignored this crucial point.[74]

An alternative way of attempting to reconcile self-entrenched referendum requirements with parliamentary sovereignty is to argue that they 'reconstitute' Parliament, by adding to it an additional element—the electorate—for the purpose of passing special laws. On this view, they change the composition of Parliament without diminishing its law-making power. This so-called 'reconstitution' argument should not be confused with a 'manner and form' argument, which focuses on Parliament's procedures and statutory forms rather than its composition.[75] But as I have shown elsewhere, when the reconstitution argument was first made in the Australian case of *Attorney General for New South Wales v Trethowan*,[76] it was 'plainly fanciful—a contrived rationalisation of a pre-determined conclusion'.[77] Moreover, 'in the United Kingdom, it would be even less plausible':

> if Parliament were to subject its power to enact certain kinds of legislation to the veto of the electorate, voting in a referendum, it would in substance severely restrict that portion of its power. Such a radical change would require a change in the fundamental rule of recognition—in the customary consensus among senior legal officials—that underpins the British constitution. The necessity for such a change could not be evaded by formalistic word magic—by labelling the change a 'reconstitution' of Parliament itself, rather than a limitation of its powers. The reality of such an enormous change in legal authority cannot be concealed, and debate about its profound philosophical and political implications evaded, by semantic game-playing.[78]

On the other hand, a self-entrenched referendum requirement in a very important statute or new written constitution could be held valid and binding if there were a radical change to the official consensus that constitutes the unwritten constitution, amounting to a repudiation of the doctrine of parliamentary sovereignty. If Parliament purported to limit itself in this way, the courts would first have to ask whether the consensus among legislators themselves had truly evolved, as

[74] Most recently, M Gordon, 'The Conceptual Foundations of Parliamentary Sovereignty: Reconsidering Jennings and Wade' [2009] *PL* 519. For references to Ivor Jennings, RTE Latham, and RFV Heuston, see Goldsworthy (n 9) 175 fn 5. See also *Jackson* (n 12) [81] (Lord Steyn), [163] (Baroness Hale).

[75] For this distinction see Goldsworthy (n 9) 139, 155–60, 167, 171–3, 198–9.

[76] (1931) 44 CLR 394 (High Court of Australia); [1932] AC 526 (Privy Council).

[77] Goldsworthy (n 9) 160. [78] Goldsworthy (n 9) 199.

distinct from one political party attempting constitutional change without broader support. Let us assume that the imposition of a referendum requirement is controversial, and vehemently opposed by one side of politics, which later gains a majority in Parliament, ignores the requirement and reasserts Parliament's sovereign authority to legislate without a referendum. In that case, it is hard to see how the judges could justify upholding the referendum requirement, given that there would clearly have been no change of consensus about its legitimacy even among legislators.

It is also hard to see how the judges could justify upholding this requirement in terms of underlying constitutional principle. If an earlier Parliament can use ordinary legislation to enact its preferred policies, why should a later Parliament not have the same liberty? To put it another way, why should the later Parliament be bound by the expression of a will that has no higher authority than its own will? This is the main justification of the orthodox view that Parliament cannot bind itself.

But the outcome should be very different if the statute imposing the referendum requirement were itself put to a referendum and approved by a majority of voters—in other words, if it complied with the principle of symmetric entrenchment.[79] That would add greatly to the case in favour of it being held legally binding. First, there is more likely to be a consensus among legislators that the will of the electorate should be respected, and another referendum required in order to amend or repeal the statute. Secondly, it is also more likely that the judges would regard enforcing the requirement as morally justified, because obtaining the approval of the voters in order to impose the requirement overcomes the principled objection just mentioned. If a referendum requirement is enacted with the approval of a majority of voters in a referendum, a future Parliament could then be said to be bound, not by an earlier will of no higher authority than its own will, but by an earlier will that does have such a higher authority—the expressed will of the people. This would surely be necessary to legitimate any new written constitution protected by a self-entrenched referendum requirement.

The consensual change thesis that I have advocated would enable the judges to accept the validity of a written constitution, approved by both Houses of Parliament and a majority of voters in a referendum, which future Parliaments could not violate without obtaining the approval of voters in another referendum. But the thesis would not require them to accept the validity of a provision making it very difficult for future Parliaments to repeal a statute passed with the support of only a small majority from one side of politics. The thesis would enable the judges to insist that only important constitutional rules or principles, which enjoy widespread, non-partisan support, may be entrenched, and only in ways that are consistent with the political sovereignty of the people.

[79] See McGinnis and Rappaport (n 72).

5

Parliamentary Sovereignty Re-defined

Alison L Young[*]

Does it really matter whether the Westminster Parliament is still sovereign, in the sense described by Dicey, or whether sovereignty has shifted in nature following the enactment of either one of, or a combination of, the Parliament Acts 1911–49, the European Communities Act 1972, and the Human Rights Act 1998? This chapter will argue that the answer to this question is 'yes', but not because it is important to know whether Dicey's description of the English constitution is correct, or because Dicey's conception of parliamentary sovereignty is a fundamental cornerstone of the English constitution that must not be shaken.[1] Instead, it will argue that there are strong normative justifications for concluding that the Westminster Parliament should not be able to bind its successors as to the procedures used to enact legislation. To make this argument this chapter will explore different accounts of parliamentary sovereignty and why these accounts matter. The European Union Act 2011 and the decision of the Supreme Court in *AXA General Insurance v Lord Advocate*[2] will be used as examples both to explain the subtle differences between competing conceptions of sovereignty and to explain why it is both more descriptively accurate and normatively justifiable to conclude that the Westminster Parliament does not, and should not, have the power to bind its successors.

A. Delineating the 'Old' and the 'New'

It is almost impossible to start a discussion of parliamentary sovereignty without providing an account of Dicey's conception of parliamentary sovereignty. The great Victorian argued that:

> The principle of Parliamentary sovereignty means neither more nor less than this, namely, that Parliament thus defined has, under the English constitution, the right to make or unmake any law whatever; and, further, that no person or body is recognised by the law of England as having a right to override or set aside the legislation of Parliament.[3]

* Fellow and Lecturer in Law, Hertford College, University of Oxford.

[1] I use 'English' here deliberately to recognize the argument that the Scottish Parliament prior to the Act of Union may never have possessed absolute legislative sovereignty, given its acceptance of the doctrine of desuetude.

[2] [2011] UKSC 46, [2012] AC 868.

[3] AV Dicey, *Introduction to the Study of the Law of the Constitution* (10th edn, Macmillan 1958) 39–40.

This is commonly referred to as the 'old' view of parliamentary sovereignty. Although Parliament can legislate on any matter it wishes, without its provisions being set aside by a court, it cannot legislate so as to bind its successors. To do so would not only limit the sovereign powers of a future incarnation of Parliament, but would also lead to a situation where a court could declare legislation invalid as the actions of a future Parliament failed to comply with the requirements of an earlier Parliament. Dicey's old view of sovereignty is in turn contrasted with the so-called 'new' (mid-twentieth-century) view that Parliament can bind its successors as to the 'manner and form' in which legislation is enacted. The new view is found in the work of Jennings[4] and Heuston,[5] who relied upon two cases to support their views: *Harris v Minister for the Interior*,[6] a decision of the Supreme Court of South Africa and *Attorney General for New South Wales v Trethowan*,[7] a decision of the Privy Council on appeal from the High Court of Australia. In both of these cases, legislation proscribed a special process for its own modification. Legislation that was enacted without adhering to this special procedure was declared invalid—it had not been enacted in the manner prescribed by earlier legislation and, therefore, was not recognized as valid legislation.

Goldsworthy's theory of sovereignty proposes a third answer, a modified version of the new view. In contrast to Dicey, he concludes that Parliament can bind its successors. However, in contrast to the new view his conclusion is not that Parliament can bind its successors as to the manner and form in which legislation is enacted. Instead Parliament can only bind its successors as to the procedures through which legislation is enacted,[8] provided that (i) the substantive power of Parliament to legislate is not restricted and (ii) the process through which legislation is enacted does not make it so difficult for Parliament to legislate that it effectively restricts the substantive power of Parliament to enact legislation.[9] For Goldsworthy, this restriction is necessary to maintain the internal coherence of any account of sovereignty. Sovereignty is assessed in terms of power, specifically in terms of the power to enact legislation. Under both the old and the new view of sovereignty, Parliament has, at least theoretically, limits on its law-making power. Under the old view, Parliament is limited as it cannot bind its successors as to the manner and form under which to enact legislation, making it hard to make long-standing commitments. Goldsworthy's conception of parliamentary sovereignty aims to resolve this difficulty.

The new view of sovereignty is faced with a different potential limit on the sovereignty of Parliament. What if Parliament were to bind its successors as to the manner and form in which legislation is to be enacted which resulted in it being impossible for Parliament to enact legislation of a particular content? For example,

[4] Sir I Jennings, *The Law and the Constitution* (5th edn, University of London Press 1959).
[5] RFV Heuston, *Essays in Constitutional Law* (2nd edn, Stevens and Sons 1964).
[6] [1952] 1 TLR 1245 (Supreme Court of South Africa).
[7] [1932] AC 526 (PC).
[8] J Goldsworthy, *Parliamentary Sovereignty: Contemporary Debates* (CUP 2010) 181.
[9] Goldsworthy (n 8) 174.

Parliament may legislate so as to make it practically impossible for legislation to be enacted that contravened the rights found in the European Convention on Human Rights ('ECHR') unless there was a 90 per cent majority vote in favour of this legislation, and an approval by a referendum. Given the range of views in Parliament as to the desirability of these rights, this requirement may effectively mean that it was impossible to ever legislate in a manner incompatible with Convention rights, essentially restricting the substantive law-making powers of Parliament.

To analyse the difference between the old view and the new view of sovereignty in terms of whether Parliament can bind its successors focuses predominantly on consequences. I have argued elsewhere that the difference between the two views is better understood in terms of different types of sovereignty.[10] First, sovereignty could be understood in terms of the power to enact primary legislation—that is rules that regulate the actions of individuals. Secondly, sovereignty can be understood in terms of the power to enact specific rules regarding the definition of Parliament, the enactment of legislation and the ability to change the definition of Parliament and how legislation is enacted. This distinction helps to illustrate a second way in which Goldsworthy's theory differs from the more traditional understanding of the new view. Jennings's theory classifies rules regarding the definition of Parliament and of valid legislation as provisions of the common law. Therefore, they could be modified by courts but also, more importantly for his theory, by Parliament if the rule is that legislative enactments override the common law.[11] The work of RTE Latham has been used to support the new view through classifying the rules regarding the definition of Parliament and of legislation as conventions that lie in the hands of the courts.[12] Courts can modify the definition of law and enable Parliament to bind its successors through recognizing a shift in the 'grundnorm' and enabling Parliament to bind its successors.[13] Goldsworthy regards this 'rule' as a Hartian 'rule of recognition'—a conventional rule that can only be modified through the officials of the legal system accepting such modification.[14]

This explanation of the differences between the new view and the old view explains my account of the old view of sovereignty, which seeks to provide a normative justification for why, in the current UK constitution, Parliament should have legally unlimited law-making power but should not be able to bind its successors; either as to substance, or as to manner and form, or as to the procedures through which

[10] I have argued elsewhere that this is to simplify the distinction between the two theories. See AL Young *Parliamentary Sovereignty and the Human Rights Act 1998* (Hart Publishing 2009); AL Young 'Sovereignty: Demise, Afterlife or Partial Resurrection?' (2011) 9 *International Journal of Constitutional Law* 163.

[11] Although, arguably, this is unstable. If the rule that 'legislative provisions override the common law' is also a principle of the common law, then it may be open to the courts to modify this provision, such that any purported legislative amendment to the manner and form in which legislation is enacted can be overturned by the courts through a modification of the common law.

[12] RTE Latham, 'The Law and the Commonwealth' in WK Hancock (ed) *Survey of British Commonwealth Affairs, Volume 1: Problems of Nationality 1918–36* (OUP 1937); P Oliver 'Law, Politics, the Commonwealth and the Constitution: Remembering RTE Latham, 1909–43' (2000) 11 *King's College LJ* 153.

[13] Goldsworthy (n 8) 175.

[14] Goldsworthy (n 8) ch 3.

legislation is enacted. I refer to this as 'continuing parliamentary legislative supremacy' for three reasons. 'Legislative supremacy' is preferred to 'sovereignty' to demonstrate that my theory is an account of the law-making powers of Parliament, not an account of the more abstract issues of 'sovereignty' analysed, for example, by Loughlin.[15] 'Supremacy' is used to recognize that the claim is relative. Legislation, when validly enacted, is the superior form of law, overriding the common law and administrative regulations. 'Continuing' refers to the fact that Parliament cannot bind its successors.

Although Parliament has continuing parliamentary legislative supremacy, it is not sovereign. When discussed at the most abstract level, it is clear that Parliament is not sovereign as 'sovereignty' is merely an abstract concept, necessary, in theory, to ground political and legal authority. As such, it does not and cannot vest in any particular institution. In addition, Parliament is not sovereign in the sense of having the authority to determine its own definition, its competences, the process through which law is made, and the way in which these rules may be modified. This is because these rules are best understood as a Hartian rule of recognition, a conventional rule whose content, although reflected in the law, is determined and modified through acceptance of the change by officials administering the legal system. When courts recognize a shift in the rule of recognition, they do so through exercising a political, as opposed to a purely legal, function.[16] Moreover, Parliament is not sovereign in terms of having the sole power authoritatively to determine the manner in which its legislative provisions are to be interpreted. Courts have wide interpretative powers and should not be restricted to merely seeking to ensure that their interpretation complies with their perception of the intention of Parliament when enacting that legislation. This does not place Parliament under a legally enforced limit as to the legislation that it can enact, given that Parliament is free to use clear and express words in legislation that can overturn an interpretation of legislation with which it disagrees. The latter two explanations of the sense in which Parliament is not sovereign can also be explained in terms of bipolar sovereignty, when understood as recognizing that both Parliament and the courts have the ability to initiate modifications to the rule of recognition,[17] or to dictate the definition of statutory provisions and,[18] when combined with other powers of Parliament and the courts, equip them with the ability to assert sovereignty,[19] even if they do not have sufficient powers to authoritatively determine these issues.[20] Courts can lay claims to sovereignty through the common law, asserting their

[15] M Loughlin, *The Idea of Public Law* (OUP 2003) 72–98.

[16] J Finnis, 'Revolutions and the Continuity of Law' in AWB Simpson (ed) *Oxford Essays in Jurisprudence* (2nd edn, Clarendon Press 1973); NW Barber 'Sovereignty Re-examined: The Courts, Parliament and Statutes' (2000) 20 *OJLS* 131.

[17] See CJS Knight, 'Bi-Polar Sovereignty Restated' (2009) 68 *CLJ* 361.

[18] See TRS Allan 'The Limits of Parliamentary Sovereignty' [1985] *PL* 614; S Sedley, 'The Common law and the Political Constitution: A Reply' (2001) 117 *LQR* 68.

[19] See N Walker, 'Sovereignty and Differentiated Integration in the European Union' (1998) 4 *ELJ* 355.

[20] See NW Barber and AL Young, 'The Rise of Prospective Henry VIII Clauses and their Implications for Sovereignty' [2003] *PL* 112.

power over the common law to modify sovereignty and to modify the rule that statutory provisions override the common law. Parliament asserts its claim to sovereignty through enacting statutes, including those modifying the procedures through which legislation is enacted,[21] or which may be interpreted as binding their successors as to the manner and form in which legislation is enacted, or through redefining the nature of the sovereign law-maker.[22] However, sovereignty, if it vests anywhere, vests in the relationship between the institutions asserting their claims to sovereignty and between these institutions and those governed by them. This is because any assertion of sovereignty by one institution can be countered by another institution, potentially leading to a constitutional crisis. Any such constitutional crisis could result in sovereignty—in the sense of the ability to finally determine statutory interpretation or the rules relating to the composition, competences, and procedures of enacting legislation—being vested either in the legislature, or the courts, or in a written constitution whose provisions are open to interpretation by the courts. This provides both with the need to err on the side of caution, as either may lose the ability to assert sovereignty.

Goldsworthy's theory of sovereignty provides a strong challenge to the traditional old and new views of sovereignty, adopting a modified new view. My account of sovereignty does not challenge the old view, but provides a different justification for its adoption. In order to assess these competing accounts we will first examine whether adopting Goldsworthy's conception of sovereignty is viable, before determining whether either conception is more desirable than the traditional old and new views of sovereignty.

B. Viability

Two possible challenges can be made to Goldsworthy's theory. First, it may be difficult to identify provisions that regulate the way in which legislation is made, but which do not restrict the substantive law-making powers of Parliament. Secondly, conceptual difficulties may arise as to the possibility of differentiating between types of rules regulating the definition of Parliament, of legislation, and the way in which these provisions are changed. Goldsworthy's theory can be defended against these challenges, but in doing so the utility and desirability of his theory of sovereignty is potentially undermined.

(1) Practical problems

To reiterate, Goldsworthy places two restrictions on the ability of Parliament to bind its successors as to the law-making process: first, it must not remove substantive law-making power from Parliament and place it in the hands of another; secondly it must not make it so difficult to legislate as to effectively restrict the

[21] eg Parliament Acts 1911–49.

[22] eg European Communities Act 1972 and the European Union Act 2011.

substantive legislative powers of Parliament. The first criterion is easy to satisfy. If legislation were to require a referendum for it to be modified, for example, then this would effectively provide the electorate with a veto power. This would take substantive legislative power away from Parliament. This would not be the case, for example, were procedural requirements of legislation to be modified in order to require a two-thirds majority vote. Parliament would still possess substantive law-making power, none of its powers being shared with another institution.[23]

However, the second requirement appears to be inherently vague.[24] It is easy to recognize that a provision that the legislature obtain the votes of 99 per cent of its members in order to enact particular legislation makes it impossible for Parliament to enact legislation, placing a significant substantive limit on its law-making powers. It is also easy to conclude that a change in the law-making process to require some legislation to be amended by the votes of a majority of those voting plus one extra vote would not normally place a significant restriction on the substantive law-making powers of Parliament. However, if the addition or removal of one vote makes no difference as to whether the substantive law-making powers of Parliament are limited, then we appear to have created a Sorites paradox, making it impossible to draw a clear line between those procedures that do, and do not, effectively restrict the substantive law-making powers of Parliament.[25]

Goldsworthy provides a neat solution to this difficulty by drawing a line between restrictive and alternative procedures, both of which he contrasts with the ordinary procedure for enacting legislation. Restrictive procedures are mandatory and limit the power of the legislature to enact substantive provisions of legislation by making it more difficult to enact legislation than it would be to use the ordinary legislative procedure. Alternative law-making procedures are not mandatory. They apply in addition to the ordinary law-making process, providing an alternative means of law-making. They do not restrict the substantive law-making powers of Parliament as the ordinary law-making process for enacting legislation is still available. If anything, the substantive powers of Parliament to enact legislation are enhanced as opposed to restricted by these alternative law-making procedures.[26] An example of an alternative law-making process that does not restrict the substantive powers of legislation of Parliament is found in the provisions of the Parliament Acts 1911–49. These provisions enable legislation to be enacted without the consent of the House of Lords thereby facilitating the resolution of legislative deadlock should the House of Lords consistently refuse to assent to legislative provisions approved by the House of Commons.

However, although this distinction may be possible to draw in theory, it may cause problems in practice. The European Union Act 2011 provides an example

[23] Goldsworthy (n 8) 175.

[24] See G Winterton, 'The British Grundnorm: Parliamentary Sovereignty Re-Examined' (1976) 82 *LQR* 591, 604–5; PC Oliver, *The Constitution of Independence: The Development of Constitutional Theory in Australia, Canada, and New Zealand* (OUP 2005) 77–9.

[25] See TAO Endicott, 'Vagueness and Legal Theory' (1997) 3 *Legal Theory* 37.

[26] Goldsworthy (n 8) 176–7.

of two types of problem that may arise: (i) problems relating to the interpretation of complex, inter-related legislative provisions and (ii) difficulties arising from the need to take context into account when interpreting legislation.[27] Section 2(1) of the Act regulates the ratification process of treaties amending the Treaty of European Union ('TEU') or the Treaty on the Functioning of the European Union ('TFEU'). Such a treaty 'is not to be ratified unless' a statement regarding such ratification has been laid before the House,[28] an Act of Parliament has approved the treaty,[29] and the 'referendum condition' has been met.[30] Section 2(2) sets out the criteria of the 'referendum condition' which includes that a referendum has taken place,[31] that a 'majority of those voting in the referendum are in favour of ratification of the Treaty',[32] and that 'the Act providing for the approval of the Treaty is not to come into force until a referendum about whether the treaty should be ratified has been held'.[33]

First, the Act illustrates the difficulties of identifying whether legislation places a restriction on the law-making process. Section 2(1), for example, on its face, does not regulate the law-making powers of Parliament, but regulates the power of the executive to ratify a treaty. Section 2(1) argues that a treaty 'is not to be ratified' unless certain criteria are met. As such, it merely controls when the executive can exercise its powers to ratify a particular type of treaty. However, this section may also indirectly limit the substantive legislative powers of Parliament. Section 2(1) can also be read as not merely *a restriction on the powers of the executive* to ratify treaties amending or replacing the TEU or the TFEU but instead as *a definition of ratification* for the purposes of these treaties.[34] If so, then this potentially restricts the substantive powers of Parliament as, were Parliament to enact a statute that purported to ratify such a treaty without matching the criteria of section 2(1), arguably this statute would be ineffective as ratification could not occur unless carried out according to the provisions of section 2(1). Even if section 2(1) were not to be interpreted as furnishing the legal criteria of ratification of these treaties, were legislation to be enacted purporting to give legal effect to a treaty amending or replacing the TEU or the TFEU without the criteria of section 2(1) being met, then the argument could be made that the legislation in question was ineffective, given that legal effect could not be given to a treaty unless ratified and, as section 2(1) had not been complied with, any purported ratification by the executive of this treaty would be unlawful as the executive had not exercised their powers of ratification according to the criteria of section 2(1). Consequently, section 2(1) may be interpreted both as a restraint on the powers of the executive and as placing a substantive restriction on the law-making powers of Parliament.

[27] The consequences of this Act for parliamentary sovereignty are discussed in the contribution of Paul Craig in Chapter 10 of this volume. See also P Craig, 'The European Union Act 2011: Locks, Limits and Legality' (2011) 48 *CML Rev* 1881.

[28] European Union Act 2011 ('EUA 2011'), s 2(1)(a).

[29] EUA 2011, s 2(1)(b).

[30] EUA 2011, s 2(1)(c).

[31] EUA 2011, s 2(2)(b).

[32] EUA 2011, s 2(2)(c).

[33] EUA 2011, s 2(2)(a).

[34] I am grateful to Julie Dickson for pointing this interpretation out to me.

Section 2(2) also provides a further conundrum for Goldsworthy's theory of sovereignty, demonstrating the difficulties of delineating between a restrictive and an alternative law-making process; one that does or does not restrict the ability of Parliament to enact substantive legislation. To see this, we need to set out the wording of section 2(2)(a) in full. Ratification of the treaties mentioned in section 2(1) requires that legislation be enacted approving the ratification of the treaty. Section 2(2)(a) regulates this legislation, requiring that:

> the Act providing for the approval of the treaty provides that the provision approving the treaty is not to come into force until a referendum about whether the treaty should be ratified has been held throughout the United Kingdom or, where the treaty also affects Gibraltar, through the United Kingdom and Gibraltar.

On one reading of section 2(2) this only provides a restriction on the law-making procedures to be followed for legislation approving a treaty modifying or amending the TEU or the TFEU. Such legislation must include a provision that it is not to come into force until a referendum has taken place. A requirement to include a section regarding when a statutory provision is to come into force does not place an overly great restriction on the law-making powers of Parliament. As such, it may appear that the provision should, according to Goldsworthy's theory, be able to bind future Parliaments such that future legislation approving a treaty that did not contain such a section was invalid.

However, it is hard to sustain this reading as, although section 2(2) may only require that legislation approving a treaty includes this 'coming into force' provision, such a section effectively precludes the Act from having legal force unless a referendum has been held. This does not technically require that a referendum be held for the statute to amount to valid legislation. However, in practice, this is the case given that legislation that has not yet been given legal effect cannot be relied upon in the courts and, in at least that sense, is not yet law. Nor could it be relied upon by the executive as satisfying section 2(1)(b) of the European Union Act 2011. When interpreted in this manner, the provision is not merely a restriction on the law-making process. Instead, the provision appears to place a substantive limit on the law-making powers of the legislature as a statute approving a treaty amending or modifying the TEU or the TFEU does not have legal effect unless approved by a referendum. If so, then section 2(2)(a) places a substantive limit on the law-making powers of the legislature as it requires that its legislation be approved by the electorate in a referendum for its legislation to have legal effect. However, it could also be argued that section 2(2)(a) only requires that a referendum be held. It does not require that the referendum approves the legislation, or approves the treaty amending the TFEU or the TEU. A referendum vote in favour of the treaty amending the TEU or the TFEU is only required for the ratification of the treaty under section 2(1)(c) and not for the coming into force of legislation under section 2(2)(a).

Given this range of possible interpretations, it may be hard to determine whether section 2(2)(a) binds future Parliaments. These complications are exacerbated by the possibility that Parliament could legislate so as to ratify a treaty amending the

TEU or the TFEU by inserting a clause in the legislation to the effect that its provisions take effect notwithstanding the provisions of section 2(2)(a). This would be sufficient to enable legislation to be enacted to ratify a treaty even without a referendum being held.

Thirdly, difficulties may arise surrounding whether a contextual approach needs to be taken to our assessment of whether significant restrictions have been placed upon the substantive law-making power of Parliament. Goldsworthy's concern is with the substantive powers of Parliament to enact legislation on any subject matter it wishes. It is possible that a treaty purporting to replace the TEU or the TFEU would place restrictions upon the ability of Parliament to enact substantive legislation, perhaps through transferring exclusive law-making power over a particular subject matter from the UK Parliament to the European Union, at least as regards the effectiveness of this legislation vis-à-vis European citizens. As such, although the requirement of a referendum may appear to be designed to limit the substantive law-making powers of Parliament, by incorporating a veto of the electorate, in reality the referendum requirement may be a means through which Parliament may be rescued from mistakenly enacting legislation that would further limit its substantive law-making powers. The need for a referendum would draw this issue to the attention of the public, forcing Parliament to take care over whether it wished to further restrict its substantive law-making powers in this manner. Far from a referendum restricting the sovereignty of Parliament, it may be a means of attempting to preserve it.

These difficulties are not restricted to the European Union Act 2011. Similar problems arise with regard to the provisions of the Parliament Acts 1911–49, particularly as regards the desirability of taking a contextual approach. Goldsworthy argues that the Parliament Acts do not place a significant restriction on the substantive powers of the legislature given that the legislation merely provides for an alternative legislative process. Moreover, it is not the power of Parliament to legislate that is restricted, rather the legislative powers of one chamber are reduced, the veto of the House of Lords being replaced by a power of delay. The context of the enactment of the Parliament Act 1911 famously stems from a legislative deadlock.[35] The solution was to limit the powers of one chamber—the House of Lords—effectively enhancing the powers of the more democratic chamber over the powers of the less-democratically composed chamber. As such, the Parliament Acts 1911–49 enhance democracy, granting more powers to the democratically composed chamber and fewer to the non-democratically composed chamber. If parliamentary sovereignty is valuable as it promotes democracy, then Goldsworthy's distinction, although a useful means of delineating between modifications to the law-making process that do and do not restrict the substantive law-making powers of Parliament, may produce results that detract from the normative justification for maintaining parliamentary sovereignty.

[35] See R Jenkins, *Mr Balfour's Poodle: An Account of the Struggle Between the House of Lords and the Government of Mr Asquith* (Collins 1968).

(2) Conceptual difficulties

Goldsworthy's conception of sovereignty empowers Parliament to modify rules relating to the process through which law is enacted, but not rules relating to the substance of its law-making powers or rules relating to the definition of the sovereign. The latter can only be modified by a shift in the rule of recognition, which could not be achieved through Parliament acting alone. Is such a distinction sustainable? Winterton's work would argue that it is not.

The new view of sovereignty empowers Parliament to bind its successors as to the manner and form in which legislation is enacted, but not as to the substance of the law. Winterton classified this theory as advocating a continuing theory of sovereignty as regards the substance of the law, and a self-embracing conception of sovereignty as regards the manner and form in which legislation is enacted. The new view requires a distinction to be made between rules as to the manner and form of legislation, or the procedure through which legislation is enacted, and rules that define Parliament or legislation. It would enable Parliament, for example, to bind its successors as to a requirement that any legislation contradicting rights found in the ECHR could only be enacted by a two-thirds majority of Parliament, but would not allow Parliament to bind its successor as to a redefinition of legislation, such that legislation enacted contrary to the rights found in the ECHR was not legally valid legislation. Winterton, relying upon the work of RTE Latham, argued that these rules are inter-connected. Rules relating to the definition of the sovereign and the way in which law is validly enacted should be of the same type as both are logical prerequisites of legislative sovereignty. Legislative sovereignty is granted to the validly enacted provisions of the sovereign law-maker. As such, courts cannot respect the wishes of the sovereign law-maker unless they are able to identify who the sovereign law-maker is and ensure that their legislative commands are obeyed.[36] Winterton's criticism relies upon a distinction between two types of rules—primary rules that are used to govern those in society and secondary rules concerning the definition of the sovereign law-making power, the process through which it enacts legislation and the rules regulating the manner in which these rules are changed. Parliament cannot, logically, have unlimited sovereign law-making power over both of these types of rules. If Parliament is sovereign over primary rules, then it must enjoy the power to modify the content of these rules, free from any restriction that may arise from a prior Parliament having exercised its sovereign powers to alter the secondary rules. Vice versa, if Parliament has the power to modify the secondary rules, then future Parliaments no longer possess a legally unlimited power to modify the content of primary rules.[37]

Goldsworthy's theory argues that Parliament can have sovereignty over secondary rules, without losing sovereignty over primary rules, but only in very narrow

[36] Winterton (n 24) 604–5.

[37] JL Mackie, 'Evil and Omnipotence' (1955) 64 *Mind New Series* 200; JW Harris 'When and Why does the Grundnorm Change?' (1971) 29 *CLJ* 103.

circumstances. His theory does escape the potential philosophical contradiction as it defines the powers of Parliament over secondary rules in such a manner so as to avoid this potential contradiction. It suggests that there may be some powers that Parliament can possess over secondary rules which would not empower Parliament to limit the scope of its power to enact primary rules. These are more akin to the way in which Parliament has the power to regulate its own internal procedures; a form of technical rule. If Parliament can determine that votes on legislation are taken through pressing the relevant buttons on an electronic handset as opposed to walking through different corridors, then surely it can also create a different law-making process that did not limit its substantive law-making powers?

However, whilst this distinction may be possible to maintain in theory, it may be difficult to maintain in practice. The method through which votes are counted when legislation is enacted is easily recognized as a technical procedure. It is not defining legislation; it is modifying one of the ways in which Parliament provides evidence that the criteria for enacting valid legislation have been met. The answer is not so clear cut when we analyse modifications to the way in which legislation is enacted, particularly when these modifications occur through the enactment of legislation as opposed to a modification of Parliament's own internal rules. How do we classify section 19 of the Human Rights Act 1998, which requires that the minister promoting a Bill either makes a statement that the Bill is compatible with Convention rights,[38] or that, despite the inability to make a compatibility statement, the government wishes to enact the legislation in question?[39] The requirement, on its face, may not appear to make it more difficult to enact legislation that has a particular substance. It seems to provide alternative law-making procedures as it is possible for a minister to make a statement and continue to enact legislation that both is and is not compatible with Convention rights. However, section 19 draws attention to potential issues of incompatibility, alerting Parliament, including the opposition, in order to ensure that the matter is fully debated. Consequently, it is at least arguable that section 19 is designed to make it harder to enact legislation that is incompatible with Convention rights, even though it is still possible for Parliament to do so. Does this mean that section 19 is no longer a mere technical rule as to how Parliament enacts legislation, given that it may make it more difficult to enact certain legislative provisions?

The potential philosophical contradiction may explain the problems of vagueness discussed in the previous section. Although the vagueness may be resolved in theory, it may be difficult to resolve in practice. This does not mean that Goldsworthy's theory is not viable. However, it is important to realize that problems may arise when his theory is applied. As such, it may provide a reason for not adopting this conception of sovereignty; the advantages gained may be outweighed by the practical problems caused by its application.

[38] Human Rights Act 1998 ('HRA 1998'), s 19(1)(a).

[39] HRA 1998, s 19(1)(b).

C. Desirability

Why should we accept one particular conception of sovereignty over another? If one were to discover a case in English law that conclusively proved that Parliament could bind its successors, this would prove the truth of the empirical statement that the Westminster Parliament could bind its successors—although disputes may arise as to whether the evidence was conclusive. The same however does not apply when determining the truth of a particular conception of sovereignty. Evidence that the Westminster Parliament can bind its successors neither proves nor disproves that sovereignty is 'sovereignty' according to the new or the old view. The evidence could either be used to demonstrate that English law adopted the new view of sovereignty, or that English law misunderstood sovereignty, had mistakenly adopted the new view and so could no longer be seen as an example of a legal system which had a sovereign Parliament.[40] In a similar manner, historical evidence may show that English law adopts a particular conception of sovereignty, but it cannot be used to prove that this is a better conception of sovereignty than other conceptions.

We may decide to adopt a conception of sovereignty because adopting a particular conception leads to particular outcomes. One potential outcome promised by Goldsworthy's theory is the ability of Parliament to enact long-standing commitments. However, although this may desirable, I will argue that it is not clear that this is not possible under other conceptions of sovereignty. In addition, conceptions of sovereignty may be adopted because they are normatively justified. It will be argued, through an analysis of practical implications, that there are stronger normative justifications for the old view of sovereignty.

(1) Long-standing commitments

Adopting Goldsworthy's conception of sovereignty should make it easier for Parliament to make long-standing commitments. Providing an alternative law-making process for these long-standing commitments will ensure that Parliament can send a clear signal that a particular legislative provision is not one that can be inadvertently overturned by future legislation. However, it is not clear that this is needed. Nor is it clear that Goldsworthy's theory will achieve this end.

The perceived need for the ability of the legislature to make long-standing commitments stems from the principle of implied repeal. Simply stated, this principle states that, where there is a conflict between earlier and later statutory provisions, the later statutory provision prevails. Understood in this simplified form, particularly when applied to manner and form as well as substantive requirements, it would appear to make it extremely difficult, if not impossible, for Parliament to make

[40] B Bix, *Jurisprudence: Theory and Context* (5th edn, Sweet & Maxwell 2012) ch 1.

long-standing commitments that cannot be accidentally overturned by future legislation. In particular, when stated in this manner, the principle seems to imply that any form of accidental contradiction of an earlier legislative provision, no matter how tangential, overrides this provision. However, closer examination of the doctrine of implied repeal reveals that this is not the case. Courts have developed principles of interpretation that protect legislative provisions from inadvertent replacement. It would perhaps be more accurate to see the principle of implied repeal as an exception as opposed to a rule.[41] The development of 'constitutional statutes', whose provisions cannot be impliedly repealed,[42] as well as the enactment of legislative provisions that instruct the courts as to how to read[43] or to give effect to[44] legislation provide an alternative means of enabling Parliament to make long-standing commitments. In addition, although the old view of sovereignty does not empower Parliament to make long-standing commitments on its own, these long-standing commitments can still be made through a modification of the rules determining the definition of Parliament or of legislation.[45] A modification of these rules may be harder to achieve, but this may be perceived as an advantage, ensuring that long-standing commitments were not made, as well as not erased, inadvertently.

Even if the ability for Parliament to make long-standing commitments were not needed, a re-interpretation of sovereignty that would make this easier, or clearer, may be advantageous. However, it is not clear that Goldsworthy's theory would achieve this goal. The above discussion suggested that it may be difficult to find a provision that enables long-standing commitments to be achieved, without also placing too great a restriction on the substantive law-making powers of Parliament. One possible example of a manner and form provision that would satisfy his theory is the alternative law-making procedure found in the Parliament Acts 1911–49. However, this provision satisfies Goldsworthy's theory not only because it is an alternative, as opposed to a mandatory, law-making process, but also because it makes it easier, as opposed to harder, for Parliament to enact legislation. Are these cumulative or alternative justifications for concluding that allowing Parliament to bind its successors as to the law-making process does not contradict legislative sovereignty? If these requirements are cumulative, then it is hard to find a way in which Parliament can make long-standing commitments without harming its substantive law-making power. To do so may only be achieved through, for example, modifying the quorum required for Parliament to vote in favour of legislation by a simple majority or by requiring MPs to walk twice through voting chambers. However, if this is the case, then problems may arise as to the ability of these mechanisms to facilitate Parliament's ability to uphold long-standing commitments. As Goldsworthy recognizes, although he may classify these provisions as 'legally binding' rules, it may be hard for these to be enforced by the courts unless parliamentary privilege is modified.[46] If these rules cannot be controlled by the courts, then Parliament

[41] Young (n 10) ch 2.
[42] *Thoburn v Sunderland City Council* [2002] EWHC 195 (Admin), (2003) QB 151.
[43] See eg HRA 1998, s 3. [44] See eg ECA 1972, s 2(4). [45] Young (n 10) ch 3.
[46] Goldsworthy (n 8) 189–96.

is essentially required to exercise self-restraint and self-police its commitment to long-standing commitments. But if these difficulties arise because of mistakes as to whether, for example, legislation is or is not contrary to human rights, it may be hard to see how these extra procedural requirements would be capable of preventing Parliament from accidentally legislating contrary to its long-standing commitments.

Even if the requirements are not cumulative and restrictions on the law-making process need only be alternative as opposed to ones that also do not make it harder for Parliament to enact legislation, this may not fully enable Parliament to make long-standing commitments that it is harder to mistakenly override. If the law-making process designed to facilitate long-standing commitments really is just an alternative law-making process, then Parliament must be free to choose between two alternative law-making processes. If applied to areas when it can be hard to discern whether a legislative proposal breaches a long-standing commitment, then it is feasible that, when exercising its choice, Parliament makes a mistake when it chooses the alternative law-making process over the ordinary law-making process and vice-versa. As such, requiring courts to determine whether Parliament breached its long-standing commitment or not through examining which legislative process was chosen by Parliament may not facilitate Parliament's ability to correct mistakes as to whether it wishes to retain its long-standing commitments.

(2) Maximizing legislative sovereignty

The strongest defence of Goldsworthy's conception of sovereignty stems from regarding legislative sovereignty as a foundational principle. His work provides an excellent and extensive account of constitutional history, demonstrating how parliamentary sovereignty, understood as the requirement for Parliament to possess legally unlimited substantive law-making powers, is a recognized foundational principle of the UK constitution. It is this historical foundation that grounds his revised new view of sovereignty, maximizing the legislative sovereignty of Parliament. Parliament is sovereign when it has 'full continuing power to change the substance of the law however and whenever it sees fit'.[47] By enabling Parliament to bind its successors and to make long-term commitments, whilst also ensuring that its power to change the substance of the law is not restricted, the legislative sovereignty of Parliament is maximized.

This approach, however, provides only a weak justification for adopting a particular conception of sovereignty. Are there reasons for adopting the legislative sovereignty of Parliament as a normative principle? Normative justifications for granting substantively unlimited law-making power to Parliament normally argue that granting such power enhances democracy. As the democratic law-making institution, democracy is enhanced if Parliament as opposed to another institution has the power to make laws. To place legal limits over the substantive law-making powers of Parliament would reduce democracy, restricting the law-making powers of Parliament. In addition, it may damage the sovereign status of Parliament.

[47] Goldsworthy (n 8) 174.

Parliament would no longer be the institution at the top of the constitutional hierarchy. Instead, a legal document—the constitution—would limit the powers of Parliament. This limitation also suggests that parliamentary sovereignty is subordinate to the rule of law and that courts are higher in the institutional hierarchy than Parliament.

Two criticisms arise. First, this is not the best interpretation of Dicey's theory, particularly given his later work where he was willing to accept the possibility of enabling Parliament to bind its successors so as to require the enactment of referendums when enacting legislation that would have serious constitutional consequences.[48] Dicey's theory is better understood as one which focuses on the need for a balance between parliamentary legislative sovereignty and the rule of law, with a focus on a more complex inter-relationship between Parliament and the courts. Far from welcoming the Parliament Act 1911, as a means through which the substantive law-making powers of Parliament can be enhanced through the provision of an alternative law-making procedure, Dicey regretted that the Act removed what he regarded as an essential check upon the power of Parliament. Without the Parliament Act, legislative deadlock could only be resolved by the dissolution of the House of Commons and an ensuing general election. This provided an effective check over the wishes of the executive whose government held power in the House of Commons. If the political party from which that executive was formed was successful in the election, then this would mark endorsement of the legislation that had been rejected by the House of Lords—and vice versa. As such, the electorate, in combination with the House of Lords, was able to provide an effective check over the actions of the Government. The Parliament Act 1911 removed this check, enabling Parliament to legislate contrary to the wishes of the House of Lords and, potentially, contrary to the wishes of the electorate, even on matters of constitutional importance. My interpretation of sovereignty preserves these checks and balances. Parliament may have continuing legislative supremacy, but is not sovereign. It cannot modify the definition of Parliament alone. In addition, were it to legislate to place limits on the substantive law-making powers of Parliament, courts would not be legally bound to accept these limits. When determining whether to accept these limits, the courts will have regard to political facts, determining whether political actors and the general public regard these substantive limits as desirable.

Secondly, to justify granting parliamentary sovereignty in terms of its enhancement of democracy requires the existence of a strict divide between law and politics. Political restrictions are preferred to legal restrictions as political restrictions represent a democratic constraint on the substantive law-making power of Parliament. It may well be that political factors prevent Parliament from legislating so as to restrict certain human rights, in a similar manner to what may be achieved were Parliament to be legally constrained by a Bill of Rights. However, such political restraints are compatible with parliamentary sovereignty as an example of a democratic restriction on the powers of Parliament. Yet, it can be difficult to separate

48 See R Weil, 'Dicey was not Diceyan' (2003) 62 *CLJ* 474.

law from politics in practice. In addition, to require such a rigid distinction misses the way in which the interaction between law and politics can help to justify constitutional arrangements,[49] particularly as regards the resolution of actual or perceived constitutional crises in a predominantly political, predominantly unwritten constitution such as the United Kingdom.[50] My justification of the old view of sovereignty recognizes the need for inter-action between legal and political actors. It recognizes that Parliament has a greater claim to legitimacy through its democratic credentials, but that also its resolutions may ignore long-standing principles, fail to recognize when broad provisions may inadvertently harm individual rights and may potentially fail to fully protect minority interests. Courts may be better placed to correct these potential mistakes. In addition, although they lack democratic legitimacy, they may be in a better position to provide rational justifications and scrutinize the reasoning of the legislature. Both need to play a role when evaluating long-standing commitments.

(3) *AXA General Insurance*

The different normative justifications of the old and the new view of sovereignty can best be explained by means of an example. Let us take the Supreme Court case of *AXA General Insurance*,[51] which concerned the enactment by the Scottish Parliament of the Damages (Asbestos-related Conditions) (Scotland) Act 2009 specifically to reverse the decision of the House of Lords in *Rothwell v Chemical & Insulating Co Ltd*.[52] The Supreme Court, with leading judgments given by Lord Hope and Lord Reed, concluded that Acts of the Scottish Parliament can be subject to judicial review not only to determine its compatibility with section 29 of the Scotland Act 1998 (lack of vires), but also on common law grounds,[53] albeit not on the grounds of irrationality, unreasonableness or arbitrariness.[54] Lords Brown,[55] Mance,[56] Kerr, Clarke, and Dyson[57] agreed with Lords Reed and Hope regarding the ability of the courts to review Acts of the Scottish Parliament on common law grounds.

Lord Hope and Lord Reed provide different justifications for their conclusions and these differences help to illustrate competing conceptions of sovereignty. One argument in common appears to provide support that both adopt a conception of sovereignty which focuses on an analysis of law-making power. The Westminster Parliament possesses absolute law-making power. It delegated some of its powers to the Scottish Parliament. As such, the Scottish Parliament can be understood, constitutionally, as a delegated law-making body. Therefore, it seems to follow that its law-making powers can be limited by the common law, as well as by statute; as a body with delegated as opposed to absolute powers, one limitation entails the possibility of others. This conclusion was reinforced by the lack

[49] Loughlin (n 15) 81–4.
[50] See JAG Griffith, 'The Political Constitution' (1979) 42 *MLR* 1.
[51] *AXA General Insurance* (n 2).
[52] [2007] UKHL 39, [2008] AC 281.
[53] *AXA General Insurance* (n 2) [47] (Lord Hope), [138] (Lord Reed).
[54] *AXA General Insurance* (n 2) [49] (Lord Hope), [147] (Lord Reed).
[55] *AXA General Insurance* (n 2) [84].
[56] *AXA General Insurance* (n 2) [97].
[57] *AXA General Insurance* (n 2) [177].

of any express exclusion of review on common law grounds by the Scotland Act 1998.[58] However, the conclusion that Acts of the Scottish Parliament can be subject to judicial review on common law grounds does not necessarily follow. First, the reasoning employed here is similar to that used to explain why the new view of sovereignty found in *Attorney General for New South Wales v Trethowan*[59] and *Harris v Minister of the Interior*[60] does not apply to the Westminster Parliament. The new view of sovereignty vests sovereignty in Parliament, but allows Parliament to bind its successors. As such, the Parliaments of New South Wales and of South Africa were able to bind their successors as to the manner and form in which to enact legislation. The situation is not the same when applied to the Scottish Parliament and *AXA General Insurance* in two regards. First, it is the Westminster Parliament that placed limits on the Scottish Parliament that the courts will enforce through section 29 of the Scotland Act 1998, not the Scottish Parliament placing limitations on its own powers. Secondly, the limitations derive from the common law, not from the enactments of the Scottish Parliament.

In addition, although the analysis of Lord Reed and Lord Hope focuses at first on an understanding of sovereignty in terms of absolute law-making power, the second justification for common law review focuses more on a conception of sovereignty based on the inability of the courts to question the express wording of Parliament. Both Lord Reed and Lord Hope refer to the fact that common law review is in play as it has not been expressly ruled out by the wording of the Scotland Act 1998. However, although a requirement that courts do not contradict the express wording of Parliament can be implied by analysing sovereignty in terms of absolute law-making power, this requirement can also be understood as part of a separate conception of sovereignty; one which focuses upon sovereignty in terms of legal rules determining the scope of the powers of Parliament and the courts. It is not clear how far these different conceptions of sovereignty are used in tandem to form one justification, or to create alternative justifications of common law judicial review of Acts of the Scottish Parliament. The two conceptions may also pull in opposite directions.

This contrast between two conceptions of sovereignty can be explained through an analysis of the tension between the ultra vires and the common law justifications of judicial review, particularly regarding their conclusion as to whether allowing courts to develop their own limits upon the power of the executive, or any other delegated law-making body, contradicts parliamentary sovereignty.[61] For advocates of ultra vires, only Parliament can determine the scope of powers delegated from Parliament to the executive. Parliament has absolute unlimited law-making powers; it delegates an aspect of those law-making powers to the executive; therefore only

[58] *AXA General Insurance* (n 2) [49] (Lord Hope), [138] (Lord Reed).

[59] *Trethowan* (n 7).

[60] *Harris* (n 6).

[61] The best overview of this debate can be found in C Forsyth (ed) *Judicial Review and the Constitution* (Hart Publishing 2000). See also TRS Allan, 'The Constitutional Foundations of Judicial Review: Constitutional Conundrum or Interpretative Inquiry?' (2002) 61 *CLJ* 87; C Forsyth and M Elliott, 'The Legitimacy of Judicial Review' [2003] *PL* 286; TRS Allan 'Constitutional Dialogue and the Justification of Judicial Review' (2003) 23 *OJLS* 563.

Parliament can ascertain the precise limits on the law-making powers of the executive and the job of the court is merely to 'police' the executive, ensuring that it does not act outside the limits of the powers conferred by Parliament. This analysis of sovereignty explains why a court-created limit that was not in line with the express or implied limits placed by Parliament contradicts parliamentary sovereignty. If only Parliament can limit the powers of the executive, then anything the executive does that has not been expressly or impliedly restricted by Parliament must, by definition, be permitted. Therefore, if the courts were to limit the powers of the executive beyond this, they would be contradicting the will of Parliament. This interpretation could explain Lord Reed's further justification of judicial review of Acts of the Scottish Parliament. Lord Reed held that the Scotland Act 1998 was to be interpreted according to the principle of legality, meaning that its broad wording could not be construed to provide specific power to the Scottish Parliament to legislate contrary to the rule of law or fundamental common law human rights.[62] The principle of legality is a principle of interpretation, recognized by the courts and forming a background principle that dictates implied intentions of Parliament. Being aware of this principle of interpretation, Parliament must have intended that the Scotland Act would have been interpreted in this manner, placing this implied limit on Holyrood's law-making powers and giving rise to judicial review on common law grounds. Interpreted in this way, Lord Reed's argument applies to the devolved Parliaments, but not to the Westminster Parliament.

For common law theorists, courts have the power to determine the content of the common law, thus empowering courts to devise common law limits on the powers of the executive. Parliamentary sovereignty is only breached if courts contradict the will of Parliament by establishing legal controls that directly undermine the express wording of legislation. Understood in this manner, the express words of Parliament may place restrictions on the powers of the executive, or may expressly empower the executive to perform specific activities. However, there is also a range of activities that are neither expressly permitted nor expressly restricted. As such, for the court to control the executive in these circumstances, they would not be contradicting parliamentary sovereignty, or perhaps more clearly, parliamentary legislative sovereignty. Parliament has not expressly stated anything; therefore there is nothing for the court to contradict. This may provide a potential explanation for Lord Hope's different reasoning, relying on the importance of the rule of law.[63] Although parliamentary legislative sovereignty and the rule of law do not conflict in practice, Lord Hope recognizes that there is a danger, given the dominance of the executive in both Westminster and Holyrood, that legislation would be passed that places a serious threat on the rule of law—namely legislation designed to 'abolish judicial review or to diminish the role of the courts in protecting the interests of the individual'.[64] For Lord Hope, '[t]he rule of law requires that the

[62] *AXA General Insurance* (n 2) 153.

[63] Although I will argue later for a different—and I believe more persuasive—interpretation of Lord Hope's reasoning.

[64] *AXA General Insurance* (n 2) [51].

judges must retain the power to insist that legislation of that extreme kind is not law which the courts will recognise.'[65] Interpreted in this way, Lord Hope's argument applies to both the devolved Parliaments and to the Westminster Parliament.

That there are weaknesses in the analysis of the Supreme Court in *AXA General Insurance* does not render the conclusion unsound. Rather, it illustrates the ways in which 'sovereignty' is often used in an under-theorized manner, casting doubt upon, but not necessarily defeating, legal conclusions. Further difficulties arise with the conclusions of the Supreme Court when we analyse its conclusions in terms of sovereignty over primary or secondary rules. Is it for the Westminster Parliament or for the courts to determine the scope of the law-making powers of the Scottish Parliament? If this power belongs to Parliament, then the lack of reference to common law limits in the Scotland Act 1998 would appear to contradict the conclusion reached by the Supreme Court. If this power belongs to the courts, through the development of principles of the common law, then there would appear to be no justification for limiting the conclusion of the Supreme Court to Acts of the Scottish Parliament. If the common law can develop judicial review over Acts of the Scottish Parliament, then surely it is also open for the common law to develop judicial review over Acts of the Westminster Parliament—as implied in Lord Hope's judgment. Yet this undermines sovereignty in a deeper sense. Parliament is not sovereign as its powers are limited by the rule of law as interpreted by the courts.

I would argue that sovereignty over secondary rules is shared between Parliament and the courts. As such, *AXA General Insurance* can be regarded as a potential shift in the rule of recognition, in a similar manner to my analysis of *R (Jackson) v Attorney General*.[66] The difference between the two cases turns on the different institutional initiation of the potential shift in the rule of recognition. As regards *Jackson*, Parliament enacted the Parliament Acts 1911-49, in the first instance as a means of resolving a potential constitutional crisis. In *Jackson* the courts were required to confirm or deny a shift in the rule of recognition. In *AXA General Insurance* the courts have initiated a shift in the rule of recognition, initiating a potential change in the definition of Acts of the Scottish Parliament so as not to include those Acts that contradict fundamental common law rights or the rule of law. As such, it would then be for Parliament (I would argue both the Westminster and the Scottish Parliament) to determine whether they do or do not accede to this shift in the rule of recognition.

It is difficult to say whether this analysis is a more accurate account of the interaction between the Scottish and Westminster Parliaments and the courts given the short time-frame. However, I would argue that support for this interpretation could be found in Lord Hope's judgment and his contribution to this volume.[67] Lord Hope does not argue that legislation that undermines the rule of law is *not law*, but that the courts *would not recognize it* as valid legislation. In addition, he argues that this should only occur in extreme circumstances—where the power of the courts to protect individual rights through judicial review is

[65] *AXA General Insurance* (n 2) [51].

[66] [2005] UKHL 56, [2006] 1 AC 262.

[67] See Chapter 6 in this volume by Lord Hope.

removed or diminished. Such legislation would undermine the delicate separation of powers between the legislature and the judiciary that underpins the constitution of the United Kingdom. I also consider this analysis easier to justify on normative grounds than the alternatives. To analyse the sovereignty issue here purely in terms of absolute law-making power places the powers of the Scottish Parliament in the hands of the Westminster Parliament. From a legal perspective, it is hard to regard the Westminster Parliament as having ultimate law-making authority, yet in addition to regard the common law as placing additional limits upon its powers. Lord Reed's use of the principle of legality can reconcile these two apparently contradictory positions—the principle of legality forming a principle of interpretation. Parliament does not legislate in a vacuum, acting instead against a backdrop of principles that govern the interpretation of legislation. However, to interpret the case in this way is to recognize the flimsy nature of the line between interpretation and repeal, questioning whether Parliament really does possess absolute law-making power if courts may interpret legislation in ways that may contradict Parliament's intentions. Do we really know whether Westminster wanted the devolved Parliaments to enact legislation that could be subject to judicial review on common law grounds? Would it not be more accurate here to regard Parliament and the courts as sharing bipolar sovereignty, in the sense recognized by Stephen Sedley and Trevor Allan,[68] the sovereignty of Parliament being tempered by the principles of interpretation developed by the courts? From a political perspective, it seems difficult to view the Scottish Parliament as entirely subservient to the whims of the Westminster Parliament—should not Holyrood also have a say as to whether its powers can, and should, be limited by the common law?

Moreover, when analysed from a legal perspective, it is hard to reconcile the legal principle of parliamentary sovereignty with a legal principle that regards the common law as determining the definition of legislation and the limits of law-making power of legislative bodies. Surely to analyse the law in this way is to place the common law above Parliament? From a normative perspective, I find it difficult to justify the role of the court in establishing fundamental principles of the common law and the rule of law. However, I acknowledge that this is due to my theory of human rights; regarding human rights as contestable I find it difficult to conclude that the court can, always, determine rights with such certainty that it is justifiable for them to impose rights to limit democratic law-making institutions. This is not to argue that the legislature alone should have a say in the determination of rights, rather that I believe there is a role for both the legislature and the judiciary.

To view both Parliament and the courts as possessing a role in determining the law-making powers of the Scottish Parliament provides a better means of protecting human rights. In addition, I would argue that this reflects the advantages of my interpretation of sovereignty in a predominantly political constitution. To vest the rules determining the scope of the law-making powers of the legislature in the hands of both Parliament and the courts is better able to ensure the legitimacy

[68] S Sedley, 'Human Rights: a Twenty-First Century Agenda' [1995] *PL* 389; TRS Allan, 'Parliamentary Sovereignty: Law, Politics and Revolution' (1997) 113 *LQR* 443.

of the legislature than if such power rests solely in the hands of the legislature or the judiciary. First, it helps to ensure that principles which determine the limits of law-making power are more likely to reflect the wishes of the people—through approval by Parliament—as well as maintaining long-standing principles developed over time by the principles of the common law. Secondly, both institutions realize that to assert full sovereignty over the other to determine the scope of the legislature's law-making powers may give rise to a constitutional crisis. This encourages a better balance of powers between the institutions. In addition, the threat of a potential constitutional crisis means that both institutions need to pay attention to the wishes of the electorate. A constitutional crisis will, ultimately, be determined by the wishes of the people. As such, neither institution will be tempted to enforce full sovereignty over the other unless there is at least some assurance that this will be supported by the people, should their actions give rise to a constitutional crisis.

6

Is the Rule of Law now the Sovereign Principle?

*Lord Hope of Craighead**

According to Dicey, the sovereignty of Parliament is the dominant characteristic of our political institutions.[1] But, like all constitutional doctrines in our system in the United Kingdom, those relating to Parliament are the result not of scholarly debate but of history. We have to remember that our revolutions, amongst which was the rejection of the absolute monarchy of the Stuart Kings and their return under a constitutional monarchy in 1688, occurred relatively early in the history of the modern State. They occurred at times when it had not become customary to complete a revolution by framing a constitution in writing, or even contemplate doing so. This is especially so in relation to the place in our constitution of Parliament. Nothing very much has been written down. There is ample room for debate.

Its current position and powers may be traced back to the struggle for supremacy with the Crown and the King's prerogative. The Bill of Rights of 1688 abolished the right that the Stuart Kings had asserted to suspend laws made by Parliament. The Act of Settlement of 1700 enshrined in our constitution the independence of the judiciary, save that *in extremis* a judge could be removed upon the address of both Houses of Parliament. And in 1716 Parliament prolonged its own existence, previously fixed at three years, to seven years by the Septennial Act. As Dicey saw it, this was at once the result and proof of Parliament as the sovereign legal power in the State.[2] In the meantime, by the Acts of Union of 1707, the Parliaments of England and Scotland had become united in the Parliament of Great Britain at Westminster. Among other provisions which protected particular aspects of Scottish society such as the church and the universities, by Article XIX it was declared that the Court of Session—the supreme court of civil jurisdiction in Scotland—was to remain in all time coming, with the same authority and privileges

* Former Deputy President of the Supreme Court of the United Kingdom. I am grateful to my judicial assistant Peter Webster for his help in preparing this chapter.

[1] AV Dicey, *Introduction to the Study of the Law of the Constitution* (ECS Wade ed, 10th edn, Macmillan 1962) 39.

[2] Dicey (n 1) 48.

as before the Union. This appeared to confer a particular status on that court, making it immune from the otherwise unlimited power of the new Parliament to do what it liked with it.[3] It may be that one should avoid reading too much into language of the kind found in that Article.[4] But it has been taken as an indication that by 1707, at least, the doctrine that the Scots Parliament enjoyed unlimited sovereignty had not yet emerged. The Inner House of the Court of Session recently described parliamentary sovereignty—looking at the matter from the Scots viewpoint, of course—as essentially a nineteenth-century doctrine.[5]

The touchstone by which one may measure sovereignty is whether there exists any competing authority which can challenge the legislative authority of Parliament.[6] It is abundantly clear that the Crown lost that right for ever in 1688. But the relationship between Parliament and the judges is, I would suggest, less clear. This is especially so from the Scottish viewpoint. As is well known, Lord President Cooper in *MacCormick v Lord Advocate*[7] had difficulty in seeing why it should be supposed that, as the principle of the unlimited sovereignty of Parliament appeared to be a distinctively English principle which had no counterpart in Scots law, the new Parliament of Great Britain should inherit all the peculiar characteristics of the English Parliament and none of the Scottish Parliament, as if all that had happened in 1707 was that Scottish representatives were admitted to the Parliament of England. Lord Russell observed in the same case that during the two centuries that had preceded the Union of the Crowns in 1603 Scotland was politically in an unsettled and disturbed State, and that there was little to suggest that by 1707 the framework of government in Scotland had been so consolidated that the Scottish Parliament enjoyed unchallengeable sovereignty.[8]

As the Lord President pointed out, the Treaty by which the new Parliament was brought into being contained some clauses, among which was Article XIX, which expressly reserve to the Parliament of Great Britain powers of subsequent modification and other clauses which either do not contain such a power or which emphatically exclude such a power by declarations that the provision shall be fundamental and unalterable in all time coming. 'I have never been able to understand', he declared, 'how it is possible to reconcile with elementary canons of construction the adoption by the English constitutional theorists of the same attitude to these markedly different types of provision.' It has been suggested by Professor Wade that the answer is that the former Parliament of England could not be understood to have given up at the union the attribute of sovereignty which it already had.[9] To Scottish ears that is not much of an answer. Professors Bradley and Ewing, in their book on constitutional law, acknowledged that it cannot be concluded from existing precedents that under no circumstances could the basic rule of legislative supremacy be qualified by judicial decision.[10]

[3] *Lord Gray's Motion* 2000 SC (HL) 46, 58.

[4] JD Ford, 'The Legal Provisions in the Acts of Union' (2007) 66 *CLJ* 106, 128–39.

[5] *AXA General Insurance Ltd Petitioners* [2011] CSIH 31, 2011 SC 662 [62].

[6] AW Bradley and KD Ewing, *Constitutional and Administrative Law* (12th edn, Longman 1998) 44, 50.

[7] 1953 SC 396 (IH) 411.

[8] *MacCormick* (n 7) 417.

[9] Dicey (n 1) lxv–vi.

[10] Bradley and Ewing (n 6) 82–3. See also *Lord Gray's Motion* (n 3) 59.

It may be that, as Wade himself thought,[11] the Lord President regarded the Act of Union itself as a fundamental part of constitutional law and that his regret was that the State of the law was such that even a fundamental provision was subject to alteration by an Act of Parliament which the courts were bound to accept. I find that view hard to reconcile with the words that the Lord President himself used. Professor TB Smith, always eloquent in his advocacy of the Scottish viewpoint, was certainly not of the same view as Wade.[12] But the Scottish courts have been reluctant to engage further in this debate.

Lord Keith, sitting as a judge in the Outer House, declined to accept as justiciable the question whether an Act of the United Kingdom Parliament which altered a particular aspect of Scots private law was or was not 'for the evident utility' of the subjects within Scotland for the purposes of Article XVIII of the Act of Union, which provided that unless that was so no alteration could be made to the laws of Scotland concerning 'private right'.[13] I myself, sitting in the Inner House as Lord President of the Court of Session, declined to deal with a similar argument which had been advanced by a litigant in person. He maintained that he was not obliged to provide information to a community charges registration officer under section 17 of the Abolition of Domestic Rates Etc (Scotland) Act 1987, which he certainly was according to the terms of the statute.[14] The introduction of the community charge, popularly referred to as the poll tax, in Scotland one year ahead of its introduction in England was hugely unpopular in Scotland. It led to the collapse of support for the Conservative party in Scotland from which it has never recovered. But that was not enough to tempt me then into the very difficult area of whether there are limits to the doctrine of parliamentary sovereignty. Sitting in the House of Lords' Committee for Privileges on an application for a declaration by that Committee that the Bill which was to abolish the right of hereditary peers to sit in the House of Lords violated the rights of the Scottish Peers under the Treaty of Union, I said that the issue as to whether the Westminster Parliament enjoyed unlimited sovereignty did not need to be resolved in that case and was ultimately for the courts to decide.[15]

My views have moved on a bit since those days, however, and I am less reluctant than I was then to engage with the subject. There are, of course, two aspects to this doctrine. First, there is the positive aspect. Is Parliament competent to legislate upon any subject matter? It appears now to be accepted that it can make or unmake any law it chooses. As it cannot bind it successors, its successors can unmake any law that it may choose to make. If it were not otherwise, the sovereignty of its successors would be limited. But there is also the negative aspect. Once Parliament has legislated, can a court or any other body pass judgment on the validity of the

[11] Dicey (n 1) lxvi. [12] TB Smith, 'The Union of 1707 as Fundamental Law' [1957] *PL* 99.

[13] *Gibson v Lord Advocate* 1975 SLT 134 (OH) 137.

[14] *Murray v Rogers* 1992 SLT 221 (IH) 226. See also *Pringle, Petitioner* 1991 SLT 330; *Sillars v Smith* 1992 SLT 539.

[15] *Lord Gray's Motion* (n 3) 59.

legislation that it has enacted? Dicey's pronouncements on these two aspects, which show how closely that are linked to each other, were unequivocal:

> The principle of Parliamentary sovereignty means neither more nor less than this, namely, that Parliament thus defined has, under the English constitution, the right to make or unmake any law whatever and, further, that no person or body is recognised by the law of England as having a right to override or set aside the legislation of Parliament.[16]

Having examined the history of the matter, including experience of legislation in respect of matters covered by the Treaties of Union with Scotland and Ireland which, to his mind, revealed the futility inherent in every attempt of a sovereign legislature to restrain the action of an equally sovereign body, he declared:

> Parliamentary sovereignty is therefore an undoubted legal fact. It is complete both on its positive and on its negative side. Parliament can legally legislate on any topic whatever which, in the judgment of Parliament, is a fit subject for legislation. There is no power which, under the English constitution, can come into rivalry with the legislative sovereignty of Parliament.[17]

His repeated use of the words 'England' and 'English' where he must surely have been referring to the Parliament and constitution of the United Kingdom is rather irritating to a Scotsman. But, as his editors Wade and Bradley point out, there was for him no definite assignable part of the law of the country which could be recorded as the constitution of the United Kingdom.[18] He would have been unshaken by the arguments that were advanced in the various Scottish cases to which I have referred in his belief that the English judges do not claim or exercise any power to repeal a statute, and that there is no legal basis for the theory that judges, as exponents of morality, may overrule Acts of Parliament.

It seems to me, however, that there is a problem about this approach. No theory about the sovereignty of Parliament can be proved, in the way that other legal concepts may be, by a chain of elucidatory decisions.[19] This is partly because the cases in which the issue may properly be raised are so rare. The Scottish cases to which I have referred illustrate this feature of the doctrine's lack of exposure to detailed and exacting judicial scrutiny. It was all too easy to find ways of dealing with the issue in some other way so as to avoid a confrontation with Parliament which, in truth, the judges would rather not have. Such precedents as there may be were decided long ago, reflecting political facts and circumstances as they were then, not those of today. Experience of the way the system has operated in practice shows that Parliament has been pre-eminent in the development of our modern constitution. It has been virtually the sole source, either directly or indirectly, of legislation and has been free from the restraints of any other system of law. In rare cases, such as under the United Nations Act 1946, the executive has power to legislate by Order in Council without the need to secure the approval of Parliament.[20] But it was Parliament itself which created this exception. It is a universal rule that in practice

[16] Dicey (n 1) 39–40. [17] Dicey (n 1) 68–70. [18] Dicey (n 1) xxx.

[19] JDB Mitchell, *Constitutional Law* (1st edn, W Green & Son 1964) 49.

[20] See *A v HM Treasury* [2010] UKSC 2, [2010] 2 AC 728; *R v Forsyth* [2011] UKSC 9, [2011] 2 AC 69.

no legislation of any kind, whether direct or indirect, may be made or enacted without the authority of Parliament. The authority of the devolved legislatures on Scotland, Wales, and Northern Ireland on matters that it decided not to reserve to itself was conferred on them by the Parliament at Westminster.

It appears then to be the case that it is simply because of the *apparent* absence of limitations that the belief has grown up that Parliament may pass any law at all whatever without any limitation. The limitations on its powers that are the result of the European Communities Act 1972 were self-inflicted, as it was its own legislation that imported the treaty obligations under the EC Treaties into domestic law. So too are the carefully circumscribed limitations which have been built into the Human Rights Act 1998 as part of the exercise of bringing home rights recognized by the European Convention on Human Rights. Those particular cases aside, as they tell us nothing about the position at common law, it is clear that the ability of Parliament to do what it likes is not confined by international law or the laws of logic or any other system of norms such as morality.[21] It could, if it wished, declare that the development of pleural plaques as a result of exposure to asbestos dust which, in the light of the agreed medical evidence, the House of Lords held gives rise to no actionable loss or damage should nevertheless sound in damages and thus be actionable.[22]

The question whether the devolved legislatures in Scotland and Northern Ireland, which had passed legislation to this effect, had legislative competence to do this was the subject of litigation in the UK Supreme Court.[23] The validity of the Damages (Asbestos-related Conditions) (Scotland) Act 2009 was challenged not only on the ground that it was outside the legislative competence of the Scottish Parliament under the powers conferred on it by statute, but also on common law grounds as an unreasonable, irrational, and arbitrary exercise of its legislative authority. The challenge failed on both grounds. The common law challenge was rejected on the ground that the mandate given to the Scottish Parliament by the electorate suggested that, while its legislation was not immune from judicial review, the judges should intervene, if at all, only in the most extreme circumstances. The opportunity was however taken to emphasize that the rule of law was the ultimate controlling factor, and that the Scottish Parliament was not free to abrogate fundamental rights. Legislation of that extreme kind, if it were to be passed, was not law which the courts would recognize.[24] But I think that no-one would regard legislation by the Westminster Parliament, if it chose to follow the Scottish example, as open to challenge at common law on the ground that it lacked the power to legislate in such terms.

There is little reason, then, to doubt the soundness of what Dicey had to say on the positive aspect of the matter. The more difficult issue is as to what he said about the negative aspect. Is it true—leaving aside the special case of legislation that is

[21] See, eg, *Mortensen v Peters* (1906) 8 F(J) 93, 100 (Lord Dunedin).

[22] *Rothwell v Chemical Insulating Co Ltd* [2007] UKHL 39, [2008] 1 AC 281.

[23] *AXA General Insurance Ltd v Lord Advocate* [2011] UKSC 46, [2012] AC 868. The Attorney General for Northern Ireland withdrew his challenge before the hearing of the appeal in the Scottish case: see [15].

[24] *AXA General Insurance* (n 23) [49]–[51], [149–53].

incompatible with EU law or with Convention rights, as to both of which the judges have an undoubted function in controlling the activities of the legislature—that no person or body has the right to override or set aside the legislation of Parliament? Here we are, I think, in uncharted territory. The traditional answer, of course, is that no judicial review of legislation enacted by Parliament is possible. In *Mortensen v Peters*[25] Lord Justice General Dunedin said: 'For us, an Act of Parliament duly passed by Lords and Commons and assented to by the King, is supreme, and we are bound to give effect to its terms.' There is Scottish authority to that effect dating from the middle of the nineteenth century,[26] which predated a forceful declaration to the same effect in England.[27] Lord Guthrie, sitting in the Outer House in *MacCormick* was quite explicit on the point. He said that no Scottish court had ever held an Act of Parliament to be ultra vires and that it had never been suggested that it could do so.[28]

But Professor JDB Mitchell, who taught constitutional law at Edinburgh University in the 1960s, was of the opinion that the authorities are not all one side on this point or consistent within themselves.[29] There is, he said, an interplay of political ideas and political facts in the creation of such ideas or rules of law as we have on this subject. Without a written constitution to guide us, a process of evolution in the development of ideas is inevitable. This is as true of the position in our constitution of the judiciary as it is of Parliament.

In the past the courts did not prove themselves to be strong bulwarks against claims by the Crown under the prerogative. It was left to Parliament to do this by asserting its authority. But it is far from clear today, when it comes to providing a bulwark against an excess of the exercise of power by the executive, that Parliament can be relied upon in a way that would make it unnecessary to look to the judges to do this for us. Under our system, as it has evolved, a party must command a majority in the House of Commons if it is to enter into government. An executive which has that majority can in theory, and usually in practice, get the House of Commons to do whatever it—the executive—likes. The sovereignty of Parliament is in the hands of the executive. The House of Lords, constrained by the Parliament Acts and by the Salisbury Convention by which it will not obstruct legislation for which the elected government sought and has obtained a mandate in its manifesto, will always give way, eventually, to the elected House. So when we think of the sovereignty of Parliament we should really be thinking of what this means about the power that this gives to the executive. The executive is, of course, subject to the will of Parliament. But in practice, nowadays, between elections we have what Lord Hailsham famously described in his 1976 Dimbleby Lecture as an 'elective dictatorship'.[30] Is the executive really to be free to pass through Parliament, which is under its control, whatever measures it likes? There may now be grounds for thinking that a shift has taken place and that the possibility of judicial review, albeit only in the most extreme circumstances, needs to be re-examined.

[25] *Mortensen* (n 21) 100–1. [26] *Middleton v Anderson* (1842) 4 D 957, 1010 (Lord Mackenzie).
[27] *Lee v Bude and Torrington Junction Railway* (1871) LR 6 CP 576, 582 (Wiles J).
[28] 1953 SC 396, 403. [29] Mitchell (n 19) 66–7.
[30] Lord Hailsham, *The Dilemma of Democracy* (Collins 1978) 9–11.

As is well known, the case of *R (Jackson) v Attorney General*,[31] in which the issue was whether the Hunting Act 2004 was a valid Act of Parliament, provided judges in the House of Lords with an opportunity of expressing views on the more general issue of parliamentary sovereignty. The real issue in that case was one of statutory interpretation, as to the effect of the Parliament Acts. But some of us said things about the broader issue which have been regarded as controversial and, by two very distinguished judges, as quite wrong. Lord Steyn said that the classic account given by Dicey about the doctrine of the supremacy of Parliament can now be seen to be out of place in the modern United Kingdom.[32] It was, he said, a construct of the common law. The judges had created the principle, and that it was not unthinkable that circumstances could arise where the courts might have to qualify a principle which had been established by the judges on a different hypothesis of constitutionalism. He took as an example an attempt to abolish judicial review or the ordinary role of the courts.[33] Scottish lawyers, recalling the words of Lord President Cooper in *MacCormick*, would take as an example an attempt by the Westminster Parliament to abolish the Court of Session in Scotland and subject Scots law to the jurisdiction of the English courts. In my speech I said that the rule of law enforced by the courts was the ultimate controlling factor on which our constitution is based.[34]

In a recent lecture the then Master of the Rolls and now President of the Supreme Court, Lord Neuberger of Abbotsbury, took issue with these propositions.[35] He concluded that the doctrine of parliamentary sovereignty remains as it was declared to be by Dicey. Although he recognized that the judges have a vital role to play in protecting individuals against the abuses and excesses of an increasingly powerful executive, he said that we cannot go against Parliament's will as expressed through a statute. That, with respect, seems to be to a dangerous doctrine unless one can be absolutely confident that the increasingly powerful executive will not abuse the legislative authority of a Parliament which, *ex hypothesi*, it controls because of the absolute majority that it enjoys in the House of Commons. I think that he is right to regard a fundamental reordering of the constitution to limit parliamentary sovereignty as a matter for a written constitution. But it is questionable whether it would require a fundamental re-ordering of the constitution for the judges to refuse to accept as law a statute which struck at the heart of the rule of law itself.

Lord Bingham of Cornhill in his celebrated book *The Rule of Law* said that he could not accept that parliamentary sovereignty was created by the common law:

> It is true of course that the principle of parliamentary sovereignty cannot without circularity be ascribed to statute, and the historical record in any event reveals no such statute. But it does not follow that the principle must be a creature of judge-made common law which the

[31] [2005] UKHL 56, [2006] 1 AC 262. [32] *Jackson* (n 31) [102].

[33] See also J Jowell, 'Parliamentary Sovereignty under the New Constitutional Hypothesis' [2006] *PL* 562, 573 where judicial review is described as a building block of our constitutional democracy.

[34] *Jackson* (n 31) [107].

[35] Lord Neuberger, 'Who are the Masters Now?' (Second Lord Alexander of Weedon lecture, 6 April 2011), available at <http://www.judiciary.gov.uk/Resources/JCO/Documents/Speeches/mr-speech-weedon-lecture-110406.pdf> (last accessed 8 April 2013).

judges can alter: if it were, the rule could be altered by statute, since the prime characteristic of any common law rule is that it yields to a contrary provision of a statute. To my mind, it has been convincingly shown that the principle of parliamentary sovereignty has been recognised as a fundamental in this country not because the judges invented it but because it has for centuries been accepted as such by the judges and others officially concerned in the operation of our constitutional system. The judges did not by themselves establish the principle, and they cannot, by themselves, change it.[36]

I cannot find fault with anything in this passage, apart from the last few words in the last sentence. But it seems to me to overlook the fact that under our legal system a law does not simply exist. It has to come from somewhere. It is either enacted law, for which Parliament is the source, or it is a product of the common law made by the judges. There is, as Lord Bingham says, no statute to which the principle can be ascribed. Parliament has not passed any law declaring, in so many words, its own sovereignty. It is because officials at the highest level, including the judges, have refrained from calling its sovereignty into question that the traditional view has grown up, which the judges have endorsed in the exercise of their common law powers, that it is a fundamental principle that Parliament's sovereignty is absolute.

But I do not think that we can ignore the fact that times have changed since Dicey. It seems to me that there is a very real question as to whether we can continue to rely on Parliament to control an abuse of its legislative authority by the executive. It is an uncomfortable fact that parliamentary sovereignty and the rule of law are not entirely in harmony with each other. So long as Parliament respects the rule of law there is no problem. But to assert that Parliament can enact whatever laws it pleases runs the risk that the rule of law will be subordinated to the will of the government. I think that Lord Bingham recognized this when he said that our constitutional settlement has become unbalanced by the fact that the power to restrain legislation favoured by a clear majority of the House of Commons has become much weakened. He accepted that this was not a problem that will go away if we ignore it. In the last paragraph of his book he wrote these words: 'One may hope that the sovereignty of Parliament and its relationship with the rule of law may be seen as a matter worthy of consideration if, as I suggest, there are some rules which no government should be free to violate without legal restraint.'[37] But the solution to this problem, as he saw it, was the substitution of a codified and entrenched constitution, not a conflict between the judges and Parliament.

Of course, conflict between the judiciary and the legislature is undesirable. But circumstances could arrive where we are left with no alternative. A government which had no regard for the rule of law, seeing it as an impediment to the action it wished to take, would hardly be likely to facilitate the enactment of a constitution that gave the rule of law pre-eminence. Politicians with an absolute majority in a democratically elected legislature who regard the rule of law as an impediment to progress may be tempted to use the mandate that their majority gives them

[36] T Bingham, *The Rule of Law* (Allen Lane 2010) 167.

[37] Bingham (n 36) 169–70.

to override its effect under the umbrella of democracy. My point in *Jackson*, and I think the point that Lord Steyn was making too, is that the ultimate safeguard against such abuses of the legislative power of Parliament lies in the power of the judges. After all, other countries such as the US, Canada, and Germany believe that rights are better protected when judges, rather than politicians, have the last word. It does no harm to our unwritten constitution for the judges to indicate to the executive arm of government that it should not assume that the sovereignty of Parliament, over which it has control, is entirely unlimited. The absence of a general power to strike down legislation which it has enacted does not mean that the courts could never fashion a remedy for use in an exceptional case where the survival of the rule of law itself was threatened because their role as the ultimate guardians of it was being removed from them.

I cannot leave this topic without acknowledging the contribution to this debate of Professor Jeffrey Goldsworthy. He has argued powerfully that sovereignty is the product of long-standing consensual practices among senior officials within our legal system, including those within the executive, which emerged from centuries-old political struggles and that it would require legislation for radical change to be brought about.[38] I think that his answer to the argument that *in extremis* the power of the judges is the ultimate safeguard is that there are things that a majority in Parliament either would not want to do or, for political reasons, would never do, and that it is not the business of the courts to add the threat of judicial invalidation to the moral and political imperatives that prevent Parliament from doing them.

I suppose that what lies between us at the end of the day is the extent to which we can be confident that those imperatives will always prevail. There is no need for a deterrent if the feared-for event will never happen. But I think that to make the assumption would be a hostage to fortune. Our constitutional arrangements are so uncertain and so fast-moving that I would rather not make it.

[38] J Goldsworthy, *The Sovereignty of Parliament: History and Philosophy* (Clarendon Press 1999); J Goldsworthy, *Parliamentary Sovereignty: Contemporary Debates* (CUP 2010).

7

Changing the United Kingdom Constitution: The Blind Sovereign

*Richard S Kay**

It has frequently been remarked that it seems to have been reserved to the people of this country by their conduct and example, to decide the important question, whether societies of men are really capable or not of establishing good government from reflection and choice, or whether they are forever destined to depend for their political constitutions on accident and force.

Alexander Hamilton *The Federalist* (No 1)

A. Introduction

In the middle of the last century, the fundamental rules governing public power in the United Kingdom could be stated succinctly and fairly uncontroversially. In AV Dicey's 1908 formulation 'Parliament' (the monarch, the House of Lords, and the House of Commons 'acting together') had the right to 'to make or unmake any law whatever' and 'no person or body [had] a right to override or set aside the legislation of Parliament'.[1] There was a necessary corollary. No individual Parliament could restrict the power of Parliament as an institution: no Parliament could bind its successors.[2]

Today, this doctrine of the 'sovereignty' of Parliament is a matter of serious doubt. Many commentators have proposed that there are some things Parliament may *not* do. My purpose in this chapter is not to question the fact, the extent, or the propriety of this change in the constitution.[3] I want rather to consider one feature of the *process* by which such change is thought to have occurred and, by inference, the

* Wallace Stevens Professor of Law, University of Connecticut School of Law. I am grateful to James Allan, Anthony Bradley, Jeffrey Goldsworthy, and Peter Oliver for helpful suggestions.

[1] AV Dicey, *Introduction to the Study of the Law of the Constitution* (8th edn, Liberty Classics 1982) 3–4.

[2] *Ellen Street Estates Ltd v Minister of Health* [1934] 1 KB 590 (CA), 597; 1 Bl Comm 93: ('Acts of Parliament derogatory from the power of subsequent parliaments bind not'). Dicey (n 1) 23–4, fn 48.

[3] My examination is limited to the criteria for producing binding rules of law. I exclude 'constitutional conventions', the rules, practices, and traditions that are, in fact, observed in the operation

process by which future constitutional change may occur in the United Kingdom: the constitution emerges from a series of specific decisions—executive, legislative, and judicial—dealing with particular political problems. We know what the constitution is by inference from these individual acts. I want to contrast this method of constitutional change with the standard model of constitutional creation and wholesale constitution reform in the rest of the world. According to that model, the 'sovereign'—in just about all modern societies this is some version of the 'people'—deliberates on and frames a set of ultimate rules that define institutions, grant them stated powers, specify necessary procedures, and impose certain limits. Constitution-making, that is, is a rule-making event. It takes place at a certain moment and it is the work of an identifiable group of people. It is a 'datable act of human will'.[4]

In Section B, I briefly outline the particular developments in UK public law that, together, point toward fundamental changes in the rules of the constitution. In Section C, I describe the more typical process of defining public power that has prevailed in constitutional States for the last two centuries—the conscious and intentional formulation of written constitutions by identifiable institutions. In Section D, I elaborate the description of developments in the United Kingdom and in Section E I raise some difficulties associated with this piecemeal kind of constitution-making. Finally, in Section F, I qualify my description of the standard model of constitution-making, using as my main example, its best known manifestation—the constitutional law of the United States. I suggest that the process of American constitutional interpretation has resulted in a kind of constitutional change not unlike the one that has prevailed in the United Kingdom.

B. Some Changes in the Constitution

Many observers believe that the simple rule of parliamentary sovereignty no longer obtains in the United Kingdom. This conclusion is based on a number of discrete developments. Each of them has been the object of extensive critical discussion. In this chapter, it is sufficient briefly to describe a few of them to show how the traditional understanding has been undermined.

The most explicit alteration has been the subordination of Acts of Parliament to European law. The European Communities Act of 1972, authorizing the United Kingdom's accession to the European Treaties, provided (consistent with the case law of the European Court of Justice) that any 'enactment passed or to be passed' would only take effect subject to applicable European law.[5] The Act thus explicitly recognized, *pace* Dicey, a body with 'a right to override… legislation of Parliament'.

of government but would not be enforceable in a court of law. See AW Bradley and KD Ewing, *Constitutional and Administrative Law* (14th edn, Pearson 2007) 20–30.

[4] L Alexander, 'Introduction' in L Alexander (ed), *Constitutionalism: Philosophical Foundations* (CUP 1998) 6. See also Section C below.

[5] European Communities Act 1972, s 2.

The effectiveness of this limitation was affirmed by dicta in the House of Lords' 1991 judgment in *R v Secretary of State for Transport ex parte Factortame (No 2).*[6] In his speech, Lord Bridge chose his words with care: it was the duty of United Kingdom courts 'to override any rule of national law found to be in conflict with any directly enforceable rule of Community law'.[7] While it is generally believed that Parliament could remove this limitation by express repeal of the European Communities Act 1972,[8] even requiring a particular form of legislative action to effect some objective constitutes a substantial chink in the Diceyan orthodoxy.[9]

Although it lacks the explicit judicial imprimatur given to the priority of European law, a further limitation on the unfettered authority of Parliament has been taken for granted for a much longer time. Parliament, over the course of the last century, relinquished its right to legislate for former colonial possessions. Section 4 of the 1931 Statute of Westminster stated that no Act of Parliament would 'extend or be deemed to extend, to a Dominion as part of the law of that Dominion, unless it is expressly declared in that Act that that Dominion has requested, and consented to, the enactment thereof'.[10] More emphatic renunciations were repeated in subsequent Independence Acts.[11] Although judicial dicta have questioned the strict legal effectiveness of such Acts,[12] courts or commentators all agree today that any attempts by the Westminster Parliament to legislate for territories to which it had granted independence would be ineffective in those jurisdictions. It is hard to find an observer willing to quarrel with Lord Sankey's observation that Parliament's power to repeal the Statute of Westminster 'is theory and has no relation to realities'.[13] Geographically, at least, Parliament has irreversibly ceded part of its power to legislate.[14]

While its impact is less direct, the radical expansion of the power of judicial review of government action is at least as significant an indication of a basic change in the constitutional allocation of power. In the past several decades, courts have invigorated their power to review and to invalidate decisions of agencies acting within the apparent scope of the authority granted to them by legislation. The

[6] [1991] 1 AC 603 (HL).

[7] *Factortame* (n 6) 659. In the case itself, the only law 'overridden' was the law concerning interim relief which predated the 1972 Act. See PP Craig, 'Sovereignty of the United Kingdom Parliament After Factortame' [1991] 11 *Yearboook of European Law* 221, 248. The dictum according supremacy to Community law over *subsequent* legislation, however, is usually accorded controlling significance. See also *R v Secretary of State for Employment, ex p. Equal Opportunities Commission and Day* [1995] 1 AC 1 (HL) (courts may issue declarations that an Act of Parliament is inconsistent with European law).

[8] See latterly European Union Act 2011, s 18.

[9] *Factortame* 'prompted even the most devoted Dicey apologist to acknowledge that the traditional theoretical order had ended'. PC Oliver, *The Constitution of Independence: The Development of Constitutional Theory in Australia, Canada, and New Zealand* (OUP 2005) 77.

[10] The Statute of Westminster recently proved relevant in the context of the Succession to the Crown Act 2013.

[11] See, eg, Kenya Independence Act, 1963, s 1(2).

[12] *Manuel v AG* [1983] Ch 77 (CA), 88

[13] *British Coal Corp v R* [1935] AC 500 (PC), 520.

[14] See Bradley and Ewing (n 3) 63. It is too early to say whether a similar conclusion can be drawn with respect to any or all of the sub-state legislatures established in the United Kingdom proper. See C Turpin and A Tomkins, *British Government and the Constitution: Text and Materials* (7th edn, CUP 2011) 241.

courts have applied a number of criteria to such actions, including requiring that procedures be minimally fair and that measures be rationally related to public aims.[15] These grounds of review usually appear nowhere in the texts of the authorizing legislation and it is widely agreed they are creations of the reviewing courts. There is an intense and voluminous literature on the legal justification for such a robust judicial role. One school suggests that the judicially imposed limits are properly attributable to a supposed parliamentary intention to restrict agencies within standards to be developed by the courts.[16] Another holds that such review is directly rooted in the common law and is, therefore, subject to judicial development with no need to refer to any implicit parliamentary authorization.[17] For our purposes, the distinction is immaterial. Under either version, certain operations of the State are not constrained solely by rules intended by Parliament. They are, rather, under the supervision of courts, acting according to judicially formulated standards and procedures.[18] Parliament might, perhaps, reassert its power in a particular case and authorize government action not meeting the judicial standards. The courts, however, have shown a marked unwillingness to acknowledge the force of such legislation.[19] Much less probably, it might, by painfully explicit enactment, attempt to strip courts, in general, of the right to regulate government action although some judges have declared that such a law should be treated as invalid,[20] suggesting that the assertive use of judicial review has laid the basis 'for a reevaluation of the concept of Parliament's legislative supremacy'.[21]

A fourth major development bearing on the extent of parliamentary authority is the jurisprudence of the Human Rights Act 1998 ('HRA'). By its terms, the Act does not purport to limit Parliament's right to legislate. A court confronting legislation that it deems in conflict with the prescribed rights is limited to issuing a 'declaration of incompatibility' that 'does not affect the validity, continuing operation or enforcement' of the law in question.[22] The government White Paper published to explain the Bill reaffirmed that 'Parliament is competent to make any law on any matter of its choosing and no court may question the validity of any Act that it passes'.[23] But another section of the HRA may have had a greater impact on

[15] See Bradley and Ewing (n 3) 725–57.

[16] See, eg, M Elliott, *Constitutional Foundations of Judicial Review* (Hart Publishing 2001).

[17] See, eg, P Craig, 'Competing Models of Judicial Review' [1999] *PL* 428.

[18] On the relationship between assertive judicial review and parliamentary sovereignty see M Elliott, 'The Demise of Parliamentary Sovereignty? The Implications for Justifying Judicial Review' (1999) 115 *LQR* 119.

[19] '[I]t is a basic rule of administrative law that even when a statutory discretion is phrased in absolute terms, the courts do not accept that the power is absolute or unlimited.' AW Bradley, 'The Sovereignty of Parliament—Form or Substance?' in J Jowell and D Oliver (eds), *The Changing Constitution* (4th edn, OUP 2000) 23, 35.

[20] See text around nn 57–61.

[21] EW Thomas, 'The Relationship of Parliament and the Courts' [2000] 31 *Victoria University, Wellington L Rev* 5, 14.

[22] Human Rights Act 1998, s 4.

[23] Home Office, *Rights Brought Home: The Human Rights Bill* (Cm 3782, 1997) reproduced in part in MW Janis, RS Kay, and AW Bradley, *European Human Rights Law: Text and Materials* (3rd edn, OUP 2008) 859, 862.

the constitutional allocation of authority. Section 3 enjoins courts, 'so far as it is possible to do so' to 'read and give effect' to primary legislation 'in a way which is compatible with Convention rights'. The received meaning of this duty was articulated in Lord Nicholls' speech in *Ghaidan v Godin-Mendoza* in 2004:

> Even if, construed according to the ordinary principles of interpretation, the meaning of the legislation admits of no doubt, section 3 may none the less require the legislation to be given a different meaning (...) Section 3 may require the court to depart from this legislative intention, that is depart from the intention of the Parliament which enacted the legislation.[24]

So long as courts adhere to this notion of interpretation, Parliament cannot 'make or unmake any law whatever', even if it expresses its intention to do so in words that 'admit of no doubt'. Again, Parliament might, in theory, reassert its plenary power by repealing the Human Rights Act and, from time to time, exactly such action has been proposed. It is hard, at this late date, however, to imagine that some form of legislatively created and judicially interpreted fundamental rights will ever be fully removed from the British legal system.[25]

The cumulative effect of these and other developments has resulted in an arrangement of governing authority markedly different from the one that prevailed in the 1950s. Their larger constitutional significance has been highlighted by academic commentators and, notably, by judges.[26] In *R (Jackson) v Attorney General,* the Law Lords rejected a challenge to the validity of the Parliament Act of 1949 extending the circumstances in which the House of Commons might legislate without the assent of the House of Lords. That Act had itself been enacted without the Lords' assent under the Parliament Act of 1911 that had specified a more restricted procedure for legislation by the Commons acting alone. The complainants' argument in *Jackson* supposed that (1) legislation under the 1911 Act, was an exercise of delegated authority and (2) the 1949 Act was an ineffective attempt by a delegate to enlarge its own power. The Lords rejected this characterization of the 1911 Act finding that it did not provide for a form of subordinate law-making. Rather it redefined the procedure for primary legislation.[27] The implications of this holding

[24] [2004] UKHL 30, [2004] 2 AC 557, paras 29–30. It is uncertain whether or not the House of Lords has adopted a more cautious approach in subsequent cases. See A Kavanagh, *Constitutional Review Under the UK Human Rights Act* (CUP 2009) 92–5 (discussing *R (Wilkinson) v IRC* [2005] UKHL 30, 1 WLR 1718). The High Court of Australia declined to follow *Ghaidan* in construing a materially similar provision in the Victoria Charter of Human Rights and Responsibilities 2006: *Momcilovic v The Queen* [2011] HCA 34, 280 ALR 221. See also, on the New Zealand Bill of Rights Act 1990, *Hansen v R* [2007] NZSC 7.

[25] See, eg, Ministry of Justice, *Commission on a Bill of Rights, A UK Bill of Rights: The Choice Before Us* (Members of the Commission on a Bill of Rights, 2012) para 12.24 ('We conclude... that mechanisms in the UK Bill of Rights should be broadly similar to those in the Human Rights Act'). But see Anthony Speaight QC, 'Mechanisms of a UK Bill of Rights' in *Commission on a Bill of Rights, A UK Bill of Rights: The Choice Before Us* (Members of the Commission on a Bill of Rights, 2012) 257–62.

[26] See especially Bradley (n 19).

[27] *Jackson* [2005] UKHL 56, [2006] 1 AC 262. For a summary and critical review of the judgments see J Allan, 'The Paradox of Sovereignty: Jackson and the Hunt for a New Rule of Recognition?' [2007] 18 *Kings College LJ* 1.

for *restricting* parliamentary power were articulated in some of the judgments. In particular, Lord Steyn asserted that Dicey's 'classic account' of a 'pure and absolute' parliamentary supremacy was 'out of place in the modern United Kingdom'. While Parliament's authority was still the presumptive rule, courts might, in exceptional cases, such as legislation 'attempting to abolish judicial review or the ordinary role of the courts', properly refuse to recognize it. Lord Hope said that 'courts have a part to play in defining the limits of Parliament's legislative sovereignty'.[28] In 1995, Stephen Sedley, then a High Court judge, had described a 'new and still emerging constitutional paradigm' claiming that Dicey's parliamentary sovereignty had morphed into a 'bi-polar sovereignty of the Crown, in, Parliament and the Crown in its courts, to each of which the Crown's ministers are answerable—politically to Parliament, legally to the courts'.[29] It has been, according to Adam Tomkins, 'one of the most fundamental realignments of the constitutional order since the end of the seventeenth century... The constitution is up for grabs, and it is the judges who are grabbing it.'[30]

As noted, my main concern is not the exact shape of the new constitution or the suitability of the arrangements it prescribes. It is rather how such a new dispensation may have come into being. A number of discrete decisions took place over many years, some by Parliament, some by the executive, and some by courts. Sometimes these institutions worked independently, sometimes in tandem, and sometimes at cross purposes. The various decisions were motivated by numerous factors including, among other things, matters of short-term politics, foreign policy, economic development, and institutional rivalry. Their impact on the long-term nature of the constitution was sometimes part of the decision-making calculus but rarely the most important part. These days, this is a funny way to make a constitution.

C. The Designed Constitution

That is, of course, because these days the British Constitution is a funny kind of constitution. The term 'constitution' in the United Kingdom legal system is often used to refer to the whole complex of rules, institutions, and practices that define the operation of government.[31] I use it here in a narrower sense, one that more closely corresponds to the usage in States with constitutional texts. The United Kingdom is usually cited as one of only two national jurisdictions that lack an authoritative constitutional text that stipulates rules at the highest level of the

[28] *Jackson* (n 27) [102] and [107]. See also *Thoburn v Sunderland CC* [2003] QB 151(DC) [60] (Laws J) (the 'scope and nature of parliamentary sovereignty are ultimately confided' to the courts). *AXA General Insurance Ltd v Lord Advocate* [2011] UKSC 46, [2012] 1 AC 868 [50] (Lord Hope) ('The question whether the principle of the sovereignty of the United Kingdom Parliament is absolute or may be subject to limitation in exceptional circumstances is still under discussion'). See, too, Chapter 6 in this volume by Lord Hope.

[29] S Sedley, 'Human Rights: A Twenty-First Century Agenda' [1995] *PL* 386, 389.

[30] A Tomkins, *Public Law* (OUP 2003) 23.

[31] See, eg, Bradley and Ewing (n 3) 4–6.

legal system.[32] Such a text creates and defines the institutions of the State, specifies the exclusive means by which they may act and, usually, imposes limits on their powers. This kind of constitution specifies those principles that are accepted as the ultimate legally binding restraints on the exercise of all forms of public power. In the United Kingdom, until recently, the unwritten counterpart of such a constitution was the single rule of parliamentary sovereignty—and the concomitant limit on Parliament's ability to bind its successors. It is that 'constitution' which appears to be changing.

In most of the rest of the world, where written constitutions are employed, there is a standard, if rather idealized, picture of how such a constitution comes into being. A political society becomes dissatisfied with existing governing arrangements. An intense form of public debate ensues and some kind of representative process emerges with a licence to speak on behalf of 'the people' of that society.[33] That process results in a plan for instituting new government with characteristics that are thought suitable for that people in that place and time. The plan is reduced to a text which is promulgated as the binding constitution.[34]

I refer to the agency that creates this constitution as the 'sovereign'. It is worth pausing to clarify this term. In the current discussion in the United Kingdom, the term 'sovereignty of Parliament' sometimes refers to the capacity of Parliament as it is defined by the existing legal system. Thus Dicey was able to describe the sovereignty of Parliament 'under the English constitution'.[35] Arguments about this kind of sovereignty are arguments *of law*, such as the claim that the judges can restrain parliamentary authority because parliamentary sovereignty is itself a rule of common law.[36] In contrast, the sovereign whose actions I described in the previous paragraph is the force that *defines the legal system*. As such, this sovereign cannot be a subject of that legal system and an assertion about its 'legal authority' is incoherent.[37]

This does not mean that the identity of this sovereign or the propriety of its decisions cannot be the subject of rational argument. But such argument must proceed

[32] The other is New Zealand. Israel's Basic Laws have been interpreted as authoritative texts that are superior to all kinds of other law but they have been passed one by one over a long period of time and do not purport to control every exercise of public power. See A Maoz, 'The Institutional Organization of the Israeli Legal System' in A Shapira and KC DeWitt-Arar (eds), *Introduction to the Law of Israel* (Kluwer 1995). They thus share some, but not all, of the peculiar features of the UK constitution-making process.

[33] See B Ackerman, *We the People: Foundations* (Belknap 1991) 6–10.

[34] PC Oliver, 'Sovereignty in the 21st Century' [2003] 14 *Kings College LJ* 137, 156.

[35] Dicey (n 1) 3.

[36] See, eg, *Jackson* (n 27) [102] (Lord Steyn); TRS Allan, *Constitutional Justice: A Liberal Theory of the Rule of Law* (OUP 2001) 271.

[37] See HWR Wade, 'The Basis of Legal Sovereignty' [1955] *CLJ* 172, 187–8, 192; compare Chapter 4 in this volume by J Goldsworthy and PC Oliver, 'Change in the Ultimate Rules of a Legal System' (2006) (*draft on file with the author*) 26. On the two kinds of sovereignty see JDB Mitchell, 'What Happened to the Constitution on 1st January 1973?' (1980) 11 *Cambrian L Rev* 69, 72–3 (contrasting the 'sovereignty of Parliament and the sovereignty of the nation or Kingdom'); AL Young, 'Sovereignty: Demise, Afterlife, or Partial Resurrection?' [2011] 9 *International Journal of Constitutional Law* 163, 169–70 (contrasting sovereignty 'in terms of lawmaking power' and sovereignty 'in terms of power over constitutive rules').

on the basis of some shared political, social, or moral values, not on the grounds of supposedly binding positive law.[38] In modern democracies, there is near universal agreement on one characteristic of a proper constitution-making sovereign: it must represent the will of 'the people'. There are, to be sure, multiple and acute problems with constructing a plausible surrogate for 'the people', capable of translating its will into defined rules.[39] But, however those problems are resolved, every model of 'the people' as a constitution-maker supposes that it can act knowingly and intentionally. The State in this vision is the product of a collective decision. So Locke saw the people 'appoint[ing] the form of the commonwealth . . . by constituting the legislative, and appointing in whose hands that shall be',[40] and Rousseau contemplated the people 'legitimately assembled' and 'decree[ing] that there shall be a governing body established in this or that form'.[41] These hypothetical exertions of popular will were translated into practical action in the constituent assemblies of the independent American states at the end of the eighteenth century. Those bodies deliberated, drafted, and revised. Their products were often further debated in the general population before final approval. In the case of the Federal Constitution of 1787–9, the arguments in *The Federalist Papers* illustrate the kind of enterprise that constitution-making was understood to be. Those tracts relied on reason, history, and comparative experience to make the case that the rules proposed by the Philadelphia Convention were, in the circumstances, suitable for the United States.[42]

This picture of the process of constitution-making fits naturally with the idea that constitutions are necessarily the acts of a 'constituent power'. For Sieyès, that power resided in the 'nation' which would be represented in an 'extraordinary representative body'. 'The community needs a common will; without singleness of will it could not succeed in being a willing and acting body.'[43] This assumption is implicit in recent debates about the minimum coherence that a population must exhibit before it is capable of uniting in a constitutional State.[44] We insist on certain commonalities because we think that only then can the actions of representatives be treated as judgments attributable to a group of human beings. According to Carl Schmitt, '[l]ike every other order, the legal order rests on a decision and not on a norm.'[45] No such decision is possible unless an aspiring

[38] See HLA Hart, *The Concept of Law* (OUP 1961) 104.

[39] See RS Kay, 'Constituent Authority' (2011) 59 *Americal Journal of Comparative Law* 715, 735–55.

[40] J Locke, *Treatise of Civil Government and A Letter Concerning Toleration* (C Sherman ed, D Appleton-Century Co 1937) 95; Locke 67: 'So that politic societies all began from a voluntary union, and the mutual agreement of men freely acting in the choice of their governors and forms of government.' See also Kay (n 39) 67.

[41] J Rousseau, *The Social Contract* (M Cranston trans, Penguin 1968) Book III, chs xiv, xvii.

[42] A Hamilton, J Madison, and J Jay, *The Federalist Papers* (Clinton Rossiter ed, New American Library 1961).

[43] EJ Sieyès, *What is the Third Estate?* (M Blondel trans, SE Finer ed, Praeger 1964) 121, 130–1.

[44] See J Weiler, *The Constitution of Europe: 'Do the New Clothes Have an Emperor?' and Other Essays on European Integration* (CUP 1999) 337.

[45] C Schmitt, *Political Theology: Four Chapters on the Concept of Sovereignty* (G Schwab trans, MIT 2005) 10.

constitutional collectivity is capable of acting as 'a person with all the attributes of personality, conscience and will'.[46]

From these ideas follows the standard assortment of constitution-making devices employed by modern societies—special legislative acts, constituent assemblies, and referendums.[47] Indeed, there is no way to create a formal constitutional text without the deliberate, methodical application of human intelligence and judgment. The logical relation between an expression of will and the creation of a constitution is often displayed in constitutional preambles. They commonly explain how the process of constitution-making was a reasonable way of expressing the will of the sovereign. So, whether promulgated by an ordinary legislature or a special constituent assembly, preambles are likely to declare the enactors' right to act for 'the people'.[48] Even more commonly, preambles will list a set of values that are supposed to inform the whole constitution, reinforcing the idea that the document is the expression of a coherent political will.

This standard model presumes that constitutions are the product of the rationalist enterprise criticized by Friedrich Hayek, one that pictured 'intelligent men coming together for deliberation about how to make the world anew'.[49] The resulting legal system, on this view, is what Hayek would later characterize as a *taxis*, a 'made order' (to be contrasted with a *cosmos* or 'spontaneous order').[50] Hayek defends the competing view, one deeply sceptical of reliance on human design of social institutions. Edmund Burke, mistrusting 'the fallible and feeble contrivances of our reason', found 'the very idea of the fabrication of a new government is enough to fill us with disgust and horror'.[51] With respect to making constitutions, however, Burke's warning would fall on deaf ears. New governments have come to be universally understood as things to be 'fabricated', purpose-made by the calculated application of human intelligence. (Hayek's own preference for rules that 'manifest themselves only by being observed' was, it should be noted, largely confined to rules of primary conduct and did not extend to public institutions and procedures which he acknowledged were fit for deliberate design).[52] Shortly after Burke published his warning about the futility of intentional design of the State, Thomas Paine published *Rights of Man,* affirming the possibility of an ever-improving human science of constitution-making. 'There is', he wrote, 'a morning of reason

[46] L Duguit, *Traité de Droit Constituionnel*, vol 1 (2nd edn, E de Boccard 1921) quoted and translated in CI Keitner, *The Paradoxes of Nationalism: The French Revolution and its Meaning for Contemporary Nation-Building* (SUNY Press 2007) 27.

[47] See Kay (n 39) 735–55.

[48] See, eg, Preamble, Constitution of the Czech Republic, 16 December 1992 (promulgation by Parliament); Constitution of Colombia 1991 (promulgation by Constituent Assembly).

[49] See FA Hayek, *The Constitution of Liberty* (University of Chicago Press 1960) 57. Interestingly, Hayek characterized the rationalist tradition as 'French' and the opposing, empirical tradition as 'British' (54–8).

[50] See FA Hayek, *Law, Legislation and Liberty: Rules and Order*, vol 1 (University of Chicago Press 1979) 28, 38.

[51] E Burke, *Reflections on the Revolution in France* (Gateway 1962) 50, 54.

[52] Hayek (n 50) 43, 124–5, 134.

rising upon man, on the subject of government, that has not appeared before.'[53] It is Paine's conception that has carried the day.

D. The Accidental Constitution

With this background, we can reconsider the apparent process of constitutional change in the United Kingdom. The standard model of constitutional renewal—the drafting of a written constitution approved by some acceptable surrogate of 'the people'—has been a minor theme in British literature on this subject. The Levellers' proposed Agreement of the People and Cromwell's short-lived Instrument of Government show that the idea of an enacted written constitution has not been entirely absent from English history.[54] More recently, the Charter 88 movement called for a 'new constitutional settlement', establishing a Bill of Rights, reforming the composition and election of Parliament, and limiting the exercise of power by the government. The last of its ten demands was for 'draw[ing] up a written constitution anchored in the idea of universal citizenship that incorporates these reforms'. Little attention was devoted to elaborating just how this document would be 'drawn up' and, in truth, the Charter's advocates appeared much more interested in substantive changes than in the proper means of defining State power.[55]

Recognition of the cumulative constitutional changes of the recent past—those outlined in Section B, as well as several others, especially the emergence of regional parliaments or assemblies in Scotland, Wales, and (again in) Northern Ireland—have stimulated further interest in deliberate constitutional reform. Several parliamentary committees have examined aspects of the subject. So far, however, none has recommended a thorough and comprehensive process for the creation of a binding written constitution. The Political and Constitutional Reform Committee of the House of Commons, for example, recently issued an equivocally positive report on the question, 'Do We Need a Constitutional Convention for the UK?' The kind of convention the committee endorsed, however, would do little more than 'discuss constitutional change' and 'consider how, in the future, our constitution can best serve the people of the UK'. As to whether or not such a process should lead to a written constitution, the committee 'believe[d] further work is necessary fully to examine this option'.[56]

[53] T Paine, *Rights of Man* (1791) reprinted in *The Life and Major Writings of Thomas Paine* (PS Foner ed, Citadel Press 1974) 396. See also J Wilson, *Lectures on Law* (1791) reprinted in *The Works of James Wilson*, vol 1 (J DeWitt Andrews ed, Callaghan 1896) 375 (The people 'have the right to mould, to preserve, to improve, to refine and to finish' the constitution).

[54] See M Loughlin, 'Constituent Power Subverted: From English Constitutional Argument to British Constitutional Practice' in M Loughlin and N Walker (eds) *The Paradox of Constitutionalism: Constitutional Power and Constituent Form* (OUP 2007) 27, 36–9.

[55] See, eg, D Erdos, 'Charter 88 and the Constitutional Reform Movement: A Retrospective' (2009) 62 *Parliamentary Affairs* 537

[56] House of Commons Political and Constitutional Reform Committee, *Do We Need a Constitutional Convention for the UK?* (HC 2012–13 371) paras 15, 53, 81. The desirability of a written constitution is to be examined in a further planned inquiry of the committee, 'Mapping the Path to Codifying—or

The current debate about the British Constitution involves a number of alternative propositions purporting to describe (or to prescribe—sometimes it is hard to say which) the set of rules replacing Dicey's ascription to Parliament of power to make any law at all. One version modifies the corollary that Parliament's power does not extend to the right to bind future Parliaments. Once this limitation is relaxed, any sitting Parliament may irreversibly alter the conditions for the effective exercise of public power. In some variations, this authority is limited to the imposition of 'manner and form' limitations. That is, Parliament might be obliged to follow any procedures laid down by a predecessor but, if it follows such a procedure, it remains free to legislate on any subject to any substantive effect. So, one Parliament could, by ordinary legislation, require that certain enactments, such as a Bill of Rights, may only be altered by a two thirds vote of the House of Commons or only by using certain formulary language.[57]

Somewhat more ambitiously, other versions have proposed that Parliament could bind its successors both procedurally and substantively: it might enact, for example, a Bill of Rights which no future statute could contravene, no matter the manner in which it was passed. If we take the Independence Acts for former colonial possessions to be legally effective, irrepealable abdications in British law, they would provide a precedent.[58]

Yet another possible description of the transformed constitution supposes that limitations on Parliament have emerged independently of any act attributable to Parliament itself.[59] Sometimes these restraints are ascribed to the 'common law'. In *Jackson*, Lord Steyn described the principle of parliamentary supremacy as 'a construct of the common law. The judges created this principle... [I]t is not unthinkable that circumstances could arise where the courts have to qualify [it].'[60]

Not Codifying—the UK's Constitution', available at <http://www.parliament.uk/business/committees/committees-a-z/commons-select/political-and-constitutional-reform-committee/inquiries/parliament-2010/mapping-the-path-to-codifying---or-not-codifying---the-uks-constitution/> (last accessed 7 July 2013). At the time of writing, no report on the latter question has been published. See also House of Lords Constitution Committee, *The Process of Constitutional Change*, paras 27–34, 58 (2011) (stressing the need for comprehensive examination of constitutional change).

[57] This seems to be the way most of the Law Lords interpreted the Parliament Act of 1911 in *Jackson* (n 27) [24] (Lord Bingham), [64] (Lord Nicholls), [91] (Lord Steyn), [163] (Lady Hale), [173] (Lord Carswell). The European Union Act 2011, s 2 prohibits UK agreement to certain changes in the European Union treaties without approval by an Act of Parliament that would itself require endorsement of the change in a referendum. If this provision is effective, Parliament must now authorize any qualifying treaty change *and* that approval can only be manifested by either (1) an enactment coupled with approval via referendum or (2) repeal of the European Union Act's requirements altogether. It is also arguable that Parliament might approve a treaty change by use of an explicit provision stating that it is to operate 'notwithstanding' the European Union Act. Recognition of such a power, however, would make the supposed authority to create 'manner and form' limits decidedly less significant. In Chapter 4 in this volume, Jeffrey Goldsworthy defends the propriety of certain form and manner requirements. See also Chapter 5 in this volume by Alison L Young.

[58] Peter Oliver regards the possible recognition of such limitations not as changes in the basic rules but as potential articulations of aspects of the existing rule of recognition which has a necessary penumbra of uncertain application. Oliver (n 37) 12–15.

[59] N MacCormick, *Questioning Sovereignty: Law, State, and Nation in the European Commonwealth* (OUP 1999) 9–10.

[60] *Jackson* (n 27) [102]. See also TRS Allan, 'Parliamentary Sovereignty: Law Politics and Revolution' (1997) 113 *LQR* 443, 445.

As matter of history, however, the claim that Parliament's power originated in the common law decisions of the judges is highly doubtful.[61] For other writers the 'common law' limitations on Parliament are more abstract. They are implicit in basic values necessarily presupposed by the legal system. According to this view, any exercise of power manifestly inconsistent with these values should be treated by courts as invalid.[62] Perhaps, we should not be too surprised that the prime example of a statute that judges have suggested would violate these principles and justify nullification is one that would abolish the power of judicial review of government action.[63]

To reiterate, I am less interested in which, if any, of these descriptions is accurate or desirable than in the process by which people believe the alteration has come or ought to come about. The discussion in Section B shows that any new United Kingdom constitution seems to have emerged one step at a time from a series of narrowly focused enactments and judgments. From these measures, more general inferences are drawn about the loci of public power. The resulting constitution is optimistically supposed to be 'an integrated expression of historical experience conferring a unified meaning on political existence'.[64] For common lawyers, this is a familiar process and, although, for the reasons stated, the basic rules cannot themselves be regarded as aspects of the common law, this way of looking at things does resemble a kind of common law process of constitution-making.[65]

Unlike actual common law, these rules are not evidenced exclusively in the process of litigation and the judgments of the courts. One of the fallacies resulting from treating the basic rules as genuine rules of common law has been to conclude that the final decision on the shape of the constitution rests with the judges. An example is Lord Steyn's dictum in the *Jackson* case that it was in the power of judges to 'qualify' the rule of parliamentary sovereignty. Somewhat more realistically, others have argued that, whatever we call it, the practical fact is that no constitutional change will be thought effective unless and until the courts accept it as binding in their decisions. RTE Latham claimed that 'the *Grundnorm* of a case-law system is simply the sum of those principles which command the ultimate allegiance of the

[61] See J Goldsworthy, *The Sovereignty of Parliament: History and Philosophy* (OUP 1999) 242–4; J Goldsworthy, 'The Myth of the Common Law Constitution' in DE Edlin (ed) *Common Law Theory* (CUP 2007) 204.

[62] TRS Allan, for example, sees the doctrine of parliamentary sovereignty as a 'doctrine of the common law' that arises from a 'substratum of constitutional principle' associated with 'the rule of law, the separation of powers…and representative democracy'. '[S]ome common law values', moreover, 'are too deeply entrenched… to be vulnerable even to explicit statutory incursion.' TRS Allan, 'Questions of Legality and Legitimacy: Form and Substance in British Constitutionalism' (2011) 9 *International Journal of Constitutional Law* 155, 157–8. Allan's understanding of the constitution is further described and criticized in Chapter 4 in this volume by Jeffrey Goldsworthy.

[63] See *Jackson* (n 27) [102] (Lord Steyn), [159] (Lady Hale); *AXA General Insurance* (n 28) [50] (Lord Hope); Lord Woolf, 'Droit Public—English Style' [1995] *PL* 57, 69. See also Chapter 6 in this volume by Lord Hope.

[64] See AW Bradley (n 19) 28–30 (quoting M Foley, *The Silence of Constitutions: Gaps, 'Abeyances' and Political Temperament in the Maintenance of Government* (Routledge 1989) 87).

[65] See M Loughlin, *Public Law and Political Theory* (OUP 1992) 232.

courts'.[66] And for HWR Wade, it was 'obvious...that this grundnorm, or whatever we call it, lies in the keeping of the judges and it is for them to say what they will recognize as effective legislation'.[67] So central were the courts for Wade that he suggested that a fundamental law could be entrenched by persuading the judges to submit to it through subscription to a modified judicial oath.[68]

More commonly, however, the emergence of fundamental rules is seen as evidenced by a combination of the actions of judicial and legislative agents.[69] A mere declaration by the highest court will be insufficient unless the political actors in the system accept it as an accurate statement of the criteria for recognition of legally binding norms. Commentators have stated something of a formula: a modification in the constitution attempted by one of these institutions that is accepted by the other is *ipso facto* valid. So the new relationship between European law and Acts of Parliament follows from enactment of the European Communities Act 1972 and acceptance of the priority it stipulated in the *Factortame* case.[70] These actors are, doubtless, critical in effecting a change in the constitution but, since we are now observing a social-political phenomenon and not an act of legislation according to some legally defined process, it makes sense to factor in the actions and reactions of all the agents involved, including the government, the opposition, the press, the academy, and other opinion-makers. It may be that, at the end, an effective change manifests itself, in acceptance of the new arrangements by the 'officials' of the system, but the reasons for that acceptance are likely to involve actions and opinions of many people, official and unofficial.[71]

E. The Blind Sovereign

The kind of constitutional change observed in the United Kingdom marks a distinct contrast to the standard process I outlined in Section C. In that model, basic rules of the legal system may be influenced by a messy assortment of social factors. But the rules themselves are produced formally by the application of human intelligence

[66] RTE Latham, *The Law and the Commonwealth* (Greenwood Press 1970) 525. See also M Gordon, 'The Conceptual Foundations of Parliamentary Sovereignty: Reconstructing Jennings and Wade' [2009] *PL* 519, 537–8.

[67] HWR Wade, *Constitutional Fundamentals* (Stevens 1980) 26.

[68] Wade (n 67) 37–8.

[69] See Oliver (n 9) 80 ('[T]here is a great difference between courts agreeing to recognize that which a Parliament has enacted...and those same courts deciding to impose limitations at their own initiative').

[70] See Oliver (n 34) 163, fn 103; D Oliver, 'The United Kingdom' in D Oliver and C Fusaro (eds) *How Constitutions Change: A Comparative Study* (Hart Publishing 2011) 329, 349–30. See also Chapter 4 in this volume by J Goldsworthy.

[71] See Hart (n 38) 113–20. One of Hart's examples illustrates the point. He describes a period in the 1950s when the rule of recognition of South Africa was in contest, as evidenced by opposing actions of the Parliament and the courts, each premised on different views of the limits of the legislative power (118–19). To restrict one's examination of that conflict to the actions of these two official institutions would provide a grossly incomplete picture of the causes of the constitutional change taking place. See M Chanock, *The Making of South African Legal Culture 1902–1936: Fear, Favour and Prejudice* (CUP 2001) 514–19; see generally B Beinart, 'The South African Appeal Court and Judicial Review' (1958) 21 *MLR* 587.

and deliberate political choice. That is, constitutional rules—like all rules of positive law—are 'laid down'.[72] The British Constitution, to be sure, is the product of a series of intentional actions. Moreover, some of those actions, particularly legislative measures, may be undertaken with some understanding of their long-term constitutional significance. But they are not part of a plan to create a coherent constitution. The sovereign is not a human agent but an uncoordinated series of largely unrelated incidents. This 'sovereign' lacks any unified vision of the resulting constitution. It is, in that sense, blind.

Not everyone finds this blind constitution-making defective. Commentators going back at least to Burke have praised the gradual, organic way in which the British Constitution has changed. In fact, the idea that a complicated and coherent order can emerge from a multitude of independent and uncoordinated actions is familiar in other contexts. The idea of a blind sovereign may call to mind the ethologist Richard Dawkins' picture of biological evolution as a 'blind watchmaker', producing what looks like a carefully designed organism through the random medium of natural selection.[73] Dawkins posited an analogous process for the evolution of cultural artefacts resulting from the 'differential survival of replicating entities' he called 'memes'.[74] Even more familiar is the analogy of the well-functioning market economy allocating resources to their best uses and maximizing the welfare of a whole society as a result of a multitude of independent, selfishly motivated transactions. Hayek, who was deeply influenced by the model of evolutionary biology as well as of market economics, thought that something like the market's invisible hand was also responsible for the production of successful rules of social conduct.[75]

Similar advantages have been noted with respect to the evolutionary development of a constitution. The step-by-step process avoids the wrenching disruptions of full scale replacement and allows each incremental reform to be tested, with limited cost, against the demands of experience. In the *Jackson* case, Lord Carswell described the constitution as a 'delicate plant... capable of being damaged by over-vigorous treatment, which may have incalculable results'.[76] Peter Oliver, arguing the value of binding incremental changes implemented by Parliament, questions the virtues of all-at-once constitutions drafted to meet the concerns of a particular moment. 'Over the coming decades and centuries the United Kingdom [can] cautiously and pragmatically develop an organic constitution making use of the full range of possibilities as appropriate.'[77] John Laws, then a High Court judge, described the constitution and the constitution-making process in terms that highlight both their virtues and their risks:

> [T]he absence of what I will call a sovereign text means that the legal distribution of public power consists ultimately in a dynamic settlement, acceptable to the people, between the

[72] AWB Simpson, 'The Common Law and Legal Theory' in AD Renteln and A Dundes (eds) *Folk Law: Essays in the Theory and Practice of Lex Non Scripta*, vol 1 (Garland 1994) 119, 122.

[73] R Dawkins, *The Blind Watchmaker* (WW Norton 1996) 4–20.

[74] R Dawkins, *The Selfish Gene* (OUP 1989) 189–201.

[75] See Hayek (n 50) 18. See also M Rutherford, *Institutions in Economics: The Old and the New Institutionalism* (CUP 1994) 83–4.

[76] *Jackson* (n 36) [176].

[77] Oliver (n 34) 156.

different arms of government. It is not written in stone; it is not even written in paper. It cannot therefore be ascertained by reference to the pages of a book whose authority is unquestioned, scriptural. The settlement is dynamic because, as our long history shows, it can change; and in the last 300 years has done so without revolution.[78]

The characteristics that have given satisfaction to these commentators, however, may equally be conceived as defects in the constitution-making process. We can identify three problems of an evolutionary constitution: (a) it definitionally lacks the benefits of deliberate design, of what Alexander Hamilton called 'reflection and choice'; (b) it leaves the constitutional rules at any moment essentially unknowable, frustrating one of the central purposes of constitutionalism; and (c) it lacks the legitimating authority of popular approval.

One observer has described the United Kingdom process as 'unique in the democratic world [in] gradually giving ourselves a constitution (...) in a piecemeal and ad hoc way, there being neither the political will to do more nor any degree of consensus as to what the final resting place should be'.[79] In general, this is not how human beings go about creating institutions that they hope will be effective or coherent in bringing about some desired State of affairs. It was for this reason that Bentham, Hume, and others thought that law reform was properly a subject of legislation rather than adjudication.[80] It has sometimes been remarked that the fundamental rules in the United Kingdom amount to a kind of customary law.[81] Customary law, by definition, is not intended by anyone. Judges and other officials contribute to changing such rules but only as 'accidental participant[s]'.[82] This kind of constitution-making recalls the effort of the Laputan professor to 'give the world a complete body of arts and sciences' by mechanically accumulating random collections of words.[83] Judicial common law law-making which is, if anything, more disciplined than the constitution-making at issue here, has often been criticized for its unsystematic quality. For Bentham, 'as a system of general rules', it was 'a thing merely imaginary',[84] and for TE Holland, 'a chaos with a full index'.[85]

It follows that the resulting constitution will end up as an uncertain guide to the permissible limits of public action. Neil MacCormick observed that 'the curiously evolutionary character of [the United Kingdom's] constitutional arrangements' has led to a 'highly flexible constitutional law'.[86] Ivor Jennings was sanguine in his

[78] J Laws, 'Law and Democracy' [1995] *PL* 72, 81.
[79] V Bogdanor, 'The Sovereignty of Parliament or the Rule of Law?', 10–11 (Magna Carta Lecture, 15 June 2006).
[80] See D Lieberman, *The Province of Legislation Determined: Legal Theory in Eighteenth-Century Britain* (CUP 1989) 239; N McArthur, 'David Hume and the Common Law of England' (2005) 3 *Journal of Scottish Philosophy* 67, 78–9.
[81] See, eg, J Goldsworthy, *Parliamentary Sovereignty: Contemporary Debates* (CUP 2010) 124
[82] J Gardner, 'Some Types of Law' in DE Edlin (ed) *Common Law Theory* (CUP 2007) 51, 64.
[83] J Swift, *Gulliver's Travels* (Rand McNally 1912) 172. See House of Lords, Constitution Committee (n 56) para 29 (the current practice of 'continuous constitutional change' may mean that 'little thought is given to the constitution as a whole').
[84] J Bentham, 'A Comment on the Commentaries', reprinted in *A Comment on the Commentaries and a Fragment of Government* (JH Burns and HLA Hart eds, Athlone Press 1977) 119.
[85] TE Holland, *Essays Upon the Form of the Law* (Butterworths 1870) 171.
[86] MacCormick (n 59) 49.

assessment of the constitution as 'a transient thing, changing like the colours of the kaleidoscope'.[87] If, however, one thinks that a central purpose of constitutional law is to provide the security that follows from knowing the circumstances in which the State may, and may not, intervene in the life plans of individuals,[88] this kind of uncertain constitution is gravely defective. Bentham thought law in general was obliged to 'mark out the line of the subject's conduct by visible directions instead of turning him loose into the wilds of perpetual conjecture',[89] a capacity even more important when the conduct to be regulated is the State's. The fact that the shape of the existing constitution continues to be a matter of deep but reasonable disagreement demonstrates this deficiency. One contemporary advocate of a 'common law' constitution believes 'the limits of legislative power' can be discovered only 'through the process of adjudication' where 'fundamental principles are tested and refined'.[90] As with the common law, 'the point... is not that everything is always in the melting-pot but that you never quite know what will go in next'.[91] This is a far cry from Thomas Jefferson's idea of a constitution: 'Our peculiar security is in the possession of a written constitution. Let us not make it a blank paper by construction.'[92]

Probably the most serious problem with continuous, ad hoc constitution-making is its doubtful political legitimacy. The ultimate rules in a legal system may not derive their force from law but that does not mean that they acquire their status with no authority of any kind. Such rules may be facts but they are not brute facts. They need to be consonant with the values of the society in which the legal system is to operate. Beyond that, they need to issue from a source that is regarded as an appropriate maker of fundamental law.[93] In modern democracies there is wide agreement that constituent authority resides in 'the people', who alone have the moral or political right to construct a system of collective coercion. This explains the standard process of constitution-making in the rest of the world. While there are many variations, all of them employ decision-making machinery that claims to represent the consent of the human population that will be subject to the system of government created. Depending on which version one adopts, the constituent process in the United Kingdom is an imperfect or a totally deficient vehicle for representing the popular will that can legitimate a constitution.

This difficulty may, in part, explain the accelerating use of referendums for approval of constitutionally significant legislation.[94] The electorate was consulted in connection with Britain's accession to the European Communities, with legislation

[87] Quoted in KD Ewing, 'Law and the Constitution: Manifesto of the Progressive Party' (2004) 67 *MLR* 734, 738. See also House of Lords Constitution Committee (n 56) para 20 ('[T]he way the UK constitutional arrangements may be changed is more flexible than in virtually any other western democracy').

[88] See RS Kay, 'American Constitutionalism', in L Alexander (ed), *Constitutionalism: Philosophical Foundations* (CUP 1998) 16, 22–4.

[89] Bentham (n 84) 95.

[90] Allan (n 36) 249ff.

[91] Simpson (n 72) 131.

[92] Letter from T Jefferson to WC Nichols (7 September 1803) in A Koch and W Peden (eds), *The Life and Selected Writings of Thomas Jefferson* (Random House 1944) 573.

[93] I elaborate these conditions in Kay (n 39).

[94] See Chapter 9 in this volume by Peter Leyland.

devolving authority on assemblies in Scotland, Wales, and Northern Ireland and, most recently, with a proposed alteration in the parliamentary electoral system.[95] The new European Union Act requires that (subject to important exceptions) changes in European treaties be approved in a referendum.[96] And 2014 will see a referendum on independence for Scotland. Whatever it says about the future, however, this isolated and irregular resort to popular sanction remains far removed from the kind of comprehensive endorsement of 'the people' underlying constitutional legitimacy in most of the world.

The political deficiency is evident if we presume that the basic rules of the constitution are, like the common law, a form of customary law.[97] Legitimacy has always been something of a problem for customary law. Its force has historically been based on the claim that it represented universally accepted practice. Hale said that common law rules 'acquired their binding power... by a long and immemorial usage and by the strength of custom and reception in this kingdom'.[98] He did not explain how the fact of an ancient and universal custom translated into a normative imperative. For a modern critic, focused on the question of authority, the argument looks very much like the simple inference of an 'ought' from an 'is'.[99] 'Consistent behavior in accordance with particular implicit rules', as Alan Watson observed, 'does not indicate that people should so behave.' Consequently, '[c]ustomary law flourishes in circumstances where law is likely to be the least theoretical.'[100]

At least two explanations have been offered by modern scholars for the normative force of customary and, in particular, common law. One holds that, whatever its political authorization, this kind of law-making is likely to produce rules that will maximize the welfare of the society that it regulates. The second suggests that, despite the absence of an explicit process of popular consent, customary law reflects widely shared values and is legitimated by the tacit approval of the population.

The first justification supposes that, since customary law arises only after a long experience of shared practice, its very longevity is a commendation. The seventeenth-century common lawyer Sir John Davies reasoned that when an act 'once done is found to be good and beneficial to the people, and agreeable to their nature and disposition, then do they use and practice it again and again, and so by often iteration and multiplication of the act becomes a custom'.[101] The resulting body of

[95] A list, complete to 2010, is found at House of Lords Constitution Committee, 'Referendums in the United Kingdom' (2010) 9–10. On the alternative voting system referendum, see <http://www.electoralcommission.org.uk/elections/referendums/referendum> (last accessed 7 August 2012).

[96] See n 57. See also Chapter 10 in this volume by Paul Craig.

[97] Goldsworthy (n 81) 124; Gardner (n 82) 63–4; N MacCormick, *Institutions of Law: An Essay in Legal Theory* (OUP 2007) 42–5.

[98] M Hale, *The History of the Common Law* (C Runnington ed, Dublin 1792) (spelling has been modernized) 23–4. See also *Ellen Street Estates Ltd v Minister of Health* [1934]; 1 Bl. Comm. 55.

[99] 'It is revolting to have no better reason for a rule of law than that so it was laid down in the time of Henry IV', OW Holmes, Jr, 'The Path of the Law' [1897] 10 *Harv L Rev* 457, 469. See Hayek (n 49) 79–82. J Kammerhofer, 'Book Review' (2012) 23 *European Journal of International Law* 583.

[100] A Watson, 'An Approach to Customary Law' [1984] *University of Illinois L Rev* 561, 561. See also TW Bennett, *A Sourcebook of African Customary Law for Southern Africa* (Juta 1991) 4 ('By an enigmatic process that has never been fully understood the "is" of custom may become the "ought" of law').

[101] Quoted in JGA Pocock, *The Ancient Constitution and the Feudal Law: A Study of English Historical Thought in the Seventeenth Century* (CUP 1987) 33; GJ Postema, 'Classical Common Law

law may be refined and perfected by learned judges but, at its core, it reflects the lived experience of society. As such, it may be easily 'incorporated into [the] very temperament' of society and provides the best basis for cooperative and productive human action.[102]

The second justification is premised on the idea that customary law 'rises up from the population'.[103] Classical common law jurists sometimes assumed that ancient practice was simply evidence of a real, explicit agreement among the people though the actual moment of that agreement preceded the reach of human memory. They also saw the day-to-day integration of the common law rules into people's daily lives as manifesting approval.[104] In a much noted passage, Blackstone quoted the Roman jurist, Salvius Julianus on the authority of unwritten law: '[W]here is the difference whether the people declare their assent to a law by suffrage or by a uniform course of acting accordingly?' Custom, said Blackstone, carried an 'internal evidence of freedom, that it probably was introduced and maintained by the voluntary consent of the people'.[105]

Neither of these attempts to legitimate customary law—that based on its intrinsic merits and that based on tacit consent—is convincing with respect to the common law as it is understood today. Both arguments assume that the law in question is, at its core, the reflection of well-settled customary practice, subject only to occasional judicial tweaking. In fact, we know that the development of the common law has always been dominated by courts and the 'reason' that has been used to adjust and refine it is not everyman's reason but the 'artificial reason' of the judges.[106] The notion that custom was the true source of the common law largely disappeared with the triumph of legal positivism at the end of the nineteenth century. 'The common law', Holmes wrote in 1917, is only 'the articulate voice of some sovereign . . . that can be identified'.[107] The idea of a law that rises up from the people, one that is thus peculiarly appropriate for them or has earned their consent cannot survive the common law's redefinition as a form of judicial legislation.

These considerations apply with at least as much force to the 'common law' process of constitution-making. The most plausible descriptions of that process see it as a series of actions and responses by various actors, notably Parliament and the

Jurisprudence (Part I)' [2002] *OUCLJ* 155, 171. See also JQ Whitman, 'Why Did the Revolutionary Lawyers Confuse Custom and Reason?' (1991) 58 *University of Chicago L Rev* 1321, 1349.

[102] Hale (n 98) 51. For a discussion of Hale's 'common law' response to Hobbes' argument that society was constructed according to abstract principles, see D Saunders, *Anti-Lawyers: Religion and the Critics of Law and State* (Routledge 1997) 41–7.

[103] Gardner (n 82) 73.

[104] GJ Postema, 'Classical Common Law Jurisprudence (Part II)' [2003] *OUCLJ* 1, 22–5.

[105] See 1 Bl. Comm. 65ff. See also Watson (n 100) 561, quoting Ulpian: 'Custom is the tacit consent of the people deeply rooted through long usage.'

[106] *Prohibitions del Roy* (1607) 12 Coke Rep 63, 77 ER 1342. See A Vermeule, 'Many-Minds Arguments in Legal Theory' [2009] 1 *Journal of Legal Analysis* 1, 25ff ('[C]alling the body of precedent produced [by the justices of the United States Supreme Court] "the work of many minds" exaggerates, at least if the comparison is to genuinely widespread social customs and traditions').

[107] *Southern Pacific Co v Jensen* 244 US 205, 222, 37 S Ct 524, 531 (dissenting opinion). See Simpson (n 72) 122–3; Simpson, himself, however, doubted that all common law rules could reasonably be described as judicial legislation (at 126).

courts. These isolated decisions of politicians and judges can in no way claim the virtues that are supposed to inhere in widespread customary practice. Unlike true customary rules, the norms inferred from them do not prove their merit by being chosen over and over again in countless individual transactions. Nor can they claim popular agreement by a 'uniform course of acting accordingly'. The participation of Parliament might impart some popular element, but it is far from the kind of expression of the will of the people associated with constitution-making in the rest of the world. Ordinary legislatures do sometimes re-write constitutions but they tend to use special procedures that are thought better to signify popular approval.[108] The version of parliamentary constitution-making observable in the United Kingdom, moreover, privileges that particular form of democratic decision-making reflected in the electoral and institutional arrangements currently in place. Consequently, 'constituent power is almost completely absorbed by constituted powers within the settled constitutional form'.[109] Furthermore, when other legislatures make constitutions, they do so comprehensively and deliberately, not as the incidental fallout of legislative initiatives that are not directed at the shape of the constitution but rather at independent political goals.[110] In any event, we still need to justify the indispensable role of the judiciary present in almost all current accounts. Almost every commentator assumes that constitutional change by parliamentary enactment is incomplete until adopted by the courts. In the case of sub-constitutional law, decisions of courts are subject to correction by the elected legislature. In this case, the contemplated judicial role is to help define the legislative power itself. Its undemocratic aspects, therefore, cannot be easily domesticated. Ultimately, the political justifications for this method of laying new foundations for the legal system remain profoundly obscure.

F. Interpretation and Constitutional Design

I have contrasted two ways in which the basic legal rules defining public power are made and re-made. In most of the world, those rules are set out in an authoritative text, promulgated in a discrete process representing the decision of the sovereign 'people'. The individuals participating in that process hammer out a set of procedures, institutions, and limitations that represent a considered view about the best way to organize public power in that society. In the United Kingdom, on the other hand, the content of those basic rules are inferred from the history of State practice

[108] See Kay (n 39) 743–5. In Chapter 4 in this volume, Goldsworthy suggests a number of devices of constitutional legislation—including referenda—that might provide a politically enhanced basis for altering the substantive scope of parliamentary authority.

[109] M Goldoni, 'Political Constitutionalism and the Value of Constitution-Making' (2013) 26 *Ratio Juris* (forthcoming). See also Chapter 4 in this volume by Jeffrey Goldsworthy noting the danger of a temporary parliamentary majority attempting permanent constitutional change.

[110] See Goldoni (n 109). Both the House of Lords Constitution Committee and the House of Commons Political and Constitutional Reform Committee have expressed concern that Parliament's piecemeal process of constitutional change means that it has neglected the coherence of the whole constitutional structure, see (n 56).

and have never been reduced to canonical form. They develop in an irregular and necessarily uncertain way. It follows that, at any given moment, there may be competing plausible descriptions of the constitution.

In practice, however, this contrast is not so clear-cut. I have described developments in the United Kingdom with reference to some of the changes that have actually taken place but I have set out the alternative model only in abstract, and therefore deceptively neat, form. In fact, the limits on State power formulated in an original constitution-making act never play out exactly as the constitution-makers planned.[111] The effectiveness of written constitutional rules depends on the existence of an agency that can, on appropriate occasions, declare when those rules have been violated, an agency whose rulings will be respected. It requires, that is, some kind of constitutional court.[112] The first job of such a court is to make out the meaning of the codified constitutional rules—to interpret them. We now have a long record and a voluminous literature on the topic of constitutional interpretation. One clear conclusion can be drawn from that record and literature. The limitations that courts, in fact, apply to the actions of public authorities deviate and sometimes deviate substantially from those that the designers of the written constitution contemplated at the time the rules were chosen.[113]

The intense American debate on the propriety of 'originalist' constitutional interpretation illustrates the point. Constitutional adjudication in the United States has from an early date commonly departed from the originally intended meaning of the rules of the constitutional text. The *Dred Scott* case of 1856,[114] the economic liberty cases of the late nineteenth and early twentieth centuries,[115] and the invention of a constitutional 'right of privacy' in the 1960s and 1970s,[116] are a few of many examples that could be cited. Uneasiness with the legitimacy of these decisions led, in the last decades of the twentieth century, to an explicit call for tethering constitutional interpretation to the 'original' meaning of the constitutional text invoked. A central argument for this 'originalist' jurisprudence was that only the originally intended rules were legitimated by the extraordinary political process that could lay claim to the endorsement of 'we the people'.[117]

Strong academic resistance to originalism has yielded over time to a substantial body of opinion agreeing that the job of courts is to apply the original constitutional meaning.[118] This victory, however, has turned out to be somewhat formal: the 'original meaning' that most current proponents of originalism promote is not the

[111] See MacCormick (n 97) 46.

[112] See Kay (n 88) 42.

[113] See RS Kay, 'Judicial Policy-Making and the Peculiar Function of Law' (2007) 26 *University of Queensland LJ* 237, 246–9.

[114] *Dred Scott v Sandford* 60 US (19 How) 393 (1857).

[115] See, eg, *Adkins v Children's Hospital* 261 US 525, 43 S Ct 394 (1923); *Lochner v New York* 198 US 45, 25 S Ct 539 (1905).

[116] See, eg, *Roe v Wade* 410 US 113, 93 S Ct 705 (1973); *Griswold v Connecticut* 381 US 479, 85 S Ct 1678 (1965).

[117] See, eg, RE Barnett, 'Scalia's Infidelity: A Critique of Faint-Hearted Originalism' (2006) 75 *University of Cincinnati L Rev* 7, 9.

[118] See LB Solum, '*District of Columbia v. Heller* and Originalism' (2009) 103 *Northwestern University L Rev* 923, 933–4.

meaning actually intended by the human beings who enacted the constitution but any meaning that would have been understood by a reasonably competent English-speaker at the time of adoption.[119] This re-formulation gives the interpreter considerable room for reaching a preferred outcome.[120] One prominent exponent is candid: this kind of originalism is 'actually a form of living constitutionalism'.[121] Some 'public meaning' originalists go a step further. They find that certain disputed questions of constitutional authority are not resolved by recourse to the original meaning, perhaps because that meaning—considered independently of the intentions of the enactors—is broad enough to be consistent with contradictory results. In such a case, it is proper for a court to engage in something called constitutional 'construction'. This allows the interpreter to decide the question based, in part, on 'considerations extrinsic to [the inadequate] meaning', such as 'one's theory of constitutional legitimacy'.[122] It should go without saying that, notwithstanding the presence on the United States Supreme Court of several self-professed originalists, their judgments have continued to be persuasively criticized as unsupported by original meaning.[123] As a theoretical matter, adherence to the original meaning continues to exert a strong appeal but, in practice, the discipline of unchanging constitutional rules that such adherence demands has proved too severe for both commentators and courts.

The consequence is that the United States (and almost every other jurisdiction with a written constitution and an active constitutional court) has gone through the exercise of deliberate and comprehensive constitution-making but has ended up living under constitutional arrangements that change over time in an unpredictable manner. They have ended up, that is, in a situation roughly equivalent to that of the United Kingdom. In fact, it is more or less a commonplace in such jurisdictions to describe the effective set of basic rules as a 'living constitution'.[124] In much cited language, Justice Holmes declared that the American founders had 'called into life a being the development of which could not have been foreseen completely (...) [T]hey had created an organism.'[125] In a series of articles, and in

[119] See, eg, A Scalia, *A Matter of Interpretation: Federal Courts and the Law: An Essay* (Princeton University Press 1997) 38.

[120] See RS Kay, 'Original Intentions and Public Meaning in Constitutional Interpretation' (2009) 103 *Northwestern University L Rev* 703, 719–25.

[121] JM Balkin, 'Original Meaning and Constitutional Redemption' (2007) 24 *Constitutional Commentary* 427, 449.

[122] RE Barnett, 'The Misconceived Assumption About Constitutional Assumptions' (2009) 103 *Northwestern University L Rev* 615, 632, 639.

[123] See, eg, GE Maggs, 'Which Original Meaning of the Constitution Matters to Justice Thomas?' (2009) 4 *New York University Journal of Law & Liberty* 494; TB Colby and PJ Smith, 'Living Originalism' (2009) 59 *Duke LJ* 239, 244–5.

[124] The phrase has its counterparts in other jurisdictions. See, eg, *Edwards v Canada (A-G)* [1930] AC 124 (PC), 136 (Sankey, LC) ('The British North America Act planted in Canada a living tree capable of growth and expansion within its natural limits'); *Pla and Puncernau v Andorra* (application no 69498/01) (13 July 2004), sec 4 ECHR 2004–VIII (2006) 42 EHRR 25, para 62 ('[T]he [European] Convention [on Human Rights] which is a dynamic text... is a living instrument, to be interpreted in the light of present-day conditions').

[125] *Missouri v Holland* 252 US 416, 433 (1920) 40 S Ct 382, 383 (1920).

a recently published book, David Strauss has described and lauded the American living constitution, 'one that evolves, changes over time and adapts to new circumstances'.[126] It is, moreover, a 'common law constitution', one to be adapted by the judges to new circumstances. The judges are not free to decide its meaning as they like. They are constrained by the common law method. They may change the rules 'only by continuing the evolution not by ignoring what exists and starting anew'.[127] His defence of this system has much in common with the Burkean justification of the gradualist, pragmatic British Constitution. 'There does not have to be one entity who commanded the law in a discrete act at a particular time.'[128] Like Burke, Strauss distrusts 'abstractions when those abstractions call for casting aside arrangements that have been satisfactory in practice, even if the arrangements cannot be fully justified in abstract terms'.[129]

The parallels with the process of constitutional change in the United Kingdom that I have described in this chapter go further. A fashionable theory of constitutional interpretation posited in various jurisdictions suggests the influence of a 'dialogue' between the courts and the political branches of government. An instance of legislation may be found constitutionally invalid in a judgment in which its particular vices are elaborated. In response, the legislature may re-enact the law in a somewhat modified form, responding to the problems identified by the court but also expressing the law-makers' own appreciation of the constitutional values at stake. By this process of iteration a satisfactory constitutional norm evolves, incorporating and compromising the positions of the various participants.[130]

It is important not to carry this argument too far. There are still some basic distinctions between the options for constitutional change in the United Kingdom and in countries with written constitutions. Certain institutional features are far more fixed in the latter and the texts even of broadly worded constitutional provisions inhibit, even if they cannot eliminate, the introduction of significant new limitations by judicial action. Nonetheless, it is reasonably accurate to say that individuals in the United States and other jurisdictions with written constitutions are subject to public authorities whose powers cannot be known with substantial certainty and have, at best, a mixed popular sanction. That is because the fundamental rules are being continuously defined and redefined in a process involving courts and political institutions, a process which is itself uncontrolled by law. Its outcome, therefore, can never be precisely predicted. If definition of political power is the prerogative of the sovereign, then these sovereigns, perhaps all sovereigns, are blind.

[126] DA Strauss, *The Living Constitution* (OUP 2010) 1. [127] Strauss (n 126) 38.

[128] Strauss (n 126) 37. [129] Strauss (n 126) 41.

[130] See L Fisher, *Constitutional Dialogues: Interpretation as Political Process* (Princeton University Press 1988) (US); P Hogg and A Bushell, 'The *Charter* Dialogue Between Courts and Legislatures (Or Perhaps the *Charter Of Rights* Isn't Such a Bad Thing After All)' (1997) 35 *Osgoode Hall LJ* 75 (Canada). The idea of constitutional dialogue is also discussed in Chapter 13 in this volume by Margit Cohn.

8

'A Sort of Farewell': Sovereignty, Transition, and Devolution in the United Kingdom

*John Morison**

A. Introduction

Most readers will be familiar with Michel Foucault's famous remark about how in political theory we have failed to cut off the King's head.[1] As the traditional conceptual framework for public lawyers, like the very idea of publicness itself, has worn increasingly thin and less serviceable over the last thirty years there may even be a general measure of agreement with the idea of diminishing the significance accorded to ideas of sovereignty and all the appurtenances of the nation-State. Those interested in a whole range of themes—globalization and the development of the European project; the future of human rights protection; and, of course, the continuing story of devolution—may well feel a sense of exasperation as the old language of sovereignty and its threadbare concepts come like uninvited guests to dominate discussion. All too often in public law theory the door has not been barred to sovereignty. The concept has been allowed in either to hold the floor while other, potentially more interesting, ideas must stand to one side or as something that must be negotiated around before the interesting part of the discussion can continue. In this contribution I will try to work through the implications of actually following up on Foucault's radical suggestion and consider the consequences of displacing sovereignty and the State from their central position within public law. I will try to develop a governmentality approach that requires a reorientation in our thinking towards wider technologies of power. The consequences of this de-centring of the State and sovereignty are explored and a different agenda for investigation is uncovered.

* Professor of Jurisprudence, School of Law, Queen's University Belfast. Thanks to Elizabeth Meehan, Paul McCusker, Edward Cooke, Sam Adelman, Gordon Anthony, Kieran McEvoy, and the editors, especially Rick Rawlings, for helpful comments.

[1] Foucault argues that what is needed is 'a political philosophy that isn't erected around the problem of sovereignty nor, therefore, around the problem of law and prohibition. We need to cut off the king's head: in political theory that has still to be done.' See M Foucault, 'Truth and Power' in C Gordon (ed) *Power/Knowledge: Selected Interviews and Other Writings, 1972–1977* (Pantheon 1980) 121.

The first section of this chapter considers the persistence of sovereignty, particularly in the area of devolution where attempts to develop different understandings for a United Kingdom constitutional order are struggling to find expression in formats that can escape the rather sterile terms in which the sovereignty debate places them. The chapter then looks more directly at what it might mean to take seriously Foucault's remark and what a turn to a governmentality approach might require. This is considered particularly in relation to what it might mean in methodological terms for developing alternative ways of looking at how power actually operates within the constitution. The resulting idea of a 'non-sovereignty' approach is then explored in the context of the Northern Ireland settlement as a particularly interesting illustration of how power operates in a whole range of emerging constitutional spaces beneath the complex, formal constitutional architecture of the Belfast Agreement. Although the conflict was often expressed in terms of sovereignty, and this is recognized in its solution, the sort of anti-foundationalist foundation provided by the wider peace process provides an excellent case study for looking at the reality of power operating beneath the formal State and conceptions of sovereignty. Finally, the wider devolution debate is returned to in order to assess briefly the potential of such an approach to broaden and deepen the debate.

B. The Persistence of Sovereignty

Although there is a big agenda of change for the British Constitution at this time, this has struggled to move beyond the language of sovereignty and, indeed, a rather Diceyean, pre-twenty-first-century view of the role of the nation-State. For instance there is the debate over the proper foundation for, and nature of, human rights that was initiated by the Prime Minister's election promise to replace the Human Rights Act 1998, which enshrines the European Convention on Human Rights in UK law, with a 'British' Bill of Rights. Discussion here has been framed, frustratingly for many, in terms of reclaiming rights from (what is invariably termed) 'a court sitting overseas', and re-establishing sovereignty.[2] The conflict within the Coalition Government over the whole issue is reflected in the Report by the Commission charged with producing a British Bill of Rights which has struggled to find a way forward in these terms.[3] In a similar way, and as a result of similar forces, the future involvement of the United Kingdom within the European Union has re-emerged in British politics and, here

[2] See the on-going efforts to attack the Human Rights Act 1998 in Parliament through a range of mechanisms including, eg, the Human Rights Act 1998 (Repeal and Substitution) Bill 2012–13.

[3] The origins of this Commission as well as, arguably, the conflicted nature of its report would seem to lie fundamentally in anxieties about whether the origin and enforcement of rights should or can be returned to domestic/sovereign level. The very framing of the debate in these terms is of course inimical to the foundations of the devolved settlements in which the Human Rights Act is formally embedded. See the Commission on a Bill of Rights, 'A UK Bill of Rights? The Choice Before Us (vols 1 and 2, 18 December 2012, available at <http://www.justice.gov.uk/about/cbr> (last accessed 26 April 2013).

again, the debate struggles to escape the language of State, super-States, and sovereignty.[4] But most significantly of all there is the continuing story of devolution. Always a rather uncertain and uncomfortable political entity, the United Kingdom is now undergoing another phase of re-alignment as the reality of the often quoted description of devolution being 'a process not an event' is being worked through and all the component parts of the United Kingdom consider their future in a post-crisis, austerity world.[5] Questions about the extent and desirability of further devolution to Scotland or independence; the fitness for purpose of a peace agreement as a design for government in Northern Ireland; and the nature of a more 'grown-up' version of devolution in Wales compete for attention with increasing concern about how the interests (and revenues) of the 75–80 per cent of the population who live in England can best be managed within the context of what might be seen as a quietly disintegrating constitutional settlement. In much of this discussion the old constitutional furniture of Parliaments and assemblies, referendums and the proper constitutional role of the judges, and, particularly, sovereignty, is being dragged about as various new constitutional futures for the United Kingdom are considered.

There are several significant indicators of the obeisance that, it seems, must be afforded to the idea of sovereignty. There was the initial squabble over who has the right to call a referendum in Scotland relating to independence that has been diverted into an essentially legal argument—as if a recondite account of how sovereignty works in theory could resolve an essentially political dispute.[6] In the courts the initially bold approach of judicial disregard for the traditional, sovereignty-bounded interpretation of statutes that reached a high water mark with *Ghaidan v Godin-Mendoza* now seems rather far away.[7] Indeed, the developing idea of constitutional statutes that was beginning to be seen as a potentially interesting way of reconciling political reality and constitutional theory,[8] has been paused. Some judges have taken a step backwards towards what may be seen as a more cautious position where sovereignty is prevalent again.[9] Indeed, the view that sovereignty remains the cornerstone of the constitution has found new expression in *Imperial Tobacco v Lord Advocate*.[10]

[4] See the Chapter 10 in this volume by Paul Craig.

[5] This phrase is attributed to the former Welsh Secretary of State Ron Davies who in 1997 described the devolution he had helped to design in these terms. For some discussion of general trends within this most recent phase of devolutionary activity see, eg, M Perryman (ed), *Breaking Up Britain: Four Nations after a Union* (Lawrence and Wishart 2009); R Wyn Jones and R Scully, *Wales Says Yes: Devolution and the 2011 Welsh Referendum* (University of Wales Press 2012).

[6] For the background to this see the House of Lords Select Committee on the Constitution Report 'Referendum on Scottish Independence' (HL Paper (2012–2013) no 263).

[7] [2004] UKHL 30, [2004] 2 AC 557. See further the discussion in Chapter 13 in this volume by Margit Cohn.

[8] See especially *Robinson v Secretary of State for Northern Ireland* [2002] UKHL 32, [2002] NI 390 and *Thoburn v Sunderland City Council* [2002] EWHC 195 (Admin), [2003] QB 151. For an account of the early evolution of this idea, see M Elliot, 'Embracing Constitutional Legislation: Towards Fundamental Law' (2003) 54 *Northern Ireland Legal Quarterly* 25. For some more recent highlights see *Somerville v Scottish Ministers* [2007] UKHL 44, [2007] 1 WLR 2734 [169]; and *R (Brynmawr Foundation School Governors) v Welsh Ministers* [2011] EWHC 519 (Admin) [70]–[73].

[9] See, eg, *AXA General Insurance v Lord Advocate* [2011] UKSC 46, [2012] 1 AC 868; see further Chapter 6 in this volume by Lord Hope.

[10] [2012] CSIH 9.

In the Court of Session Lord Reed stated that the 'democratic legitimacy of the Scottish Parliament does not...warrant a different approach to interpretation from that applicable to Acts of Parliament...Nor does it impinge upon the fact that the power of the Scottish Parliament to legislate is limited by the Act of Parliament which established it.'[11] This approach was reinforced when the case was heard in the Supreme Court. Here Lord Hope, while acknowledging that 'the purpose of the [Scotland Act 1998] has informed the statutory language', made it clear that 'the description of the Act as a constitutional statute cannot be taken, in itself, to be a guide to its interpretation. The statute must be interpreted like any other statute'.[12]

My interest here is in how we might begin to move beyond all this; in particular how we might dispense with sovereignty and consider the devolution dynamic in a more interesting and constructive way. In doing this I will consider theory and practice in turn. I will try to uncover what Foucault, and some commentators on his work, say about removing sovereignty from our consideration, and set out what this might mean for how we consider the big constitutional questions of today. This will draw upon the particular experience of constitutional change in Northern Ireland where sovereignty is simultaneously central to the conflict and its formal resolution, and bypassed by political structures, processes, and spaces where more down-to-earth expressions of everyday constitutional power can be found. Some of these will be sketched out before the account returns to consider more widely how this theory of 'non-sovereignty' might work out in relation to some of the big constitutional issues, and, in particular, the on-going processes of devolution. If we are able to think about devolution without reference to sovereignty as a primary starting point it may open ways of imagining new forms of constitutional relationships.

C. Reorienting the Approach to Sovereignty: The Turn Towards Governmentality

How can we change the way that we look at sovereignty? In order to do this, and so gain the advantages that I will argue flow from reorienting our approach to sovereignty, it is important to stop considering sovereignty as a 'thing in itself'. Instead we should try to see sovereignty as a way of thinking, and one that is connected to

[11] *Imperial Tobacco v Lord Advocate* [2012] CSIH 9 [58] (Lord Reed).

[12] *Imperial Tobacco v Lord Advocate* [2012] UKSC 61 [15]. Similarly, in a reference made by the Attorney General for England and Wales under the Government of Wales Act 2006, s 112, for a determination about whether aspects of a bill for about making local bylaws were within the legislative competence of the National Assembly for Wales, the Supreme Court was invited to consider the view that the Government of Wales Act 2006 should be seen as a constitutional enactment. Lord Hope was willing to recognize that the aim of the act was to achieve a constitutional settlement, and that it is an act of 'great constitutional significance'. However he went on to say that 'I do not think that this description, in itself, can be taken to be a guide to its interpretation. The rules to which the court must apply in order to give effect to it are those laid down by the statute, and the statute must be interpreted like any other statute.' See *Local Government Byelaw (Wales) Bill* [2012] UKSC 53, [2012] 3 WLR 1294 [80].

a wider project and exercise of government. This has the potential to change not only how we conceptualize sovereignty but also the *use* that we put the concept to as we try to understand the change in the context and scope of government marked by the current phase of constitutional development. The suggestion is that there is really no such thing as 'sovereignty' but only examples of power actually being mobilized, and then working through the consequences of this.

Thinking about governmentality directs us to ideas about the so-called 'governmentalization of the State'. We should understand that there is not necessarily such a thing platonically as 'the State', or even 'sovereignty', and we are not necessarily required to find the institution or body that accords with it in any given situation. Government too is not a single mechanism such that the State might deploy but rather a whole series of practices, and the State is really an expression or effect of the whole range of these tactics of government: it is a dynamic form and historic stabilization of societal power relations.[13] As Foucault argues, it is important to move away from 'what could be called this "institution-centric" approach' and 'attempt to free relations of power from the institution, in order to analyse them from the point of view of technologies'.[14] There are three elements to this and they all involve reorienting our focus.

First, it is important to go behind the 'institution' to discover a wider and more overall technology of power. In other words, instead of looking only, or mainly, at the structural and organizational characteristics of an institution, we should direct our attention to all the practical mechanisms, the details of the technologies of government, and all those strategies, techniques, and procedures through which different forces and groups attempt to render their programmes operable in a wider exercise of governance.[15] These involve a whole range of multiform tactics. In addition to action through law, sanctions, budgets, and administrative action, there is the important quality of the freedom of the subject (government of the self) and how this freedom is managed. In contrast to simple domination, which involves crushing the capacity for action of the dominated, government—properly understood here—involves recognizing that capacity and mobilizing it. Within this understanding, to govern is to act upon action. It involves understanding how those who are to be governed think and act, and using and shaping this in order to guide conduct in the desired direction. As Foucault expresses it, 'the exercise of power is a "conduct of conducts" and a management of possibilities'.[16]

Secondly, we should not look at something—for example, the prison—only on the basis of the functions it is expected to perform. Rather, as with Foucault's

[13] See further M Foucault, 'Governmentality' in G Burchell, C Gordon, and P Miller (eds) *The Foucault Effect: Studies in Governmentality* (Harvester Wheatsheaf 1991) 103.

[14] M Foucault, *Security, Territory and Population: Lectures at the College de France 1977–1978* (M Senellart ed, Picador 2009) 117–18. Technologies in this context refers to all the means, mechanisms, and methods used in governance; see further, M Dean, *Governmentality: Power and Rule in Modern Society* (2nd edn, Sage 2010) 269–70.

[15] See further N Rose and P Miller, 'Political Power Beyond the State: Problematics of Government' (1992) 43 *British Journal of Sociology* 173.

[16] M Foucault, 'The Subject and Power' in JD Faubion (ed) *Michel Foucault, Power: The Essential Works* vol. 3 (Allen Lane Penguin Press 2000) 341.

approach in *Discipline and Punish*,[17] we should consider more widely how the prison is involved in wider strategies and tactics of governing which encompass more than simply the straightforward function of imprisonment. Indeed, as Foucault demonstrates so vividly with the history of the prison, the exercise of power associated with an institution is not governed by the successes or failures of its functionalities, but can be seen best within an external view of the wider strategies and tactics that support it.

Thirdly, Foucault cautions, we should not allow ourselves to approach an area of inquiry, be it the prison, sexuality, or sovereignty, as a 'ready-made subject' where we can measure institutions, practices, and knowledges in terms of the criteria and norms of an already given subject. A better approach involves 'grasping the movement by which a field of truth with objects of knowledge was constituted' by means of all of these technologies of government which together have manufactured this way of seeing and dealing with an area.[18] This calls for a wider focus which does not take for granted any field or form of activity but rather seeks to explore how it has come about and how it has come to be seen as it is.

In summary, Foucault sees this approach as a triple movement transferring attention to 'the outside'. He summarizes his work on madness, delinquency, and sexuality as involving:

> the attempt to free relations of power from the institution in order to analyze them from the point of view of technologies; to distinguish them also from the function, so as to take them up within a strategic analysis; and to detach them from the privilege of the object, so as to resituate them within the perspective of the constitution of fields, domains, and objects of knowledge.[19]

This is a different way of seeing, and it is one that seeks to isolate the various elements from their usual, accepted context and perceived function in order to renew our perception of their role in wider processes. This type of orientation is something that should be applied to our understandings of the State and, indeed, sovereignty. Rather than seeing only what might be expected within a context of States and Parliaments, and hierarchies and supremacy, it is possible to see anew the actual operations of power for what they actually are, without the gestalt effect of concepts of sovereignty and State dictating the patterns that are perceived.

D. Post-sovereignty or Non-sovereignty Approaches

In an account of how Foucault responded to various Marxist critics of his work who complained that there was an underdeveloped account of the role of the State, Thomas Lemke describes how Foucault 'takes the State to be an integral part of governmental practices . . . an instrument and effect of these practices, and not their

[17] M Foucault, *Discipline and Punish: The Birth of the Prison* (A Sheridan trans, Penguin 1977).
[18] Foucault (n 14) 118. [19] Foucault (n 14) 118.

foundation or counterpart'.[20] Lemke points out how, while Foucault maintained that he refrained from pursuing a theory of the State as one would abstain from an indigestible meal, at the same time he is concerned to provide an 'analytics of government'. This theoretical perspective focuses on governmental technologies and challenges the notion of a State apparatus as confined to the structural and organizational characteristics of the State as an institutional ensemble. Instead it conceives of the State 'as an effect and instrument of political strategies and social relations of power'.[21] As Foucault himself reminds us, 'the analysis of power relations within a society cannot be reduced to the study of a series of institutions, not even to the study of all those institutions which would merit the name "political"'.[22]

Lemke develops a rather complex argument that 'the State' as such does not exist: there is only a particular exercise of power and a 'transactional reality' which entails 'a dynamic ensemble of relations and syntheses that at the same time produces the institutional structure of the State and the knowledge of the State'.[23] However the key message is about developing a Foucauldian approach that focuses on, as Lemke puts it, 'practices instead of object, strategies instead of function, and technologies instead of institution'.[24] Within such an account, government must be seen as a singular historical event; as something that has happened or is happening now, and may be occurring in any number of ways and means.[25] This means that government should be approached as a contingent political process that can be explored and explained in terms of asking questions such as how *this State now* comes to act and be seen as a coherent political force? How is this unity of the State, whereby we see all sorts of different institutions and individuals acting together in one apparently singular process, produced in practical terms? How does all the plurality of institutions and processes that are involved in some idea of an exercise of public power come to be the State? This requires us to avoid suspending or contorting our analysis of how power is actually operating in order to relate what we are seeing to some universal idea, or essence, of State or sovereignty. As Foucault puts it, 'it means making visible a *singularity* in places where there is a temptation to invoke a historical constant... to show that things "weren't as necessary as all that"; it wasn't a matter of course'.[26]

[20] T Lemke, 'An Indigestible Meal? Foucault, Governmentality and State Theory' (2007) 8 *Distinktion: Scandinavian Journal of Social Theory* 43, 56.

[21] Lemke (n 20) at 50.

[22] M Foucault 'Afterword, The Subject and Power' in H Dreyfuss and P Rabinow, *Beyond Structuralism and Hermeneutics* (University of Chicago Press 1982) 224.

[23] See further Lemke (n 20) 48. Lemke argues that Foucault does not see the State as either an object, an illusion or even an ideological effect of hegemonic practices, but rather conceptualizes the State as 'a transactional reality', without a universal or general essence. Here the issue is about examining how different governing elements and practices create something approximating to an idea of State which possesses a historical reality and structural consistency over time, and about investigating the 'historical ontology' of the State to uncover discontinuities and ruptures in the regimes of truth.

[24] Lemke (n 20) 58.

[25] As Foucault maintains, 'power exists only as exercised by some on others, only when it is put into action'. See Foucault (n 16) 340.

[26] Foucault (n 16) 226.

Of course, this does not mean that the State disappears. Foucault accepts that the State is not simply one specific form of the exercise of power, even if it is maybe the most important, but it is something that all other forms of power relations must refer to. However, and this is of central significance, this is *not* because other forms of power:

> are *derived* from it: rather, it is because power relations have become more and more under State control . . . power relations have become progressively governmentalized, that is to say, elaborated, rationalized, and centralized in the form of, or under the auspices of, State institutions.[27]

We have come to think about power in relation to the State, and indeed the State itself has become a site for strategic action as well as an instrument of strategies so that, for example, it constitutes a boundary establishing and reproducing structural gaps between private and public, and privileging some actions over others.[28] This must be acknowledged and accommodated within the way that we approach power within the constitutional sphere.

This is not necessarily a unique insight, especially as regards how political theory should treat the State. Indeed, it is a consequence of what some have termed the 'Foucault effect' more generally,[29] but it brings with it more sophisticated ways of seeing how power operates than are usually associated with lawyers thinking about sovereignty. This is reflected in Rose and Miller's claim that the governmentality perspective focuses empirically on 'forms of power without a centre, or rather with multiple centres, power that was productive of meanings, of interventions, of entities, of processes, of objects, of written traces and of lives'.[30] It involves refusing to equate government with the State, understood as a centralized locus of rule, and focuses instead on how programmes and practices of rule are applied in micro-settings, including at the level of individual subjects. Those who advance this Foucault effect seek to decompose power into political rationalities, governmental programmes, technologies, and techniques of government.[31] These operate at all points and levels, including beyond the immediate influence of State institutions. This is very much in line with Foucault's position against seeing the State as an originary, central institution in the exercise of political power but rather focusing on the actual operations of power.[32]

[27] Foucault (n 16) 345 (emphasis added).

[28] See further B Jessop, *State and Theory: Putting the Capitalist State in its Place* (Polity Press 1990); M Valverde, '"Despotism" and Ethical Liberal Governance' (1996) 25 *Economy and Society* 357; and G Agamben, *Homo Sacer: Sovereign Power and Bare Life* (Stanford University Press 1998).

[29] For discussion of this see G Burchell, C Gordon, and P Miller (eds) *The Foucault Effect: Studies in Governmental Rationality* (C Gordon trans, University of Chicago Press 1991); J Donzelot and C Gordon, 'Governing Liberal Societies—The Foucault Effect in the English-Speaking World' (2008) *Foucault Studies* 5, 48–6 and B Jessop, 'Constituting Another Foucault Effect—Foucault on States and Statecraft' in U Bröckling, S Krassmann, and T Lemke (eds) *Governmentality: Current Issues and Future Challenges* (Routledge 2010) 56–74.

[30] N Rose and P Miller, *Governing the Present* (Polity Press 2008) 9. See also N Rose and M Valverde, 'Governed by Law?' (1998) 7 *Social and Legal Studies* 541.

[31] See further the overview in N Rose, P O'Malley, and M Valverde, 'Governmentality' (2006) 2 *Annual Review of Law and Social Science* 83.

[32] As Foucault explains, 'an analysis in terms of power must not assume that State sovereignty, the form of the law, or the over-all unity of a domination, is given at the outset; rather, these are only

This de-centring of 'the State' enables us to rethink sovereignty. We will examine first how the sovereignty issue can then bypassed before looking at some methodological consequences of doing so.

Foucault talks about being able to say 'a sort of farewell to the theory of sovereignty insofar as it could—and can—be described as a method for analyzing power relations'.[33] The focus on sovereignty, and the search within each arrangement of government for a corresponding point, body, or institution where sovereignty can be said to reside, causes us to miss how power actually operates. Foucault argues that, 'rather than deriving powers from sovereignty, we should be extracting operators of domination from relations of power, both historically and empirically.'[34] This means that we should look at the actual power relations themselves as they exist and operate, the ways in which they connect and support one another, and how they reinforce each other to create both domination and subjugation, control and conformity. Instead of starting from a search for a point of sovereignty from where powers spring, and from where powers derive their legitimacy, 'we should be studying domination and not sovereignty…the manufacture of subjects rather than the genesis of the sovereign'.[35] Indeed, Foucault maintains, this search for sovereignty sets us off in the wrong direction. For Foucault the whole idea of sovereignty in this context, as well as the general enterprise of developing a theory of sovereignty as being elemental to law and relating to how a power can be constituted, should be abandoned. The sovereignty within this traditional view that is the object of Foucault's criticism is of a fundamental character. It relates to what Foucault describes as 'a certain basic legitimacy that is more basic than any law and that allows laws to function as such'.[36] A theory of sovereignty here is concerned with a cycle of legitimacy and law, and in this way it assumes, according to Foucault, the existence of three constituting elements: the subject who has to be subjectified; the unity of power that has to be founded; and the legitimacy that has

the terminal forms power takes.… [P]ower must be understood in the first instance as the multiplicity of force relations immanent in the sphere in which they operate and that constitute their own organization; as the process which, through ceaseless struggles and confrontations, transforms, strengthens, or reverses them; as the support which these force relations find in one another, thus forming a chain or a system… [and] as the strategies in which they take effect, whose general design or institutional crystallization is embodied in the State apparatus, in the formulation of the law, in various social hegemonies. Power's condition of possibility [and its role as a] grid of intelligibility of the social order must not be sought in the primary existence of a central point, in a unique source of sovereignty from which secondary and derived forms might emanate; it is the moving substrate of force relations which, by virtue of their inequality, constantly engender states of power, but the latter are always local and unstable.… Power is everywhere; not because it embraces everything, but because it comes from everywhere.' See M Foucault, *Naissance de la biopolitique—Cours au Collège de France, 1978–79* (Seuil/Gallimard 2004), quoted and translated by B Jessop, 'From Micro-powers to Governmentality: Foucault's Work on Statehood, State Formation, Statecraft and State Power' (2006) 26 *Political Geography* 37.

[33] M Foucault, *Society Must be Defended* (D Macey trans, Penguin 2004) 43. Elsewhere in the same text Foucault talks about how 'we have to bypass or get around the problem of sovereignty' (27).

[34] Foucault (n 33) 45. [35] Foucault (n 33) 46.

[36] Foucault (n 33) 44. This is seemingly about taking on Jean Bodin's ideas from the sixteenth century relating to the indispensability of sovereignty in accounting for law, and how sovereignty is 'that which gives the law'. See J Bodin, *On Sovereignty: Four Chapters from the Six Books on the Commonwealth* (CUP 1994).

to be respected. But for Foucault the enterprise of building a theory of sovereignty *presupposes these very elements even as it seeks to establish them*. As he puts it, 'subject, unitary power, and law: the theory of sovereignty comes into play…among these elements, and it both takes them as given and tries to found them.'[37]

It is because of the self-referential nature of this search, because a theory of sovereignty is seeking only to find itself in its own terms, that Foucault maintains that we should put it aside in favour of a project that is released from this strait-jacketed analysis of power. We should start with the actual power relationships themselves and draw out, both empirically and historically, exactly how 'actual relations of subjugation manufacture subjects'.[38] Next we should examine the relations of domination in all their multiplicity, difference, and specificity, looking not for a sovereignty from which source powers spring, but to show how all the various operators of dominance work to support one another, how they converge and reinforce each other, or even in some instances strive against or negate themselves. This involves looking less at the great institutions of government operating within a supposedly coherent plan of rule but at how ideas, initiatives, and ways of seeing things across a whole range of areas actually function at various levels from the very local to the global. Finally, this interest in the relations of domination rather than the source of sovereignty means that our concern is not with trying to trace the origins of power back to what might establish basic legitimacy. Instead of looking for the prerequisites of power in terms of law, unity, and subject—those elements which make sovereignty both the source of power and the basis of institutions—we must look at the way that power actually *works*. As Foucault puts it, 'the manufacture of subjects rather than the genesis of the sovereign: that is our general theme'.[39]

E. Methodological Consequences of a Non-sovereignty Approach

Foucault cautions us that:

> in order to make a concrete analysis of power relations, we must abandon the juridical model of sovereignty…rather than looking for the single form or the central point from which all forms of power derive, either by way of consequence or development, we must begin by letting them operate in their multiplicity, their differences, their specificity; we must therefore study them as relations of force that intersect, refer to one another, converge, or, on the contrary, come into conflict and strive to negate one another.[40]

For him the point is not to look at rule-governed and legitimate forms of power that have a single centre. Instead he proposes a much more detailed account of how different varieties of power are exercised at all sorts of levels by a huge range of mechanisms and by all sorts of persons and agencies. He argues that it is wrong

[37] Foucault (n 33) 44. [38] Foucault (n 33) 45. [39] Foucault (n 33) 46.
[40] Foucault (n 33) 65ff.

to try to analyse power from the inside, asking questions about who has power and what are they trying to do with it. Such questions about strategies and intentions, desires, and plans, he believes, lead into a labyrinth from which there is no escape. It is better to look at the external face of power, where real practices and applications can be seen. Foucault argues that he wants to do the opposite of what Hobbes was trying to do in *Leviathan* and, indeed, what he believes that all jurists are trying to do as they address the question that is central to their world—that is how a multiplicity of individuals and wills can be shaped into a single will or even a single body—a polity or State—that 'is supposedly animated by a soul known as sovereignty'.[41] To answer this jurists' concern involves presupposing the State as the sum of its parts, a 'coagulation . . . of distinct individuals', and imagining something at the heart of the Leviathan that constitutes it as such. That something is, of course, sovereignty, that which Hobbes sees as the soul of Leviathan but which Foucault wishes to avoid searching for, preferring instead to look at the real outworkings of power rather than for its supposed font and origin.

The methodological consequences of this turn towards governmentality and away from sovereignty are significant. In particular they require that we develop and act upon a much wider definition of power than simple State action in the form of formal law. Indeed, as argued above, we need to develop a non-sovereignty view of power where it is not regarded a phenomenon of mass or homogeneous domination by one individual or group over all others. As Foucault argues, the study of power should begin from below, in the heterogeneous and dispersed microphysics of power, explore specific forms of its exercise in different institutional sites, and then move on to consider how, if at all, these are linked to produce broader and more persistent societal configurations. One should study power where it is exercised over individuals rather than legitimated at the centre; explore the actual practices of subjugation rather than the intentions that guide attempts at domination; and recognize that power circulates through networks rather than being applied at particular points.[42]

It also means that we should lift our eyes both above and below the level of the formal constitution and its institutional outworkings. Power exists everywhere and in every interaction. It is something that circulates and, indeed, only functions when it is part of a chain passing through people rather than simply acting upon them. Power is not the sole preserve of the State or its institutions and it does not act upon people only as passive objects of rule. Indeed—and this is important—seeing power in this way gives a sense of *agency* to those who are governed and implicates and involves them within the process of governance as subjects involved in governing themselves and others. As Foucault explains, a relationship of power is a mode of action that does not act directly and immediately on others. It acts instead upon their actions. It directs, controls, and influences future

[41] Foucault (n 33) 29.

[42] See further the agenda set out in M Foucault, 'Introduction' in *History of Sexuality: Volume 1* (R Hurley trans, Allen Lane 1979) 92–102.

possible actions through 'the conduct of conduct' and 'the management of possibilities'.[43] This means that power relations are rooted in the whole network of the social—broadly conceived—and they must be sought there just as much as in the out-workings of the great institutions of State. The State may be seen as integral to government practices—an instrument and effect of these practices—but not their foundation. Indeed the 'State' itself is best seen as the outcome of all the various conflicting governmental practices from various actors. It represents the 'current State of play' as it were, among all the variable governing forces, whatever their origin or form. In this sense small spaces of governable activity—symbols, language, detailed mechanisms for organizing services or ameliorating conflict—can be just as 'constitutional' as the activities of Parliaments or assemblies. It also means that such activity is very much part of what should be examined. The local and the particular is as constitutive in its own way as the high matters of State. Indeed, perhaps this is the place where we should start. As Foucault urges, we must 'conduct an *ascending* analysis of power, starting, that is, from its infinitesimal mechanisms... and then see how these mechanisms of power have been—and continue to be—invested, colonized, utilized, involuted, transformed, displaced, extended, etc. by ever more general mechanisms and by forms of global domination'.[44]

This turn towards governmentality, and its new approach to understanding power, also suggests that the commonplace distinction between State formation and policy making loses its force, since the former is not a single event but an enduring process in which the limits and contents of State action are permanently negotiated and redefined.[45] Changes to the nature of the State—transitions, devolutions of power, and re-balancings of the role of courts—are much less about technical, foundational changes to sovereignty and more about how other forms of knowledge, political and sociological, operating with dualisms like individual and State, national and regional, play a constitutive role in the emergence and reproduction of concrete forms of statehood. As examples are developed later in this chapter, it will be shown how this approach can include a wide range of practices, methods, procedures, and mechanisms where the boundaries between the symbolic and the material, and the hard and the soft, and between formal political technologies and technologies of the self, become indistinct and of less consequence.[46]

[43] Foucault (n 16) 341.

[44] M Foucault, 'Two Lectures' in C Gordon (ed) *Power/Knowledge: Selected Interviews and Other Writings 1972–1977* (Pantheon 1980) 142.

[45] Lemke (n 20) 48–9. The State is not something that is ready made and fully, or even adequately, described in terms of its formal institutions. Rather it is something that is constantly being made and re-made, and where therefore any simple boundary between ordinary law-making and State formation disappears. The view of power that a governmentality approach entails does not see power as either static or confined to the formal institutions of government and this suggests a whole governing complex that is constantly refining its role and reach.

[46] As Lemke says, 'an analytic of government operates with a concept of technology that includes not only material but also symbolic devices... discourses, narratives and regimes of representation are not reduced to pure semiotic propositions; instead they are regarded as performative practices' (Lemke (n 20) 50).

F. Non-sovereignty in Action: The Northern Ireland Constitutional Transition

So far this account has attempted to follow through on the implications for constitutional theory of acting on Foucault's proposition about cutting off the king's head. This has suggested the beginnings of a new methodology. This involves refusing to equate government with the State and developing instead a wider view of what power is, and how it is exercised, and by whom. It necessitates developing an account that looks less at the formal institutions of Parliaments and courts and concentrates more on the actual operations of power where they occur. It takes the view that it is in a whole range of practices, programmes, and technologies that government occurs just as much as with parliamentary statutes or judicial pronouncements. It avoids looking only and exclusively at the traditional concepts of rule of law, legitimacy, and sovereignty and focuses more on all the actors who govern themselves and respond to, or as Foucault would express it, 'make themselves up', in relation to a whole range of multiform tactics of government. In short, it requires saying a 'sort of farewell to sovereignty' and thinking about the reality of how power operates in the constitution aside from the formal State and its traditional sources of authority.

Of course this does not mean that the everyday decisions of ordinary individuals can be equated in importance with an act of Parliament or that a self-help initiative is as much a part of governance as formal law. The formal State remains a significant player. But it is not the only one. Its actions alone do not constitute the only source of power and neither should all power be seen in reference to the State or its sovereignty. There is a wide agenda of action and a whole array of governmental technologies to be considered. And, of course, the role of law in all of this remains of central importance—not least to lawyers. But this is not because law is the expression of sovereign will or because law can trace its effect to some originating legitimacy. It is rather because law is one of the multiform tactics of governance. It is one that gains its effect not simply because it is a sovereign command but as a result of its role in establishing frameworks and schemes, classifications and categories, plans and programmes around which people can orient their action and make themselves up. Law is an important instrument in the management of possibilities and it can provide a significant expression of power around which people will act and react. These actions and reactions are themselves expressions of power, and the whole ensemble which together produces meanings and conduct, interventions and reactions, is what constitutes government, and is our proper subject of study. This requires that we go beyond seeing law as being simply about sovereignty and examine how it is taken up, accepted, or modified, and generally operates as part of an ongoing technology of government. To do this is to give agency to those who would otherwise be seen as merely the passive objects of rule. It involves seeing law as only one element in a more fundamentally 'constitutionalizing' process.

It may seem paradoxical to argue that the peace process in Northern Ireland is an exemplar of this wider government beyond the formal State. After all, there are few societies that are more over-governed in terms of formal institutions, bodies, commissions, councils, and inquiries, and these exist at every level from the local to the international.[47] Also the whole issue of sovereignty—expressed in terms of nationalism and unionism—is often seen as at the heart of the conflict. Indeed, it was to defuse the sovereignty issue, festering as an everyday concern across political debate, that the whole baroque edifice of the Belfast Agreement structures was erected and is maintained. However, an analysis of Northern Ireland's on-going transition provides an excellent illustration of how sovereignty is in fact displaced, as the constitution there is better explained in terms of the creation of a whole series of governable spaces where the project of governance is less dependent on the formal State and the engine of sovereign law-making than a much wider, bottom-up exercise of power.

There are a number of reasons for this. There is the very nature of the conflict, whereby politics was (and indeed remains) both broader and deeper than elsewhere, and many everyday issues—from housing to education, policing to commemorating the past, and flags to marches—are not only highly political but also indeed 'constitutional'.[48] This has the effect that any settlement not only had to successfully address the high politics of constitutional accommodation through a formal power-sharing agreement with institutions and recognition of the 'consent principle' as determinative of Northern Ireland's future within the United Kingdom, but also a whole range of other, continuing, smaller—but no less 'constitutional'—issues. The genius of the Belfast Agreement relates not only to how it managed to square the circle of high politics, and provide a place to park the big constitutional issue of Northern Ireland, but also how it was able to offer ways to defuse all these issues. The Agreement, and subsequent legislation, provides not only a variety of structures for managing the whole range of 'wicked issues' that remain 'constitutional' but also a more general paradigm for seeing how they can be worked on towards resolution.

This means that the Northern Ireland constitutional transition is not best seen—or certainly not only to be seen—as a political deal or one-off constitutional moment where a deal was brokered among elites to in some way 'solve' the Northern Ireland

[47] In addition to representation in the European and Westminster Parliaments, the Northern Ireland Assembly has 108 members (to be reduced to 96 after the next Assembly elections) and a 61 member Civic Forum (presently non-operational). There is a North–South Ministerial Council and six north–south Implementation bodies as well as the British Irish Council. There are currently twenty-six local councils (to be reduced to eleven by 2015). There is an Executive currently made up of twelve departments, a variety of executive agencies, and a separate Northern Ireland Civil Service employing about 27,000 staff. Northern Ireland's First Minister responding to an Assembly question reported that more than 100 non-departmental public bodies had been identified in a recent review. See AQO (1783/11–15), 24 April 2012. This is a generous structure of formal government for a population of some 1.6 million. See further the critique in J Morison, 'Democracy, Governance and Governmentality: Civic Space and Constitutional Renewal in Northern Ireland' (2001) 21 *OJLS* 287.

[48] See J Morison and S Livingstone, *Reshaping Public Power: Northern Ireland the British Constitutional Crisis* (Sweet & Maxwell, 1995) chs 4 and 5; and J Morison, 'Constitutionalism, Civil Society and Democratic Renewal in Northern Ireland' in M Cox, A Guelke, and F Stephens (eds) *A Farewell to Arms? Beyond the Good Friday Agreement* (2nd edn, Manchester University Press 2006) 338–53.

problem. Rather what we have is a complex and expensive structure addressing the three strands of the big 'Political Problem', namely the internal governance of Northern Ireland, the relationship between the Republic of Ireland and Northern Ireland, and the wider relationships among the islands in the British Isles, and one which enables politicians to put on hold the constitutional problem relating to the place of Northern Ireland within the United Kingdom.[49] The other 'constitutional' issues remain, and their containment or eventual resolution is dependent on the wider range of bodies, structures, and mechanisms that have been developed to accommodate them.[50] It is perhaps a feature of the high profile nature of the Northern Ireland settlement that these can be seen operating at multiple levels from the international to the national and local, and across the boundaries of the public, private, voluntary, and community sectors. There is not space here to detail the whole range of mechanisms, bodies, and modes of thinking that have been developed. However some big themes can be sketched out. This demonstrates some of the actual dynamics of governance below and beyond the formal State, and so illustrates the value of a non-sovereignty approach.

G. Post-Agreement Technologies of Governance

The very idea of a 'peace process' commands attention. It provides a 'way of seeing' and a language in which to render thinkable, and actionable, the sort of change required. The power of this concept as a governing idea capable of galvanizing action and a concept around which actors will orient their behaviour is not to be underestimated.

There is a huge intellectual industry around the ideas of peace process and conflict resolution.[51] Northern Ireland is a leading example for both the general idea and many of the sub-specialisms relating to, variously, institutional reform and reparations and prosecutions, truth recovery and commemoration, victims and ex-combatants. 'Peace process' allows an imagining and a re-imagining of the

[49] For an account of the processes leading to the new government structures see B Campbell, *Agreement! The State, Conflict and Change in Northern Ireland* (Lawrence and Wishart 2008) and for an overview of the formal structure of government in Northern Ireland see C Harvey (ed) *Human Rights, Equality and Democratic Renewal in Northern Ireland* (Hart Publishing 2001); P Carmichael, C Knox, and R Osbourne, *Devolution and Constitutional Change in Northern Ireland* (Manchester University Press 2007); and C McCrudden 'Northern Ireland and the British Constitution' in J Jowell and D Oliver (eds) *The Changing Constitution* (6th edn, OUP 2007) 227–70. For more recent updates to the original Agreement see G Anthony, 'Northern Ireland: The St Andrews Agreement and the Northern Ireland Assembly' (2008) 14 *European Public Law* 151 and G Anthony, 'Northern Ireland: The Devolution of Policing in Criminal Justice' (2011) 17 *European Public Law* 197.

[50] As Amalendu Misra describes, the 'conflict cycle', particularly where there is an ethnic dimension, is notoriously difficult to cap. See A Misra, *Politics of Civil Wars: Conflict, Intervention and Resolution* (Routledge 2008) 135–48.

[51] See generally O Ramsbottom, T Woodhouse, and H Miall, *Contemporary Conflict Resolution* (2nd edn, Polity Press 2005) and for some more specialist outworkings in terms of consociationalism or transitional justice see, eg, R Taylor (ed)*Consociational Theory McGarry and O'Leary and the Northern Ireland Conflict* (Routledge 2009), or R Teitel, 'Transitional Justice Genealogy' (2003) 16 *Harvard Human Rights Journal* 69.

past and the future to take place and, as it filters down to more everyday levels, it offers an alternative narrative of what is happening. Often this will be couched in terms of more general historical and comparative experience, and so allow the particularity of the local conflict to be overlaid by processes that can be thought more general. At a more practical level, individuals, organizations, and groups can orient themselves and their actions around the cluster of ideas contained within the concept. Organizations, both State and privately funded, exist at local, national, and international levels to support, encourage, and fund both research and practical interventions.[52] Government at every level, from the European Union and the national governments in the United Kingdom, Republic of Ireland, and elsewhere have contributed funds with the result that since 1987, Northern Ireland and the six border counties of the Republic have benefited from funding of almost £2.5 billion in total, averaging around £100 million per annum.[53] Not surprisingly there are a whole range of organizations and groups, both statutory and voluntary sector based, who will undertake work within the various programmes of action that are supported.[54] While much of this governing technology is taking place at a remove from the formal State, there is no denying that the peace process paradigm is an important governing influence within formal government too. Within the British and Irish Governments, no less than in the Northern Ireland Executive, it continues to have considerable rhetorical and practical power, and it undoubtedly guides action. It could even be argued that the concept is determining of how the courts, too, will interpret legislation as a number of challenges to the foundations of the Belfast Agreement have been denied in favour of an approach emphasizing the maintenance of the peace process.[55]

Another, perhaps less abstract, way to indicate the nature and range of the governing technology operating in post-Agreement Northern Ireland involves pointing to some big themes that were part of the Agreement negotiations and remain to be resolved beyond the extensive institutional structure of devolution that was put in

[52] eg—and it is only by way of example of what is a numerous grouping—there are local and international bodies dedicated to both developing understanding within a general conflict framework and funding practical projects within this paradigm. See the Conflict in Cities and the Divided State Project, details available at <http://www.conflictincities.org> (last accessed 26 April 2013); INCORE, The International Conflict Research Institute, details available at <http://www.incore.ulst.ac.uk> (last accessed 26 April 2013); Stanford Center on International Conflict and Negotiation, details available at <http://www.law.stanford.edu/organizations/programs-and-centers/stanford-center-on-international-conflict-and-negotiation-scicn> (last accessed 26 April 2013) and its local partner, Community Dialogue, details available at <http://www.communitydialogue.org> (last accessed 26 April 2013).

[53] See further P Nolan, *The Northern Ireland Peace Monitoring Report, Number One* (Community Relations Council, 2012) 172ff. See also P Nolan, *The Northern Ireland Peace Monitoring Report, Number Two* (Community Relations Council 2013 at p. 143.

[54] To offer just one example in a particular area, the CAIN website lists over 100 bodies and organizations providing support to victims of conflict in Northern Ireland; see <http://cain.ulst.ac.uk/victims/groups/victimgroups.html#list> (last accessed 26 April 2013).

[55] See further J Morison and M Lynch, 'Litigating the Agreement: Towards a New Judicial Constitutionalism for the UK from Northern Ireland' in J Morison, K McEvoy, and G Anthony (eds) *Judges, Transition, and Human Rights* (OUP 2007) 105–46; and G Anthony, 'Judicial Review in Northern Ireland: A Guide to the "Real" Devolution Issues' [2009] *Judicial Review* 230.

place. These issues have been rendered governable in a variety of ways. Often this has involved inquiries and commissions to conceptualize the problems within a peace process paradigm, and devise ways forward. Generally this has led to the creation of new bodies and commissions as well as often additional organizations to deliver facilities and services. These are invariably organized with different, more inclusive working methods and appointment processes ensuring wider participation. On many occasions international bodies, individuals, or exemplars have been brought in.[56] New language and new ways of conceptualizing old issues have been developed. Often, as with the Agreement more generally, a constructive ambiguity has been relied upon to allow a way forward. Although far from complete or universally agreed, this transformation has not just been institutional or organizational. It has required change across a whole range of actors involved in government in its widest sense, and indeed required active involvement not just from them but from wider society. It is an important feature of this process that the governing technology be widened and seen to come 'from below'.[57] These outstanding issues or governable spaces can be grouped under three general headings.

(1) Policing, justice, and security

Under this heading there are issues about not only the transformation of the Royal Ulster Constabulary into a new Police Service for Northern Ireland but also the new and complex governing arrangements for continuing policing. The policing issue in particular demonstrates many of the governing techniques that are prevalent. Here an international body produced a blueprint for change involving a form of positive discrimination to boost the number of Catholics recruited. The reforms involved supervision by an Oversight Commissioner and now a Policing Board, the development of a Professional Standards Department, and the creation of an independent Police Ombudsman and some twenty-six Policing and Community Safety Partnerships with extensive community involvement.[58] In terms of the justice system generally, a Criminal Justice Review has led to, among other things, an independent Criminal Justice Inspectorate and the creation of a new system for the appointment of judges. The governance of the prison regime, early release of political prisoners, and their reintegration is a theme requiring a range of sophisticated

[56] There is the influence of foreign examples and champions, particularly in the areas of decommissioning, prisoners, and prisoner release, see eg, K McEvoy and J Morison 'Beyond the Constitutional Moment: Law, Transition and Peacemaking in Northern Ireland' (2003) 26 *Fordham International L Rev* 961, 978–85.

[57] See further K McEvoy and L McGregor (eds) *Transitional Justice from Below: Grassroots Activism and the Struggle for Change* (Hart Publishing 2008) (and particularly K McConnachie and J Morison, 'Constitution-making, Transition and the Reconstitution of Society' at 75–98); and A Errikson, 'A Bottom-Up Approach to Transformative Justice in Northern Ireland' (2009) 3 *International Journal of Transitional Justice* 301.

[58] See, egs, G Ellison and C O'Reilly, '"Ulster's Policing Goes Global": The Police Reform Process in Northern Ireland and the Creation of a Global Brand' (2008) 50 *Crime, Law and Social Change* 331; and, on the idea of widening participation, B Ryan, 'Northern Ireland's District Policing Partnerships and the Participatory Ideal' (2008) 3 *Irish Political Studies* 341.

governing techniques.[59] Disarmament, demilitarization, and normalization, as well as the role of the intelligence services are important issues within a whole technology of governance involving reports, commissions, and initiatives. The devolution of justice issues to the Northern Ireland Assembly and Executive has not rendered the mechanisms of governance within this general area any less simple but rather has provided another layer.[60]

(2) Identity, culture, and the past

Under this heading are a variety of matters from victims to commemoration, citizenship to marching, and language to symbols. Each of these brings not only an often torrid political agenda but also a series of mechanisms and bodies to manage the issues. For example, even the flying of flags is subject to a complex legal and governance regime,[61] while issues such as marches require not only a framework of law, and an Independent Commission, but also a series of community group liaison mechanisms with complex agreements relating to the route walked and the amount and volume of music played.[62] The interpretation that is given to events in recent history, the way in which the past is memorialized and to how issues about 'truth' are seen is also highly problematic and strongly governed by a range of actors in various ways.[63] Issues around victims are managed by what has now become an almost standard process. Following the report of an initial Commissioner, scoping and consulting

[59] See K McEvoy, *Paramilitary Imprisonment in Northern Ireland: Resistance, Management, and Release* (OUP 2001); P Shirlow and K McEvoy, *Beyond the Wire: Former Prisoners and Conflict Transformation in Northern Ireland* (Pluto Press 2008); and K McEvoy, 'Agents of Change—Ex-Prisoners, Ex-Combatants, and Conflict Transformation in Northern Ireland' in V Dudoet, H Giesman, and A Planta (eds) *Post-War Security Transitions: Participatory Peace-Building after Asymmetric Conflicts* (Taylor and Francis 2012) 105–22

[60] See further G Anthony, 'The Devolution of Policing and Criminal Justice' (2011) 17 *European Public Law* 197.

[61] There is legislation, regulations, and a court judgment setting out the formal position (see *Murphy, Re Application for Judicial Review* [2001] NIQB 34). See further A Schwartz, 'Symbolic Equality: Law and National Symbols in Northern Ireland' (2012) 19 *International Journal on Minority and Group Rights* 339. The dispute over the Union flag flying over Belfast City Hall which at the time of writing has arisen because this governance regime covers only the practices in the Assembly Building rather than more generally in local councils—a fact which perhaps illustrates the capacity of power and politics in this context to overflow its governing structures.

[62] See C O'Kelly and D Bryan, 'The Regulation of Public Space in Northern Ireland' (2007) 22 *Irish Political Studies* 565.

[63] There is a government appointed Consultative Group on the Past which in 2009 recommended the setting up of a Legacy Commission (see Northern Ireland Affairs Committee 'The Report of the Consultative Group on the Past in Northern Ireland', HC 2008–09, available at <http://www.publications.parliament.uk/pa/cm200910/cmselect/cmniaf/171/171.pdf> (last accessed 26 April 2013); and the cross-community Healing Through Remembering Organization, details available at <http://www.healingthroughremembering.org> (last accessed 26 April 2013). For commentary on some of the wider issues, see eg D Bryan and G McIntosh, 'Symbols and Identity in the "New" Northern Ireland' in P Carmichael, C Knox, and R Osbourne (eds) *Devolution and Constitutional Change in Northern Ireland* (Manchester University Press 2007) 125–37; B Rolston, ' "Trying to Reach the Future through the Past": Murals and Commemoration in Northern Ireland' (2010) 6 *Crime Media and Culture* 285; and P Lundy 'Commissioning the Past in Northern Ireland' (2010) 15 *Review of International Affairs* 101.

on the issues, there is now a statutory Commission for Victims and Survivors and a host of informal bodies in what is a highly politicized area where perceived nationalist, unionist, and cross-community organizations struggle to create and resist a hierarchy of victims as they deliver services to victims.[64] In terms of culture, there is a plethora of arts and sports based projects and initiatives.[65] A particularly good example is the Re-imaging Communities consortium, which involves a wide range of authorities and groups led by the Arts Council of Northern Ireland in a project to replace the 2,000 or so paramilitary murals and insignia with less threatening expressions of a new post-conflict identity.[66] There are bodies created and funded to promote both the Irish language and the (re)invented language of Ulster Scots,[67] and a whole discourse and mechanics to manage whether people wish to identify as British, Irish—or both.[68]

(3) Rights, equality, and good relations

The important practical technologies arising out of the framework of rights and equality provided in and around the Peace Process are very significant. Here is a highly developed and sophisticated governing mechanism that offers a framework within which government must operate, and which is available to a whole range of individuals and organizations. It also provides a series of concepts and a language in which conflicts can be expressed and worked upon in non-violent ways. It allows people to see things in different terms and regard themselves and others in alternative ways.

The rights and equality regime in Northern Ireland, with its various bodies and commissions, is one of the most developed and extensive in the world.[69] There is a

[64] See the initial report, K Bloomfield, '"We Will Remember Them": Report of the Northern Ireland Victims Commissioner, Sir Kenneth Bloomfield' (April 1998) available at <http://cain.ulst.ac.uk/issues/violence/victims.htm> (last accessed 26 April 2013). For the work of the new Commission, see Commission for Victims and Survivors, details available at <http://www.cvsni.org> (last accessed 26 April 2013) and the list of more than 100 community bodies working with victims provided, available at <http://cain.ulst.ac.uk/victims/groups/victimgroups.html> (last accessed 17 June 2013).

[65] See eg the Community Arts Partnership which describes itself as 'committed to championing community arts in the belief that they can positively transform our society' (Community Arts Partnership, details available at <http://comartspartner.org/?page_id=60> (last accessed 26 April 2013). For an overview of the role of sport in this context, see Nolan (n 53) 129–39 and J Sugden, *Sport and Peace Building in Divided Societies: Playing with the Enemy* (Routledge 2013).

[66] See further Arts Council of Northern Ireland available at <http://www.artscouncil-ni.org/award/re-imaging_communities.htm> (last accessed 26 April 2013). See also B Roulston '"Trying to Reach the Future through the Past": Murals and Commemorations in Northern Ireland' (2010) 6 *Crime, Media and Culture* 285; and A Hill and A White, 'Painting Peace? Murals and the Northern Ireland Peace Process' (2012) 27 *Irish Political Studies* 71.

[67] There are a number of bodies to promote the Irish language including *Foras na Gaeilge*, funded by the Northern Ireland Department of Culture, Arts and Leisure (DCAL) which is an agency of the North/South Language Body, formed as a cross-border implementation body under the Belfast Agreement. DCAL also funds the Tha Boord o Ulstèr-Scotch.

[68] See further J McAuley and J Tonge, 'Britishness (and Irishness) in Northern Ireland since the Good Friday Agreement' (2009) 63 *Parliamentary Affairs* 266.

[69] See further C Harvey, 'Contextualised Equality and the Politics of Legal Mobilisation: Affirmative Action in Northern Ireland' (2012) 21 *Social & Legal Studies* 23; C Harvey and A Schwartz (eds) *Rights*

statutory duty on public authorities to promote equality of opportunity between persons of different religious belief, political opinion, racial group, age, marital status, or sexual orientation.[70] There are also duties to produce and review equality schemes, conduct equality impact assessments, and include consultation as an integral part of the policy-making process. The Equality Commission of Northern Ireland operates within a framework of more than sixty pieces of devolved, national, and European legislation to monitor, encourage, and police an agenda of equality. Fair employment legislation requires most employers to monitor the religious composition of their workforces, and individuals must allow themselves to be recorded as perceived 'protestant' or perceived 'catholic'—irrespective of their actual religious beliefs, with a category called 'other' reserved only for those from outside Northern Ireland, again designated without regard to any actual belief.[71] This mirrors a similar designation process in the Assembly for voting purposes and is indicative of a wider method of approaching conflict resolution.[72]

Less ostensibly successful has been the good relations agenda. In some ways this has offered a contradictory technology of governance, focused as it is less on the assertion of rights and more on ideas of sharing resources and encouraging communities to get along with one another through the development of, for example, neutral workspaces.[73] Section 75(2) of the Northern Ireland Act 1998 requires public authorities to have regard to the desirability of promoting good relations between persons of different religious belief, political opinion, or racial group. However, beyond this there have been efforts to overcome the high degree of segregation in Northern Ireland society and a tendency for services to be provided separately. This was manifested in a policy document titled *A Shared Future*, introduced during a suspension in devolved arrangements in 2005.[74] This offered another blueprint for tackling the visible manifestations of sectarianism and racism, reclaiming shared space, reducing tensions at interface areas, supporting good relations through cultural diversity, and developing shared workspaces. However, with the restoration of devolved government in 2007, the *Shared Future* policy agenda was abandoned and replaced instead by a promise in the Executive's Programme for Government

in Divided Societies (Hart Publishing 2012); C McCrudden, R Ford, and A Heath, 'Legal Regulation of Affirmative Action in Northern Ireland: An Empirical Assessment' (2004) 24 *OJLS* 363.

[70] See Northern Ireland Act 1998, s 75(1).

[71] See further the Fair Employment and Treatment (Northern Ireland Order) 1998 and the Fair Employment (Monitoring) Regulations Northern Ireland 1999 which makes failure to comply a criminal offence with a fine of up to £5,000 on conviction. The Equality Commission offers a fifty-page guide on relevant matters.

[72] See Northern Ireland Act 1998, s 4 as amended by the St Andrew's Agreement Act 2006 and the Standing Orders of the Assembly as amended in March 2010. More generally see the consociationalist approach and its critics in R Taylor (ed) *Consociational Theory: McGary and O'Leary and the Northern Ireland Conflict* (Routledge 2009).

[73] See the Equality Commission of Northern Ireland, *Promoting a Good and Harmonious Working Environment* (2009).

[74] See Office of the First Minister and Deputy First Minister, *A Shared Future: Policy and Strategic Framework for Good Relations in Northern Ireland* (March 2005) available at <http://www.ofmdfmni.gov.uk/asharedfuturepolicy2005.pdf> (last accessed 26 April 2013).

2008–11 that a new *Programme for Cohesion, Sharing and Integration* would be developed.[75] A public consultation on this finished in 2010 but it was not until May 2013 that a plan was produced.[76] This adds 'good relations' to 'equality' as a principal aim of government, and builds upon the familiar elaborate technology of reports and consultations with two agencies dedicated to developing this area with extensive programmes of operation.[77] These extend across a whole range of areas and enlist a wide variety of groups and agencies. Sometimes they involve celebrating one or other culture but perhaps one of the more interesting areas relates to work attempting to detoxify certain traditional celebrations and re-package them as wider communal events or even tourist attractions, where the conflict can be relegated safely to the past.[78]

These examples could be multiplied and a larger history of successful and less successful, and often contradictory, schemes, plans, and actions could be produced. The role of law in various formats in establishing, underwriting, enabling, and actioning all of these would be set out further. This would exist alongside a narrative describing all the choreography of handshakes, royal, and presidential visits and other political and cultural initiatives. Such an account would include the history and role of important governing ideas, such as 'parity of esteem', 'mutual respect', and of course the idea of 'consent' which is a vital governing concept for dealing not only with the big self-determination issue but much else besides. The role of language as a technology, an indicative conceptual apparatus and a way of seeing that allows the imagining and re-imaging of ways of living in order that conflict may be ameliorated and governed, would be elaborated. The importance of funders and their particular programmes would be fully considered. The role of international parties and exemplars would be taken into account, as would the engagement of national, local, and community bodies and actors. The processes by which issues, plans, and programmes for action have been reviewed and consulted upon, and devolved to a range of agencies and bodies would be charted. So too would the way in which the governing process has been widened out to include a full range of community actors to ensure that the business of government has the

[75] See *Programme for Cohesion, Sharing and Integration* available at <http://www.ofmdfmni.gov.uk/reformatted_final_print_version_csi_-_26.07.10.pdf> (last accessed 26 April 2013).

[76] See *Together: Building a United Community* available at <http://www.ofmdfmni.gov.uk/together_building_a_united_community.pdf> (last accessed 5 July 2013).

[77] The Community Relations Unit is located within the Equality and Strategy Directorate of the Office of the First Minister and deputy First Minister (see <http://www.community-relations.org.uk> (last accessed 26 April 2013)). There is also a Community Relations Council which is an independent charitable body funded in part by the Northern Ireland Executive and established to fund community relations work, establish expertise, and provide advice (see <http://www.ofmdfmni.gov.uk/index/equality/community-relations.htm> (last accessed 26 April 2013)).

[78] See, eg, the efforts by various bodies to transform the protestant Twelfth of July celebrations into a safer, community-funded 'Orangefest' celebration of history (see <http://gotobelfast.com/whats-on/event/orangefest-twelfth-of-july-celebrations> (last accessed 26 April 2013)) and, from the other community, a re-badging of Saint Patrick's Day where non-sectarian events will be supported (see <http://www.gotobelfast.com/whats-on/event/st-patricks-festival> (last accessed 26 April 2013)). See further T Crowley, 'The Art of Memory: The Murals of Northern Ireland and the Management of History' (2011) 7 *Field Day Review* 22.

widest possible base of engagement. This effort to provide a bottom-up approach is intended to bring increased legitimacy to governance in a contested society but it also has the effect of engaging and responsibilizing more people in what can be seen clearly in this context as an effective and ambitious technology of governance operating beyond the notion of sovereignty.

Of course while this governance technology is more clearly observable in the context of a hugely governed society undergoing a significant transition, such governing processes and technologies are occurring everywhere. Indeed, even in Northern Ireland there is an agenda of 'normal' governance and, neither in Northern Ireland or elsewhere, is this adequately explained by reference only to sovereignty. However it is perhaps in relation to issues of devolution that this non-sovereignty approach can be applied most readily. It is to this that we must now turn briefly, and by way of conclusion.

H. Non-sovereignty and Devolution: A Research Agenda

This chapter has argued that we should set aside sovereignty in order to achieve a better understanding of how constitutional power actually operates within a wider and more complex idea of governance than is appreciated in traditional constitutional theory. The important changes in any polity are brought about not only by formal changes in the formal governance structures but by a whole wider range of what we should properly regard as constitutional actors making themselves up in new ways in order to govern themselves within a variety of constitutional spaces. Some indication of the various technologies of governance deployed across a number of these spaces in Northern Ireland has been offered under three general headings, encompassing legal and other mechanisms. These technologies involve the traditional institutions and agents of the State but also bring with them a much wider agency. A whole range of other actors are enlisted directly within the wider processes of governance through the extended range of bodies, commissions, and consultation processes. Beyond them a wider society is required to 'make themselves up' differently in relation to new governing ideas. This may range from the direct and personal, such as a victim having to accept an early release prisoner returning to a small community as a 'peace-building measure', to a more abstract engagement with ideas such as parity of esteem between the two traditions and the outworkings of such concepts in human rights and equality measures. Northern Ireland as a society in transition sharply illustrates this broader notion of governance but of course the idea applies to how all societies are constituted at all times and in all ways.[79]

[79] See for an earlier attempt to provide a governmentality style analysis of the role of the community and voluntary sectors in the delivery of public services across the United Kingdom, J Morison, 'The Government—Voluntary Sector Compacts: Governance, Governmentality and Civil Society' (2000) 27 *Journal of Law and Society* 98.

The continuing story of devolution in the United Kingdom is a particularly fertile place to develop further such a non-sovereignty approach. In any polity such as Scotland or Wales that is undergoing a continuing transition the distinctions between simple policy-making and the constitution and re-constitution of the idea of the polity are blurred as the two processes are interlinked. As new forms of governance are being developed to deal with the range of governable issues that are increasingly appearing as pertinent on a Scottish or Welsh footing, rather than only on a UK basis, it is possible to see both new structures and mechanisms of governance and new ideas and language supporting them. These are not irreducibly linked to sovereignty and indeed often flourish well out of sight of the high politics of Westminster.

For this reason it is important to develop an approach that both recognizes the limits of the devolution debate in its present sovereignty terms and offers another, alternative, 'way of seeing'. As noted earlier, Foucault cautions us that we should not approach any area of study as a 'ready-made subject' where all the elements are pre-given and our search is only to find them using the measures and criteria of the given subject. As the continuing story of devolution is examined we should not look simply for the traditional elements of legislative competence, executive independence, and overall legitimacy from Westminster. Devolution in this sense, expressed in terms of sovereignty, with all its attendant paraphernalia of referendums, reserved powers, and parliamentary hierarchy, is really only one way of seeing; and it is one that is inextricably tied up with seeing power as having only one centre from which all other legitimate outworkings of power can be traced and understood. The non-sovereignty approach suggests that we put aside this way of seeing and develop instead an approach that allows us to consider a much wider process where power is seen as being exercised across a whole range of constitutional spaces and with greater agency involving more actors and processes and in a way that amounts to a re-constitution of the polity and the power relations there.

What does this actually mean? First, the whole idea of a devolution debate is simply a way of seeing. For some it is a means by which bigger processes of governance, change, and self-determination may be subsumed within the safety of a debate about sovereignty. After all, discussions about Parliaments, assemblies, and the continuing role of the Queen are arguably a more manageable way of thinking about governance than dealing with a more underlying sense of discontinuity and a need for change. However, of course, for others even the very idea of devolution is a contestable concept and a range of formal alternatives are being offered in its place. Indeed, the referendum debate in Scotland is as much one over policy divergence and symbols, language and culture, finance and social policy, and defence and Europe, as it is about formal limits on law-making or further tax-raising powers. The same is true to a degree in Wales. Some of this will play out in terms of the Silk Commission review in Wales,[80] and the devolution versus independence debate

[80] The Commission on Devolution in Wales (the Silk Commission) was established to review the present financial and constitutional arrangements in Wales. Its work is proceeding in two parts, dealing first with fiscal powers before turning to review the powers of the National Assembly.

in Scotland, but much is already happening on these fronts and will continue to do so irrespective of the publication of the second volume of the Silk review in spring 2014 or the outcome of the referendum on independence for Scotland in autumn 2014.

We could track various topics and processes, such as, for example, the efforts in both countries to gain greater fiscal autonomy without devolution to allow devolved countries to resource their policy choices.[81] The document called *Key Issues for the Fourth Assembly* produced for the National Assembly of Wales encompasses a whole range of matters, from transport to the digital divide, and from food security to child poverty.[82] Many of these have little to do with formal devolution as such, and further devolution and issues of sovereignty are at best only one possible part of a number of possible answers. In Scotland the political as opposed to governmental work of the Scottish Nationalist Party would provide a fertile place to examine how ideas of independence are made thinkable in ways that do not immediately invoke debates about sovereignty as such. We could consider how, as in Northern Ireland, human rights discourse in Scotland and Wales is increasingly becoming the way to operationalize change.[83] There is much else besides.

Of course this does not mean that the issue of a formal transfer of power to a Scottish Parliament or the conclusions of the Silk Commission are without interest. But it does mean that the arrangement of legislative power, the detailed outworkings of sovereignty in a newly constituted United Kingdom, will not exhaust interest in how public, *constituting* power is organized in the changing agenda of constitutionalism in the United Kingdom. There is much above and below the level of sovereignty that needs to be explored in order to understand how the new polities within the changing United Kingdom are being 'constituted'. It is here that the value of the non-sovereignty approach comes in.

This is not to suggest that everything is now somehow 'constitutional' and a suitable object of study to understand how power operates to constitute society. Rather it is the role and action of law that remains our subject. However, it is now to be seen within the context of a wider governing project, in the form typically of rights and regulatory regimes where we can see how law underpins, constitutes, supports, operationalizes, and validates a whole range of wider governing techniques and strategies. This does not downgrade the importance of law in the governing process—on the contrary. Although such an approach may demur from claiming originating, foundational status for law as derived from its relationship to

[81] For a discussion of some these, albeit mainly in a devolution context, see the Silk Commission, *Empowerment and Responsibility: Financial Powers to Strengthen Wales* (November 2012) available at <http://commissionondevolutioninwales.independent.gov.uk/files/2012/11/English-WEB-Executive-Summary.pdf> (last accessed 25 April 2013).

[82] See National Assembly for Wales Research Service, *Key Issues for the Fourth Assembly* (2011).

[83] In Scotland the SNP has put forward proposals for a written constitution enshrining rights to education and housing. See WE Bulmer, *A Model Constitution for Scotland: Making Democracy Work in an Independent State* (Luath Press 2012). Wales is also developing a rights-based approach, particularly in the area of children's rights: see *The Children's Rights Scheme* (March 2012) available at <http://wales.gov.uk/docs/phhs/publications/120418rightsofchildrenen.pdf> (last accessed 26 April 2013).

sovereignty, it does in fact elevate law to a more central role in understanding how power really works in the changing constitution.

Back in 1993 Neil MacCormick, to whom any discussion on sovereignty must revert, reflected with approval on those who 'pointedly criticised mainstream jurisprudence of unreflectively privileging State-law over all other forms of law, as though really the only law that counts is that of the (presumably) sovereign and independent State'.[84] He maintained that 'looking from this one-State point of view can be distorting', and that 'there is no compulsion to regard "sovereignty", or even hierarchical relationships of super-ordination and subordination, as necessary to our understanding of legal order'.[85] MacCormick was at this time considering mainly the European legal order, and addressing his thoughts to issues about the value of ideas of the State and sovereignty in what we now see as post national constitutionalism or post national public law.[86] However, his conclusion, if not all of the reasons for arriving at it, is one that can be endorsed now in the context of devolution below the level of the national State. The fact that the continuing devolution process is happening requires us to think more carefully about what is really going on. I contend that it is only by saying 'a sort of farewell to sovereignty' that we can begin to do so.

[84] See N MacCormick, 'Beyond the Sovereign State' (1993) 56 *MLR* 1. See also M Hunt, 'Reshaping Constitutionalism' in J Morison, K McEvoy, and G Anthony (eds) *Judges, Transitions and Human Rights* (OUP 2007) 467–78 for a discussion of some of this literature.

[85] MacCormick (n 84) 10.

[86] See further N Walker, 'Postnational Constitutionalism and Postnational Public Law: A Tale of Two Neologisms' (2012) 3 *Transnational Legal Theory* 61.

9

Referendums, Popular Sovereignty, and the Territorial Constitution

Peter Leyland[*]

A. Introduction

The referendum which will be held on 18 September 2014 to determine the matter of independence for Scotland not only draws attention to a pivotal constitutional issue, but also illustrates the controversy that frequently surrounds the use of referendums.[1] It will be argued in this chapter that the role of the Westminster Parliament and the wider democratic process at devolved and local government level is in danger of being redefined by the growing use of referendums as a substitute for traditional politics under the banner of 'popular sovereignty'.

The British electoral system traditionally embodied the idea of a choice of representatives at parliamentary or local government level selected to speak for their communities. Referendums are an alternative mechanism for the expression of popular sovereignty which permit the people to have an input by measuring the aggregation of individual wills in relation to a single question, or series of questions. This form of participation allows rational citizens to engage in the collective task of governing themselves.[2] Different types of referendums have become a familiar part of British constitutional practice in recent times: both binding and advisory referendums have been accepted as a means to enable citizens to make what are meant to be regarded as authoritative choices.[3]

Although referendums are used as a method of ascertaining the popular will of the people they may be abused in obvious ways. Voters tend to respond to the set question or questions put to them and the debate may be orchestrated by

* Professor of Public Law, London Metropolitan University.

[1] See House of Lords Select Committee on the Constitution, *Agreement Between the United Kingdom Government and the Scottish Government on a Referendum on Independence for Scotland*, Edinburgh, 15 October 2012 (HL Paper (2012–13) no 62).

[2] R Katz, *Democracy and Elections* (OUP 1997) 28.

[3] The Parliamentary Voting System and Constituencies Act 2011, s 1 provided for a binding referendum to determine the voting system for parliamentary elections while the Local Government Act 2000, ss 34–6 provided for advisory referendums on changes to the form of executive arrangements for a local authority.

organized factional interests. In the United Kingdom the Political Parties, Elections, and Referendums Act 2000 provides many important procedural controls on the conduct of referendums. As we will see later when considering the referendum for an independent Scotland, the Election Commission is placed under a duty to advise on the intelligibility of any referendum questions[4] and the legislation also establishes control over donations and expenses[5] and many other issues.[6] However, no clear rules have emerged to determine under what precise constitutional conditions referendums can be held. Another important question that needs to be decided in advance of constitutional referendums is whether the validity of the result should be linked to the level of voter turnout. The Scotland Act 1978 and Wales Act 1978 both lapsed in 1979 because of a failure to meet a threshold which required approval from 40 per cent or more of registered electors. While no such threshold has been set for subsequent referendums and there is no turnout requirement for other types of election, it is difficult to claim a mandate for major constitutional change on a marginal vote in favour with a low turnout, for example less than 50 per cent of the electorate.[7]

Referendums undoubtedly have a constitutional role to play, not least in relation to such fundamental events as the foundation of a new State, the creation of a new constitution, the radical change of an existing constitution, the transfer of sovereign powers from the State to international institutions, and the introduction of new forms of substate autonomy. Such changes are likely to call for popular approval precisely because they affect the sovereign relations between the wider electorate and the institutions of government.[8] Constitutional referendums may be distinguished from legislative referendums on the basis that the latter do not impact upon the location and distribution of sovereign power within the State.[9] But in the absence of a codified constitution in the United Kingdom, ordinary legislation is employed to introduce changes at different levels of governance and thus what may be counted as constitutional for this purpose may be difficult to define with precision.

Referendums have often been used in other States with codified constitutional systems as a form of legitimation to demonstrate popular support, but without clear rules referendums can be manipulated politically. The referendum might sanction a transfer of powers but at the same time undermine the claim to represent an

[4] See Political Parties, Elections, and Referendums Act 2000 ('PPERA 2000'), s 104(2).

[5] PPERA 2000, ss 119–23.

[6] eg, the referendum period, date of poll, and referendum questions (PPERA 2000, ss 102–04); designation of organizations to whom assistance is available (ss 108–10); referendum expenses (ss 111–18); restrictions on the publication and subject matter of promotional materials (ss 125–6); and referendum campaign broadcasts (s 127).

[7] Constitution Committee, *Referendums in the United Kingdom* (Twelfth Report) (HL Paper (2009–10) no 99) paras 180–9. See also in relation to other jurisdictions the Canadian Supreme Court in the Secession Reference Case [1998] 2 SCR 217 arising from the 1995 referendum in Quebec, which recognized the importance of democratic legitimacy. See also S Tierney, *Constitutional Law and National Pluralism* (OUP 2004) 258.

[8] S Tierney, 'Constitutional Referenda: A Theoretical Enquiry' (2009) 72 *MLR* 360, 361.

[9] Tierney (n 8) 364.

expression of the popular will. To take a famous example, President De Gaulle in 1961 and 1962 deployed referendums unilaterally in France to engage directly with the electorate over crucial constitutional issues outside the terms set by the constitution.[10] After such a referendum had resolved the matter in favour of the President the people were deprived of their sovereignty on these issues which now resided with the President. In similar fashion, plebiscites have provided a form of purported legitimacy for the internal constitutional manoeuvrings of autocratic regimes.

In regard to the question of territoriality and the recognition of local interests and identities all constitutions are susceptible to claims of substate nationalism if they fail to reflect the depth of plurality within the State. Tierney points out that:

> the sub-State challenge, particularly when it tries to mobilise the referendum as a vehicle of legitimacy, tests not only the authority of a given constitution, but the almost universally accepted understandings of the monistic demotic environment within which liberal constitutionalism plays out.[11]

In other words, constitutional referendums are recognized as a form of direct democracy appropriate for deliberation on matters of nation building potential which are capable of influencing the constitution as the supreme source of law but without strict controls there is potential for the device to be abused to obtain political advantage or it may lead to the unbounded rule of public opinion.

The classic counter argument to resorting to referendums in a democracy is founded on the basis that elected politicians are better placed to make decisions on behalf of the people.[12] They are elected to parliaments, assemblies, or local councils with procedures for debate and possess the expertise and experience to make decisions on behalf of the electorate. At the same time they are equipped to take into account the complexity and interrelatedness of controversial public policy questions.[13] On the other hand, ordinary voters may be prone to make ill-informed choices without adequate deliberation. Further, the resort to referendums on a routine or unprincipled basis will tend to marginalize the elected institutions and thereby undermine fundamental assumptions about the role of representative democracy.

Nonetheless, referendums have emerged as an increasingly common feature of constitutional practice in the United Kingdom. The first nationwide referendum on continued membership of the European Economic Community in 1975 was held after the United Kingdom had joined under the previous government without any direct consultation of the wider electorate. Prime Minister Harold Wilson opted for a referendum on the renegotiated terms as a means of keeping the Labour party in power and in one piece. This was achieved by negotiating an 'agreement

[10] S Boyron, *The Constitution of France: A Contextual Analysis* (Hart Publishing 2013) 60–2.

[11] S Tierney, *Constitutional Referendums: The Theory and Practice of Republican Deliberation* (OUP 2012) 139.

[12] Constitution Committee (2009–10) (n 7) para 50ff.

[13] Tierney (n 11) 29, 37.

to differ' between divided factions within the party up to and including cabinet ministers during the referendum campaign.[14]

Since 1975 there has been an increasing reliance on referendums to settle political questions including the type of electoral system and the introduction of devolved government. They are not only an alternative to representative democracy but have the potential to modify basic assumptions concerning legislative institutions and constitutional principles. For instance, the European Union Act 2011 potentially impacts on parliamentary sovereignty as it includes referendum provisions which make it more difficult for Parliament to legislate in certain circumstances. The legislation achieves this end by specifying that any future Act which includes the transfer of significant additional powers to the European Union will not come into force until the proposed legislation containing it has been approved by a majority in a national referendum.[15] In effect, until such time as the European Union Act 2011 is repealed, consent in a referendum forms part of the legislative process for this category of legislation.[16]

In many nations referendums are subject to constitutional regulation which stipulates when they can be used and precisely under what conditions. The danger of abuse has been recognized by the House of Lords Constitution Committee:

> [T]he referendum, in countries with a codified constitution, is intended to constrain the government of the day. In Britain, by contrast, if the use of the referendum lies at the discretion of government, it can be used to augment the power of government rather than limiting it, by allowing a government to bring the people into play against Parliament...The referendum could then become a tactical device, 'the Pontius Pilate' of British politics.[17]

Rather, the holding of referendums should be determined by constitutional rules and their use confined to constitutional matters. Indeed, pressing issues such as the adoption of a European Constitution, a proposal to join the euro currency, or independence for Scotland generate legitimate demands for resolution by referendum. Given the practice since the early 1970s this is arguably a matter which is already governed by convention. Judged in terms of the Jennings criteria for the creation of conventions (precedents, supporting reasons, and feelings of obligation among political actors) it would appear that some rules have emerged to support a convention relating to the holding of referendums.[18] The Constitution Committee concluded that referendums should be confined to fundamental constitutional issues but it also recognized that in the absence of a written constitution such issues are difficult to define.[19]

[14] P Hennessy, *The Prime Minister: The Office and Its Holders Since 1945* (Penguin 2000) 369.

[15] European Union Act 2011, part I. See also P Craig, 'The European Union Act 2011: Locks, Limits and Legality' (2011) 6 CMLR 1915, and also Chapter 10 in this volume by Paul Craig.

[16] V Bogdanor, 'Imprisoned by a Doctrine: The Modern Defence of Parliamentary Sovereignty' [2011] *OJLS* 179, 188. In Chapter 4 in this volume, Jeffrey Goldsworthy discusses the implications of special requirements relating to referendums designed to secure constitutional entrenchment.

[17] Constitution Committee (2009–10) (n 7) para 70.

[18] G Marshall, 'The Constitution: Theory and Interpretation' in V Bogdanor (ed) *The British Constitution in the Twentieth Century* (OUP 2003) 62

[19] Marshall (n 18) para 95.

While State sovereignty has been traditionally conceived in terms of the power of the State to exercise supreme authority over its territory,[20] the focus of this chapter is on the role of popular sovereignty in regard to the configuration and operation of territorial governance. The discussion begins by surveying the challenges to constitutional questions of sovereignty with reference to Ireland and Scotland under what might be regarded as the traditional model of the Constitution which depended on having a parliamentary mandate from an elected government. We then proceed to consider how referendums have been increasingly employed as mechanisms of participatory democracy to sanction more recent changes in sub-national governance. It will be argued that in the absence of ground rules governing their application that they have not only been used pragmatically but also with an alarming lack of consistency. The result is that the intensity of democratic participation in the United Kingdom has varied strikingly depending on both nation and locality. Recent measures regarding local government can be regarded as an extreme example of this trend. Nevertheless, it is further argued that referendums should have a significant constitutional role and that it is possible to formulate broad guidelines to determine when they should be held, either as part of a codified constitution or as part of a special constitutional statute.

B. Constitutional Expansion and Contraction: Two Historical Experiences

(1) Ireland

From an English standpoint Dicey claimed that none of the limitations imposed by law on the absolute authority of Parliament had any real existence. [21] They would not only lack any legal recognition in the statute-book but also would not be recognized by the courts. Moreover, he argued that the Acts of Union with Scotland (1707) and with Ireland (1800) demonstrated the inherent futility of any attempt by one sovereign body to restrain the actions of another equally sovereign body.[22] Even at the time this account was something of a misrepresentation. In Ferdinand Mount's words:

> Nor again are ideas of devolutionary or federal bodies as utterly unfamiliar as Dicey liked to pretend. From feudal times, through the century of the two parliaments and the brief life of Grattan's Parliament in Ireland, down to the separate legal and ecclesiastical governments in Scotland and the great white Parliament on Stormont Hill, we have experience of a huge variety of chartered, independent bodies exercising a huge degree of self-government.[23]

[20] See Chapter 15 in this volume by Joanne Scott.

[21] AV Dicey, *An Introduction to the Study of the Law of the Constitution* (10th edn, Macmillan 1958) 68–70.

[22] Dicey (n 21) 66.

[23] F Mount, *The British Constitution Now* (Mandarin 1992) 84.

Dicey himself later changed his tune on the absolutism of parliamentary sovereignty as it had been explained in the *Law of the Constitution*. He believed that the Irish Home Rule Bill, which he personally opposed, lacked constitutional authority because it had not been confirmed at an election. He commented that the 'institution of a Referendum would simply mean the formal acknowledgement of the doctrine that lies at the basis of English democracy—that a law depends at bottom for its enactment on the assent of the nation as represented by the electors'.[24] Any Home Rule Bill had to be stopped outright or put to the people of England (not Ireland) in a referendum. [25]

No referendum was held by the British government over Irish independence. The procedure eventually adopted for seeking a constitutional settlement was to call a Speaker's Conference on devolution which was followed by the introduction of the Government of Ireland Bill. The proposals were then enacted by the Westminster Parliament as the Government of Ireland Act 1920 which was meant to work on the basis of temporary partition of Ireland. In 1921, however, the Anglo-Irish treaty was negotiated between the British Prime Minister and Irish leaders which allowed the twenty-six counties to become a self-governing dominion referred to as the Irish Free State. In other words, as Hadfield explains:

> The legal force of the Anglo-Irish Treaty in British constitutional law…derives from the enactment by Westminster of the incorporating Act [the Irish Free State (Agreement) Act 1922] [which] recognises…the twenty six county Irish Free State.[26]

Northern Ireland was allowed to opt out of this arrangement and so have her own home rule legislature which became operational in 1921.[27] Subsequently, in 1937, the Irish Free State approved an Irish Constitution which was enacted after a referendum organized by the Irish government in Ireland. This Constitution was highly controversial as it recognized the pre-eminence of the Roman Catholic Church and made claim to the whole island of Ireland.[28] The final vestiges of formal association with the United Kingdom were extinguished in 1948 when the Irish Free State became the Republic of Ireland outside of the Commonwealth.

The process demonstrates the capacity of the Westminster Parliament to limit on an irrevocable basis the legislative competence of its successors.[29] The crucial point to recognize is that the Westminster Parliament, exercising its sovereign powers, was able to redefine the United Kingdom by giving up twenty-six of its counties and by conferring dominion status to a substantial part of its empire.[30]

[24] AV Dicey, *A Leap in the Dark: A Criticism of the Principles of Home Rule as Illustrated by the Bill of 1893* (2nd edn, John Murray 1911) 199.

[25] I McLean, *What's Wrong with the British Constitution* (OUP 2010) 121.

[26] B Hadfield, 'The United Kingdom as a Territorial State' in V Bogdanor (ed) *The British Constitution in the Twentieth Century* (OUP 2003) 603.

[27] Government of Ireland Act 1920, s 1.

[28] See art 44.1.2 and arts 2 and 3.

[29] Under the Statute of Westminster 1931, s 4, the Westminster Parliament limited its powers to legislate in relation to Australia, New Zealand, Canada, and South Africa without their consent. See G Marshall, *Parliamentary Sovereignty and the Commonwealth* (Clarendon Press 1957) 76.

[30] C Munro, *Studies in Constitutional Law* (2nd edn, Butterworths 1999) 149.

Such changes were not dependent on referendums called under the auspices of the British government.

(2) Scotland

In Neil MacCormick's words: 'There was one essential Act of Union that extended the sway of Parliament over Scotland on agreed terms.'[31] Nevertheless from a Scottish perspective the Diceyan view of legal sovereignty has always been contested. It has been claimed that the guarantees contained in the Treaty of Union 1707 continued to have a binding effect on the Westminster Parliament.[32] While there is an absence of any court decisions which directly recognize legal support for this view,[33] MacCormick drew attention to what he called:

> 'The Scottish anomaly' at the heart of the British State. The Union encompasses both an English constitution and a special dispensation for Scots law, Scots Courts, Scottish education, and Scottish local government. It also provides for a separate church establishment, and this has been matched by separate hierarchies in Catholic and Episcopal churches. . . . This concatenation of circumstances made possible just such appeals to a continuing background constitutional tradition of popular sovereignty rather than Parliamentary sovereignty as that which the Scottish Convention recited in the 'Claim of Right'.[34]

The acknowledgment of a latent popular sovereignty underpinning Scottish constitutionalism also meant that 'it would be quite erroneous to speak of "British law" or "United Kingdom" law, for no such system exists. If the sovereign State with which we are dealing is the United Kingdom, it nonetheless comprises three distinct systems.'[35] This has left us with 'a federalism of political management and judicial separation rather than a federalism of constitutional form'.[36] In effect, even before the Scottish Constitutional Convention was formed in 1989 to work on proposals for devolution and legislative devolution in the form of the Scotland Act 1998, there was already administrative devolution in operation north of the border.[37] The structural features in place included a Scottish educational system, a Scottish form of local government, and a Scottish legal system.

In constitutional terms legislative devolution is different from federalism as a method for dealing with territorial governance because it is based on the assumption that sovereignty will be retained at national level by the Westminster Parliament.[38] In other words law-making capacity is granted to new institutions while at the same time preserving parliamentary sovereignty. The devolution legislation goes

[31] N MacCormick, *Questioning Sovereignty: Law, State and Nation in the European Union* (OUP 1999) 58.

[32] A Bradley, 'The Sovereignty of Parliament: Form or Substance' in J Jowell and D Oliver (eds) *The Changing Constitution* (7th edn, OUP 2011) 58.

[33] Lord President Cooper held that the Union of 1707 constituted fundamental law in *MacCormick v Lord Advocate* 1953 SC 396. See also Chapter 6 by Lord Hope in this volume.

[34] MacCormick (n 31) 60. [35] Munro (n 30) 15. [36] MacCormick (n 31) 60.

[37] The role of the Convention is discussed further in Section C.

[38] P Leyland, 'The Multifaceted Constitutional Dynamics of UK Devolution' (2011) 9 *International Journal of Constitutional Law* 251, 253.

to considerable lengths to achieve this end. In a formal sense the Westminster Parliament remains sovereign. The statutes, including the Scotland Act 1998, which establish devolution set in place procedures of pre-legislative and post-legislative scrutiny to prevent the devolved legislatures from exceeding their powers.[39] Nevertheless, prior to devolution it was recognized that there might be occasions where notwithstanding that the devolved body had the power to legislate it might chose not to do so. It was recognized that what has become known as the 'Sewel Convention' would be likely to develop allowing the Parliament or Assembly to pass what have since been termed legislative consent motions. The effect of such motions is for the devolved Parliament or Assembly to permit the Westminster Parliament to pass legislation on its behalf. Legislative consent motions have been regularly used since the introduction of devolution.[40]

In practice, the sovereign power of Westminster is modified while devolution remains in place. It follows from the fact that there are now devolved legislatures that the Westminster Parliament no longer routinely legislates for the devolved parts of the United Kingdom such as Scotland. In this political and practical sense the sovereignty of the Westminster Parliament has shrunk and this shrinkage is a feature of the Constitution for as long as devolution remains a significant part of the constitutional landscape.[41] Moreover, the devolution legislation, while not directly affecting the continuing sovereignty of the Westminster Parliament, provides what some commentators have regarded as the equivalent of constitutions for the devolved parts of the United Kingdom. As Lord Hoffmann put it in relation to the Northern Ireland Act: 'The 1998 Act is a constitution for Northern Ireland, framed to create a continuing form of government against the background of the history of the territory.'[42] In its wake devolution has provided scope for the further development of distinct constitutional identities for Scotland, Wales, and Northern Ireland.

Enough has been said to underscore the significance of 'the Scottish anomaly'. As Bogdanor observes, the continuing sense of Scottish distinctiveness has meant that:

> There is . . . some degree of conflict between the idea of sovereignty of Parliament and the idea of the sovereignty of the Scottish people. From this point of view the Scotland Act

[39] See, eg, Scotland Act 1998, ss 31–3. In the first example of such pre-legislative scrutiny, the UK Supreme Court recently confirmed that provisions in the Local Government Byelaws (Wales) Bill 2012 fell within the legislative competence of the Welsh Assembly. See *Local Government Byelaws (Wales) Bill—Reference by the Attorney General for England and Wales* [2012] UKSC 53, [2013] 1 All ER 1013.

[40] See B Winetrobe, 'A Partnership of the Parliaments? Scottish Law Making Under the Sewel Convention at Westminster and Holyrood' in R Hazell and R Rawlings (eds) *Devolution Law Making and the Constitution* (Imprint Academic 2005); G Anthony and J Morison, 'Here, There, and (Maybe) Here Again: The Story of Law Making for Post-1998 Northern Ireland' in R Hazell and R Rawlings (eds) *Devolution Law Making and the Constitution* (Imprint Academic 2005).

[41] Neil Walker, in Chapter 2 in this volume, also notes the progressive questioning of sovereignty buttressed by devolution, with the Scottish Government regarding devolution as a staging post on a journey towards an independent sovereign State. See the Scottish Government, *Scotland's Future: From the Referendum to Independence and a Written Constitution* (February 2013).

[42] *Robinson v Secretary of State for Northern Ireland* [2002] UKHL 32, [2002] NI 390 [25] (Lord Hoffmann).

[1998] represents a self-generated constitution... rather than, as the term devolution implies, one imposed by Westminster.[43]

The upshot was that, even prior to the contemporary debate over independence for Scotland, sovereignty already represented something different in Scotland (as it also did in Northern Ireland). Popular support in Scotland for these Scottish institutions meant that the scope for Westminster to change fundamental assumptions relating to Scotland had practical limitations. Professor Hadfield goes even further by suggesting that as a result of the referendum process which preceded its introduction a principle of 'necessary popular consent' has been built into the foundations of devolution. Such a view runs counter to the traditional doctrine of the sovereignty of Parliament and it follows from this that the formative principles of devolution should not be unilaterally amended by the Westminster Parliament.[44]

(3) The referendum on independence for Scotland

From the standpoint of the challenge to sovereignty the question of Scottish independence raises constitutional questions which have obvious parallels with the situation in Ireland post-1920. Following its success in the 2007 election for the Scottish Parliament, the Scottish National Party ('SNP'), which as the largest party went on to form a minority government, were keen to allow the Scottish people to express their view on independence in a referendum. Although the SNP government launched a debate in the form of a 'National Conversation' supported by a White Paper on independence,[45] without a majority in the Scottish Parliament it was not possible to fulfil that commitment. In any event the Scotland Act 1998 specifies that reserved matters for Westminster include aspects of the constitution affecting the union of the Kingdoms of Scotland and England.[46] In consequence, legislation introduced in the Scottish Parliament by the Scottish Government proposing a referendum which was intended to go beyond consultation could have been challenged under section 29 of the Scotland Act 1998 as falling outside its legislative competence. The political situation changed in May 2011 when the Scottish Nationalist Party, with a similar manifesto commitment to hold a referendum on independence, secured an overall majority in the Scottish Parliament. But a unilateral decision by the Scottish Government to hold such a referendum would no doubt have led to litigation.[47] In the event, the government at Westminster entered into direct negotiations with the Scottish Government on the holding of such a

[43] See V Bogdanor, 'Devolution and the Territorial Constitution', Gresham Lecture, 2005, available at <http://www.gresham.ac.uk/lectures-and-events/devolution-and-the-territorial-constitution> (last accessed 23 April 2013).

[44] B Hadfield, 'Devolution: A National Conversation?' in J Jowell and D Oliver (eds) *The Changing Constitution* (7th edn, OUP 2011) 218.

[45] The Scottish Government, *Your Scotland, Your Voice: A National Conversation*, November 2009, available at <http://www.scotland.gov.uk/Publications/2009/11/26155932/0> (last accessed 27 April 2013).

[46] See Scotland Act 1998, sch 5, para 1(1)(b).

[47] Select Committee on the Constitution, *The Agreement on a Referendum on Independence for Scotland* (Seventh Report) (HL Paper (2012–13) no 62) paras 15–25.

referendum. However, while the Scottish electorate had been consulted twice on the issue of independence before entering these negotiations, the Conservatives and the Liberal Democrats had no such authority from the UK electorate and the UK electorate were not being offered the opportunity to be consulted either in a general election or a referendum.

The Scottish Government entered the negotiations seeking a referendum featuring two questions.[48] The first would have been on the issue of an independent Scotland and the second question would have concerned so-called 'Devolution Max'. In other words Scottish voters would have the opportunity to express a second preference for an enhanced form of devolution as a fall-back position. The varying definitions of Devolution Max considerably overlap with the measures contained in the Scotland Act 2012 granting additional tax-raising powers and additional devolved powers to the Scottish Parliament.[49] Despite the persuasive constitutional reasons for holding a referendum on extending devolution, the second question on Devolution Max was dropped as a part of the political negotiations between the two governments. Had the Scottish electorate voted yes on the first question of independence, the second question would have been redundant. On the other hand, the second question would have been an opportunity for the Scottish electorate to vote on the extension of powers under the Scotland Act 2012 or otherwise proposed by the SNP. Following the Edinburgh Agreement between the Scottish Government and the Westminster Government in October 2012 for a legally binding referendum, an order in council under section 30 of the Scotland Act 1998 was made. This has allowed legislation to be introduced in the Scottish Parliament for a single question referendum to be held on Scottish independence on 18 September 2014.[50] The Scottish Government had proposed: 'Do you agree that Scotland should be an independent country?' The House of Commons Scottish Affairs Committee believed that this referendum question was biased.[51] Moreover, the House of Lords Constitution Committee and the Scottish Affairs Committee were in no doubt that the Electoral Commission was the oversight body suited to apply the criterion of intelligibility through evidence-based analysis and that the Commission should be involved in reviewing the wording of referendum questions as 'an important constitutional check on executive power, one that clearly facilitates parliamentary scrutiny'.[52] In any event, the Commission concluded that the formulation 'Do you agree…' could lead people towards voting 'yes' and its

[48] Select Committee on the Constitution (n 47) (2012–13) paras 1–14.

[49] The Scottish Parliament will be able to set its own income tax rates, introduce a land tax, and landfill tax, as well having borrowing powers of up to £2 billion.

[50] See Scottish Independence Referendum (Franchise) Bill 2013 (which prescribes the rules for who can vote in a referendum on Scottish independence) and the Scottish Independence Referendum Bill 2013 (which prescribes the rules for voting and sets out the rules for how the poll should be conducted).

[51] Scottish Affairs Committee, *The Referendum on Separation for Scotland: Do You Agree this is a Biased Question?* (Eighth Report) (HC Paper (2010–12) no 1942).

[52] Constitution Committee, *Referendum on Scottish Independence* (Twenty-fourth Report) (HL Paper (2010–12) no 263) ch 3, paras 8 and 48; Scottish Affairs Committee, *The Referendum on Separation for Scotland: The Proposed Section 30 Order—Can a Player Also be the Referee?* (Sixth Report) (HC Paper (2012–13) no 863) para 36.

recommendation of a more neutral wording has been accepted by the Scottish Government.[53] The question to be put will be: 'Should Scotland be an independent country? Yes/No.'[54]

The electoral success of the SNP resulted in agreement on the principle of holding a referendum on the question of independence but further difficulties arise in promoting an informed debate over the precise terms of independence.[55] At one level this involves the practical task of regulation to ensure fair practice and the dissemination of accurate information by both camps in advance of the referendum.[56] At another, the debate itself is limited because the two governments are effectively precluded from entering any pre-negotiation on the terms for independence. Until the result of a referendum suggests otherwise, UK government ministers must represent the whole of the United Kingdom, including Scotland, and must continue to serve the interest of all UK citizens. In consequence, not only the timetable and process but also crucial issues, such as international treaty obligations, the future currency of an independent Scotland, and disposition of the armed forces, can only be agreed by the UK and Scottish Governments following a referendum result in favour of independence.[57] Voters in Scotland must therefore decide on their future without knowing the answers to many pivotal questions.

(4) Franchise issues

The construction of the franchise in relation to referendums is a natural point of controversy. For example, the re-launch of devolution in Northern Ireland was made dependent on referendums held both in the Republic of Ireland and in Northern Ireland. By contrast, in Scotland and Wales the referendums were confined to the electorates within the devolved entities rather than extended to include the electorate of the United Kingdom. The failure to consult the English electorate appears

[53] I Jack, 'Scotland's Independence Referendum Question is Set, But Who Does it Favour?' *The Guardian*, London, 8 February 2013.

[54] The Electoral Commission, *Referendum on Independence for Scotland: Advice of the Electoral Commission on the Proposed Referendum Question*, January 2013, available at <http://www.electoralcommission.org.uk/__data/assets/pdf_file/0007/153691/Referendum-on-independence-for-Scotland-our-advice-on-referendum-question.pdf> (last accessed 23 April 2013).

[55] It was agreed on 15 October 2012 by both governments as part of the Edinburgh agreement that the election should be fair and command the confidence of both sides of the debate. The subsequent section 30 order under the Scotland Act 1998 allowed the Scottish Parliament to legislate on the organization of matters relating to the referendum. The Bill was introduced 11 March 2013 as the Scottish Independence Referendum (Franchise) SP Bill (2013, session four) ss 4–10.

[56] The PPERA places legal constraints on donations but the advisory role of the UK Electoral Commission as an impartial referee on such matters of campaign funding was not explicitly accepted by the Scottish Government. See House of Commons, Scottish Affairs Committee, *The Referendum on Separation for Scotland: The Proposed Section 30 Order—Can a Player Also be the Referee?* (Sixth Report) (HC Paper (2012–13) no 863) para 16.

[57] See Scotland Office, HM Treasury, and Cabinet Office, *Scotland Analysis: Devolution and the Implications of Scottish Independence* (Cm 8554, 2013) para 2.45. The Scottish Government has set out its own vision for Scotland in *Scotland's Future: From the Referendum to Independence and a Written Constitution*, February 2013, available at <http://www.scotland.gov.uk/Resource/0041/00413757.pdf> (last accessed 25 April 2013).

to neglect the fact that any change sanctioned by a referendum would be certain to impact England. The case for a UK plebiscite is that Scotland, Wales, and Northern Ireland belong to a larger entity and all the people should therefore have a voice in deciding the future shape of the United Kingdom. Although the secession of Scotland has profound consequences for the United Kingdom, the electorate in England, Wales, and Northern Ireland would have exercised no democratic input into the decision. In particular, there has been no general election where the matter of holding a referendum or indeed any policy relating to Scottish independence has been placed directly before the UK electorate. In the light of the debate over a referendum on Scottish independence it is worth stating again that Ireland's change of constitutional status did not derive from a British cession of territory but from an assertion by the Irish people of their nationhood.[58] On the other hand, when devolution was introduced in 1998 the view of the wider UK electorate had a direct mandate in the Westminster Parliament. Labour and Liberal Democrats MPs were elected in 1997 on a platform of devolution and then Parliament passed the devolution legislation after appropriate parliamentary deliberation.[59] From a somewhat different perspective, there might have been a case for extending the franchise in an independence referendum to allow Scottish nationals living outside the territory to participate. The idea of consulting a wider electorate was rejected on the grounds of an interest test. It was reasoned that only residents would be bound by the laws enacted at a devolved level and contribute financially to taxes at the devolved level.[60] Lastly, the wider franchise for the 2014 independence referendum follows the precedent of the 1997 devolution referendum and is on the same basis as for Scottish parliamentary and local government elections but the Edinburgh agreement in 2012 conceded responsibility for regulating the franchise to the Scottish Government which provides scope for them to lower the voting age to 16. The commitment to achieve this end required the enactment of special provisions to allow for the registration of all eligible 16- and 17-year-old voters.[61]

C. The Popular Will and Devolution: New Forms of Legitimation and Their Consequences

Against this backdrop, let us now consider the broader implications of the use of referendums in the context of devolution. The referendums which were held in 1979 in Scotland and Wales to confirm the devolution legislation passed in

[58] Hadfield (n 26) 603.

[59] As constitutional statutes the committee stage of the devolution legislation was considered by a committee of the whole house rather than a standing/Public Bill committee.

[60] Tierney (n 11) 77.

[61] See Scottish Independence Referendum (Franchise) Act 2013 (n 55) ss 4–10, and the associated Policy Memorandum available at <http://www.scottish.parliament.uk/S4_Bills/Scottish%20Independence%20Referendum%20Franchise%20Bill/b24s4-introd-pm.pdf> (last accessed 25 April 2013).

1978 under the Labour government,[62] and then again in 1997 to secure approval for devolution under the Blair government, support the view that a convention has been established indicating that constitutional changes of this magnitude relating to the de-centralization of sub-national governance require a referendum.[63] Devolution was founded on a new kind of politics which was intended to bring government closer to the people.[64] Although in Wales ideas tended to be developed as an internal party issue within the Welsh Labour Party[65] in Scotland the process of democratic participation as a prelude to devolution in 1999 originated with an all-party campaign for a Scottish Assembly in 1980. Later this was followed by the establishment of a Scottish Constitutional Convention in 1989.[66] The Convention was responsible for developing concrete proposals for legislation and it took the view that the powers of any future Scottish Parliament should not be altered without the consent of the Scottish Parliament representing the people of Scotland.[67] The work of the Scottish Constitutional Convention was fed into the drafting of a White Paper that established principles later to be incorporated in the Scotland Act 1998.[68] Not surprisingly the Scottish Parliament was described by Donald Dewar, former Secretary of State for Scotland and initial incumbent as First Minister, as 'the settled will of the Scottish people'.[69]

The devolution arrangements introduced under the Labour Government elected in 1997 can be regarded as an expression of a form of popular sovereignty since in each case the legislation was preceded by this process of consultation and its introduction then depended on a referendum. Popular sovereignty was consolidated because the local electorates in Scotland, Wales, and Northern Ireland were consulted in advance of the implementation of the devolution bills. Admittedly in Wales there was only a marginal vote in favour of the bill, reflecting tepid enthusiasm for devolution,[70] but in May 1998 there were separate referendums on the same day in the Irish Republic and Northern Ireland which demonstrated support for the Good Friday Agreement. Here, it was important to be able to show the approval of nationalists north and south of the border as well as a majority among unionists.[71] In Scotland following the publication of the White Paper the electorate were asked whether a Scottish Parliament should be established and whether it should have tax-raising powers. Although there was stronger endorsement for the

[62] The result in Scotland was 51.6 per cent in favour and 48.3 per cent against of a 63.8 per cent turnout, and in Wales 20.26 per cent in favour and 79.74 per cent against with a turnout of 58 per cent. Both bills failed as a threshold of 40 per cent of all voters were required to support devolution.

[63] Hadfield (n 44) 221.

[64] R Rawlings, *Delineating Wales: Constitutional, Legal and Administrative Aspects of National Devolution* (University of Cardiff Press 2003) 36.

[65] Rawlings (n 64) 34.

[66] The convention included representatives from mainstream political parties with the exception of the Scottish Nationalists.

[67] *Scotland's Parliament, Scotland's Right* (Scottish Constitutional Convention 1995).

[68] The Scottish Office *Scotland's Parliament* (Cm 3658, 1997).

[69] McLean (n 25) 161.

[70] Rawlings (n 64) 48.

[71] C McCrudden, 'Northern Ireland and the British Constitution since the Belfast Agreement' in J Jowell and D Oliver (eds) *The Changing Constitution* (6th edn, OUP 2007) 235.

Scottish Parliament there was also a decisive 'yes' vote for tax-raising powers.[72] This initial endorsement by referendum of what might be regarded as constitutions for the devolved territories of the United Kingdom also suggests that the powers granted to the devolved Parliaments and Assemblies should not be significantly modified without the consent of the same electorate that originally sanctioned its introduction.[73] Nevertheless, it remains the case that any Act of the Westminster Parliament, including foundational devolution legislation, can be repealed or amended without any formal referendum requirement.[74] Since 1998 there have been several examples of legislation with referendum provisions relating to devolution, regional government, and local government.[75] In practice, the Scotland Act 2012 makes very significant changes to the Scotland Act 1998 and although the Scottish Parliament was consulted before the statute was enacted at Westminster, no referendum was held to gain the approval of the electorate in Scotland.

The shortcomings in the initial arrangements for Welsh devolution under the Government of Wales Act 1998 were partly addressed by the Richard Commission.[76] In taking forward the Commission's recommendations, the Government of Wales Act 2006 brought into effect the legal separation of the executive branch (Welsh Assembly Government) and the parliamentary branch (National Assembly of Wales).[77] Further, in order to overcome the problem of securing the passage of legislation required for Wales through the Westminster Parliament, the 2006 Act allowed the Assembly to make, with the approval of Westminster, a new form of delegated legislation termed a 'legislative competence order'.[78] The same Act specified that a referendum would be required before the National Assembly of Wales assumed full legislative powers. Such a referendum would be called if instigated by the Welsh Assembly Government and a two-thirds majority of the Assembly then voted in favour of holding one. At this point a request would be made to the Secretary of State for Wales who would lay the draft order before each of the Houses of Parliament or give notice in writing for refusing to do so.[79] Such a referendum was triggered in 2010 and after the Welsh electorate, in March 2011, voted 63.5 per cent in favour, the Assembly has full powers to legislate over matters listed in Schedule 7 of the Government Wales Act 2006. Not only does the use of a referendum emphasize the sovereignty of the people in determining the legislative powers of the National Assembly,[80] but it also provides 'statutory reinforcement of the established convention that any major change to devolution must be endorsed by the electorate as well as by the Assembly and the UK Parliament'.[81]

[72] N Burrows, *Devolution* (Sweet & Maxwell 2000) 17.

[73] We saw above that this was identified by Professor Hadfield as a 'principle of necessary popular consent'; see Hadfield (n 44) 218.

[74] Munro (n 30) 91.

[75] eg, Local Government Act 2000, part 2; Regional Assemblies (Preparations) Act 2003; and Government Wales Act 2006.

[76] See Richard Commission, *Powers and the Electoral Arrangements of the National Assembly for Wales*, 2004.

[77] R Rawlings, 'Hastening Slowly? The Next Phase of Welsh Devolution' [2005] *PL* 824.

[78] Government of Wales Act 2006, s 93. See also T Jones, 'Wales, Devolution and Sovereignty' (2012) 33 *Statute L Rev* 151.

[79] Government of Wales Act 2006, part 4.

[80] Jones (n 78) 152ff.

[81] Hadfield (n 44) 228.

The recommendations by the Calman Commission granting the Scottish Parliament enhanced tax-raising powers were incorporated into the Scotland Act 2012.[82] As mentioned, the measures included in the Scotland Act 2012 go some way towards achieving Devolution Max. In consequence, there are obvious reasons why the Westminster Parliament might have been expected to have included a referendum provision in relation to the legislation as a condition for its introduction. First, in terms of substance, the effect of the Scotland Act 2012 was to alter fundamentally the variable tax rate, a feature of Scottish Devolution that had been put to the electorate as a separate question back in 1998. Secondly, a referendum requirement might have been included on the basis that the Government of Wales Act 2006 establishes a precedent by requiring a referendum to be held in advance of making further far-reaching constitutional changes at the devolved level.[83] Thirdly, the need for consultation in a referendum might have been justified on the basis that a major redefinition of devolved powers related to revenue raising should be regarded as equivalent to a constitutional amendment for Scotland which, therefore, needed to be approved by the Scottish electorate.[84] Had there been a second question on Devolution Max on the ballot paper for the referendum on Scottish independence the electorate would have been given the opportunity to vote on the principle of the extension of powers.[85] The Commission on Devolution in Wales which recently reported on further fiscal powers for the devolved government provides further support for this approach. The Commission considers that a referendum should be held in advance of the Welsh Government and Assembly assuming responsibility for income tax given that this would represent a major change in the relationship between the citizen and the devolved administration.[86]

Viewed in the round, the experience of devolution demonstrates that there has been much more than a general trend towards participatory decision-making. The practice of holding referendums as a prelude to introducing devolved institutions has been established as a constitutional convention. This convention means, for example, that it is difficult to envisage any political attempt to dismantle or replace the main institutions of devolution without first gaining approval from the local electorate in Scotland, Wales, or Northern Ireland. However, at the same time the

[82] Commission on Scottish Devolution, *Serving Scotland Better: Scotland and the United Kingdom in the 21st Century* (Final Report) June 2009, recs 3.1–3.7 available at <http://www.commissiononscottishdevolution.org.uk/uploads/2009-06-12-csd-final-report-2009fbookmarked.pdf> (last accessed 25 April 2013).

[83] The change which prompted the 2011 Welsh referendum was the conferral of law-making powers as opposed to tax-raising powers but the Scotland Act 2012 also transfers more functions to the Scottish Parliament and confers other tax-raising powers.

[84] See Hadfield (n 44) 218.

[85] The Northern Ireland (St Andrews Agreement) Act 2006 is another significant piece of devolution legislation which might have been endorsed by referendum but there would have been a clear political risk in holding one.

[86] See Commission on Devolution in Wales, *Empowerment and Responsibility: Financial Powers to Strengthen Wales* (November 2012), ss 8.2.8 and 8.2.2.9, available at <http://commissionondevolutioninwales.independent.gov.uk/files/2012/11/English-WEB-Executive-Summary.pdf> (last accessed 25 April 2013). The Silk Commission on Devolution in Wales was established in October 2011 by the Secretary of State for Wales to review the case for the devolution of fiscal powers to the National Assembly of Wales and to review the powers of the National Assembly for Wales.

divergence in practice between the Government of Wales Act 2006 and the Scotland Act 2012 over the holding of referendums demonstrates a lack of consistency. In Section D of this chapter further anomalies are shown to arise concerning the use of referendums in the context of local government which have similar constitutional implications.

D. Popular Sovereignty and the Redefinition of Local Democracy

In political terms the Localism Act 2011 has been presented as an important vehicle for the delivery of the Coalition Government's 'big society' agenda,[87] but it is discussed here as a statute which has far reaching legal and constitutional implications for local governance. The Act not only transforms the legal relationship between central and local government, but it also employs referendums as a means for policy delivery in a novel fashion which has profound implications for local democracy. The Act was drafted to implement an agenda of decentralization under which 'power should be held at the lowest possible level, whether this is individuals, communities, neighbourhoods, local institutions, or local government'.[88] But it has also been criticized for attempting to further centralize power.[89]

The localism White Paper and the original Bill had advocated using local referendums as a means of validating new forms of citizen empowerment.[90] In any neighbourhood, community groups (comprising citizens, voluntary organizations, and businesses) seeking to take on services traditionally in the hands of local government would have been able to petition the local community to hold a referendum on this community right to challenge or right to bid. A positive result would not have been binding but would have provided authority for the transfer of functions to the community.[91] Although a community right to challenge and a community right to bid to deliver such services are retained as part of the Act, the particular proposal to stage referendums has been dropped as this device could have been exploited by community groups dominated by powerful individuals or by sectional interests.[92]

[87] V Lowndes and L Pratchett, 'Local Governance under the Coalition Government: Austerity, Localism and the "Big Society"' (2012) 38 *Local Government Studies* 21, 22; MJ Smith, 'From Big Government to Big Society: Changing the State-Society Balance' (2010) 63 *Parliamentary Affairs* 818.

[88] Communities and Local Government Committee, *Localism* (Third Report) (HC Paper (2010–11), no 547) para 15.

[89] Communities and Local Government Committee (2010–11) paras 49 and 69 by Professors George Jones and John Stewart. See also J Crowe, 'The Government's Plans for Decentralisation and Localism: A Progress Report' (2011) 82 *The Political Quarterly* 651, 656.

[90] Department for Communities and Local Government, *Decentralisation and the Localism Bill: An Essential Guide*, December 2010, 11, available at <https://www.gov.uk/government/publications/decentralisation-and-the-localism-bill-an-essential-guide--2> (last accessed 23 April 2013).

[91] T Bovaird, 'Community Rights to Challenge and Take Over Services and to Buy Public Assets' in J Raine and C Staite (eds) *The World Will Be Your Oyster?* (Institute of Local Government Studies, University of Birmingham, 2011).

[92] *Decentralism and the Localism Bill* (n 90).

In a different context, the Secretary of State has powers under the Localism Act 2011 to call referendums in regard to local governance arrangements. The powers under the Act have since been used to compel England's largest cities to hold referendums on adopting a revised system of governance based upon a directly elected Mayor and Cabinet model.[93] Where these referendums turn out in favour of a directly elected Mayor the governance structure of the authority in question must be modified accordingly. This degree of intervention by the Coalition Government can be contrasted with the approach of the previous Labour Government. It had also responded to what was regarded as a crisis in local government by setting out a variety of revised arrangements for the governance structure of councils but it allowed each local authority to decide whether to call a referendum on its own initiative.[94] A piecemeal approach on a region by region basis was also applied by Labour in 2003 to the attempted implementation of proposals for regional government. This scheme depended on a referendum triggered by the Secretary of State in each of the designated regions to approve the principle. The proposals were subsequently abandoned after being overwhelmingly rejected by voters in the North East region referendum in November 2004.[95]

From a constitutional standpoint, the most obvious failing under these pieces of legislation, and now under the Localism Act, is the failure to require a referendum to be held nationwide on the broad principle of the form that democratically elected regional or local government should take, rather than leaving the Secretary of State or local authorities with a wide discretion to decide upon the referendum arrangements.

Under the Localism Act 2011, local authorities in England proposing to increase the level of council tax above a limit set by the Secretary of State will be compelled to hold a referendum to gain approval from local electors.[96] The new scheme replaces the previous regimes of rate capping operating under successive governments since the 1980s.[97] The revised approach has been presented as an extension of democracy.[98] Councils are now required by gaining direct approval to demonstrate the support of local people for any such increase. The onus is thus shifted onto any local authority which plans to exceed the centrally set levels of spending to convince its electors that the rise is justified. The council in question

[93] This requirement would have applied to the twelve largest cities in England but Leicester elected its first mayor in May 2011 and Liverpool City Council pre-empted the holding of a referendum when the council voted overwhelmingly to opt for a directly elected mayor in February 2012. See A Bounds, 'Elected Mayor to Run Liverpool' *Financial Times*, London, 8 February 2012.

[94] eg, Department of Transport, Local Government, and Regions, *Modern Local Government: In Touch with the People* (White Paper, Cm 4014, 1998).

[95] See the Regional Assemblies (Preparations) Act 2003, which, for example, enabled the government to specify the region(s) able to hold a referendum on an elected regional assembly and to fix the date of the poll. It also allowed the government to set out the questions to be asked and determine those eligible to vote in such a referendum. See P Leyland, 'Post Devolution: Crystallising the Future of Regional Government for England' 56 (2005) *Northern Ireland Legal Quarterly* 435, 453.

[96] Localism Act 2011, s 72 and sch 5.

[97] See Local Government Finance Acts 1982, 1987, 1988, and 1992.

[98] I Leigh, 'The Changing Nature of Local and Regional Democracy' in J Jowell and D Oliver (eds), *The Changing Constitution* (7th edn, OUP 2011) 248.

is faced with the task of organizing and funding the referendum triggered in its locality. Failure to achieve a majority will result in the automatic implementation of a pre-prepared substitute budget which is in compliance with the principles set by the Secretary of State.[99]

The minister is here given a formidable delegated power. While the Act specifies conditions under which a referendum must be called, namely when the authority has exceeded the limit set, the parameters for triggering the referendum are essentially determined by the Secretary of State. It is the minister who sets a uniform national set of principles annually in a report laid before the House of Commons.[100] A local authority must then either apply the substitute calculations which conform to the national policy or gamble on the outcome of a referendum. The result of the referendum is binding and it applies on a bare majority without any regard to the level of turnout.[101] In addition, the local authority is penalized as it is required to pay for the cost of the referendum. For the first year of its implementation (2013–14) 150 council had agreed to a freeze. Nevertheless, in order to remain within the 2 per cent threshold and avoid the prospect of having to hold a referendum, a number of local councils increased their council tax by 1.99 per cent. Only sixteen councils proposed increasing their spending beyond this figure and thus requiring a local referendum to be held.[102]

The new capping procedure has to be judged against the background of sweeping cuts to local government budgets. In a wider sense the provision for capping referendums can be regarded as a mechanism for consolidating the centralization of power.[103] By setting the principles under which an increase is determined as being excessive it is the Secretary of State, on behalf of central government, who determines the general level of council tax without having to take account of conditions relating to each and every authority. Until such time as the Act is amended or repealed the referendum provision relating to excessive council tax increases is set in place as a new type of limitation on power which is activated without any direct intervention from the Secretary of State and with minimal recognition of base national standards in services needed to protect the most vulnerable in society.[104] Moreover, although the principles for setting council tax must be laid before Parliament there is no formal provision for detailed scrutiny of the wider implications of the spending limits.

The fact that referendums are required after an elected council has taken a decision obviously calls into question the democratic credibility of local democracy. What is the point of having elected local councillors to take such decisions if the outcome

[99] Localism Act 2011, s 72 and sch 5, new chapter, 52ZQ. Under the Act the Secretary of State is empowered to make regulations for the conduct of these 'council tax' referendums after consulting the Electoral Commission which are then laid before Parliament in draft form.

[100] Localism Act 2011, sch 5; Local Government Finance Act 1992, new chapters 4ZA, 52ZC/D.

[101] Localism Act 2011, sch 5, new chapter 52ZH.

[102] C Hope and R Winnett, 'Defiant Councils Planning Tax Rises' *Daily Telegraph*, London, 14 February 2013.

[103] See G Jones and J Stewart, 'Reflections on the Localism Bill' in J Raine and C Staite (eds) *The World Will Be Your Oyster?* (Institute of Local Government Studies, University of Birmingham 2011) 100.

[104] *Localism* (n 88) para 75.

is overridden by a minority of the local electorate in a referendum? But an even more pressing concern, viewed against the backdrop of the post-Second World War universal welfare State, is one of fragmentation of the delivery of policy. It has been widely recognized that '[c]ommunities can be exclusive, on grounds of race or gender. They can actually erode the promotion of equality and rights.'[105] With no turnout threshold established under the Act, the majority against the council tax rise could consist of a small minority of those entitled to vote. There is strong evidence to suggest that the pursuit of social justice requires an active central State. The employment of referendums on an uncertain basis in different parts of the country to regulate local government spending and council tax levels could lead to considerable discrepancies in welfare provision. In this context, the façade of democratization provided by referendums to encourage financial restraint is clearly at the expense of the autonomy of elected councils to decide spending levels and local tax rates. In consequence, the new power amounts to a perverse exercise in popular sovereignty.

E. Conclusion

This chapter has reflected on a growing tension between the well-established forms of representative democracy and the exercise of popular sovereignty through referendums in the context of the territorial constitution. The development bears testimony to the evolution of a new style of constitutionalism in the United Kingdom. Only recently has Parliament regarded the need to demonstrate popular support as a pre-condition for the introduction of reform. Referendums were used to provide legitimation for devolved government, both for the aborted attempt in the 1970s, and then to approve the current settlement in the 1990s. This important element of popular sovereignty experienced at the level of sub-national government has allowed direct citizen participation through the holding of referendums. Moreover, this form of consultation has been recognized as a convention of the contemporary constitution. In place of the traditional political sovereignty of the electorate expressed through an elected Parliament, referendums concerning devolution, and other sub-national changes to governance, demonstrate a shift towards promoting direct citizen involvement in decision-making at a constitutional level. But it will also be apparent from this discussion that any claim that referendums are a valid legitimating device indicating the consent of the majority depends upon the conditions under which they are held.

Indeed, while the case of territorial governance demonstrates a welcome extension of popular sovereignty it also illustrates the potential for abuse. In the absence of a general set of constitutional rules governing their use, referendums have been employed under a variety of statutes on a pragmatic basis. We have seen that the lack of regulation has opened up the potential for manipulation of referendums, and with the Localism Act there is a further danger of undermining fundamental assumptions underpinning the

[105] R Hattersley and K Hickson, 'In Praise of Social Democracy' (2011) 83 *The Political Quarterly* 8.

welfare State. From a constitutional standpoint, the degree of inconsistency in the availability of referendums is simply anomalous and unsupportable.

An advantage of adopting a codified constitution is that the text would be likely to contain rules limiting the application of referendums to a set of situations which have been foreseen, or fit a given set of rules. This type of regulation would prevent the device from being easily manipulated by politicians. In a proposed draft constitution for the United Kingdom, Richard Gordon links the holding of referendums to obtaining approval for constitutional amendments. Otherwise, there are strict rules attached. In particular, a threshold of 20 per cent of voters petitioning the House of Representatives (the body replacing the House of Commons in this draft constitution) would be required before a referendum could be triggered on a specified list of topics.[106]

Another possibility would be to link restrictions on the holding of constitutional referendums to proposals for constitutional changes. But how would these be defined in relation to the UK Constitution? Laws LJ in *Thoburn v Sunderland City Council*[107] explained the meaning of constitutional in statutory terms as being when the legislation either conditions the legal relationship between the citizen and State in some general, overarching manner, or enlarges or diminishes the scope of what are regarded as fundamental constitutional rights.[108] Although it would be difficult to achieve any strict categorization, it is possible to recognize matters which qualify as constitutional by considering the potential constitutional effects. Any list would now include fundamental questions concerning national sovereignty, entry to, or continued membership of, supra-national commitments such as the EU or European Convention on Human Rights, changes to democratic principles such as electoral reform, changes to law-making powers, changes to the structure and fundamental powers at the level of territorial governance, and changes to fundamental constitutional rights. A test to establish whether a referendum would need to be held would ask, first, whether there is an established precedent for having one, and secondly, whether the change can be justified given the political and constitutional context without first consulting the wider electorate on the issue.

As there is no sign on the horizon of the promulgation of an entrenched constitution a dedicated piece of constitutional legislation is called for to regulate referendums. This statute would itself need to be legitimated by referendum to make it more difficult to repeal. First and foremost, such a 'Constitutional Referendum Act' should set out conditions for the constitutional use of referendums. It is envisaged that the Act would set up an independent commission with responsibility for drafting rules to determine when referendums might be called and how, in practice, they should be managed. The rules would not only recognize established convention, but they would apply to legislation associated with constitution-building or which affects the location and distribution of sovereign power within the State.

[106] R Gordon, *Repairing British Politics: A Blue Print for Constitutional Change* (Hart Publishing 2010) 161.

[107] *Thoburn v Sunderland City Council* [2002] EWHC 195 (Admin), [2003] QB 151.

[108] *Thoburn* (n 107) 186 para 62.

10

The United Kingdom, the European Union, and Sovereignty

*Paul Craig**

A. Introduction

This chapter explores the relationship between the United Kingdom, the European Union, and sovereignty. It is not however the standard legal account, much beloved or hated, by first year law students asked to consider how far the traditional Diceyan conception of parliamentary sovereignty has or has not been affected by UK membership of the EU. The chapter is built instead around three principal legislative and political initiatives of the Coalition Government led by David Cameron that have had, or will have, a marked impact on the relationship with the EU, and reflects on what they have to tell us about UK sovereignty. This focus has the virtue of chiming with real world events that affect the relationship between the United Kingdom and the EU.

The discussion begins with the major legislative initiative that constrains the giving of new power to the EU, the European Union Act 2011, inquiring as to what we can learn from this about Parliament, referendums, and the body politic. It is followed by examination of the government's initiative to repatriate power in the area of policing and criminal justice by invoking an opt-out contained in the Lisbon Treaty. This then sets the scene for the final section of the chapter, which analyses the more general demands for repatriation of power that are already being pressed by Conservative Party Eurosceptics in advance of the referendum promised by the Prime Minister David Cameron after renegotiation of the United Kingdom's terms of membership.[1] It will be seen that each of these events reveals interesting insights, normative as well as political, into UK sovereignty and membership of the EU.

* Professor of English Law, St John's College, University of Oxford.

[1] D Cameron, EU Speech at Bloomberg, 23 January 2013, available at <http://www.number10.gov.uk/news/eu-speech-at-bloomberg> (last accessed 20 April 2013).

B. Sovereignty and 'Giving Power': Referendums and the European Union Act 2011

(1) The genesis of the legislation

The European Union Act 2011 was the initial, 'high visibility' legislative initiative from the Coalition Government, in which it staked its ground for subsequent dealings with the EU. The promise of legislation enshrining a referendum lock was contained in the Coalition's Plan for Government,[2] but its inclusion and subsequent passage is credited in part at least with the Prime Minister's perceived need to offer something tangible to Tory Eurosceptics, who had been pressing for an in/out referendum on UK membership of the EU. David Cameron's stance for some considerable time after the election was that this was neither necessary, nor desirable. What became the European Union Act 2011 was thus designed to appease restless and potentially rebellious backbenchers by giving them a concrete measure curbing growth in EU power. This is of course somewhat paradoxical, since the Prime Minister subsequently conceded on the referendum desired by the Eurosceptics.

The European Union Act 2011 is predicated on the assumption that the UK government of the day supports an increase in the EU's power, since if it was opposed it would veto the change, which could not then be made because the requisite unanimity would be lacking. The 2011 legislation stipulates that such an increase in EU power cannot be achieved merely through an affirmative vote in Parliament. This is a necessary, but not sufficient, condition for such change. There must also, subject to limited exceptions, be a positive vote in a referendum.[3] The legislation is strengthened by the broad range of changes that trigger the need for a referendum. Thus any conferral of a new competence, or extension of an existing competence, has this effect,[4] and a referendum is demanded also for a plethora of other EU decisions, such as those which invoke passerelle provisions in the Lisbon Treaty, in order to move from, for example, a requirement of unanimity to one of qualified majority.[5] There are in addition provisions requiring EU decisions to be approved by Act of Parliament,[6] or some other form of parliamentary control.[7]

This is not the place for detailed exegesis on the legislation, and the difficulties involved therewith. This can be found elsewhere.[8] The objective is rather to focus on the conception of sovereignty in the European Union Act 2011. This is at its most fundamental predicated on the precept that power should reside with the UK Parliament, and that any transfer thereof should be subject to the twin constraints of approval by Act of Parliament and a positive vote in a referendum. This was

[2] *The Coalition: Our Programme for Government*, 20 May 2010, available at <https://www.gov.uk/government/publications/the-coalition-documentation> (last accessed 18 April 2013).

[3] European Union Act 2011, ss 2–3. [4] Section 4. [5] Section 6.

[6] Sections 7–8. [7] Sections 9–10.

[8] P Craig, 'The European Union Act 2011: Locks, Limits and Legality' (2011) 48 *CML Rev* 1881.

reinforced by the very imagery of 'referendum lock' used in the political documentation.[9] The remainder of Section B explores this conception.

(2) Referendums and the UK constitution

It is helpful in terms of perspective to reflect on the use of the referendum in the United Kingdom, before considering the schema in the 2011 Act. There has been considerable debate about the desirability of referendums.[10] It is not possible in this chapter to traverse this terrain, nor is it necessary, because the House of Lords' Select Committee on the Constitution recently produced an admirable report, which contained a balanced summary of the contending arguments.[11]

The arguments favouring referendums were that they enhanced the democratic process, made it difficult to reverse a policy that had demonstrable public support, fostered citizen political engagement, and were popular with voters. The arguments against were that referendums were often used as tactical devices by the government, they were dominated by elite groups, they could be a block on progress, they were ill-suited to complex issues, voting was often not about the issue put to a referendum, they were costly, and voter participation was frequently rather low.

The Committee concluded that on the balance of the evidence there were significant drawbacks to referendums,[12] but that if they were to be used it should be in relation to issues of constitutional importance.[13] While the Select Committee acknowledged the difficulty of defining what was of fundamental constitutional importance, it nonetheless produced a non-exhaustive list of matters that it felt should qualify in this regard.[14]

It should be noted when reflecting on the constitutional background to the referendum requirements in the European Union Act 2011 that no such requirement is stipulated, or has been argued for, in relation to UK ratification of the approximately 14,000 other international treaties to which the United Kingdom is a party.[15] Nor is this required in relation to any extension of the powers of such bodies. Now it might of course be argued that the EU is different in this respect because of the reach and potency of EU law. Thus on this view the supremacy of EU law, combined with direct effect, give it a peremptory force within the United Kingdom that other treaties lack. There is some force in this argument, although space precludes detailed examination of the complex conceptual premises that underpin it.

[9] *Programme for Government* (n 2) 19.

[10] S Tierney, *Constitutional Referendums: A Theory and Practice of Republican Deliberation* (OUP 2012). See also Chapter 9 in this volume by Peter Leyland.

[11] Select Committee on the Constitution, *Referendums in the United Kingdom* (HL Paper (2009–10) no 99.

[12] *Referendums in the United Kingdom* (n 11) 209.

[13] *Referendums in the United Kingdom* (n 11) 210.

[14] *Referendums in the United Kingdom* (n 11) 210: abolishing the monarchy; leaving the EU; secession from the United Kingdom by one of the constituent nations; abolishing either House of Parliament; changing the electoral system for the House of Commons; adopting a written constitution; and changing the United Kingdom's system of currency.

[15] Foreign and Commonwealth Office 'UK Treaties' available at <http://www.fco.gov.uk/en/publications-and-documents/treaties> (last accessed 16 April 2013).

We should nonetheless keep this argument in perspective and not allow it to blind us to reality. The idea that all or most of the extensions of EU power for which a referendum is required by the 2011 Act entail greater constriction on national power than that contained in many other treaties that the government accedes to, subject only to parliamentary ratification, does not withstand examination. A mere glance at the treaties concluded by the executive since 1999 reveals the breadth, variety, and depth of such binding obligations, with subject matter ranging from crime to the environment, health to extradition, drugs to labour, and fisheries to trade.[16]

It should also be noted when thinking about referendums against the general UK constitutional background that there is commonly an asymmetry, in formal terms at least, between giving power and taking it back. The commonplace assumption is that a referendum is required 'more' when power is 'given away', than when it is 'taken back' through exit from an international treaty obligation. Thus, for example, there is no evidence that members of the Conservative Party who desire an exit from the European Convention on Human Rights ('ECHR') believe that the legitimacy of this change should be predicated on a referendum.

The obvious rejoinder is that the asymmetry is apparent rather than real, precisely because the two situations are not analogous. To give power away to an international organization based on treaty entails correlative limits on what national governments can do, given minimal assumptions of *pacta sunt servanda*. To take power back is, on this view, to increase national freedom of action, in the sense that government and Parliament can exercise their power unencumbered by pre-existing constraints, and the voters can express their approval or not of the way that the power is exercised through the traditional ballot box. There is some force in this view, but it is a good deal less secure than might initially be thought.

It is axiomatic that governments acting on behalf of the people sign international agreements, and Parliament ratifies them, because they believe that such agreements serve important purposes and are beneficial to the United Kingdom. The constraint on autonomous national action is felt to be worthwhile, given the benefits of collective action pursuant to the treaty. The treaties thus ratified do not moreover merely constrain national freedom. They also commonly constrain other States and thereby bring benefits to the United Kingdom through obligations relating to, for example, free movement, or extradition.

The dichotomy between 'giving power' and 'taking power back' nonetheless continues to exert a powerful force on the political imagination. It is thrown into sharp relief by the promise of an EU referendum after the next UK general election. The focus of such a referendum is noteworthy in this respect. It is assumed that it will be about whether the government has secured enough by way of repatriation of power to justify the United Kingdom's continued membership of the EU. The in/out referendum will be conducted against this backdrop. There is no hint that the UK public will be asked directly whether it believes that the government should seek to repatriate particular powers at all. Thus while supporters of the European

[16] UK Treaties (n 15).

Union Act 2011 zealously maintain that any grant of power to the EU, howsoever small, should require a referendum, they are equally zealous in the belief that any repatriation of power, howsoever large, does not. Government and Parliament are not entrusted to take the former decisions without positive assent from the people, but they can take the latter, even if it is arguable that the consequences for the UK national interest and power will be negative.

(3) Referendums and the European Union Act 2011

The Select Committee on the Constitution drew on the reasoning in its Referendums Report when it produced its Report on what became the European Union Act 2011.[17] The Committee noted 'the complex and highly technical nature of the referendum lock provisions',[18] which hindered transparency and accessibility in the law. It noted that the referendum requirements in what became the 2011 Act were 'wholly unprecedented in UK constitutional practice'.[19] The Committee applied its criterion from the earlier Report to the effect that referendums should in general be restricted to instances that were of constitutional significance, and concluded that the great majority of the instances where a referendum was mandatory under the 2011 Act were not of this nature. It concluded that:

> [in] specifying over 50 policy areas where a referendum would be or might be required, the European Union Bill is a radical step-change in the adoption of referendum provisions...[20] In our judgement, the resort to referendums contemplated in the European Union Bill is not confined to the category of fundamental constitutional issues on which a UK-wide referendum may be judged to be appropriate. Furthermore, many of the Bill's provisions are inconsistent with the Government's statement that referendums are most appropriately used in relation to fundamental constitutional issues.[21]

This is surely correct. The Committee's conclusion can be reinforced by reflecting on the 2011 Act in the light of the pros and cons of referendums adumbrated above. A moment's reflection reveals that the arguments in favour of referendums—that they enhance the democratic process, make it difficult to reverse a policy that has public support, foster citizen political engagement, and are popular with voters—are all predicated on the assumption that citizens exercise their right to vote in a referendum. If the numbers voting are small then the arguments favouring a referendum are undermined, and the legitimacy of the result, whatsoever it might be, is thereby diminished.

We cannot of course know the numbers that would turn out for a referendum under the 2011 Act, and the answer may of course differ depending on the particular change in EU power that triggers the referendum. We can nonetheless make an educated guess that in many instances the turnout will be very low, often embarrassingly so.

[17] Select Committee on the Constitution, *European Union Bill* (HL Paper (2010–11) no 121).
[18] Select Committee on the Constitution (n 17) 27.
[19] Select Committee on the Constitution (n 17) 28.
[20] Select Committee on the Constitution (n 17) 37.
[21] Select Committee on the Constitution (n 17) 38.

The idea that people will be flocking to the polling booths to vote for or against some technical extension of an existing EU competence does not withstand serious examination. The idea that they will do so for a referendum triggered by a passerelle clause that changes EU voting rules beggars belief. Low voter turnout would not fulfil the posited advantages associated with referendums, nor would it cloak the result with much by way of legitimacy.

All actions have consequences, and in this context they are both internal and external. In terms of internal domestic politics, it is likely that there would be popular backlash at the costs of holding a referendum, more especially in a period of financial stringency, in which there have been significant cuts in public services. They include the costs associated with explaining to the electorate what the proposed change in EU competence actually is, its significance in the more general schema of EU power, as well as the direct expenditure entailed by the actual running of the referendum in terms of voting sites, personnel, and the like. It is doubtful that the populace would view with equanimity what might amount to upwards of £50 million spent on a referendum,[22] given the opportunity costs involved in alternative uses of such funding. In terms of external politics, the Prime Minister would face considerable difficulties in explaining to colleagues in the European Council that the United Kingdom could not accede to a treaty amendment desired by the other Member States because the 'people' had spoken in a referendum with a very low turnout. It is doubtful in the extreme that other Member States would regard this result with equanimity, nor would they believe that it was cloaked with any real legitimacy. The potential backlash against the United Kingdom could take many forms, ranging from loss of influence to the blocking of other EU initiatives favoured by the United Kingdom.

C. Sovereignty and 'Taking Power Back': The Opt-Out

(1) The Treaty provisions

The European Union Act 2011 represents one response by the Coalition Government to sovereignty and the EU, by conditioning any extension of EU power on a referendum. The proposal to exercise a treaty opt-out from EU measures concerning the Area of Freedom, Security, and Justice ('AFSJ') indicates the desire to repatriate power. A brief background to the complex legal provisions is necessary.

The Lisbon Treaty contains transitional provisions relating to Union courts and enforcement as they pertain to some AFSJ measures.[23] Article 10(1) of the Protocol on Transitional Provisions specifies two limits to the powers of the institutions

[22] The 2011 referendum on the UK voting system was estimated by the Electoral Commission to have cost £75 million; The Electoral Commission, *The Costs of Running a UK-wide Poll Published for First Time*, 19 December 2012, available at <http://www.electoralcommission.org.uk/news-and-media/news-releases/electoral-commission-media-centre/news-releases-reviews-and-research/costs-of-running-a-uk-wide-poll-published-for-first-time> (last accessed 18 April 2013).

[23] Protocol (no 36) on Transitional Provisions [2008] OJ C115/322, Art 10.

with respect to acts of the Union in the field of police and judicial cooperation in criminal matters that were adopted before the entry into force of the Lisbon Treaty. First, the Commission's enforcement powers under Article 258 TFEU are not applicable and, secondly, the powers of the Court of Justice of the European Union ('CJEU') under what was the Third Pillar of the Maastricht Treaty remain the same, including where Member States accepted the preliminary ruling jurisdiction under what was Article 35(2) EU. These limits cease to have effect five years after entry into force of the Lisbon Treaty.[24] The limits are also inapplicable if a Third Pillar act is amended after the Lisbon Treaty enters into force.[25]

Article 10(4) of the Protocol is relevant to the United Kingdom. It states that at the latest six months before the expiry of the five year transitional period, the United Kingdom may notify to the Council that it does not accept, with respect to the Third Pillar acts passed before the Lisbon Treaty, the powers of the institutions referred to in Article 10(1) as set out in the Treaties. If the United Kingdom makes such a notification then Third Pillar acts adopted prior to the Lisbon Treaty cease to apply to it from the expiry of the transitional period. This is subject to the caveat that a Third Pillar act amended after the Lisbon Treaty enters into force that is applicable to the United Kingdom remains so. Article 10(5) of the Protocol however leaves the door open to the United Kingdom to notify the Council of its wish to participate in acts which have ceased to apply to it pursuant to Article 10(4). If the opt-out is exercised it operates in relation to all such measures, subject to the possibility that it can opt back in later, with the agreement of the other EU players.

The scope of the opt-out should be clarified to avoid confusion. It is only applicable to police and criminal justice measures adopted prior to the Lisbon Treaty and hence does not apply to new measures adopted thereafter, insofar as these apply to the United Kingdom. Protocol 21 of the Lisbon Treaty provides that the United Kingdom is not bound by measures adopted under the AFSJ Title, including those on crime and police cooperation, but that it can signify that it wishes to take part in the adoption of a proposed measure, and it can also opt-in after an AFSJ measure has been adopted.[26] There have been a number of new measures on EU criminal justice and policing measures and the United Kingdom has chosen to participate in most of them. It should moreover be noted that exercise of the opt-out in Article 10(4) of Protocol 36 would not remove the jurisdiction of the CJEU in all matters related to policing, crime, and criminal justice. Thus the CJEU has jurisdiction in relation to post Lisbon measures, and in relation to measures enacted under Treaty provisions to which Protocol 21 does not apply. It also has jurisdiction if the United Kingdom opts-in to measures that it had opted-out from.

[24] Protocol (no 36) (n 23) Art 10(3), which ends on 1 December 2014.

[25] Protocol (no 36) (n 23) Art 10(2).

[26] Protocol (no 21) On the Position of the United Kingdom and Ireland in respect of the Area of Freedom, Security and Justice.

(2) Sovereignty and politics

The political rationale underlying what became Article 10(4) of Protocol 36 is not free from doubt, but the best explanation is that the '"game plan" at the time was to preserve Maastricht, not to destroy it'.[27] Thus on this view the objective was not an escape route from the entirety of EU criminal justice, but preservation of the Maastricht principles that Third Pillar measures required unanimity and were not subject to the jurisdiction of the CJEU. The Lisbon Treaty removed both of these features, which were problematic, but this did not please the United Kingdom, hence the negotiation of the opt-out. The fact that the opt-out was cast in all or nothing terms was at the insistence of other Member States, who wished 'to discourage the United Kingdom from exercising the opt-out lightly, and also to avoid recurrent disruptions from the United Kingdom opting out of measures one by one'.[28]

The final decision as to whether to exercise the opt-out will is by Parliament. The Coalition Government has signalled its intent to make use of this legal power, but will seek to opt back in to some of the AFSJ measures including the European Arrest Warrant.[29] The Treaty demands that a decision whether to exercise the opt-out has to be made six months before the end of the transitional period, but the activation of the power was nonetheless inextricably involved with Conservative Party politics and the Prime Minister's need to appease the Eurosceptic wing of his party, by throwing it some further 'EU red meat'. The force of their view can be gauged from the Manifesto of the Fresh Start Group,[30] which is composed largely of Tory Eurosceptics. It advocates exercise of the block opt-out; no opting back in to any of these measures; operational cooperation with EU partners via other means, such as international agreements, memoranda of understanding, and voluntary cooperation on a case-by-case basis; and Treaty change to allow the United Kingdom to opt-out of those EU laws on police and criminal cooperation that it has opted in to since the Lisbon Treaty entered force. The pressure for exercise of the opt-out was further fuelled by inaccurate press coverage framed in terms of the Commission's ambitions for some pan-European criminal code, which is a myth,[31] and by equally inaccurate arguments in the other direction, to the effect that the EU should concentrate its efforts on practical cooperation to fight terrorism, drugs, human trafficking, and the like, which is in reality what the measures that would be lost by exercise of the opt-out are designed to do.[32]

[27] A Hinarejos, JR Spencer, and S Peers, 'Opting Out of EU Criminal Law: What is Actually Involved?' [2012] 1 CELS Working Paper, New Series 12.

[28] Hinarejos, Spencer, and Peers (n 27) 14.

[29] Letter from Home Secretary to the Chairman of the House of Lords Select Committee on the EU, 21 December 2011, available at <http://www.parliament.uk/documents/lords-committees/eu-sub-com-f/cwm/protocol36optout.pdf> (last accessed 18 April 2013); Decision Pursuant to Article 10 of Protocol 36 of the Treaty on the Functioning of the European Union (Cm 8671, July 2013); Council of the European Union, UK notification according to Article 10(4) of Protocol No 36 to the TEU and TFEU, 12750/13, 26 July 2013.

[30] Fresh Start Project, *Manifesto for Change, A New Vision for the UK in Europe*, January 2013, available at <http://www.eufreshstart.org/downloads/manifestoforchange.pdf> (last accessed 18 April 2013).

[31] Hinarejos, Spencer, and Peers (n 27) 17–18.

[32] Hinarejos, Spencer, and Peers (n 27) 17.

(3) Sovereignty and the national interest

Sovereignty as traditionally conceived has commonly been associated with State power. The State has both power and authority to enact laws and it was felt that this was the optimal way to serve and protect the national interest. The conjunction between exclusive State authority and optimal preservation of the national interest was always subject to exceptions, and these have become more pronounced over time. We should therefore be mindful of the rationale for what was the Pillar system introduced by the Maastricht Treaty.

The Member States wished for some degree of international cooperation in foreign and security policy, and justice and home affairs, but were not ready for the application of the full supranational machinery which operated in the Community Pillar. Thus the Second and Third Pillars gave the Member States an institutionalized forum in which to discuss these matters, without subjecting themselves to supranational controls. The Member States believed that such cooperation would be beneficial for reasons articulated by international relations theorists.[33]

The Member States wished for some established mechanism through which they could cooperate in these areas. Setting up *ad hoc* meetings to discuss such matters is cumbersome, time consuming, and involves heavy 'transaction costs', more especially as the number of players expands. The sensitive nature of the subject matter, touching closely as it did at the heart of traditional conceptions of sovereignty, meant however that Member States preferred the 'default position' of intergovernmentalism, thereby retaining maximum control in their own hands. The cost-benefit analysis of having supranationalism, with its attendant delegation of power to Commission and Court of Justice was therefore negative, in the sense that the benefits attendant on supranationalism in these areas were felt by the Member States to be outweighed by the costs.

The passage of time led to the Member States being more willing to accept that the Third Pillar should be subject to the normal process of EU decision-making, and this culminated in the Lisbon Treaty.[34] The rationale for EU involvement nonetheless remains at its most fundamental now that the cross-border nature of crime, terrorism, and the like requires cross-border measures that can be best enacted and applied through EU law. Any such form of collective action necessarily entails some sacrifice of State autonomy, in the sense that each Member State must apply the precepts agreed to by all the players, even if it might have chosen slightly different criteria if it had been making the choice entirely of its own volition. The very decision to engage in close collaboration is however predicated on the assumption

[33] A Moravcsik, 'Preferences and Power in the European Community: A Liberal Intergovernmentalist Approach' (1993) 31 *Journal of Common Market Studies* 473; A Moravcsik, *National Preference Formation and Interstate Bargaining in the European Community, 1955–86* (Harvard University Press 1992); M Pollack, *The Engines of European Integration: Delegation, Agency and Agenda Setting in the EU* (OUP 2003); M Pollack, 'International Relations Theory and European Integration' [2000] EUI Working Papers, RSC 55.

[34] J-C Piris, *The Lisbon Treaty: A Legal and Political Analysis* (CUP 2010); P Craig, *The Lisbon Treaty, Law, Politics and Treaty Reform* (OUP 2010).

that some diminution of autonomy is deemed to be a price worth paying in terms of the more efficacious dealing with cross-border crime, terrorism, and the like, through measures such as exchange of information, mutual recognition, and institutionalized police cooperation.

It is for this very reason that commentators from a broad arena are concerned about the impact of the opt-out,[35] including the devolved administrations, which raised issues relating both to the lack of timely consultation and the substantive wisdom of the opt-out. The House of Lords Select Committee conducted a detailed investigation into the matter, with many of those giving evidence expressing serious disquiet at the possible opt-out.[36] Now to be sure not all of the 130 measures covered by the opt-out are important, but many are, none more so than the European Arrest Warrant[37] ('EAW') which was introduced because the pre-existing system of extradition was expensive, protracted, and difficult to use. The EAW is not without its difficulties, but it has reduced the time to hand over a wanted person very significantly.[38] The idea that the ends served by the EAW and many other measures could be achieved without supranational legislation is premised on vague injunctions that we should, for example, offer to continue practical cooperation on criminal records checks, and offer operational cooperation with Europol, or that we should negotiate bilateral international treaty arrangements on extradition to and from other EU countries.[39] The House of Lords European Union Committee was very clear in its conclusions:[40] it found that many of the arguments in favour of the opt-out were based on unfounded assumptions; that the overwhelming legal view was that the opt-out would have negative implications for the United Kingdom; it was unconvinced by the government's arguments in favour; it found that the opt-out from criminal justice measures would have significant adverse negative repercussions for the internal security of the United Kingdom; and it did not believe that alternative arrangements posited by the government would work.

[35] See, eg, Hinarejos, Spencer, and Peers (n 27); H Brady, *Britain's 2014 Justice Opt-Out, Why it Bodes Ill for Cameron's EU Strategy* (Centre for European Reform, 2013). Compare S Booth, C Howarth, and V Scarpetta, 'An Unavoidable Choice: More of Less EU Control over Policing and Criminal Law' [2012] *Open Europe* available at <http://www.europarl.org.uk/ressource/static/files/jha2014choice.pdf> (last accessed 20 April 2013).

[36] House of Lords European Union Committee, *EU Police and Criminal Justice Measures: The UK's 2014 Opt-Out Decision* (HL Paper (2013–14) no 159.

[37] Council Framework Decision 2002/584/JHA of 13 June 2002 on the European arrest warrant and the surrender procedures between Member States [2002] OJ L190/1; Council Framework Decision 2009/299/JHA of 26 February 2009 amending Framework Decisions 2002/584/JHA, 2005/214/JHA, 2006/783/JHA, 2008/909/JHA, and 2008/947/JHA, thereby enhancing the procedural rights of persons and fostering the application of the principle of mutual recognition to decisions rendered in the absence of the person concerned at the trial [2009] OJ L81/24.

[38] Hinarejos, Spencer, and Peers (n 27) 97.

[39] *Fresh Start Project* (n 30).

[40] House of Lords European Union Committee (n 36) [277]–[319].

D. Sovereignty and 'Taking Power Back': Repatriation and Referendum

(1) Varieties of Euroscepticism

Those of a Eurosceptic persuasion hope that the Protocol 36 opt-out will be but a foretaste of things to come. The Prime Minister conceded the referendum so desired by backbenchers in his long awaited speech on the EU,[41] but not surprisingly refrained from specifying details as to what he believes the UK should seek by way of renegotiation before the referendum takes place, which will be after the next general election. We shall consider this crucial issue further, but before doing so it may be helpful to say a few words more generally about Euroscepticism.

The academic literature distinguishes between hard Euroscepticism, which captures principled opposition to the EU and European integration, and soft Euroscepticism, which covers qualified opposition to the EU.[42] The classic work also distinguishes between Euroscepticism within political parties, with limited contestation connoting the fact that the major parties are generally committed to European integration, with the corollary that there is a limited role for European integration in party competition, as in Germany and France. Open contestation captures the scenario where a major party has adopted Eurosceptic positions, and EU integration is thus a more important component of party competition, as in the United Kingdom and Denmark. Constrained contestation is used to describe the situation in Central and East European States, where there is some evidence of Euroscepticism, but it is less likely to affect party competition in a direct manner. There is moreover interesting work that reveals four independent types of Euroscepticism, utilitarian, sovereignty-based, democratic, and social.[43]

It is customary to acknowledge that the United Kingdom is more Eurosceptic than most other Member States, and there may be some truth in this, although the picture is rather more complex than appears at first sight. Thus study has shown a large information deficit about what the EU actually does, with a real link between knowledge of the EU and how well it is perceived: those who know a considerable amount about the EU are twice as likely to hold favourable opinions. It is also of interest that when asked more specific questions there are often more positive answers about the EU. For example in one survey, majorities agreed that the EU was good for consumers (69 per cent); improved working conditions (55 per cent); benefited environmental protection (55 per cent); strengthened global trade

[41] See n 1.

[42] A Szczerbiak and P Taggart (eds) *Opposing Europe? The Comparative Party Politics of Euroscepticism, Volume I: Case Studies and Country Surveys, Volume II: Comparative and Theoretical Perspectives* (OUP 2008).

[43] C Sørensen, 'Love me, Love me not... A Typology of Public Euroscepticism' [2008] SEI Working Paper 101.

negotiations (58 per cent); improved regulation of financial markets (55 per cent); and improved detection of criminals (70 per cent).[44]

Few would be willing to predict the mood of the UK public in 2016 or 2017, more especially because it can change markedly in a short space of time, as exemplified by the fact that the split between those pro and anti EU membership actually became more equal after the Prime Minister's EU speech, with 39 per cent in favour and 39 per cent against, as compared to 28 per cent in favour and 49 per cent against a short time earlier.[45]

(2) 'Fresh Start' and Euroscepticism

(a) The 'Fresh Start' manifesto

The Prime Minister is unlikely to reveal a fixed shopping list of demands from the EU prior to negotiations. He was cheered by his backbenchers after the speech promising the referendum, but this will turn to pressure to yield concrete concessions in terms of repatriation of power. Whereas nothing will satisfy the United Kingdom Independence Party ('UKIP') other than complete withdrawal from the EU, it is helpful in seeing how events might unfold to consider the demands of Conservative Party Eurosceptic MPs and what these tell us about the United Kingdom, the EU, and sovereignty.

There is good evidence of these demands in the manifesto for 'Fresh Start', which is a cross-party group with the objective of recasting the United Kingdom's relationship with the EU. Although the group is open to MPs of all parties,[46] as well as think tanks and the like, it is predominantly a vehicle for Conservative Party Eurosceptics. It makes interesting reading in terms of the demands that Tory MPs seek to fulfil through 'renegotiation' of the Lisbon Treaty. Fresh Start produced a *Manifesto for Change, A New Vision for the UK in Europe* in January 2013, with a foreword written by William Hague.[47] The manifesto contains some sensible suggestions for reform to the Common Agricultural Policy (CAP) and the Common Fisheries Policy ('CFP'). It is however not fortuitous that detailed discussion of these and other issues is preceded by a list of 'five significant revisions' that are sought to the Treaties:[48]

- An emergency brake for any Member State regarding future EU legislation that affects financial services.
- The EU should repatriate competence in the area of social and employment law to Member States. Several EU members are already finding their attempts at structural reform are hampered by inflexible EU bureaucracy, and we should work with them to negotiate change. Failing that, we should seek an opt-out

[44] J Litobarski, 'Britain: Euroconfused not Eurosceptic', 17 March 2011, available at <http://www.leftfootforward.org/2011/03/britain-is-more-confused-about-europe-than-sceptical> (last accessed 18 April 2013).

[45] *The Independent*, 1 March 2013.

[46] See generally Fresh Start Project (n 30).

[47] Fresh Start Project (n 30).

[48] Fresh Start Project (n 30) 3.

for the United Kingdom from existing EU social and employment law, and an emergency brake for any Member State regarding future EU legislation that affects this area.

- An opt-out for the United Kingdom from all existing EU policing and criminal justice measures not already covered by the Lisbon Treaty block opt-out.
- A new legal safeguard for the single market to ensure that there is no discrimination against non-Eurozone member interests.
- The abolition of the Strasbourg seat of the European Parliament, the Economic and Social Committee, and the Committee of the Regions.

The members of Fresh Start also seek significant reforms that can be achieved within the current treaty framework, 'either by the UK on its own (such as improving scrutiny in the UK Parliament, removing "gold-plating", invoking the block opt-out for some policing and criminal justice measures) or following negotiation with other Member States (such as reforms in the EU Budget, in CAP and CFP, and repatriating regional policy)'.[49] The architects of the manifesto insist that it is not about cherry picking, but that 'its goal is rather to articulate the necessary reforms that would lead to a more sustainable relationship for the UK in the EU'.[50] The analysis will focus on features of the manifesto that are central to it and central also for discussion of sovereignty and the EU. Most important in this respect is the balance between the 'economic' and the 'social'.

The economic is the *raison d'être* for United Kingdom membership of the EU for signatories of the manifesto. Thus they acknowledge that the United Kingdom's access to the single market is an important reason why the United Kingdom 'is the second most favoured global destination for foreign direct investment ('FDI') and the first choice among global corporations for the location of their European HQs'.[51] The manifesto continues by stating that 'the benefits of the single market, to UK exports and to FDI, are generally accepted to be the reason Britain entered the EU and the main reason for our remaining a member'.[52] It considers the possibility that the costs of membership might be held to outweigh the benefits, but concludes that the alternative models of a trading relationship with the EU have been found wanting. The alternative models are joining the European Economic Area, as in the case of Norway; negotiating a series of free trade agreements, as in the case of Switzerland; or negotiating a new customs union relationship with the EU, as in the case of Turkey. The Prime Minister in his recent speech rejected all three options,[53] and the framers of the manifesto do likewise. They conclude that such arrangements whereby the United Kingdom would be bound by trading rules in relation to which they had no input would be a 'disastrous position for the UK in terms of services trade'.[54] This then provides the frame for the subsequent proposals about trade, which are focused on lobbying for liberalization of the single market

[49] Fresh Start Project (n 30) 3.
[50] Fresh Start Project (n 30) 4.
[51] Fresh Start Project (n 30) 5.
[52] Fresh Start Project (n 30) 5.
[53] Cameron (n 1).
[54] Fresh Start Project (n 30) 6.

in services, new legal safeguards for the single market to ensure that EU institutions and Eurozone members cannot discriminate against non-Eurozone member interests, and encouraging the EU to complete more free trade agreements with other players, such as the United States, Canada, India, and Mercosur.[55]

The manifesto's approach to social and employment policy is starkly different.[56] EU social and employment law is said to have imposed increasing regulatory financial burdens on British businesses, to have impeded development of the United Kingdom's flexible labour model,[57] and to have forced a uniform labour model on all Member States, which is neither desirable nor necessary.[58] The manifesto's primary objective is for treaty change whereby competence over social and employment law should be returned from the EU to Member States. If this proved unavailing then the United Kingdom should seek to build an alliance of European partners to 'call for a substantial lessening of the regulatory burden by repealing legislation and a re-evaluation of the EU's powers in this area'.[59] If this too was unsuccessful then the 'UK should seek to negotiate a complete opt-out of all existing EU social and employment legislation,[60] and to introduce an emergency brake to cover future legislation in this field'.[61] The emergency brake would:

> allow any Member State that considers a proposal that affects social and employment law to be a threat to subsidiarity or to an important national interest to refer that proposal to the European Council where unanimity, and hence a national veto, would apply.[62]

The strength of feeling is manifest in the final paragraph of the section on social and employment policy in which it is suggested that 'if negotiation to repatriate these powers failed, we should consider the unilateral disapplication of EU social and employment law in Britain through an Act of Parliament'.[63] The manifesto accepts that this could lead to fines or suspension of obligations from other EU nations, but maintains that such unilateralism 'would not be a petulant act, but rather a signal that this is a red line issue for the UK'.[64]

(b) 'Fresh Start' and the political reality of treaty renegotiation

A week is a long time in politics. Five years is considerably longer. Predicting the outcome of treaty negotiations across such a time frame is at best fraught with difficulty, at worst downright foolhardy. It is nonetheless extremely unlikely that the package of proposals contained in the manifesto will gain agreement from other Member States.

This is more especially so when it is recognized that the overall 'wish list' of desired changes, whether involving treaty revision, amendment of EU legislation,

[55] Fresh Start Project (n 30) 6. [56] Fresh Start Project (n 30) 20–2.
[57] Fresh Start Project (n 30) 20–1; the Working Time Directive and the Temporary Agency Workers Directive come in for particularly heavy criticism.
[58] Fresh Start Project (n 30) 21. [59] Fresh Start Project (n 30) 20.
[60] Fresh Start Project (n 30) 21, Arts 19 and 145–161 TFEU.
[61] Fresh Start Project (n 30) 20. [62] Fresh Start Project (n 30) 21.
[63] Fresh Start Project (n 30) 22. [64] Fresh Start Project (n 30) 22.

or change of EU policy, is in fact very long. There are detailed changes proposed on areas as diverse as immigration and energy, defence and regional policy, financial services and policing and criminal justice, social and employment law and EU institutions, and common agriculture and common fisheries policy.

It is this very fact that serves to blur the line between hard and softer forms of Euroscepticism. The framers of the Fresh Start manifesto would likely position themselves in the softer camp, at least by way of comparison to UKIP. There is force in this relative comparison, which is further reinforced by the fact that Fresh Start seeks to engage with the EU about its future direction in a way that UKIP manifestly does not. It is nonetheless the case that the greater the list of demands emanating from avowedly soft Eurosceptics and the more far reaching those demands are as compared to the status quo ante, the less likely they are to prove acceptable.

This then leads to choices for those in Fresh Start that are never fully faced. The tension is evident in the manifesto, but never resolved. It is unclear whether if some, perhaps many, of the important demands are not met the members of Fresh Start will campaign for a no vote in a referendum on whether the United Kingdom should remain in the EU, given that Fresh Start's manifesto is predicated on the centrality of membership of the single market for UK economic health and given also its acceptance that alternatives such as membership of the EEA would be seriously deficient in this respect. If they do campaign for a no vote then they will therefore face some awkward tensions. They will have to argue that failure to secure the changes that they desire means that the United Kingdom should leave the EU, even though they have acknowledged the centrality of the single market for the United Kingdom's economic health, and even though they have no alternative solution as to how the ensuing economic loss could be made good, since they correctly recognize that 'solutions' based on the Norway, Swiss, or Turkish models will not work for the United Kingdom.

This reveals moreover an ultimate paradox in the balance between the economic and the social that pervades Eurosceptic thinking. It is the prioritization of the economic over the social that drives this branch of Eurosceptic thought. It is the belief that the EU should not meddle with the social that is central to their very Euroscepticism. It is the strength of this feeling that could fuel a campaign for a no vote if the demands are not met. If however such a campaign were to be successful the cost would be loss of access to the single market and the forgoing of the very economic benefits of EU membership that Eurosceptics regard as so important in their vision of a liberalized market economy. Anger at their inability to purge the EU of its social dimension expressed through support for a no campaign would thus close the door on the economic dimension of membership that is so central to their thinking.

(c) 'Fresh Start' and the normative balance between the economic and the social

We express ourselves by and through language. It has power and symbolism. This is nowhere more apparent than in the language of Fresh Start itself. It carries the threefold implication that the EU needs a radical overhaul, that it should be cast in the mould suggested by the manifesto, and that this is the legitimate boundary of the EU's terrain. These assumptions are however contestable.

The reality is that the balance between the economic and the social within the EU has been debated in detail over many years. The tension initially came to prominence with the 'completion' of the internal market, in the years following the Single European Act 1986. There were some who defended the market orientation in the Rome Treaty, viewing it as a mechanism through which autonomous economic agents expressed their utility preferences across a European-wide market.[65] The normative underpinnings of their view were often explicitly Hayekian. They acknowledged that the original Treaty contained non-market elements, principally in the common policies for agriculture, iron and steel and the like, but they deprecated such interventions in the market order, which they regard as a failure.

There was nonetheless increased concern at the dominance of the economic over the social within the EU. The priority accorded to the four freedoms interpreted predominantly in economic terms, coupled with renewed emphasis on positive economic integration through harmonization, fuelled these concerns. They were exacerbated by the normative force accorded to EU law through the concepts of direct effect and supremacy, which imbued EU economic doctrine with considerable power in the domestic legal orders. This then was the foundation for the concern about the balance between the economic and the social, which played out from the mid-1980s onwards. It was the fear that the equilibrium between the two fashioned in differing ways in the Member States would be unbalanced in favour of the economic, thereby jeopardizing valued national conceptions of the mixed market economy.

Scharpf's voice was especially influential, speaking of the 'zealots of undistorted competition',[66] and the need for liberation from 'the tyranny of regulatory competition'.[67] He argued that the EU was premised on asymmetrical treatment of the economic and social spheres.[68] The economic order predominated, as evidenced by the Treaty provisions, and the primacy accorded to completion of the single market with the attendant priority placed on market and competitive principles. Scharpf contended that it would have been possible when the Rome Treaty was framed to have made harmonization of social protection a pre-condition for market integration, given that the welfare regimes of the original six Member States were closer than they have since become. If the Rome Treaty had been cast in this form then the debates at EU level about the interplay between social protection and the market mechanism

[65] M Streit and W Mussler, 'The Economic Constitution of the European Community—From Rome to Maastricht' in F Snyder (ed) *Constitutional Dimensions of European Economic Integration* (Kluwer Law International 1996) 109–49.

[66] F Scharpf, *Governing in Europe: Effective and Democratic?* (OUP 1999) 167.

[67] Scharpf (n 66) 180.

[68] F Scharpf, 'The European Social Model: Coping with the Challenges of Diversity' (2002) 40 *Journal of Common Market Studies* 645 and 'Legitimate Diversity: The New Challenge of European Integration', in T Borzel and R Cichowski (eds) *The State of the European Union, Volume 6: Law, Politics and Society* (OUP 2003) 79–104.

would have replicated similar discourse at national level. Matters developed very differently. The Treaty focus was heavily on markets, with the consequence that there was a decoupling of economic integration and social protection. This led to constitutional asymmetry. Whereas at national level economic and social policy had the same constitutional status, it was economic policy that predominated at the EU level. The very predominance afforded to economic policy reduced the Member States' ability to influence their own economies or to 'realize self-defined socio-political goals'.[69] EU law doctrines of direct effect and supremacy made these constraints even firmer.

Similar thoughts were expressed by other writers. Thus Heller expressed concern that it would be 'shocking if the contemporary nation states of Europe which have spent so much political blood and effort in the development of sophisticated modes of organizing the labour, capital, and transfer markets of mass industrial economies, were now to abandon that path in the embrace of the liberal constitution'.[70] Weiler emphasized that completion of the single market went beyond the mere removal of technocratic obstacles to trade, and embraced 'a highly politicized choice of ethos, ideology and political culture: the culture of "the market"'.[71] The removal of barriers to free movement was a means to maximize utility, premised on the assumption of formal equality of individuals, in which market efficiency was prized above other competing values.[72]

The preceding concerns were a significant factor in driving various EU policies from the 1980s onwards, in which the common element was the desire to re-balance the relative emphasis between the economic and the social within the EU. This is evident in the inclusion in the Single European Act package designed to expedite market harmonization through what became Article 114 TFEU, of provisions concerning the Structural Funds used for regional development in order to quieten fears of the weaker economic Member States that they would suffer inordinately from market liberalization. Commentators echoed the need for a strong regional policy to balance the effect of market integration on the weaker economies.[73]

It is evident too in amendments to the Maastricht and Amsterdam Treaties that created new heads of social competence, or modified those existing hitherto, in areas such as the environment, employment, industry, social policy, and the like, which were in no small measure the result of the perceived need to re-balance the economic and social orders within the EU. Political leaders, and European Commission President Jacques Delors, came to see the necessity for an increase in European social policy in order to retain the support of workers.[74]

[69] Scharpf (n 68) 648.

[70] T Heller, 'Comments by Thomas Heller' in F Snyder (ed) *Constitutional Dimensions of European Economic Integration* (Kluwer Law International 1996) 161.

[71] J Weiler, 'The Transformation of Europe' (1991) 100 *Yale LJ* 2403, 2478.

[72] Weiler (n 71) 2478.

[73] R Dehousse, 'Completing the Internal Market: Institutional Constraints and Challenges' in R Bieber, R Dehousse, J Pinder, and J Weiler (eds) *1992: One European Market?* (Nomos 1988) 336.

[74] M Kleinman, *A European Welfare State? European Union Social Policy in Context* (Palgrave 2002) 82–3, 86–7.

It is evident yet again in the way in which the EU political organs consciously re-conceptualized the internal market in more holistic terms, to embrace not only the traditional economic sphere, but also a wider range of social, environmental, and consumer concerns.[75] The Commission and the European Council consciously reconfigured the single market in a broader, more holistic, manner. Consumer welfare, social policy, and environmental policy were regarded as important facets of the internal market strategy. The Lisbon European Council constituted an important stage in the changing internal market agenda. The meeting focused on employment, economic reform, and social cohesion. It set a 'new' strategic goal: the Union was to become 'the most competitive and dynamic knowledge-based economy in the world, capable of sustainable economic growth with more and better jobs and greater social cohesion'.[76] Completion of the internal market was one way of achieving this strategy.[77] The modernization of the European social model through the building of an active welfare State was to be another. This was crucial to ensure that 'the emergence of this new economy does not compound the existing social problems of unemployment, social exclusion, and poverty'.[78] This objective was further particularized in terms of better education, an active employment policy, modernizing social protection, and promoting social inclusion.[79] These commitments were reiterated at later European Council meetings.[80]

There is of course no *a priori* reason why the current disposition between the economic and the social should not be open to challenge. There is in that sense nothing wrong with Fresh Start shaking the established order. Any such challenge should however be predicated on the facts, which includes in this respect the historical discourse that has shaped the current range of EU powers. There are three dimensions to this discourse that are especially pertinent to the emerging UK debate.

From an EU perspective, Member States may have had differing visions of the balance between the economic and the social, but these have been resolved through the very processes for determination encapsulated in the Rome Treaty as amended over time. The Member States have been central to this process, since they debated and agreed the Treaty amendments that brought more social policy into the Treaty. It was the Member States once again that were willing to enact EU legislation to carry forward the Treaty imperatives in these areas. It is of course the case that the legislation was proposed by the Commission pursuant to its right of legislative initiative, and true also that the EU courts played a role in interpretation of both the Treaty provisions and EU legislation. This does not alter the fact that Member

[75] P Craig, 'The Evolution of the Single Market' in C Barnard and J Scott (eds) *The Law of the Single European Market, Unpacking the Premises* (Hart Publishing 2002) ch 1.

[76] Lisbon European Council Meeting, 23–4 March 2000 at 5, available at <http://www.european-council.europa.eu/council-meetings/conclusions/archives-2002-1993> (last accessed 20 July 2013).

[77] Lisbon European Council Meeting (n 76) 5, 16–21.

[78] Lisbon European Council Meeting (n 76) 24.

[79] Lisbon European Council Meeting (n 76) 25–34.

[80] See, eg, Feira European Council Meeting, 19–20 June 2000 at 19–39, 44–9; Nice European Council Meeting, 7–9 December 2000, available at <http://www.european-council.europa.eu/council-meetings/conclusions/archives-2002-1993> (last accessed 20 July 2013).

States were central to the amendments that brought social provisions into the Rome Treaty as amended and they were central also in the subsequent legislative process. Treaty change requires unanimity, and even though much EU legislation is subject to qualified majority voting under the ordinary legislative procedure this commonly operates through consensus.[81] The idea that EU social policy has been foisted on unwilling Member States may be 'good' political propaganda for those minded to oppose the EU, but it is nonetheless simply fantasy. A particular State may not like the balance between the economic and the social embodied in the Treaty, but then the very essence of a treaty regime comprising twenty-eight Member States is that you cannot have it all your own way. Collective political action means that the players forgo some individual decisional autonomy for the gains that are felt to be forthcoming from membership of the club.[82] The reality is moreover that concerns that the EU pays too much attention to the social have been outweighed by worry that it still pays too little.[83]

From an internal UK perspective, the simple but uncomfortable fact for the adherents to Fresh Start is that the United Kingdom does not unswervingly adhere to its policy precepts in this regard. On the contrary, the Labour Party has traditionally supported social policy, as exemplified by the Blair Government's ending of the UK opt-out from the Social Protocol. So too have the Liberal Democrats. This is of course to State no more than that the balance between the economic and the social is one of the fault lines that run through national politics. It does however have a somewhat less obvious but special resonance for debates about the United Kingdom's terms of EU membership. It may be termed the paradox of sovereignty, and can be explicated as follows. It is unlikely in the extreme that the Member States will agree to treaty amendment removing all the provisions on social/labour policy. Nor is it likely that there will be wholesale repeal of legislation enacted under the existing provisions of the Lisbon Treaty, which is sufficient to satisfy adherents of Fresh Start. So, that leaves negotiation of a UK opt-out from the social provisions. It is once again doubtful whether the Member States would accede to this request. However even if they did the logic of an opt-out is that it does not thereby preclude a later opt-in. This would to be sure be subject to the European Union Act 2011, but that does not change the point made here. The classic UK ideal of continuing sovereignty, whereby Parliament is omnipotent save for the fact that it cannot bind its successors, is the blessing and curse for those minded to repatriate power. It is the blessing since it provides the conceptual foundation for the very claim that powers should be returned to Parliament to enable it to make the choices in the salient areas. It is the curse precisely because sovereignty is continuing, thereby leaving open the real possibility that a subsequent government will be persuaded that it is in the best interests of the United Kingdom that certain

[81] Arts 289, 294 TFEU.

[82] J Buchanan and G Tullock, *The Calculus of Consent: Logical Foundations of Constitutional Democracy* (University of Michigan Press 1962); M Olson, *The Logic of Collective Action: Public Goods and the Theory of Groups* (Harvard University Press 1965).

[83] Sørensen (n 42).

powers should be exercised in a supranational forum. It is thus an 'awkward' but undeniable facet of the sovereignty argument deployed by the Eurosceptics that others who hold the legitimate reins of elected power in the United Kingdom may choose to exercise it in very different ways.

From a substantive policy perspective, it is easy to forget the close linkage between debates about repatriation of power and strongly held political preferences. It is a point made neatly in an Economist blog.[84] It posits a new political party, the Honesty Party, with three 'punchy, distinctive policies': fewer regulations for the City; fewer laws protecting workers against long hours and other impositions; and making it harder to extradite people accused of crimes. The Honesty Party is imaginary and is likely to remain so, given that the three policies would generate considerable opposition, not support. However while the Party is not real, its manifesto is, as the author of the blog states, in effect what Eurosceptics want, as expressed in their Fresh Start Manifesto. It is true that the manifesto speaks in terms of national parliaments being 'best placed to decide on the appropriate social, employment, and health and safety regulations for each Member State, and we are confident the UK Government will retain appropriate domestic legislation in the UK'.[85] It is nonetheless clear where their policy preferences lie, as captured succinctly by the Economist blog:

> The Fresh Start folks (mostly Tory MPs) do not actually say they want weakened employment laws, for example. But it is not hard to join the dots. They complain about how the European Working Time Directive is a burden on business and constricts Britain's labour market. They could easily add that Parliament should replace the European regulation with a British one offering similar protections. But they don't. It sounds like they want to get rid of it entirely. [86]

E. Conclusion

The United Kingdom has always 'enjoyed' a somewhat equivocal relationship with the EU, and it has become more turbulent in recent years. The next few years will be challenging, both for the EU as it seeks to recover from the euro crisis, and for the United Kingdom as it seeks to clarify and chart its relationship with the EU. There is no guarantee that a referendum on UK membership will be held after the next election, given that a Conservative Party victory is by no means a foregone conclusion. Whether the Labour Party would choose to hold one remains unclear. Nick Clegg, the Deputy Prime Minister and leader of the Liberal Democrats, has made it clear that his vision for the EU and the

[84] *The Economist*, 'Paradox of Euroscepticism', 1 February 2013, available at <http://www.economist.com/blogs/blighty/2013/02/british-politics> (last accessed 18 April 2013).

[85] Fresh Start Project (n 30) 21.

[86] *The Paradox of Euroscepticism* (n 84).

United Kingdom is starkly different from that advanced by the Conservative Party Eurosceptics.[87] What is clear is that the issues discussed in this chapter will not go away, whichever party or parties form the government after the next general election. The United Kingdom's relationship with the EU, and the conception of sovereignty that shapes, and is shaped by it, will continue to occupy the political terrain.

[87] N Clegg, 'A Vision for the UK in Europe' (Chatham House, transcript, 1 November 2012) available at <http://www.chathamhouse.org/sites/default/files/public/Meetings/Meeting%20Transcripts/011112Clegg.pdf> (last accessed 18 April 2013).

11

European Restatements of Sovereignty

*Damian Chalmers**

A. Introduction: The Sovereign Puzzle

Sovereignty, it can appear, is part of the DNA of the EU. Its attachment to the European integration project has led to the latter being seen as an exemplar of a new way of organizing life beyond the nation-State.[1] That most prominent of Europeans, Jacques Delors, thus stated that the project was 'building a community whose member states jointly exercise a measure of pooled sovereignty through fully-fledged common policies'.[2] Over twenty years later, Commission President Barroso reiterated this by calling for a 'democratic federation of nation states that can tackle our common problems, through the sharing of sovereignty in a way that each country and each citizen are better equipped to control their own destiny'.[3] However, if Delors assosciated pooled sovereignty with a pooled government, Barroso's vision had sovereignty as enabling self-government to flourish.

The beneficiary of this self-government is unclear, however. Euro-Federalists argue that the true sovereigns in Europe are its citizens. They argue that the *raison d'être* of the European project is the regaining of sovereignty, by which they mean giving European citizens back 'control over the world in which they live'.[4] By contrast, opponents of European integration see sovereignty as simply a property of States. The Charter of the European Freedom and Democracy political grouping 'favours an open, transparent, democratic and accountable co-operation among sovereign European States and rejects the bureaucratisation of Europe…'[5] If sovereignty is a

* Professor of European Union Law, London School of Economics and Political Science.

[1] RO Keohane, 'Ironies of Sovereignty: The European Union and the United States' (2002) 42 *Journal of Common Market Studies* 743, 756–7; J Ruggie, 'Territoriality and Beyond: Problematising Modernity in International Relations' (1993) 47 *International Organisation* 139, 171–2.

[2] J Delors, 'European Integration and Security' (1991) 33 *Survival* 99, 103.

[3] JMD Barroso, 'State of the Union Address 2012', Plenary Session of the European Parliament, Strasbourg, 12 September 2012, available at <http://europa.eu/rapid/press-release_ SPEECH-12-596_en.htm> (last accessed 1 February 2013).

[4] G Verhofstadt, speech on the decision by the German Constitutional Court and the ESM Treaty, Hannover, 18 September 2012, available at <http://www.alde.eu/press/press-and-release-news/press-release/article/verhofstadt-sovereignty-is-better-pooled-at-eu-level-than-lost-in-a-global- world-39742/> (last accessed 21 April 2013).

[5] Europe of Freedom and Democracy, Group in the European Parliament, 'Our Charter', available at <http://www.efdgroup.eu/about-us/who-we-are/charter.html> (last accessed 21 April 2013).

property of States which cannot be acquired by anybody else, it can still be threatened by the Union.

This sense that parties are talking about different things when they talk of sovereignty is reinforced by a further position, which is expressed in the Lithuanian Constitution. Under that Constitution, sovereignty belongs to the Lithuanian nation, and nothing can restrict or limit that sovereignty.[6] That 'nothing' includes EU law. When Lithuania acceded to the Union, a Constitutional Act was passed providing for primacy of EU law over Lithuanian law.[7] This does not limit Lithuanian sovereignty, per se, with sovereignty seen rather as a structure which requires all institutions to act in the interest of the Lithuanian nation and allows for Lithuanians to rise up where this does not take place.

These frequent and diverse usages arise because sovereignty is one of those terms through which actors make sense of their legal and political worlds and express strong beliefs about the organization of political life. Sovereignty mediates the type of associative tie needed to sustain political community, the role of government within modern life and, most fundamentally, the nature of the relationship between rulers and ruled. A failure to engage with these different usages is both a failure to engage with these worlds and a failure to be true to the tradition of sovereignty: a concept whose meaning has changed significantly over time.[8]

This chapter will argue that EU law shifted understandings of sovereignty by presenting it as something to be justified. Sovereignty had to be asserted against the claims of EU law. To prevail, it now had to present a value which it brought to the polity and its citizens. This led to a fragmentation of sovereignty as parties relied on different traditions of the relationship between sovereignty and government to assert this value. This relationship was handled in three different ways.

In the first, sovereignty is presented as a human order to be protected from EU law. This human order is presented as those activities most intimately connected with a vision of domestic society as an eternal, indivisible body constructed around a shared lived experience. These activities include welfare provision, foreign policy and defence, criminal justice, fundamental rights, and those legal institutions traditionally concerned with relating collective values and narratives to local lives, be these family, religious or educational law. If this vision was historically used to emphasize the constrained nature of government and the presence of human activity and other forms of rules beyond it, within EU law it has been used, over-formalistically, to ring-fence a series of activities from scrutiny on the basis that they are too central to making us who we are.

[6] Constitution of the Republic of Lithuania 1992, Arts 2, 3.

[7] Constitutional Act of the Republic of Lithuania on Membership of the European Union 2003, para 2. It is believed that EU law has precedence over all Lithuanian law other than the Constitution. P Ravluševičius, 'The Enforcement of the Primacy of European Union Law: Legal Doctrine and Practice' (2011) 18 *Jurisprudencija* 1369.

[8] On the steady change in the meaning of the term see J Bartelson, *A Genealogy of Sovereignty* (CUP 1995) 88–236; B Teschke, 'Geopolitical Relations in the European Middle Ages: History and Theory' (1998) 52 *International Organization* 325, 350–5.

In the second tradition, the sovereign ordains government. National sovereigns authorize EU law, and it governs by virtue of their blessing. EU law is granted a different quality of power from national law in that it is derived and oriented to particular problems whereas national law is general and original in nature. Sovereignty becomes associated with a series of external democratic controls to be imposed on EU law by national law. The challenge with this tradition is that the sovereign only steps in occasionally; more to grant a democratic blessing to government than to hold it rigorously to account.

The third vision is the most troubling. In this, sovereignty is deployed not to check EU power but to justify greater administrative power for the Union than would otherwise be allowed. Such a vision sees sovereignty and government coming fully together so that the sovereign actively governs. Typically, this is done through the active involvement of national Parliaments in forms of European integration allowing the Union to claim that it is acting out the sovereign will of EU citizens or peoples, and thereby engaging in self-government. However, this is something of a slippage. In other words, the Union uses sovereignty as a legitimation strategy, whereby its claim to involve sovereigns—be they Parliaments, peoples, or citizens—in its government grants the European integration process a general power of sovereign rule that largely stands outside the law.

B. The Justification of Sovereignty as a Counterpoint to EU Government

The EU 'sovereign question' is often cast as one of possession. The central issue is who possesses sovereignty as sovereignty is, in this debate, the ultimate authority over rule. It can, thus, only be exercised by one body at any time over any field of activity. This characterization of sovereignty makes questionable assumptions. Sovereignty is seen as a fungible property which can be transferred from one context to another with no real change in its qualities, other than who possesses it. Alongside this, any limits on national sovereignty, to be effective, must endow the other legal order with equivalent qualities, as otherwise the latter will operate under the shadow of the sovereign and never have sufficient power to act as an independent legal order.

Van Gend en Loos is the entry point for this debate.[9] It set out a formulation about the relationship between EU law and sovereignty which has been reiterated constantly since, most notably in *Opinion 1/09*:

> the founding treaties of the European Union, unlike ordinary international treaties, established a new legal order, possessing its own institutions, for the benefit of which the States have limited their sovereign rights, in ever wider fields, and the subjects of which comprise not only Member States but also their nationals... The essential characteristics of the European Union legal order thus constituted are in particular its primacy over the laws of the Member

[9] Case 26/62, *NV Algemene Trasporten Expeditie Onderneming van Gend en Loos v Nederlandse Administratie der Belastingen* [1963] ECR 1.

States and the direct effect of a whole series of provisions which are applicable to their nationals and to the Member States themselves.[10]

This line of reasoning does not see sovereignty as transferrable or fungible but distinguishes between two sources of legal authority: that of EU law and that of national sovereignty. Asymmetry is central to understanding the relationship as no sovereignty is claimed for EU law. The central challenge becomes that of identifying those qualities of EU law which give rise to and characterize its authority and relating those to ideas of State sovereignty. As a consequence, and problematically for many accounts, whilst there are clearly some similarities between this authority and sovereignty there are also a number of differences. Like a sovereign, the EU claims a power to found a rule of law for itself which generates individual rights and obligations. If sovereignty claims a unity for a legal order and its political system,[11] the characterization of the EU as a new legal order suggests this for the Union and EU law too. However, other similarities are missing, notably the most fundamental quality associated with a sovereign, the 'right to let live'.[12] EU law claims no equivalent for itself. Furthermore, the justification for its authority is grounded on a different calculus. The traditional justification for sovereignty is that it represents the unity and autonomy of the body politic.[13] *Van Gend en Loos* justifies EU legal authority in the bringing together of human beings for collective purposes and the establishment of institutions with powers of rule to secure these purposes. If one is based on the claim of a timeless community, the other rests on the claim of common purpose.

Van Gend en Loos presented sovereignty, instead, as something which required justification rather than as something to be acquired by the Union. Its displacement of sovereignty by EU legal authority put sovereignty into competition with EU law as it begged the question as to why, or when, each should prevail at the expense of the other.[14] *Van Gend en Loos* suggested that resolution of this question lies in the relative value of sovereignty and EU law. In particular, it associated sovereignty with two forms of value. It is granted an *end value*. It is valuable in itself to be sovereign, and holders of sovereignty hold it only by virtue of certain valued attributes which enable them to be sovereign. Thus, only the sovereign has original power and only she is able to speak as representative of the State.[15] *Van Gend en Loos* recognizes this end value in the tacit admission that something of real value is being limited

[10] *Opinion 1/09 on a unified patent litigation system* [2011] ECR I-1137, para 65.

[11] H Lindahl, 'Sovereignty and Representation in the European Union' in N Walker (ed) *Sovereignty in Transition* (Hart Publishing 2003) 87–90, 101–10.

[12] G Agamben, *Homo Sacer: Sovereign Power and Bare Life* (D Heller-Roazen trans, Stanford University Press 1998) 142.

[13] M Loughlin, *Foundations of Public Law* (OUP 2010) 186–96.

[14] The description of the Treaty limiting national sovereignty was in line with a number of constitutional provisions sets up after the Second World War which provided for limitation of sovereignty to enable international cooperation. B de Witte, 'The European Union as an International Legal Experiment' in G de Búrca and JHH Weiler (eds) *The Worlds of European Constitutionalism* (CUP 2012) 26–8.

[15] On this debate within the context of US independence see A Reed Amar, 'Of Sovereignty and Federalism' (1986) 96 *Yale LJ* 1425, 1435–7.

by the EU, and, more explicitly, by the statement that sovereignty is something which only the States themselves can limit. Sovereignty is also given a *use value*. It allows its holder to do other things of value. The sovereign can generate the conditions for, for example, collective wealth, security, social solidarity, and realization of individual freedoms. EU law recognizes this by seeing sovereignty as something to be traded, through the placing of limits on it, to allow Member States to pursue a number of collective goods, notably the single market.

These values fit with traditionalist understandings in which the sovereign is granted both an end value in the form of a special status (ie only the sovereign can speak in the name of the State) and a use value in that, as representative of the body politic, it has to act in the common good.[16] However, these traditions had historically been deployed to reinforce a unitary political agency, the State.[17] By contrast, EU law seeks to fragment this political agency. Two systems, the EU and the Member State, are established with each having a right to govern or rule. Sovereignty moves from being a concept which consolidates and integrates rule to becoming a terrain for competition between different spheres of rule and government. If this led to some competition over the end value of sovereignty in the form of debates over who has original power to found legal authority within the Union, this competition is largely symbolic.[18] This power is, alone, a hollow power. It grants a status without offering up anything more finite about the scope or intensity of that power. One can be a sovereign over a classroom or the world. It can be a power noted for not being exercised or for being used intensely. Alongside this, the absolute notion of the end value, namely that it claimed a special status for the sovereign to rule and was silent about other forms of rule, was unhelpful in regulating a relationship between sovereignty and other forms of power. The end value of sovereignty could found legal rule within a territory yet, insofar as wide-ranging legal authority could then be transferred to the Union, the end value of sovereignty had nothing to say on the limits or operation of such authority.

The use value came increasingly to be deployed by both proponents and opponents of EU legal authority as a condition for determining the presence of sovereignty. Reference was nearly always made to the use value of sovereignty, and what further goods it enabled, as something to bolster the respective arguments. And this shift to the presence of use value to justify the presence of sovereignty is the real revolution of EU law. It led some to claim that, as sovereignty had insufficient use value, we were moving to an age without it.[19] More commonly, it has led to sovereignty becoming increasingly configured around the value of what it enables.

[16] Q Skinner, 'The Sovereign State: A Genealogy' in H Kalmo and Q Skinner (eds) *Sovereignty in Fragments: The Past, Present and Future of a Contested Concept* (CUP 2010) 37.

[17] On the importance of this B Van Roermund, 'Sovereignty: Popular and Unpopular' in N Walker (ed) *Sovereignty in Transition* (Hart Publishing 2003) 42–5.

[18] See, eg, European Union Act 2011, s 18. This provision, which emphasizes that the supremacy of EU law is derived from the European Communities Act 1972, is seen as largely symbolic even within the notes to the Act; see Explanatory Notes, para 109.

[19] D Kostakopoulou, 'Floating Sovereignty: A Pathology or a Necessary Means of State Evolution?' (2002) 22 *OJLS* 135; A Jakab, 'Neutralizing the Sovereign Question—Compromise Strategies

In some instances, sovereignty has been gauged against how far it advances or restricts ideas of freedom. In its *Lisbon Treaty* judgment, the German Constitutional Court stated that sovereignty stood within the German constitutional order for a 'freedom that is organised by international law and committed to it'.[20] It was compatible with this sovereignty to enter arrangements which advanced this freedom internationally—be it through securing peace, transnational collective goods, or transnational democratic arrangements—but it must do so in a manner which did not unduly restrict domestic collective and individual freedoms. By contrast, the Polish Constitutional Tribunal and Czech Constitutional Court in their *Lisbon Treaty* judgments looked not at whether sovereignty advanced freedom in a generic manner but whether it advanced the practical freedom of the State. Both argued that by allowing the State to do things it would otherwise not be able to do, EU law was enlarging its freedom and therefore extending its sovereignty.[21] In other cases, sovereignty becomes something to be curtailed to secure other fundamental values. The Estonian Supreme Court has therefore stated that the core essence of Estonian sovereignty is 'the right of discretion in all matters, irrespective of external influences'.[22] This autonomy can quite easily be restricted by EU law. These restrictions will only be lawful if they advance other Estonian constitutional values and the Union does it in a proportionate manner. In this manner, sovereignty becomes a prism through which to assess the scope and worth of Union action.

The duty to justify the presence of sovereignty in terms of its use value only exists when a claim has been made that EU law should limit national sovereignty. The *incidence* of EU law will, therefore, determine when this happens. EU law will also frame the *manner* of justification. The reasons for EU legal authority are reasons why it should exercise greater authority than national law. The sovereign justification is a response to this. It is a response, moreover, which centres around showing either that EU legal authority can be accommodated, that EU law carries unacceptable costs, or that national sovereignty provides something not offered by EU law. In all cases, this will be informed by *particular traditions* of sovereignty as these provide the vocabulary for formulating such responses. The central tradition in this regard is the historical distinction between sovereignty and government. This distinction is now territorialized. EU law is cast, in this regard as a governmental order: a particular conception and ordering of legal and political power.[23] The sovereign is the national legal order.

in Constitutional Argumentations before European Integration and Since' (2006) 2 *European Constitutional L Rev* 375.

[20] *Re Ratification of the Treaty of Lisbon* (Germany) [2010] 3 CMLR 13, para 223.

[21] See respectively K 32/09 *Lisbon Treaty* (Polish Constitutional Tribunal, 24 November 2010) para 21–2; Pl ÚS 19/08 *Lisbon Treaty I* (Czech Constitutional Court, 26 November 2008) para 107.

[22] Case 3–4–1–6–12 *Request of the Chancellor of Justice to declare Article 4(4) of the Treaty establishing the European Stability Mechanism in conflict with the Constitution* (Estonian Supreme Court, 12 July 2012).

[23] The idea of government traces its roots to *oikonomia* in which the metaphor of the household (*oiko*) is seen as something to be enjoyed in common (*koinon*). Government sees political communities in the image of a family whose everyday affairs have to be taken care of by a 'gigantic, nation-wide administration of housekeeping'. H Arendt, *The Human Condition* (University of

C. Sovereignty as a Human Order Protected from EU Law

(1) Sovereignty and the domestic human order

Formally, EU law claims an unconstrained power to limit national sovereignty: the latter cannot be invoked as a defence against the requirements of EU law.[24] This led a current leading member of the Court of Justice to declare that there is simply no nucleus of sovereignty that Member States can invoke against the Union.[25] Sovereignty becomes, on this view, what EU law leaves behind for Member States. However, this is too crude. For most of its life, the activities of EU law have been limited. They have not constituted the norm of legal life within the Member States but the exception. In the long period prior to Maastricht, the EU legal system focused predominantly on addressing market externalities.[26] This regulation did not intrude on politically sensitive institutions. The single market, at least up until the mid-1990s, did not seek to establish those institutions of market building more central to domestic political economies, such as property rights or governance mechanisms involving direct rule.[27] In like vein, there was not much direct regulation of relations between private parties. The most wide-ranging instrument, the Directive, was unable, directly or indirectly, to impose obligations on private parties until 1990.[28]

The pressure placed on national legal autonomy was thus confined. Furthermore, EU law was accepted in many national legal systems precisely on this basis. This shaped understandings of sovereignty. National sovereignty became a reserved sphere not to be touched by EU law. This reserved sphere was, moreover, not something residual but rather that sphere of action which provided a central source of meaning by 'touch[ing] on the intelligibility of the social world more generally, on one's sense of coherence, continuity and vibrancy of the form of life into which one is inscribed and from which one derives one's most basic sense of orientation in the world'.[29]

In 1973, in *Frontini*, the Italian Constitutional Court stated that EU measures could not violate fundamental rights protected by the Italian Constitution because of the limited powers of the Union. Powers had been transferred to the Union on the basis of a 'precise criterion of division of jurisdiction by subject matter'.[30] The

Chicago 1958) 28. Its rule is administrative and impersonal. Its focus is behaviour, which concerns how individuals relate to particular conformities rather than to other individuals (at 38–49). See also G Agamben, *The Kingdom and the Glory* (Stanford University Press 2011) 16–52.

[24] See, eg, Case C-196/04 *Cadbury Schweppes v IRC* [2006] ECR I-8031, para 40. At more length Case C-141/07 *Commission v Germany* [2008] ECR I-6935, Opinion of AG Bot, paras 88–9.

[25] K Lenaerts, 'Constitutionalism and the Many Faces of Federalism' (1990) 38 *American Journal of Comparative Law* 205, 220.

[26] G Majone, 'The Rise of the Regulatory State in Europe' (1994) 17 *West European Politics* 77.

[27] N Fligstein and I Mara-Drita, 'How To Make a Market: Reflections on the Attempt to Create a Single Market in the European Union' (1996) 102 *American Journal of Sociology* 1.

[28] Case C-106/89 *Marleasing v La Comercial* [1990] ECR I-4135.

[29] E Santner, *The Royal Remains: The People's Two Bodies and the Endgames of Sovereignty* (University of Chicago 2011) 3.

[30] *Frontini v Ministero delle Finanze* [1974] 2 CMLR 372, para 9.

transferred subject matter was confined to economic relations with it 'difficult to form even abstractly the hypothesis that a [Union] Regulation can have effect in civil, ethno-social or political relations through which provisions can conflict with the Constitution'.[31] A similar ethos, albeit more cryptically phrased, is present in the reasoning of the German Constitutional Court in *IHT*. It characterizes the Union as not a State but as both a *sui generis* community and an inter-State institution.[32] It is, in other words, an association of human beings which have come to be governed. The EU, moreover, is only a settlement which governs. Article 24 (the then relevant provision of the German Basic Law) allowed for a transfer of sovereign rights to inter-State institutions, but, was not according to the Court, to be read literally. The State's exclusive right to rule remained intact with the provision merely requiring German law to open itself up not to EU law rule but to 'the direct effect and applicability of law from another source'.[33] The Union, moreover, is something which does not go to the deeper political imaginary of Germany constitutional democracy. It is not to do anything, therefore, which 'encroach[es] on the structures which go to make the [German Constitution] up'. These structures are not to be seen exclusively in formal terms but rather encompass those understandings which go to the identity of the Constitution: its sense of what it is about. We find similar language used in *Cohn Bendit*, the well-known decision of the French Conseil d'Etat refusing to grant direct effect to Directives. This decision was justified partly on a literal reading of the Treaty, which did not provide in the Conseil's view for direct effect. However, a prior reason was given, namely that EU law, notably Article 56 of the Treaty,[34] excluded EU law-making over the 'ordre public':[35] that concept in French law, wider than public policy, which comprises that body of laws which allow 'life in society and the organisation of the Nation'.[36]

What was to be the subject-matter of this reserved space? Within the Westphalian model, territory was used to establish the parameters of national sovereignty. This could not be the case here as EU law clearly had authority in national territories over certain fields of activity. Instead, resort was had to the idea that the distinctive identity of different political communities relies on some idea of human existence to describe and sustain their terms and foundations in a way that allows them both to be recognizable to and distinguishable from other political communities.[37] Charles Taylor has observed that with the onset of modernity, this idea of existence became vested in:

> a picture of human order... which sees us as historical agents, bodies in a material world, which move towards modes of common life in which our individuality is respected.[38]

[31] *Frontini* (n 30) para 21.

[32] *IHT v Einfuhr und Vorratsstelle für Getreide und Futtermittel* [1974] 2 CMLR 540, para 19.

[33] *IHT* (n 32) para 22.

[34] Now Consolidated Version of the Treaty on the Functioning of the European Union [2010] C83/47 (TFEU), art 52.

[35] *Cohn-Bendit v Ministre de l'Intérieure* [1980] 1 CMLR 543.

[36] Available at <http://www.toupie.org/Dictionnaire/Ordre_public.htm> (last accessed 21 April 2013).

[37] PW Kahn, *Political Theology: Four New Chapters on the Concept of Sovereignty* (Columbia University Press 2011) 39–45.

[38] C Taylor, *A Secular Age* (Harvard University Press 2007) 279.

This idea of a human order has been encapsulated in a number of terms: people, nation, public, or society. In all cases, it is used to justify the unity and authority of the domestic political system. Its normative qualities, thus, enable law-making and the exercise of institutional power, [39] but also act as a constraint insofar as institutions must be guided by these qualities and not violate them. Beyond this, the human order also grants the political system an identity. It sets out a representation of a way of life which that political community is deemed to have inherited and whose mission it is to act out. This way of life, moreover, is something that the political community can never transcend but can only develop insofar as it goes to what that community is and what it holds sacred.

The vesting of sovereignty in this human order emphasized its centrality to the organization and identity of domestic political life. It also set it out as something to be protected. However, most fundamentally, it set out the contours and qualities of this human order. As a sovereign, it inherited the qualities and shape of the metaphor of its predecessor, which had performed an analogous role: that of the King's Bodies.[40] This led to this human order, and modern ideas of political community, having four dimensions, in particular.

It is *organological*. Its elements can be only properly understood in the light of their relationship to the whole.[41] It had *temporal persistence*, so that it was granted an eternal, secular, political life.[42] It was to be granted *dignity and acclaim* in that its qualities were to be seen as both singular to it and as sufficiently special in their own right to be worthy of lionization.[43] It represented a *lived experience* through laying down its own history, traditions, and myths.[44]

Lastly, as a sovereign, this human order marks itself out from government in two important regards. First, it sets out a different form of association. Individuals form part of this order merely by virtue of their co-presence. Their simple being is sufficient to generate ties between them and other members of this order. Government, by contrast, is dedicated to establishing associative ties for common purposes. Individuals are recognized insofar as they relate to this common purpose or activity and to others participating in such a venture.

The second difference goes to the quality of power enjoyed and exercised. The sovereign possesses a power to reign or, in modern parlance, to rule. This is an absolute and transcendental power. It contrasts with ordered power, which is the power necessary to execute the objectives of those holding authority.[45] Law, as the

[39] Loughlin (n 13) 184–9.

[40] In the Middle Ages, the sovereign was the King's Bodies: the physiological body of the monarch and the body politic, comprising the totality of the subjects, social relations, institutions, and moral ends of a political system. If the former allowed a particular individual to rule, the latter enabled continuity of rule, and marked out the qualities and contours of the political community. See EH Kantorowicz, *The King's Two Bodies: A Study in Medieval Political Theology* (Princeton University Press 1997) 207ff.

[41] Kantorowicz (n 40) 199–203. [42] Santner (n 29) 41.

[43] Kantorowicz (n 40) 383–5; Agamben (n 23) 167ff. [44] Kahn (n 37) 26.

[45] Agamben locates this division in theological roots. Sovereign power is a divine power vested in the King and the Kingdom. The origins of governmental power are vested in angels whose role is to praise the sovereign, contemplate, act as role models for subjects, and administer the affairs of the kingdom. See Agamben (n 23) 68–82, 144–60.

institutional expression of sovereign command, has come to occupy this place of reign. This is most vividly expressed in the idea of the rule of law, which sees law, *in toto*, as something which can extend itself to rule anything it wishes. This raises a curiosity about EU law. If the treaties claim that the rule of law is a value on which the Union is founded,[46] there has never been a claim to a *rule of EU law* over anybody other than the EU Institutions.[47] If EU law rules over these, it is only granted attributes to enable it to have sufficient ordering force over discrete spheres of activities: autonomy, effectiveness, and the fidelity principle in Article 4(3) TEU which requires EU Institutions and Member States to secure the tasks which flow from the treaties.

(2) The formalization and ring-fencing of the human order

The deployment of this tradition of sovereignty to mark out a space reserved from EU law led to its formalization. If, previously this human order had stood for a symbolic order, a way for individuals to understand how things are done and their place in the world,[48] it was now associated with boundary-marking between EU and national law and differentiation and categorization of different fields of activity.

(a) The organological qualities of social policy and criminal justice

Domestic laws encapsulating a vision of the national society as a collective, indivisible body which generates mutual commitments between citizens are protected from EU law.[49] Social laws are one example with the grounds for entitlements typically fused together, so that citizens acquire these partly by reason of their membership of the body politic, partly by reason of their human needs and partly by ideas of what society, as a body, can sustain.[50] A similar logic is applied to criminal law which can be represented as, on the one hand, a series of mutual commitments between individuals and the body politic not to harm one another, and, on the other, a series of common ties binding citizens together as a body oriented around common ideas of harm. This leads not just to an aversion to EU law governing significant aspects of criminal law[51] but also to certain elements of criminal law—notably the idea that other States should try a State's own citizens—being seen as elements of citizenship which should not be disrupted excessively by EU law.[52] The

[46] Consolidated Version of the Treaty on European Union [2010] OJ C83/13 (TEU) art 2(1)

[47] Most recently see Case C-336/09 P *Poland v Commission* (Grand Chamber, 26 June 2012) para 36.

[48] Santner (n 29) 2–32.

[49] On mechanical solidarity, E Durkheim, *The Division of Labour in Society* (L Coser trans, Macmillan 1984) chs II and III.

[50] *Admenta et al v Federfarma et al* [2006] 2 CMLR 47; Pl ÚS 5/12 *Slovak Pensions* (Czech Constitutional Court, 31 January 2012).

[51] *Ratification of Lisbon Treaty* (Germany) (n 20); *Assange v Swedish Prosecution Authority* [2012] UKSC 22, [2012] 2 AC 471; *Re Enforcement of a European Arrest Warrant against Tzoannos* (Greek Court of Appeal) [2008] 2 CMLR 38.

[52] *Re Enforcement of a European Arrest Warrant* (Polish Constitutional Tribunal) [2006] 1 CMLR 36; *Re Constitutionality of Framework Decision on the European Arrest Warrant* (Czech Constitutional Court) [2007] 3 CMLR 24; *Cyprus v Konstantinou* [2007] 3 CMLR 42.

organological metaphor brings out a further element to the relationship between EU and national law. As the body has some resilience, harm to the parts does not necessarily mean that the integrity of the body is being challenged. Problems are only generated where *significant* parts of social, criminal, or citizenship law are governed by EU law. It is only where the intrusion is sufficiently meaningful—be it in terms of the range of activities or resources involved or their resonance—that the integrity of the body politic is placed in doubt.[53]

(b) Temporal persistence and fundamental rights

The idea of temporal persistence has been identified most strongly with fundamental rights laws. These are presented as a series of values around which strangers can constellate.[54] These impersonal qualities can be presented as something eternal, connecting the past and the present, and as something universal, stretching across space. Fundamental rights are presented, therefore, as something which does not belong to a particular territory but a European heritage shared by the Union and member States which are universal in nature.[55] These qualities, in turn, allow them to be seen as something which forms not just part of the national body politic but can carry over into EU law.[56] However, this occurs only symbolically. It is predominantly the ideational elements which carry over, namely the important idea that the Union observes EU law. A host of national legal systems have emphasized that fundamental rights go to the stability, meaning, and worth of their particular political community.[57] This bond is not to be disrupted by EU law. Insofar as EU law touches on controversial debates about conflicts between fundamental rights or about the limits of these rights, the Court of Justice is quick to say that the question of whether a breach has occurred, is one for the national judicial system not it.[58] It is manifested, in like vein, in the territoriality of national constitutional courts over the interpretation of fundamental rights with very few references being made to the Court of Justice on the interpretation of these. National settlements have also been fiercely protective of rights which are regarded as fundamental within their constitutions but which do not carry that pedigree across the rest of the EU.[59]

[53] A variety of formulations are used. These includes matters 'inherent' to national sovereignty (see *Re Ratification of the Lisbon Treaty* (French Constitutional Council) [2010] 2 CMLR 26, paras 7–9); 'material core' (*Re Czech Sugar Quotas* [2006] 3 CMLR 15, paras 109–110); 'sufficient space…for the political formation of the economic, cultural and social living conditions' (*Ratification of Lisbon Treaty* (Germany) (n 20) para 249).

[54] MJ Sandel, *Liberalism and the Limits of Justice* (CUP 1982) 143.

[55] Preamble to the TEU (n 46), alinea 2.

[56] TEU (n 46) Art 6(1).

[57] See also *Ratification of the Lisbon Treaty* [2010] 1 CMLR 42 (Latvia); *Decision 17/04 regarding Agricultural Surpluses* (Hungarian Constitutional Court, May 2004); Pl ÚS 50/04 *Sugar Quotas III* (Czech Constitutional Court, 3 March 2008); K 32/09 *Lisbon Treaty* (Poland) (n 21).

[58] In the case of EU instruments, the administration of these is seen as a matter for national authorities and therefore to be resolved by national courts See Case C-540/03 *Parliament v Council* [2006] ECR I-5769. Similarly, it is national courts which have to rule whether a national measure which falls within the field of EU law violates fundamental rights. See Case C-260/89 *ERT v DEP* [1991] ECR I-2925.

[59] Protocol on Article 40.3.3 of the Constitution of Ireland [2004] OJ C310/377; Protocol No. 7 Act of Accession of Malta to the European Union (2003); Declaration 61 to the Treaty of Lisbon by

(c) *The dignity and singularity of territory, citizenship, and political authority*

The dignity and singularity of the King's Bodies lay, in part, in their being seen as bringing the political system into being and enabling it to persist. In the modern day, dignity and singularity is granted to those elements of the State seen as necessary for uniting territory, subjects, and government into a unitary conception of political life and which enable the political system to retain its autonomy and authority (its dignity) vis-à-vis other spheres of life.[60] Territory, the social contract, and the authority of public office are seen as giving rise not simply to the State but to the presence of the public qualities of political life. As a consequence, the monopoly of State authority over these is recognized.

With regard to territory, EU law does not affect national competences to demarcate borders.[61] This vision also extends to States retaining control over central elements of foreign policy, insofar as these, like territory, mark out political identity within international society.[62] Further, the social contract between State and citizen is viewed through the prism of the nationality relationship.[63] Described as a bond creating a 'special relationship of solidarity and good faith',[64] the establishment and termination of this relationship is a matter for national law.[65] The reciprocal entitlements and responsibilities seen as going to its special qualities are also protected from the full force of EU law. These include the right to be tried by one's own State,[66] rights to vote and stand in national elections,[67] right to hold high public office,[68] and duties to pay taxes.[69] Finally, those qualities of public office or the public space which are seen as granting it a public and distinctive status are

the Republic of Poland on the Charter of Fundamental Rights of the European Union [2000] OJ C364/1.

60 Loughlin (n 13) 186–96.

61 TFEU (n 34) art 77(4); Protocol on External Relations of The Member States with Regard to the Crossing of External Borders [2004] OJ C310/361; Case C-16/05 *R v Secretary of State for the Home Department, ex p. Tum & Dar* [2007] ECR I-7415.

62 Protocol on the Position of Denmark [2004] OJ C310/356, Art 5; Protocol on the Concerns of the Irish People on the Treaty of Lisbon [2013] OJ L60/131, Art 3.

63 On how migration and naturalization problematize this, most notably in relation to electoral rights, see J Shaw, 'Sovereignty at the Boundaries of the Polity' in N Walker (ed) *Sovereignty in Transition* (Hart Publishing 2003).

64 Case C-1135/08 *Rottmann v Freistaat Bayern* [2010] ECR I-1449, para 51.

65 *Rottmann* (n 64). The hypothetical possibility is held out that a Member State cannot extinguish nationality in such a way that it violates EU law but this will not be the case where these qualities are not considered present in the relationship (ie nationality acquired by dishonesty or, one assumes, insufficient connection to the State of nationality).

66 See the case law in n 51.

67 These rights are excluded from EU citizenship rights in TFEU (n 34) Arts 20, 22. To be sure, some States' constitutions saw municipal electoral rights as part of this prior to Maastricht (*Re Treaty on European Union* (Decision 92–308) JORF 1992, No 5354); *Re Treaty on European Union* (Spanish Constitutional Court) [1994] 3 CMLR 101.

68 Member States may reserve these for their own nationals by virtue of the TFEU (n 34) Arts 45(4), 51.

69 To be sure, all fiscal residents are subject to liability to pay tax. However, only nationals can be prevented from leaving the territory on these grounds (Case C-434/10 *Aladzhov* (Judgment of 17 November 2011)). Similar reasoning would no doubt apply to jury or conscription duties.

protected: be these the secular qualities of the French State[70] or those entitlements granted particularly to Heads of State.[71]

(d) *The human order as a lived experience*

There is concern to emphasize that the order underpinning the State system is a human one, rather than a moral one. In *Brunner*, for example, the German Constitutional Court talks of the protection of a 'living democracy' in Member States.[72] There is concern to ring-fence structures which relate ideas of the good and the right with the lives of a particular society: be these charities, educational, or religious institutions.[73] Similar treatment is accorded to the home. There is much EU law preventing national laws or practices disrupting family or private law. However, it governs far less certainly those experiences which go to the make-up of this private life. The right to marriage or to found a family are to be determined in accordance with national law.[74] There is no right to housing within EU law.[75] Likewise, various States have insisted on Protocols or Declarations to protect their understandings of family life.[76]

(3) The dangers of having, and not having, a domestic human order

This tradition of sovereignty emphasizes that government power should be constrained. This constraint requires governmental authority to be justified by reference to those qualities we associate with authority figures: capacity, expertise, wisdom, and fairness. Sovereignty also acts to restrain those pathological features of government which see life too much through a monocular prism of realizing a common purpose or ideal State. It emphasizes the presence and value of other types of community and tie, and that space must be found for these. However, this tradition of sovereignty has a dark side. Excessive sanctity granted to this human order allows its conservatism not only to be unchallenged but transgression not to be tolerated, as its sanctification requires that it be given effect over everything else. It becomes quickly a fascistic artefact.[77]

Elements of this have emerged within the EU debate. Insofar as sovereignty has been deployed in this way, it has been used for a very practical task, namely to protect domestic activities from EU intrusion. This has led to this idea of human

[70] *Re European Union Constitutional Treaty and the French Constitution* [2005] 1 CMLR 750.

[71] Case C-364/10 *Hungary v Slovak Republic* (Grand Chamber, 16 October 2012) para 35.

[72] *Brunner v TEU* [1994] 1 CMLR 57, para 107.

[73] Protocol on the concerns of the Irish people (n 62) Art 1.

[74] EUCFR (n 59) Art 9.

[75] There is talk merely of the right to housing assistance (EUCFR, Art 34(3)).

[76] Protocol on the concerns of the Irish people (n 62) Art 1; Declaration 61 to the Lisbon Treaty (Poland) (n 59).

[77] On how this happens within the work of Carl Schmitt see H Lindahl, 'Constituent Power and Reflexive Identity: Towards an Ontology of Collective Selfhood' in M Loughlin and W Neil (eds) *The Paradox of Constitutionalism: Constituent Power and Constitutional Form* (OUP 2006) 21–4.

order becoming too formalized. It has become associated with a particular set of activities with little regard to how central these activities are to making us who we are. A bigger problem, however, is the dichotomization which takes place. If any activity falls within this ring-fenced field belonging to the sovereign (ie social policy, criminal law, fundamental rights, etc.) it is not to be significantly troubled by EU law. This stops EU law realizing its potential as a vehicle for political communities to re-imagine themselves. There is a whole tradition associating EU law with providing a vehicle for giving under-represented interests voice or enabling us to transcend what we have at the present or to recognize more fully the singularity of others.[78] This is not realizable if those activities perceived as most central to collective identity formation are insulated from this purview. As a consequence, this vision of sovereignty often also has a peculiar impoverished vision of domestic political community.

However, dangers are also evident in those States who have not followed this tradition. This occurs in those States which allow international treaties to limit their sovereignty but place no counter-check on the international treaty. EU law thereby takes precedence over all national law including the constitution.[79] This leads to weak restraints on EU government. It is allowed to go wherever EU law's purposes lead it and to have as much as force as is necessary to realize these purposes.

States following this path have, therefore, adopted a variety of routes to counter this. In Ireland for example, this authorization of power by the external sovereign is taken to be something only the people and not the government can do.[80] All treaty amendments have, thus, been subject to referendums and all EU treaty amendments have been characterized by a series of exceptions to protect the Irish vision of this tradition of sovereignty.[81] Another approach has been to fret about the quality of governmental process offered by the Union. Dutch courts, for example, have refused to follow Court of Justice rulings where they believe it oversteps the proper role of a court.[82] Likewise, Austrian courts have emphasized the importance of fundamental rights as a check on EU government.[83] With these latter approaches, if there is not to be a continual second-guessing of EU processes and controls, a

[78] JHH Weiler, 'To be a European Citizen—Eros and Civilization' (1997) 4 *JEPP* 495; J Kristeva, *The Crisis of the European Subject* (Other Press 2000) ch 3. U Beck and E Grande, *Cosmopolitan Europe* (Polity Press 2007) 6–9, 225–40; R Gasché, *Europe, or the Infinite Task: A Study of a Philosophical Concept* (Stanford University Press 2009) 342.

[79] *Connect Austria*, VfSlg 15.427/1999 (Austria); *Minister for Economic Affairs v Fromagerie Franco-Suisse 'Le Ski'* [1972] CMLR 330; *Orfinger v Belgium* [2000] 1 CMLR 612 (Belgium); Constitution of the Kingdom of the Netherlands 2002, Arts 91–3.

[80] *Crotty v An Taoiseach* [1987] IR 713 (Irish Supreme Court) [62] (Walsh J).

[81] Protocol on the Irish Constitution (n 59); Protocol No 4 on the position of the UK and Ireland [2007] OJ C340; Declaration of the Seville European Council on the National Declaration of Ireland (Nice concerning defence) POLGEN 52 13463/02; Protocol on the Concerns of the Irish (n 62).

[82] S Garben, 'Sky-High Controversy and High-Flying Claims? The Sturgeon Case Law in the Light of Judicial Activism, Euroscepticism and Eurolegalism' (2013) 50 *CML Rev* 15, 30–3. For similar debates in Belgium, see M Melchior and P Vandernoot, 'Contrôle de constitutionnalité et droit communautaire derivé' (1997) *Revue Belge de Droit Constitutionnel* 3.

[83] See the current preliminary reference from that court to the Court of Justice, Case C-594/12 *Seitlinger et al*, EU Council, *Information Note*, 5 March 2013, 7115/13.

considerable deference has still, however, to be granted to the Union. Furthermore, nothing is in place to counter the expansion of government. It can dominate, under this ethos, all forms of activity and way of life, and there would be nothing unproblematic to this.

D. Sovereignty as Ordainment

(1) The European multiplication of ordainment

The tradition of sovereignty as ordainment is traceable back to William of Ockham who, noting that God and Christ did not involve themselves with daily rule, observed that ordainment took place of those, the Church, who were to do this in their name.[84] This was replicated in the distinction between the sovereign power of the King and those who administered on his behalf. As monarchy disappeared with modernity, this became a simple distinction between sovereign and government. If the sovereign was general and transcendent and government derived and concrete each relied on the other for its coming into being. Without the presence of government, sovereign power could not be realized in daily life. Conversely, government relied for its authority on some blessing by the sovereign.[85] The presence of a single providential order required that the sovereign had a power of ordainment which linked and coordinated the two.

The onset of EU law led once again to a formalization of this tradition. The sovereign, be it the Member States or some other being or institution, became something which had put the Union into being. It had authorized the Union and, thereby, bequeathed it with authority. As a consequence, the Union enjoyed a fiduciary relationship with regard to it. It was to act on its behalf. It was not to abuse that trust by exceeding anticipated limits on what it can do or acting in an abusive or procedurally improper way. In this way, sovereignty becomes a watchdog over EU governmental activity.

This tradition emerged, first, in the *Matter* doctrine: the French approach to the authority of EU law prior to 1975. Under this doctrine, as treaty law, EU law was authorized by the French Parliament to apply within France. In cases of conflict with subsequent French laws, French courts were to reconcile differences by interpreting EU law and the French statute to be mutually compatible wherever possible.[86] If this were not possible, the French statute was to prevail. Formally, this was because it occupied a hierarchically superior position to EU law.[87] Ideationally, however, this was because the French statute was seen as expressing a general will (*volonté*

[84] F Maiolo, *Medieval Sovereignty: Marsilius of Padua and Bartolus of Saxoferrato* (Eburon 2007) 151–3; JB Elshtain, *Sovereignty: God, State and Self* (Basic Books 2008) 33–40.

[85] Agamben (2011) (n 23) 109–43.

[86] For a similar approach in the United Kingdom see *Macarthys Ltd v Smith* [1981] 1 QB 180 (CA).

[87] On the *Matter* doctrine see J Plötner, 'Report on France' in A-M Slaughter, A Stone Smith, and JHH Weiler (eds) *The European Court and National Courts: Doctrine and Jurisprudence* (Hart Publishing 1998) 44–6.

générale) which should have precedence over laws without these qualities, and were therefore transgressing the leeway granted to them by this general will.

Brunner, the decision of the German Constitutional Court reviewing the constitutionality of the Maastricht Treaty, marked a step change in this reasoning. Sovereignty is not vested in the State or in an institution, but in the human order which is being ruled, and is now granted the power to authorize government.[88] This was followed through, and made more explicit in the subsequent *Lisbon Treaty* judgment of the German Court where it stated 'sovereign statehood stands for a pacified area and the order guaranteed therein on the basis of individual freedom and collective self-determination'.[89] A doctrine of democratic sovereignty was, thereby, introduced into the EU debate with a sovereign human order both authorizing governmental power and holding it accountable.[90]

This begs the question as to the nature of the human order which can be deployed to authorize government and hold it to account. *Brunner* sets out one as a people with its own independent metaphysical presence which exists in some way prior to the presence of any political settlement. The presence of this people is, in turn, a precondition for the presence of democracy (the *No Demos* thesis). This was rightly eviscerated on the grounds of its ethno-centric bias.[91] However, others have observed that this human order could have other traits. It could simply be all those affected or anticipated to be affected by a rule. In this manner, it could become a transnational or global constituency which gives rise to transnational or cosmopolitan rule.[92] Democratic sovereignty, under this vision, allows for a dissipation of institutional power and political community away from the State. De-anchored from statehood or particular institutions, the sovereign can divide itself and multiply. The power of ordainment now acquires an active jurisgenerative capacity to authorize and put in play new patterns of rule, which it did not have previously.

Less frequently observed is the effect of *Brunner* on sovereignty's ordaining powers over government. Historically, this ordainment emphasizes government's contingency and insufficiency.[93] Sovereign power is set out as something conferring, indivisible, and transcendental whilst governmental power is characterized as derived, discrete, and material. *Brunner* recasts this, by allowing the sovereign to authorize not just government but also the transfer of sovereignty.[94] It was thus, stated that Member States established the Union to exercise part of their '[government] function in common and to that extent to exercise their sovereignty in common'.[95]

[88] *Brunner* (n 72) paras 35, 40.

[89] *Ratification of Lisbon Treaty* (Germany) (n 20) para 224.

[90] On this debate in Germany see A von Bogdandy, 'Globalization and Europe: How to Square Democracy, Globalization, and International Law' (2004) 15 *EJIL* 885, 887–8, 901–2.

[91] JHH Weiler, 'Does Europe Need a Constitution? Demos, Telos and the German Maastricht Decision' (1995) 1 *European Journal of International Law* 219, 224–31.

[92] S Benhabib, 'Claiming Rights across Borders: International Human Rights and Democratic Sovereignty' (2009) 103 *American Political Science Review* 691; J Habermas, *The Crisis of the European Union: A Response* (Polity 2012) 42ff.

[93] Lindahl (n 11).

[94] This idea of sovereignty being transferred to the Union has been followed in Slovenia (Constitution, Art 3a); Latvia (*Ratification of the Lisbon Treaty* [2010] 1 CMLR 42, para 210) and the Czech Republic (Pl ÚS 19/08 *Lisbon Treaty I* (Czech Republic) (n 21) para 105).

[95] *Brunner* (n 72) para 52.

The distinction between the ordaining sovereign and the ordained government is therefore put in doubt.

This doubt was reflected in the establishment of the *Kompetenz-Kompetenz* which had to establish a relationship between the ordaining and ordained sovereign. This recreated the distinction between sovereignty and government, albeit with the national sovereign taking the role of the former and the European sovereign the latter. All traditions involved, thus, found national sovereignty had an original and ordaining quality which European sovereignty did not possess. The establishment of this role required the national sovereign to become actively engaged in the business of government through patrolling the democratic quality of EU government. This brief for national sovereignty was to reduce it to a form of administrative law.

(2) Sovereignty as European administrative law

This administrative law function involved a number of patrolling elements. The first goes to the limit of Union powers. The Union is to operate under a doctrine of limited powers and only have powers whose ambit is 'sufficiently foreseeable'.[96] This applies not just to the Union as a whole but also to particular institutions. EU Institutions are not to exceed their anticipated brief or adopt a measure not seen as in keeping with their institutional function. The most notable example, *Slovak Pensions*, concerned a refusal by the Czech Constitutional Court to follow a Court of Justice judgment which declared that a scheme compensating Czech citizens who received lower Slovak pensions under the agreement dissolving Czechoslovakia illegal insofar as these benefits were only granted to Czechs resident in the Czech Republic, and therefore discriminated against other EU citizens. The Czech Court stated that the Court of Justice had acted ultra vires insofar as it failed to account for the complexity of arrangements dealing with State dissolution or their centrality to Czech history by treating it simply in terms of free movement of EU citizens.[97]

The second field of concern is to the quality of policy-making. In *European Stability Mechanism Treaty* the Estonian Supreme Court found that the treaty compromised Estonian financial sovereignty by allowing significant financial assistance from euro area States, including Estonia, to be granted in emergencies by Qualified Majority to States with financing difficulties.[98] It held that the measure would be lawful if it was for legitimate purposes and proportionate. It considered the stability of the euro area to be such a purpose, but then considered whether the instrument was proportionate. It looked, first, at whether the measure was appropriate. For this it looked at how the European Stability Mechanism ('ESM') balanced efficient

[96] *Brunner* (n 72) para 33; *Ratification of Lisbon Treaty* (Germany) (n 20) para 322.

[97] *Slovak Pensions* (n 50). The Court of Justice judgment is Case C-399/09 *Landtová* [2011] ECR I-5573. For further analysis see J Komárek, 'Playing with Matches: The Czech Constitutional Court Declares a Judgment of the Court of Justice of the EU Ultra Vires' (2012) 8 *European Constitutional Law Review* 323.

[98] Case 3–4–1–6–12 (n 22).

decision-making with protecting Estonian influence. It then looked at whether the measure was reasonable by assessing the size of the Estonian contribution.

The third element is securing institutional oversight. The institutions necessary to secure democratic control vary according to national preferences. The German Constitutional Court has argued that increasingly intrusive measures require greater involvement by the European Parliament.[99] The Danish and Estonian Courts argue, by contrast, that involvement and effective influence of the national government in the Council is necessary to protect national sovereignty.[100] In *Slovak Pensions*, a feature in the Czech Constitutional Court's decision that the Court of Justice had acted illegally was the failure by the latter to allow the Czech court to submit an amicus curiae brief outlining the consequences for the Czech legal system. It considered the lack of domestic judicial involvement a failure of due process. If the institutions vary, however, their role is invariably cast as a prudential one in which they review or advise EU government in order to block or limit its adverse effects.

The final ground for patrol is respect for fundamental rights. It has already been mentioned that fundamental rights are characterized as forming part of the national human order which is to be protected from EU law. This protection extends not merely to resistance to an EU fundamental rights law which would submerge national fundamental rights law but to transgressions of national fundamental rights by EU Institutions or EU law. This, combined with arguments of democratic control, pushed for a national sovereign who ensured that EU government did not violate fundamental rights.[101] A number of national courts—German, Italian, Hungarian, Czech, Polish, Latvian, and Estonian—have, thus, made EU observance of fundamental rights a precondition for the authority of EU law.[102]

(3) Sovereignty as democratic acclaim for EU government

EU law acceded to the demands that democratic controls be placed over EU government by replicating these controls within its structures. As a ground of review, fundamental rights were incorporated into EU law, and then granted the same formal status as the TEU.[103] There was similarly a commitment to conferred powers and to EU Institutions observing the proportionality principle.[104] And, finally, over time, mimicking national models, parliamentary involvement increased in both EU law-making and over review of EU administrative activities.[105] It is unclear how rigorous these are as controls. There is only one instance of any provision of a

[99] *Brunner* (n 72) para 40.

[100] *Carlsen v Rasmussen* [1999] 3 CMLR 854, para 9.9; Case 3–4–1–6–12 (n 22) para 184.

[101] As a consequence, within the Union there is not really an EU human rights policy. Focus is instead on EU Institutions and implementing national measures, as an extension of this government, not violating fundamental rights. This is in stark contrast to EU external policies which pursue very active human rights agendas; A Williams, *EU Human Rights Policies: A Study in Irony* (OUP 2004) ch 4.

[102] See Santner (n 29), and the cases referred in n 57.

[103] TEU (n 46) Art 6(1).

[104] TEU (n 46) art 5(1).

[105] On how these paralleled each other as legitimating strategies see B Rittberger, *Building Europe's Parliament: Democratic Representation beyond the Nation State* (OUP 2005) ch 6.

Directive being struck down because it violates fundamental rights[106] and only one clear instance of EU Institutions having exceeded the doctrine of conferred powers.[107] The proportionality principle, similarly, grants considerably latitude to the EU legislature which will only be found to have violated the principle where the legislation is 'manifestly inappropriate'.[108] Finally, whilst national parliamentary input within EU decision-making has increased, it is confined to consultation by the Commission and to policing the subsidiarity principle.[109]

This begs the question as to why national sovereignty has not been asserted more aggressively to limit EU government. Agamben has argued that sovereign controls of this ilk are, in reality, a form of acclaim: something on which government has always relied.[110] This acclaim has a ceremonial function of legitimating government by granting it a certain glory. In modern times, government becomes through this something sanctioned by the public as democratic. This acclaim struggles, however, to limit or control government.

All this raises the question as to whether the autonomy of EU law sets out conditions where it is all but impossible for sovereign controls to do anything but sanctify EU government. As a tool of government, EU law claims to realize three benefits which, in turn, allow it a freedom from sovereign controls. The first is the provision of collective goods. The second benefit is that (EU) law establishes associative ties between people who would otherwise be strangers. Finally, (EU) law enables social ordering by setting clear parameters about permissible behaviour. This allows parties to realize things for themselves by planning their lives with a certain degree of certainty and idea of what is possible.[111]

These benefits make it very difficult to disapply an established EU law. Even if parties object to the way in which it secures one of these benefits (ie the goods it pursues) there is still the problem about what to do with the other two elements. Suspending a disliked law generates problems about what to do with the relationships that have settled around it and raises issues of legal uncertainty. Furthermore, this creates as much uncertainty for domestic law as for EU law as it is unclear when the latter is to prevail over EU law and when not. In terms of associative ties, it can destabilize trust by piercing a regulatory reality which has established self-perceptions and perceptions about other parties. Finally, it can undermine law's claim to authoritative settlement. Many might claim that EU law is morally bankrupt, but, without some substitute vision to replace the space left by EU law, it is a claim that no law is better than this law.

[106] Case C-236/09 *Association Belge des Consommateurs Test-Achats v Conseil des Ministres* [2011] ECR I-00773.

[107] Case C-355/10 *Parliament v Council and Commission* (Grand Chamber, 5 September 2012). The European Union's proposal to accede to the ECHR was also found to exceed its powers but the measure was just a draft at that stage *Opinion 2/94 Re Accession to the ECHR* [1996] ECR I-1759.

[108] See, eg, Case C-309/10 *Agrana Zucker v Bundesminister für Land- und Forstwirtschaft, Umwelt und Wasserwirtschaft* (28 July 2011); Case C-59/11 *Association Kapokelli v Baumaux* (12 July 2012).

[109] See, eg, TEU (n 46) Art 12(a)–(b).

[110] Agamben (n 23) 194–6, 253–9.

[111] On law as a planning tool see SJ Shapiro, *Legality* (Harvard University Press 2011) chs 6 and 7.

These arguments exert a powerful pull where there is any settled EU law as they go to the power of law as an institution of government. One sees this where there is a settled EU law in practice no equivalent substitute domestic law that can be introduced relatively seamlessly. This is best shown by a comparison of *ex ante* adjudication by national courts which looks at EU laws not yet in force and *ex post* adjudication where national courts are called on to disapply EU laws. *Ex ante* regulation typically occurs on a State's accession to the Union, consideration of treaty amendments or international treaties related to the integration process, such as that on the European Stability Mechanism. In the event, a host of *ex ante* judgments condition the authority of EU law.[112] To be sure, courts are induced to address this question at such a moment. However, they could choose just to repeat prior jurisprudence. That they do not is testament to both their having a particular freedom at such moment and to the concerns raised by EU law.

The approach with *ex post* judgments is very different. The overwhelming majority accept the authority of EU law. Opposition, when expressed, is formulated in a subversive form so as not to challenge the authority of EU law directly. A variety of techniques are deployed to present challenges as sporadic and ad hoc rather than as a basis for the authority of EU law. These include targeting implementing domestic legislation rather than the EU law itself;[113] deciding the matter under national law rather than EU law;[114] narrow interpretation of EU legal norms;[115] or referring the matter back to the domestic political process to sort out the difficulties wherever legal consonance is not possible.[116] When there are explicit disapplications, moreover, it is telling that they always relate to either a well-established national law[117] or to targeting an administrative measure.[118]

This difference is also apparent in the reasoning of constitutional courts. The Hungarian and Polish Constitutional Courts thus both gave judgments on, or prior to, accession suggesting both a sceptical posture to the claims of the Court of Justice and a disposition to give only limited authority to EU law.[119] Confronted with an EU law already in force, they both took a far more deferential approach.[120] The most striking example, however, is that of German Constitutional Court with regard

[112] See, eg, *Ratification of Lisbon Treaty* (Germany) (n 20); *Re Lisbon Treaty* (Latvia) [2010] CMLR 24; K 32/09 *Lisbon Treaty* (Poland) (n 21); *Ratification of the Lisbon Treaty* (France) (n 53).

[113] *Constitutionality of German Law Implementing the Framework Decision on a European Arrest Warrant* [2006] 1 CMLR 16.

[114] *AG v X* [1992] 2 CMLR 277; *Tzoannos* (n 51); *Assange* (n 51).

[115] See, eg, the actions against the Italian Supreme Court of Cassation and the Austrian Administrative Court in Case C-12/00 *Commission v Italy* [2003] ECR I-4637; Case C-224/01 *Köbler v Republik Osterreich* [2003] ECR I-10239. In a similar vein see *AG of Cyprus v Konstantinou* [2007] 3 CMLR 24.

[116] *Re Enforcement of a European Arrest Warrant* [2006] 1 CMLR 36 (Polish Constitutional Tribunal).

[117] *Re Value Added Tax Directives* [1982] 1 CMLR 427; *Admenta et al* (n 50); *Slovak Pensions* (n 50).

[118] *Internationale Handelsgesellschaft v Einfuhr und Vorratsstelle für Getreide und Futtermittel* [1974] 2 CMLR 540; *Minister of the Interior v Cohn-Bendit* [1980] 1 CMLR 543.

[119] *Decision 30/1998 invalidating Article 62 of the 1994 Europe Agreement* (Hungarian Constitutional Court, 25 June 1998); *Decision 17/04 regarding Agricultural Surpluses* (Hungarian Constitutional Court, 25 May 2004); K 18/04 *Polish Accession to the European Union* (Polish Constitutional Court, 11 May 2005).

[120] K 3/08 *Competence of every Polish Court to make a Preliminary Ruling* (Polish Constitutional Court, 18 February 2009); Decision 143/2010 (VII 14) *Constitutionality of the Act of promulgation of*

to the Lisbon Treaty. In its *Lisbon Treaty* judgment, prior to German ratification of the Lisbon Treaty, the Court was adamant about the doctrine of limited powers applying to the Union in such a way that the Union only has sufficiently precise powers.[121] The Court would not just monitor this but also observance of the subsidiarity principle[122] and that Union competencies were not developed with resort to any methods of interpretation beyond those of *effet utile* or implied powers.[123] However, a year later in *Honeywell,* a case right at the edge of Union powers[124] the Court took a different approach, both substantively and procedurally. Substantively, it stated that it would not revise measures of the Union which were ultra vires but only measures where the exceeding of powers was drastic and obvious.[125] Even this would be insufficient to lead domestic review as this would threaten the uniformity and precedence of EU law. National judicial control could only take place where the Court of Justice had first been given an opportunity to consider the matter itself and had failed to hold the measure invalid.[126]

E. European Sovereign Government

(1) The *folies de grandeur* of European democratic sovereignty

The dynamics of these two debates on sovereignty generated a third mode of thinking about sovereignty, that of European sovereign government. Within it, the human order, be it the people or the democratic order, is no longer seen as limiting government or rendering it contingent. Instead, government is now taken to be synonymous with the will of the sovereign. Institutions have to be aligned to reflect this, and to allow the sovereign to be actively involved with its discharge of government. There is said to be correspondingly less need for external controls on the range of governmental activities or on the manner in which they are exercised.

The idea of a European sovereign government was put most fully into play by the *Lisbon Treaty* judgment of the German Constitutional Court, which had to consider what political conditions would support a move to a European federal State. This, it was said, would not require a *Demos* but that Union powers enjoyed sufficient 'democratic legitimation'.[127] A European federation could only occur where it was 'fully consistent with the requirements for the democratic legitimation of a union of rule organised by a State':[128] when EU legal and institutional structures 'create an

the Lisbon Treaty (Hungarian Constitutional Court, 12 July 2010) (The Lisbon Treaty was already in force when this was adopted).

[121] *Ratification of Lisbon Treaty* (Germany) (n 20) para 236.

[122] *Ratification of the Treaty of Lisbon* (Germany) (n 20) para 240.

[123] *Ratification of the Treaty of Lisbon* (Germany) (n 20) para 242.

[124] Decision 2 BvR 2661/06 *Honeywell* (German Constitutional Court, 6 July 2010). The case concerned whether Directives could generate obligations for private parties prior to the transposition date. The Federal Labour Court had considered that this exceeded Union powers.

[125] *Honeywell* (n 124) para 61.

[126] *Honeywell* (n 124) paras 58–60.

[127] *Ratification of the Treaty of Lisbon* (Germany) (n 20) para 264.

[128] *Ratification of the Treaty of Lisbon* (Germany) (n 20) para 263.

independent people's sovereignty for all Union citizens'.[129] This would require the Union to have a 'democratic core' in which the 'decision of the people is the focal point of the formation and retention of political power'. Legislative office must, in particular, be based on the presence of elections in which all citizens are treated as free and equals.[130]

The Court then went on to consider the institutional conditions for when the Union could enjoy democratic sovereignty, and thus enjoy general powers of government. Democratic legitimation could not, it believed, be provided by any EU Institutions.[131] Democratic legitimation could however be provided through the involvement of national Parliaments in its decision-making as these possessed the mandate to be seen as democratic representatives of this human order.[132]

The implications of this were spelt out by the Court in most detail in its *ESM Treaty (Temporary Injunction).*[133] The judgment concerned a challenge to the treaty between the euro area States establishing the ESM,[134] which exposed States to unprecedented public expenditure liabilities and moved the Union much more aggressively into budgetary policy. Financial support could only be offered if States met certain conditions, typically balancing their public finances and economies. These conditions typically involve a mixture of privatizations, tax rises, and public spending cuts. The ESM thus also moves European integration into the field of fiscal and welfare policy.

The Court indicated that decisions on public expenditure and revenue were a 'fundamental part of the ability of a constitutional State to democratically shape itself'.[135] Significant budgetary decisions, such as the ESM Treaty, went in other words to a State's sense of its democratic identity. They were so fundamental that they could not be seen as a limited power. However, what makes these measures more fundamental than measures in other fields? The idea of democratic self-shaping conveys the idea of a human order which needs to be able to rule certain activities to have a sufficient form to be whole. Taxation is one of these activities, insofar as it lies at the heart of the social contract which allows citizens to be represented not merely as a group of individuals but as a collective being (a people or public) and finances those policies, which are most intimately associated with the metaphor of the human order as a collective human being (ie, social policy, foreign and defence, criminal justice). For the German Constitutional Court, EU government was

[129] *Ratification of the Treaty of Lisbon* (Germany) (n 20) para 281.

[130] *Ratification of the Treaty of Lisbon* (Germany) (n 20) paras 270–1.

[131] *Ratification of the Treaty of Lisbon* (Germany) (n 20) paras 287, 297.

[132] These include the amendment procedures; TFEU (n 34) art 352. *Ratification of the Treaty of Lisbon* (Germany) (n 20) paras 301–28. On the subsequent procedures put in place see D Jancic, 'Caveats from Karlsruhe and Lisbon: Whither Democracy after Lisbon?' (2010) 16 *Columbia Journal of European Law* 337. This requirement of domestic parliament approval has been followed in the United Kingdom. See European Union Act 2011, s 8.

[133] Case 2 BvR 1390/12 et al *ESM Treaty Temporary Injunction* (German Constitutional Court, 12 September 2012).

[134] See J Tomkin, 'Contradiction, Circumvention and Conceptual Gymnastics: The Impact of the Adoption of the ESM Treaty on the State of European Democracy' (2013) 14 *German LJ* 169.

[135] *ESM Treaty Temporary Injunction* (n 133) para 194 (all references are to the English translation).

therefore to be extended to a field normally reserved for sovereign rule provided this government was controlled by the representative of this order, the German Bundestag. The Bundestag had, therefore, to retain control over all 'fundamental budgetary decisions'.[136] Furthermore, in exercising this control, it must enjoy complete autonomy and be 'free of other-directedness on the part of the bodies and of other Member States of the EU and remain(s) permanently "the master of its decisions"'.[137] As a dominant arm of EU government, Bundestag involvement is to be gradated according to the perceived budgetary importance of the activity. In principle, its involvement, in particular its powers of financial approval and monitoring, must increase in proportion to the size of the financial liability or spending commitment.[138] In particular, the Bundestag must be able to approve every large scale aid measure. It must have sufficient influence over the manner in which the funds are spent. Finally, the Bundestag must be provided with sufficient information about the workings of the Mechanism to be able to assess the basis for and the consequences of any decision.[139]

This reasoning abolishes the distinction between sovereignty and government so that they become one. The people, qua individual citizens, only become sovereign insofar as they govern through national Parliaments. Government only enjoys authority insofar as it involves the sovereign. This joinder justifies EU government in areas previously protected from it, and subject to sovereign rule. As EU government now involves the sovereign, it has the power to rule all those fields which are traditionally ruled by the sovereign. The German Court, therefore, talks of the strengthening of the position of national Parliaments in EU structures to 'use their (national parliaments') reservoir of legitimation to benefit European processes'.[140] Such a power is, moreover, subject only to the constraints of parliamentary assent and those which the EU places on itself. There is no need to impose external controls on EU government. Instead, as the sovereign is now seen as fully involved in the activity of government so that she is governing herself (or -selves),[141] these external controls become otiose.

(2) A Schmittian Europe?

The bringing together of sovereignty and government harks back to a darker tradition, the Schmittian one in which the sovereign both founds legal authority and governs it. For Schmitt, the central mission of any political order was to provide public safety and order. The sovereign was the body which could provide that order.[142]

[136] *ESM Treaty Temporary Injunction* (n 133) para 195.
[137] *ESM Treaty Temporary Injunction* (n 133) para 197.
[138] *ESM Treaty Temporary Injunction* (n 133) para 196.
[139] *ESM Treaty Temporary Injunction* (n 133) paras 198–9.
[140] *ESM Treaty Temporary Injunction* (n 133) para 226.
[141] M Wendel, 'Judicial Restraint and the Return to Openness: The Decision of the German Federal Constitutional Court on the ESM and the Fiscal Treaty of 12 September 2012' (2013) 21 *German LJ* 21, 31–40.
[142] C Schmitt, *Political Theology: Four Chapters on the Concept of Sovereignty* (C Schwab trans, MIT 1985) 6.

The mode of association was, therefore, not one of mutual recognition or of realizing common projects. It was rather securing the interests of the political order and of ensuring no threat to stability. As a consequence, sovereignty was vested in the body or capacity best placed to secure this rather than in any broader justification. It lay in that body's ability to produce and guarantee a State of affairs.[143] Now Article 3 of the ESM Treaty states:

> The purpose of the ESM shall be to mobilise funding and provide stability support under strict conditionality... to the benefit of ESM Members which are experiencing, or are threatened by, severe financing problems, if indispensable to safeguard the financial stability of the euro area as a whole and of its Member States.

The ESM's mission is to safeguard the euro area and national financial stability. The associative ties established by it are not concerned with securing mutual recognition of citizens or of realizing common purposes. They are to secure order and the survival of the system: a European *raison d'état* in which the latter becomes not simply a value in itself but possibly the highest value. Other forms of associative tie are consequently downgraded relative to this mission. The rationale for the ESM lies, furthermore, in its power to secure this order and save the system: its capacity to harness the financial resources provided by national governments. This is reflected in the political structures of the ESM where voting weights are calibrated according to the financial contribution of the government.[144] The powers of the EU Institutions within this body are also, correspondingly, fluid and novel. The central decision-making body, the Board of Governors, comprizes euro area finance ministers.[145] Its composition is identical to the Council of Ministers when it considers euro area matters of monetary policy, but it now exercises another function, namely to lend financial support and approve the terms of that support: set out in Memorandum of Understanding between the ESM and the State concerned.[146] If the Council has become a banker, the Commission and European Central Bank negotiate and supervise the conditions which have to be met by the debtor State.[147] This is a new task, in particular, for the European Central Bank. Its dominant task has, historically, been setting short-term interest rates. It is now negotiating and supervising welfare and fiscal reform. The reason for these new tasks, in all cases, is a belief in the capacity of the institution. It can realize the objectives set of it. Thus, the ECB and the Commission ask for assistance from the IMF in negotiating conditions and monitoring their implementation precisely because this will augment their capacity.[148]

The second feature of the Schmittian sovereign is the power of decision. The sovereign decides what constitutes public order and security, and this power

[143] Schmitt (n 142) 13.

[144] Treaty establishing the European Stability Mechanism, T/ESM 2012/en 1, Art 4(7). For criticism see M Dawson and F de Witte, 'Constitutional Balance in the EU after the Euro-Crisis' (2013) 76 *MLR* (forthcoming).

[145] TESM (n 144) Art 5(1).

[146] TESM (n 144) Art 13(4). This is formally signed by the Commission.

[147] TESM (n 144) Art 13.

[148] TESM (n 144) Arts 13(1)(a), 13(7).

founds the political system.[149] As a foundational power, this decision precedes law, thereby giving a prior power to the administration. The power of decision operates in a qualified way within the ESM. The ESM and the government seeking support decide the measures necessary to restore stability, notably the level of financial support and the conditions to be attached. These are set out in a Memorandum of Understanding rather than any law.

However, to what extent does this decision precede the law? The ESM has been characterized by the Court of Justice as an international agreement which exists independently of the EU Treaties. It can enjoy competencies beyond those set out in those Treaties. EU Institutions can be granted powers by it that are not granted to them by the EU Treaties. Finally, as it operates beyond the aegis of EU law, the checks and balances and fundamental rights checks provided by EU law do not apply to the exercise of powers under the ESM.[150] The only checks on institutional power, beyond the financial resources available to the ESM, are that it must obey the ESM Treaty, the substantive requirements of EU law, and powers granted to EU Institutions was not to alter the 'essential character' of the powers enjoyed under the Treaties.[151] None of these checks are meaningful. The only substantive constraint imposed by the ESM Treaty on the Memorandum of Understanding which governs a debtor States fiscal and welfare policy is that it must reflect the 'severity of the weaknesses' addressed.[152] Similarly, as the funding arrangements extend beyond the remit of EU law, it imposes few limits on what can be demanded or offered. In looking at the powers granted to the EU Institutions, the Court did not examine whether these were performing radically new tasks but rather at the governmental objectives to which these contribute. It noted that the European Central Bank was required to support the economic policies of the Union and that the Commission was to promote the general interest of the Union under the ESM Treaty, and this was sufficient.[153] Finally, the legal quality of the conditions to be met by the State in this Memorandum is unclear for it is not a treaty or instrument of EU law. It is a decision outside the law. However, it is also a decision which gives rise to law, insofar as both creditor and debtor States will have to take legal measures to implement it.

The final feature of the sovereign is that it decides who constitute members of the political community. For Schmitt, this goes to the political quality of the sovereign. It is to decide who is outside the political community and, therefore, the enemy of that community. This goes to the question of that community's existence.[154] If the ESM Treaty is silent on this, EU government is not. The President of the Commission has indicated that overcoming the crisis represented 'a fight for European integration itself'.[155] Alongside this, the crisis is presented as one of systemic risk whereby the whole European political economy could collapse as a consequence of the ripple

[149] Schmitt (n 142) 8–9.
[150] Case C-370/12 *Pringle v Ireland* [2013] All ER (EC) 1 (ECJ).
[151] *Pringle* (n 150) para 158.
[152] TESM (n 144) Art 13(3).
[153] *Pringle* (n 150) paras 162–9.
[154] C Schmitt, *Constitutional Theory* (J Seitzer trans, Duke University Press 2008) 389.
[155] JM Durão Barroso, Speech to the European Parliament during the Debate on the Economic Crises and the Euro, Plenary Session of the European Parliament, Strasbourg, 14 September 2011,

effects from either a sovereign debt default or a bankruptcy of a large commercial bank.[156] To refuse aid or to default is to be an enemy not simply of the euro but, presented like this, of Europe itself. It is not clear what possibility for membership of the Union exists for States who default.

Wisely, the German Constitutional Court never explicitly vests sovereignty in the ESM in its *ESM (Temporary Injunctions)* judgment. It is seen, however, as the next worse thing: an exercise of democratic sovereignty. This is used to legitimate an EU governmental machine which claims if not a general right to rule, then certainly an open-ended power of government. It is to govern those activities seen as central to generating ties of solidarity within domestic societies in which the needs and aspirations of citizens are supported not because they contribute to some policy or goal but because they allow a collective dignity and flourishing. In a sovereign governmental world, these ties matter less than the central concern of sustaining sovereign power. Insofar as governmental rule rests on sustaining external activities as a series of well-functioning orders, and these activities are more often than not marked by instability and disjuncture, sovereign government becomes a normative imperative to secure ever wider rule not merely to secure the good functioning of the external activities that is the business of government but to safeguard the (perceived) survival of the political system.[157]

F. Conclusion

The genius and the folly of EU debates on sovereignty lie in their fluidity. The need for different interlocutors to justify sovereignty leads to different justifications and, in turn, different uses being found for it. This has led to a revitalization of sovereignty as a concept: EU debates engage with the term like no other debates. Further, sovereignty is granted an emancipatory potential. It is difficult to explain its appeal if it is not a tool of self-assertion and protest. One root of this appeal lies in sovereignty emphasizing the multiplicity of associative ties which sustain any political community. If government brings people together to realize common purposes, these will never be sufficient and will inevitably have divisive qualities insofar as the common purpose generates winners and losers. The rule of the sovereign emphasizes that

available at <http://europa.eu/rapid/press-release_SPEECH-11-572_en.htm?locale=en> (last accessed 21 April 2013).

[156] Council Regulation (EC) 1174/2011 of 16 November 2011 on enforcement measures to correct excessive macroeconomic imbalances in the euro area [2011] OJ L306/8, esp Art 3(2).

[157] To secure 'genuine' economic and monetary union, an extension of EU government has been called for. Contracts between each euro area State and the EU Institutions will be made governing all fields of activity covered by the ESM Treaty (ie welfare policy, labour, capital and service market regulation, fiscal policy). These will apply to all euro area States and will be indefinite. There will be accountability to national parliaments and the European Parliament for content and implementation. It is not clear, however, that these will be involved in the formulation of these non-legislative documents. President of the European Council Report, 'Towards a Genuine Economic and Monetary Union', Brussels, 2012, 13–16.

another form of association is necessary for political communities in which ties are built simply on co-presence and mutual recognition on one's equality before the sovereign. If it has many limits, it can nevertheless better capture the singularity of subjects and ideas of kinship. The other root of sovereignty's appeal lies in the contingency and limited materiality it ascribes to governmental power. It captures the need for government to be seen as perennially insufficient in what it can offer: be these limits in the government's resources, its cognitive blinkers, its potential for abuse or simply its confined materiality.

The deployment of the term has, nevertheless, been fraught and unsatisfactory. In large part this is because, as sovereignty asserts a strong power, it has habitually been used by the powerful to consolidate power. This consolidation has taken the form of its rendering national rulers unaccountable or its being used to justify centralized EU intervention. This might be simply innate to the term. It lacks insufficient safeguards to prevent its abuse. However, something else has taken place within the EU debate. The unity of the relationship between rulers and ruled, which sovereignty has traditionally signified, has been lost. This unity involves subjects submitting themselves to the rule of the sovereign but the quid pro quo is that the sovereign rules for the benefit of its subjects. In contrast, in EU debates sovereignty has become a terrain for competition over which administration rules. In this arm wrestle between administrations, the quid pro quo made with subjects is forgotten. In principle, national or EU administrations govern for the ruled. If this were brought more to the fore, this would entitle the ruled, whether as a national political community or pan Union one, to say to any administration 'Enough! This does not work for us the sovereign!' In short, sovereignty in EU debates should emphasize more the political limits of all rule. This is the message from the Lithuanian Constitution which is quoted in the Introduction. It is a pity that EU debates about sovereignty don't take place more often in Lithuanian.

12

Sovereignties in Strasbourg

David Feldman[*]

A. Introduction

Much has been written about States' constitutional mechanisms for controlling the impact of international law on municipal legal and political orders. Little attention has been paid to the reverse process, whereby international tribunals take account of States' internal structures when developing international law. International lawyers tend to assume the normative superiority of international over municipal law, and so are less interested than they might be in ways of making international law responsive to a State's constitutional or political imperatives. Yet such mechanisms do exist, usually seen as resulting from a clash between national sovereignty and international law. This chapter examines them in the context of the approach of the European Court of Human Rights to applying the Council of Europe's Convention for the Protection of Human Rights and Fundamental Freedoms 1950 ('ECHR'). It distinguishes between three forms of sovereignty—national or State sovereignty, constitutional sovereignty, and legislative sovereignty—and argues that, while they are largely irrelevant to international legal theory concerning the relationship between international and national law, there are sometimes good reasons of both prudence and principle for international institutions to give thought to the constitutional and political realities of life within States before extending the substance of States' obligations. The argument is illustrated with examples of issues which have given rise to tension between the Strasbourg Court and national authorities.

B. National, Constitutional, and Legislative Sovereignty in International Law

We must first distinguish between three doctrines which are often described by the term 'sovereignty'. The first is State sovereignty, a concept of international law.

* Rouse Ball Professor of English Law, University of Cambridge.

The second is constitutional sovereignty, a creature of national, constitutional law and theory. The last is legislative sovereignty, which may take many forms and is a creature of national, constitutional law.

State sovereignty in public international law is not concerned with hierarchical ordering either within or between States. On the contrary: it asserts the essential equality of States before international law. Simply being a State under international law carries with it the idea of sovereign equality. In principle, every State is equal in its sovereignty.[1] This makes it the equivalent of equality before the law as a principle of the rule of law in domestic legal and political orders. The existence within a territory of governmental bodies collectively exercising effective control over the territory is one of the indicators that there is a State on that territory.[2] States do not readily recognize other entities as States unless there is that degree of control. It follows that for a territory to constitute a State its government must be able to operate to some degree independently of the will of governments of other States. Hence international law requires, as a basic principle, that States do not (without lawful justification) interfere in the internal affairs of other States.

State sovereignty thus recognizes a State's right, in general, to determine its own internal structure and policies by procedures which it chooses for itself. That right can never be absolute, for three reasons. First, States have interests, and policies adopted by a State can easily affect neighbouring States and, sometimes, more distant States. Those States, with their own sovereignties and interests to protect, are legitimately interested in policy choices of other States. Secondly, in order to minimize the risks arising from conflict between States when their interests clash, or to allow States to cooperate in advancing interests which overlap, States can agree with each other to act or not to act in certain ways, or to establish inter-State or supra-State institutions for collaborative or independent policy-making. International law treats these inter-State agreements (treaties) as capable of imposing obligations on States which may be legally enforceable or subject to supranational arbitration or mediation. States (like contracting parties in domestic law) are required to submit to the obligations and dispute-resolution processes to which they have themselves agreed. Adhering to the principle *pacta sunt servanda* makes possible secure inter-State relations. Thirdly, international intervention in a State's internal affairs may be authorized in exceptional circumstances by an invitation from the State itself (as in Mali in 2013), by international humanitarian law, or by resolution of the UN Security Council made under Chapter VII of the UN Charter to preserve international peace and security.

Except in relation to intervention in one of those ways, international law is not generally concerned with constitutional and legislative structures within a State. International lawyers are principally concerned with rules governing the behaviour of States in their dealings with other States. Nevertheless, when States agree to

[1] Charter of the United Nations 1946, Art 2.1; International Law Commission, *Draft Declaration on the Rights and Duties of States 1949*, Arts 1, 3, 5.

[2] On the criteria of statehood, see J Crawford, *The Creation of States in International Law* (2nd edn, OUP 2006) chs 1–5 (on effective control, see particularly ch 2).

behave in specific ways the principle *pacta sunt servanda* means that they limit the range of the internal policy choices and laws which they can make without violating their obligations to other States in international law. State sovereignty does not excuse or justify a breach of a State's treaty obligations, except in carefully circumscribed circumstances. A State's internal structures, such as the foundations of constitutionalism or the location of constitutional or legislative sovereignty within the State, are thus normally irrelevant to a State's international obligations. International tribunals are blind to them, save that they expect States to arrange and operate their internal structures (whatever form they take) so as to enable them to comply with their obligations in international law.[3]

Sometimes, however, a State's internal structures may make it difficult or impossible for it to comply with the State's international obligations. For example, there may be practical, political, constitutional, or legal obstacles to complying with a treaty obligation to treat people in a particular way. The risk of a clash between internal and international obligations is greatest in two circumstances. First, there is a serious tension between international law and State sovereignty when international law imposes an obligation to behave in a way that is contrary to a State's perception of its own interests. Secondly, there may be a tension between dominant political forces within a State and the demands of public international law. Such difficulties are particularly likely when international law imposes obligations on a State in respect of its treatment of individuals, groups or corporations. The law of the World Trade Organisation, refugee law, treatment of combatants and civilians in time of war, and human-rights law regularly give rise to problems of this sort.

Constitutional sovereignty, the idea that a State's constitution is supreme over its law and must be obeyed by all State institutions, is a creature of constitutional theory, not international law. The constitution of the United States is paradigmatic. But it is important to bear in mind two points. First, some States do not distinguish clearly between constitutional and other norms. The United Kingdom is an example of this.[4] Secondly, even States which do make the distinction systematically may treat constitutional norms as inferior to some or all norms of international law or supra-national organizations such as the EU, and do not necessarily regard municipal legal norms as invalid if they conflict with constitutional norms. The Netherlands offers an example of this.[5] Constitutional sovereignty in the US sense is, therefore, far from universal, though it is considerably less uncommon than it once was.

[3] See, eg, International Law Commission's Articles on State Responsibility, Art 4; *Armed Activities on the Territory of the Congo* (*Democratic Republic of the Congo v Rwanda*) (Jurisdiction and Admissibility) ICJ Rep [2006], p 27, [46]–[47]; *Application of the International Convention on the Elimination of All Forms of Racial Discrimination* (*Georgia v Russia*) (Preliminary Objections) ICJ Rep [2011], p 18, [37]. I am grateful to William Bateman for drawing the significance of these judgments to my attention.

[4] See, eg, P Leyland, *The Constitution of the United Kingdom: A Contextual Analysis* (2nd edn, Hart Publishing 2012) 26–32; House of Lords Constitution Committee, *The Process of Constitutional Change* (HL Paper (2010–12) no 177) [3]–[15]; D Feldman, 'The Nature and Significance of "Constitutional" Legislation' (2013) 129 *LQR* 343–58.

[5] Constitution of the Kingdom of the Netherlands, Arts 94, 120, available at <http://legislationline.org/documents/section/constitutions/country/12> (last accessed 19 April 2013).

The location and meaning of *legislative sovereignty* within a political and legal order is a matter for the members of that polity. Sovereignty here signifies the hierarchical superiority of legislation produced by a particular person, institution, or group over legislation produced by other people, institutions, or groups. It operates for the purpose of establishing priorities between norms of that polity's legal system, and has no implication for the relationship between norms of that system and norms of other systems, such as international law.

C. State Sovereignty and the ECHR

The ECHR is a multilateral, international treaty. Under Article 1, each of the 'High Contracting Parties' (ie States Parties to the Convention, of which there are currently forty-seven, with a total population of about 800 million people) gave an undertaking to all the others to secure the rights in the Convention, including those Protocols to which the State in question is a party, to everyone within its jurisdiction. The United Kingdom was one of the original High Contracting Parties. The Convention and Protocol No. 1 took effect in relation to the United Kingdom in 1953. One of the unusual features of the Convention was that it established two special, international bodies (the European Commission of Human Rights and the European Court of Human Rights ('ECtHR')) to resolve allegations that States had violated people's Convention rights. The Commission was to investigate petitions from States or, where a State had accepted its jurisdiction so to do, from individuals complaining that a State had violated their rights under the Convention. The Commission operated behind closed doors, and was initially very cautious about finding violations by States in its reports. It had power to refer cases to the ECtHR for a formal adjudication, but rarely did so.[6] On the rare occasions when it was called upon, the Court, while deliberating in private, could hold public hearings, delivered its judgments in public, and was sometimes more outspoken in criticizing States than the Commission typically was.[7] The Court and the Commission had different roles. The Commission saw itself as developing compliance with the Convention, and considered that it should develop the trust of States to that end in order to encourage them to grant the right of individual petition and accept the jurisdiction of the Court in relation to them. The Court saw itself as an adjudicative body with a duty to stand above all the parties.[8] Where cases were not referred to the Court, the Committee of Ministers of the Council of Europe, a political, inter-governmental body, decided whether to uphold a report of the Commission finding a violation. If the Court or the Committee of Ministers established a violation, the Committee was responsible for overseeing, by political and diplomatic

[6] E Bates, *The Evolution of the European Convention on Human Rights From its Inception to the Creation of a Permanent Court of Human Rights* (OUP 2010) 191–225.

[7] Bates notes the high quality of the judges of the Court and their frustration at having so few cases referred to them. See Bates (n 6) 179–84.

[8] Bates (n 6) 215–25 and also at 179–84.

means, the respondent State's implementation of the judgment of the Court or decision of the Committee.

It would be hard to exaggerate the concern of States at the prospect of an adverse decision by the Court having serious diplomatic and reputational consequences for them.[9] The Commission's caution built up States' confidence in the system. When the United Kingdom accepted the compulsory jurisdiction of the Commission and Court in respect of individual petitions in 1965 (taking effect in 1966), no State had been held by the Court to have violated a Convention right. The first judgments establishing violations were delivered in 1968, a full fifteen years after the Convention had come into operation.[10] Forty years later, the work of the Court had developed in ways which caused some political leaders in the United Kingdom to characterize its case-law as infringing the United Kingdom's national sovereignty. This concern is linked to UK parliamentarians' concern that judgments of the Court adverse to the United Kingdom have infringed parliamentary sovereignty in the United Kingdom by effectively forcing Parliament to legislate in ways of which a majority of members of the House of Commons disapprove, for example in relation to prisoners' voting rights.

Those concerns arise from the way in which the Court has interpreted the Convention, extending States' obligations in unexpected directions. The Court treats the Convention as a living instrument, and does not consider itself bound to interpret it in accordance with the intentions of its framers or the original High Contracting Parties. As a result, there has been a steady expansion in the scope of several of the rights, in the coercive powers asserted by the Court, and in the territorial reach of States' Convention obligations. Dissatisfaction in the United Kingdom with the effects of the Court's interpretation of the Convention sometimes spills over into dissatisfaction with the Court itself, and even with the Convention, leading to threats to denounce the Convention in order to reassert national and parliamentary sovereignty. Subsequent sections of this chapter will explore these matters. At this point, however, we should clarify how State sovereignty operates in the field of international treaties generally and the ECHR in particular.

By virtue of its sovereignty in international law, the United Kingdom is entitled to enter into treaties. It did so: the ECHR and those of its Protocols to which the United Kingdom is a party are the result of an exercise by the United Kingdom of its sovereignty. The United Kingdom did not immediately accept the jurisdiction of the Court (and originally the European Commission of Human Rights) over applications by individuals who complain that a State has violated their rights under the ECHR. That was at first optional. When the United Kingdom's government declared in 1965, under what was then Article 25 of the ECHR, that it would accept the jurisdiction of the Court in relation to individual complaints, the decision was temporary: the declaration remained in force for only five years unless it was renewed. Successive UK governments had to decide whether to renew

[9] AWB Simpson, *Human Rights and the End of Empire: Britain and the Genesis of the European Convention* (OUP 2001) 678–9, 718–20, 723–30, 1082–99.

[10] Bates (n 6) 185–91, 248–51.

it, and did renew it, every three years until 1972, then every two years until 1976, then every five years until Protocol No 11 came into operation in 1998.

Protocol No 11 thoroughly renovated the ECHR's procedural rules. The Commission ceased to exist, and the Court became a permanent, full-time body. When negotiating Protocol No 11, the United Kingdom agreed with all the other States which were parties to the ECHR that States should all accept, permanently, the right of individual petition and the jurisdiction of the Court over cases brought against the States by individuals. By signing and ratifying Protocol No 11, the United Kingdom's government as a High Contracting Party voluntarily accepted what became Article 34 of the ECHR:

> The Court may receive applications from any person, non-governmental organisation or group of individuals claiming to be the victim of a violation by one of the High Contracting Parties of the rights set forth in the Convention or the protocols thereto. The High Contracting Parties undertake not to hinder in any way the effective exercise of this right.

As a High Contracting Party to the ECHR, the United Kingdom also voluntarily accepted what are now Article 44 (providing that a judgment of a Chamber of the Court becomes final after three months if not referred to the Grand Chamber—earlier if the respondent State indicates that it will not seek to refer the case to the Grand Chamber—and that judgments of the Grand Chamber are always final) and Article 46.1: 'The High Contracting Parties undertake to abide by the final judgment of the Court in any case to which they are parties.'

This makes it clear that the Convention and the work of the Court result from the United Kingdom's exercise of its State sovereignty. The Court decides cases brought against the United Kingdom because the United Kingdom (among other High Contracting Parties) told it to do so. The Court's judgments bind the United Kingdom in international law because the United Kingdom (together with other High Contracting Parties) decided that they should be binding. This all came about as a direct result of an exercise by the United Kingdom of its State sovereignty in international law. It is no more (but no less) a limitation of that sovereignty than any other set of treaty obligations which the United Kingdom voluntarily assumes. Like any other contract, a treaty is made to be obeyed: *pacta sunt servanda* is an important principle of international law, as it is of domestic law. A State, having agreed with others to an international, judicial body's determining disputes authoritatively and finally, should not complain about the process when a decision goes against it.

Nevertheless, since international law can be effective only if States are by and large willing and able to give effect to it, international tribunals should minimize disincentives to compliance by not imposing excessively heavy burdens on them. Unlike much of public international law, human-rights treaties directly impose obligations on States with regard to their treatment of people *within their own jurisdictions*.[11] The effectiveness of the ECHR relies primarily on States' willingness to take action to secure the rights domestically. The role of the ECtHR is necessarily secondary and residual, as both the Court and the High Contracting Parties to

[11] See, eg, Convention for the Protection of Human Rights and Fundamental Freedoms 1950, Art 1.

the Convention recognize.[12] The Court must therefore be conscious of the limits to what a State can practically achieve. If a judgment makes unmanageable demands, it is liable to weaken the State's commitment and loyalty to the Convention system as a whole:

International human-rights law can function effectively only if it maintains the consent of the states which are subject to it. This has to be borne in mind by international judges. Failing to respect the dignity of states threatens the delicate thread linking a state's self-interest with its commitment to human rights and the international rule of law on which depends the efficacy of international human-rights adjudication. The state's continuing consent to be ruled by an international tribunal in human-rights matters is crucial to the effectiveness of the remedial regime of the ECHR. If states did not voluntarily comply with judgments of the Court, it would not be possible to force them to do so.[13]

This is not a purely pragmatic (or prudential) consideration. State sovereignty is one of the foundations of international law, and international tribunals put their own legitimacy at risk if they undermine it. If international tribunals develop international law in directions which make it difficult for States' institutions to ensure compliance because of constitutional, political, or legal arrangements, States cannot be expected to be able simply to change those arrangements, especially in functioning democracies which have to take account of public opinion and in States whose constitution is enforceable and lexically superior to ordinary laws. International law itself regards democratic and constitutional government as highly desirable: some would say it is mandatory;[14] but it comes at a price in terms of reliable compliance with developing international law.

That claim is not as simple as it sounds, because legitimacy is more complex than is often realized. There are many possible dimensions to legitimacy, and many possible criteria in each dimension. The dimensions include the legal, the political, the social, and the moral. In each dimension, relevant criteria may, or may not, include fidelity to constitutional principles, fidelity to basic rights, fidelity to ideas of the good, and fidelity to ideas of democracy. States' consent to the establishment of fundamental rights through treaty-making, and submission to the ECtHR's jurisdiction, are the source of the Court's legal legitimacy in international law (although legal legitimacy in international law is not wholly dependent on States' consent, as the doctrine of *ius cogens* and the operation of rules of international law *erga omnes* show). The court's political legitimacy, as a matter of international politics and diplomacy, requires that:

the decisions of the institutions should be reasonably capable of being accommodated within the mainstream of law within the State to which it applies, without causing violence

[12] *High Level Conference on the Future of the European Court of Human Rights* ('Brighton Declaration') (20 April 2012) paras 3, 4, 7, 9, 10 available at <http://hub.coe.int/20120419-brighton-declaration> (last accessed 21 April 2013).

[13] D Feldman, 'Establishing the Legitimacy of Judicial Procedures for Protecting Human Rights' (2001) 13 *European Review of Public Law* 139, 146.

[14] See, eg, the discussions in GH Fox and BR Roth (eds), *Democratic Governance and International Law* (CUP 2000); Crawford (n 2) 150–5, 333.

to the state's constitution, so that one can reach a position in which State compliance with decisions of the institutions becomes more or less routine.[15]

On the other hand, the moral and social legitimacy of international human-rights institutions is secured:

partly by virtue of their contribution to advancing the values of human rights, including those which support advanced forms of democracy. This dimension of legitimacy does not turn on the attitude of states towards the international institutions, but on the capacity and willingness of the institutions to translate the values of human rights into practical reality, which will depend crucially on appropriate procedures being available to fix states with liability for human-rights violations.[16]

The ECtHR can therefore properly adopt a dynamic approach to interpreting Convention rights. But this poses a dilemma:

There are ample opportunities for states to restrict their obligations, and it is not reasonable to allow them to complain about the enforcement of obligations to which they have agreed. However, there may be more substance to complaints that adjudicative bodies are interpreting the treaty obligations in ways which were not reasonably foreseeable when the treaty was drawn up. Where a court desires to adopt a dynamic style of interpretation, it becomes very important to the legitimacy of the judicial action that states should be able to continue to accept their developing obligations.[17]

These considerations produce a complex relationship between States and international institutions which allows room for the ECtHR to bolster its moral and social legitimacy by innovating in setting the content of human-rights standards as long as the court does not over-stretch its political legitimacy by eroding the patience and practical capacity of States. Tensions are inevitable, and they have to be managed by mutual sensitivity and usually tacit accommodations in order that States remain willing to accept and implement the court's judgments.[18]

The main doctrinal method of mediating between Strasbourg and national authorities in this respect is the 'margin of appreciation'. This is a subsidiarity principle: the ECtHR accepts that national authorities, being closer to local society than an international tribunal, are in a better position to assess social and moral conditions within the State. The court therefore respects assessments by national authorities of the needs of local communities as long as they can be shown to be objectively reasonable and rationally related to the legitimate aim of a measure which infringes a Convention right.[19] But the opportunity to use the margin of appreciation to add flexibility to the system is not always available. As it relates only to the assessment of States' justifications for interfering with rights, it does not apply to absolute rights for which no justification for interference is possible. Nor is it available if

[15] Feldman (n 13) 146–7. [16] Feldman (n 13) 147. [17] Feldman (n 13) 140–1.

[18] Feldman (n 13) 141.

[19] *Handyside v United Kingdom* (1979–80) 1 EHRR 737 [19], [22]–[23]; G Letsas, *A Theory of Interpretation of the European Convention on Human Rights* (OUP 2007) ch 4; D Harris, M O'Boyle, C Warbrick, and E Bates, *Law of the European Convention on Human Rights* (2nd edn, OUP 2009) 349–59.

the State fails to reach the stage of offering a reasoned justification because the interference is not prescribed by, or in accordance with, the law. Even when the margin of appreciation is available, the court's review function requires the State to show that a municipal authority genuinely assessed competing rights and interests; the court will respect a municipal assessment only if there has been one. This can lead the court to take an interest in acts and decisions of State institutions other than the executive, and as we shall see causes tension between the court and States.

D. National Constitutions and the ECHR

Constitutional sovereignty within a State is a matter of national law and political theory, usually considered to be of no interest to international law as long as national, constitutional principles do not breach, or prevent a State from meeting, its international legal obligations. But what happens if the ECHR is applied in such a way as to produce an obligation in international law which, for a combination of constitutional and political reasons, it is impossible for a State to comply with? This was the position when the ECtHR decided that constitutional privileges for the three Constituent Peoples of Bosnia and Herzegovina (BiH)—Bosniacs (Muslims), Croats, and Serbs—guaranteed by the Dayton Agreement which ended the war in former Yugoslavia in 1995 and reflected in the Constitution of Bosnia and Herzegovina, which formed Annex 4 to the Agreement, discriminated unjustifiably against Others (ie those who do not identify themselves as Bosniacs, Croats, or Serbs) in connection with their right to stand for election to the Presidency and House of Peoples of the State. When a related challenge was brought before the Constitutional Court of Bosnia and Herzegovina, the Court held that it lacked competence to deal with a claim that part of the Constitution which the court had a constitutional duty to uphold was unconstitutional. Nevertheless, at least one of the judges considered that the need to provide security for the Constituent Peoples as a condition for the peace agreement continued to provide an objective and rational justification for the unfavourable treatment of Others.[20]

When the issue was considered by the ECtHR in the context of human rights law rather than constitutional law, that court, unconstrained by the need to uphold the constitution, rejected the State's argument that the special arrangement was still justified, and found a violation of Article 14 taken together with Protocol 1, Article 3 of the ECHR in relation to the House of Peoples and a violation of Article 1 of Protocol 12 in relation to elections to the Presidency.[21] Unfortunately, the

[20] Case No U–5/04, *Request of Mr Sulejman Tihić* (Constitutional Court of Bosnia and Herzegovina, 31 March 2006). See also Case No U–13/05, *Request of Mr Sulejman Tihić* (Constitutional Court of Bosnia and Herzegovina, 26 May 2006), separate opinion of Judge Feldman, both available at <http://www.ccbh.ba/eng> (last accessed 21 April 2013).

[21] *Sejdić and Finci v Bosnia and Herzegovina*, Apps nos 72996/06 and 34836/06 (ECtHR, 22 December 2009). For extended evaluation and critique of the judgment, see C McCrudden and B O'Leary, *Courts and Consociations: Human Rights versus Power-Sharing* (OUP 2013) esp chs 6–8.

Court's reasoning failed to address seriously the problems still afflicting BiH, the issue of justification, or the use of the margin of appreciation in transitional States. The effect of the decision was to require the State to amend its Constitution. This has so far proved impossible, despite repeated deadlines set by the Committee of Ministers of the Council of Europe. That is not a surprise to anyone familiar with the political problems in the country. It was entirely predictable, given the lack of consensus on fundamental constitutional and political issues and the suspicion with which politicians from each Constituent People regard those from other Constituent Peoples. The difficulty of securing consensus among Peoples and parties is tellingly illustrated by the fact that, after the General Election in October 2010, it took over fourteen months to secure enough consensus among members of the House of Representatives to elect a Council of Ministers to govern the country. The Strasbourg Court's unrealistic expectations of BiH have reduced its authority among the political elite in that country.

This does not mean that the Court should have regarded the application as non-justiciable or treated the difference of treatment between Constituent Peoples and Others as not being in need of justification. To do so would have relativized Convention rights to a point at which there would be no common standard for Council of Europe nations. The problem arose because the Strasbourg Court, having held that principles governing the right under Protocol 12 to the ECHR to be free of discrimination in the enjoyment of legal rights were the same as those developed in relation to Article 14 of the ECHR, gave insufficient attention to its own case-law holding that the right under Article 14 (and the right to stand for election to the legislature under Article 3 of Protocol 1 to the ECHR) are not absolute rights.[22] These rights are not typical of public international law (or even of human rights in general) in this respect, because there is no express limit to the grounds on which a State may restrict them as long as there is an objective and rational justification for the restriction and it is not disproportionate to the legitimate aim of the measure. The Court said that, in relation to racial and ethnic discrimination, the grounds for justification must be interpreted as narrowly as possible. In this context, it was impressed by the fact that fourteen years had passed since the end of the war in former Yugoslavia, and eight years since Bosnia and Herzegovina had joined the Council of Europe and taken on obligations in international law under the ECHR. In the Court's view, the State had had ample time to bring its Constitution into line with the requirements of the Convention.[23] That, however, does not adequately deal with the complexity of the case. Bosnia and Herzegovina's obligations under the ECHR depended on whether there was an objective and rational justification for treating Others differently from Constituent Peoples in the political system. By refusing to take seriously the real problems which continued

[22] See, eg, *Belgian Linguistic* (1968) 1 EHRR 252; *Zarb Adami v Malta* (2006) 44 EHRR 49, para 73 on Art 14; *Mathieu-Mohin and Clerfayt v Belgium* (1987) 10 EHRR 1, para 52 on Protocol 1, Art 3.

[23] *Sejdić and Finci* (n 21) paras 44–56.

(and continue) to afflict the country and its peoples, the Court failed to make a proper assessment of the justification for a measure which was fundamental to the existence of the State, and had indeed been imposed on the State in 1995 by the international community through the Dayton Agreement in order to secure peace.

The saga provides a telling example of the dangers for the perceived legitimacy and authority of the Convention system when an international tribunal fails to have regard to political and social reality when deciding whether a State has a sufficient justification for interfering with a Convention right. It is legally as well as politically illegitimate for the Court to refuse to engage seriously with a State's problems when assessing whether an interference with or restriction of a qualified right is justified. Qualifications are permitted to allow States to take account of local needs. If ever there was a case that required careful assessment of proportionality in the light of a margin of appreciation as a condition for both the legitimacy and the effectiveness of the Court's judgment, this was it.

E. Legislative Sovereignty in Strasbourg

Section D argued that there are good reasons for international tribunals generally, and the ECtHR in particular, to think hard before delivering judgments which require States to amend their constitutions with regard to fundamental, structural characteristics of the State. This section turns the spotlight from constitutional provisions concerning the institutional structure of the State to legislative provisions which are not concerned with core, institutional structures. From the viewpoint of international law the executive, not the legislature, is usually regarded as representing the State on the international plane.[24] This reflects State practice. For example, treaty-making in the United Kingdom is a prerogative of the Crown, exercised by (typically) ministers. They are accountable to Parliament for their actions, and sometimes an Act of Parliament may be needed in order to discharge the obligations which arise from treaties, but ministers' authority to make treaties does not depend on parliament. That is one reason why constitutional law in the United Kingdom does not allow treaty provisions to create rights or obligations in domestic law without legislation.[25] By the same token, nothing contained in an Act of Parliament can affect the obligations which bind the United Kingdom in public international law. Nevertheless, as we have seen, an international tribunal which fails to take account of political and legal reality within a State puts its own effectiveness and authority at risk.

[24] *Application of the International Convention on the Elimination of All Forms of Racial Discrimination* (*Georgia v Russia*) (Preliminary Objections) ICJ Rep [2011], p 18, [37]. We shall see, however, that international tribunals sometimes look beyond the executive when assessing justifications for interfering with human rights.

[25] D Feldman, 'The Internationalization of Public Law and its Impact on the UK' in J Jowell and D Oliver (eds) *The Changing Constitution* (7th edn, OUP 2011).

We can illustrate this by reference to national provisions restricting aspects of the right to free elections to the legislature under Article 3 of Protocol 1 to the ECHR. In the United Kingdom, people convicted of felonies and treason were disenfranchised by the Forfeiture Act 1870. When the distinction between felonies and misdemeanours was abolished by the Criminal Justice Act 1967, the disfranchisement was applied to all convicts serving prison sentences, a position maintained by the Representation of the People Act 1983. In the case of the United Kingdom, litigation in Strasbourg has precipitated something approaching an impasse between the ECtHR and the United Kingdom. The clash has been presented in the United Kingdom as a result of the failure of the Strasbourg Court to take proper account of the legislative sovereignty of the United Kingdom's Parliament, which ought not to be compelled by international law to legislate in a manner contrary to the view of a majority of its members.[26]

The United Kingdom's doctrine of parliamentary sovereignty is, from one viewpoint, of no concern to international law. As we have seen, the Strasbourg Court deals only with States' obligations under the Convention as a matter of public international law. It decides whether a *State*, not an institution within a State, has violated a person's Convention right. Once the Court is satisfied that the events of which the applicant complains engage the responsibility of the State (rather than of individuals or substate institutions) in international law, the identity and constitutional powers of particular institutions or individuals within the State who made the impugned decision or took the action of which the applicant complains is irrelevant. States are free to organize their constitutional and institutional structures as they will, but international law requires that, however organized, States do not violate international law. From another perspective, however, we have seen that, for reasons of both effectiveness and legitimacy, international institutions cannot afford to ignore States' internal structures and political realities. The United Kingdom has been particularly concerned about the effect of some of the Court's decisions. One area of particular concern has related to prisoners' voting rights.[27]Article 3 of Protocol 1 of the ECHR provides:

> Right to free elections
> The High Contracting Parties undertake to hold free elections at reasonable intervals by secret ballot, under conditions which will ensure the free expression of the opinion of the people in the choice of the legislature.

[26] On 4 July 2013, the First Section of the Strasbourg Court decided two similar complaints relating to the Russian Federation: *Anchugov and Gladkov v Russia*, App nos 11157/04 and 15162/05 (not yet reported). In the case of Russia, the problem is complicated by the fact that the prohibition is contained in the Constitution. Art 32, which gives to citizens of the Federation the right to elect and be elected to State bodies and participate in referendums (Art 32.2), also deprives of that right citizens recognized by a court as legally unfit, and those kept in places of confinement pursuant to a court sentence (Art 32.3). Nevertheless, the Strasbourg Court, applying *Hirst* and *Scoppola (No 3)*, decided that the prohibition violated Art. 1.3 of Protocol 1 to the ECHR. The Court did not consider the domestic implications of the prohibition having constitutional status, as to which see Section D. Two further challenges have been lodged with the Court and are pending: *Kuchmara v Russia*, App No 4664/10; *Bolsunovskiy v Russia*, App No 16824/10. I am grateful to Dr Anton Burkov for drawing my attention to this.

[27] S Briant, 'Dialogue, Diplomacy and Defiance: Prisoners' Voting Rights' [2011] *EHRLR* 243. Another problematic area is the government's ability to remove immigrants from the United Kingdom

This does not expressly confer a right to vote or stand for election. One could conceivably satisfy the terms of Article 3 by holding parliamentary elections by way of focus groups or an electoral college of the kind required to elect a President by Article II of the US Constitution, as long as electors were chosen to provide a reliable cross-section of the opinion of the people. This, however, would be out of step with modern notions of democracy, as illustrated by Article 25 of the International Covenant on Civil and Political Rights of 1976:

Every citizen shall have the right and the opportunity, without any of the distinctions mentioned in article 2 and without unreasonable restrictions:

(a) To take part in the conduct of public affairs, directly or through freely chosen representatives;
(b) To vote and to be elected at genuine periodic elections which shall be by universal and equal suffrage and shall be held by secret ballot, guaranteeing the free expression of the will of the electors;
(c) To have access, on general terms of equality, to public service in his country.

The Strasbourg Court has accordingly interpreted Article 3 of Protocol 1 as conferring both a right to vote and a right to stand in elections conducted at regular intervals on the basis of free, universal, adult franchise, with a secret ballot in which each person's vote counts equally. At the same time, the Court is sensitive to the fact that there are many different models for such elections, and each State must be able to adopt a system which is appropriate for its political culture and circumstances.[28]

In the United Kingdom, however, section 3 of the Representation of the People Act 1983, as amended, provides:

3.—Disfranchisement of offenders in prison etc.

(1) A convicted person during the time that he is detained in a penal institution in pursuance of his sentence or unlawfully at large when he would otherwise be so detained is legally incapable of voting at any parliamentary or local government election.
(2) For this purpose—
    (a) 'convicted person' means any person found guilty of an offence (whether under the law of the United Kingdom or not), including a person found guilty by a court of a service offence within the meaning of the Armed Forces Act 2006, but

in pursuit of its immigration, extradition, and national security policies. This concern is of long standing; see, eg, *Soering v United Kingdom* (1989) 11 EHRR 439 (on extradition to the United States); *Chahal v United Kingdom* (1997) 23 EHRR 413 (on removal of a suspected Tamil terrorist to India). The United Kingdom has attempted (without notable success) to persuade the Court to relax the Convention's requirements in such cases: see *Saadi v Italy*, App no 37201/06 (Grand Chamber, 28 February 2008), (2009) 48 EHRR 730, in which the United Kingdom intervened; *Othman (Al Qatada) v United Kingdom*, App no 8139/09 (ECtHR, 17 January 2012), (2012) 55 EHRR 1; *Babar Ahmad and ors v United Kingdom*, App no 24027/07 (ECtHR, 10 April 2012), (2013) 56 EHRR 1.

[28] *Mathieu-Mohin* (n 22); *Sadak and ors v Turkey (No 2)*, App no 25144/94 (ECtHR, 11 June 2002); *Russian Conservative Party of Entrepreneurs v Russia*, Apps nos 55066/00 and 55638/00 (ECtHR, 11 January 2007) para 70; Harris et al (n 19) ch 20.

not including a person dealt with by committal or other summary process for contempt of court; and

(b) 'penal institution' means an institution to which the Prison Act 1952, the Prisons (Scotland) Act 1952 or the Prison Act (Northern Ireland) 1953 applies; and

(c) a person detained for default in complying with his sentence shall not be treated as detained in pursuance of the sentence, whether or not the sentence provided for detention in the event of default, but a person detained by virtue of a conditional pardon in respect of an offence shall be treated as detained in pursuance of his sentence for the offence.

(3) It is immaterial for the purposes of this section whether a conviction or sentence was before or after the passing of this Act.

Section 3A makes similar provision for prisoners who are detained in mental institutions.

In a series of cases, convicted prisoners in the United Kingdom argued that their disfranchisement violated their rights under Article 3 of Protocol 1. In England and Wales, the Divisional Court held that the 1983 Act was not incompatible with Article 3, because the State had a wide margin of appreciation under Article 3 and the court accepted that the legislation served a legitimate aim (marking society's disapproval of criminals) and was proportionate to it.[29] When a Chamber of the European Court of Human Rights considered the case, however, it reached a different conclusion. The Court accepted (with slight scepticism) that a blanket ban on prisoners' voting might be rationally related to the legitimate aim of discouraging crime, but the indiscriminate nature of the ban made it difficult to regard it as proportionate to that aim. The United Kingdom argued that the Court should allow it a wide margin of appreciation in deciding who should vote, but the Court rejected that claim as there was no evidence that the proportionality of the ban had ever been considered by a national authority, including Parliament, during the passage of the Representation of the People Bill. A margin of appreciation in assessing whether a measure pursues and is proportionate to a legitimate aim recognizes that national authorities, being more closely in touch with morality and social conditions locally, are usually better placed than an international tribunal to evaluate those matters. But an international tribunal should not respect a national authority's judgment if there is no evidence of any such judgment having been made. That being so, the Chamber thought that it was disproportionate to have a ban imposed without reference to the circumstances of the offender or the offence.[30]

At the instance of the United Kingdom's government, the Chamber's judgment was referred to the Grand Chamber, which reached the same conclusion as the Chamber although on rather narrower grounds.[31] The Court focused on the indiscriminate nature of the ban. While accepting that a State could properly have a general rule, the majority considered that, to be proportionate, such a rule should

[29] *R (Pearson) v Secretary of State for the Home Department; Hirst v Attorney General* [2001] EWHC 239 (Admin), [2001] HRLR 39.

[30] *Hirst v United Kingdom* (2004) 38 EHRR 40.

[31] *Hirst v United Kingdom (No 2)* (2005) 42 EHRR 41.

distinguish on some relevant ground between convicted criminals whose right to vote was suspended and those whose right was not suspended. Reliance on one offender having been sent to prison, for however short a period, while another might have received a lengthy community penalty or large fine was not sufficiently related to the legitimate aim of discouraging crime to be proportionate to it. For this apparent arbitrariness to be justified, it would have been useful to know what reasons had been given for imposing disfranchisement in the form adopted in the 1983 Act. In the absence of information about those reasons, the Court had to make its own assessment of proportionality from a purely objective standpoint and without any reasoned input from the State. In those circumstances, the Court was not persuaded that the measure had an objective, rational, and proportionate justification.

This judgment caused great unhappiness to politicians in the United Kingdom. There were three main reasons for this. First, taking account of the absence of debate on and justification for the ban when the Bill was before Parliament was inconsistent with the normal approach in the United Kingdom, where (subject to the possible exception of using Hansard as an aid to construing a statute, established in *Pepper v Hart*[32]) courts will not examine proceedings in Parliament (an element of parliamentary privilege derived from Article IX of the Bill of Rights 1689, providing that 'freedome of speech and debates or proceedings in Parlyament ought not to be impeached or questioned in any court or place out of Parlyament'). The Court's reasoning was seen as a challenge to the dignity of the two Houses of Parliament, and particularly that of the House of Commons. Secondly, people saw the judgment of the Court as a challenge by international (European) law and judges to national democracy. Thirdly, British politicians had for about twenty-five years competed with each other to be seen as toughest on crime, which usually meant simply being tough on criminals. The retributive attitude of politicians and much of the British media towards criminals was different from a more rehabilitative view in many continental European countries, and also out of step with the stated purpose of the United Kingdom's prison system, which Rule 3 of the Prison Rules 1999 defines as follows: 'The purpose of the training and treatment of convicted prisoners shall be to encourage and assist them to lead a good and useful life.'

The first and second of these concerns have been touched on in Sections B and C of this chapter. The third, being an aspect of a claim to political autonomy within the State, is closely related to them. As we have seen, there is an inevitable tension between the idea of national autonomy (including democratic authority and accountability for national policy) and the idea in international law that the State is bound by treaties into which it enters by exercising its State sovereignty. There is also a tension between domestic constitutional law, including the idea of parliamentary privilege in the United Kingdom, and the systematic blindness of international law and tribunals to national (including constitutional) law. These tensions cannot be resolved, but are inherent in the desire of States to enter into treaties with each other and the drive for efficacy in international law.

[32] [1993] AC 593 (HL).

In relation to prisoners' voting rights, it should have been easy to amend the 1983 Act to provide a suitably differentiated approach to the impact of different offences on the Convention right while preserving a fairly broad disfranchisement of prisoners and, perhaps, some other convicted people. Nevertheless, political pressure within Parliament made it difficult for the government to amend the law to accommodate the Court's judgment in this way. The Labour Government delayed taking action, instead instituting a two-stage consultation process: stage 1 in 2006–7 considered the principle involved; stage 2 never happened, as the government started a more wide-ranging consultation on constitutional reform in July 2007 with the publication of its Green Paper, *The Governance of Britain*,[33] and decided to deal with prisoners' voting in the context of that consultation's review of rights and responsibilities of citizenship.[34] The consultation was interrupted by the General Election in May 2010, and the Coalition Government has not continued it.

Meanwhile, courts in the United Kingdom and Strasbourg were considering the matter in the light of the Grand Chamber's judgment in *Hirst (No 2)*. In Scotland, the Registration Appeal Court made a declaration under section 4 of the Human Rights Act 1998 that section 3 of the Representation of the People Act 1983 was incompatible with prisoners' right to vote under Article 3 of Protocol 1 to the ECHR.[35] In April 2010, a Chamber of the Strasbourg Court interpreted the *Hirst* judgment as meaning that only an individualized decision by the sentencing court in each case to limit a convict's voting rights could be a proportionate interference with the rights.[36] Later that year in England and Wales, the Court of Appeal refused to make a declaration of incompatibility, on the ground that the government and Parliament fully understood the position and nothing would be gained by a further declaration.[37]

After the 2010 General Election, the new Conservative Prime Minister, David Cameron, and his supporters in the House of Commons showed no sympathy with the ECtHR or with prisoners. Indeed, the Conservative Party's manifesto for the General Election had included a promise to repeal the Human Rights Act 1998, partly in reaction against all things European and partly because the party saw the ECHR and the Court as interfering unduly with the United Kingdom's freedom to deport criminals and suspected terrorists and to impose restrictions on convicted prisoners, including that on their right to vote. As their Coalition partners the Liberal Democrats were the party most fully committed to protecting human

[33] Lord Chancellor's Department, *The Governance of Britain* (Green Paper, Cm 7170, 2007).

[34] Written answers by Lord Hunt of Kingsheath, Parliamentary Under-Secretary of State, Department of Justice, HL Deb, 6 May 2008, vol 701, cols WA59–WA60.

[35] *Smith v Scott* [2007] CSIH 9, 2007 SC 345.

[36] *Frodl v Austria* (2010) 52 EHRR 267.

[37] *R (Chester) v Secretary of State for Justice* [2010] EWCA Civ 1439, [2011] 1 WLR 1436. A challenge based on EU law failed in Scotland in *McGeogh v Lord President of the Council* [2011] CSOH 65, 2011 SLT 633, where Lord Tyre rejected an application for judicial review of a refusal to register a prisoner to vote on the ground that the prisoner should have proceeded by way of statutory appeal to the Registration Appeal Court. In case the matter went further, however, he opined that rights under EU law added nothing to the case, because the right to take part in elections under EU law applied only to EU citizens in EU Member States where they were non-national residents.

rights in the United Kingdom and to the Convention mechanism, the government compromised by establishing a Commission in March 2011 to consider whether there should be a Bill of Rights to replace or supplement the Human Rights Act 1998, but continued commitment to the Convention system was outside the Commission's terms of reference.[38]

Lack of progress with reform led a Chamber of the Court, in November 2010 in *Greens and MT v United Kingdom*,[39] to invoke the pilot judgment procedure against the United Kingdom on account of the United Kingdom's continued failure to implement the judgment in *Hirst*. The Court uses the procedure, under Rule 61 of its Rules of Court, when cases demonstrate that a High Contracting Party has a systemic failing which prevents it from securing a right to people within its jurisdiction. As part of the Court's strategy for controlling its caseload and preventing a backlog of repeat cases raising the same issue, the Court instructs the State to take appropriate measures within a certain period and stays its consideration of other, similar cases. The Chamber gave the United Kingdom six months to introduce legislative proposals to comply with its obligations.

This went beyond holding that legislation was incompatible with a Convention right, amounting instead to an instruction to the United Kingdom to introduce amending legislation, an obligation which the United Kingdom had in international law but which, when presented in that stark form, seemed to many MPs to trespass on parliamentary sovereignty. Instead of seeking to introduce amending legislation, the Prime Minister, David Cameron, decided to grandstand his opposition to the Court's action. On 3 November 2010 he had told the House of Commons, 'It makes me physically ill even to contemplate having to give the vote to anyone who is in prison.'[40] The Strasbourg Court refused a request from the United Kingdom for the *Greens* judgment to be referred to the Grand Chamber, but deferred the deadline until six months after judgment in another case, *Scoppola v Italy (No 3)*,[41] which raised similar issues to those in *Greens*, to allow the United Kingdom's government to intervene in that case to advance arguments against the decisions in *Hirst* and *Greens*.

Meanwhile MPs sought a way of evading the effect of the *Hirst* judgment without changing the law. As the Court in *Hirst (No 1)* had drawn attention to the absence of any parliamentary consideration of the need for or desirability of disfranchising prisoners when considering the Bill which became the 1983 Act, MPs tried to repair the omission by holding a debate on 10 February 2011 on the following motion:

> That this House notes the ruling of the European Court of Human Rights in Hirst v the United Kingdom in which it held that there had been no substantive debate by members of the legislature on the continued justification for maintaining a general restriction on the right of prisoners to vote; acknowledges the treaty obligations of the UK; is of the opinion that legislative decisions of this nature should be a matter for democratically-elected lawmakers;

[38] For the inconclusive report, see Commission on a Bill of Rights, *A UK Bill of Rights? The Choice Before Us* (Commission on a Bill of Rights, 2012) 2 vols.

[39] (2011) 53 EHRR 21.

[40] HC Deb, 3 November 2010, vol 517, col 921.

[41] (2013) 56 EHRR 19.

and supports the current situation in which no prisoner is able to vote except those imprisoned for contempt, default or on remand.[42]

After a debate lasting nearly five and a half hours, the motion was passed by 234 votes to 22. But there was remarkably little discussion of the merits of disfranchising prisoners. By far the greater part of the debate was occupied by speakers talking about who should decide whether prisoners would be allowed to vote, not the merits of allowing prisoners to vote. As a result, the debate will offer little assistance to the ECtHR if it again has to evaluate the justifications for the ban on prisoners' voting rights.[43]

Meanwhile, in mid-November 2011, the United Kingdom took over the chairmanship of the Committee of Ministers of the Council of Europe for a six-month term of office, which it used to press for changes to the relationship between the Strasbourg Court and States. The government planned a high-level conference on the future of the Strasbourg Court, to be held at Brighton on 19–20 April 2012. This was one of a series which had been held to address the logistical problems caused by the Court's huge back-log of cases and the growing number of applications to it. At the end of 2011, 151,600 cases were awaiting a hearing by a judicial formation (single judge, three-judge committee, or seven-judge Chamber). Judicial formations had decided 52,188 cases in 2011. Protocol 14, further streamlining the Court's procedure, had started to have an effect, and by the end of 2012 the Court was making significant inroads into its backlog.[44] Nevertheless, at the beginning of 2012 the United Kingdom's government could credibly present its argument for the Court to leave more to States as a contribution to the task of relieving pressure on the Court.

In the run-up to the Brighton Conference, British diplomats and ministers tried to persuade representatives of other Council of Europe States to put pressure on the Court to give greater respect to States' policy decisions, exploiting widely shared concerns about the effect of the Court's decisions on immigration and anti-terrorism strategies to argue for greater flexibility in the Court's application of Convention standards. But the Court's President, Sir Nicolas Bratza (by coincidence British), and NGOs put up a stout defence of the Court, and, as a result, the Brighton Declaration adopted at the High Level Conference did not give the United Kingdom everything her government had hoped for. The States of the Council of Europe reaffirmed their commitment to the Convention, to the right of individual petition, and to the position of the Court as the authoritative interpreter of the Convention.[45] They also accepted that they shared with the Court responsibility for implementing the Convention and securing people's rights by providing effecting national remedies.[46] The United Kingdom government's diplomatic effort was not, however, entirely

[42] HC Deb, 10 February 2011, vol 523, cols 493–584.

[43] D Nicol, 'Legitimacy of the Commons Debate on Prisoner Voting' [2011] *PL* 681.

[44] For the statistics, see the Court's website, available at <http://www.echr.coe.int/ECHR/EN/Header/Reports+and+Statistics/Statistics/Statistical+data/> (last accessed 19 April 2013).

[45] *Brighton Declaration* (n 12) paras 1–2, 10, 13.

[46] *Brighton Declaration* (n 12) paras 3, 4, 7, 9c.

unsuccessful. In relation to the margin of appreciation, the States recognized that the jurisprudence of the Court itself was the source of:

> the margin of appreciation in how they apply and implement the Convention, depending on the circumstances of the case and the rights and freedoms engaged. This reflects that the Convention system is subsidiary to the safeguarding of human rights at national level and that national authorities are in principle better placed than an international court to evaluate local needs and conditions. The margin of appreciation goes hand in hand with supervision under the Convention system. In this respect, the role of the Court is to review whether decisions taken by national authorities are compatible with the Convention, having due regard to the State's margin of appreciation.[47]

As the Declaration went on to assert, 'Consistency in the application of the Convention does not require that States Parties implement the Convention uniformly.'[48] This is unproblematic. At the same time, however, the States seemed to want the Court to broaden the margin of appreciation, encouraging it 'to give great prominence to and apply consistently these principles in its judgments' and inviting the Committee of Ministers 'for reasons of transparency and accessibility' to draft a treaty by the end of 2013 to amend the Convention by including 'a reference to the principle of subsidiarity and the doctrine of the margin of appreciation as developed in the Court's case law' in the Preamble to the Convention.[49] To complement this, the Declaration pressed the Court to interpret the time limits for petitions more strictly and to change its Rules to ensure that only the Grand Chamber could decide to adopt novel interpretations of the Convention, reiterated 'the importance of the Court applying fully, consistently, and foreseeably all the admissibility criteria including the rules regarding the scope of its jurisdiction, both to ensure the efficient application of justice and to safeguard the respective roles of the Court and national authorities', and concluded that the Committee of Ministers should draft an amending treaty to remove the provision in Article 35(3)(b) of the Convention that no case may be rejected as inadmissible on the ground that the applicant has not suffered significant disadvantage if the case has not been duly considered by a domestic tribunal. The Declaration affirmed that an application should be rejected as manifestly ill-founded 'to the extent that the Court considers that the application raises a complaint that has been duly considered by a domestic court applying the rights guaranteed by the Convention in light of well-established case law of the Court including on the margin of appreciation as appropriate, unless the Court finds that the application raises a serious question affecting the interpretation or application of the Convention', encouraged the Court 'to take a strict and consistent approach in declaring such applications inadmissible, clarifying its case law to this effect as necessary', and invited the Court 'to develop its case law on the exhaustion of domestic remedies so as to require an applicant, where a domestic remedy was available to them, to have argued before the national courts or tribunals the alleged violation of the Convention rights or an equivalent

[47] *Brighton Declaration* (n 12) para 11.
[48] *Brighton Declaration* (n 12) para 23.
[49] *Brighton Declaration* (n 12) paras 12(a)–12(b).

provision of domestic law, thereby allowing the national courts an opportunity to apply the Convention in light of the case law of the Court'.[50]

This provoked President Bratza, in his address to the conference, to remind delegates:

> The principal characteristic of a court in a system governed by the rule of law is its independence. In order to fulfil its role the European Court must not only be independent; it must also be seen to be independent. That is why we are, I have to say, uncomfortable with the idea that Governments can in some way dictate to the Court how its case-law should evolve or how it should carry out the judicial functions conferred on it. . .
>
> The doctrine of the margin of appreciation is a complex one about which there has been much debate... It is a variable notion which is not susceptible of precise definition. It is in part for this reason that we have difficulty in seeing the need for, or the wisdom of, attempting to legislate for it in the Convention, any more than for the many other tools of interpretation which have been developed by the Court in carrying out the judicial rule entrusted to it.[51]

The unusual feature of this exchange is not that the tension arose, but that each side addressed it publicly and expressly. Some matters are normally better when understood but left unsaid. Nevertheless, as the Declaration was quickly followed by the unanimous[52] judgment of the Grand Chamber of the Court in *Scoppola (No 3)*, in which several States including the United Kingdom had intervened to argue for that *Hirst* had been wrongly decided, the judgment can be seen as a partial response by the Court to the Declaration.

The Court first reaffirmed that, as stated in *Hirst (No 2)*, the right to vote is crucial to establishing and maintaining a truly democratic regime, and that it is a right, not a privilege. There is a presumption that the primary principle is that of universal, adult suffrage.[53] Nevertheless, the right is not absolute, and States enjoy a margin of appreciation in relation to limiting it. The role of the Court is to assure itself that limitations do not reduce the right to the point where its essence and effectiveness are lost, that restrictions pursue a legitimate aim and that the means employed are not disproportionate, as the Court had stated in *Mathieu-Mohin and Clerfayt v Belgium*.[54] Council of Europe States had divergent approaches: twenty-five of the forty-seven States of the Council of Europe permitted some restriction of voting rights for at least some convicted criminals, and in eleven of those the sentencing court assessed the appropriateness for including some restriction as part of the sentence. There was therefore a margin of appreciation. The Court noted that the United Kingdom's legislation was without nuance, and deprived a great number of people of the right to vote automatically and in an indiscriminate manner, thus

[50] *Brighton Declaration* (n 12) paras 15(b)–15(d), 15(g), 23, 25(c)–25(d).

[51] *Brighton Declaration* (n 12), Address to the Conference by President N Bratza, available at http://echr.coe.int/Documents/Speech_20120420_Bratza_Brighton_ENG.pdf > (last accessed 7 July 2013) 2, 5–6. See also N Bratza, 'The Relationship Between the UK Courts and Strasbourg' [2011] *EHRLR* 505.

[52] Judge David Thor Björgvinsson agreed with the Court's general reasoning, which he thought followed prudently and logically from the judgment in *Hirst (No 2)* (n 31), though he dissented on the application of the principles to the circumstances of *Scoppola* (n 41) itself.

[53] *Scoppola* (n 41) para 82.

[54] *Scoppola* (n 41) paras 83–4.

exceeding the State's margin of appreciation.[55] It was permissible to limit the right of convicted prisoners to vote in order to prevent crime, and to strengthen civic responsibility and respect for the rule of law. But the United Kingdom's legislation was not proportionate to that aim. The Court reaffirmed its conclusion in *Hirst (No 2)* that, whilst there was no clear consensus among Council of Europe States as to the appropriate approach, Article 25 of the International Covenant on Civil and Political Rights reflected an evolving global consensus opposed to automatically depriving convicted prisoners of their right to vote, without regard to the length of their sentences, the nature or gravity of their offence, or their personal circumstances.[56]

Nevertheless, the Court would not direct States as to the precise measures to be taken to achieve proportionality. Whilst an individualized assessment by the sentencing judge of the appropriateness of depriving someone of the right to vote by way of penalty would certainly suffice to ensure proportionality, the Chamber in *Frodl v Austria*[57] had gone too far in suggesting that that was necessary.

To that limited extent, the judgment in *Scoppola (No 3)* was less prescriptive than the United Kingdom might have feared. On the other hand, it created more difficulty for the United Kingdom in another direction. Whilst recognizing that States have a margin of appreciation, the Court's reasoning made it clear that the United Kingdom could not bring itself within it merely by holding votes on the subject in the House of Commons to reassert MPs' preference for a blanket ban on voting by convicted prisoners. The absence of reasoned debate on the ban during the passage of the Representation of the People Bill in 1982–3 made it more difficult for the Chamber in *Hirst (No 1)* to find arguments for the proportionality of the ban, but the Grand Chamber in *Scoppola (No 3)* held that a blanket, indiscriminate ban could never be objectively proportionate, however many times the Commons might debate it.

The Grand Chamber gave judgment in *Scoppola (No 3)* on 22 May 2012, so the United Kingdom had to introduce its legislative proposals to Parliament to amend the 1983 Act by 23 November 2012. The Prime Minister continued to resist. On 24 October 2012, two hours after his Attorney General, Dominic Grieve QC, had told the House of Commons Select Committee on Justice that the United Kingdom should comply with the Strasbourg Court's rulings,[58] David Cameron said on the floor of the House of Commons:

> The House of Commons has voted against prisoners having the vote. I do not want prisoners to have the vote, and they should not get the vote—I am very clear about that. If it helps to have another vote in Parliament on another resolution to make it absolutely clear and help put the legal position beyond doubt, I am happy to do that. But no one should be in any doubt: prisoners are not getting the vote under this Government.[59]

[55] *Scoppola* (n 41) paras 85–6, 101.
[56] *Scoppola* (n 41) paras 90, 95, 96.
[57] *Frodl* (n 36).
[58] House of Commons Select Committee on Justice, *The Work of the Attorney General: Oral Evidence* (HC Papers (2012–13) no 644–i), Questions 24–32.
[59] HC Deb, 24 October 2012, vol 551, cols 922–3.

Nevertheless, the government complied with its immediate obligation to produce legislative proposals just in time. On 22 November 2012 it published the Voting Eligibility (Prisoners) Draft Bill, and asked the two Houses to set up a Joint Select Committee to scrutinize and report on it.[60] The Draft Bill offers a choice between three options: allowing prisoners to vote if sentenced to terms of less than four years; allowing prisoners to vote if sentenced to terms of less than six months; and retaining the current ban. The government accepted that the last option would leave the United Kingdom in breach of its international obligations, although it asserted that this would be politically justified in order to uphold parliamentary sovereignty. A Joint Select Committee of the two Houses of Parliament was appointed in May 2013 and is in the process of taking evidence prior to reporting on the Draft Bill. The government will then consider the report, prepare a Bill, introduce it to Parliament, and allow Parliament to make the final decision. It seems unlikely, though it is possible, that a Bill will be introduced to Parliament before the General Election due to take place in May 2015.

F. Conclusion

We started by evaluating the claim that judgments of the ECtHR, dynamically interpreting the ECHR, had in some cases infringed States' national sovereignty in international law or their constitutional or legislative sovereignty in national law. It was argued that national sovereignty, at the level of doctrine in international law, is something of a red herring, and that international institutions have no duty under international law to respect States' internal, constitutional, or legal arrangements; the only question for an international tribunal is whether the State has acted in accordance with its international legal obligations. Nevertheless, it was suggested that, in order to maintain conditions in which they can rely on States' cooperation in upholding international law and giving effect within States to those obligations, international bodies should not ignore the ways in which constitutional and, sometimes, even legislative sovereignty operate within a State. There are two reasons for this. First, international institutions usually rely on States to give effect to measures adopted outside the State, and too extreme a dissonance between their demands and the constitutional structure of a State may make it impossible for a State to do so. Secondly, one (though not the only) source of continuing legitimacy for international institutions is their ability to reinforce moral and social values such as respect for rights and democracy. Side-lining democratic decision-making within States without reasons which are accepted within the States as persuasive will ultimately undermine either respect for those values or respect for, and hence the legitimacy of, the international institution, if not both. On the other hand, we saw how allowing morally sound and socially persuasive concerns of States' governments to be taken into account in the process of applying international law could

[60] HC Deb, 22 November 2012, vol 553, cols 745–6 (statement by the Lord Chancellor and Secretary of State for Justice, Chris Grayling).

enhance the effectiveness and perceived legitimacy of an international institution's decisions and judgments.

This was illustrated by reference to the treatment by the ECtHR of concerns which, for States' governments, were compelling on social, political, or constitutional grounds, particularly in relation to the right to participate in elections in BiH and the United Kingdom. If we strip away the language of sovereignty, which seems to be unhelpful in illuminating what is going on, we find a complicated relationship between national authorities and the Court in which the legitimacy of each depends to some extent on the actions of the other. This reality of inter-institutional politics cannot be wholly excluded from the development and implementation of doctrines of international human-rights law. National authorities and the ECtHR have to be sensitive to different dimensions and sources of legitimacy: constitutional, legal, political, social, and moral, which do not always pull in the same direction. Each institution, whether municipal or international, has its own functions, and in pursuing them is involved in inter-institutional politics. An international, human-rights institution such as the ECtHR cannot allow States to dictate the content of rights or to insist on rights being given different meanings in different States. On the other hand, where a right is qualified and an interference with it capable of justification, international institutions must take account of conditions within the State concerned when considering whether a proffered justification is acceptable. If an international institution fails to give sufficient weight to local conditions, it will undermine its own legitimacy and authority.

Where a State's reasons for resisting change are fundamental to the structure of the State and its constitution, as was the case in Bosnia and Herzegovina in *Sejdić and Finci*, they should be given great weight. By contrast, when a State's objection is based on mere preference and is of no deep significance, as is the case in relation to prisoners' voting rights in the United Kingdom, it should be given little weight. States and international institutions should be cautious about picking fights with each other. They should not make an issue about things that are not fundamentally important, or they undermine their own authority; but they should each be aware of the issues which the other regards as being of fundamental importance, and should conduct themselves accordingly when evaluating justifications for interfering with rights.

The complexity of relationships of this kind is not limited to human rights. It can be seen also in the growth of resistance by national and supra-national authorities (especially courts) to the practice of the UN Security Council in 'listing' people and organizations as suspected terrorists without due process.[61] I suggest that this study of the ECtHR and the role of different kinds of sovereignty in its relationships with States can be seen as a case-study for international institutions more generally, and as indicating why and how the international sphere is gradually having to respond to promptings by States' institutions to improve their practices while maintaining the integrity of their core activities.

[61] C Harlow, 'Composite Decision-Making and Accountability Networks: Some Deductions from a Saga' (2012) *Jean Monnet Working Paper* 04/12, available at <http://centers.law.nyu.edu/jeanmonnet/papers/12/documents/JMWP04Harlow.pdf> (last accessed 8 April 2013).

13

Sovereignty, Constitutional Dialogues, and Political Networks: A Comparative and Conceptual Study

*Margit Cohn**

A. Introduction

This chapter links two discourses; that of sovereignty and that of constitutional dialogue. The link has been forged before, but only in the context of juridical accounts of the ways competences and powers are allocated in State structures. Such analysis typically focuses on the use of the 'dialogue' metaphor, first in Canada and later in the United Kingdom, and is part of a normative attempt to alleviate concerns about the supremacy of the judiciary once the former structure was replaced, or revamped, by the Canadian Charter in the first case and by the Human Rights Act 1998 ('HRA') in the second. The term 'sovereignty' is not always explicitly mentioned, but this emerging literature has clearly been a response to arguments about the breakdown of former understandings over domestic sovereignty structures.

The chapter broadens the sphere of dialogue discourse and its link with sovereignty discourse in several directions. First, it highlights parallel dialogue analyses in other systems; secondly, it incorporates an entirely different version of dialogue theory developed in the United States; thirdly, drawing on the literature that expands the notion of sovereignty and reveals the variety of meanings attached to the term, it identifies a corresponding variety of conceptions of dialogue that go far beyond the hierarchical, power-allocation meaning. Finally, it explores the possible links, or affinities, between these two concepts.

Adopting a distinction between classical-hierarchical and political versions of sovereignty, it is argued that 'dialogue' in fact connotes two distinct structural arrangements: formal and implied, the latter straddling the legal and the political. Analytically,

* Senior Lecturer, Faculty of Law and Federmann School of Public Policy and Government, Hebrew University of Jerusalem; Visiting Professor of Law, Columbia Law School, 2012–13. Research was supported by the Israel Science Foundation (Grant No. 160/09). I thank participants at the WG Hart Legal Workshop that took place in June 2011 for their comments. Opinions and errors are mine alone.

override clauses and limitation clauses, both presented as dialogue mechanisms, are seen to be entirely different forms of dialogue, and both are removed from dialogues that are not directly based on an explicit constitutional provision. This distinction, which draws on the literature from Canada and the United States, is employed in an analysis of so-called dialogue mechanisms in the United Kingdom and elsewhere.

Exploring the concept of 'political' modes of dialogue, the chapter also draws on a parallel strand of dialogue theory that has emerged in the United States, one that celebrates the political nature and the complexity of the constitutional decision-making sphere. This involves a move from bipolarity and two-player interactions to networks. While analyses of formal dialogical structures are useful, excessive emphasis on the purely legal aspects of dialogue deflects attention from the complexity of the decision-making process in the public sphere. The implications of each conception for the concept of sovereignty are addressed in the conclusion.

B. Sovereignty: In the Middle of a Continuum

For many, UK-style 'sovereignty' has almost been interchangeable with 'parliamentary sovereignty'. This is but one aspect of a more general tendency to search for the 'sovereign' in the domestic arena by identifying the ultimate decision-maker, be it Parliament, the judiciary, or the executive. This type of search is based on a hierarchical vision of the public sphere: there must always be a 'bearer of the last word'. Although much of this type of debate has been held in common law systems, the notion that sovereignty is hierarchical is not limited to the common law world.[1]

The well-known UK challenges to this hierarchical model, resulting first from the United Kingdom's membership of the European Union and then by enactment of the HRA, have been extensively treated in this volume and elsewhere.[2] These analyses often remain on the legal/juridical level, and are concerned with the allocation of powers within the constitutional framework.

Martin Loughlin presents an entirely different notion of sovereignty, as a political concept 'devised for the purpose of giving expression to the distinctively political bond between a group of people and its mode of governance'.[3] In this volume, Loughlin further develops the notion of sovereignty as a concept, a symbol of the autonomous entity that is the State which, even as a legal concept, is indivisible.[4] This chapter returns to the aspect of sovereignty, Loughlin nevertheless admits is

[1] Notably, Carl Schmitt's 'sovereign is he who decides on the exception', pointing at the executive as the ultimate wielder of power in extreme contingencies; see C Schmitt, *Political Theology: Four Chapters on the Concept of Sovereignty* (Chicago University Press 1985) 5.

[2] See, eg, N Walker (ed) *Sovereignty in Transition* (Hart Publishing 2003); A Young, *Parliamentary Sovereignty and the Human Rights Act* (Hart Publishing 2009); J Goldsworthy, *Parliamentary Sovereignty: Contemporary Debates* (CUP 2010); see Chapters 4, 5, and 6 in this volume by Jeffrey, Goldsworthy, Alison L Young, and Lord Hope respectively.

[3] M Loughlin, 'Ten Tenets of Sovereignty' in Walker (n 2); M Loughlin, *The Idea of Public Law* (OUP 2003).

[4] See Chapter 3.

often discussed, which focuses on competences and their allocation. The notion of sovereignty as the search for a single dominant power within several government branches is challenged here; remaining, however, in the context of allocation, a non-hierarchical vision of the meaning of sovereignty on the domestic level is presented.

In this respect, 'sovereignty' can be configured into different structures, both formal and informal. The different conceptions of domestic 'sovereignty', explored in several contributions to this volume, can be placed on a continuum ranging from descriptive accounts of the minutiae of the ordering of State powers to considerations of sovereignty as an abstract concept, embedded in a national political ethos and serving as its justification. This chapter is predicated on a meaning of sovereignty placed in the middle of this continuum. On the one hand, it goes beyond the purely juridical. Searches for sovereignty that focus on law as the single basis for analysis are misdirected. Such accounts deflect attention from complex realities, in which law is but one social ordering mechanism. Setting law above society's forces, politics, and public opinion cannot capture the intricate web that constitutes the decision-making process in modern reality. Hence, no formal legal structure can offer a complete and robust account of sovereignty. In other words, juridical accounts of sovereignty are more likely to be overly rigid: excessive focus on structure comes at the price of ignoring sovereignty-in-action.

On the other hand, I do not limit the concept of 'sovereignty' to the political. Although law is not the single mechanism that grants meaning to, and shapes the social sphere, its force as an important mechanism is beyond doubt.

As for sovereignty as an aggregate versus sovereignty as a unified concept, I agree with Loughlin that discussions of sovereignty as divisible deflect attention from the conceptual notion of State entity, but this need not mean that the former should be removed from the debate. Indeed, the term 'sovereignty' carries many meanings, and care is required when distinguishing between these meanings. But this is exactly what they are: different meanings of one term. The ambiguity of 'sovereignty' is not singular: consider the even fuzzier 'rule of law'. Research, such as the works collected in this volume, can assist in understanding what 'sovereignty' can connote. Rather than choosing one meaning, all conceptions should be embraced and distinguished.

The meaning discussed here, then, draws its life from both law and politics, but is not a purely abstract concept: it thus explores the allocation of competences but meshes the political with the legal. Against this backdrop, I find 'dialogue' a useful epistemological tool for the fleshing out of this conception of shared domestic sovereignty, just as it has been useful for the juridical accounts.

C. 'Dialogue': An Overture

The term 'dialogue' has become a fashionable keyword in analyses of constitutional structures, often paired with the adjective 'constitutional' or 'democratic'. It carries different meanings, as will be discussed further. The usages of the term I am interested in are based on a shared assumption: the term is used to express distinct ways of decision-making in constitutional matters that involve the participation of more than one actor.[5] Dialogue analysis has spread across continents, and can be found inter alia in Canada,[6] the United Kingdom,[7] the United States,[8] Australia,[9] Israel,[10] and South Africa.[11] The definition adopted in many discussions of this concept is that of Hogg and Bushell. Writing in the late 1990s in the context of the Canadian Charter, they considered it 'meaningful to regard the relationship between the court and the competent legislative body as a dialogue' when 'a judicial decision is open to legislative reversal, modification, or avoidance'.[12] In such a situation, 'the legislative body is in a position to devise a response', one that is respectful to the values recognized by the court but also 'accomplishes the social or economic objectives that the judicial decision has impeded'.[13] When the constitutional structure offers such venues for legislative responses, the problem of democratic legitimacy or, in our words, the seeming threat to the sovereignty of Parliament, is resolved, or at least alleviated. The Canadians did not remain alone for long. In the United

[5] I am thus not interested in the usage of terms such as 'constitutional dialogue' or 'dialogue' in passing, or without the intent of defining a distinct mode of decision-making.

[6] First was the groundbreaking work of Hogg and Bushell: PW Hogg and AA Bushell, 'The Charter Dialogue between Courts and Legislators (Or Perhaps the Charter of Rights Isn't a Bad Thing after All)' (1997) 35 *Osgoode Hall LJ* 75, 79. For mere examples of the exceptionally rich literature see CP Manfredi and JB Kelly, 'Six Degrees of Dialogue' (1999) 37 *Osgoode Hall LJ* 513; K Roach, *The Supreme Court on Trial: Judicial Activism or Democratic Dialogue* (Irwin Law 2001); PW Hogg, AA Bushell Thornton, and WK Wright, 'Charter Dialogue Revisited—Or Much Ado About Metaphors' (2007) 45 *Osgoode Hall LJ* 1, opening a special issue dedicated to 'The Charter Dialogue: Ten Years Later'.

[7] See, eg, TRS Allan, 'Constitutional Dialogue and the Justification of Judicial Review' (2003) 23 *OJLS* 563 (not discussed in the context of the HRA; for implications on the HRA see Section F); R Clayton, 'Judicial Deference and "Democratic Dialogue": The Legitimacy of Judicial Intervention under the Human Rights Act 1998' [2004] *PL* 33; TR Hickman, 'Constitutional Dialogue, Constitutional Theories and the Human Rights Act 1998' [2005] *PL* 306; TR Hickman, 'Judges and Politicians after the Human Rights Act 1998: A Comment' [2008] *PL* 84; Young (n 2) ch 5.

[8] 'Dialogue' emerged as a distinct metaphor for constitutional analysis in the late 1980s; see L Fisher, *Constitutional Dialogues: Interpretation as Political Process* (Princeton University Press 1988); B Friedman, 'A Different Dialogue: The Supreme Court, Congress and Federal Jurisdiction' (1990) 85 *Northwestern University L Rev* 1; B Friedman, 'Dialogue and Judicial Review' (1992) 91 *Michigan L Rev* 577; C Bateup, 'The Dialogic Promise: Assessing the Normative Potential of Theories of Constitutional Dialogue' (2006) 71 *Brooklyn L Rev* 1109.

[9] See, eg, L McDonald, 'New Directions in the Australian Bill of Rights Debate' [2004] *PL* 22; B Batross and P Webb, 'Accountability for Torture Abroad and the Limits of the Act of State Doctrine: Comments on *Habib v Commonwealth of Australia*' (2010) 8 *Journal of International Criminal Justice* 1153.

[10] Y Dotan, 'A Constitution for Israel? The Constitutional Dialogue after the "Constitutional Revolution"' (1997) 28 *Mishpatim* 149 (in Hebrew); G Dor, 'Constitutional Dialogues in Action: Canadian and Israeli Experiences in Comparative Perspective' (2000) 11 *Indiana International & Comparative L Rev* 1; A Barak, *The Judge in a Democracy* (Princeton University Press 2006) 236–40. 'Dialogue' has been used in other contexts, for example in David Scharia's analysis of judicial dicta as directive messages (D Scharia, *The Pure Sound of the Piccolo: The Supreme Court of Israel, Dialogue and the Fight Against Terrorism* (Harry and Michael Sacher Institute for Legislative Research and Comparative Law, Hebrew University of Jerusalem 2012) (in Hebrew)).

[11] R Dixon, 'Creating Dialogue About Socioeconomic Rights: Strong-Form versus Weak-Form Judicial Review Revisited' (2007) 5 *International Journal of Constitutional Law* 391.

[12] Hogg and Bushell (n 6) 79. A few pages further, the authors are ready to accept as dialogue all cases in which 'some action' could be found (Hogg and Bushell (n 6) 82).

[13] Hogg and Bushell (n 6) 79–80.

Kingdom, this form of 'dialogue' discourse has exponentially grown in volume in the post-HRA era.[14] The same form of dialogue has a strong transnational hold.[15]

Two elements are central to this definition. First, 'dialogue' occurs between two actors—the judiciary and the legislature. Hence the recurring use of the adjective 'bipolar' in this respect,[16] presented as one that offers a better-fitting explanation of the reformed structures that offered new modes of interaction between the legislature and the judiciary. The second is the original focus on single events of dialogue or response, which fits less well with the concept of 'dialogue'. Hogg and Bushell's initial analysis did not discuss continuous modes of interaction between the State actors; rather, 'dialogue' presented an option for a single response. This was amended later, to allow a second judicial consideration of a statute amended after the first event of judicial review.[17] Yet the term was not designed to connote prolonged, multidimensional processes and, as such, was limited in scope.[18]

As previously mentioned, dialogue analyses were originally used as responses to the rising criticism against seemingly omnipotent courts, operating under constitutional structures that allow them some mode of interference with the legislature. Designed then to minimize, if not obliterate, the democratic criticism of judicial review, these analyses also rejected the linked notion that, since judicial review empowered the judiciary to invalidate legislation, pre-existing sovereignty structures were challenged. Indeed, much of the literature that developed and relied on this keyword wished to advance a variety of normative arguments that supported judicial participation while showing that their contribution was always only part of the story.[19] However, 'bipolarity', expressed in the recognition of the constitutionality of legislative response, may support arguments for judicial deference to the legislature. The very fact that dialogue offers legislatures an option to respond may signal to judges that they should tread carefully in the constitutional thicket. Normatively, then, the theory can be helpful to both sides of the constitutional debate over the role of the judiciary.[20]

I am not concerned here with normative elements, or normative implications of the theory; rather, I wish to unpack the concept itself. Participants in this discussion are actually talking about different forms of dialogue-inducing mechanisms, which range from the formal-institutional to the purely political. The recognition

[14] See, eg, Allan (n 7); Clayton (n 7); Hickman (n 7); Hickman (n 7); Young (n 2) ch 5.

[15] See McDonald (n 9); Batross and Webb (n 9); Dotan (n 10); Dor (n 10); Barak (n 10) 236–40; Scharia (n 10); Dixon (n 11).

[16] For analyses of bipolar sovereignty see S Sedley, 'Human Rights: A Twenty-First Century Agenda' [1995] *PL* 386, 389; CJS Knight, 'Bi-Polar Sovereignty Restated' (2009) 68 *CLJ* 361.

[17] Hogg later recognized that 'dialogue' may continue when an amended legislation is challenged in court; see PW Hogg, 'Discovering Dialogue' (2004) 23 *Supreme Court L Rev* (2d) 3, 5.

[18] On this point see also Hickman (n 7) 84 fn 3.

[19] eg, Hogg and Bushell's subtitle, ('Or Perhaps the Charter of Rights Isn't a Bad Thing after All') (Hogg and Bushell (n 6)). Hogg later conceded that he and his coauthor 'should not have claimed that we had answered the counter-majoritarian objection to judicial review' as 'this went too far'. However, the claim that the decisions of the court were 'not usually the last word' remained. Hogg (n 17) 4.

[20] See Christine Bateup's highly detailed survey of dialogue theories, which places them on a normative ↔ positive (or prescriptive ↔ descriptive) continuum (Bateup (n 8)).

of these different forms opens up the discussion of the nature of constitutional deliberation which moves beyond two-player structures, better expresses the realities of decision-making in the public sphere, and offers novel insights into the nature of sovereignty.

D. Two Concepts of Constitutional Dialogue

(1) Formal dialogue

In their seminal 1997 article, Hogg and Bushell, who studied the Canadian Charter, identified several dialogue-enabling mechanisms. First, there was the override clause in section 33, which opens as follows:

> (1) Parliament or the legislature of a province may expressly declare in an Act of Parliament or of the legislature, as the case may be, that the Act or a provision thereof shall operate notwithstanding a provision included in section 2 or sections 7 to 15 of this Charter.

At first glance, this provision does not seem to offer much of a dialogue: the override clause enables Parliament to impose its choice on the court, despite recognition that the statute flagrantly contravenes the values enshrined in the constitution. The insertion of an override clause can therefore be a preventive, rather than responsive, measure. Yet Hogg and Bushell assume that reliance on section 33 will occur after a court had struck down a statute. To this effect, the following dialogue occurs: (a) Parliament enacts; (b) the court strikes down; (c) in response, Parliament re-enacts, invoking the override clause; (d) if the conditions in the override clause are met, this is the end of the matter, for the period specified in the override clause. This type of override clause[21] thus creates a formal structure, 'a legal mechanism for interaction between the judiciary and the legislature'.[22] It enables the legislature to respond to a judicial decision and annul its implications to the legality of a statutory arrangement.

(2) Implied dialogue

Although Hogg and Bushell's article is still considered the progenitor of dialogue theory in common law systems, the term 'constitutional dialogue' was used earlier in the United States. Hogg and Bushell were not unaware of this parallel literature, and other participants in the Canadian debate have granted it some attention,[23] but this offering of a multiplayer structure of decision-making was structured in an

[21] For a similar example, see the one adopted in Israel's Basic Law: Freedom of Occupation, s 8.

[22] Young (n 2) 117. My use of the adjective 'formal' differs from Dor (n 10), where it connotes a multiparticipant debate not led by a mutual will to find a solution, in distinction from 'substantive' dialogue, which does.

[23] First in Hogg and Bushell (n 6) 79 fn 12 (although the central US dialogue literature available at the time and discussed in this section was not mentioned); A Petter, 'Taking Dialogue Theory Much Too Seriously (Or Perhaps Charter Dialogue Isn't Such a Good Thing After All)' (2007) 45 *Osgoode Hall LJ* 147, 157–60.

entirely different fashion. The differences between these two types of dialogue warrant careful attention, since in some analyses both types are discussed indiscriminately.

Louis Fisher published his book, *Constitutional Dialogues*, in 1988. Fisher was not the first to recognize the ongoing multiple-member process of rule-making, but he gave this idea a new focus.[24] Many have succumbed to the assumption that the United States Constitution, as interpreted by the court in *Marbury v Madison*[25] and accepted since, grants the court the final word.[26] Fisher argued that, in reality, supremacy is mitigated by dialogue.

Indeed, it would be incorrect to claim that judicial decisions delivered in the United States have no post-decision life. Clearly, any decision delivered by the courts of the United States generates a range of possible responses. In this way, dialogue is part of the life of the constitutional sphere of the United States just as it is elsewhere. This dialogue is generated by the very structure of the Constitution and its allocation of powers between government branches, which enables the legislature to make laws, sometimes following an interpretation of the Constitution rendered by the judiciary, rather than from any specifically created mechanism.

Barry Friedman's work on dialogue leads to a similar insight. In a series of articles that addressed the nature of judicial review through the concept of 'dialogue', he challenged the 'faulty premises' of the counter-majoritarian difficulty. Friedman emphasized that it would be wrong to assume that all judicial decisions are in fact final and are never thwarted by political forces.[27] In 1990, Friedman was concerned with congressional power over the determination of the scope of jurisdiction of federal courts. Positing two competing visions, the first granting Congress full power of determination, the second allowing for some judiciary discretion, Friedman argued that since the Constitution provided no clearly defined rules on the matter, 'the issue is subject of an ongoing dialogue between those two branches'.[28] In 1992, a similar argument was made in the context of the decades-long debate over the legitimacy of judicial review (in US parlance, the invalidation of statutes by courts for non-constitutionality), expressed inter alia, under the title 'the counter-majoritarian difficulty'. To answer the constitutional difficulty inherent in the grant of power to strike down legislature to independent, unelected judges, Friedman redefined the judicial contribution as one that 'is significantly more interdependent and interactive than generally described'.[29] To make the point slightly differently, a decision may not be the end of a matter, but rather a new beginning, or better put, one stage in a lengthy process of multiparticipant decision-making. Any response to a

[24] For Alexander Bickel's reference to 'interplay', or a 'continuing colloquy' between government branches see A Bickel, *The Least Dangerous Branch* (Bobbs-Merril 1962) 206. See also M Minow, 'Interpreting Rights: An Essay for Robert Cover' (1987) 96 *Yale LJ* 1860, 1875–6 (discussing the development of a discourse over the protection of a right as a 'communal dialogue').

[25] *Marbury v Madison* 5 US 137 (1803).

[26] This reading of the United States Constitution is also common in the United Kingdom; see, eg, Clayton (n 7) 41.

[27] Friedman (n 8) 643–53. The other fallacy is found in simplistic accounts of the nature of majoritarian legitimacy, an aspect I do not need to deal with.

[28] Friedman (n 8) 10. [29] B Friedman (n 8) 653.

decision may elicit further response from other actors in the public sphere, which can generate subsequent responses in a possibly endless process or, as others see it, until an equilibrium is reached.[30]

This type of dialogue analysis is clearly different from the one embedded in the override clause. It emerged in the context of a constitution that offers no formal mechanism for the overriding of judicial decisions except, of course, the amendment of the Constitution which, understandably, no longer receives substantive attention.[31] But dialogue it is, as the input of the judiciary is recognized as amenable to reshaping. This then is a second type of dialogue. It is not rooted in a provision that expressly offers the legislature a path for reaction; rather, it derives from the constitutional structure itself and the grant of power to the judiciary to interpret and thereby to reshape, if not make, law. No distinct, formal legal mechanism for response, such as Canada's override clause, exists in this context. This second form is appropriately labelled 'implied' dialogue as it draws on the political division between government branches set in the Constitution.

E. Limitation Clauses as Inducers of Implied Dialogue

One could adduce that two separate dialogue discourses exist—implied dialogue in the United States and the Canadian-rooted one, which is simply more limited in scope. Yet let us now consider Hogg and Bushell's other examples of Charter dialogue. Several Charter clauses are presented as essentially allowing interference with protected rights under defined conditions, the most famous and popularly used being section 1, under which:

> The Canadian Charter of Rights and Freedoms guarantees the rights and freedoms set out in it subject only to such reasonable limits prescribed by law as can be demonstrably justified in a free and democratic society.[32]

For Hogg and Bushell, this provision offers a dialogical process. Assuming that a statute is found lacking under the requirements of the section:

> [T]he reviewing court will explain why the section 1 standard was not met, which will involve explaining the less restrictive alternative law that *would* have satisfied the section 1 standard. That alternative law is available to the enacting body and will generally be upheld.[33]

These dynamics, it is claimed, are similar in nature to the dialogue generated by section 33. The authors explain the process as follows. When a law is found to impair a Charter right and found unconstitutional for choosing an overly restrictive

[30] Such lengthy processes are often fuelled by interest group action; see, eg, C Harlow and R Rawlings, *Pressure Through Law* (Routledge 1992); AJ Nownes, *Intererest Groups in American Politics: Pressure and Power* (2nd edn, Routledge 2012).

[31] On this point see, eg, Friedman (n 8) 650–1.

[32] The others are the qualified rights (Candian Charter of Rights and Freedoms, ss 7, 8, 9, and 12) and the guarantee of equality rights (s 15(1)). All set standards that, when met, can allow an interference with a right (Hogg and Bushell (n 6) 82).

[33] Hogg and Bushell (n 6) 85.

measure, 'the invalidity of the law could be corrected by the enactment of a new law that is more respectful to the Charter' which is, shall we say, instructed by the terms of the judicial decision.[34] Similar analyses are offered with regard to the other provisions that qualify rights provisions. Section 8, for example, prohibits only 'unreasonable' search and seizure; when a court rules on the reasonableness of a process introduced in a statute, this can be followed by a new law that satisfies the court's standard.[35]

But is the process arguably generated by limitations clauses really similar to the one created by override mechanisms (in section 33 of the Canadian Charter)? Clearly, responses to a judicial decision are part of the dynamics that are the outcome of *any* decision in the constitutional sphere. A rights-protecting constitutional provision, once interpreted and applied, will always offer possibilities for post-decision response. In fact, this type of 'dialogue', if this would be a suitable title, is a potential part of any post-decision dynamics in any field of the law. If we wish to follow the definition laid out in the Canadian literature, it would mean that all rules of legal status generate a dialogue, as long as they are open and subject to judicial interpretation and application.

Under a more restricted reading, one that draws on the distinction discussed in this Section, only provisions such as section 33 offer a significant form of dialogue, by creating a formal path of dialogue that operates beyond the merely interpretative. The limitation clauses and other interpretable constitutional provisions, once interpreted and applied, may lead to legislative reaction, but in a fashion not different from other cases of post-decision dynamics. This type of dialogue is thus closer in nature to the dialogue generated by any judicial interpretative exercise, as discussed in the United States. This type of 'dialogue' is no more, but certainly no less, than the normal interaction between government branches that may occur, and often does, after a court delivers a decision.

F. The UK Dialogue Mechanisms Re-examined

This leads us to the HRA, familiarly seen as the source of two dialogue mechanisms.[36] How do they fit the above distinction between formal and political dialogue?

Section 3, which grants the judiciary power to interpret legislation against its original grain and, to a certain extent, contrary to its wording, is correctly recognized as a dialogue-generating device. But the dialogue it offers is similar to the dialogue generated by limitation clauses. Like them, section 3 expands the role of the judge and offers new grounds for decision-making, but response to judicial use of section 3 relies on the traditional interaction between the court and other players in the

[34] Hogg and Bushell (n 6) 87. See also K Roach, 'Dialogic Judicial Review and Its Critics' (2004) 23 *Supreme Court L Rev* (2d) 49, 57.

[35] Hogg and Bushell (n 6) 88. For a similar analysis on equality rights see Hogg and Bushell (n 6) 90–1.

[36] Allan (n 7); Clayton (n 7); Hickman (n 7); Hickman (n 7); Young (n 2) ch 5.

constitutional sphere. Indeed, by empowering the judiciary to interpret a statute against the text, in order to render the statute compatible with the Convention, judicial reliance on section 3 may limit the range of possible responses by Parliament, and may also make it harder to justify responses that are relatively distanced from the core judicial reading. Further, one may argue that in essence section 3 still enables Parliament to enact statutes that are incompatible with the Convention, while section 1 of the Canadian Charter merely offers Parliament the option of proposing a more refined balance between the protection of the right and competing interests or rights. However, informal dialogue, under the distinction proposed here, emerges under myriad permutations: what is shared here is that this type of 'dialogue' emerges as an outcome of legislative provisions that set limits on government action, without the provision of a dedicated form of response. It is no more than the usual State-of-affairs since courts began to review government power. As such, this section opens no new institutional challenge to sovereignty.

Section 4, which authorizes the court to issue a declaration of incompatibility when a statute is found to be non-compliant with the provisions of the ECHR incorporated into domestic law through the Act ('Convention rights'), opens up several alternative possibilities. These include parliamentary inaction, in which case, the legislation emerges unscathed; the issuing of a remedial ministerial order; or the amendment or repeal of the branded statute by Parliament.[37]

Since competences are formally allocated under section 4, dialogue, in its one-step form defined by Hogg and Bushell, seems a well-fitting metaphor; no wonder that UK commentators have joined the dialogue discourse.[38] But only the second option, the making of a ministerial remedial order, is explicitly found in the Act (section 10). As such, it creates a novel mechanism of formal dialogue, one that turns away from the classical two-player analysis offered by Hogg and Bushell. Inaction, the first option available to the legislature, is implicit in section 4(6), which stipulates that a declaration 'does not affect the validity, continuing operation or enforcement of the provision in respect of which it is given'. Amendment by Parliament is available as a matter of course under the pre-existing constitutional structure ('parliamentary sovereignty'). As such, one could argue that amendment by Parliament and parliamentary inaction are two examples of a political dialogue, similar to section 3, while only the remedial ministerial order should qualify as a novel formal mechanism that resembles the override clause.

G. Formal or Implied: Why Distinguish?

The distinction between formal constitutional mechanisms that offer distinct venues of response and other existing mechanisms that have always been part of the

[37] Human Rights Act 1998, ss 4, 10. A section 10 remedial order may be made only for 'compelling reasons', and can also be the result of a finding of the ECtHR.

[38] Allan (n 7); Clayton (n 7); Hickman (n 7); Hickman (n 7); Young (n 2) ch 5. For a comparison between sections 3 and 4, leading in a different direction but encompassing a similar argument, see Hickman (n 7) 326–7. See also Hickman (n 7) 98–9.

public sphere has received little or no attention in the dialogue literature. But is it important? Does it offer constitutional theorists an insight into constitutional workings that is of value?

In my view it does. First, the distinction offers a basis for analysis of constitutional drafting options, directing attention to embedded dialogue processes as distinct from dedicated institutional structures. Secondly, it highlights the limitations of dialogue theory based solely on formal institutional structures, since it offers a glimpse into the values of analysis based on political structures.

In its formal legal sense, dialogue is limited only to the bodies or branches granted an explicit role, and their role is limited and set by the constitutional script, be they the legislature or, in the case of section 10 of the HRA and the accompanying Schedule, government ministers and Parliament. Such analysis is sufficient when exploring the formal structure of a constitution. Reliance on such a theory has enabled discussants to substantiate their normative vision, either one that wished to justify constitutional judicial review (or at least to contain and minimize the dreaded counter-majoritarian problem), or one that calls for judicial deference as the proper outcome of the grant of venues for legislative response. But at the same time this type of analysis deflects attention from the complex workings of the constitutional sphere, expressed in parallel discussions of multi-participant, open-ended and ever-revolving offer decision-making processes. No judicial decision in the public sphere involves only the court and the government. Perhaps first in importance is the applicant: the initiator of the judicial process, the person or body whose rights or interests were allegedly interfered with. Further, a case brought before court can be but one expression of a hotly debated social issue. In short, the debate over formal dialogue makes much sense when placed in the purely legal sphere. Moving to the socio-politico-legal sphere, more is required.

H. Hierarchies, Dialogue, and Networks: The Full-Fledged Political Version of Dialogue

Dialogue theory has broken down previous hierarchical conceptions, under which constitutional structures necessarily grant the power of the last word to one body. Let us now consider the value of moving from mere dialogue analysis to the study of multi-layered, multi-member, political ongoing processes of decision-making.

As previously mentioned, Hogg and Bushell were not unaware of the variety of inter-branch political interaction; they were simply less interested in this variety and preferred to focus on the structures offered in the Charter. Indeed, as stated in one of Kent Roach's important contributions, 'dialogic review' 'focuses on issues of constitutional design and the constitutional rejection of both judicial and legislative supremacy. It does not capture all the dialogue that actually occurs'.[39] Roach offers Bruce Ackerman's theory of constitutional moments as a prime example of an

[39] Roach (n 34) 55–6.

excluded dialogue, and he moves to address other 'sophisticated sub-constitutional devices used in the United States to encourage dialogues between courts and legislators'.[40] The distinctive nature of dialogic judicial review is that it 'combines constitutional decisions of courts with legislative revision or rejection of these decisions by means of ordinary legislation'.

The link of public law to politics, well recognized by many,[41] offers another aspect of dialogue. The issue here is not only the focus on the limited number of participants.[42] Much more can be garnered from Louis Fisher and other participants in the debate as it evolved in the United States. In *Constitutional Dialogues*, Fisher pointed at the political, rather than structural, elements of the constitutional sphere in general and of dialogical processes in particular. Starting from the argument that the assumption that the court has been given the final word is thus wrong, he submitted that the Constitution undergoes constant interpretation and reinterpretation. The political nature of dialogue derives not only from the absence of a formal dialogical mechanism, an aspect discussed; dialogue is essentially conducted between many actors, rather then two. Fisher points at the legislature as partner to the dialogue with the court, but also at the executive and beyond. In fact, his dialogue collapses into pure politics:

> Each decision by a court is subject to scrutiny and rejection by private citizens and public officials. What is 'final' at one stage of our political development may be reopened at some later date, leading to revisions, fresh interpretations, and reversals of Court doctrines.[43]

Barry Friedman's 'dialogue' is similarly redefined:

> The Constitution is not interpreted by aloof judges imposing their will on the people. Rather, constitutional interpretation is an elaborate discussion between judges and the body politic. The American body politic consists of numerous constituencies clamoring to be heard... the court mediates the views of various people. The process is interactive... Simply put, our process of constitutional interpretation is a dialogue.[44]

But there is more to dialogue than that. Studying the responses to judicial decisions, Friedman recognized that some of them are to be found on 'a continuum of non-enforcement'.[45] Some types of response do remain within the constitutional structure, for example, when Congress re-enacts a statute that conforms, at least in its key elements, to the decision. But Friedman recognized, as others have done, different ways in which decisions may be unimplemented. This is an important point as it challenges the argument that in the United States the judiciary reigns supreme; it shows that 'strong form' review is not politically omnipotent. For Friedman, 'non-enforcement' includes downright failure to comply, as in Lincoln's reaction to *Ex p. Merryman*,[46] 'foot-dragging', as in the school segregation cases,[47]

[40] Roach (n 34) 56. [41] See, eg, Loughlin (n 3).

[42] S Lakin, 'How to Make Sense of the HRA 1998: The Ises and Oughts of the British Constitution' (2010) 30 *OJLS* 399, 415.

[43] Fisher (n 8) 275. [44] Friedman (n 8) 653–5. [45] Friedman (n 8) 645.

[46] 17 F Cas 144 (CCD Md) (1861).

[47] *Brown v Board of Education* 347 US 483 (1954). For analysis of the aftermath of this, and subsequent decisions concerned with school segregation, see, eg, JT Patterson, *Brown v Board of Education: A Civil Rights Milestone and Its Troubled Legacy* (OUP 2001).

and, most telling in the context of dialogue theory, lengthy processes of 'testing the finality of judicial lawmaking', as in the aftermath of *Roe v Wade*.[48] Similar studies of US post-decision dynamics have shown that constitutional realities are messy, and include cases of partial accommodation, evasion, and sometimes downright defiance.[49] Such post-decision interactions only loosely derive from constitutional scripture. They also feed on political and social forces; despite the seemingly weaker pedigree of such forces, their vitality may be just as strong, if not stronger, in comparison to legal and constitutional-based forces.

Recognition of the political multilayered nature of the decision-making process is not absent in the United Kingdom either. For example, Nick Barber argues that it is best to consider the constitutional structure of the United Kingdom (and elsewhere) as one that balances 'multiple unranked sources of power',[50] which draws on the political. Indeed, the constitutional framework is more accurately depicted as one that legitimizes a multi-actor network that enables a joint and ongoing process of decision-making and consensus formation. This process is generated by many: in addition to Parliaments and courts, government ministries, government agencies, individuals, interest groups, the media, and other members of society continuously interact to produce a social solution under constantly changing tensions and coalitions of interest.[51]

Further, judicial decisions and statutes alike should be assessed not only on their date of birth. They are both subject to the dynamics of subsequent implementation or rejection by other members of the network. A decision may be just one component of an ongoing social debate, and should thus be assessed as such, rather than as a single event. This is more of a conversation than a dialogue, in that government branches, interest groups, political parties, individuals—in short, any locus of power—can potentially participate and influence the (possibly temporary) settlement of a debate. When 'dialogue' becomes 'conversation', the search for the ultimate sovereign is replaced by the recognition that social decision-making is complex, multiparticipatory, and ever-evolving.

I. The Multiple Forms of Dialogue and Sovereignty: Conceptual Affinities

How should these three types of 'dialogue' be considered, and what is their link to sovereignty analysis? True formal dialogue mechanisms, such as override clauses

[48] 410 US 113 (1973). For a reference to the above three examples see Friedman (n 8) 645–8.

[49] See, eg, WN Eskridge, 'Overriding Supreme Court Statutory Interpretation Decisions' (1991) 101 *Yale LJ* 331; KE Whittington, 'James Madison Has Left the Building' (2005) 72 *Chicago L Rev* 1137. For another type of dialogue, embodied in techniques used by courts to effectively remand the decision back to the decision-maker, essentially by considering processes rather than content, see DT Coenen, 'A Constitution of Collaboration: Protecting Fundamental Values With Second-Look Rules of Interbranch Dialogue' (2001) 42 *William and Mary L Rev* 1575.

[50] NW Barber, 'Sovereignty Re-Examined: The Courts, Parliament, and Statutes' (2000) 20 *OJLS* 131.

[51] See M Cohn, 'Judicial Activism in the House of Lords: A Composite Constitutionalist Approach' [2007] *PL* 95 at 106 (argued in the context of analysis of judicial activism).

and provisions empowering the judiciary to issue declarations of incompatibility, can indeed be viewed as dialogue-inducers and, thereby, creators of potential crises for those who wish to maintain the hierarchical vision of sovereignty. Under these mechanisms, sovereignty has indeed been compromised, if not broken. Those who challenge these reforms may view them as a threat for sovereignty and a threat to the polity itself; those who celebrate them may present this as bipolar sovereignty or, in its most accommodating version, composite sovereignty, as one that carries more promise for the protection of rights without overly compromising the legislature.

Regarding 'implied dialogue', this chapter has argued that as far as the nature of power-allocation between parliament and the judiciary, nothing new has emerged with the emergence of limitations clauses, broad interpretation provisions such as section 3 of the HRA, and the like. The difference is one of degree, not of substance. In these situations, as in other interpretable statutory and constitutional provisions, courts are offered the interpretative power, while State bodies manoeuvre around these interpretations, often creating revamped arrangements to accommodate the interpretation, in varying degrees of fidelity. This type of interaction has nothing to do with 'dialogue' in any meaningful way, at least not with the concept introduced in the current dialogue literature. Similarly, this type of interaction has little to contribute to the discussion of sovereignty, unless the dialogue turns in reality to a de facto monologue. If legislatures systematically disregard or misapply judicial decisions, or judicial interpretation always wins the day, the polity no longer remains within the sphere of dialogue, and one is led back to the good old concept of hierarchical sovereignty.

Political dialogue, however, fits well within the sovereignty discussion, this time, in its political form. Essentially, a vision of a multiparty, ongoing interaction, which fluctuates between formal structures and informal politics, has much in common with versions of sovereignty that emphasize more than mere juridical allocations of power. The notion of sovereignty as a political expression of the general will rejects formalist accounts of structural frameworks by wedding the legal with the political. So does my political version of dialogue, which may be considered, in this context, as but one expression of this version of sovereignty.

J. Conclusion

Linkage of the discussion of sovereignty with the parallel concept of constitutional/democratic dialogue requires a better understanding of the various meanings of the latter well-worked metaphor. Unpacking the different meanings of 'dialogue', this chapter first set aside 'implied' forms of dialogue, found for example in limitation clauses. Such provisions may redesign the extent of judicial review, but not its nature: as in the case of pre-existing frameworks, their implementation requires judicial interpretation, and no novel type of interaction is introduced in such cases. Conceptually, then, they are marginal to the dialogue discussion itself. This led to a focus on the distinction between formal and political dialogue. The former is expressed in its purest form in the override clause and in one of the possible responses to a declaration of incompatibility under section 4 of the HRA. The latter finds its place within political, network analyses of decision-making. Each is linked with one of the two visions of sovereignty, as briefly discussed. If sovereignty is political, and I consider it better described as such, reliance on 'dialogue' in its political form enhances this reading. In turn, dialogists can benefit from the parallel discussion on sovereignty, allowing for a broader concept of dialogue, as explicated in this chapter.

14

Sovereignty: A View from the International Bench

*Sir Christopher Greenwood**

For some the concept of sovereignty (or, more accurately, concepts, for there is more than one) is a standard around which to rally—'the sovereignty of Parliament', 'the sovereign nation', 'loyalty to the sovereign'. For others it has become something outmoded, an obstacle to reform, whether in the form of democratization at home or greater international cooperation abroad. For the international judge, however, sovereignty is neither totem nor torment but an inescapable fact of life, part of the landscape within which judgments have to be made. The purpose of this chapter is briefly to survey sovereignty as it is seen from the international bench and to hazard a few comments thereon. In doing so, I am mindful of Herbert Hart's warning, given more than fifty years ago, that:

> an uncritical use of the idea of sovereignty has spread similar confusion in the theory both of municipal and international law, and demands in both a similar corrective.... The question for municipal law is what is the extent of the supreme legislative authority recognized in this system? For international law it is: what is the maximum area of autonomy which the rules allow to States?[1]

My focus is necessarily upon sovereignty as part of the international order, rather than sovereignty in the sense in which it is used by constitutional lawyers and, for the most part, by legal philosophers, although it will be necessary to say something about that latter notion of sovereignty the better to understand the international concept of sovereignty.

Section A, will therefore begin with the distinction between sovereignty in the internal sense of power and authority *within* the State and sovereignty in its international sense of power and authority *between* States, each of which is sovereign. Section B, will examine the effect of sovereignty in this latter sense upon the

* Judge, International Court of Justice.

[1] HLA Hart, *Concept of Law* (Oxford: OUP, 1961) 218.

substance of international law. Section C will turn to some aspects of the effect of sovereignty upon jurisdiction in international law. Lastly, Section D will return to the relationship between internal and international concepts of sovereignty to see how that relationship has become more complicated over time.

A. Internal and International Concepts of Sovereignty

When lawyers speak of sovereignty in its internal (or domestic) sense, they are generally referring to the constitutional allocation of power and authority within the legal system of the State. It is in that sense that we speak, for example, of the 'sovereignty of Parliament' in the United Kingdom. In Dicey's conception, the sovereignty of Parliament meant that Parliament (or, more precisely, the Queen-in-Parliament) could always have the last word in making law. Since the Constitution of the United Kingdom acknowledged no authority higher than Parliament, its enactments were necessarily the highest form of law within the legal system of the United Kingdom.[2] To speak in this way of the sovereignty of Parliament is, of course, quintessentially British; most other States possess written constitutions which impose limitations on the powers of their legislatures. Nevertheless, that means merely that their concept of internal sovereignty is different from that of the United Kingdom, not that they lack such a concept. The constitution may, for example, have been an expression of the will of the 'sovereign people', through a plebiscite or a constitutional assembly, the regular legislature being given only limited or delegated powers and the judicial system being empowered to ensure that the legislature keeps within the confines of the constitution. In many federal States, sovereignty is considered to be divided between the federation and the component states or provinces. In such cases, the description of the domestic sovereign will be different from that in the United Kingdom but the concept of domestic sovereignty is just as significant.

Today, anyone discussing the sovereignty of Parliament must, of course, take account of the effects of European Union law which prevails, even before United Kingdom courts, over inconsistent provisions in an Act of Parliament. Within the United Kingdom legal order, however, that supremacy of European Union law is the result of an exercise of sovereignty by Parliament in Section 2 of the European Communities Act 1972 and United Kingdom constitutional theorists have traditionally reconciled the supremacy of European Union law with the continuing sovereignty of Parliament by maintaining that Parliament has the power to repeal or amend the 1972 Act.[3] While there are obvious practical obstacles to such repeal, there is no legal impediment within the United Kingdom legal order, so the

[2] Professor Vernon Bogdanor has written that the British concept of the sovereignty of Parliament can be summed up in eight words: 'what the Queen-in-Parliament enacts is law'; V Bogdanor, 'Our New Constitution' (2004) 120 *LQR* 242, 259.

[3] See, eg, Lord Bingham, *The Rule of Law* (Allen Lane, 2010) 163–6. See also now, European Union Act 2011 (c 12) s 18, and see further Chapter 10 in this volume by Paul Craig.

concept of the sovereignty of Parliament is preserved. It is important, however, to note the limits which follow from the phrase *within the United Kingdom legal order*. Within the legal order of the European Union, the answer might be quite different.[4] The sovereignty of the United Kingdom Parliament extends only to the law of the United Kingdom; its enactments are undoubtedly law within that legal system but they may not produce legal effects within other legal systems.[5]

The same is true of the relationship between English law and international law. When Lord Justice Diplock famously remarked that 'the sovereign power of the Queen, in 'Parliament extends to breaking treaties',[6] he did not mean that, because Parliament was sovereign, it could break a treaty without violating international law but only that Parliament's sovereign power within the English legal system meant that if Parliament legislated contrary to a treaty binding upon the United Kingdom, the English courts were obliged to give effect to the will of Parliament. He recognized that, in those circumstances, the United Kingdom would be in breach of international law and might therefore be called to account in another forum outside the United Kingdom.

There follows another important feature of the internal concept of sovereignty. That concept is primarily concerned with the relations between the different organs of the State and those who are subject to their authority and with the relations of those subjects *inter se*. The subjects of the sovereign are not themselves possessed of individual sovereignty, although they may have a share in the collective concept of the sovereign people or a right to elect the members of the sovereign Parliament.

The international concept of sovereignty is quite different. For the international lawyer, sovereignty means the sovereignty of the State itself and the principal concern of international law is not with the allocation of power between the institutions or territorial units within that State but the relations between that State and other States, each of which is also sovereign.[7]

Perhaps the clearest aspect of the international concept of sovereignty is the sovereignty of the State in relation to its own territory. Sovereignty in this sense was described in 1928 by Max Huber, President of the Permanent Court of International Justice, sitting as a sole arbitrator in the *Island of Palmas Case*[8] between the Netherlands and the United States of America, in the following terms:

[4] This is not the place to debate whether, as a matter of EU law, a Member State has the power to withdraw from the European Union without the consent of the Union itself, or of its other Member States; suffice it to say that a European Union lawyer might well give a less unequivocal answer than did Lord Bingham.

[5] The legal systems of the few remaining British overseas territories are an exception and there remains a debate about the existence of residual powers for the United Kingdom Parliament under the Statute of Westminster.

[6] *Salomon v Commissioners of Customs and Excise* [1967] 2 QB 116, 143 (CA).

[7] At the time of writing there were 193 States which were members of the United Nations. International law today also deals with relations between States and international organizations, as well as individuals and other non-state actors, but relations between States remain at the core of the international legal order.

[8] *Island of Palmas Case* (*Netherlands v USA*) (1928) 2 United Nations Reports of International Arbitral Awards 829.

Sovereignty in the relations between States signifies independence. Independence in regard to a portion of the globe is the right to exercise therein, to the exclusion of any other State, the functions of a State. The development of the national organization of States during the last few centuries and, as a corollary, the development of international law, have established this principle of the exclusive competence of the State in regard to its own territory in such a way as to make it the point of departure in settling most questions that concern international relations.[9]

Despite the importance which it attaches to the concept of sovereignty, the *Palmas* award also indicates some of the limits of that concept. Huber was speaking in the context of a dispute between two States, each of which claimed that the disputed territory (an island lying between the then Dutch East Indies, modern day Indonesia, and the Philippines, at that time governed by the United States) fell within their sovereignty. The award (which found that the Netherlands had the superior claim) makes clear that a dispute of this kind cannot be resolved by reference to the fact of sovereignty; it is international law which determines which of two competing sovereigns has the better claim to the territory. Indeed, it necessarily follows that if any difference between two States is to be resolved by law, reference to the sovereign status of the competing parties gets one nowhere. Since a fundamental principle of international law is the sovereign *equality* of States,[10] neither party to the dispute can gain any priority by referring to its sovereign status. A legal resolution of the dispute can thus be achieved only by reference to principles of law which exist, and which take effect, independent of that sovereign status.

Moreover, although sovereignty over an area of territory is described by Huber as exclusive, it is not unlimited. The sovereignty of a State over its territory does not entitle it to perform therein actions which are contrary to its international law obligations towards other States. An early instance of this limitation being enforced can be found in the *Alabama* arbitration between the United States of America and the United Kingdom in 1872.[11] The case concerned ships built for the Confederacy in a British shipyard during the American Civil War. Although ostensibly constructed as merchant ships, they were in fact raiders designed to prey on Union shipping. After the British government failed to act on a United States request to prevent the ships from sailing, they were fitted out with weaponry after leaving British waters and did extensive damage during the latter part of the War. In one of the first major cases between two States, the five member arbitration tribunal awarded the United States damages of $15.5 million (then equivalent to £3.25 million) for the breach of neutrality which it held the United Kingdom had committed.[12] The damage

[9] *Island of Palmas Case* (n 8) (1928) 8.

[10] One of the governing principles in the Charter of the United Nations is that of the 'sovereign equality' of States (art 2(1)).

[11] JB Moore, *History and Digest of the International Arbitrations to which the United States has been a Party*, vol 1 (Washington GPO) 495.

[12] The United States, which maintained that the raiders had caused the War to last far longer than it would otherwise have done, had claimed a much larger sum. Even so, the sum awarded is the equivalent of some $160 million today and constituted five per cent of the UK budget in 1872; a similar percentage today would amount to more than £150 billion; R Jenkins, *Gladstone* (Macmillan, 1995) 359; T Bingham, 'The Alabama Claims Arbitration' (2005) 54 *ICLQ* 1.

done by the raiders took place on the high seas and in American waters but the wrongful conduct for which the United Kingdom was found liable—permitting the vessels to be built and then to sail—took place in British territory.

The *Palmas* and *Alabama* cases afford us an interesting insight into the difference between the international concept of sovereignty and its domestic counterpart. While the passage quoted from *Palmas* speaks of one aspect of the international concept of sovereignty in terms which have some similarity to sovereignty in the domestic context, the fact that the case concerns the competing claims of two sovereigns demonstrates that the two concepts are distinct. There is no room in domestic law discussion of sovereignty for a principle like the sovereign equality of States. The differences are even more apparent in the *Alabama* case. In that case, not only did the sovereign status of the United Kingdom not save it from a finding of liability and the award of substantial damages, the Tribunal held that the United Kingdom was liable even though, under English law, the British government had had no power to stop the construction of the ships for the Confederacy or to prevent them from sailing. In reaching that conclusion, the Tribunal laid down an important principle, to which it will be necessary to return in Section D, namely that a State may not rely upon its own internal law as a justification for failure to comply with its international obligations. In other words, whatever the sovereign Queen-in-Parliament might enact as law within the United Kingdom legal order made no difference to the obligation of the United Kingdom, as a sovereign State, to comply with the international law of neutrality.

The *Alabama* arbitration award also highlights another, related point. Whereas the domestic law concept of sovereignty is concerned with the allocation of sovereign powers to the different organs within a State, the award treated that allocation as irrelevant to international law. For the Tribunal, the sovereign which was the respondent in the proceedings was the State itself (ie the United Kingdom) which it treated as one and indivisible. How that sovereign chose to allocate power to its different organs was neither a matter of concern to international law nor one which international law could take into account. Thus, the fact that the government of the United Kingdom (which was responsible for the conduct of the arbitration proceedings) was not empowered to prevent the departure of the ships unless Parliament conferred such power upon it was immaterial since the international obligation to prevent their departure was imposed by international law upon the State of the United Kingdom. How the United Kingdom chose to comply with that obligation and which organ of State it entrusted with that task was a matter for the United Kingdom alone.

B. Sovereignty and the Substance of International Law

States can no longer be regarded as the only subjects of international law. The last century has seen the emergence of more than 2,000 international organizations which are also undeniably subject to international law, possessing rights and obligations under that law and deriving their legal personality from it. Moreover, since the Second World War at least, it has become established that international law confers rights and imposes obligations upon individuals, as the rapidly expanding law of human rights and international humanitarian law make clear. Nevertheless, it is fair to say that States remain the principal subjects of international law. Since each State is sovereign and the sovereign equality of States is a fundamental principle of international law, it is necessary to ask what effect that sovereignty has upon the rules of international law.

If we begin with the substantive rules of international law, for many commentators there is an immediate dilemma: how can sovereigns become subject to legal obligations?[13] If law can emanate only from an exercise of sovereignty (as many constitutional theorists tend to assume), then it would appear that only two answers are possible. Either there exists in the international order some higher form of sovereign power hierarchically superior to States, or the rules of international law must be a product of the exercise by States of their sovereignty in such a way as to impose obligations upon themselves.

The first approach immediately encounters the obstacle that, subject to one important qualification, there is no institution in international law remotely equivalent to a sovereign Parliament. It is true that there are numerous international organizations, some of which have the power to create rules.[14] Each such organization, however, derives that power from its constituent treaty, an agreement freely entered into by those States which choose to become members of the organization and the decisions of the organization are binding only upon those members. Moreover, in the majority of cases, a member State may avoid the application of a rule adopted by the organization either because the rule is contained in a treaty drawn up by the organization to which its members are free to become party or not, as they please, or because there is some process by which a member can opt out of the effects of a particular rule adopted by the organization. The rules drawn up by such organizations may thus have some of the characteristics of legislation but they are a far cry from the legislation adopted by the parliament of a State.

The one qualification that has to be entered concerns the United Nations. The Charter of the United Nations ('the Charter') the constituent treaty of the United Nations Organization, is an agreement between the 193 Member States of the United Nations. It is, however, somewhat more far-reaching than other constituent treaties. Chapter VII of the Charter gives the Security Council (one of the six principal organs of the United Nations) the power to take 'measures' necessary to address threats to international peace and security, breaches of the peace and acts of aggression.[15] According to Article 48 of the Charter:

> The action required to carry out the decisions of the Security Council for the maintenance of international peace and security shall be taken by all the Members of the United Nations or by some of them, as the Security Council may determine.

[13] For discussion of this question, see Hart (1961) (n 1) ch 10.

[14] The International Labour Organization is a particularly important example; see H Sauer, 'International Labour Organization' in *Max Planck Encyclopedia of Public International Law*, vol V (Oxford: OUP, 2012) 810.

[15] Charter of the United Nations, arts 39, 41, and 42.

Such decisions are legally binding upon every United Nations Member State,[16] irrespective of whether it was a member of the Security Council at the time the decision was taken,[17] or, if it was a member of the Security Council, whether it voted for or against the particular decision.[18]

While decisions of this kind were rare before 1990, since that date the Council has used its powers under Chapter VII to impose economic and political sanctions, to override contractual obligations, to establish international criminal tribunals and a compensation commission, and to provide for the delimitation of an international frontier.[19]

Although the emphasis has been upon establishing the means for ensuring compliance with existing rules of international law,[20] rather than adopting new rules of general application, the decisions of the Security Council adopted under Chapter VII of the Charter have imposed upon States a number of obligations to which they would not otherwise have been subject and from which they have no capacity to withdraw while remaining Members of the United Nations. Moreover, while Articles 25 and 48 of the Charter speak only of the obligations of States which are members of the United Nations, it has to be remembered that, during the last twenty years or so, the United Nations has had universal or near-universal membership. In addition, Article 2(6) of the Charter [21] has frequently been interpreted as providing that non-members may be required to comply with decisions of the Security Council so far as is necessary for the maintenance of international peace and security, although this interpretation has been controversial.[22]

[16] Charter of the United Nations, art 25.

[17] There are fifteen members of the Security Council, five of which are permanent members, while the other ten are elected for two-year terms (art 23 of the Charter). According to art 27(3) of the Charter, a decision on a non-procedural matter requires nine affirmative votes 'including the concurring votes of the permanent members', although the last part of this provision has long been interpreted as requiring only that none of the five permanent members actually votes against the measure under consideration, so that a decision which attracts nine affirmative votes will be adopted irrespective of abstentions by permanent members.

[18] Security Council resolution 955 (1994), creating the International Criminal Tribunal for Rwanda and imposing on all Member States obligations of cooperation with the Tribunal including the duty to surrender suspected offenders to it, was adopted despite the negative vote of Rwanda, which was an elected member of the Security Council in 1994.

[19] See, eg, the sanctions imposed upon Iraq following the invasion of Kuwait (Security Council resolution 661 (1990)) and the subsequent establishment of the United Nations Compensation Commission and a mechanism for determining the frontier (Security Council resolution 687 (1991)). The Security Council first used its Chapter VII powers to establish an international criminal tribunal when it created the International Criminal Tribunal for the Former Yugoslavia in 1993 (Security Council resolution 827 (1993)).

[20] The Security Council stated, for example, that the resolutions by which it created the International Criminal Tribunal for Yugoslavia and the International Criminal Tribunal for Rwanda did not create new substantive rules of law but merely directed the tribunals to apply certain existing international law rules.

[21] Article 2(6) of the Charter provides that the United Nations shall ensure that States which are not Members of the United Nations act in accordance with the principles on which the United Nations is based 'so far as may be necessary for the maintenance of international peace and security'.

[22] Thus the United Nations and a majority of commentators have interpreted this provision as meaning that the United Nations may require non-members to comply with decisions of the Security Council under Chapter VII if their compliance is necessary for the maintenance of international

These powers of the Security Council therefore come closer to providing for a form of international legislation than anything else in international law and show that, in certain circumstances, legal obligations can be imposed upon a State (given Article 2(6) of the Charter, perhaps even if it is not a Member of the United Nations) notwithstanding its active opposition.

The second approach, which explains the rules of international law as the product of State sovereignty, has received considerable support. As the Permanent Court of International Justice put it, in its judgment in *SS Lotus (France v Turkey)* ('the *Lotus* Case') in 1927:

> International law governs relations between independent States. The rules of law binding upon States therefore emanate from their own free will as expressed in conventions or by usages generally accepted as expressing principles of law and established in order to regulate the relations between these co-existing independent communities or to the achievement of common aims. Restrictions upon the independence of States cannot therefore be presumed.[23]

This is the classic statement of the approach that rules of law must emanate from the exercise of the sovereignty of states.

Although it is today the subject of severe academic criticism,[24] the statement of the Permanent Court retains a great deal of force. The two main sources of international law—treaties and customary international law—can both be seen as the product of the free will of sovereign States. That is manifestly the case with treaties.[25] A treaty is an agreement voluntarily negotiated and entered into by States. With the possible exception of peace treaties imposed upon a defeated State (now largely a thing of the past), no State is obliged to enter into a treaty if it does not wish to do so, nor does it violate any legal obligation if it chooses not to become a party. The United States, for example, was—and is—under no legal obligation to become party to the Statute of the International Criminal Court (which, despite its name, is a treaty to which, at the time of writing, 122 States were parties). Moreover, in the case of a multilateral treaty, unless the treaty either expressly or by necessary implication prohibits reservations, a State may make its participation in the treaty subject to special conditions set out in a reservation at the time that it deposits its instrument of ratification or accession to the treaty. So long as other parties accept—or at least do not object to—that reservation, its effect is to modify the provisions of

peace and security. That claim has not always been accepted. Switzerland, before it joined the United Nations in 2002, always stated that its compliance with such decisions was voluntary and not a matter of legal obligation.

23 *SS Lotus (France v Turkey)* (1927) PCIJ Series A no 9, 18.

24 For a summary of the debate regarding the decision, see A von Bogdandy and M Rau, 'The Lotus' in *Max Planck Encyclopedia of International Law*, vol VI (Oxford: OUP, 2012) 946

25 Confusingly, treaties go by several different names—agreements, conventions, protocols, exchanges of notes being only some of the names in current use. Nevertheless, art 2(a) of the Vienna Convention on the Law of Treaties 1969 (n 26) defines a treaty as 'an agreement concluded between States in written form and governed by international law, whether embodied in a single instrument or in two or more related instruments and whatever its particular designation'. Apart from the fact that treaties may also be concluded by international organizations, this definition reflects current international practice.

the treaty as between the reserving State and other parties.[26] Since treaties, as such, bind only their parties, they are a source of law which is very much the product of the exercise of State sovereignty, rather than something superimposed upon States notwithstanding that sovereignty.[27]

Thus, treaty obligations are binding upon a State because that State has exercised its sovereign power to adhere to the treaty in question. For that reason, appeals to sovereignty are of no avail for a State accused of violating a treaty obligation. As the Permanent Court of International Justice put it in its first judgment in 1923:

> The Court declines to see in the conclusion of any Treaty by which a State undertakes to perform or refrain from performing a particular act an abandonment of its sovereignty. No doubt any convention creating an obligation of this kind places a restriction upon the exercise of the sovereign rights of the State, in the sense that it requires them to be exercised in a certain way. But the right of entering into international engagements is an attribute of State sovereignty.[28]

Customary international law is less straightforward. Rules of customary international law are traditionally said to be the product of widespread and uniform State practice, together with *opinio juris*. State practice may take many different forms and includes action by the legislature and judiciary, as well as the executive of a State.[29] *Opinio juris* is generally defined as a sense of legal obligation,[30] although it might be better seen as the acceptance of a legal obligation or the assertion of a legal right which others had the obligation to respect. For a rule of customary international law to exist, the two elements must coexist, that is to say there must be sufficient State practice and it must be accompanied by an acceptance that the practice is required by international law or, in the appropriate case, constitutes the exercise of a right under international law.

Seen in this way, customary international law also appears to emanate from the free will of States and was clearly viewed as such by the Permanent Court of International Justice in the *Lotus* case. Customary international law is certainly produced by the exercise of State sovereignty; both the elements which are necessary for

[26] Vienna Convention on the Law of Treaties 1969 arts 19–23. A State may not, however, enter a reservation which is incompatible with the object and purpose of the treaty. Some important modern treaties, such as the United Nations Convention on the Law of the Sea (1982), do not allow reservations.

[27] That is not to say that particular rules embodied in a treaty may not bind non-parties. They will do so if they reflected customary international law at the time of the adoption of the treaty or if they come to do so as a result of State practice following the adoption of the treaty. In both cases, however, what is binding on the State which does not become party to the treaty is not the treaty provision as such but the rule of customary international law of which the treaty provision has come to be an authoritative statement. See *North Sea Continental Shelf Cases* (*Federal Republic of Germany v Denmark; Federal Republic of Germany v Netherlands*), ICJ Reports, 1969, p. 3, 44.

[28] *SS Wimbledon*, PCIJ Series A no 1, 17 August 1923, 25.

[29] See, eg, the discussion of State practice on jurisdictional immunities in the 2012 judgment of the International Court of Justice in *Jurisdictional Immunities (Germany v Italy)* (2012) 51 *International Legal Materials* 563, in which the Court referred to national court judgments, national legislation, and executive action as instances of State practice.

[30] That was the definition employed by the International Court of Justice in *North Sea Continental Shelf Cases* (1969) (n 27), p. 44.

the creation of a rule of customary international law involve that exercise of the sovereign powers of States. Yet that is not to say that a particular State is bound by a rule of customary international law because it has exercised its sovereign will to become bound (as is the case with a treaty rule). Unlike treaties, which require a deliberate act of acceptance to become binding upon a State, no such act is required for a State to become subject to a rule of customary international law.

First, in contrast to a treaty, which is binding only upon the States that choose to become party to it, customary international law is, in principle, binding upon all States. The creation of a rule of customary international law requires widespread, but not universal, State practice and a State may, therefore, find itself bound by a rule even though its own practice has not contributed to its formation. The effect is mitigated by the principle that a State which has persistently objected to an emerging rule from before the time when that rule crystallized into customary international law will not be bound by it.[31] However, the extent of the persistent objector principle is not entirely clear and, even when it applies, it excludes the application of a rule of customary international law only in the case of a State which has actively and consistently opposed that rule from before its incorporation into customary international law; it is far more limited than the principle that a State is not bound by a treaty rule unless it takes active steps to become a party to that treaty.

Secondly, it is now generally accepted that each new State, on attaining statehood, becomes bound by the entirety of the existing customary international law. The very act of attaining statehood—and thus sovereignty—is automatically accompanied by the assumption of obligations under rules of customary international law. In some respects it might be likened to the fact that each new member of the European Union is bound by the existing body of European Union law (the *acquis*) but with an important difference. Membership of the European Union is voluntary; a State may choose whether to join or not, just as it may choose whether or not to join the United Nations. But it is not possible to exist as a State without becoming subject to customary international law. To describe this process as a voluntary exercise of will by the new State is surely artificial. Yet it is a very widely recognized feature of international law and is almost certainly indispensable for the role of law in international society.

Thirdly, both courts and writers have been willing to accept certain rules as customary international law on the basis of comparatively little in the way of State practice if those rules have also been embodied in texts—whether treaties or instruments such as resolutions of the United Nations General Assembly—which have achieved very widespread acceptance, at least as long as there is very little in the way of contrary practice.[32]

[31] The origins of this principle are generally thought to lie in the judgment in the *Fisheries Case (United Kingdom v Norway)*, ICJ Reports, p. 116, p. 131.

[32] See, eg, the reference to resolutions of the General Assembly by the International Court of Justice in *Military and Paramilitary Activities in and against Nicaragua (Nicaragua v United States of America)* ICJ Reports, 1986, p. 3, and by the sole arbitrator in *Texaco/Calasiatic v Libya* (1977) 53 ILR 389. See

Lastly, once a State has become bound by a rule of customary international law, it can cease to be bound only if it can bring about a change in the law such that the rule in question ceases to be part of the law. There is no scope for a State which has become bound by a rule of customary international law to withdraw from it. That is in marked contrast to the position with most treaties from which States are free to withdraw. There is no equivalent of the argument, considered in Section B, that the sovereignty of Parliament is not compromised by the United Kingdom's membership of the European Union because Parliament can legislate for the withdrawal of the United Kingdom from the European Union.

Two other features of contemporary international law also require mention here. The first is the phenomenon, already noted, of binding decisions of the United Nations Security Council. Such decisions, especially if part of a pattern, may have an effect upon the generally applicable rules of international law, even though they originate with an institutional decision rather than an exercise of State sovereignty in the classical sense.

The second is what is known as rules of *jus cogens* or peremptory norms. A rule of *jus cogens* is defined by the Vienna Convention on the Law of Treaties as a rule 'accepted and recognized by the international community of States as a whole as a norm from which no derogation is permitted and which can be modified only by a subsequent norm of general international law having the same character'.[33] The concept of *jus cogens* had its origin in that part of international law known as the law of treaties, which came to recognize that a treaty was void if it conflicted with a rule of *jus cogens*.[34] It is now accepted as having a broader application.[35] While there is great controversy about which rules have the status of *jus cogens,* some, such as the prohibition of aggression and of torture, are now generally accepted as such. A rule can only acquire the status of *jus cogens* if the international community recognizes it as such. Since the international community is generally thought to mean, in this context, the collectivity of States, the recognition of a rule as one of *jus cogens* entails the exercise of State sovereignty. However, universal recognition is not required and there is no persistent objector principle where *jus cogens* is concerned. Moreover, whereas two States can always agree by treaty that a particular rule of customary international law will not apply as between themselves, a rule of *jus cogens* cannot be set aside in this way as any treaty to that effect would be void.

It follows, therefore, that while most obligations imposed by international law are created by the exercise of State sovereignty, it is no longer true (if, indeed, it ever was) to say that the international law obligations which bind a State do so only

also the discussion in M Mendelson, 'The Formation of Customary International Law' (1998) 272 *Receuil des Cours* 159.

[33] Vienna Convention on the Law of Treaties 1969 (n 26) art 53.

[34] Vienna Convention on the Law of Treaties 1969 (n 26) art 53.

[35] See, eg, its incorporation into the law of State responsibility by the International Law Commission, Articles on State Responsibility, art 26. The commentary to that provision makes clear that the International Law Commission considered the definition of *jus cogens* in art 53 of the Vienna Convention on the Law of Treaties 1969 (n 26) to be applicable in the law of State responsibility and not as confined to the law of treaties.

because of the free will of that State. Statehood entails at least some obligations which are not the choice of the State concerned. Our understanding of sovereignty in its international sense has to take that fact into account.

C. Sovereignty and Jurisdiction

Both in international law and national law it was often considered to be a feature of sovereignty that the sovereign could not be called to account in court. In most systems of national law, that aspect of sovereignty has long disappeared or, at least, been substantially ameliorated. In international law, however, it has had a more enduring legacy. The concept of State sovereignty was traditionally held to entail that a State could not be required to defend itself before a court—whether an international court or the court of another State—without its consent. In the case of proceedings against one State before the courts of another, this principle stemmed from the notion that one sovereign could not exercise sovereignty over another (*par in parem non habet imperium*) and was given effect by what we now know as the doctrine of sovereign (or State) immunity.[36] In the case of proceedings before an international court or tribunal, the requirement of consent had a more complicated history but was generally thought to be an attribute of State sovereignty and became a fundamental principle of jurisdiction. Both situations require closer examination.

In the case of proceedings before national courts, the traditional 'absolute' doctrine of State immunity, which barred the exercise of jurisdiction over a foreign State unless that State gave its consent to the specific proceedings, gave way during the twentieth century to a 'restrictive' doctrine in which there was no immunity if a foreign State was sued for acts of a commercial, as opposed to a sovereign, character.[37] At first glance, there is no conflict between the concept of State sovereignty and the restrictive theory of immunity; a State is immune from the jurisdiction of foreign courts when it acts in a sovereign capacity but not when it acts in a commercial, non-sovereign manner.[38] Closer inspection, however, reveals that the

[36] The United States Supreme Court has described this principle as merely one of comity, rather than law; see *Republic of Austria v Altmann* (2004) 541 US 677, 147 ILR 681. That view is not, however, shared by the courts of other States or by the International Court of Justice, which recently held that States have a legal obligation to accord immunity to other States in certain circumstances; *Jurisdictional Immunities (Germany v Italy)* (2012) (n 29) para 56.

[37] The evolution of the law in this regard was traced by the International Law Commission in a series of reports on State immunity which culminated in the adoption of the United Nations Convention on the Jurisdictional Immunities of States (2004); see A Watts, *The International Law Commission*, vol 3 (Oxford: Oxford University Press, 1999) 1999–2103; and A Pronto and M Wood, *The International Law Commission*, vol 4 (Oxford: Oxford University Press, 2010) 13–73. See also the judgment of the International Court of Justice in *Jurisdictional Immunities (Germany v Italy)* (n 29).

[38] In *Jurisdictional Immunities (Germany v Italy)* (n 29) para 60, the International Court of Justice held that war crimes committed by German forces during the Second World War had to be regarded as sovereign, rather than commercial, acts.

restrictive theory makes more of an inroad into the sovereignty of a defendant State than might be thought.

First, the distinction between sovereign and commercial acts is widely (though not universally) taken to be based upon the nature of the transaction in question, rather than its purpose. Consequently, a contract for the sale of goods is generally treated as a commercial matter, irrespective of whether the goods in question are souvenirs for the State's tourism department to sell to visitors or military equipment for use by the State's army.[39] Moreover, if the original transaction is a commercial one, it is now generally established that the fact that a State might break a contract for reasons of high policy (for example because of the need to safeguard its currency during a financial crisis) will not entitle it to immunity.[40] The result is that States may often find themselves subject to the jurisdiction of foreign courts for acts which have at least an element of sovereignty about them.

Secondly, beginning with the *Pinochet* case in 1998–9, a number of national courts have held that a foreign State is not entitled to immunity for even its senior officials and former officials if they are the subject of criminal proceedings for certain violations of international law, such as torture.[41] The extent to which those decisions have brought about a change in the law is controversial.[42] Moreover, it is noticeable that the House of Lords in the *Pinochet* case based its conclusion that the former President of Chile was not immune from extradition proceedings initiated by Spain relating to certain offences of torture on the fact that Chile, Spain, and the United Kingdom had all chosen to become parties to the United Nations

[39] That was the approach taken by the English courts when they applied common law (considered for these purposes to include customary international law), *Trendtex Trading Corporation v Central Bank of Nigeria* [1977] 1 QB 529 (Court of Appeal) and *I Congreso del Partido* [1983] 1 AC 244 (House of Lords) (following the judgment of the Federal Constitutional Court of the Federal Republic of Germany in the *Empire of Iran Case* (1963) 45 ILR 57). The matter is now governed by the State Immunity Act (1978) s 3, which adopts the same approach, as does the legislation adopted in most States which have dealt with the matter by statute. The United Nations Convention on the Jurisdictional Immunities of States and their Property (2004), which is not yet in force but which is widely regarded as an authoritative statement of customary international law on most points, also relies primarily on the nature of the transaction, though it allows for some reference to its purpose; see art 2(1)(c).

[40] See, eg, *Trendtex Trading Corporation v Central Bank of Nigeria* [1977] and *I Congreso del Partido* [1983] (n 39). Art 10 of the United Nations Convention provides that a State which engages in a commercial transaction is not immune as regards proceedings 'arising out of that commercial transaction'; it makes no provision for an exception relating to the State's purpose in breaching the contract.

[41] *R v Bow Street Metropolitan Stipendiary Magistrate,* ex parte *Pinochet Ugarte* [2000] 1 AC 61 and 147, (2000) 119 ILR 1. By the time of the proceedings against him, General Pinochet had ceased to be President of Chile. A serving Head of State is immune from the jurisdiction of the courts of other States. Like the Head of Government, Foreign Minister, and a small number of the most senior ministers, the Head of State is treated as an ambassador and accorded immunity *ratione personae*; see the judgment of the International Court of Justice in *Arrest Warrant (Democratic Republic of Congo v Belgium),* ICJ Reports, 2002. On the position of other officials, see the judgment of the Divisional Court in *Khurts Bat v Investigating Judge of the German Federal Court* [2011] EWHC 2029 (Admin), (2011) 147 ILR 633.

[42] See, eg, *Arrest Warrant* (n 41), para 61. The House of Lords considered, moreover, that the principle laid down in the *Pinochet* case was confined to criminal proceedings and did not extend to civil proceedings against the officials of a State; *Jones v Saudi Arabia* [2007] 1 AC 270.

Convention Against Torture or other Cruel, Inhuman or Degrading Treatment or Punishment 1984 ('Convention Against Torture'). Nevertheless, since States can act only through individuals, the possibility that those individuals may face criminal charges in another country for acts which involved the execution of State policy is a considerable departure from the traditional approach to questions of sovereignty and jurisdiction.

The principle that a State is not subject to the jurisdiction of an international court or tribunal unless it has consented to subject itself to that jurisdiction remains a cornerstone of international law. In its 1995 judgment in the *East Timor Case*, the International Court of Justice recalled that 'one of the fundamental principles of [the] Statute [of the Court] is that it cannot decide a dispute between States without the consent of those States to its jurisdiction'.[43] The same approach has been followed by other international courts and tribunals.

Again, however, this principle requires some qualification. First, consent need not be contemporary; it is sufficient that the States concerned have at some previous time given their consent to the jurisdiction of the Court, provided that the consent extends to the type of dispute before the Court and is still extant at the date on which proceedings are commenced. The International Court of Justice has thus exercised jurisdiction on the basis that the States concerned had given their consent by becoming party to a treaty such as the Vienna Convention on Diplomatic Relations,1961, and its Protocol on Dispute Settlement.[44] Moreover, Article 36(2) of the Statute of the Court provides that States may make a declaration by which they consent in advance to the Court hearing any dispute between themselves and any other State which makes a similar declaration, thus creating a form of 'compulsory jurisdiction' to which States may 'opt in'.

Secondly, an increasing number of treaty regimes now require acceptance of some form of international dispute settlement for any State which wishes to become a party to that treaty. Thus, European States wishing to be parties to the Convention for the Protection of Human Rights and Fundamental Freedoms (ECHR) must now accept the jurisdiction of the European Court of Human Rights, something which used to be optional.[45] The United Nations Convention on the Law of the Sea (1982) gives States a choice between the jurisdiction of the International Court of Justice, the International Tribunal for the Law of the Sea, and arbitration but, for certain types of dispute, requires acceptance of one or other of these methods.

Thirdly, in both the human rights and investment law fields, recent developments have led to a vast expansion in the scope for individuals and corporations to

[43] *East Timor Case (Portugal v Australia)*, ICJ Reports, 1995, p. 90, 103.

[44] Thus, when the United States brought proceedings against Iran over the seizure of the American Embassy in Tehran and the detention of the diplomatic staff there, the International Court of Justice had jurisdiction under the Optional Protocol to the Vienna Convention, because both the United States and Iran were parties to the Protocol, notwithstanding Iran's refusal to recognize the jurisdiction of the Court; *United States Diplomatic and Consular Staff in Tehran (United States of America v Islamic Republic of Iran),* ICJ Reports 1980, p. 3.

[45] The change was introduced by Protocol No 11 to the Convention, which entered into force in 1998.

bring proceedings against States. In each case this has come about because treaties concluded between States have provided for the possibility of individuals or corporations bringing proceedings against those States either before a standing court or tribunal (in the case of human rights treaties) or in arbitration (in the case of the many investment treaties).[46]

These are qualifications of, rather than exceptions to, the principle of consent. They depend upon the State concerned choosing to become party to the treaty in question or to make the Article 36(2) declaration accepting the jurisdiction of the International Court of Justice. Nor should their importance be overstated. Although the number of States making declarations under Article 36(2) has increased in recent years, for example, it nonetheless represents a far smaller percentage of the international community than had made the corresponding declaration accepting the jurisdiction of the Permanent Court of International Justice before the Second World War.[47] In addition, many of those declarations are subject to reservations limiting their scope.

Nevertheless, the last thirty years have seen an enormous increase in the number of cases brought before international courts and tribunals. Whereas inter-State cases were rare before the 1980s and cases brought against States by individuals or other non-State entities were almost unknown, they are now commonplace and the jurisprudence which they have generated has had a dramatic effect upon many areas of international law and State activity.

Moreover, there is one area of international jurisdiction that has seen a major departure from the principle of consent as the basis for jurisdiction. As described in Section B, the United Nations Security Council has established both criminal tribunals (the International Criminal Tribunals for the Former Yugoslavia and Rwanda) and a civil system of compensation (the United Nations Compensation Commission established to hear claims against Iraq for compensation arising out of the Iraqi invasion of Kuwait) which exercise jurisdiction on the basis of a mandate from the Security Council, rather than consent. Even the International Criminal Court, established by consent of the 122 States parties to its Statute, has a degree of jurisdiction over nationals of States which are not parties, since offences committed by such persons may fall within its jurisdiction if committed on the territory of a State party to the Statute or if they occur as part of a situation referred to the Court by the United Nations Security Council.

These developments in international jurisdiction have led to a lively debate about the approach which an international court should adopt to provisions by which States accept jurisdiction. Since that debate sheds some light on the significance of sovereignty in contemporary international law, it requires brief mention. For many decades it has been argued by some that, since acceptance of the jurisdiction of an international court or tribunal is a limitation on the sovereignty of the State, provisions accepting jurisdiction should be restrictively construed so as

[46] See Chapter 16 in this volume by Peter Muchlinski.

[47] At the beginning of 2013, 69 States out of the 193 States entitled to do so had an extant declaration, whereas 42 out of 55 States had made such a declaration in 1939.

to keep to the minimum the intrusion upon sovereignty. More recently, other commentators, especially in the field of human rights law, have countered that limitations upon jurisdiction should be regarded as the exception and that, in order to ensure better enforcement of international law and to achieve the purpose of the treaties that provide for jurisdiction, such provisions should in principle be given a broad construction and that exceptions and limitations, such as reservations entered by some States, should be given a restrictive interpretation. These competing approaches illustrate two very different concepts of the role which sovereignty should play in modern international law. Yet neither is very convincing. Except in those cases previously mentioned, consent remains a prerequisite for international jurisdiction, so an approach which treats as axiomatic that the instruments by which such consent is given must be the subject of the broadest interpretation the text might possibly allow (and for some writers even that qualification is too much) cannot be accepted. On the other hand, while being subjected to the jurisdiction of an international court may be seen as a limitation of sovereignty, since it is based upon consent it is also an exercise of sovereignty, so the presumption in favour of restrictive interpretation is equally unacceptable. The correct approach is surely that provisions giving consent to jurisdiction should be subjected to the same principles of interpretation as any other treaty provision, that is to say they should be interpreted in good faith in accordance with the ordinary meaning to be given to the terms used in their context and in the light of the object and purpose of the treaty concerned,[48] without any presumption in favour of either a broad or a restrictive outcome.

D. The Relationship between Internal and International Concepts of Sovereignty Revisited

Having explored some of the implications of the international concept of sovereignty for both substantive and jurisdictional law, it is necessary to return to the relationship between that concept of sovereignty and its internal counterpart. Since the two concepts are largely concerned with different matters, this relationship should not be problematic. The discussion in Section A suggested that that relationship is based upon three principles. First, it is international law which determines over what territory, which people and what activities each State possesses jurisdiction. Secondly, how each State allocates between its different organs the power to exercise that sovereignty is a matter for the State, not for international law which treats the State as a single entity and holds it accountable for the acts of all those organs, whether federal or provincial, political or judicial. Thirdly, it follows that a State may not rely upon the way in which it has exercised its sovereignty internally to excuse a failure to comply with its international law obligations; it must meet those obligations irrespective of how power is distributed within the State.

[48] Vienna Convention on the Law of Treaties, 1969, (n 26) art 31.

These three principles are all well established in international law and appear to be generally understood and accepted in most systems of national law. In a world of nearly two hundred independent States—the legacy of the Treaty of Westphalia which ushered in the modern State system in Europe—it is difficult to see how a peaceful international order could function without them. Yet certain developments in the last fifty years or so suggest that their application is becoming more difficult than it was in the past.

The first such development is that international law increasingly imposes obligations regarding the way in which States behave within their own territories. That is most evident in the field of human rights. The network of universal and regional human rights treaties, ranging from agreements of broad, general scope (such as the International Covenant on Civil and Political Rights and the ECHR and its counterparts in other regions) to specialized agreements (such as the Convention against Torture and the UN Convention on the Rights of the Child, 1989), have brought about a considerable change in the landscape of international law since the time when Huber described territorial sovereignty in the *Palmas* award. Today's international law regulates—to an extent unimaginable at the time of the *Palmas* award—what a State may do in the exercise of its sovereignty within that portion of the globe in which it has the right to exercise the functions of a State. Huber, of course, did not say that the State's sovereignty within that portion of the globe was unfettered, only that it was exclusive in the sense that no other State might exercise sovereignty there. Nevertheless, he wrote in the context of a society in which the limitations international law imposed upon the State's exercise of its sovereignty within its own territory were few and in which those that did exist were almost always designed to protect the interests of other States (as with the laws of neutrality considered in the *Alabama* arbitration) rather than to benefit the State's own people. The horrors of the middle decades of the twentieth century should leave no room for doubt that the prohibition by international law of genocide, torture, murder, and a host of other abuses is not only beneficial but necessary. Yet the result is that there is greater scope for tension between international law and the domestic concept of sovereignty, not least because the greater involvement of international law in matters such as human rights means that questions of international law—and its possible conflicts with domestic law—now come more frequently before national courts.

The second development is, in many ways, the mirror image of the first. Just as international law has encroached on matters which were once regarded as internal to each State, so a significant number of States have increasingly sought to apply their laws to activities taking place outside their borders. Thus many States have legislated to make terrorist activities, cross-border frauds, or antitrust activities occurring outside their territory unlawful under their law. In addition, a somewhat smaller group of States have sought to extend their jurisdiction to activities abroad on the ground that those activities are contrary to international law.[49]

[49] The most noticeable example has been the jurisprudence of the United States courts under the Alien Tort Claims Act.

The result has been to increase the potential for conflicts between different national sovereigns, a subject which international law seeks to address.

Finally, the first two developments, together with a greater insistence in many countries upon the accountability of governments for the conduct of foreign affairs and an insistence upon the separation of powers, have brought international law into debates over the allocation of power within States. That issue has been particularly prominent in federal States, where the power to conclude treaties is usually vested in the federal institutions but the subject-matter of many modern treaties is frequently concerned with matters which those federations entrust to the states. The extent to which the power to conclude treaties carries with it, as a matter of constitutional law, the power to implement those treaties notwithstanding that they deal with subjects in which the federal authorities would normally lack competence has been the subject of much discussion in Australia for example.[50] A related issue has arisen in the United States[51] where the Supreme Court held that the President's power to conduct foreign relations did not extend to requiring courts in Texas to reconsider death sentences, even though the International Court of Justice had required the United States to ensure that the defendants,[52] who had not been accorded the consular access to which they were entitled under international law, were not executed without such reconsideration.[53] The Supreme Court did not reject the decision of the International Court of Justice but held that its implementation in the United States could only be accomplished by Congress and not by the Executive.

None of these developments should cause any departure from the three principles outlined above but they do make the application of those principles less straightforward. Hart's warning about the confusion which the concept of sovereignty can cause remains as important today as it was fifty years ago.

[50] See, eg, *Commonwealth v Tasmania* (1983) 68 ILR 266.

[51] *Medellin v Texas* (2008) 128 S Ct 1346; (2008) 136 ILR 689.

[52] The term, 'United States' means, in this context, the United States of America as one of the States of the international community, not the United States as a synonym for the federal authorities, a sense in which the expression is often used by United States courts.

[53] *Avena and other Mexican Nationals (Mexico v United States of America)*, ICJ Reports 2004, p. 12.

15

Territorial Sovereignty and Territorial Extension in an Inter-Connected World

Joanne Scott[*]

A. Introduction

Territory has traditionally assumed a central place in thinking about sovereignty, with State sovereignty being conceived principally as the power of the State to exercise supreme or final authority over persons and things within its territory; 'territorial supremacy' in Oppenheim's terms.[1] However, this close association between State, sovereignty, and territory is increasingly called into question on two principal grounds.

First, we see many examples in which sovereignty as territorial supremacy no longer accords with the practice of States. States are sometimes willing to relinquish claims to final authority; substate, supra-State, and non-State actors are increasingly willing to assert claims to final authority; and there is often contestation over which claims to final authority should succeed.[2] Secondly, there is recognition that formal sovereignty should not be equated with 'real' power. The capability or 'autonomy' of sovereign States to define and achieve their own policy goals is powerfully eroded as they are buffeted by events and countervailing forces from the outside;[3] and the more so in an age of globalization and inter-connection.

* Professor of European Law, University College London.

[1] R Jennings and A Watts (eds) *Oppenheim's International Law, Volume 1: Peace* (9th edn, OUP 2008) 171. Oppenheim also includes the State's supreme authority over its citizens (personal supremacy) as part of State sovereignty. Many other commentators have made a similar point concerning the centrality of territory. See, eg, K Jayasuriya, 'Globalization, Law, and the Transformation of Sovereignty: The Emergence of Global Regulatory Governance' (1999) 6 *Indiana Journal of Global Legal Studies* 425, who understands the Westphalian model of sovereignty as being predicated upon the idea that 'sovereignty is linked with exclusive territorial jurisdiction' (431).

[2] This point draws heavily on TJ Biersteker, 'State, Sovereignty and Territory' in WE Carlsnaes, T Risse, and BA Simmons, *Handbook of International Relations* (Sage 2012). Biersteker adopts a constructivist approach to sovereignty arguing that it is fruitful for us to focus on 'the practices of making and recognizing claims to authority' and that by so doing we will be able 'to gauge significant change in the meaning of sovereignty' (167).

[3] David Held distinguishes between sovereignty and autonomy arguing that '[s]overeignty refers to the entitlement of a state to rule over a bounded territory, while autonomy denotes the actual power a nation-state possesses to articulate and achieve policy goals independently'. See D Held, *Democracy*

While much of the literature on sovereignty captures a picture of transformation, there is one element of our shifting sovereignty landscape that is often left out. This concerns on-going efforts by at least some States (and non-State polities such as the European Union) to re-configure the manner in which they exercise claims to final authority over territory, creating the possibility that the nature and place of territorial jurisdiction in the sovereignty matrix may be subject to change.

In keeping with this, and using the example of the EU's Aviation Directive, this chapter will examine territorial jurisdiction as a source of *global* power. It will do so by highlighting a phenomenon that may be called 'territorial extension'. The concept of territorial extension is distinct from the concept of extra-territoriality.[4] Whereas the latter captures efforts by a State to regulate the foreign conduct of persons not present within its territory, territorial extension occurs when the application of a State's law rests upon a territorial 'trigger' in that it requires conduct or presence within the territory of the regulating State. However, the application of the law having been triggered, territorial extension will be present when the State's regulatory determination is influenced as a matter of law by conduct and/or circumstances abroad.

The concept of territorial extension may be illustrated by reference to one non-specific example. The EU may make the importation of a product conditional upon the manner in which the product has been produced and upon the legal framework that the country of origin has in place. In this example, the application of the law rests upon a territorial trigger (the importation of the good into the territory of the EU) but the EU's regulatory determination is influenced by conduct (production process) and circumstances (legal framework) abroad. Here, market access is made conditional upon conduct and circumstances outside the EU and territorial jurisdiction is exercised with a view to incentivizing or provoking third country behavioural and legal change.

The focus on territory in this chapter is not intended to refute the existence of broader transformations in the configuration of global authority. It is intended rather to suggest that territory as a constituent element of sovereignty remains important and that, as with the other constituent elements, territory and territorial jurisdiction may also be subject to transformation.

and the Global Order (Princeton University Press 1995) 100. For an influential early example of work in this vein see S Strange, *The Retreat of the State: The Diffusion of Power in the World Economy* (CUP 1996). For a critique of this argument as giving rise to a 'descriptive fallacy' see N Walker, 'Late Sovereignty in the European Union' in N Walker (ed) *Sovereignty in Transition* (Hart Publishing 2003). Walker accepts that the pressure globalization places on States' real regulatory capacity does have implications for sovereignty, in that this sometimes leads to the formation of non-state polities such as the EU and UN.

[4] I will leave aside in this chapter the question of whether 'effects-based' jurisdiction represents territorial jurisdiction or not. However, it is important to stress, as Hannah Buxbaum observes, that notions of territoriality and extra-territoriality are legal constructs that are used to resist or re-enforce claims to authority. See HL Buxbaum, 'Territory, Territoriality and the Resolution of Jurisdictional Conflict' (2009) 57 *American Journal of Comparative Law* 631, 635. Or, as Richard Ford puts it: 'the assertion that an individual 'belongs' to a particular jurisdiction for a particular purpose relies on a host of potentially controversial premises and arrives through scores of leaps of faith and logic' (RT Ford, 'Law's Territoriality (A History of Territoriality)' (1999) 97 *Michigan L Rev* 843, 904).

The discussion that follows will focus on one example: the decision of the EU to include international aviation in its 'domestic' emissions trading scheme (the EU Aviation Directive). As will be seen, while this EU measure is not extra-territorial it does give rise to territorial extension. This chapter forms part of a broader research project that focuses upon the territorial reach of EU law. It is already clear from the preliminary findings of the project that there are numerous examples of territorial extension in EU law. Thus, this one example is used to highlight some of the issues arising as a result of a feature that is increasingly widespread in EU law.

B. The EU's Decision to Include Aviation in its Emissions Trading Scheme

In 2008 the EU decided to include aviation in its emissions trading scheme.[5] It enacted a Directive requiring airlines to acquire emission permits to cover the carbon dioxide emitted during EU-arriving and EU-departing flights. While some of these permits would be issued free on the basis of an airline's historic emission levels, the remainder would have to be bought at auction, thus imposing a cost on the airlines concerned. This Directive required airlines to surrender permits to cover emissions generated during the entirety of the relevant flight, including during those parts that take place outside of EU airspace, over the High Seas and the territory of other States.

While the first allowances were due to be surrendered by airlines on 30 April 2013, an amendment to the directive has been proposed that would, if passed, delay the Directive's application in relation to third country departing or arriving flights until 2014.[6] This postponement has been justified by the Commission on the basis that it will serve to facilitate recent progress achieved in the International Civil Aviation Authority (ICAO) in elaborating a *global* market-based framework for aviation emissions.[7] Hence, the Commission has agreed to 'stop the clock' pending the outcome of deliberations at the ICAO Assembly in 2013. The Commission had made it clear that, should the 2013 ICAO General Assembly fail to make the necessary progress, the EU Emmission Trading System ('ETS') legislation would be applied in full again to all flights, including those to and from non-EU Member States.

The EU's Aviation Directive is characterized by three particular traits. It is unilateral, it gives rise to territorial extension, and it is contingent in its application. Each of these three traits will be elaborated below.

[5] Council Directive 2008/101/EC of 19 November 2008 amending Directive 2993/87/EC so as to include aviation activities in the scheme for greenhouse gas emission allowance trading within the Community [2008] OJ L8/3 (the Aviation Directive).

[6] Commission 'Proposal for a Decision of the European Parliament and of the Council derogating temporarily from Directive 2003/87/EC of the European Parliament and of the Council establishing a scheme for greenhouse gas emissions allowance trading within the Community' COM (2012) 697. A 'third country' is for this purpose a country not included in the EU emissions trading scheme for aviation (ie not an EU Member State or Iceland, Liechtenstein, and Norway).

[7] COM (2012) 697 (n 6) 2, recital 2.

(1) Unilateral measure

International aviation emissions are essentially unregulated at an international level.[8] While the Kyoto Protocol States that developed countries shall pursue limitation or reduction of international aviation emissions working through ICAO,[9] to date no meaningful progress has been achieved.[10] In view of this sustained lack of progress in achieving *international* regulation of aviation emissions the EU, after fifteen years of waiting, decided to go it alone. In order to ensure that EU airlines were not placed at a competitive disadvantage and to enhance the environmental ambition of the scheme, all flights arriving in or departing from an EU airport are covered in the scheme.[11] Because of its broad scope, the European emissions trading scheme has the potential to cover around 60 per cent of international aviation emissions. The EU's Aviation Directive is unilateral in the sense that the EU is acting alone to address the global challenge of aviation-related climate change *and* because the EU is acting alone in a policy domain in which authority to act had previously been vested in an organ of the UN (ICAO).[12]

(2) The EU Aviation Directive is contingent in its application

The EU's Aviation Directive is 'contingent' in the sense that its application is, at least in part, contingent upon there not being adequate climate change mitigation measures in place elsewhere. An airline operator may be exempted from the requirement to surrender emissions allowances for flights departing from a third country and landing in the EU where the airline comes from a country which has itself taken measures to reduce the climate change impact of flights departing from it which land in the EU.[13] Exemptions may be granted following consultation with

[8] International aviation produces around 2–3 per cent of global greenhouse gas (GHG) emissions, and aviation emissions are rising rapidly at a rate of around 3–4 per cent per year.

[9] Article 2(2) of the Kyoto Protocol to the United Nations Framework Convention on Climate Change 1997 (UNFCCC).

[10] Though ICAO has endorsed an 'aspirational goal' of annual fuel efficiency improvements in aviation of 2 per cent, still no binding emission targets have been agreed. For a taste of the limited progress so far, see ICAO: Resolution A37/19, Consolidated statement of continuing ICAO policies and practices related to environmental protection.

[11] It has been suggested that non-EU interests were under-represented in the EU's Aviation Working Group that played an important role in shaping the content of the Aviation Directive; see R Martella, G Francke, and N van der Meulen, 'Lessons Learned: The EU and its Aviation Directive' (Trends 2012). Also available at <http://www.sidley.com/files/Publication/84e7a07e-59b3-4e4f-a82e-59c09ab8a35e/Presentation/PublicationAttachment/dc908ebe-4fe5-4ed4-964a-5ae63608d0bc/Martella_Franck_van%20der%20Meulen_Trends%20March%20April2012.pdf> (last accessed 21 April 2013).

[12] Drawing on the definition of unilateralism put forward by Malone and King: 'a tendency to *opt out* of a multilateral framework (whether existing or proposed) or to *act alone* in addressing a particular global or regional challenge, rather than choosing to participate in collective action'. See DM Malone and YF Khong, 'Unilateralism and US Foreign Policy: International Perspectives' in DM Malone and YF Khong (eds) *Unilateralism and US Foreign Policy: International Perspectives* (Lynne Rienner 2003) 3.

[13] Consolidated Version of Council Directive 2003/87/EC of 13 October 2003 establishing a scheme for greenhouse gas emission allowance within the Community and amending Council Directive 96/61/EC [2003] OJ L275/32, Art 25a.

the third country concerned and the EU has insisted that it is 'ready to engage constructively in such consultations so as to reach agreement'.[14] The emissions trading directive also provides that if a global agreement to reduce greenhouse gas emissions from aviation were to be concluded, the Commission shall consider whether amendments to the directive are required.[15] The Aviation Directive thus sets out circumstances in which it is possible to 'escape' from the application of EU law because adequate third country 'measures' or an appropriate international agreement is in place.

The Commission's recent decision to seek a postponement to the application of the Aviation Directive in respect of third country arriving or departing flights re-enforces the contingent character of the Aviation Directive.[16] Pending the possible conclusion of an international agreement in ICAO in 2013, the EU has essentially exempted third country departing *and* third country arriving flights from inclusion in the scheme.

Due to the contingent quality of the Aviation Directive, it is possible to argue that the EU should be viewed as a reluctant unilateralist, deploying contingent unilateralism as a means of incentivizing urgently needed climate action elsewhere. For all that, the EU's approach remains controversial. While there is virtually universal agreement that action to mitigate climate change is required and that airlines should contribute to achieving the climate mitigation goal, there is no agreement at present about how to allocate responsibility for causing climate change between States and about how the burden of mitigating against climate change should be shared. By acting unilaterally, the EU has taken it upon itself to make an autonomous determination on sensitive issues of this kind. Contingent unilateralism would be yet more controversial if it were deployed in a policy domain where no agreement on the need for global action had been achieved and in an area in which deep disagreements between States remain.

(3) The EU Aviation Directive gives rise to territorial extension

As noted in the introduction, a measure may be considered to be extra-territorial when its application is triggered by something other than a territorial connection with the regulating State. By contrast, a measure will not be genuinely extra-territorial but will give rise to territorial extension when its application is triggered by a territorial connection with the regulating State *and* where the regulating State's regulatory determination is influenced as a matter of law by conduct or circumstances abroad.

[14] See 'Written Statement of Reservation by Belgium on behalf of the EU, its 27 Member States, and the 17 Other States Members of the European Civil Aviation Conference on Resolution A37–17/2: Consolidated Statement of continuing ICAO policies and practices related to environmental protection—climate change (8 October 2010) available at <http://www.icao.int/Meetings/AMC/Assembly37/Documents/ReservationsResolutions/10_reservations_en.pdf> (last accessed 9 July 2013).

[15] Directive 2003/87/EC (n 13) Art 25a(1).

[16] See COM (2012) 697 (n 6) and Decision 377/2013/EU of 24 April 2013 (2013) OJ L113/1.

As such, the EU's Aviation Directive gives rise to territorial extension. It only applies to aircraft which take off from or land in an EU Member State, and hence its application is triggered by a territorial connection. Nonetheless, in applying the Aviation Directive, the EU will be influenced by both conduct and circumstances abroad. Most obviously, the EU's regulatory determination will be influenced by how many tonnes of carbon dioxide have been emitted during the relevant EU-arriving or EU-departing flight, including emissions that were generated abroad. Here, the EU is influenced by conduct relating to a specific flight. This may be labelled 'transaction-level' territorial extension. In addition, however, the contingent character of the Aviation Directive means that the EU will also be influenced by the content of third country law and by the possible existence of a global agreement to reduce greenhouse gas emissions from aviation. Here, 'country-level' or 'global-level' territorial extension (higher-level territorial extension) applies, in that the EU is influenced by conduct or circumstances in a third country or in terms of the entire globe.

The phenomenon of territorial extension in relation to this example is captured by the table below:

Table 1. Territorial Extension in the EU Aviation Directive

Measure	Territorial Trigger	Level of Territorial Extension
Dir 2008/101/EC	Landing in or taking off from EU airport	Transaction, Country, Global

C. Reactions to the EU's Decision to Include Aviation in its Emissions Trading Scheme

The EU's Aviation Directive has provoked strong reactions, both in favour of it and against. Three types of reaction are particularly relevant and interesting from a sovereignty perspective: the launching of litigation to challenge the lawfulness of the Aviation Directive, the enactment by the United States of a 'blocking statute' to resist the application of the measure to US airlines, and the use by aircraft leasing companies of compliance-oriented contract terms. Each of these three types of reaction will be examined in more detail below before turning to assess the significance of the Aviation Directive and of these reactions to it from a sovereignty perspective.

(1) Litigation to challenge the lawfulness of the EU Aviation Directive

In a judgment of 21 December 2011, the Court of Justice of the European Union ('CJEU') upheld the validity of the Aviation Directive in a challenge brought by the Air Transport Association of America.[17] The CJEU assessed the validity of the Directive from the point of view of principles of customary international law and from the point of view of international treaties that are binding on the EU and which satisfy the conditions for justiciability it has laid down.[18]

In upholding the validity of the Aviation Directive, the CJEU rejected the argument that it infringed the principle of territoriality or the sovereignty of other States.[19] It did so because the only flights subject to inclusion in the EU's emissions trading scheme are those that result in aircraft being physically present in the territory of the EU, in that that they take off from or land in an airport in an EU Member State. Because these aircraft are in that sense physically present in the EU, they are 'subject on that basis to the unlimited jurisdiction of the European Union'.[20] In this setting, the CJEU accepted that unlimited jurisdiction can serve to justify the regulation of events that occur partly outside EU territory, at least where these events give rise to effects that are felt inside the EU.[21] There is ambiguity in the judgment as to whether the Court might have reached a different conclusion if the EU measure in question had given rise to territorial extension in the *absence* of EU-felt effects.

(2) The enactment by the United States of a 'blocking statute' to resist the application of the EU Aviation Directive to US airlines

Towards the end of 2012, and shortly after the European Commission had put forward its proposal to 'stop the clock' on the international aspects of its aviation in emissions trading scheme, President Obama signed the European Union Emissions Trading Scheme Prohibition Act 2011. This empowers the US Secretary of Transportation to prohibit operators of US civil aircraft from participating in the EU's emissions trading scheme where he or she makes a determination that this is in the public interest.[22] Further, the Secretary of Transportation, the Administrator of the Federal Aviation Administration, and other US governmental officials shall take such other actions that are in the public interest to hold operators of US civil aircraft 'harmless' from the EU emissions trading scheme. While the concept of 'harmless' is not explained, it may be assumed that this would include measures that prevent US airlines from having to incur costs as a result of being included in the

[17] Case C–366/10, *Air Transport Association of America and ors v Secretary of State for Energy and Climate Change* (2011) ECR I–000. See also the opinion of AG Kokott, 6 October 2011.

[18] The CJEU is willing to review the validity or legality of an EU act on the basis of an international agreement where the nature and the broad logic of the international treaty does not preclude the Court from so doing and where the treaty provisions in question are sufficiently unconditional and precise. See *Air Transport* (n 17) paras 52–5.

[19] *Air Transport* (n 17) para 125.

[20] *Air Transport* (n 17) para 125.

[21] *Air Transport* (n 17) para 129.

[22] European Union Emissions Trading Scheme Prohibition Act 2011, s 2(a). In making this determination, the Secretary of Transport shall take into account impacts on US consumers, air carriers, and operators; impacts on the economic, energy, and environmental security of the United States; and impacts on US foreign relations, including existing international commitments.

EU scheme.[23] These authorities should also, as appropriate, use their authority to conduct international negotiations to pursue a worldwide approach to aircraft emissions.[24]

The adoption of this 'blocking statute' by the United States marks the culmination of sustained opposition to the international aspects of the EU's emissions trading scheme.[25] On 20 September 2011, twenty-six ICAO members signed the 'Delhi Declaration' opposing the EU initiative and calling on the EU to refrain from including third-country arriving and departing flights in its scheme and to work collaboratively for an international solution.[26] Then in February 2012, representatives of the United States and twenty-two other countries meeting in Moscow produced a joint declaration urging the EU to desist from applying its emissions trading scheme to international aviation and calling on the EU to participate in negotiations in ICAO to reach a global solution to aviation emissions.[27]

The EU has also stated that there has been 'systematic non-reporting' of emissions data by Indian and Chinese airlines in breach of the demands of the EU's emissions trading scheme.[28] It is reported that ten airlines failed to submit the required data by the due date of 31 March 2011.

(3) Use by aircraft leasing companies of compliance-oriented contract terms

Firms leasing aircraft are beginning to take steps to protect their interests in relation to the compliance burden associated with the emissions trading scheme. It is reported that they are beginning to include provisions in their leases providing that those leasing or sub-leasing aircraft must comply with the terms of the EU ETS.[29] Relevant contract terms also aim to ensure that the burden of non-compliance with the ETS falls on the airline operators leasing the aircraft. We see these developments reflected in legal advice to the aviation industry from, for example, international law firm DLA Piper suggesting that:

> Lessors and financiers will want to ensure that aircraft operators comply with the obligations placed upon them pursuant to the UK Regulations by drafting compliance undertakings

[23] European Union Emissions Trading Scheme Prohibition Act 2011, s 3(a)(2). This does not, however, allow the authorities to pay the 'taxes' (the costs associated with acquiring emission allowances) or penalties imposed by the EU pursuant to its emissions trading scheme.

[24] European Union Emissions Trading Scheme Prohibition Act 2011, s 3(a)(1).

[25] For an overview see 'Report of the Committee on Commerce, Science, and Transportation on S.1956', 2 August 2012 (Senate Report 112-195).

[26] This was approved by the ICAO Council on 22 November 2011.

[27] On 16 December 2011, Secretary of State Hillary Clinton and Secretary of Transportation Ray LaHood sent a letter to the European Commission expressing strong opposition to the application of the EU scheme to third country airlines.

[28] Bloomberg News, '10 Airlines Snub Europe's Emissions Rules', *New York Times*, 15 May 2012, available at <http://www.nytimes.com/2012/05/16/business/global/10-airlines-snub-europes-emissions-rule.html?adxnnl=1&adxnnlx=1366560547-oV+Q8kDfPMpEEsVOV9apnA> (last accessed 21 April 2013).

[29] Testimony of Annie Petsonk, a lawyer at the Environmental Defense Fund, before the US Senate Committee on Commerce, Science and Transportation on 6 June 2012, available at <http://commerce.senate.gov/public/index.cfm?p=Hearings&ContentRecord_id=3cfc8134-0ee8-4296-b0de-93d28b9f086c> (last accessed 21 April 2013).

into transaction documents, including an obligation for the lessee to identify itself as operator to the Regulator. Lessors and financiers may also consider undertakings for aircraft operators to promptly discharge any penalties incurred for non-compliance and remedy failures to comply within set time periods taking all steps necessary to avoid detention of the aircraft by the Regulator.[30]

It has been pointed out that certain countries that are resisting compliance with the EU law are heavily dependent upon leased aircraft. For example, India is said to have prohibited its airlines from complying with the EU Aviation Directive and, as already observed, there has been systematic under-reporting of emissions data by Indian airlines. However, '[w]ith the exception of State-owned Air India, almost all the aircraft used by cash-strapped Indian airlines belong to leasing companies, according to India's Directorate General of Civil Aviation'.[31]

D. Sovereignty and Territorial Extension

As a preliminary point, it is important to observe that in the EU aviation example it is the intensity of 'global flows',[32] in the form of people and cargo being transported by air, that serves to extend the global reach of EU law. It is only because of the volume of these flows that the EU's Aviation Directive can reach around 60 per cent of international aviation emissions. Far from undermining the EU's regulatory capacity, the volume of air traffic to and from the EU augments its regulatory capacity in a rather dramatic way. This stands in contrast to the usual claim that 'the territorial jurisdiction of the modern State over economic life is increasingly constrained by the globalization of economic and social relations'.[33] Thus, when combined with the practice of territorial extension, global flows can serve to enhance rather than undermine a State or polity's global regulatory power.

The adoption by the United States of a blocking statute reflects the US concern that the EU's Aviation Directive impinges on the sovereignty of other States. In the aviation example, both the EU and the United States express a sovereignty claim.[34] These sovereignty claims overlap for two reasons. First, the EU and United States choose different premises to support their claims. The EU uses territory as the basis of its claim to sovereignty and consequently its Aviation Directive applies to foreign airlines, including US airlines, when these airlines make use of airports

[30] D Erni and S Humpleby, 'EU Emissions Trading Scheme for the Aviation Industry', DLA Piper, 2 September 2012, available at <http://www.dlapiper.com/files/Publication/46fc0a0f-1de0-4de5-96a3-b364d42a89ed/Presentation/PublicationAttachment/d381be2b-8f4f-495f-ad50-b8e34bf15d0d/EU_Emissions_Trading_Scheme_Aviation.pdf> accessed 21 April 2013.

[31] B Lewis and V Volcovici, 'Aircraft Owners Seek Shelter from EU-ETS Law Breaches', *Reuters*, 12 August 2012, available at <http://www.reuters.com/article/2012/08/10/us-eu-aviation-idUSBRE87912620120810> (last accessed 21 April 2013). This article reports that around one-third of the total aircraft fleet is leased and that this is expected to continue to rise until 2015.

[32] Jayasuriya (n 1) 433–4.

[33] Jayasuriya (n 1) 434.

[34] It is irrelevant for the purpose of this argument whether the EU does so acting as an agent for the Member States or whether it enjoys autonomous sovereign powers of its own.

situated in the EU. The United States, by contrast, uses nationality or personality as the basis for its sovereignty claim, and consequently its 'blocking statute' applies to US airlines, including when they are not present in the United States. Secondly, as already emphasized, the EU engages in a practice of territorial extension in designing and applying its Aviation Directive. This has the result that, once the territorial trigger has been pulled because an aircraft lands in or takes off from an EU airport, the Aviation Directive applies also to activities—carbon dioxide emissions—that take place outside the EU. Thus, even if the United States had emphasized territory as the basis for its sovereignty claim, overlapping sovereignty claims would still occur because both the EU and the United States would make sovereignty claims in respect of some emissions that occur in US territory.

In the aviation in emissions trading example, both the EU and the United States make *credible* sovereignty claims. In keeping with Neil Walker's conception of sovereignty as a 'speech act',[35] each is engaging in discursive practices that seek to shape our understanding of how the boundaries of a sovereign State are presently, and how they should be, drawn. This gives rise to conflict as well as to overlap and raises the question of how (if at all) overlapping and conflicting claims are to be managed or resolved. At present, this conflict is being managed in a number of different ways.

First, there was recourse to the judiciary as an arbiter of the EU's claim to final authority. The European Court of Justice emphasized both the existence of a territorial nexus and the presence of EU effects, finding emphatically in favour of the EU's sovereignty claim. Subsequently, the EU was able to assert that its legislation *is* compatible with international law and that it 'infringes neither the principle of territoriality, nor the sovereignty of third countries'.[36] Needless to say, there were many who disagreed. The CJEU's judgment was dismissed as representing a 'triumph of politics over law',[37] and the possibility of seeking recourse to alternative forums for the 'resolution' of the dispute was discussed.[38] Given the existence of multiple forums with jurisdiction to hear disputes of this kind, no single court or tribunal could claim to speak the definitive truth about the limits of territorial sovereignty in law.[39]

Secondly, there is the role played by 'private ordering' in adjudicating between the EU, the United States, and the airlines in this contest over sovereignty.[40] As

[35] Walker (n 3) 7.

[36] European Commission, 'Inclusion of Aviation in the EU ETS' available at <http://ec.europa.eu/clima/policies/transport/aviation/index_en.htm> (last accessed 21 April 2013).

[37] BF Havel and JQ Mulligan, 'The Triumph of Politics: Reflections on the Judgment of the Court of Justice of the European Union Validating the Inclusion of Non-EU Airlines in the Emissions Trading Scheme' (2012) 37 *Air and Space Law* 3.

[38] Among these was the possibility of launching proceedings under Art 84 of the Chicago Convention on International Civil Aviation and the taking of appropriate action in the WTO; see 'Joint Declaration of the Moscow Meeting on Inclusion of Civil Aviation in the EU-ETS', *Russian Aviation*, 22 February 2012, available at <http://www.ruaviation.com/docs/1/2012/2/22/50> (last accessed 21 April 2013).

[39] This is a familiar situation. For a discussion of one of the most famous conflicts between different forums see R Churchill and J Scott, 'The Mox Plant Litigation: The First Half-Life' (2004) 53 *ICLQ* 643.

[40] See P Zumbansen, 'Introduction: Private Ordering in a Globalizing World: Still Searching for the Basics of Contract' (2007) 14 *Indiana Journal of Global Legal Studies* 181.

noted, by shaping the content of relevant contractual terms, aircraft leasing companies are playing an important role in allocating risk by, in this case, promoting compliance with EU law.

Nonetheless, despite the entry into law of the US blocking statute, the US Secretary of Transportation has not yet issued any order prohibiting the participation of any US air carriers in the EU emissions trading scheme. Thus, US air carriers have not yet been forced to confront the ultimate dilemma: namely whether to comply with the EU measure or with conflicting US law. It is likely that in confronting this dilemma, the strength of the sanctions contemplated under each national regime will play an important role. While no sanctions were elaborated in the US blocking statute, heavy sanctions for non-compliance are included in the EU's Aviation Directive. A failure to comply with the Aviation Directive would result in a fine of 100 Euro per tonne of carbon dioxide emitted and the shortfall in terms of allowances would anyway have to be made up in the following year.[41] Ultimately, if the regulatory authorities of the relevant EU Member State were to be faced with persistent non-compliance even after the levying of fines, the European Commission could in principle decide to impose an operating ban on the airline concerned; a sanction that might be thought to lack credibility at least in relation to airlines originating in the United States.[42]

Thirdly, the boundary conflict between the EU and the United States has been managed through dialogue and compromise. US condemnation of the EU measure has been matched by an insistence on the appropriateness of a global response to the challenge of regulating international aviation emissions. In keeping with this, some recent progress towards the adoption of a global market-based mechanism in ICAO has been achieved, and senior EU and US climate change officials are participating in a newly established high-level panel with a view to facilitating further progress in relation to this.[43] Also, despite its firm talk, the EU has also demonstrated a willingness to compromise, postponing the inclusion of international aviation in its emissions trading scheme pending the results of negotiations in ICAO in 2013.

E. Appraising Territorial Extension

The phenomenon of territorial extension has been greeted with disagreement, and ambivalence, by legal scholars. This is especially apparent in discussions about what are known as 'production process methods' ('PPMs'). These are controversial in international trade law where the propensity of rich countries to make the importation of goods dependent upon the way in which the goods have been produced has given rise to suggestions that the World Trade Organization ('WTO') is taking

[41] Directive 2003/87/EC (n 13) Art 16.

[42] Directive 2003/87/EC (n 13) Art 16(5).

[43] B Lewis, 'Top Obama Men Join UN Quest to Curb Airline Emissions', *Reuters*, 10 December 2012, available at <http://www.reuters.com/article/2012/12/10/us-eu-icao-idUSBRE8B90RA20121210> (last accessed 21 April 2013).

steps to 'occlude' developed country protectionism while permitting it nonetheless.[44] In the area of environmental protection, it has been suggested that a strategy of territorial extension through the adoption of unilateral PPMs is not only substantively and procedurally unfair but potentially counterproductive. Chimini warns that 'unilateral trade sanctions tend to weaken the support for environmental protection within the poor world [as] the objective of environmental protection comes to be associated with the hegemonic objectives of the developed world'.[45]

But for all these criticisms of territorial extension through PPMs, there is ambivalence nonetheless, even in the writings of those who seek to defend the interests of the 'third world'.[46] Thus, while Chimini condemns the decision of the United States to make the importation of shrimp depend upon the manner in which they were caught, he suggests that it is appropriate for consumers to assert their 'sovereignty', by boycotting goods produced by transnational corporations 'that do not abide by minimum human rights standards'. Likewise, Ugo Mattei, in charting the emergence of what he terms 'imperial law' observes (rightly) that:

> Most of the externalities, most of the social costs dumped in the backyard of our weaker neighbors of the South, are created during the process of producing commodities that are consumed mainly by the roughly 300 million people that make up the European market…Either European consumers pay too little for their commodities, because their prices do not reflect the true social costs of production (environmental damage, labor exploitation, and so forth) and European capitalism is once again subsidized by former colonies, or multinational corporate logo-lords…make unfair profits pocketing the value of such social costs. In both cases, such an economic reality should be a concern for the European policymaker drafting the rules of the game.[47]

Why is it, he asks, that EU law serves to protect children in Europe who are injured by toys but not children in the developing world who are injured in the production of these toys which are played with by children inside the EU. While Mattei is thinking principally about the remedies available to those injured as a matter of private law, when we are talking about social costs associated with environmental protection and labour exploitation one might reasonably conclude that *ex ante* regulation to mitigate the likelihood of harm is preferable to *ex post* compensation once the harm has occurred.

Disagreement between scholars, and the apparent ambivalence of individual scholars, is indicative of the normative challenge that territorial extension implies.

[44] BS Chimini, 'WTO and Environment: The Shrimp-Turtle and EC-Hormones Cases' (2000) 35 *Economic and Political Weekly* 1757.

[45] Chimini (n 44) 1760. Chimini suggests that unilateral PPMs are substantively unfair in that they respond to developed country concerns in the WTO without offering poor countries advantages, such as improved market access or financial/technological transfers in return. He suggests that they are procedurally unfair in that unilateral measures will contain a natural bias in favour of the domestic interests represented in the decision-making process.

[46] I use the term 'third world' in keeping with the critical movement called 'Third World Approaches to International Law'. Here, the 'third world' is understood to be a group of States which, though economically and culturally diverse, are united in their common history of colonialism.

[47] U Mattei, 'A Theory of Imperial Law: A Study on US Hegemony and the Latin Resistance' (2003) 3 *Global Jurist Frontiers* 1, 54 (footnotes omitted).

There are good reasons why a State may wish to use the fact of conduct or presence within its territory to shape patterns of behaviour abroad. In the same vein as Mattei, a State legislature may feel that consumers within its territory should take more responsibility for the harms that their consumption generates abroad. If carbon dioxide emissions 'embodied' in products imported into the EU were included on the EU's carbon account, EU emissions would be deemed to have risen dramatically rather than as having declined.[48]

It may also be that the protection of interests within the territory of the regulating State can only be achieved by regulating foreign conduct. In management-based regulation, for example, food safety is secured by governing the manner in which the food product is produced.[49] Where the food product is imported, the importing State will insist upon compliance with these process-based regulations by food producers operating abroad. Physical spillovers between States also occur in relation to climate change, where there is an element of spatial dislocation between the place in which greenhouse gas emissions are generated and the place in which the consequences currently, and will in the future, occur. Furthermore, Chimini's protests notwithstanding,[50] there are reasons to think that unilateral measures giving rise to territorial extension may sometimes stimulate the formation of regional or global regimes.[51] The recent progress achieved in ICAO in relation to aviation emissions is at least suggestive of this.

For these and other reasons, it may be concluded that an understanding of sovereignty conceived as territorial supremacy without the possibility for territorial extension would be ill-suited to our profoundly inter-connected world. An absolute exclusion on measures that give rise to territorial extension would also ignore the fact that sometimes the presence of territorial extension serves to soften, rather than exacerbate, the external effects of the measure concerned. This point can be illustrated by reference to a recent controversy arising in EU law.

When the Netherlands, acting pursuant to EU law, seized a batch of generic pharmaceuticals that were in transit in the EU en route between India and Brazil, it did so regardless of whether the pharmaceuticals were subject to patent protection in the country of production (India) or in the country of destination (Brazil).[52]

[48] See, eg, SJ Davis and K Caldeira, 'Consumption-based Accounting of CO2 Emissions' (2010) 107 *Proceedings of the National Academy of Sciences of the United States of America* 5687.

[49] C Coglianese and D Lazer, 'Management-Based Regulation: Prescribing Private Management to Achieve Public Goals' (2003) 37 *Law and Soc Rev* 691. Particularly important in this respect is the system of 'Hazard Analysis and Critical Control Points' that adopts a preventive approach to food safety by putting in place processes to identify and mitigate hazards.

[50] Chimini suggests that 'unilateral measures do not serve as catalysts for arriving at international agreement around a particular issue area'; see Chimini (n 44) 1760.

[51] For one compelling example surrounding the tuna/dolphin litigation in the WTO, see RW Parker, 'The Use and Abuse of Trade Leverage to Protect the Global Commons: What Can We Learn from the Tuna-Dolphin Conflict?' (1999) 12 *Georgtown International Environmental L Rev* 1.

[52] See B Mercurio, '"Seizing" Pharmaceuticals in Transit: Analysing the WTO Dispute that Wasn't' (2012) 61 *ICLQ* 389. The decision to seize the goods in transit was deemed to be unlawful by the CJEU in Joined Cases C-446/09 and C-495/09 *Philips Electronics NV v Lucheng Meijing Industrial Co Ltd* and *Nokia Corportation v HM Commissioners of Revenue and Customs*, judgment of 1 December 2011. However, the legislature is fighting back. See COM(2013) 162 final to approximate the laws of the Member States relating to trade marks.

Although the pharmaceuticals in question were not intended to be placed on the EU market, the fact that the pharmaceuticals in question were subject to patent protection in the EU was regarded as sufficient to justify their detention.

In this situation, the application of EU law was triggered by a territorial connection with the EU: namely, the fact that the pharmaceuticals were in transit through its territory in the course of international trade. The measure did not give rise to territorial extension in that the decision of the regulator was not influenced as a matter of law by conduct or circumstances abroad. The mere fact that the pharmaceuticals were subject to patent protection inside the EU was enough.

It would, by contrast, have been open to the Netherlands to justify the seizure of pharmaceuticals not on the basis that they were protected in the EU, where they were merely in transit; but on the basis that the pharmaceuticals were subject to patent protection in either the State of production or in the destination State. Had it done so, the measure would have given rise to territorial extension in that the Dutch/EU regulator would have been influenced in its determination by circumstances abroad, namely by the patent status of the pharmaceuticals in a third country. While the decision of the Dutch authorities to seize the pharmaceuticals would still have been controversial, in view of its consequences for public health,[53] the presence of territorial extension would on this occasion have eliminated one prominent source of complaint. Many commentators have criticized the EU for not taking into account the patent status of the pharmaceuticals in the production or destination States. They have done so on the basis that recourse to EU standards of patent protection seems manifestly inappropriate given the transient nature of the connection between the pharmaceuticals and the territory of the EU.[54]

None of this is to suggest that the phenomenon of territorial extension does not present challenges and dilemmas or that, as a legal technique, it is not open to abuse by powerful States or non-State polities such as the EU. It is not, however, to suggest that these challenges and dilemmas are not best addressed by seeking to draw a bright line that would imply an automatic condemnation of measures on the basis that they give rise to territorial extension. Although not easy to elaborate or to achieve, a more nuanced approach is required; one which balances the reasons for and against specific actions giving rise to territorial extension. The EU's Aviation Directive is suggestive of a number of criteria that could be used to appraise territorial extension in this way. Five such criteria will be adumbrated here. Each of these criteria militates in favour of the EU's aviation initiative, suggesting that *on this occasion* territorial sovereignty should be conceptualized in a manner that is permissive of territorial extension.

First, the EU's Aviation Directive serves to further attainment of an objective, the importance and urgency of which has been internationally recognized and

[53] See FM Abbott, 'Seizure of Generic Pharmaceuticals in Transit Based on Allegations of Patent Infringement: A Threat to International Trade, Development and Public Welfare' (2009) 1 *The WIPO Journal* 43.

[54] eg Abbott observes that 'The European Union has elected to disregard the sovereign rights of foreign WTO Members by refusing to give effect to their decisions as to patent status by the use of force—the seizure and detention by customs authorities of goods in transit.' See Abbott (n 53) 49.

agreed. Among the many examples that could be offered, this is reflected in the first recital of the Durban Action Programme that climate change presents an urgent and potentially irreversible threat that must be addressed urgently by all parties.[55]

Secondly, as the CJEU has emphasized,[56] the EU's Aviation Directive is intended to address a global challenge that threatens the environmental integrity of the EU. Carbon dioxide emitted outside the EU will contribute to global climate change the effects of which will be felt inside as well as outside the EU. The Aviation Directive is intended to respond to this *physical* threat as well as to the competitiveness (economic) disadvantages that would otherwise flow from acting alone.

Thirdly, the EU's Aviation Directive is intended to address a global challenge that will impact more harshly on the poor than on the rich.[57] At the same time, the costs of complying with the EU measure will fall predominantly on the rich.[58] While this is not to step back from the criticism that the EU should have designed the Aviation Directive in a manner that treats poorer countries more favourably, for example by dedicating the money raised by the auctioning of emission allowances to mitigation activities within developing countries,[59] it is to acknowledge that, by contrast to the seizure of pharmaceutical measures in the transit example referred to above, the measure is not conspicuously skewed in favour of the global rich.

Fourthly, in *Shrimp-Turtle* the WTO Appellate Body condemned the US prohibition on the importation of shrimp on the basis that only shrimp that originated in a country with essentially the same policies as the United States could be imported.[60] Even if an individual shipment of shrimp had been caught in a manner that was entirely friendly to sea turtles, the shrimp could not be imported into the United States, if the *country* had not put the requisite policies in place.[61] In the language of territorial extension, this US measure gave rise to 'country-level' territorial extension.

The Aviation Directive also gives rise to country-level territorial extension but here it operates in a different way. Airlines which originate in a country that has not adopted its own measures to reduce the climate change impact of flights can still access the market of the EU by meeting the demands of the EU's emissions

[55] 'Establishment of an Ad Hoc Working Group on the Durban Platform for Enhanced Action' (Dec. 1/CP17 adopted by the UNFCCC Conference of the Parties on 15 March 2012).

[56] *Air Transport* (n 17) para 129.

[57] See A Costello et al 'Managing the Health Effects of Climate Change' (2009) *The Lancet*, vol 373, issue 9676, 1693.

[58] See European Commission, Impact Assessment of the inclusion of aviation activities in the scheme for greenhouse gas emission allowance trading within the Community SEC(2006) 1685 (20 December 2006) 36, where the Commission argues that the costs imposed by the Aviation Directive will fall on wealthier segments of the population, both within the EU and globally.

[59] For a full discussion of the argument that the principle of Common but Differentiated Responsibility and Respective Capabilities applies and should be respected in this setting see J Scott and L Rajamani, 'EU Climate Change Unilateralism' (2012) 23 *EJIL* 469.

[60] *United States—Trade Restrictions on Shrimp and Shrimp Products* (WT/DS58/AB/R) para 165.

[61] The Appellate Body also objected to the fact that the United States insisted upon third countries putting in place policies that were essentially the same as those prevailing in the United States. The US standards were therefore too 'rigid and unbending' in that they did not provide space to take into account circumstances in the exporting States (see especially *Shrimp and Shrimp Products* (n 60) paras 163–5).

trading scheme. While the Aviation Directive seeks to encourage third countries to enact legislation to address climate change, it does not prevent market access for airlines that come from countries that have not adopted measures of this kind. On the contrary, the Aviation Directive constructs three different compliance routes, enabling airlines to achieve compliance, and EU market access, even in the absence of third country or global policy change. They are not at the mercy of governments, and can themselves take the requisite steps to satisfy the EU's demands, regardless of third country or global policies in place.

Fifthly, and finally, the EU's Aviation Directive is unilateral but it is unilateralism with a twist. As has already been suggested, the EU Aviation Directive is 'contingent' in its application. It gives rise to a form of contingent unilateralism that seeks to combine recognition of the urgency of confronting the climate change challenge with respect for policy initiatives adopted or agreed by other States. The EU insists upon its own entitlement to move forward unilaterally, but also on the importance of recognizing the competing sovereignty claims of other States. Hertogen captures the normative salience of my concept of contingent unilateralism very well.[62] Drawing on my previous work, she argues that this concept:

> expresses the idea of relative sovereignty, according to which State sovereignty is limited by the equal sovereignty of other states. Contingent unilateralism ensures that states that currently do not regulate in response to a specific problem retain not only the legal but also the political capacity to regulate later without fear of adding to the regulatory compliance costs of companies that already fall within the scope of another state's regulation.[63]

Taken together, these five characteristics of the Aviation Directive imply that from the perspective of sovereignty and territorial extension, it constitutes a relatively easy case. More difficult cases will, and indeed do, arise when one or more of these five characteristics is not present or is present in a markedly different form. For example, the regulating State may experience only economic effects as a result of the activity abroad that is associated with the territorial extension, rather than both economic and physical effects as is the case with global climate change. Also, country-level territorial extension may be required rather than incentivized in the sense that no transaction-level route to attain compliance is made available, with market access depending in all cases upon the law or policy prevailing in the relevant State.

The intention here is not to offer a definitive guide as to when and on what basis territorial sovereignty should be capable of accommodating territorial extension. It is rather to suggest that the matter needs to be determined on a case-by-case basis and to begin (or more accurately continue) a conversation about which characteristics, in which form, are relevant to an assessment of this kind.

[62] A Hertogen, 'Sovereignty as Decisional Independence over Domestic Affairs: The Dispute Over Aviation in the EU Emissions Trading Scheme' (2012) 1 *Transnational Environmental Law* 281. Hertogen draws on Scott and Rajamani (n 59).

[63] Hertogen (n 62) 298.

F. Conclusion

The EU has been a forceful critic of US extra-territoriality in the past, yet today it is itself engaging in a practice of territorial extension. The EU is seeking to use the presence of a territorial connection as a lever to influence law, policy, and behaviour in other States. The phenomenon of territorial extension presents a challenge for the concept of territorial sovereignty. The concept of territorial extension seems familiar in that it relies upon territorial jurisdiction and upon the existence of a territorial nexus as a basis for regulation. But it is novel in that it also seeks to extend the regulatory perimeter, using the existence of a territorial connection to shape conduct or circumstances abroad. At its most extreme, territorial extension may rest on a 'thin' territorial connection and at the same time seek to leverage far-reaching global change. For powerful States and non-State polities with large markets, there is a danger that territorial extension will encourage them to seek to 'rule the world'. Using the example of the EU's Aviation Directive, this chapter has argued that the practice of territorial extension can only be evaluated on a case-by-case basis having regard to the specific context and characteristics of the measure at hand. The chapter has taken a first step in identifying the kind of criteria that may be considered to be relevant in making a contextual assessment of this kind.

16

Sovereignty and Private Corporate Power: The Case of Multinational Enterprises

*Peter Muchlinski**

A. Introduction

When Neil MacCormick published *Questioning Sovereignty*[1] in 1999 the process of economic globalization was well under way.[2] The year of publication was also the time of the Seattle protests against the World Trade Organization and globalization.[3] Indeed, at that time, a number of developments highlighted concern over transnational private corporate power exercised by multinational enterprises ('MNEs'). For example, in 1998, Amnesty International went beyond its traditional concern over the civil and political rights of individuals and published its *Human Rights Guidelines for Companies*.[4] This was one aspect of a wider movement among non-governmental organizations ('NGOs') to add to their agendas the effects of MNEs on human rights, labour rights, and sustainable development,[5] spurred on, in part, by their opposition to negotiations on a Multilateral Agreement on Investment ('MAI'). The MAI failed when France pulled out on the ground that the provisions on the protection of foreign investors, and their right to challenge national policy decisions before international arbitral tribunals, represented too great an inroad into national sovereignty over economic policy.[6] Despite this

* Professor in International Commercial Law, School of Oriental and African Studies, University of London.

[1] N MacCormick, *Questioning Sovereignty: Law State and Practical Reason* (OUP 1999).

[2] See generally JA Scholte, *Globalisation: A Critical Introduction* (2nd edn, Palgrave Macmillan 2005).

[3] On which see J Vidal 'Real Battle for Seattle' *The Observer*, 5 December 1999 at 20; G de Jonquieres and F Williams 'A Goal Beyond Touch' *Financial Times*, 6 December 1999 at 18; Editorial, 'Disaster in Seattle' *Financial Times*, 6 December 1999.

[4] Amnesty International UK Business Group, *Human Rights Guidelines for Companies* (Amnesty Interantional, 1 January 1998) available at <http://www.amnesty.org/en/library/asset/ACT70/ 001/1998/en/8d6c82f3-e81c-11dd-9deb-2b812946e43c/act700011998en.pdf> (last accessed 21 April 2013).

[5] On which see M Yaziji and J Doh, *NGOs and Corporations: Conflict and Collaboration* (CUP 2009).

[6] On the MAI see MAI Negotiating Text (as of 24 April 1998) available at <http://unctad.org/sections/dite/iia/docs/Compendium/en/96%20volume%204.pdf> (last accessed 21 April 2013). For background

historical context, there is relatively little explicit discussion on the role of transnational corporate power in MacCormick's thesis. It is the purpose of this chapter to consider how MacCormick's approach to sovereignty can be adapted to allow for this type of power to be taken into account. The chapter will in turn examine new approaches to the resolution of the issue of private corporate power and popular democratic and national State sovereignty.

B. MacCormick's Theory of Sovereignty and Corporate and Economic Power

MacCormick analysed sovereignty through recognition of 'institutional normative orders' which can exist beyond the State and the law, permitting him to criticize the traditional 'Statist' notion of law-based sovereignty espoused by legal positivists. As regards corporations, citing the early institutionalist writers Gierke and Hauriou, MacCormick notes that:

> the idea that recognition of corporate status was something wholly and arbitrarily in the gift of the State was . . . anathema in terms of political morality and misleading in terms of social history and contemporary social reality.[7]

Following the institutionalists, MacCormick sees corporate existence as a social rather than a legal phenomenon. In this he is at one with enterprise-based theories of the corporation which do not mix up the legal form of the corporate entity with its underlying social existence.[8] Three regulatory implications flow from this. First the impact of the distinction between the legal entity and the social reality of the enterprise must be considered more fully. This lies at the heart of the historical debate on the relationship between the corporation and the State in that, as MacCormick points out, the type of normative order (positivist or pluralist) will dictate the approach to incorporation and to the nature of corporate action. Secondly, the relationship between public and private law must be more fully considered as the realities of economic globalization led by MNEs and the rise of the 'market-State' create greater interplay between them.[9] Thirdly, the territoriality of nation-State-based legal orders is at odds with the transnational business structure

see OECD, *Towards Multilateral Investment Rules* (OECD Publishing, 1996); PT Muchlinski, 'The Rise and Fall of the Multilateral Agreement on Investment: Where Now?' (2000) 34 *International Lawyer* 1033.

[7] MacCormick (n 1) 77.

[8] On which see especially PI Blumberg, *The Multinational Approach to Corporation Law* (OUP 1993); PT Muchlinski, *Multinational Enterprises and the Law* (2nd edn, OUP 2007) ch 8; P Muchlinski, 'Limited Liability and Multinational Enterprises: a Case for Reform?' (2010) 34 *Cambridge Journal of Economics* 915.

[9] The market-state is used here to denote a State that espouses the current trend towards the outsourcing of public functions to private providers, the increased use of public–private partnerships to deliver public services and infrastructure, the privatization of public enterprise, and the liberalization and deregulation of markets and firms. See further C Crouch, *Post-Democracy* (Polity Press 2004); C Crouch, *The Strange Non-Death of Neo-liberalism* (Polity Press 2011).

of the MNE, raising public international law questions as to the legality of extraterritorial legal regulation and private international law questions concerning the proper conduct and limits of transnational litigation.[10] Clearly such issues need to be taken into consideration in any theory of sovereignty that includes MNEs as relevant actors.

In addition to the normative institutional approach, MacCormick's notion of sovereignty is rooted in the concept of subsidiarity, the idea that sovereign power should be exercised at the most local level possible taking into account the function involved.[11] In relation to economic decision-making the concept of 'market-subsidiarity' may play a significant role. This concept sees the use of rational, market-based, choices as a method of 'optimising aggregate outcome in terms of general-interest satisfaction'.[12] That requires the collective decision-making process to 'secure legal and institutional conditions for the flourishing of free and fair markets'.[13] Thus, market subsidiarity helps to secure 'in a fair way legal conditions for the fair conduct of commercial and industrial activity, without partisan distortion or pork-barrel factionalism'.[14] MacCormick terms this 'rational legislative subsidiarity'.

MacCormick sees market subsidiarity as applying only to market goods. The market itself, and the legal-political institutions that constitute and secure markets, do not fall into this category.[15] They are necessarily holistic and society-wide and so can be the subject of, 'discourse, deliberation and decision-making of the collectivity'.[16] These deliberations will focus on market efficiency in relation to market goods but the goods that markets generate will be enjoyed for non-market purposes as well. This requires a form of 'communal subsidiarity' which MacCormick defines as 'the need to have a rich and varied range of institutions within which self-realization can be fostered and developed'.[17] These will pursue goods other than market goods and constitute elements of civil society and not necessarily constitute a part of the State.

The relationship between State sovereignty and the facilitation of good corporate activity through 'market subsidiarity' raises the question of the extent to which, in facilitating market activity, the State will be 'captured' by corporate interests and will trade off non-market goals in favour of market facilitating goals. As will be elaborated further, this question lies at the heart of the contemporary debate on MNEs and State sovereignty. It has special resonance in relation to the question whether the pursuit of corporate facilitation by the democratic State can lead to the suppression of popularly legitimated policies, which may inhibit corporate interests, and also result in the undermining of equal respect for individuals and their human rights as legally conferred economic liberties create increasing disparities in wealth.[18]

[10] On which see Muchlinski (2007) (n 8) ch 4.

[11] See especially Consolidated Version of the Treaty on European Union (2010) OJ C83/13, Art 5(3).

[12] MacCormick (n 1) 152.

[13] MacCormick (n 1) 151.

[14] MacCormick (n 1) 153.

[15] MacCormick (n 1) 152.

[16] MacCormick (n 1) 152.

[17] MacCormick (n 1) 152.

[18] On which see MacCormick (n 1) 174–7.

C. The State and Transnational Corporate Power

(1) The corporation, the State, and normative institutions

Normative institutionalism requires further examination of the relationship between State and corporation through corporate law theory. This lies at the heart of the relationship between the regulatory form of the enterprise, the incorporated entity, and its social form, the collective business enterprise. It also raises the question of corporate belonging arising out of the national nature of incorporation and corporate freedom to cross borders arising out of the transnational network of the MNE.

MacCormick's perspective is both a help and a hindrance to understanding the relationship between transnational corporate and State power. It is a hindrance in that MacCormick appears to underestimate the act of legal incorporation as an act of regulation as opposed to an act of creation. As a result the role of the State in the regulatory function is not fully worked out, while the limited role of the State in creating collective entities by law is overemphasized. MacCormick's theory needs to be supplemented by a better historical understanding of the role of the act of incorporation so that the regulatory subordination of the corporation to the sovereign power of the State is better seen. On the other hand, MacCormick's institutionalism is helpful when contrasting the relationship between the legal form of the corporation and its institutional reality. Here it is important to return to the institutional conception of the corporation as the transnational network that comprises the MNE. This is invisible as a legal phenomenon and effective regulation will be inhibited if this remains the only view taken.

(2) Sovereignty and incorporation

Historically, incorporation is the legal moment when the State legitimizes the collective enterprise and gives to it a legal form that facilitates its commercial actions. It is also the moment when the corporation becomes a regulated collective in that its lawful existence as a corporation requires conformity to the rules upon which it is established. Incorporation is located in the legal response to the rise of long distance inter-continental trade in Western Europe. This developed from the middle of the fifteenth century and reached its apogee in the eighteenth and nineteenth centuries.[19] The need was for a means of permitting groups of traders to organize their expeditions effectively and to reduce their risks. At the time there was little doubt that the autocratic monarchic State, typical of the Western European States of the period, would have a controlling role. The answer lay in the royal grant of incorporation. This could legitimate collective action that might otherwise be

[19] See JH Parry, *The Establishment of the European Hegemony 1415–1715: Trade and Exploration in the Age of the Renaissance* (Harper and Row 1961); JH Parry, *The Age of Reconnaissance: Discovery, Exploration and Settlement, 1450–1650* (Phoenix Press 2000); JH Parry, *Trade Dominion: The European Overseas Empires in the Eighteenth Century* (Phoenix Press 2000).

viewed as a conspiracy to monopolize a particular trade and could offer a regulatory and institutional framework for the administration of that trade.[20]

The resulting chartered corporation was a creature of public law, based on its own unique legal instrument, the charter or *Octroi*, which covered both the public law and private law aspects of the company's operations.[21] The former pertained to the extent (if any) that the company could engage in public administration of overseas territories and to use private military force, while the latter regulated the administration of the company and the merchant adventures to be undertaken through its trading monopoly. It is here that the joint stock principle of risk spreading could be found as well as detailed provisions on company administration and management.[22]

The State grant of incorporation was a general principle of law recognized by all European systems until the development of modern general incorporation laws. It remained at the heart of the French *Code de Commerce* of 1807 which is widely seen as the first general corporation law in the world.[23] This allowed for incorporation by way of a more normative and permissive system of concession by the State and offered limited liability.[24] In practice the concession system was restrictive of new incorporations and the number of incorporated enterprises remained small.[25] However this restrictive approach to incorporation could not survive the pressure in the nineteenth century to grant general freedom of incorporation coming from European industrial entrepreneurs who sought to harness the utility of the corporate form with limited liability to their business needs.

By the 1880s all the major European commercial powers adopted general incorporation laws.[26] Automatic incorporation was accepted through registration upon the conclusion of a corporate contract, or articles of association, that conformed to the normative requirements prescribed by the law. The State had withdrawn from the direct establishment of the corporation. The corporation had become 'privatized'

[20] The counter-example was the Dutch United Provinces where the formation of independent companies by traders was only later regulated by the State by the establishment of the United Dutch East India Company in 1602 so as to end the competitive chaos of the original eleven privately formed companies (AB Levy, *Private Corporations and their Control: Volume I* (Routledge Keegan and Paul 1950) 17–20).

[21] Levy (n 20) 21–30. See also SR Brown, *Merchant Kings: When Companies Ruled the World 1600–1900* (Conway Books 2010). For a classic legal analysis in German see K Lehmann, *Die Geschichtliche Entwiklung des Aktienrechts bis zum Code de Commerce* (Karl Heymenns Verlag 1895).

[22] For the English East India Company, see P Lawson, *The East India Company: A History 1600–1857* (Longman 1993) 20–1.

[23] H Coing, 'Rechtsvergleichung als Grundlage von Gesetzgebung im 19 Jahrhundert' in *Ius Commune VII* (Max Planck Institute for European Legal History 1978) 168, available at <http://data.rg.mpg.de/iuscommune/ic07_coing.pdf> accessed 21 April 2013.

[24] See further Levy (n 20) 53–7; CE Freedeman 'Joint-Stock Business Organization in France 1807–1867' (1965) 39 *Business History Review* 184.

[25] Levy offers an excellent summary of the limits of incorporation by charter or Act of Parliament in England, France, and Germany (Levy (n 20)). In England and France many companies were formed without incorporation. Germany had fewer incorporations because it was still a highly agrarian society and in Prussia there was a high level of unease with corporations.

[26] For example, England and France moved towards freedom of incorporation with limited liability, respectively, under the English Companies Act 1862 and the French *Loi sur les Sociétés a Responsabilité Limite* of 1863, while Germany followed suit in the Corporate Laws (*Aktiengesetze*) of 1870 and 1884.

in law and corporate law developed on the basis of the need to protect the property of shareholders in the corporation while the control of monopolization would be achieved through the eventual adoption of competition laws.

By the early twentieth century, through internal growth and merger, large corporate groups had emerged in all the main industrial States. Equally industrial concentration had created large combines of powerful industrial interests. [27] This led to the development of new legal concerns over the accountability of the firm. The large modern business corporation was perceived as belonging to the wider business environment of the country and working in the wider social interest, not merely in the narrow financial interests of the shareholders. Consequently, it could no longer be seen as a private law entity but one that required a new legal basis in public interest concerns.[28] According to Adolf Berle and Gardner Means:

> The future may see the economic organism, now typified by the corporation, not only on an equal plane with the State, but possibly even superseding it as the dominant form of social organisation. The law of corporations, accordingly, might well be considered as a potential constitutional law for the new economic State, while business practice is increasingly assuming the aspect of economic statesmanship.[29]

Such public law-based ideas were to find their most extreme expressions in the corporatism of Nazi Germany where by Article 70 (1) of the Corporation Law (*Aktiengesetz*) 1937 the management board (*Vorstand*) was made the central organ of the corporation and was tasked with the management of the corporation in the interests of the employees, the *Volk* and the *Reich*.[30] However the Nazi system never denied the private character of share ownership and so did not go as far as the Soviet system where all property in corporate enterprises was vested in the State and where the State controlled enterprise activity through the central planning process.[31]

In the modern era of free incorporation, the aim of the State is to establish the limits of limited liability, protect vulnerable investors at the moment of corporate promotion, protect minorities of investors against powerful majorities during the life of the corporation and develop duties of care and trust for the conduct of corporate management. While the act of incorporation is not a necessary condition for the existence of the enterprise it is a necessary condition for its lawful conduct in society in return for the privileges of separate legal existence and limited liability and for identifying the holder of legal responsibilities on behalf of the collective

[27] See further AD Chandler *Scale and Scope: The Dynamics of Industrial Capitalism* (Harvard Belknap 1990); N Horn and J Kocha, *Recht und Entwicklung der Grossunternehmen im 19. und fruhen 20 Jahrhundert; Law and the Formation of Big Enterprises in the 19th and Early 20th Centuries* (Vandenhoeck and Ruprecht 1979).

[28] W Rathenau, *Vom Aktienwesen: eine Geschichtliche Betrachtung* (S Fischer Verlag 1918) 38–9.

[29] AA Berle and GC Means, *The Modern Corporation and Private Property* (Harvest Books, revised edn, 1968) 313.

[30] Corporation Law (*Aktiengesetz*) 1937, Art 70: '(1) Der vorstand hat unter eigener Verantwortung die Gesellschaft so zu leiten, wie dass Wohl des Betriebes und seiner Gefolgschaft und der gemeine Nutzen von Volk und Reich es forderen.'

[31] See PB Maggs, 'Soviet Corporation Law: The New Statute on the Socialist State Production Enterprise' (1965) 14 *American Journal of Comparative Law* 478.

entity. Such normative ordering cannot come from within the corporation itself but must arise from State action on behalf of society at large.

(a) Sovereignty and transnational corporate organization

A further consequence of incorporation is that the enterprise acquires a 'nationality'. This has significant consequences when MNEs are concerned. As Claire Cutler has shown, corporate actors have been excluded as subjects of international law as a result of the divide between private international law, dealing with the legal implications of private international transactions for national legal systems, and public international law, which deals mainly with the legal implications of inter-State interactions.[32] This creates a legal fiction whereby the MNE exists only as a locally incorporated entity, subject to the private municipal law of the State in which it is incorporated and not as a transnational network of production. Rather, the corporation is assimilated to a natural person and has no constitutional significance other than as a beneficiary of constitutional rights.[33]

It is hard to deny that the corporation should be properly treated by governmental authorities and that arbitrary deprivations of corporate assets cannot be permitted in a market economy. So much is clear from the emerging principles of international investment law.[34] That said, it is essential that this fiction is ignored and that the corporation is seen as an enterprise and an institution as suggested by MacCormick. Then it can become a visible subject of regulation in its own right, and not merely as a localized creature of municipal corporate law, and regulatory responses will be more in tune with its actual organization and behaviour.

The MNE as a transnational institution creates the problem of extraterritoriality whereby, in order to regulate effectively, the national regulator may need to apply their national laws and legal claims to entities and events arising outside the regulator's home jurisdiction, thereby infringing the sovereignty of the target jurisdiction. Historically that has led to conflicts of jurisdiction in a wide range of areas including competition, tax, securities, and financial services.[35] Conflicts are liable to flare at any time where the regulating jurisdiction perceives that activity in a target jurisdiction is infringing its regulatory policy goals and there is no direct territorial nexus between the activities and the regulating jurisdiction.[36]

[32] AC Cutler, *Private Power and Global Authority: Transnational Merchant Law in the Global Political Economy* (CUP 2003) 36, citing M Janis, 'Individuals and Subjects of International Law' (1984) 17 *Cornell Journal of International Law* 61, 62.

[33] See further Blumberg (n 8) 30–45 (discussing the civil rights of US corporations under the US Constitution). On the position of corporate human rights in the European Convention on Human Rights see M Emberland, *The Human Rights of Companies: Exploring the Structure of ECHR Protection* (OUP, 2006).

[34] See J Salacuse, *The Law of Investment Treaties* (OUP 2010).

[35] On which see further P Muchlinski (2007) (n 8) ch 4; JA Zerk, 'Extraterritorial Jurisdiction: Lessons for the Business and Human Rights Sphere from Six Regulatory Areas' (2010) Harvard Corporate Social Responsibility Initiative WP No 59, available at <http://www.hks.harvard.edu/m-rcbg/CSRI/publications/workingpaper_59_zerk.pdf> (last accessed 21 April 2013).

[36] A distinction is made between pure extraterritoriality, where the targeted actor has no direct or indirect presence or assets in the regulating jurisdiction, and the territorial exercise of jurisdiction with

Such concerns generated the 'sovereignty at bay' debate in the 1970s, named after the title of Raymond Vernon's famous book of 1971.[37] Some versions of this approach foresaw the end of the nation-State. In the words of Charles Kindleberger, writing in 1969, 'the nation-State is just about through as an economic unit'.[38] Books with alarming titles appeared such as 'Global Reach: The Power of Multinational Corporations', 'The Sovereign State: The Secret History of ITT', and 'Silent Surrender: The Multinational Corporation in Canada', to name but a few.[39] The constitutional implications of the rise of MNEs appeared colossal, giving further credence to the view that they had to be controlled if State sovereignty was not to be lost to an unaccountable coalition of the executive branch of government and the management of MNEs.[40] Vernon's own work was more of a historical account of the rise of US MNEs which were then the dominant type of MNE, than an alarmist exposition of an apparent conspiracy against the nation-State. Vernon did not advocate the restriction of transnational capital flows through MNEs.[41] Indeed none of the protagonists in this debate ever considered banning Foreign Direct Investment ('FDI') by MNEs. That stance was only taken by the more Marxian elements in the 'Dependency School' of international economic relations.[42]

Vernon's main concern was to deal with the issue of extraterritorial regulation. Accordingly, he recommended greater international cooperation over taxation issues and in resolving the problem of overlapping regulatory jurisdictions between the States in which the MNE operated. Solutions to this problem have tended to arise from the self-restraint of regulators, given the potential political costs of taking regulatory action against activities located in another jurisdiction especially if they are lawful under the local law, and from increased regulatory cooperation on the basis of bilateral treaties that further the principle of comity between the signatories.[43]

overseas impacts, where the targeted actor is present in the regulating jurisdiction, or has assets there, and the actor and/or the assets are involved in foreign conduct unlawful under the regulating State's law. See further Zerk (n 35).

37 R Vernon, *Sovereignty at Bay: The Multinational Spread of US Enterprises* (Penguin Books 1971). For a useful analysis see SJ Korbin, 'Sovereignty@Bay: Globalization, Multinational Enterprise, and the International Political System' in AM Rugman (ed) *The Oxford Handbook of International Business* (2nd edn, OUP 2010).

38 CP Kindleberger, *American Business Abroad* (Yale University Press 1969) 207. See also GW Ball, 'COSMOCORP: The Importance of Being Stateless' (1968) 6 *Atlantic Community Quarterly* 163.

39 K Levitt, *Silent Surrender: The Multinational Corporation in Canada* (first published 1970, McGill-Queen's University Press 2002); A Sampson, *The Sovereign State: The Secret History of ITT* (Coronet 1973); RJ Barnet and RE Muller, *Global Reach: The Power of Multinational Corporations* (Simon and Schuster 1976).

40 See, eg, AS Miller, 'The Multinational Corporation and the Nation-State' (1973) 7 *Journal of World Trade Law* 267. By contrast, Seymour Rubin denied that MNEs challenged the nation-state; rather they appeared to be well controlled by it. However, Rubin also accepted the need for at least an international forum in which the operations of MNEs could be discussed. See SJ Rubin 'The Multinational Enterprise at Bay' (1974) 68 *AJIL* 477.

41 Vernon (n 37) 260–71. See also R Vernon, 'Sovereignty at Bay: Ten Years after' (1981) 35 *International Organization* 517, 517.

42 On which see Muchlinski (2007) (n 8) 95.

43 See, eg, European Communities–United States Agreement on the Application of Their Competition Laws 30 ILM 1487 (1991), as supplemented by the 1998 European Communities–United States Agreement on the Application of Positive Comity Principles in the Enforcement of Their Competition Laws Agreement of 37 ILM 1070 (1998).

Vernon and others also considered the possible establishment of some supranational body to which MNEs could be accountable.[44] The most tangible result in policy terms was the establishment in the UN of the Commission on Transnational Corporations ('TNCs') (TNCs are the UN terminological equivalent of MNEs)[45] and the Centre on Transnational Corporations ('UNCTC').[46] These bodies were tasked with negotiation of a new binding Code of Conduct for TNCs and to offer legal and policy advice to developing countries in their dealings with MNEs. The proposed Code of Conduct floundered by the early 1990s when neo-liberal ideas gained ground that saw it as an unwarranted interference with corporate freedom and the need for investment in host countries. The UN TNC bodies were downgraded and restructured as a research branch of the United Nations Conference on Trade and Development ('UNCTAD') without any negotiating mandate.[47] At the national level, as illustrated in the case of Canada, national sovereignty concerns led eventually to the adoption of pre-entry screening laws, permitting the executive branch the discretion to prohibit a proposed major investment, on public interest economic grounds.[48] Such laws have remained in use though, as UNCTAD research shows, the overwhelming trend since 2000 has been to liberalize investment controls.[49]

A further solution to the problem of limited territorial sovereignty is to create a new level of regulatory space at the supranational level. In effect this is one of the aims of the EU—its larger territorial reach allows for a reduction of the mismatch. This is an example of MacCormick's 'post-sovereignty' in action in that the Member States have shifted their sovereign power to the EU institutions to allow for Europe-wide regulation to emerge. This has had significant impacts on corporate regulation particularly in the fields of competition law and the development of harmonized principles of corporate law including the establishment of supranational corporate entities such as the European Economic Interest Grouping ('EEIG') and the *Societas Europea* ('SE').[50] On the other hand such thinking is coming under increased scrutiny from Eurosceptic perspectives which fear that transfers of sovereignty of this kind reduce the ability of the nation-State to regulate effectively or to act in the interests of its corporate actors.[51] MacCormick dismissed such concerns by saying that the

[44] Vernon (n 37) 271; Rubin (n 40). See also PM Goldberg and CP Kindleberger, 'Toward a GATT for Investment: A Proposal for Supervision of the International Corporation' (1970) 2 *Law and Policy in International Business* 295.

[45] On which see Muchlinski (2007) (n 8) 6.

[46] See UN Secretary General's Group of Eminent Persons Report on the Role of MNEs on Development and International Relations 1974 UN Doc E/5500/Add l (Part I), 24 May 1974: 13 ILM 800 (1974).

[47] P Muchlinski, 'Attempts to Extend the Accountability of Transnational Corporations: The Role of UNCTAD' in MT Kamminga and S Zia-Zariffi (eds) *Liability of Multinational Corporations under International Law* (Kluwer Law International 2000).

[48] On Canadian FDI law and policy see Muchlinski (2007) (n 8) 206–12 and sources cited there.

[49] See, eg, UNCTAD, *World Investment Report 2012* (United Nations, 2012) 76–83, where the main trend remains towards liberalization with some sector specific exceptions though the high point of liberalization was between 2003 and 2006.

[50] Muchlinski (2007) (n 8) ch 10, 72–5.

[51] As argued by David Cameron when he vetoed the eurozone pact in December 2011 on the grounds that he was defending City of London financial interests against excessive regulation; see

centralized sovereignty of the nation-State is no less threatening to local popular sovereignty than is the shared sovereignty of the EU institutions, which offer a degree of indirect democratization at the EU level.[52]

(b) 'Market subsidiarity': the 'new corporate accountability'

This section addresses the issues of distributional justice at the heart of MacCormick's theory. That requires an understanding of the competing ideologies of political economy which inform the debate on the corporation, State, and society. The main elements of the 'neo-liberal ascendancy' that began in the 1980s and which has resulted in the currently dominant political paradigm of the 'market-State' are very familiar and need no repetition here.[53] The reaction to the neo-liberal ascendancy began around the late 1990s when a new wave of academic and popular literature emerged—critical of the power of MNEs—one which is still developing. Like 'sovereignty at bay' this 'new corporate accountability' literature also expresses alarm at the impact of global business practices on the sovereignty of States. Again alarming titles have appeared such as 'When Corporations Rule the World', 'The Silent Takeover: Global Capitalism and the Death of Democracy', and 'Post-Democracy'.[54]

This literature foretells the possible end of popular democracy in the West as a result of the hollowing out of popular power by the ever-closer association of corporations and politicians, of all major persuasions, who accept that the furtherance of corporate interests is the main objective of contemporary governance, to the exclusion of alternative aims, and to the benefit of an increasingly unaccountable elite of the super-rich.[55] Great weight is placed on the ability of major firms to lobby the political process, especially in the United States, thereby threatening the balance of democratic pluralism.[56] This is seen as being reinforced by the power of MNEs to set agendas of consumption through mass marketing and branding, creating the illusion that a good life can be achieved through individualistic consumerism.[57]

The threat to popular democracy has an apparent ring of truth when it is taken into account that mass democracy, where it actually exists, is limited to citizens and/or permanent residents of the nation-State.[58] On the other hand the reach and interests of MNEs are transnational and so such firms may not be very interested in the needs of local communities (which is, as will be argued, open to debate).

I Traynor, N Watt, D Gow, and P Wintour, 'David Cameron Blocks EU Treaty with Veto, Casting Britain Adrift in Europe' *Guardian*, 9 December 2011.

[52] MacCormick (n 1) 133–4, 145–9.

[53] On which see Crouch (2004) (n 9); Crouch (2011) (n 9).

[54] See DC Korten, *When Corporations Rule the World* (2nd edn, Berrett-Koehler 2001); N Hertz, *The Silent Takeover: Global Capitalism and the Death of Democracy* (Arrow Books 2002); Crouch (2004) (n 9).

[55] For a recent expression of this view see G Monbiot 'Our Economic Ruin Means Freedom for the Super-rich' *Guardian*, 31 July 2012.

[56] Korten (n 54) ch 10; Crouch (2011) (n 9) 124–34; G Palast, *The Best Democracy Money Can Buy: An Investigative Reporter Exposes the Truth about Globalization, Corporate Cons and High Finance Fraudsters* (Constable and Robinson 2003).

[57] Korten (n 54) ch 11; N Klein, *No Logo* (Harper Collins 2000).

[58] Crouch (2011) (n 9) 110–11.

Where popular involvement in the democratic process is on the wane, and general interest in politics is weak, the risk of an abuse of power by transnational corporate actors appears very real.[59] The 'new corporate accountability' position looks to the rise of a 'civil society' that can challenge the influence of MNEs in the political process as a remedy.[60] A case in point is the environmental movement which has achieved a degree of success in this regard.[61] Equally, the recent concerns raised in Parliament about tax avoidance by retailing corporations in the United Kingdom arose out of civil society actions.[62] According to Crouch, civil society:

> usually denotes those organisations and informal groupings that concern themselves with public affairs but which operate outside the power of both State and firm. Significantly, they have become known by the nonsensical name 'non-governmental organisations' (NGOs). Better is the German term *Burgerinitiativen* 'citizen's initiatives'...It is oriented towards public conflict, discourse, compromise and understanding, recognising plurality, difference and tension as legitimate, operating non-violently. This is a space in which value oriented critique of market State and corporation can be conducted in contemporary democracies.[63]

The conversational space identified by Crouch is fraught with problems for a new popularly focused conception of sovereignty. These problems will be addressed in the next section.

(3) 'The New Sovereignty': coordinating MNEs, States, and communities

The previous two sections have already noted instances where 'market subsidiarity' may be countered by 'communal subsidiarity' and 'rational legislative subsidiarity'. Here the concept of 'market subsidiarity' and its relation to 'communal subsidiarity' will be further considered. This requires, first, examination of the limitations of the 'new corporate accountability' perspective and its reliance on civil society as the main counterpoise to private corporate power; and, secondly, further investigation of how a 'new sovereignty' might evolve that takes into account not only State and corporate power but also popular democratic will in its delimitation of 'market' and 'communal' subsidiarity.

[59] On the weakening of popular interest and participation in political process in the United Kingdom, see S Wilks-Heeg, A Blick, and S Crone, *How Democratic is the UK? The 2012 Audit* (Democratic Audit, 2012) available at <http://www.democraticaudit.com/the-uk-audit-1> (last accessed 21 April 2013). On corporate influence and the decline of demcoracy, see Crouch (2004) (n 9).

[60] Korten (n 54) ch 23; Crouch (2011) (n 9) ch 7.

[61] See further P Utting (ed) *The Greening of Business in Developing Countries: Rhetoric, Reality and Prospects* (Zed Books, 2002); DL Levy and PJ Newell, *The Business of Global Environmental Governance* (MIT Press 2005); P Utting and J Clapp (eds) *Corporate Accountability and Sustainable Development: Ecological Economics and Human Well-Being* (OUP 2008).

[62] House of Commons Committee of Public Accounts, *HM Revenue & Customs: Annual Report and Accounts 2011–12* (HC Papers (2012–13) no 716) 7–11.

[63] Crouch (2011) (n 9) 153.

(a) Limits of the 'new corporate accountability' model

As noted, the 'new corporate accountability' approach relies on civil society to coordinate private corporate power given the inability of the market-State to do so. Crouch's above-mentioned definition of civil society raises numerous problems. First, there is the separation of civil society from private business. For example, where corporate interests fund an NGO favourable to the pursuit of pro-corporate interests does this fall outside 'civil society' because of its business funding? Similarly, where are we to place formally constituted bodies such as chambers of commerce, industry associations and sectoral bodies? Surely they too are a part of this system of regulatory conversation?[64] As Kofi Annan, the former UN Secretary-General, has stated:

> When I speak about civil society I don't mean only non-governmental organisations, though they are an important part of it. I also mean universities, foundations, labour unions and yes—private corporations.[65]

Secondly, NGOs raise issues as to their legitimacy given that they are not subject to democratic accountability, being in practice self-selecting communities of common interest. How are we to know which NGOs should be given voice and which ignored? There is a great deal here to be clarified.[66] In particular the relationship between NGOs and media corporations, as vehicles for highlighting corporate abuses, raises an important question of control over the corporate accountability agenda. It may expose NGOs to collaboration in a media driven selection of causes, which may not reflect genuine public interests but rather the interests of the NGO (eg, profile raising, increasing membership) and the media corporation (eg, audience share) in covering a particular cause.

Thirdly, the 'new corporate accountability' critique dismisses the possibility that the democratic process might require democratically elected leaders to apply policies which increase inward investment by MNEs as the basis for greater employment and growth.[67] The assumption appears to be that if the leaders, following the people, come to this decision they must all be being duped by corporate propaganda.[68] A further assumption is that MNEs can only be vehicles of exploitation and oppression, engaging national polities in a competitive 'race to the bottom' that diminishes the living standards of the many in favour of the few. This position is open to empirical doubt and so should be treated more carefully as a starting point for a critique

[64] On which see J Black, 'Regulatory Conversations' (2002) 29 *Journal of Law and Society* 163.

[65] Secretary General, 'Economic Growth about People—Their Health, Education, Security' (Opening Address to the World Focus on Social Development, Geneva 25 June 2000), cited in S Zadek *The Civil Corporation* (Earthscan 2007) 17.

[66] See Yaziji and Doh (n 5) 25–6.

[67] See further NM Jensen, *Nation-States and the Multinational Corporation: A Political Economy of Foreign Direct Investment* (Princeton University Press 2008).

[68] This can be seen as an example of middle class contempt for less educated working people. See further O Jones, *Chavs: The Demonization of the Working Class* (Verso Books 2011).

of MNEs.[69] As will be shown, the capacity for constructive engagement between corporations and local communities is a much more complex process in which negative social outcomes are not inevitable.

A fourth problem is that the power of uncoordinated (and potentially disputing) groups of people to come together and form a coherent countervailing power to corporate and State interests is overestimated. That some leading NGOs have influence is no longer in doubt.[70] The very best NGOs have high levels of subject-specific expertise at their disposal, are able to organize that into usable published and Internet-based outputs and have sufficiently wide public support and respect to earn the right to be heard. These are products of specific conjunctions of political, economic, social, and technological conditions that allow NGOs to develop in particular places at particular times.[71] However, NGOs lack the necessary power to do much more than express an opinion, or offer advice, in their current organizational form.[72]

The best way to deal with excessive corporate power would still appear to be electing a political party to a parliamentary majority so that it can pass laws for this purpose. As Crouch asserts, political parties are 'vital to civil society and essential channels for any attempt to contest corporate power within that system'.[73] However, Crouch fears that political parties can become 'polluted channels' if they restrict their concerns only to those already approved of by the leadership. If a party follows the idea of an exclusive strategy of gaining power through its traditional organization and function in the political process, given that the State has now been successfully captured by corporate power, 'parties that continue to follow it become the tools of State and corporation and thus the enemies of civil society'.[74]

This is an understandable reaction to the naively pro-business line taken by New Labour and other West European social democratic parties when in office.[75] The role of NGOs would be to act as a corrective to this problem. They could ally themselves with a sympathetic political party and provide the information, arguments, and public attention and commitment so that a more independent policy on corporate regulation can emerge. In the longer term, NGOs could eventually follow the example of the trade union movement of the twentieth century and establish political parties in their own right, as is already the case with Green parties arising out of the environmental movement.

[69] Jensen (n 67) offers an empirical critique of the 'race to the bottom' thesis, which stresses that the sunk costs of inward foreign investment actually weaken the ability of MNEs to make viable threats to governments that do not offer favourable policies (something also noted by Vernon (n 37) and Rubin (n 40)).

[70] For an analysis of methods, see Yaziji and Doh (n 5) pt II.

[71] Yaziji and Doh (n 5) 26–31.

[72] As John Kenneth Galbraith wisely warned, 'By forming an organisation, issuing statements, having access to television, [or the Internet] people can believe they have power... No one in a democracy should be in doubt as to the real effectiveness of organised opposition to concentrated power. But all must have an acute understanding of the weakness arising from the diffusion of power and the difference between illusion and practical effect' (JK Galbraith, *The Anatomy of Power* (Hamish Hamilton 1984) 185, 188). This is a very good way to describe the recent Occupy Movement, on which see <http://occupywallst.org/> (last accessed 21 April 2013).

[73] Crouch (2011) (n 9) 154.

[74] Crouch (2011) (n 9) 155.

[75] Which Crouch laments; see Crouch (2004) (n 9) 63–5.

Thus, centre left political parties espousing a social democratic programme, or, indeed, centre right parties that return to a more honest and historically accurate version of liberalism, are still a good bet to control corporate excess. The room for political manoeuvre may in fact be wider than the pessimism of the 'new corporate accountability' approach suggests, even for a social democratic party.[76] Ultimately this is what Crouch appears to favour despite his unease at the State of contemporary political parties.[77]

(b) 'Market subsidiarity', 'communal subsidiarity', and transnational corporate power

The 'new corporate accountability' approach offers a 'pessimistic' view that sees State and corporate power as a zero sum game with one winner. MacCormick's theory of sovereignty offers an 'optimistic' view which allows for an accommodation between the possible dilution of traditional State sovereignty, in the face of the twin challenges of internal devolution and economic globalization, through a pluralistic concept of sovereignty. This can be shared at a number of levels from the local, the regional, the national to the supranational. The key question is how to allocate the various exercises of sovereignty to their most appropriate level. This is achieved through the idea of subsidiarity, a concept that allows for considerable market freedom for corporate actors but which is delimited by communal concerns based on a social democratic ideal of equality.

The 'new corporate accountability' approach would no doubt point out that MacCormick is being naïve about the State as a redistributor of wealth, given its capture by corporate interests. However, as pointed out in the last subsection, this may not necessarily be an accurate picture of democratic State power, even in relation to the market-State. For example the recent US regulatory intervention against Standard Chartered bank for alleged violations of US sanctions against Iran shows that even the market-State will control corporate power where vital public interests are in issue.[78] The protection of the poor from the power of the rich may not be very high on its agenda, or at least not through direct State action, but that does not mean that the power to do so is also absent.

In the meantime the countervailing power of civil society could be brought to bear so as to challenge this situation. This is entirely compatible with MacCormick's view of liberty and the need for social groups to establish 'communal subsidiarity'. As noted above, MacCormick accepts that collective institutions geared towards the realization of non-market goods 'belong quite as much to civil society as to the State'.[79]

[76] A Przeworski and M Wallerstein, 'Structural Dependence of the State on Capital' (1988) 82 *American Political Science Review* 11; A Przeworski, *Democracy and the Market: Political and Economic Reforms in Eastern Europe and Latin America* (CUP 1991) 14.

[77] Crouch (2011) (n 9) 177–80.

[78] See 'Stan Chart Pays Hefty Price for "Small Errors"' *Financial Times*, 16 August 2012, 17. Arguably this power is being exercised against Standard Chartered and other London-based banks in an attempt to shift business to New York (J Treanor, 'US Regulators have Britain's "Wild West" Bank Culture in their Sights' *Guardian*, 8 August 2012, 22–3).

[79] Crouch (2011) (n 9) 152.

In particular, in accordance with MacCormick's scepticism about contractarian narratives of popular sovereignty, it is essential to avoid contractarian ideas of sovereignty, based on traditional State institutions, and to embrace a more diversified notion of 'sovereignty' which can help to re-define it away from the legitimation of elite power towards its relocation in the 'people', and away from the mystical authority of 'markets' and 'wealth creators' towards communities and persons. The latter are more than a reserve supply of labour; they are dignified holders of fundamental rights and freedoms that include personal freedoms defined by human dignity and not corporate interests.

So how are these beliefs to be translated into effective civil society controls over the risk of corporate human needs and rights abuses? Here two distinctive perspectives have to be considered. The first is how the corporation itself can change to make it more responsive to human needs and rights. The second is how civil society can engage with corporate actors to help achieve these objectives. In the background the State is not rejected because, as noted in the previous subsection, the State political system and parliamentary political parties can be engaged as a part of the regulatory conversation. Their power to control corporations has not ended: it is merely restrained in the market-State.

(i) Internal corporate change

As to internal corporate change, recent developments in the business and human rights field can be used as an illustrative example. The debate on the legal and ethical responsibilities of MNEs to respect human rights has become one of the most significant recent developments in the wider field of corporate social responsibility ('CSR').[80] That debate has been fuelled by the *Guiding Principles on Business and Human Rights* endorsed in 2011 by the UN Human Rights Council for implementing the UN 'Protect, Respect and Remedy' Framework ('Guiding Principles').[81] The Guiding Principles assert that:

> States must protect against human rights abuse within their territory and/or jurisdiction by third parties, including business enterprises. This requires taking appropriate steps to prevent, investigate, punish and redress such abuse through effective policies, legislation, regulations and adjudication.[82]

The State duty to protect is supplemented by a non-binding responsibility to respect human rights on the part of business enterprises.[83] The key element in the corporate

[80] See further Zerk (n 35); J Ruggie, *Just Business: Multinational Corporations and Human Rights* (WW Norton and Co 2013).

[81] UN Human Rights Council, *Guiding Principles on Business and Human Rights Implementing the United Nations 'Protect, Respect and Remedy' Framework* (21 March 2011) (Guiding Principles) available at <http://www.ohchr.org/documents/issues/business/A.HRC.17.31.pdf> (last accessed 21 April 2013) (adopted by Resolution 17/4 of the Human Rights Council on 16 June 2011, UN Doc A/HRC/RES/17/4, 6 July 2011).

[82] Guiding Principles (n 81) principle 1.

[83] This duty is non-binding as the UN Guidelines are rooted in international law under which corporate actors do not have legal personality and so cannot hold positive international law duties (see text around n 32).

responsibility to respect is the concept of human rights due diligence. This covers adverse human rights impacts that the business enterprise may cause or contribute to through its own activities, or which may be directly linked to its operations, products, or services by its business relationships. Its extent will vary according to the size of the business, the risk of severe human rights impacts, and the nature and context of its operations. It is a continuing process as human rights risks may change over time.[84] The due diligence standard has the capacity to develop into a legally binding duty of care in municipal law.[85] Equally, a wider conception of director's duties, used in an increasing number of municipal legal systems, which permits directors to take into account the social and environmental impacts of their business when making decisions, can allow for human rights considerations to be an integral part of corporate decision-making.[86]

(ii) External impacts on corporate behaviour

Here the most important legal developments have arisen out of struggles for 'subaltern legality': the process by which excluded and marginalized groups can use existing laws in a counter-hegemonic way to undermine the dominance of institutions and practices that seek to further the interests of the minority of social actors who benefit from globalization.[87] This is exemplified by the rise over the last twenty or so years of 'foreign direct liability' litigation that 'aims to hold parent companies legally accountable in developed country courts for negative environmental, health and safety, labour or human rights impacts associated with the operations of members of their corporate family in developing countries'.[88] Such litigation has had notable successes in bringing to light corporate malpractices in developing countries where legal remedies are ineffective. It has been a product of activist lawyers and civil society groups.[89] The development and institutionalization of such litigation into the legal order of States is an aspect of the State duty to protect human rights in

[84] Guiding Principles (n 81) principle 17. On human rights due diligence, see OECD, *Guidelines for Multinational Enterprises* (25 May 2011) ch IV; International Finance Corporation, *Guide to Human Rights Impact Assessment and Management* (Washington DC: International Finance Corporation, 2010) available at <http://www1.ifc.org/wps/wcm/connect/8ecd35004c0cb230884bc9ec6f601fe4/hriam-guide-092011.pdf?MOD=AJPERES> (last accessed 13 April 2013).

[85] P Muchlinski, 'Implementing the New UN Corporate Human Rights Framework: Implications for Corporate Law, Governance and Regulation' (2012) 22 *Business Ethics Quarterly* 145.

[86] Muchlinski (2007) (n 8) 157–60. See further United Nations, 'Corporate Law Project: Overarching Trends and Observations' (United Nations, 2010) 14, available at <http://www.reports-and-materials.org/Ruggie-corporate-law-project-Jul-2010.pdf> (last accessed 21 April 2013).

[87] See B de Sousa Santos, *Toward a New Legal Common Sense* (Butterworths Lexis-Nexis 2002) ch 9; B de Sousa Santos and César A Rodríguez-Garavito, 'Law, Politics and the Subaltern in Counter-Hegemonic Globalization' in B de Sousa Santos and César A Rodríguez-Garavito (eds) *Law and Globalization from Below: Towards a Cosmopolitan Legality* (CUP 2005) 12–18.

[88] H Ward, 'Governing Multinationals: The Role of Foreign Direct Liability' Chatham House Briefing Paper, February 2001, available at <http://www.chathamhouse.org/sites/default/files/public/Research/Energy,%20Environment%20and%20Development/roleoffdl.pdf> (last accessed 21 April 2013).

[89] See further P Muchlinski and V Rouas, 'Foreign Direct Liability Litigation: Towards the Transnationalisation of Corporate Legal Responsibility' in Gretchen Bellamy, Lara Blecher, and Nancy Kaymar Stafford (eds) *Business and Human Rights* (American Bar Association) (forthcoming). The most

the UN Guiding Principles, which stress access to effective remedies as the third element of the human rights and business framework.[90]

A further important avenue for influence arises out of the process of 'experimental governance'.[91] This highlights the complex web of institutions and actors that seek to manage the global economic system in the absence of global government. It involves the internal management systems of MNEs and inter-firm supply chains, the various normative standards developed by inter-governmental organizations, States, and substate entities with legislative and regulatory powers, and the activities of NGOs and other civil society bodies. This approach is also termed 'civil regulation'.[92] It has come about as a result of a perceived 'regulatory gap' between traditional legal regulation by the territorial State and the increasingly transnational character of business activities.

As already noted, the market-State has consciously retreated from its regulatory role leaving much to self-regulation by firms. Such regulatory self-limitation will be compounded in developing countries that have little or no experience as regulators, and which have few resources to devote to such tasks, but which have espoused market-based approaches to corporate regulation. The 'gap' is then filled by various civil society groups, including the major transnational NGOs, to create a sense of accountability that may have been lost in the process of de-regulation. NGOs can be said to fill the 'democratic deficit' that the increasing marketization of public economic functions might create.[93] Such an approach has been particularly prominent in the environmental protection field with the Forest Stewardship Council being the best example.[94]

The role of corporate actors in this process arises out of their expertise in the sectoral field involved. However it is wrong to see their activities as monolithic and only concerned with profit. The day to day reality is that the headquarters is often completely ignorant of what the subsidiaries are doing, while the subsidiaries operate within their local networks of training, expertise, labour, and business bodies as well as being major employers in their communities.[95] Thus tensions can arise between the aims of the parent company and those of its affiliates.

significant cases have arisen in the United States under the Alien Tort Claims Act; see S Joseph, *Corporations and Transnational Human Rights Litigation* (Hart Publishing 2004).

[90] See Guiding Principles (n 81) principles 25–8. By principle 26 'States should take appropriate steps to ensure the effectiveness of domestic judicial mechanisms when addressing business-related human rights abuses, including considering ways to reduce legal, practical and other relevant barriers that could lead to a denial of access to remedy.' The Guiding Principles also consider non-judicial State-based grievance mechanisms (principle 27) and non-state-based grievance mechanisms (principle 28).

[91] See further PH Kristensen and J Zeitlin, *Local Players in Global Games: The Strategic Constitution of the Multinational Corporation* (OUP 2005) chs 11, 12; J Zeitlin, 'Pragmatic Transnationalism: Governance Across Borders in the Global Economy' (2011) 9 *Socio-Economic Review* 187.

[92] See further J Bendell and DF Murphy, 'Towards Civil Regulation: NGOs and the Politics of Corporate Environmentalism' in P Utting (ed) *The Greening of Business in Developing Countries: Rhetoric, Reality and Prospects* (Zed Books 2002) and see also Zadek (n 65) ch 5.

[93] Muchlinski (2007) (n 8) 550.

[94] Muchlinski (2007) (n 8) 551; see also Zeitlin (n 91) 196–200.

[95] Kristensen and Zeitlin (n 91), who identify such management problems in the British-based food and drink processing systems MNE, APV, in its relations with three acquired subsidiaries in the United States, Denmark, and the United Kingdom.

In the case of APV, the drivers for short-term financial gain conditioned by the demands of the City actively undermined efforts in the subsidiaries to develop coherent business strategies. This resulted in them effectively ignoring instructions from the London-based parent, which would not be concerned so long as the subsidiaries were profitable. In this process the subsidiaries engaged actively with local bodies and became part of a system of 'experimental governance' that was geared towards the development of the business in the local community. Also important was the development of what Kristensen and Zeitlin call a 'multinational public' for the corporation to hear.[96] This emerged out of the various works councils in the European side of the business. However unless there is legal sanction for such structures to be set up (as there is in the EU), the development of such a 'public' will depend on autonomous action by the corporation and its employees and other relevant stakeholders.[97]

The key point about such processes is that the pessimism of the 'new corporate accountability' movement should not be the last word in the debate. It dwells in the 'critical' campaigning strategy of civil society, where the uncovering and condemnation of corporate abuses is central. However, if this is the final point of campaigning the situation necessarily looks bleak and hopeless. In response, the 'experimental governance' or 'civil regulation' approach offers a 'liberal' strategy creating a cooperative approach that may lead to joint standard setting and to NGO/civil society–business partnerships devoted to the pursuit of particular policy goals and/or the realization of particular projects.[98] In this context it is important to remember that there exist 'management gaps' in MNE networks where the centrifugal forces that tend towards binding subsidiaries to their communities can develop networks of cooperation which lead to genuine social responsiveness in the subsidiary. Equally the possibility of corporations evolving into what Zadek calls 'civil corporations', capable of social involvement and positive contributions to their communities, ought not to be dismissed as naïve nonsense or a threat to free enterprise.[99] The corporate responsibility to respect human rights under the UN Guiding Principles offers a recent model of how civil behaviour can be pursued by firms.

The main problem remains that of the control of the parent company over financial returns where that parent is based in a financial market that is geared towards short-term returns. That was the case with APV for example.[100] This will require reforms in the way that stock markets operate so as to reduce the incentives towards the financialization of business and to return business to its original mission—the

[96] Kristensen and Zeitlin (n 91) ch 11.

[97] In this regard the institution of corporate-based informal operational level grievance settlement systems may be valuable as a method of tracking human rights impacts and avoidance and mitigation strategies (see Guiding Principles (n 81) principles 20, 29–31; IFC Guide (n 84) chs 6, 7).

[98] On 'critical' and 'liberal' civil society strategies see P Newell, 'Environmental NGOs, TNCs and the Question of Governance' in D Stevis and V J Assetto (eds) *The International Political Economy of the Environment: Critical Perspectives* (Lynne Reiner Publishers 2000).

[99] Zadek (n 65) pt 3.

[100] Kristensen and Zeitlin (n 91) 309–12.

provision of socially useful and rewarding goods and services.[101] If transnational stock markets do not achieve this transformation then alternative channels of corporate finance that actually serve the community and its productive enterprises are needed. In this regard regional credit unions and industrial investment banks are one option.[102] Another option is to rely more on local economic systems and on small and medium sized firms (SMEs), rather than the subsidiaries of MNEs unless they are capable of being locally responsive. It should be noted that such a policy is already well tried and tested in Germany, where regional banks and local SMEs form the backbone of the economy, though even here pressures to move towards a financialized system of business are increasing.[103]

D. Conclusion

This chapter has surveyed the pressing issue of corporate power in the globalized economy. It has shown that the traditional positivist notion of the sovereign territorial State is no longer the core paradigm of sovereignty. Using MacCormick's approach to sovereignty, it has sought to accommodate corporate power into a liberal, social democratic, model of pluralistic sovereignty in which ideas of subsidiarity can help in locating the best level at which decisions affecting the application of power should be made. It has outlined key issues in the State–corporation relationship and has examined a number of 'pessimistic' critiques of the relationship between public State power and private corporate power exercised by MNEs. In response, it has sought to use MacCormick's approach to work towards a more 'optimistic' view of how corporate power can be seen, and suggests that engagement between corporations, governments, and communities can be a socially enhancing process provided that the logic of financialization, which can lead to an exaggerated degree of corporate engagement in purely financial activities, is overcome. Given the increased concern over corporate abuses in recent times greater corporate engagement in socially useful business activities may be politically possible. The task is to mould business to fit society not to mould society to fit business.

[101] Financialization 'has been used to describe the rise of financial markets, over traditional bank lending, as the main source of investment capital, the seeking of profits though financial transactions as opposed to more traditional forms of manufacturing, services or primary goods industries, as well as to changes in corporate governance theory that place enhanced shareholder value at their heart' (P Muchlinski, 'The Changing Face of Transnational Business Governance: Private Corporate Law Liability and Accountability of Transnational Groups in a Post-Financial Crisis World' (2011) 18 *Indiana Journal of Global Legal Studies* 665, 670).

[102] Kristensen and Zeitlin (n 91) 318–22.

[103] On the pressures towards financialized business in Germany see A Dignam and M Galanis *The Globalization of Corporate Governance* (Ashgate Publishing 2010) ch 8, who assert that the German system may survive intact as a good response to the current crisis.

17

Sovereignty and Liberty in the Internet Era

Perry Keller[*]

A. The Media and the State in the Communications Revolution

In a few short decades, the world has been transformed. Satellite television and broadband Internet have enabled a global flow of digitized information that has overturned long standing conceptions of media law and policy. Before this revolution, States could realistically hope to maintain effective control over their national public information spheres. Yet new communications technologies, which were always a force for greater liberty of expression since the invention of clay tablets, have now seemingly overwhelmed the capacity of the State to determine the limits of public speech.[1] Even the most determined and well-resourced States have not managed to stay firmly in control of this ongoing transformation of the media.[2] The spread of wired and wireless broadband Internet with its omnipresent delivery of digitized information and images, coupled with the liberalization of trade rules and other market-based public policies, have consequently made the realization of a workable, networked global public sphere seem increasingly possible.[3]

This global revolution in communications is not just expanding the sphere of personal and collective liberty, it is also demolishing the historic relationship between the media and the State. That relationship came into being through the early mass distribution of printed books, pamphlets, and posters, which governing authorities of the time reacted to with alarm and determined measures.[4] Since that

* Senior Lecturer, Dickson Poon School of Law, King's College London.

[1] See generally, M Castells, *The Rise of the Network Society: Information Age: Economy, Society, and Culture* (2nd edn, Wiley-Blackwell 2009); A Murray, 'Internet Regulation', in D Levi-Faur (ed) *Handbook on the Politics of Regulation* (Edward Elgar 2011).

[2] See J Scotton and W Hachten, *New Media for a New China* (Wiley-Blackwell 2010), and R MacKinnon, *Consent of the Networked: the Worldwide Struggle for Internet Freedom* (Basic Books, 2012), ch 3.

[3] On the concept of a networked public sphere see Castells (n 1). See also Y Benkler, *The Wealth of Networks: How Social Production Transforms Markets and Freedoms* (Yale University Press 2006), ch 2; S Dutta, W Dutton, and G Law, *The New Internet World: A Global Perspective on Freedom of Expression, Privacy, Trust and Security Online*, INSEAD Working Paper No 2011/89/TOM, 24 August 2011.

[4] L Febre and H-J Martin, *The Coming of the Book: The Impact of Printing 1450–1800* (Verso 2010).

formative period, the media–State relationship has played a key part in defining and constituting the institutions of the modern State and the ideas that underpin its existence, including the multiform question of State sovereignty.[5] Over several centuries, State authorities have worked to prevent their populations from accessing information and entertainment content deemed harmful or offensive, while also encouraging them to consume preferred content. Controlling public access to media content has thus been an essential task of the modern State, underpinning not just its security and authority, but also its legitimacy. While a repressive State's censorship of the media may well harm its legitimacy in the eyes of the public, the State that fails to restrain the publication of extreme pornography and violent imagery, incitements to hatred, libellous allegations, and serious disclosures of private information may lose its legitimacy just as easily.

This is not to suggest that States necessarily dominate or direct the media–State relationship. There are an abundance of powerful economic, political, and other interests that have driven the publication and distribution of information and entertainment content since antiquity, constantly pushing against State or other restrictions. State authorities are thus engaged in an unceasing battle to restrict or channel these forces in their efforts to determine the nature and boundaries of the public information environment. Whether attempting to restrict or to foster public access to media content, governments have sought effective leverage over the key individuals who produce or distribute content within their borders as well as the key communications facilities they use.[6] Historically, this has required the use of legal and regulatory measures fastening on individuals and facilities present within national territory as well as others aimed at securing national borders against the import of banned publications.

Yet governments have most often waged this struggle on the back foot. As good as any law or other measure might be at the moment, new technologies and methods in the hands of inventive producers and distributors have continually eroded or punctured that effectiveness. The territorial boundaries of all States have, therefore, always been somewhat porous to the flow of media content, even where control measures are extreme.[7] Many States have also lacked the institutional capacities needed to comprehend and master the vulnerabilities of new communications technologies or methods. In the Internet era, this struggle has become much harder and the notion that the State can enfold its citizens within a distinct public information sphere seems ever further from reality.[8]

Nonetheless, the contemporary State has shown an extraordinary resilience in the face of new communications technologies. The more resourceful are bringing

[5] P Keller, *European and International Media Law: Liberal Democracy, Trade and the New Media Law* (OUP 2011) ch 1.

[6] Keller (n 5).

[7] See, eg, C Chen, K Ko, and J Lee, 'North Korea's Internet Strategy and its Political Implications' (2010) 23 *Pacific Review* 649.

[8] On the consequences of the waning capacities of the nation-state, see, W Brown 'We are all Democrats Now' (2010) 13 *Theory & Event* Issue 2; and J Trachtman, *The Future of International Law: Global Government* (CUP 2013).

their considerable powers to bear on the individuals and facilities that enable digital communications and media services.[9] Consequently, national authorities, rather than being mere bystanders in their own demise, are making their national boundaries a significant presence in the global flow of digitized information and ideas. Indeed, some are not only effective interveners in new communications and media services, but are essential nodes of control and support for global electronic networks.[10]

B. The Diversity of Freedom of Expression

When seeking to impose their territorial boundaries on the global flow of published information and ideas, States have historically structured their controls over media publication and distribution around the fundamental characteristics of territorial sovereignty. At the same time, when restricting and fostering public access to media content for reasons of authority and legitimacy, many States have also addressed the burgeoning demands of popular sovereignty. Media law and policy is consequently tightly bound into the liberal democratic State's considerable problems in upholding a fundamental commitment to personal liberty that accommodates conflicting conceptions of the good within a single public sphere. The question that is now pressed with ever greater force is how a liberal democratic conception of the public sphere might be best established on a global basis.[11] That, however, presumes that there is a sufficient consensus on the core principles needed to underpin a constitutionalized international public order, including not least those concerning restrictions on the free flow of information and ideas. Plainly, liberalism's fundamental adherence to individual freedom and equality provides a general compass bearing towards legitimate forms of media law and regulation. No properly democratic State would, for example, seek to emulate China's restrictions on public access and use of the Internet.

That said, liberal democracy is at best a loose array of both complementary and contending arguments about the individual, society, and the State. There is undoubtedly a set of linked arguments, founded on the primacy of personal and collective liberty, that define liberal democracy in terms that are both relatively coherent but also radically distinguish it from alternative forms of political order. These arguments encompass an intense opposition to State restrictions on speech and publication and a forceful commitment to transparency, scrutiny, and critical comment in public affairs. They are also frequently associated with scepticism towards claims that expression per se causes harm and a view that, where expression

9 See, eg, Home Office, *Draft Communications Data Bill. Part 1: Ensuring or Facilitating Availability of Data* (Cm 8359, 2012).

10 On the core role of the United States, see D Thomas, R Waters, and J Fontanella-Khan, 'The Internet: Command and Control' *Financial Times*, 27 August 2012, available at <http://www.ft.com/cms/s/2/fab58818-e63a-11e1-ac5f-00144feab49a.html#axzz2Re4aR3bW> (last accessed 27 April 2013).

11 See, eg, A Stone Sweet, 'A Cosmopolitan Legal Order: Constitutional Pluralism and Rights Adjudication in Europe' (2012) 11 *Journal of Global Constitutionalism* 53.

genuinely causes direct injury, its victims must sometimes bear that harm as the price of maintaining a free society.[12] On that robust view, the liberal virtue of tolerance demands that individuals and communities tolerate expression that they find grossly offensive or even harmful. Most importantly, these arguments also embrace market-based liberties concerning rights to property, which are not just seen as the engine of social and political liberty, but also as being indivisible from those forms of personal freedom. This, in other words, is a conflation of the *laissez faire* market with the marketplace of ideas.[13]

While there is no clear continuum of ideas across the breadth of liberal democratic thought, there are well developed, alternative arguments regarding the legitimacy of restrictions on public expression.[14] These alternatives are also less distinctively removed from non-liberal democratic conceptions of political order. They certainly emphasize the importance of personal liberty but also draw on other concepts of human worth and well-being, in particular human dignity, which both sustain and also limit the liberty to speak and publish.[15] From this perspective, the potential for expression to cause harm is more often accepted and legal protections from that harm, or even gross offence, are consequently more often deemed legitimate.[16] In this vein, liberal tolerance frequently demands sensitivity and forbearance by speakers and publishers as much as it requires a willingness by others to bear offence or harm. Less welcoming of market derived analogies, these arguments also tend to afford the State a greater role in maintaining laws or regulatory regimes that respect the autonomy and dignity of citizens as well as promoting the conditions that sustain them.

Profound differences in liberal democratic concepts of free speech are irresolvable but also to be welcomed. Finding acceptable compromises between the need for liberty and transparency and the need for prohibition and restraint is an ongoing, vital task for these societies. Indeed, the fractious clash of liberty and dignity based arguments forces democratic societies to re-examine their principles and find workable responses to the formidable challenges of harmful and offensive expression in the Internet era.[17] While formally committed to similar principles of individual liberty and equality, including the protection of open public debate, national political

[12] F Schauer, 'Harm(s) and the First Amendment' (2011) *Supreme Court Review* 81.

[13] See the dissent of Holmes J in *Abrams v United States* 250 US 616, 630 (1919). See also N Whitmore, 'Facing the Fear: A Free Market Approach for Economic Expression' (2012) 17 *Communication Law and Policy* 21; and J Schonsheck, 'The "Marketplace of Ideas": A Siren Song for Freedom of Speech Theorists' in D Golash (ed) *Freedom of Expression in a Diverse World* (Springer International 2010) 27.

[14] The work of Jürgen Habermas frequently takes up this critical perspective. For discussion, see D Ingram, *Habermas: Introduction and Analysis* (Cornell University Press 2010) 268–72; and J Heath 'System and Lifeworld' in B Fultner (ed) *Jürgen Habermas: Key Concepts* (Acumen 2012) 74.

[15] See, eg, M Rosen, *Dignity: Its History and Meaning* (Harvard University Press 2012); J Habermas, 'The Concept of Human Dignity and the Realistic Utopia of Human Rights' (2010) 41 *Metaphilosophy* 464; and J Waldron, 'Is Dignity the Foundation of Human Rights?' (2013) NYU School of Law, Public Law Research Paper No 12-73.

[16] See, eg, *R (on the application of Gaunt) v Office of Communications* [2011] EWCA Civ 692, [2011] 1 WLR 2355.

[17] See, eg, *Chambers v Director of Public Prosecutions* [2012] EWHC 2157 (Admin), [2013] 1 All ER 149.

communities are thus able to arrive at distinctively different positions through their own forms of collective agency. This moreover underscores the primary importance of community, locality, and collective agency in finding solutions to the problem of limiting public expression in a liberal democratic society.

The purpose of the liberal democratic State is precisely to provide a secure forum in which a community, inevitably arbitrary in its definition and boundaries, can confront and resolve its collective problems.[18] Those plainly include the question of whether and how to limit harmful or offensive expression while also safeguarding freedom of expression. Within such a territorially bounded community, the institutions of State and society enable the collective agency of liberal democracy, sustained by the legitimacy of popular sovereignty.[19] Despite its many faults and waning capacities, the State survives because, among other reasons, it offers the possibility of a secure public sphere that does not depend on religious or ethnic homogeneity. It is, in principle, a society in common that is capable of holding and reconciling diverse beliefs and interests within its boundaries.[20]

The communications revolution has if anything increased the global importance of bounded communities capable of collective agency. While demonstrating the universality of human desires for personal liberty, the spread of the Internet has highlighted the strength of particular beliefs and loyalties. As one recent study has concluded, 'When it comes to core Internet values, users generally want it all. They desire an online environment where they can simultaneously express themselves freely, protect their personal data and privacy, trust the people and information they find, and feel safe.'[21]

The world has ever expanding numbers of networked communities. What these regional and global networks have yet to provide are effective alternative forums for decision-making and collective agency that can substitute for the territorially bounded communities of the liberal democratic State. At present, they are highly transparent, networked communities and audiences of choice that are primarily enabled by and resident on commercially operated platforms.[22] They have become integral to contemporary political and social life, but they are institutionally weak with limited capacities for informed deliberation and decision-making.[23]

[18] See Brown (n 8) and Habermas (n 15).

[19] M Loughlin, *Foundations of Public Law* (OUP 2010) 174.

[20] Loughlin (n 19) 175–6.

[21] Dutta, Dutton, and Law (n 3) 29.

[22] See W Oremus, 'Twitter Backtracks After Muzzling Journalist Who Criticized NBC's Olympics Coverage' *Slate*, 31 July 3012, available at <http://www.slate.com/blogs/future_tense/2012/07/31/guy_adams_twitter_reinstates_independent_journalist_who_criticized_nbc_coverage.html> (last accessed 27 April 2013).

[23] The Palo Alto Group, 'Democracy and the Smart Mob' (2012) 29 *New Perspectives Quarterly* 13; M Castells, *Networks of Outrage and Hope: Social Movements in the Internet Age* (Polity Press 2012); R Benkirane, 'The Alchemy of Revolution: The Role of Social Networks and New Media in the Arab Spring' (2012) Geneva Centre for Security Policy, GCSP Policy Paper No 2012/7, available at <http://gcsp.ch/Regional-Capacity-Development/Middle-East-North-Africa/Publications/GCSP-Publications/Policy-Papers/The-Alchemy-of-Revolution-The-Role-of-Social-Networks-and-New-Media-in-the-Arab-Spring> (last accessed 27 April 2013).

C. Defining European Freedom of Expression

Supranational law, both regional and international, has long promised to overcome the deficiencies of the State through ambitious forms of constitutionalized regional and global public order.[24] Over the past half century, supranational regimes have grown dramatically in their institutional powers and legal authority, setting increasingly dense, prescriptive standards for the legitimate exercise of State power. Indeed, in the overlapping fields of economic and human rights law, supranational rules affecting the publication and distribution of media content have come to exemplify the constitutionalist vision of universally applicable, autonomous legal norms. It takes little imagination to see that there is a profoundly liberal democratic, universalist vision at work not just in the development of supranational rights to freedom of speech and publication but also in the liberalization of trade and investment in media goods and services.

The major Western democracies may no longer unilaterally set the international economic and political agenda, but in the long decades of the Cold War, and the brief moment of US global supremacy that followed, these States collectively established the institutional and legal architecture that now frames contemporary supranational media law. The aspiration to supranational constitutionalism thus originates in the related, but distinctly different, legal and political traditions of the US and the major European democracies. It is however in the United States that the relationship between the media and the State was first constitutionalized. This occurred, at least formally, with the adoption of the First Amendment to the United States Constitution, which more than a century later provided the basis for an extraordinary flowering of free speech doctrine in the American appellate courts.[25]

Almost all constitutional understandings of freedom of expression in the liberal democratic world have consequently emerged downstream of the American experience. Even as national and supranational courts have articulated their own visions of that shared ideal, they have frequently worked on conceptual and practical problems first considered in US courts.[26] The American model is moreover an international exemplar of comparative openness to diverse and even threatening public speech and debate.[27] It is oriented towards an expansive conception of permissible speech and publication, which US courts have continued to strengthen, using the First

[24] M Loughlin, 'What is Constitutionalization?' in M Loughlin and P Dobner (eds) *The Twilight of Constitutionalism* (OUP 2010) 47; J Habermas, 'The Crisis of the European Union in the Light of a Constitutionalization of International Law' (2012) 23 *European Journal of International Law* 335.

[25] E Volokh, *The First Amendment and Related Statutes, Problems, Cases and Policy Arguments* (4th edn, Foundation Press 2011) pt 1.

[26] See, eg, the discussion of public figure status in *Lingens v Austria* [1986] 8 EHRR 407.

[27] *New York Times v Sullivan* 376 US 254 (1964), 'Thus, we consider this case against the background of a profound national commitment to the principle that debate on public issues should be uninhibited, robust, and wide-open, and that it may well include vehement, caustic, and sometimes unpleasantly sharp attacks on government and public officials.' See S Gardbaum, 'The Myth and The Reality Of American Constitutional Exceptionalism' (2008) 107 *Michigan L Rev* 391 and F Schauer, 'Freedom of Expression Adjudication in Europe and America' in G Nolte (ed) *European and US Constitutionalism* (CUP 2005).

Amendment as a tool to strip away government intervention in old and new places.[28]

Despite the global influence of American constitutional law regarding freedom of speech, in creating the world's leading model for supranational, constitutionalized public order Europe has approached the problem of public expression differently. Its increasingly integrated rules governing economic freedoms and fundamental human rights harbour a relatively coherent conception of the liberty to publish and distribute media content that draws primarily on Europe's own constitutional traditions.[29] Like the United States and all other liberal democracies, European law contains strong protections for expression affecting democratic politics, public affairs, and other matters of significant common interest.[30] That protected sphere of public debate is however a more limited one than that secured by the US First Amendment.

In the more politically and culturally diverse international sphere, constitutionalized public order has developed much more slowly, following but not always embracing, European innovations in multilateralism. Few international institutions or multilateral agreements possess the unalloyed liberal democratic character of their European counterparts and the major international treaty obligations that concern the media are more limited in scope and less well defined. In addition, institutional and doctrinal divisions between international economic and human rights legal regimes remain largely in place. Nevertheless, especially in the field of trade law, juridical constitutionalism is gaining ground.[31]

For liberal democracies, the fitful movement towards supranational public order has had a deep and sometimes dramatic impact on their domestic media laws and policies. Inter-governmental cooperation on shared objectives, such as the prevention of cross-border communication of child pornography or incitement to violence and other harmful information and images, has enabled a degree of effective, collective content regulation.[32] In this way, States have successfully leveraged themselves into wider spheres that would otherwise be beyond their unilateral capacities. On the other hand, States have also become subject to new forms of collective authority and agency, including regional and international courts of exclusive jurisdiction. When they act within the authority of these courts, liberal democracies have found that they are no longer the masters of the multilateral obligations they once created to promote and sustain their economic and political ends.[33]

[28] See, eg, *United States v Stevens* 559 US __, (2010) 130 SCt 1577; *Snyder v Phelps* 562 US __ (2011), 131 S. Ct. 1207; *Citizens United v Federal Election Commission* 558 US 50 (2010).

[29] Note, for example, the close connection between the protection of human dignity in European Union law (Treaty on European Union, art 2; Charter of Fundamental Rights, art 1, and Case C-36/02 *Omega Spielhallen* [2004] ECR I-9609) and its central place in German constitutional law (see *Grundgesetz für die Bundesrepublik Deutschland* ('Basic Law') pt 1: Basic Rights, art 1).

[30] See, eg, *Otegi Mondragon v Spain*, App no 2034/07, (15 March 2011).

[31] K Alter, 'The Global Spread of European Style International Courts' (2012) 35 *West European Politics* 15.

[32] An independent report by Dr Weixiao Wei commissioned by the Internet Watch Foundation and funded by the Nominet Trust was published in May 2011. Available at <https://www.iwf.org.uk/resources/independent-report> (last accessed 26 July 2013).

[33] On the expanding scope of the ECHR art 8 right to respect for private and family life, see R Walker, 'The Indefinite Article 8', Thomas More Lecture, Lincoln's Inn, 9 November 2011.

In this manner, supranational rule-making has gradually broken into the once exclusive relationship between the media and the State, which has been a core domestic concern since the media first emerged out of the hands of seventeenth-century printers, pamphleteers, and bill posters. It is however the growing juridical constitutionalism of European and international law that has cut most deeply into the sphere of territorial and popular sovereignty in which the media–State relationship has long existed. This invasive judicial power stems not just from the authority of supranational courts to interpret the primary treaty obligations of States not to restrict the publication and distribution of media content without legitimate justification. It is the combination of case specific fact finding and reasoning together with the extensive use of necessity and proportionality principles to determine the legitimacy of restrictions on the media that can involve supranational courts in a fine grained review of domestic law and policy.[34]

From a constitutionalist perspective, much of this is to be welcomed. To achieve more effective governance, on this view, the world must discard the anachronistic notion that regional and international public order rests on the primacy of State sovereignty and the limits of State consent and embrace a properly supranational alternative.[35] The constitutionalist alternative is both juridical and cosmopolitan, underpinned by courts wielding exclusive authority over the interpretation of universal rights and duties, which are in turn imbued with a liberal democratic ethos.[36] There is, as a result, an overlapping consensus spanning national, regional, and international law in which State sovereignty is legitimated by adherence to that ethos.[37]

Cosmopolitan constitutionalism has yet to find a fully convincing answer to the problem of weak democratic legitimacy faced by virtually all supranational organizations.[38] Yet, in embracing principles of individual liberty and equality, it does offer protection from the illiberal and arbitrary risks of their majoritarian democracies. The argument for supranational constitutionalism has also shifted to accommodate its pluralist critics, taking a positive view of the overlapping, divergent, and fragmented claims to authority occurring throughout regional and international law and relations.[39] As Matthias Kumm argued, the world of public law is now imagined as constituted and held together through a shared commitment to constitutional

[34] On proportionality analysis, see R Alexy 'The Construction of Constitutional Rights' (2010) 4 *Law & Ethics of Human Rights* 1; and, M Cohen-Eliya and I Porat, 'Proportionality and the Culture of Justification' (2011) 59 *American Journal of Comparative Law* 463.

[35] See, eg, A Guzman, 'Against Consent' (2012) 52 *Virginia Journal of International Law* 747; and E-U Petersmann, 'Methodological Pluralism and Its Critics in International Economic Law Research' (2012) 15 *Journal of International Economic Law* 921.

[36] Stone Sweet (n 11).

[37] M Kumm, 'How does European Union Law Fit into the World of Public Law?' in J Weiner and A Neyer (eds) *Political Theory of the European Union* (OUP 2011); see S Besson 'Sovereignty, International Law and Democracy' (2011) 22 *European Journal of International Law* 373.

[38] R Dahl, 'Can International Organizations Be Democratic? A Skeptic's View', in I Shapiro and C Hacker- Cordón (eds) *Democracy's Edges* (CUP 1991).

[39] G de Búrca, 'The European Court of Justice and the International Legal Order after Kadi' (2010) 51 *Harvard International LJ* 1. See also Stone Sweet (n 11) and M Maduro, N Walker, NJ Baquero

principles, which provide the mediating principles for a deeply pluralist structure of public law.[40] In Europe, this commitment to common values has enabled not just the sharing or pooling of sovereignty to create new forms of collective sovereignty, but also the re-distribution of that sovereignty back to Member States.[41]

In this telling, constitutional pluralism enfolds the media–State relationship in ways that maintain a universal commitment to freedom of expression, but also allow different, even divergent, interpretations of that commitment within States. Conflicts about whether and how to restrict harmful or offensive expression are thus kept to the diverse margins of liberal democracy and do not arise in its universalist core. This is not however an explanation of, or aspiration towards, supranational public order that withstands close inspection. Cosmopolitan constitutionalism, even leavened by a pluralist account of relations between national and supranational regimes, pretends to a unity that does not exist in the broad intellectual and political traditions of liberalism or democracy. There is, in short, no core understanding of freedom of expression that is sufficiently thin to be universally shared and sufficiently thick to determine when and how States ought to limit harmful or offensive expression in a meaningful way.[42] As the following discussion demonstrates, even the universal liberal democratic commitment to open debate regarding political and other matters of general concern is in practice a thin and ambiguous basis for any common understanding of free speech.

It is in the detail, rather than the reassuring generalities, that the cosmopolitan constitutionalist balance between universal norms and domestic autonomy begins to break down. Consider, for example, the European experience, where the European Court of Human Rights ('ECtHR') has taken the lead role in interpreting the evolving meaning of the liberty to publish and distribute media content as a human right, principally under Article 10 of the Convention for the Protection of Human Rights and Fundamental Freedoms ('ECHR') as well as indirectly under the European Charter of Fundamental Rights.[43] There is consequently a basic consistency of purpose that runs on both sides of the narrowing divide between European economic and human rights law. As the European Commission demonstrated in its recent confrontation with the Hungarian government, the EU is willing to enforce the rules of free movement to protect Europe's political as well as its economic foundations when media freedoms are restricted.[44]

Cruz, and M Kumm in M Avbelj and J Komárek (eds) *Four Visions of Constitutional Pluralism* (2008) EUI Working Paper Law No 2008/21.

[40] Kumm (n 37).

[41] Stone Sweet (n 11); see also N Walker, 'Surface and Depth: The EU's Resilient Sovereignty Question' in J Wiener and A Neyer (eds) *Political Theory of the European Union* (OUP 2010) 91.

[42] On the problems of thin and thick universality, see N Walker, 'Universalism and Particularism in Human Rights: Trade-Off or Productive Tension?' (2010) Edinburgh School of Law Research Paper No 2012/10.

[43] S Douglas-Scott, 'The European Union and Human Rights after the Treaty of Lisbon' (2011) 11 *Human Rights L Rev* 645.

[44] *Commission Vice-President Kroes welcomes Amendments to Hungarian Media Law*, European Commission, MEMO/11/89, Brussels, 16 February 2011.

Over several decades, the ECtHR has created a doctrinal framework that attempts to balance the universality of ECHR freedom of expression obligations with national autonomy in the media sector. Where expression relates to a matter of public interest or general concern, a broad category centred on democratic electoral politics, but extending as far as welfare issues of concern to particular communities,[45] a State Party must justify any restrictions on such expression by satisfying the Court's rigorous tests, which include clear demonstrations of necessity and proportionality.[46] These tests are applied less rigorously for other categories of public expression, such as artistic or commercial works.[47] At the bottom of this hierarchy, States need only minimally justify restrictions on expression that has no purpose other than to arouse the senses through images of sex or violence or expression that is purely intended to cause gross offence or incite hatred and even violence.[48] National autonomy, secured through a flexible 'margin of appreciation', is in other words greatest at the bottom of this hierarchy and comparatively restricted at the top.

In practice, however, national autonomy in the area of offensive and harmful expression is much more limited and uncertain than this doctrinal hierarchy suggests. The Court has defined matters of general concern as broadly as possible, no doubt in part to avoid the criticism that the determination of the legitimate public interest in a democracy should be left as much as possible to the public and not appropriated by State or supranational authorities.[49] It has nonetheless narrowed the heavily protected core area of public expression in other ways. In the Court's case law, the critical question is not simply whether the expression at issue is connected to a matter of legitimate general concern, but whether it also *contributes* to public debate on that matter. Famously, in *Otto Preminger Institut v Austria,* it was of no help to the applicants that their film seized by Austrian authorities was an attack on the Catholic faith and therefore fell within a wide category of public interest. In the view of the Court, the seizure fell within the principle that those who exercise the Article 10 right to freedom of expression have 'duties and responsibilities' that may legitimately include, in the context of religious opinions and beliefs, 'an obligation to avoid as far as possible expressions that are gratuitously offensive to others and thus an infringement of their rights, and which therefore do not contribute to any form of public debate capable of furthering progress in human affairs'.[50]

The Court's purposive interpretation of Convention rights and routine resort to balancing multiple factors to determine the priority of relevant rights and legitimate interests renders the issue of whether a particular restriction on public expression

[45] See *Selisto v Finland* (2004) 42 EHRR 144, which concerned allegations of drunkenness regarding a hospital surgeon.

[46] On the margin of appreciation see *Mouvement Raëlien Suisse v Switzerland* [2012] ECHR 1598, para 61.

[47] Keller (n 5) 194.

[48] See, eg, *Perrin v United Kingdom*, App no 5446/03 (18 October 2005).

[49] See the arguments put forward by Justice Marshall, US Supreme Court in *Rosenbloom v Metromedia Inc* 403 US 29, 79 (1971). See also, *Gertz v Robert Welch, Inc* 418 US 323, 345–6 (1974).

[50] *Otto Preminger Institut v Austria* (1994) 19 EHRR 34, para 49. See also, *Mouvement Raëlien Suisse v Switzerland* (2012) 32 BHRC 646, para 62.

violates Article 10 more uncertain.[51] In offensive expression cases, the Court may, for example, weigh the importance of the matter of general concern, the extent of any contribution to public debate, the degree of offence or harm risked or resulting, the identity of the person or group offended and the type of media involved.[52] Where other Convention rights are engaged—such as Article 8 (right to respect for private and family life)—national autonomy may be marginal due to positive obligations to protect interests covered by those rights.[53] Even where other Convention rights are not engaged, the protection of human dignity remains a background factor, of variable strength, where individuals or communities suffer grossly offensive expression relating to their race, ethnicity, gender, sexuality, or religious beliefs.[54]

A determination by the Court that a restriction on expression does not violate Article 10 therefore gives the misleading impression that the matter is open to State Parties. In principle, a State could adopt a more robust view of tolerance and allow greater liberty for abusive expression where no other Convention rights are at issue. The rhetoric of the Court is however not neutral on how national autonomy is exercised in the margin of appreciation. By weighing the relevant factors and finding in favour of the respondent State, the Court gives explicit and often detailed support for the restrictive measures it has employed.[55] While no other State Party is compelled to adopt those measures, the Court's language can be an open invitation to do so.

The European test of whether the expression at issue makes a contribution to public debate contrasts sharply with US constitutional law, where the principle of content neutrality prevents government authorities from selectively restricting expression because of its particular content.[56] That principle more than any other has sustained the substantial divide between European and US law on the restriction of hate speech (expression that goes beyond the gratuitously and grossly offensive to incite hatred). The European Court of Human Rights has not only found severe restrictions on incitement to hatred based on race, ethnicity, religion, and other aspects of identity to be permissible under Article 10(2), but in a few instances relating to denial of the Holocaust has also found that such incitement to hatred

[51] *R (Animal Defenders International) v Secretary of State For Culture, Media and Sport* [2008] UKHL 15, [2008] 1 AC 1312 [52].

[52] See, eg, *Féret v Belgium*, App no 15615/07 (16 July 2009); *Leroy v France*, App no 36109/03 (2 October 2008).

[53] On the relationship between art 8 positive obligations and ECHR art 10 see *Caroline von Hannover v Germany* (2012) 32 BHRC 527 and *Axel Springer v Germany* (2012) 32 BHRC 493.

[54] Without a clear textual point of reference in the ECHR, the Court's references to human dignity are by no means systematic, although the fundamental importance of the concept is not in doubt; see, eg, *Erbakan v Turkey*, App no 59405/00 (6 June 2006), para 56.

[55] This is especially evident where hate speech is at issue, even with regard to groups not yet protected by European prescriptive obligations, such as homosexuals (see *Vejdeland and ors v Sweden* [2012] ECHR 1813/07, (2012) 32 BHRC 474) or alternatively where the protection of children is at issue (see *Müller and ors v Switzerland* (1988) 13 EHRR 212).

[56] See, eg, *RAV v City of St Paul* 505 US 377 (1992); and see, L Barnett Lidsky, 'Incendiary Speech and Social Media' (2011) 44 *Texas Tech L Rev* 147.

constitutes an attack on the foundations of democratic society and merits no protection whatsoever under the Convention.[57]

In 1997, following acts of genocide at Srebrenica and elsewhere in former Yugoslavia, the Council of Europe adopted guidance to its Member States urging them to take measures to combat hate speech and later sponsored the Additional Protocol to the Convention on Cybercrime 2003, which obliges the criminalization of hate speech committed through electronic networks.[58] More significantly, the European Union has deployed its more formidable legislative powers to create rules that oblige its Member States to regulate and to criminalize incitement to hatred.[59] Despite this hardening of European law regarding hate speech, US First Amendment principles regarding incitement to hatred and violence[60] continue to be highly influential in European public debate, regularly featuring for example in concurring and dissenting judicial opinions in ECtHR judgments.[61] These judicial views reflect the ongoing lively debates occurring in European societies about legal restrictions on harmful and offensive speech in which the Court has come to occupy a controversial position.

D. Conflicting Versions of International Public Order

The cosmopolitan constitutionalist ideal, founded on the relative successes of European public order, is still a distant aspiration in the fragmented international sphere. Unlike Europe, international law as it affects the publication and distribution of media content remains structurally divided between international human rights and economic legal regimes with little bridging between them. International human rights law, which is centred on a sprawling array of United Nations human rights treaties and other instruments, may no longer be caught up in bitter Cold War rivalries, but is still politically divided between liberal democracies, quasi-democracies, and other States. Competing liberal democratic ideas about the proper meaning and application of the right to freedom of expression, especially those articulated in US and European constitutional law, are also prominent in international legal discourse.

[57] See, eg, *Garaudy v France*, App no 65831/01 (24 June 2003).

[58] Council of Europe, *Committee of Ministers Recommendation on 'Hate Speech'* (1997) Rec (97) 20; Additional Protocol to the Convention on Cybercrime concerning the criminalization of acts of a racist and xenophobic nature committed through computer systems (CETS No 185) (2003), arts 2 and 3–8.

[59] Directive 2012/13/EU Audiovisual Media Services [2010] OJ L95/1, art 6; Council Framework Decision 2008/913/JHA on combating certain forms and expressions of racism and xenophobia by means of criminal law [2008] OJ L328/55.

[60] *Brandenburg v Ohio* 395 US 444 (1969), in which the Court held that a State cannot forbid or proscribe advocacy of the use of force or of law violation except where such advocacy is directed to inciting or producing imminent lawless action and is likely to incite or produce such action.

[61] See, eg, the Concurring Opinion of Judge Bonello, *Sürek and Özdemir v Turkey*, App no 23927/94 & 24277/94 (8 July 1999): and see the Dissenting Opinion of Judge Pinto de Albuquerque, *Mouvement Raëlien Suisse v Switzerland* (n 50).

Articles 19 of the 1948 Universal Declaration on Human Rights and the 1966 International Covenant on Civil and Political Rights ('ICCPR'), especially the latter, sit in parallel to Article 10 of the ECHR. The Human Rights Committee, established by the ICCPR,[62] while not enjoying the authority or exclusive jurisdiction of a supranational court, has gained considerable influence over the interpretation of the ICCPR in many State Parties.[63] In recent years, benefiting perhaps from a favourable membership and the freedom that comes with a lack of enforcement powers, the Committee has shifted its interpretation of the Article 19 right to freedom of expression away from some conclusions of the ECtHR and closer to those of the United States Supreme Court. The centrepiece of its recent work on Article 19 is the Committee's General Comment No 34,[64] adopted in September 2011, which describes the right to freedom of expression in broad terms[65] and emphasizes the role of the media in securing its democratic purposes.[66]

In tone and in many specific points, the General Comment stresses the importance of liberty from the State and eschews discussion of significant competing principles, including the right to human dignity which now plays such a significant role in European public order. In this statement of principles, the Committee also rejects the notion of a margin of appreciation, reserving to itself the power to assess whether, in every specific set of facts before it, a restriction on freedom of expression is necessary and proportionate.[67] This assertive position on the right to freedom of expression has been followed by the UN Special Rapporteur on the right to freedom of opinion and expression exercised through the Internet, who in 2012 reported to the General Assembly that 'there should be as little restriction as possible to the flow of information on the Internet, except under a few, very exceptional and limited circumstances prescribed by international law for the protection of other human rights.'[68]

On the specific question of restrictions on harmful or offensive expression relating to race, ethnicity, and other aspects of identity, the Human Rights Committee has shifted away from its earlier and more European position. In defining the meaning of the 'rights of others, the protection of which is a legitimate ground for restrictions on expression under Article 19(3)', the Committee has for example narrowed its interpretation of 'others' to include only 'individual members of a community defined by its religious faith or ethnicity',[69] In its well-known 1996 decision in the

[62] On the powers of the Committee under the ICCPR, see Y Tyagi, *The UN Human Rights Committee: Practice and Procedure* (CUP 2011).

[63] Tyagi (n 62) ch 6.

[64] Human Rights Committee, General Comment No 34: Article 19—Freedoms of Opinion and Expression (CCPR/C/GC/34), 102nd session, 12 September 2011.

[65] General Comment No 34 (n 64) para 11: 'every form of idea and opinion capable of transmission to others', which includes artistic expression, religious discourse, and possibly commercial advertising.

[66] General Comment No 34 (n 64) para 13. 'A free, uncensored and unhindered press or other media is essential in any society to ensure freedom of opinion and expression and the enjoyment of other Covenant rights. It constitutes one of the cornerstones of a democratic society'; see also para 38.

[67] General Comment No 34 (n 64) para 36.

[68] Special Rapporteur Frank La Rue: A/66/290 Report of the Special Rapporteur to the General Assembly on the right to freedom of opinion and expression exercised through the Internet, para. 12.

[69] General Comment No 34 (n 64) para 28.

Faurisson v France communication, the Committee defined the 'rights of others' more broadly to include, 'the interests of other persons or those of the community as a whole'.[70] In addition, the General Comment sets out a restrictive interpretation of 'public morals', another legitimate ground under Article 19(3) for restrictions on expression, declaring that 'the purpose of protecting morals must be based on principles not deriving exclusively from a single tradition'.[71]

Finally, the Committee has taken a narrow view of Article 20(2) of the ICCPR, which requires that State Parties prohibit by law any advocacy of national, racial, or religious hatred that constitutes incitement to discrimination, hostility, or violence.[72] The General Comment reiterated the Committee's position that Article 20 may be considered *lex specialis* with regard to Article 19 only insofar as it requires prohibition by law. Any measures adopted by a State Party under Article 20 are thus subject to the necessity and proportionality requirements of Article 19(3). This approach is also reflected in the work of the Special Rapporteur on the right to freedom of opinion and expression exercised through the Internet, whose 2012 report states that the protected freedom 'to scrutinize, openly debate and criticize, even harshly and unreasonably, ideas, opinions, belief systems and institutions, including religious ones' may only be restricted where expression 'advocates hatred that incites hostility, discrimination or violence against an individual or a group of individuals'.[73] In contrast to European principles, restrictions on expression that is merely gratuitously and grossly offensive are evidently not permitted under Article 19.

While United Nations human rights bodies have struggled to assert their authority over international human rights law, the trade law regime of the World Trade Organization ('WTO') has been comparatively more successful in developing the rudiments of supranational constitutionalism.[74] Unlike the ICCPR Human Rights Committee, the WTO Appellate Body and panels have explicit authority to make interpretations of the WTO treaties that are binding on Member States.[75] Breach of their decisions, or other trade obligations, carries moreover a high risk of meaningful bilateral or multilateral counter-measures.

This greater effectiveness has meant that trade obligations are often seen as attractive vehicles for the achievement of wider foreign policy objectives, including political change through the liberalization of trade in media goods and services. In effect, this is a strategy that uses the liberalization of market forces to enable the

[70] *Faurisson v France*, Comm No 550/1993, UN Doc CCPR/C/58/D/550/1993, 8 November 1996, para 9.6.

[71] General Comment No 34 (n 64) para 32.

[72] On becoming a State Party to the Covenant in 1992, the US Government adopted a reservation to nullify the effect of art 20: 'That article 20 does not authorize or require legislation or other action by the United States that would restrict the right of free speech and association protected by the Constitution and laws of the United States.'

[73] A/66/290 Report (n 68) para 30.

[74] S Lester, 'The Role of the International Trade Regime in Global Governance' (2012) 16 *UCLA Journal of International Law and Foreign Affairs* 209; and G Shaffer and J Trachtman, 'Interpretation and Institutional Choice at the WTO' (2012) 52 *Virginia Journal of International Law* 103.

[75] I Van Damme, *Treaty Interpretation by the WTO Appellate Body* (OUP 2009)

marketplace of ideas. Not surprisingly, the possibility for political liberalization through the operation of trade commitments has been widely discussed in the United States, where First Amendment principles have sustained a long standing openness to cross border flows of information and entertainment content that does not distinguish between economic and political liberty.[76] In the Internet era, this has included strong support for the rapid spread of social media and other new communications services, both nationally and globally.[77] Indeed, the chief concern in the United States is more often that these new services will bring the chilling effects of foreign restrictions on expression into the domestic US media.[78]

Despite the synergy between economic and political liberty, international trade law has so far had a modest impact on the media sector in most WTO Member States. Not only does the General Agreement on Tariffs and Trade 1994 ('GATT') contain an important exemption for discriminatory screen quotas imposed on foreign films,[79] but its importance to the media has dwindled as the delivery of content has shifted from physical forms (goods) to electronic networks (services).[80] Yet the scope of the General Agreement on Trade in Services 1995 ('GATS') in the media sector is unclear.[81] Nearly twenty years after its adoption, WTO Member States remain divided on key issues relating to trade in media services, such as the treatment of audiovisual services or electronic commerce under trade in services commitments.[82] In addition, the trade obligations of the GATT and the GATS are comparatively shallow, requiring non-discrimination in the treatment of foreign goods or services rather than the removal of unwarranted barriers to trade as is generally required by EU law.[83] As a result, they do not reach many national measures that prohibit harmful or offensive expression where there is no discrimination between domestic and similar foreign goods or services, although highly specific content prohibitions may amount to de facto discrimination.

[76] See T Wu, 'The World Trade Law of Censorship and Filtering' (2006–7) 7 *Chicago Journal of International Law* 263; L Bollinger, *Uninhibited, Robust and Wide Open: A Free Press for a New Century* (OUP 2010) ch 4.

[77] In its landmark case concerning restrictions on Internet-based content, *Reno v ACLU* (1997) 521 US 844, the United States Supreme Court described the Internet not only as 'a unique and wholly new medium of worldwide human communication' and 'a new marketplace of ideas', but also as constituting '"cyberspace"—located in no particular geographical location but available to anyone, anywhere in the world, with access to the Internet'. Scholarly discussion is similarly broad in scope; see, eg, J Balkin, 'The Future of Free Expression in a Digital Age' (2009) 36 *Pepperdine L Rev* 427.

[78] See, eg, Securing the Protection of our Enduring and Established Constitutional Heritage, (SPEECH) Act 2010, Public Law 111–223, codified at 28 USC §§ 4101–5 (which is intended to protect public speech in the United States against foreign libel actions); see also T Zick, 'Falsely Shouting Fire in Global Theater: Emerging Complexities of Trans-Border Expression' (2012) 65 *Vanderbilt L Rev* 125.

[79] General Agreement on Tariffs and Trade 1994 (incorporating GATT 1947) 33 ILM 1153 (1994), art IV.

[80] Despite the declining relevance of the GATT to trade in media content, one of the most significant WTO disputes affecting the media arose in a case of mixed goods and services elements: *Canada—Certain Measures Concerning Periodicals*, AB-1997-2, WT/DS31/AB/R (WTO Appellate Body) (30 July 1997).

[81] General Agreement on Trade in Services (GATS) 33 ILM 1167 (1994).

[82] Keller (n 5) ch 5.

[83] C Barnard, *The Substantive Law of the EU: The Four Freedoms* (3rd edn, OUP 2010) ch 1.

The potential impact of multilateral trade rules on the media sector is however enormous. Despite the failures of the Doha Round, the WTO remains institutionally committed to further and deeper liberalization of trade, which must in principle include a further liberalization of trade in media goods and services. While the European Union has determinedly defended a broad interpretation of the Uruguay Round compromise over audiovisual services,[84] its position is increasingly unsustainable in open market economies where consumers have easy access through broadband Internet connections to foreign entertainment services. The possibility of a horizontal necessity test governing the domestic regulation of services is also on the WTO agenda, which would bring non-discriminatory restrictions on media content within the scope of trade law.[85]

WTO trade disciplines may currently have limited application to trade in media goods and services for most Member States, but this is not the case for China, which agreed to significant exceptional or 'WTO-plus' obligations when it acceded to the organization and its treaties.[86] Contrary to the expectations of the Chinese government, these obligations have since been found to affect the domestic publication, distribution, or provision of media goods and services.[87] China's contemporary media regime rests on a complex mix of criminal law prohibitions; myriad licensing requirements for every aspect of media content publication and distribution; State ownership of most major media outlets; as well as Party control or supervision of key editorial positions throughout the media sector.[88] The Communist Party's Central ('CCP') Propaganda Department sits at the apex of this system, directing a daily flow of instructions on major events or issues that helps to maintain CCP authority over all major editorial decisions.[89] This system of control is highly flexible and largely opaque to the public. It also necessarily excludes foreign entities from ultimate control over editorial functions and distribution channels, reserving these for governmental or commercial entities embedded in the Propaganda Department's national network that runs within Party hierarchies. It is in short, nakedly and necessarily discriminatory.

[84] Keller (n 5) 474–7.

[85] On the GATS VI negotiations out of which a horizontal necessity test might eventually arise, see Keller (n 5) ch 5. See also P Delimatsis, 'Due Process and "Good" Regulation Embedded in the GATS—Disciplining Regulatory Behaviour in Services through Article VI of the GATS' (2006) 10 *Journal of International Economic Law* 13. On the flexibility of the GATT and GATS non-discrimination tests, see N Diebold, 'Standards of Non-Discrimination in International Economic Law' (2011) 40 *ICLQ* 831.

[86] *Protocol on the Accession of the People's Republic of China*, WT/L/432 (10 November 2001); see also J Qin, '"WTO-Plus" Obligations and Their Implications for the World Trade Organization Legal System: An Appraisal of the China Accession Protocol' (2003) 37 *Journal of World Trade* 483.

[87] China's media sector has been the subject of a growing list of WTO disputes, including *China—Measures Affecting Financial Information Services and Foreign Financial Information Suppliers* DS373; *China—Measures affecting Trading Rights and Distribution Services for Certain Publications and Audiovisual Entertainment Products*, WT/DS363/AB/R, (December 2009).

[88] M Brady, *Marketing Dictatorship: Propaganda and Thought Work in Contemporary China* (Rowman & Littlefield 2008) ch 2.

[89] Brady (n 88) ch 2.

Nevertheless, China assumed several obligations under its Accession Protocol that have brought its media sector partially under WTO non-discrimination disciplines, enabling its trade partners, the United States in particular, to resort to the WTO dispute settlement procedures in their efforts to secure the benefits of these obligations.[90] The most important event so far has been the *China—Audiovisual Publications* case, decided on appeal to the WTO Appellate Body ('AB') in 2009.[91] In rejecting China's defence under the general exception provisions of GATT Article XX that discriminatory import controls were necessary to protect public morals, the AB found that China had failed to show that its discriminatory rules were 'necessary'.[92] The litigation probed but never directly addressed the more fundamental issue that these import restrictions are part and parcel of Communist Party rule in China.

Much of the current debate over the authority of the WTO concerns the AB's methods of assessing whether a State may legitimately shelter domestic measures that violate WTO trade disciplines under the general exception provisions of the GATT or the GATS.[93] This has become a critically important interface for the evolving relationship between trade disciplines and domestic, non-market public policy objectives, including the diverse policy goals at work in national media laws and regulations. Here, the AB has adapted elements of proportionality analysis from European law to create a method to address the 'necessity' condition that must be demonstrated before a State may invoke a public morals or public order exception. The current flexibility and uncertainty in how the AB's composite necessity test should be satisfied has given this supranational court powerful, but unpredictable, leverage over domestic public policy.[94]

China presents an extraordinary test for the development of these supervisory rules. China acceded to the organization as a one-party State, which means either that its WTO commitments should be interpreted in that light or that China's membership is essentially incompatible with the rules of the organization. On one level, this is simply a question about the wider consequences of particular legal obligations, which arises continually in relation to the trade disciplines of the GATT and GATS.[95] Where trade in media goods and services can be liberalized through specific trade commitments, a degree of increased political or social liberty may well follow. However, the questions of global public policy at issue in the expanding WTO legal regime are not the mere incidental effects of faithfully rendering textual language. China's membership has brought to the surface long

[90] *China—Publications and Audiovisual Entertainment Products* (n 87).

[91] *China—Publications and Audiovisual Entertainment Products* (n 87).

[92] *China—Publications and Audiovisual Entertainment Products* (n 87) paras 300–11. See GATT (n 79) art XX; See also GATS (n 81) art XIV.

[93] Shaffer and Trachtman (n 74); P Eeckhout, 'The Scales of Trade—Reflections on the Growth and Functions of the WTO Adjudicative Branch' (2010) 13 *Journal of International Economic Law* 3.

[94] Shaffer and Trachtman (n 74); see also M Du, 'Autonomy in Setting the Appropriate Level of Protection under the WTO Law: Rhetoric or Reality?' (2010) 13 *Journal of International Economic Law* 1077; and M Fakhri, 'Reconstruing WTO Legitimacy Debates' (2011) 64 *Notre Dame Journal of International and Comparative Law* 64.

[95] In relation to trade in cultural goods and services, see Keller (n 5) 471–7.

standing assumptions that WTO trade law is imbued not only with market-based economic values but also corresponding liberal democratic political ones.[96]

Plainly, that aspiration cannot include China in its current form, which is neither liberal nor democratic, and whose domestic political and legal order is not remotely juridically constitutionalized.[97] To pursue a vision of a unified global economy based on the liberty to own and trade property freely is moreover a particular strand within the wider liberal democratic tradition described above. As Robert Howse and Joanna Langille argue, the WTO currently risks imposing a secular, materialist, instrumentally rational worldview on its Member States, ignoring the point that the organization is founded on a fundamental acceptance of great moral, religious, and cultural diversity in the grounds on which WTO Members may legitimately regulate.[98] While they concede the necessity for any supranational regime to impose or locate boundaries for the legitimate conduct of its Member States within its sphere of competence, Howse and Langille see the WTO as a participant in a wider international public order in which human rights claims must be resolved, but not the arbiter of those claims.[99]

E. Conclusion

There is always a desire, especially in times as uncertain as the present, for legal scholarship not just to cast critical light over contemporary problems, but also to identify a conceptual framework to take us forward. Cosmopolitan constitutionalism satisfies that demand, describing a regional and even wider framework based on fundamental rights and supranational courts. In the sphere of public expression, constitutionalized supranational public order replaces the territorially bounded media–State relationship with a universal adherence to freedom of speech centred on open debate regarding public figures, affairs, and institutions. In the process the essential sovereignty of the State over its public information environment is shared, pooled or even dispersed.

Supranational constitutionalism, especially when imbued with cosmopolitan universalist aims, has however so far failed to offer a workable alternative to the

[96] There is a powerful intuitive sense to those assumptions, given the sensitivity of WTO judicial decision-making to the broader international community. See Shaffer and Trachtman (n 74) 103. On reconciling liberal democratic and other forms of State and society within the rules of the WTO, see C Wright, 'Censoring the Censors in the WTO: Reconciling the Communitarian and Human Rights Theories of International Law' (2010) *Journal of International Media and Entertainment Law* 17.

[97] G Zhu, 'Constitutional Review in China: An Unaccomplished Project or a Mirage?' (2010) 43 *Suffolk University Law Review* 625; S Zhu, 'The Party and the Courts', in R Peerenboom R (ed) *Judicial Independence in China: Lessons for Global Rule of Law Promotion* (CUP 2010) 63. On non-liberal democratic trends in contemporary Chinese political debate, see Q Jiang, D Bell, R Fan, and E Ryden (eds) *A Confucian Constitutional Order: How China's Ancient Past can Shape its Political Future* (Princeton University Press 2012).

[98] R Howse and J Langille, 'Permitting Pluralism: The Seal Products Dispute and Why the WTO Should Permit Trade Restrictions Justified by Non-Instrumental Moral Values' (2012) 37 *Yale Journal of International Law* 367.

[99] Howse and Langille (n 98).

State in resolving the key problems of public expression. Even amongst liberal democracies, there is no convergence towards a sufficiently thick set of values and principles necessary to ground a common supranational legal regime governing public expression. The division between economic and human rights law in regional and international law has also made it difficult for supranational courts to address the contentious link between economic and political liberty in relation to the media.

The communications revolution has certainly rendered national boundaries vastly more porous. States may have a long history of adapting successfully to new communications technologies and re-imposing their territorial boundaries on the global flow of information and ideas, but they have only achieved these successes through ever increasing technological inventiveness and financial costs. Nonetheless, the media–State relationship survives in part because territorially bounded, popular sovereignty expressed through the collective agency of the State remains the most effective legal and political form to address the ongoing challenges of the Internet era: notably including the role of public authority, the rules for co-existence for conflicting beliefs and values and, not least, the role of market forces.

There is consequently no overarching legal order capable of replacing this form of collective agency. Supranational constitutionalism will undoubtedly continue to grow in importance as multilateral cooperation expands to address regional and global problems, including the challenge to public authority and order from Internet-based expression that incites or causes violence and other harms.[100] The direct and indirect influence of supranational fundamental rights on domestic law, even in non-democracies like China, is likely to continue. Yet, once supranational law moves from broad generalities to specific confrontations between the liberty to speak and publish and the protection of individuals from harm or gross offence, it inevitably loses its universality and provides particular answers taken from the broader liberal democratic palette of ideas.

In the muddled evolution of national and supranational authority and law, networked relationships will continue to cross cut public and private institutions, diminishing their authority and capacities while also strengthening or creating new communities that challenge the authority and legitimacy of existing forms of public order. These ubiquitous networks of individuals and associations, catalysed by the communications revolution, are a powerful disruptive global force. They are however still far from offering platforms for collective agency capable of displacing the State or supranational regimes. Their largely commercial character not only limits their capacity to serve as neutral forums or the basis for collective agency, but renders them institutionally biased towards the argument that freedom of expression is both derived from and defined by market freedom. That bias may well signal the direction in which global debates over freedom of expression will continue to move. If there is any argument about the proper nature of free speech

[100] Trachtman (n 8).

that persists almost everywhere in the contemporary global patchwork of public and private order, it is some form of the instrumental, market-based understanding of liberty. Whether that is indeed an acceptable or appropriate common understanding of freedom of expression needs however to be addressed at the level of community and locality, where the consequences of liberty are experienced.

Index

absolutism 34, 42–4, 96, 150, 262–3
abuse of power 296, 300, 303–4
accountability
  democracy 297
  foreign affairs, conduct of 268
  government 12, 40
  institutions, acts of 266–7, 268
  multinational enterprises 291, 294, 295–9, 303
  new corporate accountability 295–9, 303
Ackerman, Bruce 246–7
Act of Settlement of 1700 89
Acts of Union of 1707 89–91
ad hoc and piecemeal development of British constitution 13–14, 99, 107–17, 119
administrative law 188, 202–3
advisory referendums 145
***Alabama* arbitration** 254–5, 267
Allan, Trevor 54–5, 87
ambiguities of sovereignty 39–40
Amsterdam Treaty 181
anachronism, sovereignty as an 36
Anglo-centricism 3, 7–9, 10
Anglo-Irish treaty 150
Annan, Kofi 297
area of freedom, security and justice (AFSJ), opt-outs from 165, 170–4
arrest 172, 174
assemblies or conventions 59, 148, 151, 157, 159–60, 163, 164
***Attorney General for New South Wales v Trethowan* (1931) 44 CLR 394** 66, 69, 84
Austin, John 2, 46
Australia 34, 66, 69, 84, 239, 268
Austria 199, 233, 314
authority
  absolutism 35, 43–4
  allocation 101–2
  claiming 12
  competing authorities 90
  concept of sovereignty 34–5, 38
  conservatism 27
  delegated authority 102–3
  EU restatements/models of sovereignty 14–15, 188–91, 197–201, 203–5, 208–9
  external sovereignty 27
  finality 20, 269–70, 278
  formal authority 269
  freedom of expression 307
  higher scale of authority, emergence of 25
  impersonal authority 20
  internal authority of the State 44–5
  internal sovereignty 27
  international law 15–16, 251–2
  late sovereignty 26–7
  legal authority 39–40, 42
  parliamentary sovereignty 30–2
  partial authority 24
  pluralism 26
  political authority 23–5, 38, 197–8
  potestas (exercise of rightful authority) 39–40, 42–3
  self-reproduction 26
  senior officials, consensus of 56–60
  systemic conservatism 27
  ultimate authority 44–7
  unlimited authority 50
autocracies 147
Aviation Directive and territorial extension
  Air Transport Association of America 274–5
  contingency in application 271, 272–3, 284
  customary international law 275
  Delhi Declaration 276
  developing countries 283
  EU Emissions Trading Scheme Prohibition Act 2011 (US) 274, 275–9, 282–5
  exemptions 272–3
  extraterritoriality 273–4
  ICAO 271–3, 276, 279, 281
  Kyoto Protocol 272
  lawfulness, litigation challenging 274–5, 278
  private ordering, role of 278–9
  reactions 274–7
  sanctions 279
  systematic non-reporting 276, 277
  territorial extension 16, 270–9, 282–5
  third country departing or arriving flights, application to 271–5, 277–9, 283–4
  treaties and conventions 275
  unilateral, as 271, 272–3, 284
  United States, enactment of blocking statute by 274, 275–9
***AXA General Insurance v Lord Advocate* [2011] UKSC 46** 68, 83–8

banks 209–11, 299, 304
Barroso, José Manual 186
Belfast Agreement 13–14, 120, 133–41, 157
Belgium 25, 232
Bentham, Jeremy 112–13
big society agenda 160
Bill of Rights of 1688 89–90, 227

bind its successors, parliament cannot
changes in constitution 104
common law 108–9
continuing sovereignty 71
Dicey 98
entrenchment 50
European Union 28, 183
grundnorms 70
Human Rights Act 1998 28
manner and form limitations 108
negative aspect (no body can trump Parliament) 91–3
procedure 54, 108
re-definition of parliamentary sovereignty 12–13, 68–88
referendums 67, 82
rule of law 13
rule of recognition 70
self-embracing sovereignty 54
substance 12–13, 69–82, 108
binding referendums 145, 150–1
Bingham, Tom (Lord Bingham of Cornhill) 95–6
bipolar sovereignty 12–13, 29, 71, 103, 237, 240–1, 249
Blackstone, William 115
Blair, Tony 157, 183
Bodin, Jean 20, 22, 39, 43
Bogdanor, Vernon 152–3
Bosnia and Herzegovina 221–3, 235
Bradley, AW 90, 92
Bratza, Nicolas 230, 232
Brazil 7–8, 25
BRIC (Brazil, Russia, India, and China) States 7–8, 25
British bill of rights, proposal for 121, 229
British constitution *see also* **parliamentary sovereignty**
ad hoc and piecemeal development 13–14, 99, 107–17, 119
changes 50–67, 98–103
claiming 11–12, 19
comparative analysis 98–119
constitutionalism 33, 50
democracy 55
designed constitutions 13–14, 99, 103–7, 111, 116–19
dualism 1
framing 11–12, 19
international law 1
interpretation 13–14, 116–19
judicial review, expansion of 100–1
Parliament Acts of 1911 and 1949 102–3
popular sovereignty 99
process of change 98–9
public law developments 99–103
Queen-in-Parliament 22
referendums 145
rule of law 95
rule of recognition 66
unwritten constitution, as 32, 50–2, 57, 66, 83, 97, 103–4
written constitutions 107
Brunner v TEU **[1994] 1 CMLR 57** 198, 201–2
Burke, Edmund 106, 111, 119
Bushell, AA 239–43, 245–6

Cabinet, cities and Mayor model of governance 161
Calman Commission 159
Cameron, David 121, 165–6, 175–7, 228, 233
Canada
Charter of Rights and Freedoms 65, 236, 239, 243–4, 246
dialogue 236–7, 239–46
free trade agreements 178
judicial review 65, 97
multinational enterprises 294
notwithstanding clauses 65
override clause 241, 243–4
quasi-federalism 25
capture of State 288
censorship 306
Central and Eastern Europe 5, 8, 175
central government *see* **government**
Charter 88 movement 107
Charter of Fundamental Rights of the EU 313
Chimini, BS 280
China 7–8, 25, 276, 307, 320–2
China-Measures affecting Trading Rights and Distribution Services for Certain Publications and Audiovisual Entertainment Products **WT/DS363/AB/R, (December 2009)** 320
church law 45
cities, Mayor and Cabinet model of governance 161
citizens
assemblies or conventions 59
European Union 186–7, 195–6, 207
civil society 16, 288, 296, 297–303
Claim of Right 4
claiming and framing 18–24, 29
classical-hierarchical sovereignty 15, 236–7
Clegg, Nick 184–5
climate change *see* **Aviation Directive and territorial extension**
codification 146–7, 149, 164
Cohn-Bendit v Ministre de l'Intérieure **[1980] 1 CMLR 543** 193
Cold War 310, 316
collective action 14, 24, 168, 173, 289–90
collective goods 190, 204
comity 293
Common Agricultural Policy (CAP) 176, 177
common fisheries policy (CFP) 177

common law
ad hoc and piecemeal development of British constitution 108–10
constitutionalism 29, 57–8
customary law 114–16
dialogue 237, 241
European Communities Act 1972 64–5
grundnorm 109–10
judicial construction of a constitution 60
judicial review 101
parliamentary sovereignty 29, 54–60, 71–2, 85–8, 95–6, 104, 108–9
United States Constitution 119
Commonwealth 3, 100
communal subsidiarity 288, 299–304
comparative analysis
British constitution 98–119
designed constitutions 103–7, 116–19
dialogue 236
EU restatements/models of sovereignty 14–15, 186–212
parliamentary sovereignty 98–119
competition 180–1, 291, 294
***Concept of Law, The*. Hart, HLA** 2
concept of sovereignty 34–49
abandonment of concept 35–7, 40, 48–9
absolutism 34–5
abstract entity of the State 34
academic writings 35–7
adjective qualifiers, increase in 37
anachronism, sovereignty as an 36
authority 34–5, 38
confusion over sovereignty 35–42
constituent people, differentiation from 34
constitutionalism, federalism, rights and other values, incompatibility with 35
contested concept, sovereignty as 12, 38
de jure sovereignty 36–7
divine law 34
erosion of sovereignty 48–9
European Union 45–7, 48
external sovereignty 12, 34, 36–7
framing 11–12, 21, 22
function of concept 34–5
globalization 12
government
power 35–6, 38–40, 42
sovereignty distinguished from 38–40, 48
governmentality 123–4
higher authority, lack of 34
institutions 34
internal sovereignty 12, 34, 36–7
international concepts of sovereignty 252–5
interpretive theory of law 53, 54–7
judiciary 54–5, 56
language, misuse of 38
legal dimension 35–8, 40–4, 47–8
modernity 35
natural law 34
negative conceptions of sovereignty 36–7
office-holders, differentiation from 34
parliamentary sovereignty 52–7
political dimension 35, 36–8, 43–4
positive conceptions of sovereignty 36–7
public law 35–6, 42, 49
reciprocity of State and sovereignty 34
socio-economic change 37–8
sovereign, concept of 42–5, 47–8
sovereignty-in-practice 37
sovereignty-in-principle 37
State-centred view 12
supremacy 34
temporalization 37
territorial communities, existence of 12
ultimate source of law, State as 34
use of term, abandonment of 35–7, 40, 48–9
usefulness of term 11–12, 21, 22
Western rationalism 34
conferred powers, doctrine of 203–4
conflict of laws 288, 292
consent 12, 115, 140, 262–6
conservatism 27, 198
Constitution Act 1916 (Queensland) 51
constitutional crises 72, 88
***Constitutional Dialogues*. Fisher, Louis** 242, 247
constitutional long-stop 13
constitutional referendums 146–8, 164, 167
constitutional sovereignty 15, 213–16, 235
constitutionalism
absolutism 35
common law 29, 57–8
cosmopolitanism 312–13, 316
government power, sovereignty confused with 35
institutions 41
judicial review 95
legal constitutionalism 55
living constitutionalism 118–19
new constitutionalism 163
parliamentary sovereignty 29, 32–3, 50, 95
politics 55
positivism 55
referendums 163
supranationalism 16, 310–12, 318, 322–3
unknowable, rules as 112–13
constitutions *see also* **British constitution; written constitutions**
amendments 223
constituted authorities 43–4
Constitutional Treaty (EU), failure of 8
designed constitutions 13–14, 99, 103–7, 111, 116–19
European Court of Human Rights 221–3
evolutionary constitutions 13–14, 99, 107–13
hierarchy 82
internal sovereignty 2

constitutions (*cont.*):
Ireland 150
legal dimension to political dimension, relation of 40–1
Lithuania 187
preambles 106
procedure for making constitutions 104
rule-making event, constitution-making as 99
Scotland Act 1998 as a constitution 152–3, 157–8
United States 13–14, 22, 33, 105, 117–18, 216, 241–2
contested concept, sovereignty as a 12, 17, 38
contingent unilateralism 273, 284
continuing sovereignty 12–13, 50–1, 71, 183–4
continuity and change 9–11, 15–16
conventions or assemblies 59, 148, 151, 157, 159–60, 163, 164
corporate law theory 289
corporate social responsibility (CSR) 300–1, 303
corporatization 43
cosmopolitanism 42, 312–13, 316
council tax increases 161–3
credit unions 304
criminal justice 14, 165, 171–2, 195–6
Cromwell, Oliver 107
culture 13–14, 25, 27, 137–8, 322
customary law 54, 57–61, 112, 114–16, 258, 259–61, 275 *see also* ***pacta sunt servanda***
customs unions 177, 179
Cybercrime Convention, Protocol to 316
Czech Republic 191, 202–3

Damages (Asbestos-related Conditions) (Scotland) Act 2009 83–8, 93
Davies, John 114–15
Dawkins, Richard 111
Dayton Agreement 221–3, 235
de facto **sovereignty** 1, 36–7
De Gaulle, Charles 147
de jure **sovereignty** 1, 36–7
death penalty 268
decentralization 37, 160
decentring of the State 19, 24, 128
declarations of incompatibility 101, 245, 249–50
definition of parliamentary sovereignty *see* **parliamentary sovereignty, re-definition of**
definition of sovereignty 1–3, 11–12, 18–19
delegated authority 103
Delhi Declaration 276
Delors, Jacques 181, 186
democracy
accountability 297
deficit 302
dialogue 15, 238–40, 249
European Court of Human Rights 219–20, 225, 232, 234
European Union 169–70, 175, 295
Euroscepticism 175
restatements/models of sovereignty 14–15, 188, 198, 201–8, 211
legislative sovereignty 81–2
local government 160–3
majoritarian democracies 312–13
multinational enterprises 296–7
Parliament Acts 1911 and 1949 76
parliamentary sovereignty 55, 82–3
pluralism 295
plurinational democracies 10–11
politics and law, divide between 82–3
popular sovereignty 295–6, 300
prisoners' voting rights 225
referendums 16–4, 167, 169–70
representative democracy, role of 147–8, 163
rule of law 97
rules of change 57–8
Denmark 175, 203
designed constitutions 13–14, 99, 103–7, 116–19
developing countries 279–80, 283, 294, 301–2
devolution
ad hoc and piecemeal development of British constitution 107
Devolution Max 154, 159
England 122, 155–6
Foucault 123, 142
governance 141–3
non-sovereignty 13–14, 123, 141–4
Northern Ireland 8, 28–9, 122–3, 149–50, 152
parliamentary sovereignty 93
persistence of sovereignty 121–3
popular sovereignty 156–60
process not an event, as 122
referendums 8, 14, 113–14, 142, 148–63
Scotland 8, 28–9, 122–3, 142–3, 151–2, 154, 157–9
self-determination 142
State sovereignty 299
Wales 8, 28–9, 122, 142–3, 155–8
Dewar, Donald 157
dialogue 236–50
bipolarity 237, 240–1, 249
classical-hierarchical sovereignty 15, 236–7
common law 237, 241
comparative analysis 236
definition of dialogue 236, 238–9, 247
democratic dialogue 15, 238–40, 249
formal mechanisms 15, 236–7, 240–1, 243–50
government 119
hierarchical vision of sovereignty 15, 237–8, 246–9

Human Rights Act 1998 236–7, 244–6, 249–50
implied forms 15, 236–7, 241–6, 249
interpretation 119, 242, 244–5, 247, 249
judicial review of legislation 15, 240, 242, 249
judiciary 9, 15, 119, 236, 240, 245–7
legal decision-making 15
legislative supremacy 246
limitation clauses 237, 243–4, 249
mechanisms 237, 240–3
multiple-member processes 242, 246, 249
multiple forms of dialogue 248–9
network analyses of decision-making 15, 236, 246–8
override clauses 15, 237, 241, 243, 245, 248–50
parliamentary sovereignty 237–40
political decision-making 15
political dialogue 237, 240–1, 245–50
political sovereignty 15, 236–8
power-allocation 15
rule of law 238
social ordering 238
State sovereignty 15, 236, 238
structural arrangements 15, 236–7, 240–3
United States 236–7, 239, 241–4, 247–8
Dicey and parliamentary sovereignty
absolutism 149–50
Acts of Union 149, 151
Anglo-centricity 3–4, 7, 9–10
bind its successors, Parliament cannot 1, 13, 28, 62–3, 68–9, 82, 91–4, 98–100, 108
common law 95
definition of parliamentary sovereignty 104
European Union 99–100, 165
highest form of law, Parliament's pronouncements of 252
Ireland 149–50
legislative supremacy 2, 10
nation-state, role of 121
negative aspect (no body can trump Parliament) 92, 98
parliamentary sovereignty 82, 89, 252
persistence of parliamentary sovereignty 121
reciprocity between State and sovereignty 6
re-definition of parliamentary sovereignty 68–9, 92
rule of law 96
Scotland 149, 151
Unionism 3
dignity 194, 197–8, 203–6, 308, 315, 317
direct effect 180–1, 189, 193
Discipline and Punish. **Foucault, Michel** 125
discrimination 136, 138–9, 177–8, 221–3, 235, 319–21
distributional justice 16, 295, 300–1
divided sovereignty 37, 46, 252
divine law 34
division of sovereignty 20, 37, 39, 43, 45–6, 48, 238, 252
Dred Scott v Sandford **60 US (19 How) 393 (1857)** 117
dualism 1, 131
duration of Parliament 89
Dworkin, Ronald 41, 53–7

East Timor Case (Portugal v Australia) **ICJ Reports, 1995** 264
Eastern Europe 5, 8, 175
economics
economic liberties 16, 117
European Union 177, 179–84
globalization 7
government 7
market economics 111
marketization of public economic functions 302
power 287–9
transnationalism 27
EEA (European Economic Area) 177, 179
EEIGs (European Economic Interest Groupings) 294
elections *see also* **voting**
elective dictatorship 94
Electoral Commission 146, 154–5
franchise 148, 155–6
referendums 148, 155–6
reform 114
Scotland 146, 154–5
emissions trading *see* **Aviation Directive and territorial extension**
empiricism 45–6
employment
European Union 176–7, 178, 181–2
labour rights 286, 301
Northern Ireland 139
policy 176–7, 178, 181–2
works council 303
England
devolution 122, 155–6
failure to consult on referendums 155–6
local government 14, 145, 158, 160–4
referendums 155–6, 158, 160–4
entrenchment
absolute majority requirement 61, 63
amendment or repeal, protection from inadvertent 61–4
bind its successors, Parliament cannot 50
controversial bills to public attention, bringing 61
customary law 60–1
European Communities Act 1972 64–5
examples of requirements 61
express repeal requirements 64–6
functions of two Houses, differentiation between 61

entrenchment (*cont.*):
implied repeal doctrine 62–3, 64–5
interpretive rule 64
judicial oaths, by modified 110
notwithstanding clauses 61, 65
Parliament Acts 1911 and 1949 60, 63
parliamentary sovereignty 12, 50–1, 58–65
purposes of form requirements 61
quorum requirement 61, 63
referendums 65–6
revolution 59
self-entrenchment 62–4
Standing Orders of HC and HL 60, 63
substantive continuing sovereignty 62–3, 65
super majority requirements 61–2
symmetric entrenchment 65
environment *see also* **Aviation Directive and territorial extension**
European Union 182
Forest Stewardship Council 302
marketization of public economic functions 302
multinational enterprises 296, 298, 301–2
political parties 298
production process methods 280
epistemology 21, 22, 26, 40, 55, 238
equality of States 214, 254–5
ESM Treaty Temporary Injunction (German Constitutional Court, 12 September 2012) Case 2 BvR 1390/12 et al 207–8, 211
Estonia 191, 202–3
ethics *see* **morality**
ethnic or cultural homogeneity 25
EU law *see* **EU restatements/models of sovereignty; European Union**
EU restatements/models of sovereignty 186–212
administrative law, sovereignty as EU 188, 202–3
authority 14–15, 188–91, 197–201, 203–5, 208–9
citizens 186–7, 195–8, 207
collective goods 190, 204
comparative study 14–15, 186–212
conferred powers, doctrine of 203–4
Court of Justice 196, 199, 205–6, 210
criminal justice, organological qualities of 195–6
democracy 14–15, 188, 198, 201–8, 211
dignity and acclaim 194, 197–8, 203–6
direct effect 189, 193
European Freedom and Democracy political grouping, Charter of 186–7
Eurozone crisis, official responses to 14–15
formalization and ring-fencing of human order 195–9
fragmentation of political agency 190
fungible, sovereignty as 188–9
government 14–15, 198–9, 201–2, 206–12
human order protected from EU law, sovereignty as 14–15, 187, 192–200, 203
human rights 14–15, 196, 199, 203–4
institutions 187–9, 192–5, 200, 202–10
integration 186, 188, 207, 210–11
interpretation 205–6
justification of sovereignty as counterpoint to EU government 187, 188–91
legitimation strategy, sovereignty as a 14–15, 188
limited powers, doctrine of 202, 206
Lisbon Treaty 206
lived experience, human order as 194, 198
Maastricht Treaty 192, 195, 201, 203
manner of justification 191
members of political community 210–11
national parliaments, active involvement of 188, 207
ordaining government, sovereignty as 14–15, 188, 200–6
organology 194–6
political authority, dignity and singularity of 197–8
property of States, sovereignty as 186–7
proportionality 203
public and collective activities making up domestic human order 14–15, 187
regulation 205
rule of law 189
Schmitt 14–15, 208–11
self-government 186, 188
social policy, qualities of 195–6
State sovereignty 189, 191–4, 202–4
subsidiarity 204
supremacy of EU law 187, 188–9, 206
temporal persistence of sovereignty 194, 196
territory, dignity and singularity of 197–8
transferable, sovereignty as 188–9, 201
use of term sovereignty 186
value of sovereignty 187, 189–91
Van Gend en Loos 188–9
European Arrest Warrant (EAW) 172, 174
European Central Bank (ECB) 209–10
European Communities Act 1972
ad hoc and piecemeal development of British constitution 110
common law 64–5
constitutional statute, as 64–5
entrenchment 64–5
Factortame No 2 case 4–5
parliamentary sovereignty 68, 93
repeal or amendment 100, 252–3
supremacy of EU law 3, 99–100, 110
European Convention on Human Rights *see also* **European Court of Human Rights**
Conservative Party 168
European Commission of Human Rights 216–17
European Court of Human Rights 213, 216
freedom of expression 313–17

Human Rights Act 1998 93, 121
interpretation 314–15
judicial review 4, 94
living instrument, as a 217
manner and form doctrine 70, 77
obligations imposed on States within own territories 267
parliamentary sovereignty 28–9, 70
Preamble 231
referendums 70, 164, 168

European Court of Human Rights 6, 213–35
adverse decisions 217
backlog of cases 230
Brighton Declaration 2012 230–2
Committee of Ministers of the Council of Europe 216–17
constitutional and other norms, distinguishing between 215
constitutional sovereignty 15, 213–16, 235
constitutions 221–3
democracy 219–20, 225, 232, 234
discrimination 221–3, 235
dispute resolution 214
effectiveness 15
equality of States 214
European Convention on Human Rights 213, 216
exhaustion of local remedies 231–2
final judgments, abiding by 218
freedom of expression 16, 313–17
implementation of judgments 217, 230
individual petitions 216–18, 230
institutions 213, 220, 235
internal affairs of other States, non-intervention in 214
internal structures 213–15, 224
international law 15, 213–16, 218–19, 221–4, 234–5
Internet 16, 313–17
interpretation 217, 220, 230–1, 234
inter-State institutions 214
jurisdiction 216–18
justification for interference 221–3, 231, 235
legislative sovereignty 15, 213–16, 223–35
legitimacy 15, 219–20
manifestly ill-founded applications 231
margin of appreciation 220–3, 226, 231–3
morally sound concerns of national government 15, 234–5
national authorities, tension with 15, 213, 215, 220
national constitutions 221–3
obligation of States to take action 218–19
pacta sunt servanda 214–15, 218
petitions 216
prisoners' voting rights 217, 224–30, 232–5
procedural rules 218
proportionality 223, 226–8, 233
Protocol No 11 218
protocols 216–18, 222
public hearings 216
reverse process 15, 213
Security Council (UN) 235
socially persuasive concerns of national government 15, 234–5
State sovereignty 15, 213–21, 234
States, petitions from 216
subsidiarity 231
supra-State institutions 214, 235
territorial reach 217
time limits 231

European Economic Area (EEA) 177, 179

European Freedom and Democracy political grouping, Charter of 186–7

European Stability Mechanism (ESM) 202–3, 205, 207–11

***European Stability Mechanism Treaty* Case 3-4-1-6-12 (Estonia)** 202–3

European Union 165–85, 237 *see also* **Aviation Directive and territorial extension; EU restatements/models of sovereignty; European Communities Act 1972; Euroscepticism**
accession 5, 8, 113–14
Anglo-centricity 7
Amsterdam Treaty 181
area of freedom, security and justice, opt-outs from 165, 170–4
autonomy 173–4
backlash against EU 170
bind its successors, Parliament cannot 28, 183
central role of member states 14
Charter of Fundamental Rights of the EU 313
Coalition Government 165–85
collective action 24
common fisheries policy, reform of 177
competences 8, 47
competition 180–1, 294
concept of sovereignty 45–7, 48
Conservative Party 165–85
Constitutional Treaty, failure of 8
continuing sovereignty 183–4
Court of Justice 46–7, 171, 173
criminal justice powers, repatriation of 14, 165, 171–2
customary international law 260
customs union relationships 177, 179
decentring of sovereignty 120
democracy 169–70, 175, 295
dialogue 237
direct effect 180–1
discrimination against non-Eurozone member interests 177–8
divided sovereignty 46
economic sphere 177, 179–84
employment policy 176–7, 178, 181–2
environmental policy 182
European Arrest Warrant 172, 174

European Union (*cont.*):
European Economic Area, joining the 177, 179
Europol 174
Eurozone 7, 8
external sovereignty 31, 45
extradition 174
federalism 46–7
financial services legislation, emergency brake for 176
foreign and security policy, cooperation in 173
foreign direct investment 177
free trade agreements, negotiating 177–8, 179
freedom of expression 316, 320
Fresh Start Group 172
future of UK involvement 121–2
giving power referendums 165–70
global financial crisis 7, 8
globalization 17
government 4, 46–7
in/out referendum, proposal for 14, 168–9
integration 10–11, 17, 175, 180–1
internal sovereignty 31, 45–6
judicial sphere, developments in 11
judicial review 94
legal dimension to political dimension, relation of 45, 48
Lisbon Treaty 8, 165–6, 170–7, 183
Maastricht Treaty 73–6, 172–3, 181, 192, 195, 201, 203
member states and EU, relations between 45
national interest 173–4
new legal order 46–7
opt-outs 165, 170–8, 183
parliamentary sovereignty 28–9, 31–2
police and judicial cooperation in criminal matters 171–2, 177
police powers, repatriation of 165
politico-legislative sphere, developments in 11
politics 172, 178–9, 183–5
popular sovereignty 8, 169, 295
positivism 45–6
post-sovereignty 45, 294–5
preliminary rulings 171
public law 45–6
ratification process 73–6
realists 45
referendums 14, 74–6, 147–8, 164–70, 175–84
regional autonomy 26
regulation 205, 277
repatriation of power 14, 165, 168–84
Rome Treaty 180–2
Second Pillars 183
seizure of goods in transit 281–3
single currency 7
Single Market programme 5, 177–82
social sphere 176–7, 178–84
State sovereignty, withering of 17
Strasbourg seat of European Parliament, Economic and Social Committee and Committee of the Regions, abolition of 177
Structural Funds 181
subsidiarity 5–6
substate nations 26
supremacy of EU law 3, 26–7, 99–100, 110, 167, 180–1, 187–9, 206, 252–3
territorial exclusivity 26–7
territorial extension 16, 270–85
Third Pillars 171, 183
Treaty on the Functioning of the EU 73–6
Treaty renegotiation, political reality of 178–9
ultimate authority 46–7
welfare policy 182
withdrawal, possibility of 46–7
European Union Act 2011 165–70, 183
contextual approach 76
executive, limiting powers of 74
genesis of legislation 165–6
notwithstanding clauses 76
parliamentary sovereignty 68, 73–4
procedure, binding Parliament through 73–6
ratification, definition of 74
referendums 74–6, 114, 148, 165–70
restrictive procedures 74–6
Select Committee on the Constitution 169
statutory interpretation 74–6
Europol 174
Euroscepticism 5, 14, 175–85
Central and Eastern Europe 175
democracy 175
Denmark 175
France 175
Fresh Start Group 172, 176–84
Germany 175
information deficit 175–6
integration 175
referendums 165–6, 170–4
repatriation of power 176
varieties 175–6
Eurozone 7, 8, 14–15
evolutionary constitutions 13–14, 99, 107–17, 119
executive *see also* **government**
delegation 84–5
dialogue 237
elections 94
European Act 2011 74
Northern Ireland 135, 137, 139–40
Parliament Acts 1911 and 1949 82
parliamentary sovereignty 94–5, 97
exhaustion of local remedies 231–2

expression, freedom of *see* **Internet and freedom of expression**
extension of territory *see* **territorial extension**
external sovereignty
authority 27
concept of sovereignty 12, 34, 36–7
dualism 1
European Union 31, 45
hierarchy of sources of law-making 31
internal sovereignty 2, 10–12, 27, 31, 36–7
international courts 11
judicial challenges 11
legal dimension 45
overlap, interlock, and mutual interference 24
parliamentary sovereignty 31–2
political dimension 45
post-Westphalian age 24
regional courts 11
sovereign States, relationship between 2
written constitutions 31
extradition 174
extraterritoriality
Aviation Directive 273–4
international law 15–16, 288
multinational enterprises 288, 292, 293–4
regulation 293–4
territorial extension 270, 285
United States 285

Factortame **litigation** 4–5, 64, 110
fairness 14, 101
Faurisson v France **Comm No 550/1993, UN Doc CCPR/C/58/D/550/1993, 8 November 1996** 318
federalism 25–6, 35, 39, 42, 46–7, 151–2, 252, 268
Federalist Papers 105
financial services legislation 176
financialization 303–4
Fisher, Louis 242, 247
'fit' criterion 55–6
foreign and security policy, cooperation in 173
foreign direct investment (FDI) 177, 293
foreign direct liability litigation 301–2
Foucault, Michel 120–1, 123–32, 142
foundational constitutionalism 23, 30
founding norms 41–2
fragmented sovereignty 6, 18, 37, 187
framing and claiming 18–24, 29
France
eighteenth-century constitutional settlement 19
direct effect 193
droit politique 44
EU restatements/models of sovereignty 193, 200–1
Euroscepticism 175
incorporation 290
language 23
Multilateral Agreement on Investment 286–7
national sovereignty 22
ordre public 193
popular sovereignty 22
referendums 147
franchise 148, 155–6
free trade agreements (FTAs), negotiating 177–8, 179
freedom as sovereignty 191
freedom of expression *see* **Internet and freedom of expression**
freedom, security and justice (AFSJ), area of 165, 170–4
Fresh Start Group 172
Friedman, Barry 242, 247–8
Frodl v Austria **(2010) 52 EHRR 267** 233
Frontini v Ministero delle Finanze [1974] 2 **CLMR 372** 192–3
fundamental rights *see* **human rights**

General Agreement on Tariffs and Trade (GATT) (WTO) 319–21
General Agreement on Trade in Services (GATS) 319–21
genocide 267
Germany
European Union 47, 191, 193, 198, 201, 203, 205–8, 211
European Stability Mechanism 207–8, 211
Euroscepticism 175
restatements/models of sovereignty 191, 193, 198, 201, 203, 205–8, 211
federalism 25
freedom as sovereignty 191
human rights 203
judicial review 97
language 23
Nazi Germany 291
Staatsrecht 44
Ghadian v Godin-Mendoza [2004] **UKHL 30** 102, 122
giving power referendums 165–70
global financial crisis 7, 8
globalization
claiming 11–12, 19
classical international law 9
concept of sovereignty 12
decentring of sovereignty 120
European Union 17
framing 11–12, 19
identity 10
multinational enterprises 286–7, 301
State sovereignty 299
territorial extension 269
World Trade Organization 286
Goldsworthy, Jeffrey 69–70, 72–3, 75–81, 97

Good Friday Agreement 13–14, 120, 133–41, 157
Governance of Britain **Green Paper** 228
government *see also* **executive; governmentality; local government**
ability to govern 39–40
absolute authority 43–4
acclaim 204
accountability 12, 40
conflation with sovereignty 6
constitutionalism 35
constraints 198–9
dialogue 119
division of sovereignty 39
economic globalization 7
erosion of sovereignty 48–9
European Union 4
federalism 35, 39
fluidity and interconnectedness of governmental relations 19
historical distinction between sovereignty and government 191
human order 198–9, 201–2
institutions 43–6
judiciary 119
marks of sovereignty 38–9
ordaining government, sovereignty as 14–15, 188, 200–6
parliamentary sovereignty 60
potentia (actual ability to govern) 39–40
potestas (exercise of rightful authority) 39–40, 42–3
power 28, 35–6, 38–40, 42, 47
prior to government, sovereignty as 21
public law 39–40
right to govern 39
socio-economic changes 38
sovereignty distinguished 35–6, 38–40, 46–8
unity 38–9
Government of Ireland Act 1920 150
Government of Wales Act 1998 158
Government of Wales Act 2006 158, 159–60
governmentality 123–9
analytics of government 126
concept of sovereignty 123–4
decentring the State 128
Foucault 121, 124–9
governmentalization of the State 124
institutions 124–8
non-sovereignty 125–31
Northern Ireland 13–14, 133–41
post-sovereignty 125–9
power relations 127–31
State, theories of the 126–7
technologies of power 120, 124–6, 132
use of concept of sovereignty 124
gradualism 59–60
Greens and MT v United Kingdom **(2011) 53 EHRR 21** 229
Grieve, Dominic 233
Grotius, Hugo 20
grundnorm 70, 109–10
Guiding Principles on Business and Human Rights. **Human Rights Council (UN)** 300–3

Hadfield, B 150, 153
Hague, William 176
Hailsham of St Marylebone, Lord (Hogg, Quintin) 94
Hale, Matthew 114
Hamilton, Alexander 112
Harris v Minister for the Interior **[1952] 1 TLR 1245** 69, 84
Hart, HLA 1–11, 54, 57, 70–1, 251, 268
hate speech 306, 315–19
Hayek, Friedrich 106, 111, 180, 181
hereditary peers, abolition of 91
Hertogen, A 284
Heuston, RFV 69
hierarchy 15, 31, 82, 216, 237–8, 246–9
Hirst v United Kingdom **(2004) 38 EHRR 40** 229, 232–3
Hirst v United Kingdom (No 2) **(2005) 42 EHRR 41** 228–9, 232–3
historicization of natural law 43–4
Hobbes, Thomas 20, 130
Hoffmann, Leonard (Lord Hoffmann) 142
Hogg, PW 239–43, 245–6
Holmes, Oliver Wendell 115, 118–19
Holocaust denial 315–16
home rule 14, 150
Honeywell **(German Constitutional Court, 6 July 2010) Decision 2 BvR 2661/06** 206
Huber, Max 253–4, 267
human order 14–15, 187, 192–200, 203
human rights *see also* **European Convention on Human Rights; European Court of Human Rights; Human Rights Act 1998; Internet and freedom of expression**
Canadian Charter of Rights and Freedoms 65, 236, 239, 243–4, 246
Charter of Fundamental Rights of the EU 313
EU restatements/models of sovereignty 14–15, 196, 199, 203–4
Human Rights Committee (UN) 16, 317–18
Guiding Principles on Business and Human Rights. Human Rights Council (UN) 300–3
institutions 24
International Covenant on Civil and Political Rights 16, 225, 233, 267, 317–18
international law 7, 256
interpretation 31
jurisdiction 264–6

multinational enterprises 16, 286, 288, 300–3
parliamentary sovereignty 28, 31, 87–8
privacy 117
Scotland 143
Wales 143

Human Rights Act 1998
alternative law-making procedure 78
bind its successors, Parliament cannot 28
British Bill of Rights, proposal to replace with 121, 229
Canada 236, 239, 243–4, 246
constitutional allocation of authority 101–2
declarations of incompatibility 101, 245, 249–50
dialogue 236–7, 244–6, 249–50
European Convention on Human Rights 93, 121
express repeal requirements 65
judicial review 8
jurisprudence 101–2
parliamentary sovereignty 28, 68, 78
reading in 102
remedial orders 245
repeal 102, 228–9
statements of compatibility 78
statutory interpretation 102

***Human Rights Guidelines for Companies.* Amnesty International** 286
human security 7
Hume, David 112
Hungary 203, 205–6
Hunting Act 2004 95

ICAO (International Civil Aviation Organization) 271–3, 276, 279, 281
identity 10, 13–14, 24–5, 137–8
***IHT v Einfuhr und Vorratsstelle für Getreide und Futtermittel* [1974] 2 CMLR 540** 193
***Imperial Tobacco v Lord Advocate* [2012] CSIH 9** 122–3
implied repeal doctrine 51, 62–3, 64–5, 79–80
India 7–8, 25, 178, 276
individuals
European Court of Human Rights, petitions to 216–18, 230
human rights 216–18, 230, 256
international humanitarian law 256
international law 256
regulation of actions 70, 77
industrial investment banks 304
information and communications technology (ICT) 7 *see also* **Internet and freedom of expression**
institutions
absolute authority 43–4
accountability 266–7, 268
allocation of tasks 44–5, 48, 266–8
balance of power 12–13, 82, 88
concept of sovereignty 34
constituted authorities 43–4
constitutionalism 41
contractarianism 16
decentring of the State 24
diversity 28
EU restatements/models of sovereignty 187–9, 192–5, 200, 202–10
European Court of Human Rights 213–14, 220, 235
government 43–6
governmentality 124–8
human rights 24
institutionalization 30
international law 7
legitimacy 220
marginalization 147–8
multinational enterprises 287
Northern Ireland 135–6
pluralism 5
popular sovereignty 30
positivism 287
referendums 147–8
regions 24
security, provision of 24
State, accountability of the 266–7, 268
supra-State institutions 214, 235
technologies of power 124
transnationalism 27

Instrument of Government 107
instrumentality of law 43–4
inter-connection 16, 269, 281 *see also* **Internet; Internet and freedom of expression**
internal affairs of other States, non-intervention in 214
internal sovereignty
accountability 266–8
authority 24, 27
comprehensive, sovereignty as 24
concept of sovereignty 12, 34, 36–7
constitutions 1
dualism 1
European Union 45–6
external sovereignty 2, 10–12, 27, 31, 36–7
extraterritoriality 267–8
federal states 268
hierarchy of sources of law-making 31
institutions, allocation of power between 266–8
international courts 11
international law 15–16, 251–5, 266–8
judicial challenge 11
legal dimension 45
obligations imposed on States within own territories 267
parliamentary sovereignty 31–2, 78
partial authority 24
political dimension 45

internal sovereignty (*cont.*):
post-Westphalian age 24
regional courts 11
territorial jurisdiction 266–7
International Atomic Energy Agency (IAEA) 24
International Civil Aviation Organization (ICAO) 271–3, 276, 279, 281
international concepts of sovereignty 252–5
International Court of Justice (ICJ) 264–5, 268
International Covenant on Civil and Political Rights (ICCPR) 16, 225, 233, 267, 317–18
International Criminal Court (ICC) 265
International Criminal Tribunal for Rwanda (ICTR) 265
International Criminal Tribunal for the former Yugoslavia (ICTY) 265
international humanitarian law 214, 256
international law 1–2, 251–68
adjudication, missing element of 2
allocation of power between States 15–16, 253, 255
authority within and between States 15–16, 251–2
centralized sanctions, missing element of 2
classical international law 9
continuity and change 15–16
cosmopolitan theory 42
customary international law 258, 259–61
dualism 1
equality of States 254–6
European Court of Human Rights 213–16, 218–19, 221–4, 234–5
extraterritoriality 15–16, 288
federal states, division of sovereignty in 252
founding norms 41–2
global environment 7
human rights 310–13, 315–18, 322–3
human security 7
individuals, rights and duties of 256
institutions, development of 7
internal sovereignty within the State 15–16, 251–5, 266–8
international concepts of sovereignty 252–5
international organizations 255–6
jurisdiction, effect of State sovereignty on 15–16, 262–6
jus cogens 261
legislation, missing element of 2
limitations of sovereignty 44–5, 48
marginalization 45
missing or limited elements 2
monism 41
multinational enterprises 288, 292
parliamentary sovereignty 93
popular sovereignty 252–3
power within and between States 15–16, 251–2
realism 45
State-centred approach 3–4
State, law of a 41–2
State sovereignty 41, 251–5, 258–62
substance of international law, effect of State sovereignty on 15–16, 251–2, 255–62
territorial sovereignty 253–4
treaties and conventions 258–61
United Nations 256–8
United States 253–5, 258
written constitutions 252
international organizations *see also* **particular organizations**
constituent treaties 256
subjects of international law 255–6
Internet 7, 24, 298 *see also* **Internet and freedom of expression**
Internet and freedom of expression 305–24
authority 307
bonded territorial and popular sovereignty 16
bounded communities 309
censorship 306
Charter of Fundamental Rights of the EU 313
child pornography 311
chilling effect of foreign restrictions 319
China 307, 320–2
collective agency 309, 323
collective sovereignty 313
community and locality, importance of 16
control and restrictions 305–24
cosmopolitan constitutionalism 312–13, 316
cultural diversity 322
definition 310–16
discrimination 319–21
diversity of freedom of expression 307–10
European Convention on Human Rights 313–17
European Court of Human Rights 16, 313–17
European freedom of expression, defining 310–16
European Union 316, 320
GATS 319, 321
GATT 319–21
global communications revolution 16, 305–7, 323
harm 307–9, 313, 317–18
hate speech 306, 315–19
hierarchy 314
historic relationship between media and State 305–7, 312
Human Rights Committee (UN) 16, 317–18
inter-governmental cooperation 311
International Covenant on Civil and Political Rights 317–18
international human rights law 310–11, 313, 315–18, 322–3

international law 312, 316–17
interpretation 312–18
legitimacy 306, 307–8, 312–13, 323
liberal democratic states 16, 307–13, 316–17, 322–3
liberalization of trade 318–22
majoritarian democracies 312–13
margin of appreciation 314, 317
national boundaries 306–7
necessity 312, 314, 317–18, 320–1
networked communities 309
offensive speech 309, 313–19
pluralism 312–13
popular sovereignty 16, 307, 312
pornography 306, 311, 314
private information, disclosure of 306
proportionality 312, 314, 317–18, 321
protected sphere 311
public interest 314
public order 307, 310–13, 316–22
religion 314
State sovereignty 306–7, 322
supranational constitutionalism 16, 310–12, 318, 322–3
territorial sovereignty 16, 306–7, 312, 322–3
tolerance 308, 315
United Nations 316
United States 310–11, 315–19, 321
Universal Declaration of Human Rights 317
universalism 309–10, 312–14, 322–3
violent imagery 306, 311, 314
World Trade Organization 16, 318–22

Internet Corporation for Assigned Names and Numbers (ICANN) 24

interpretation
amendment or repeal, protection from inadvertent 80
content of law, disagreements on 55–6
designed constitutions 13–14, 116–19
dialogue 119, 242, 244–5, 247, 249
EU restatements/models of sovereignty 205–6
European Convention on Human Rights 314–15
European Court of Human Rights 217, 220, 230–1, 234
European Union 74–6, 196, 205–6
'fit' criterion 55–6
freedom of expression 312–18
human rights 31, 102, 217, 220, 230–1, 234, 314–18
Human Rights Act 1998 102
intention of Parliament 31
International Covenant on Civil and Political Rights 317–18
interpretive rule 64
judicial review 8, 31
jurisdiction 266
legality, principle of 87
living constitutionalism 118–19
Northern Ireland 135
objectivity 54–5, 56
official consensus 56–7
originalism 117–18
Parliament Acts 1911 and 1949 95
parliamentary sovereignty 13–14, 28, 31, 53, 54–7, 71–2, 116–19
Pepper v Hart 227
positivism 56–7
reading in 102
referendums 122–3
Scotland Act 1998 85–6, 122–3
treaties and conventions 266
United States 13–14, 117–18, 242, 244
written constitutions 13–14, 116–19

investment 177, 264–5, 286–7, 293

Iraq 265

Ireland
Anglo-Irish treaty 150
Constitution 150
Government of Ireland Act 1920 150
home rule 14, 150
nationhood, assertion of 156
Northern Ireland, relations with 134
popular sovereignty 150
referendums 14, 149–51, 155–6, 199
Speaker's Conference 150

***Island of Palmas Case (Netherlands v USA)* (1928) 2 UN Expert of International Arbitral Awards 829** 253–5, 267

Israel 239

Italy 192–3, 203

Jefferson, Thomas 113

Jennings, Ivor 3, 69–70, 112–13, 148

judicial review
abolition 103, 109
bipolar sovereignty 103
British constitution 100–1
common law 101
constitutionalism 95
dialogue 15, 240, 242, 249
European Convention on Human Rights 4, 94
European Union 94
expansion 100–1
fairness 101
Human Rights Act 1998 8
interpretation 8, 31
legislative sovereignty 103
legislative supremacy 101
parliamentary sovereignty 83–8, 94–7
positivism 2
rationality 101
rule of law 95–7
Scotland 93
strong judicial review 65
United States 97

judiciary *see also* **judicial review**
competing authorities 90
dialogue 119, 240, 245–7
entrenchment 110
European Union 11
external sovereignty 11
government, dialogue with 119
gradualism 59–60
independence 89
internal sovereignty 11
interpretation 119
law-making 52, 54–5, 82, 112, 116
legislative supremacy 90–1
parliamentary sovereignty 29–30, 52, 54–6, 59–60, 71–2, 82–3, 104
politics and law, divide between 82–3
rule of law 13, 29
Scotland 90–1
secondary rules 54
sub-constitutional law 116
supremacy 15, 236, 246–7
Westminster Parliament 8, 13, 30–2, 50, 87–8, 96–103, 239–42, 249, 252
Julianus, Salvius 115
juridical concept, sovereignty as a 6, 39, 48
jurisdiction
consent 262–6
European Court of Human Rights 216–18
human rights 216–18, 264–6
international courts and tribunals 264–6
international law 15–16, 262–6
interpretation 266
investments 264–5
multinational enterprises 292
plurinational democracies 10–11
reservations 266
State immunity 262–6
State sovereignty 15–16, 262–6
territorial jurisdiction 16, 266–7, 269–85
jus cogens 261

Kelsen, Hans 40–2
***Key Issues for the Fourth Assembly*. National Assembly for Wales Research Service** 143
Kindleberger, Charles 293–4
Kumm, Mattias 41–2, 312–13
Kyoto Protocol 272

labour rights *see* **employment**
language 23, 25, 27, 38, 138
late sovereignty 26–7, 37
Latham, RTE 70, 77, 109–10
Latvia 203
Laws, John 111–12
legal dimension of sovereignty 35, 36–8, 40–4, 47–8, 151
legality, principle of 41, 85, 87
legislative referendums 146
legislative sovereignty
amendment of constitutions 223
democracy 81–2
European Court of Human Rights 15, 213–16, 223–35
foundational principle of constitution, as a 81
hierarchical superiority of legislation 216
judicial challenges 10
judicial review 103
legislative supremacy distinguished 71
long-term commitments 81
manner and form limitations 77
maximizing 81–3
national law 214
rationality 296
rule of law 82
self-embracing sovereignty 58
substantive law-making powers 81–2
legislative supremacy 1–4, 6, 12–13, 71, 90–1, 101, 246
legitimacy
customary law 114–15
EU restatements/models of sovereignty 14–15, 188
European Court of Human Rights 15, 219–20
freedom of expression 306, 307–8, 312–13, 323
institutions 220
monopoly of legitimate political power, State's 45
political legitimacy 113
Lemke, Thomas 125–6
Leveller's Agreement of the People 107
***Leviathan*. Hobbes, Thomas** 130
lex specialis 318
liberal democratic states 16, 307–13, 316–17, 322–3
liberalization of trade 318–22
limited liability 290
limited powers, doctrine of 202, 206
Lincoln, Abraham 247
Lisbon Treaty 8, 165, 170–7, 183, 191, 206
***Lisbon Treaty* K 32/09 (Polish Constitutional Tribunal, 24 November 2010)** 191
***Lisbon Treaty I* PI ÚS (Czech Constitutional Court, 26 November 2008)** 191
Lithuania 187, 212
living constitutionalism 118–19
living instrument, European Convention on Human Rights as a 217
living law, marginalization of 45
local government
cities, Mayor and Cabinet model of governance for 161
conditions for referendums 162
council tax increases 161–3
decentralization 160

democracy, redefinition of local 160–3
England 14, 145, 158, 160–4
fragmentation of policy delivery 162–3
Localism Act 2011 160–4
Mayor and Cabinet model of governance 161
petitions for referendums 160
recognition of local interests 147
referendums 14, 145, 147, 158, 160–4
Local Government Byelaw (Wales) Bill [2012] UKSC 53 123, 152
Localism Act 2011 160–4
Locke, John 105
London 6–7, 10
long-standing commitments, ability of Parliament to enact 79–81, 83
***SS Lotus (France v Turkey)* (1927) PCIJ Series A no 9, 18** 258–60
Loughlin, Martin 21, 71, 237–8

Maastricht Treaty 73–6, 172–3, 181, 192, 195, 201, 203
MacCormick, Neil 1–11, 17
absolute sovereignty 46
contractarianism 300
devolution 14
end of sovereignty 6, 27–8, 45
European Union 5, 7–10, 15, 45–6, 48, 144, 294
flexibility of constitutional law 112–13
globalization 7, 11
Hart 1–11
multinational enterprises 16, 286–8
non-sovereignty 14
post-sovereignty 4, 7–8, 144, 294
Scotland 151
subsidiarity 16, 288, 295, 299
transnational corporate power 286–9, 292, 294–5, 299–300, 304
***MacCormick v Lord Advocate* 1953 SC 396** 90, 94–5
majoritarianism 73, 312–13
manner and form limitations 3, 12–13, 69–71, 77–80, 84, 108
***Marbury v Madison* 5 US 137 (1803)** 242
margin of appreciation 220–3, 226, 231–3, 314, 317
marks of sovereignty 22–3, 26, 30–2, 39, 43
Marxism 125–6, 293
***Mathieu-Mohin and Clerfayt v Belgium* (1987) 10 EHRR 1** 232
Mattei, Ugo 280–1
Mayor, cities and Cabinet model of governance 161
***McCawley v R* [1920] AC 691** 51
Mercosur 178
***Merryman, Ex p.* 17 F Cas 144 (CCD Md 1861)** 247–8
Mitchell, JDB 94
mixed sovereignty 37
models of sovereignty *see* EU restatements/models of sovereignty
modernity 24–8, 35
monism 41
monopolies 20–1, 24, 26, 45, 291
morality
justification criteria 55–6
law, of 41
national governments, morally sound concerns of 15, 234–5
parliamentary sovereignty 55–6, 93
politics 59
***Mortensen v Peters* (1906) 14 SLT 227** 94
multi-ethnic federations 25
multinational enterprises (MNEs) 286–304
abuse of power 296, 300, 303–4
accountability 291, 294, 295–9, 303
bilateral treaties 293
capture of State 288
chartered corporations 290
civic corporations, evolution into 303
civil society 288, 296, 297–303
code of conduct (UN) 294
combinations 291
comity 293
Commission on Transnational Corporations (UN) 294
communal subsidiarity 296
concessions 290
conflict of laws 288, 292
consumption agendas 295
contractarian ideas of sovereignty based on State institutions 16
coordination of MNEs, States, and communities 296–304
cooperation 293
corporate law theory 289
corporate power and public interests, reconciling 16
corporate social responsibility 300–1, 303
democracy 296–7
developing countries 294, 301–2
distributional justice 16, 295, 300–1
due diligence standard 301
economic power 287–9
environmental movement 296, 298, 301–2
experimental governance 302–3
external impacts on corporate behaviour 301–4
extraterritoriality 288, 292, 293–4
financialization 303–4
foreign direct investment 293
foreign direct liability litigation 301–2
general principles of law 290
globalization 286–7, 301
good corporate activity 16
Guiding Principles on Business and Human Rights. UN Human Rights Council 300–3

multinational enterprises (MNEs) (*cont.*):
human rights 16, 286, 288, 300–3
incorporation 289–96
institutionalists 287
internal corporate change 300–1
internal management 302
international law 288, 292
jurisdiction 292
labour rights 286, 301
legally conferred economic liberties 16
legitimation of elite power 16
limited liability 290
management gaps 303
market subsidiarity 288, 295–6
marketization of public economic functions 302
monopolization, control of 291
nationality 292
new corporate accountability 295–9, 303
new forms of cooperative action between firms, communities and civil society 16
new sovereignty 296–304
non-governmental organizations 286, 296–8, 302–3
non-market goals and market-facilitating goals, trade-off between 16
normative institutional approach 287–9
parents and subsidiaries, tensions between 302–4
pluralism 16, 295
political parties 298–9, 300
popular democracy 295–6, 300
popular sovereignty 300
post-sovereignty 294–5
private corporate power 286–304
public interest 16, 291
public/private law dichotomy 286, 290
rational legislative sovereignty 296
registration 290–1
regulation 292–4, 302
self-regulation 302
social impacts of business 301, 304
social interests 16, 291, 295, 298–301
social phenomenon, corporate existence as a 287
State sovereignty 287–8, 293–4, 299, 304
subaltern legality 301
subsidiarity 16, 288, 295–6, 299–304
sustainable development 286
tax avoidance 296
territorial sovereignty 287–8, 294
transnational corporate organizations 292–5
transnational corporate power 289–304
United States 293, 295, 299
wealth, disparities in 16
Multilateral Agreement on Investment (MAI) 286–7
multiple sovereignty 10, 37
nation state, end of the 293
'National Conversation' 153
national identity 25
national sovereignty *see* **State sovereignty**
nationalism 32–3, 134, 138, 157
nationality 197, 278, 292
natural law 34, 43–4
Nazi Germany 291
necessity 312, 314, 317–18, 320–1
negative aspect (no body can trump Parliament) 1, 13, 28, 36–7, 91–3, 98, 110
neo-liberalism 295
Netherlands 199, 215, 281–2
networks 15, 236, 246–8, 309
new view of parliamentary sovereignty 3, 11–12, 19, 68–72, 83–4
no body can trump Parliament (negative aspect) 1, 13, 28, 36–7, 91–3, 98, 110
non-governmental organizations (NGOs) 286, 296–8, 302–3
non-intervention principle 214
non-sovereignty 13–14, 123, 125–31, 141–4
Northern Ireland
alternative narratives 135
anti-foundationalist foundation of peace process 121
Belfast Agreement 13–14, 120, 133–41, 157
Commission for Victims and Survivors 138
conflict resolution 134–5
consent, idea of 140
constitutional accommodation 133
Criminal Justice Inspectorate 136–7
culture 13–14, 137–8
demilitarization 137
devolution 8, 122–3, 149–50, 152
disarmament 137
equality 138–9
Equality Commission of Northern Ireland 139
executive 135, 137, 139–40
fair employment 139
flags, flying of 137
formal State, beyond the 132–3
franchise issues 155–6
funding 135, 140
good relations agenda 139–40
governmentality 13–14, 133–41
home rule 150
identity 13–14, 137–8
inquiries and commissions 136–7
institutions 135–6
internal governance 134
Ireland, relationship with 134
justice 13–14, 136–7
language 138
law, role of 140
marching 137–8
murals and insignia, replacement of 138

nationalism 134, 138
non-sovereignty approach 13–14, 121, 132–4
normalization 137
Northern Ireland Act 1998 139, 152
Northern Ireland Assembly 137, 139
organizations in peace process, involvement of 135–6, 138
past, the 137–8
peace process 122, 132–41
policing 136–7
popular sovereignty 157
positive discrimination 136
power-sharing 133
public authorities, duties of 138–40
referendums 8, 149–50, 157, 159–60
Reimaging Communities consortium 138
religious discrimination 136, 139
rights and equality regime 138–9
segregation 139
statutory interpretation 135
symbolism 137
technologies of government 134–41
unionism 134, 138
United Kingdom, place within the 134
victims 137–8
Norway 177, 179
notwithstanding clauses 61, 65, 76
***NV Algemene Trasporte Expeditie Onderneming Van Gend en Loos v Nederlandse Administratie der Belastingen* [1963] ECR 1 C26/62** 188–90

Obama, Barack 275
officials of system 34, 53–60, 63, 66, 70–1, 96–7, 110, 112, 263
old view of parliamentary sovereignty 68–72, 79–80, 83
Oliver, Peter 51, 111
operationalization of sovereignty 22, 32
opinio juris 259
opt-outs 165, 170–8, 183
ordainment 14–15, 188, 200–6
Orders in Council 92
ordre public 193
organology 194–6
originalism 117–18
***Otto Preminger Institut v Austria* (1994) 19 EHRR 34** 314
overrides 12, 15, 237, 241, 243, 245, 248–50

pacta sunt servanda 168, 214–15, 218
Paine, Thomas 106–7
parents and subsidiaries, tensions between 302–4
Parliament Acts 1911 and 1949
bipolar sovereignty 103
contextual approach 76
delegated authority 102–3
democracy, enhancement of 76
entrenchment 60, 63
executive 82
Hunting Act 2004 95
judicial review of legislative sovereignty 103
parliamentary sovereignty 68, 73, 76, 82, 94–5
statutory interpretation 95
Parliament, definition of 70, 72, 80, 82
parliamentary privilege 80–1
parliamentary sovereignty *see also* **bind its successors, Parliament cannot; parliamentary sovereignty, re-definition of**
absolute, as 96
ad hoc and piecemeal development of British constitution 13–14, 99, 107–17, 119
authority 30–2
blind sovereign metaphor 13–14, 110–16, 119
branches of government, acquiescence of 60
changes 13–14, 51, 99–103
citizens assemblies or conventions 59
common law 29, 54–60, 71–2, 85–8, 95–6, 104, 108–9
comparative analysis 98–119
conceptual overload 31
consensual change based on will of people 12
constitutional change in UK 50–67
constitutionalism 29, 32–3, 50, 95
consultation with public 58
contested, as 17
continuing sovereignty 50–1
control or limitation of law-making authority 12
customary rules, changing 57–60
definition 32
designed constitutions 13–14, 99, 103–7, 111, 116–19
devolution 28–9, 31, 93
dialogue 237–40
dual or bipolar principle, as 29
entrenchment 12, 50–1, 58–65
European Communities Act 1972 93
European Convention on Human Rights 28–9
European Court of Human Rights 217, 229, 234
European Union 28–9, 31–2, 93
executive 94–5, 97
express amendments 12
external sovereignty 31–2
foundational constitutional settlements 30
framing and claiming 29
human rights 28, 31
implied repeal doctrine 51
initiation of change 58–60
institutionalization 30
internal sovereignty 31–2
international law 93

parliamentary sovereignty (*cont.*):
interpretation 13–14, 28, 31, 53, 54–7, 71–2, 116–19
judicial review 94–7
judiciary 29–30, 52, 54–6, 59–60, 71–2, 82–3, 104
limitation of authority 50
manner and form limitations 3
mark of parliamentary sovereignty 30–2
morality 93
nationalism 32–3
nature of doctrine of parliamentary sovereignty 52–7
negative aspect (no body can trump Parliament) 28
new view 3
non-coercive constitutional change 59–60
obstacle to constitutional change, parliamentary sovereignty as 50–2
official consensus, changes to 58–60, 63, 66
overrides 12
Parliament Acts 94–5
personal, dynastic, and singular to impersonal, corporate and internally 30
political morality 59
popular sovereignty 30, 59
positivism 53
prerogative powers 30
prize-fighting dimension 32
procedural sovereignty 51, 58
procedure and form of legislative enactments 12, 60–5
Queen-in-Parliament, attribution of power to institutional complex of 28–31
referendums 59, 65–7, 73
reform 12, 50, 58, 65–6
repeals 12, 51
revolution 58–9
rule of law 8, 29, 59, 95–6
Scotland 94
self-embracing sovereignty 51–2, 54, 57–8, 66
self-entrenched referendum requirement 12, 65–7
single mark of parliamentary sovereignty 30–1
statutory interpretation 28, 31
substantive sovereignty 51, 58
territorial integrity 32–3
territorial relations 17
unity 30
unlimited authority 50
unwritten constitutions 50–2, 97
written constitutions 12, 58–9, 67, 95–6
parliamentary sovereignty, re-definition of 68–88
amendment or repeal, protection from inadvertent 80
AXA General Insurance case 83–8
balance of power 12–13, 82, 88
bind its successors, Parliament cannot 12–13, 68–88
bipolar sovereignty involving Parliament and judiciary 12–13, 71
common law 71–2
competences 12–13, 71–2
constitutional crises 72, 88
continuing parliamentary legislative supremacy, normative justification for 12–13, 71
definition of Parliament 70, 72, 82
democracy 82–3
Dicey 68–9, 82
European Communities Act 1972 68
European Convention on Human Rights 70
European Union Act 2011 68, 73–4
Goldsworthy's theory of sovereignty 69–70, 72–81, 97
Human Rights Act 1998 68, 78
individuals, regulation of action of 70, 77
internal procedures 78
judicial review, abolition of 103, 109
judiciary 71–2, 82–3
legislative supremacy 12–13, 71
limitations on sovereignty 68–70
long-standing commitments, ability of Parliament to enact 79–81, 83
manner and form, binding Parliament through 12–13, 69–71, 77–80, 84
maximizing legislative sovereignty 81–3
new view of parliamentary sovereignty 68–72
old view of parliamentary sovereignty 68–72, 79–80, 83
Parliament Acts 1911 and 1949 68, 73, 76, 82
primary legislation 70, 77–8
procedure, binding Parliament through 12–13, 69, 72–81
referendums 73
rule of law and parliamentary legislative sovereignty, balance between 82
rule of recognition 86
secondary rules 77–8
statutory interpretation 71–2
substance 69–82
viability 72–8
parliamentary supremacy *see* **parliamentary sovereignty**
patent protection 281–2
path-dependence 21
Pepper v Hart **[1993] AC 593** 227
Permanent Court of International Justice (PCIJ) 265
persistence of sovereignty 121–3
persistent objector principle 260–1
personality as basis for sovereignty 278
piecemeal and ad hoc development of British constitution 13–14, 99, 107–17, 119

Pinochet, Augusto 263–4
pluralism 5, 11, 16, 26, 148, 295, 299, 312–13
plurinational democracies 10–11
Poland 191, 203, 205–6
police
European Union 165, 171–2, 177
Europol 174
Northern Ireland 136
police and judicial cooperation in criminal matters 171–2, 177
Political Parties, Elections and Referendums Act 2000 146
politics
absolutism 35, 43–4
authority 23–5, 35, 38, 43–4, 197–8
autonomy of law 35, 40–1, 47–8
concept of sovereignty 35, 36–8, 43–4
constitutionalism 55
dialogue 15, 236–8, 240–1, 245–50
European Union 11, 172, 178–9, 183–5
fragmentation of political agency 190
identity 13, 24
law and politics, divide between 82–3
legal dimension 35, 36–8, 40–5, 47–8
legitimacy 113
monopoly of legitimate political power, State's 45
morality 59
normative theory of sovereignty 40–2
political parties 298–9, 300
prior to political systems, sovereignty as 21
public law 35, 44
symbolic locus, State as 24
pooled sovereignty 6, 28, 37, 186, 322
popular sovereignty *see also* **will of the people**
British constitution 99
designed constitutions 105
devolution 156–60
European Union 8, 169
France 22
freedom of expression 16, 307, 312
institutionalization 30
international law 252–3
Ireland 150
multinational enterprises 300
Northern Ireland 157
parliamentary sovereignty 30, 59
post-sovereignty 295
referendums 8, 14, 145–64, 167, 252
Scotland 3, 8, 151, 157
Wales 157
pornography 306, 311, 314
positive aspects of sovereignty 36–7 *see also* **bind its successors, Parliament cannot**
positive discrimination 136
positivism
anti-positivism 41
commands of a sovereign 2
constituted authorities 43–4
constitutionalism 55
customary law 115
empiricism 45–6
European Union 45–6
framing 21
institutionalists 287
interpretive theory of law 56–7
judicial review 2
legal dimension to political dimension, relation of 43–4
natural law 43–4
parliamentary sovereignty 53
sovereign, concept of 43–6
sovereignty with sovereign, conflating idea of 45–6
State sovereignty 304
post-sovereignty 4, 11–12, 37, 45, 125–9, 294–5
post-Westphalian age, sovereignty in a 24–8
comprehensiveness 24
external sovereignty 24
federalism 25–6
internal sovereignty 24
modernity 24–8
mutual exclusivity24
substate national recognition or protection 26
universality 24–6
potentia **(actual ability to govern)** 39–40
potestas **(exercise of rightful authority)** 39–40, 42–3
power
abuse of power 296, 300, 303–4
allocation of power between States 15–16, 253, 255
BRIC countries 25
claiming 12
corporate power and public interests, reconciling 16
dialogue 15
economic power 287–9
global power, territoriality as a source of 16, 270
government 28
governmentality 129–31
international law 15–16, 253, 255
monopoly of legitimate political power, State's 45
multinational enterprises 289–304
non-sovereignty 129–31
Northern Ireland 133
power-distributive, legal strand as 44
power-generational, political strand as 44
private corporate power 286–304
public power 99, 103–7, 109
real power 269
regional powers 25
relations 127–9
repatriation of power 165, 168–9, 175–84

power (*cont.*):
residual sovereign powers of states 22
States, within and between 15–16, 251–2
technologies of power 120, 124–6, 132
United States 25
practice, sovereignty in 37
preambles to constitutions 104
preliminary rulings 171
primitive law 45
prison, function of the 124–5
prisoners' voting rights 217, 224–30, 232–5
privacy, right to 117
private information, disclosure of 306
private international law 288, 292
privilege 80–1
procedure for change
absolute majority requirement 61, 63
alternative procedures 73, 75–6
bind its successors, Parliament cannot 54, 108
binding Parliament through procedure 12–13, 69, 72–81
designed constitutions 104
entrenchment 12, 60–5
European Act 2011 73–6
express amendments 12, 64–6
implied repeal doctrine 51, 62–3, 64–5, 79–80
inadvertent amendment or repeal, protection from 61–4, 80
initiation of change 58–60
manner and form limitations 3, 12–13, 69–71, 77–80, 84, 108
notwithstanding clauses 61, 65, 76
parliamentary sovereignty 12, 51, 58, 60–5
quorum requirement 61, 63, 80
rules of change 57–8
production process methods (PPMs) 279–80
***Programme for Cohesion, Sharing and Integration.* Office of First Minister and Deputy First Minister** 140
proportionality
EU restatements/models of sovereignty 203
European Court of Human Rights 223, 226–8, 233
freedom of expression 312, 314, 317–18, 321
prisoners' voting rights 226–8, 233
public interest 16, 291, 314
public international law *see* **international law**
public law
British constitution, changes in 99–103
concept of sovereignty 35–6, 42, 49
constitutionalism, practice-conception of 41
cosmopolitan paradigm 41
epistemological crisis 40
European Union 45–6
govern, ability to 39–40
government, sovereignty distinguished from 39–40
legal dimension 35, 41, 44–5
paradigm shift 41
positive law 44
sovereign, concept of the 43, 47–8
public opinion, unbounded rule of 147
public order 307, 310–13, 316–22
public power 99, 103–7, 109
public/private law dichotomy 286, 290
pure theory of law 40–1

quasi-federalism 25
Queen-in-Parliament 22, 28–31
***Questioning Sovereignty.* MacCormick, Neil** 6–7, 45, 286
questions in referendums 146, 154–5
quorum requirement 61, 63, 80

***R v Bow Street Metropolitan Stipendiary Magistrate, ex parte Pinochet Ugarte* [2000] 1 AC 61** 263
***R v Secretary of State for the Home Department, ex p Simms* [2000] 2 AC 115** 64
***R v Secretary of State for Transport, ex parte Factortame (1)* [1990] 2 AC 85** 4–5, 110
***R v Secretary of State for Transport ex parte Factortame (2)* [1991] 1 AC 603** 4–5, 64, 100
***R (Jackson) v Attorney General* [2006] 1 AC 262** 57, 86, 95, 97, 102, 108–9, 111
race to the bottom 298
***Ratification of the Treaty of Lisbon, Re* (Germany) [2010] 3 CMLR 13** 191, 201, 206
rationality 34, 101, 106, 288, 296
realism 45, 56
reciprocity 6, 34
recognition, rule of 66, 70–1, 77, 86
reconstitution of Parliament 66
re-definition of parliamentary sovereignty *see* **parliamentary sovereignty, re-definition of**
referendums 145–64
abuse 14, 145–8, 163–4, 167
ad hoc and piecemeal development of British constitution 113–14
advisory referendums 145
age qualification for voting, lowering of 156
autocracies 147
Belfast Agreement 157
bias 154–5
bind its successors, Parliament cannot 82
binding referendums 145, 150–1
codification 146–7, 149, 164
codified constitutional systems 146–7
commission, proposal for an independent 164
conditions 148
constitutional act, proposal for dedicated 164
constitutional convention, holding referendums as a 148, 159–60, 163, 164

constitutional referendums 146–8, 164, 167
constitutionalism 163
contraction 149–56
democracy 14, 149, 160–4, 167, 169–70
devolution 8, 14, 113–14, 122–3, 142–3, 148–63
Devolution Max 154, 159
EEC, continued membership of 147–8
elected politicians 147
elections 114, 148, 155–6
England 155–6, 158, 160–4
entrenchment 65–6
European Convention on Human Rights 70, 164, 168
European Union 8, 14, 114, 148, 164–70, 175–84
  EEC, continued membership of 147–8
  European Union Act 2011 74–6, 114, 148, 165–70
  Euroscepticism 165–6, 170–4
  supremacy of EU law 167, 180–1
expansion 149–56
expenditure 146, 170
factional interests 146, 160, 167
fairness 14
franchise 155–6
House of Lords' Select Committee 167
human rights 143
institutions, marginalization of 147–8
interest test 156
interpretation 122–3
Ireland 14, 149–51, 155–7, 199
legislative referendums 146
Lisbon Treaty 166
local government 14, 145, 147, 158, 160–4
locks 8, 167, 169
'National Conversation' 153
Northern Ireland 8, 149–50, 152, 155–7, 159–60
parliamentary sovereignty 59, 65–7, 73
petitions 160
pluralism 147
Political Parties, Elections and Referendums Act 2000 146
popular sovereignty 8, 14, 145–64, 167, 252
procedural controls 146
propriety 14
public opinion, unbounded rule of 147
questions 146, 154–5
regional government 158
repatriation of power 14, 165, 168–84
representative democracy, role of 147–8, 163
right to call a referendum 122–3
Rome Treaty 180–2
rules on use 14, 148, 164
Scotland 8, 17, 145, 149, 151–60
  Edinburgh agreement 2012 156
  Electoral Commission 146, 154–5
  independence 3, 8, 17, 122–3, 142–3, 146, 153–9
  questions 146, 154–5
  Scotland Act 1978 146
  Scotland Act 1998 122–3, 153
  Scotland Act 2012 154
  Scottish National Party 143, 153–5
  Scottish Parliament 143, 153–4
  United Kingdom electorate, lack of consultation of 156
self-embracing sovereignty 66
self-entrenchment 12, 65–7
social sphere 176–7, 178–84
State sovereignty 149
Structural Funds 181
sub-national governance 149, 157, 163
substate nationalism 147
supremacy of EU law 167, 180–1
territorial constitution 147, 149–64
treaties and conventions 167–8
voter turnout threshold 146, 167
Wales 146, 155–8, 159–60
welfare policy 182
Westminster Parliament 145, 150, 153–4, 157–8
written constitutions 148
refugee law 215
regions 11, 24, 26, 304 *see also* **local government**
regulation
  European Union 205, 277
  ex ante regulation 205, 280
  extraterritoriality 293–4
  gap 302
  multinational enterprises 292–4, 302
  self-regulation 302
  supranationalism 7
  territorial extension 16, 269–85
  transnational regulatory regimes 38
religion 25, 34, 136, 139, 314
remedial orders 245
repatriation of power 165, 168–9, 175–84
reservations to treaties 258–9, 266
restatements/models of sovereignty *see* **EU restatements/models of sovereignty**
Richard Commission 158
***Rights of Man*. Paine, Thomas** 106–7
Roach, Kent 246–7
Robinson v Secretary of State for Northern Ireland [2002] UKHL 32 29
***Roe v Wade* 410 US 113 (1973)** 248
***Rothwell v Chemical & Insulating Co Ltd* [2007] UKHL 39** 83
Rousseau, Jean-Jacques 105
Royal Ulster Constabulary (RUC) 136
rule-making event, constitution-making as 99
rule of law
  bind its successors, Parliament cannot 13
  British constitution 95
  constitutional long-stop 13
  democracy 97
  dialogue 238

rule of law (*cont.*):
equality of States 214
EU restatements/models of sovereignty 189
judicial review 95–7
judiciary 13, 29
legislative sovereignty 82
negative aspect (no body can trump Parliament) 13
parliamentary sovereignty 8, 29, 59, 82, 85–6, 95–6
Scotland 13, 93
sovereign principle, as the 89–97
strike-down power, absence of a general 13
unwritten constitution 89
Westminster model 13
Rule of Law. **Bingham, Tom** 95–6
rule of recognition 66, 70–1, 77, 86
Russia 7–8, 25

sanctions 2, 279–80
Scharpf, F 180
Schmitt, Carl 14–15, 105–6, 208–11
Scoppola v Italy (No 3) **(2013) 56 EHRR 19** 229, 232–3
Scotland
Acts of Union of 1707 89–91
age qualification for voting, lowering of 156
bias 154–5
Calman Commission 159
Damages (Asbestos-related Conditions) (Scotland) Act 2009 83–8
devolution 151–2, 154, 157–9
Devolution Max 154, 159
Claim of Right 4
Court of Session 89–90, 95
Damages (Asbestos-related Conditions) (Scotland) Act 2009 93
delegated law-making body, Scottish Parliament as 83–5
Edinburgh agreement 2012 156
Electoral Commission 146, 154–5
expenses of referendums 146
federalism 151–2
franchise issues 156
human rights 143
independence, referendum on 3, 8, 17, 122–3, 142–3, 146, 153–9
interest test 156
judicial review 93
judiciary, relationship with Parliament of 90–1
legal sovereignty 151
legislative supremacy 90–1
'National Conversation' 153
parliamentary sovereignty 8, 83–8, 95–6
popular sovereignty 151, 157
questions in referendum on independence 146, 154–5
referendums 8, 17, 145, 149, 151–60
Edinburgh agreement 2012 156
Electoral Commission 146, 154–5
questions 146, 154–5
Scotland Act 1978 146
Scotland Act 1998 122–3, 153
Scotland Act 2012 154
Scottish National Party 143, 153–5
Scottish Parliament 143, 153–4
United Kingdom electorate, lack of consultation of 156
rule of law 13, 93
Scotland Act 1978 146
Scotland Act 1998 83–6, 122–3, 151–3, 157–8
Scotland Act 2012 154, 159–60
Scottish Constitutional Convention 151, 157
Scottish National Party 143, 153–5
Scottish Parliament 83–5, 143, 153–4, 157–8
Sewel Convention 152
statutory interpretation 85–6, 122–3
taxation 157–8, 159
ultra vires 94
United Kingdom electorate, lack of consultation of 156
unlimited sovereignty of Parliament 90
Westminster Parliament 83–95, 151–4, 156, 158–9
Security Council (UN)
binding decisions 261
Chapter VII 256–8
consent 265
internal affairs of other States, non-intervention in 214
maintenance of peace and security 256–8
sanctions 257
terrorists, listing of suspected 235
Sedley, Stephen Sir 87, 103
seizure of goods in transit 281–3
Sejdić and Finci v Bosnia and Herzegovina, **Apps nos 72996/06 and 34836/06 (ECtHR, 22 December 2009)** 235
self-determination 142
self-embracing sovereignty 51–2, 54, 57–8, 66, 77
self-entrenchment 12, 62–7
self-government 186, 188
self-regulation 302
self-reproduction 21, 26
Septennial Act of 1716 89
shared sovereignty 37
Shrimp-Turtle **case** 283
Sieyès, EJ 105
Silk Commission 142–3
single market 5, 7, 192
Slovak Pensions **(Czech Constitutional Court, 31 January 2012)** 202–3
small and medium-sized enterprises (SMEs) 304

social conduct 111
social interests and business 16, 291, 295, 298–301
social ordering 204, 238
social policy, qualities of 195–6
Societas Europea (SE) 294
socio-economic changes 37–8
sociology of political power 27
South Africa 55, 69, 84, 239
sovereign
abstract quality of sovereign 20
changing the definition 77
commands of a sovereign 2
concept of sovereignty 42–8, 77, 104–5
sovereignty with sovereign, conflating idea of 45–6
Spain 25
specialist transnational organizations 24
speech acts 22
State immunity
absolute immunity 262–3
commercial and State acts, difference between 263
consent 263–6
investments 264–5
jurisdiction 262–6
Torture Convention 263–4
treaties and conventions 264–6
Vienna Convention on Diplomatic Relations 1961 and Protocol 264
State practice 117, 259–60
State sovereignty
customary international law 259–60
devolution 299
dialogue 15, 236, 238
emergence of higher scale of authority 25
EU restatements/models of sovereignty 189, 191–4, 202–4
European Court of Human Rights 15, 213–21, 234
European Union 17, 189, 191–4, 202–4
freedom of expression 306–7, 322
globalization 299
international law 41, 251–5, 258–62
jurisdiction 15–16, 262–6
Multilateral Agreement on Investment 286–7
multinational enterprises 287–8, 293–4, 299, 304
overlapping claims 277–8
pluralism 299
positivism 304
post-national views 9
property of State, sovereignty as 186–7
referendums 149
speech act, as 278
substance 15–16, 251–2, 255–62
territorial extension 269–70, 277–8
treaties and conventions 258–60
statements of compatibility 78
States *see also* **State sovereignty**
abstract entity, as an 34
accountability for institutions 266–7, 268
capture of State 288
decentring of the State 24
equality of States 214, 254–6
external independence 44
formation 131
governmentalization 124
hybrid public/private entities 24
immunity 262–6
institutions 24, 44–5, 48, 266–7, 268
internal authority 44–5
international law 3–4, 41–2, 44
law and State as same thing 40
limitations on authority 44–5, 48
monopoly of legitimate political power 45
sovereign States, relationship between 2
State-centred concept of sovereignty 34
State practice 259–60, 269
theories of the State 126–7
ultimate source of law, as 34, 44–5
unitary State 3, 7, 9–10
Statute of Westminster 1931 3, 100
statutory interpretation *see* **interpretation**
sub-constitutional law 116
subsidiarity
communal subsidiarity 288, 296, 299–304
EU restatements/models of sovereignty 204
European Court of Human Rights 231
European Union 5–6, 204
federalism 42
margin of appreciation 220
market subsidiarity 288, 295–6, 299–304
multinational enterprises 16, 288, 295–6, 299–304
neo-liberalism 296
popular democracy 295
rational legislative subsidiarity 288
sub-national governance 149, 157, 163
substance
bind its successors, Parliament cannot 12–13, 69–82, 108
continuing sovereignty 62–4
international law 15–16, 251–2, 255–62
judicial law-making 82
manner and form limitations 77
parliamentary sovereignty 51, 58, 69–82
State sovereignty 15–16, 251–2, 255–62
substate national recognition or protection 26
substate nationalism 147
super majority requirements 61–2
supranationalism 7, 9, 16, 214, 235, 310–12, 318, 322–3
supremacy
EU law 3, 26–7, 99–100, 110, 167, 180–1, 187–9, 206, 252–3
judiciary 15, 236, 246–7

supremacy (*cont.*):
legislative supremacy 1–4, 6, 12–13, 71, 90–1, 101, 246
territorial supremacy 16, 269, 281
use of word 71
sustainable development 286
Switzerland 177, 179
symbolism 22–3, 24, 33, 43, 137
systemic conservatism 27

tax 157–9, 161–3, 296
technology *see also* **Internet and freedom of expression**
governance, technologies of 134–41
information and communications technology (ICT) 7
power, technologies of 120, 124–6, 132
transnationalism 27
temporality 37, 194, 196
territorial communities, existence of 12
territorial extension 269–85 *see also* **Aviation Directive and territorial extension**
appraisal of territorial extension 279–84
contextual evaluation 16, 271–9, 281–5
country-level territorial extension 274, 283
Durban Action Programme 283
Emissions Trading Scheme (ETS), inclusion of aviation in EU 16, 271–9, 282–5
European Union 16, 270–85
extraterritoriality 270, 285
final authority, claims to 269–70, 278
food safety 281
formal authority 269
global-level territorial extension 274
global power, territorial jurisdiction as a source of 16, 270
globalization 269
inter-connection 16, 269, 281
international jurisdictional reach 16
policy 269
production process methods (PPMs) 279–80
regulation 16, 269–85
scholars, disagreements between 279–81
spillovers 281
State practice 269
State sovereignty 269–70, 277–8
territorial jurisdiction 16, 269–85
territorial sovereignty 16, 269–85
territorial supremacy 16, 269, 281
transaction-level territorial extension 274
triggers 270
United States 274, 275–8, 283, 285
World Trade Organization 279–80
territory *see also* **territorial extension**
dignity and singularity 197–8
European Court of Human Rights 217
European Union 26–7
integrity 32–3
international law 253–4
jurisdiction 16, 266–7, 269–85
parliamentary sovereignty 17
referendums 147, 149–54
sovereignty 16, 269–87, 294, 306–7, 312, 322–3
State 44
supremacy 16, 269, 291
terrorists, listing of suspected 235
Thoburn v Sunderland City Council **[2003] QB 151** 64–5, 164
Tomkins, Adam 103
torture 263–4, 267
transferable, sovereignty as 188–9, 201
transnational enterprises *see* **multinational enterprises (MNEs)**
transnationalism 9, 27
treaties and conventions *see also* **particular treaties**
Aviation Directive 275
bilateral treaties 293
breach 259
consent 264
customary international law 260–1
dispute settlement mechanisms, acceptance of 264–5
federal states 268
international law 258–61
international organizations 256
interpretation 266
reservations 258–9, 266
specialized treaties and conventions 267
State immunity 264–6
State sovereignty 258–60
United Kingdom 223
withdrawal 261
Treaty Establishing the European Stability Mechanism (ESM Treaty) T/ESM/2012 (EU) 207–8, 211
Treaty on European Union (TEU) 73–6, 172–3, 181, 192, 195, 201, 203
Treaty on the Functioning of the European Union 73–6
Treaty of Lisbon (Establishing the Treating on the Functioning of the European Union) 8, 165, 170–7, 183, 191, 206
Turkey 177, 179, 258–60

UKIP (UK Independence Party) 176, 179
ultra vires 84–5, 94, 206
UNCTAD (UN Conference on Trade and Development) 294
unilateralism 271, 272–3, 284
unitary State 3, 7, 9–10
United Kingdom constitution *see* **British constitution**
United Nations (UN) *see also* **Security Council (UN)**
Charter 256–7
codes of conduct 294

collective action 24
Commission on Transnational Corporations 294
Compensation Commission 265
end of sovereignty 9
freedom of expression 316
Guiding Principles on Business and Human Rights. Human Rights Council 300–3
Human Rights Committee 16, 317–18
international law 256–8
Internet 316
public goods 24

United States 3, 274–9
eighteenth-century constitutional settlement 19, 25
Aviation Directive, blocking statute on 274, 275–9
common law 119
Constitution 13–14, 22, 33, 105, 117–18, 216, 241–2
constitutional sovereignty 216
death penalty 268
democratic pluralism 295
designed constitutions 105
dialogue 236–7, 239, 241–4, 247–8
economic liberty cases 117
EU Emissions Trading Scheme Prohibition Act 2011 (US) 274, 275–9, 282–5
extraterritoriality 285
Federal Constitution of 1787–9 105
federalism 25
Federalist Papers 105
foreign affairs, conduct of 268
free trade agreements 178
International Criminal Court, Rome Statute of 258
international law 253–5, 258
Internet 16, 310–11, 315–19, 321
interpretation 13–14, 117–18, 242, 244
judicial review 97
living constitutionalism 118–19
multinational enterprises 293, 295, 299
nationality 278
neutrality, breach of 254–5
originalism 117–18
personality as basis for sovereignty 278
Philadelphia Convention 105
power 25
residual sovereign powers of states 22
sacred quality of Constitution 33
State sovereignty 277–8
symbolism 33
Tenth Amendment to Constitution 22
territorial extension 274, 275–8, 283, 285
territorial sovereignty 253–4
UN Compensation Commission 265
will of the people 33
written constitutions 23

***United States—Trade Restrictions on Shrimp and Shrimp Products* (WT/DS58/AB/R)** 283
Universal Declaration of Human Rights 317
universalism 24–6, 309–10, 312–14, 322–3
unwritten constitutions 32, 50–2, 57, 66, 83, 97, 103–4
utilitarian Euroscepticism 175

value of sovereignty 187, 189–91
***Van Gend en Loos* case** 188–90
Vienna Convention on Diplomatic Relations 1961 and Protocol 264
Vienna Convention on the Law of Treaties 1969 261
voting *see also* elections
age qualification for voting, lowering of 156
European Court of Human Rights 217, 224–30, 232–5
majoritarianism 73, 312–13
prisoners, rights of 217, 224–30, 232–5
referendums, turn-out for 146, 167, 169
Scotland 156
Voting Eligibility (Prisoners) Draft Bill 234

Wade, William Sir 58, 90–2, 110
Waldron, Jeremy 56
Wales
Commission on Devolution for Wales 159
devolution 8, 122, 142–3, 155–8
franchise issues 155–6
Government of Wales 1998 158
Government of Wales 2006 158, 159–60
human rights 143
Key Issues for the Fourth Assembly 143
legislative competence orders 158
popular sovereignty 157
referendums 146, 155–8, 159–60
Richard Commission 158
taxation 159
Wales Act 1978 146
Welsh Assembly 158, 159
war, treatment of combatants and civilians in 215
Weiler, J 181
welfare maximization 114
Western rationalism 34
Westminster Parliament *see also* devolution; parliamentary sovereignty
Acts of Union of 1707 89–91
challenges to power 29, 68
colonies 100
constitutional long-stop 13
Court of Session 90
judiciary, relationship with 8, 13, 30–2, 50, 87–8, 96–103, 239–42, 249, 252
referendums 145, 150, 153–4, 157–8
rule of law 13
Scotland 83–95, 151–4, 156, 158–9

Westphalian model 5, 24–8, 267
WG Hart Legal Workshops 6–8, 9–11, 16
will of the people 23, 43, 48, 105–6, 112–13, 115–17 *see also* **popular sovereignty**
William of Ockham 200
Wilson, Harold 147–8
Winterton, G 77–8
World Trade Organization (WTO)
  Appellate Body 321–2
  China 320–2
  decentring of the State 24
  freedom of expression 16, 318–22
  GATS 319–21
  GATT 319–21
  globalization 286
  late sovereignty 26
  national authorities, tension with 215
  production process methods 279–80
  Shrimp-Turtle case 283
  supranational regulation 7
  territorial extension 279–80
  United States 321
written constitutions
  ad hoc and piecemeal development of British constitution 107
  designed constitutions 13–14, 99
  external sovereignty 31
  internal sovereignty 31
  international law 252
  interpretation 13–14, 116–19
  parliamentary sovereignty 12, 58–9, 67, 95–6
  public power 99, 103–7
  referendums 148
  United States 23
WTO *see* **World Trade Organization (WTO)**